LEARNING MATHEMATICS IN ELEMENTARY AND MIDDLE SCHOOLS

Third Edition

W. George Cathcart
University of Alberta

Yvonne M. Pothier
Mount Saint Vincent University

James H. Vance
University of Victoria

Nadine S. Bezuk
San Diego State University

Merrill
Prentice Hall

Upper Saddle River, New Jersey
Columbus, Ohio

This edition is dedicated to my husband, Steve, and my son, Peter,
whose encouragement and support made this work possible.

—N.S.B.

Library of Congress Cataloging-in-Publication Data

Learning mathematics in elementary and middle schools/W. George Cathcart_[et al.].—3rd ed.
   p. cm.
  Includes bibliographical references and index.
  ISBN 0-13-048343-5
   1. Mathematics—Study and teaching (Elementary) 2. Mathematics—Study and teaching (Middle school) I. Title: Learning mathematics. II. Cathcart, W. George.

QA135.6.L43 2003
372.7—dc21

                                                  2002016545

Vice President and Publisher: Jeffery W. Johnston
Editor: Linda Ashe Montgomery
Editorial Assistant: Evelyn Olson
Development Editor: Hope Madden
Production Editor: Linda Hillis Bayma
Design Coordinator: Diane C. Lorenzo
Photo Coordinator: Valerie Schultz
Production Coordination and Text Design: Cliff Kallemeyn, Clarinda Publication Services
Cover and Insert Designer: Ceri Fitzgerald
Cover art: Stephen Schildbach
Production Manager: Pamela D. Bennett
Director of Marketing: Ann Castel Davis
Marketing Manager: Krista Groshong
Marketing Coordinator: Tyra Cooper

This book was set in Times by The Clarinda Company. It was printed and bound by Courier Kendallville, Inc. The cover was printed by The Lehigh Press, Inc.

Earlier editions © 1997, 2000, entitled *Learning Mathematics in Elementary and Middle Schools,* by Prentice Hall, Canada Inc.

Excerpts from *Principles and Standards for School Mathematics* (2000), copyright by the National Council of Teachers of Mathematics, Reston, VA. Used with permission.

Photo Credits color insert: p. A-1, D. Berry/PhotoDisc; pp. A-3 and C-3, Anthony Magnacca/Merrill; p. B-1, Bill Aron/PhotoEdit; p. B-3, David Young-Wolff/PhotoEdit; p. C-2, Silver Burdett Ginn; p. D-1, Gary Conner/PhotoEdit; p. D-3, Tony Freeman/PhotoEdit; p. E-1, Todd Yarrington/Merrill; p. E-2, Frank Siteman/PhotoEdit.

Pearson Education Ltd.
Pearson Education Australia Pty. Limited
Pearson Education Singapore Ptd. Ltd.
Pearson Education North Asia Ltd.
Pearson Education Canada, Ltd.
Pearson Educación de Mexico, S.A. de C.V.
Pearson Education—Japan
Pearson Education Malaysia Pte. Ltd.
Pearson Education, *Upper Saddle River, New Jersey*

10 9 8 7 6 5 4 3 2 1
ISBN: 0-13-048343-5

Preface

This book is about learning mathematics—about children learning mathematics. It is also about teachers creating a learning environment that supports and encourages children to build understandings, make connections, reason, and solve problems.

About the Audience

Preservice teachers will develop an understanding of the content of school mathematics programs and formulate a teaching methodology for the meaningful learning of mathematics. Inservice teachers who wish to explore current thinking about mathematics teaching and learning will find the book a valuable source of theoretical and practical ideas for involving children in meaningful problem-solving tasks and for having children reflect, talk, and write about mathematics.

Teachers will be challenged to reflect on their personal views of mathematics, on how children learn mathematics, and on classroom environments that help children understand mathematics. The more the reader becomes actively involved with the activities, problems, video, and children's literature features in this book, the greater the quality of the reflection will be and, ultimately, the more the reader will learn.

About Our Approach to Mathematics Learning

The vision of mathematics learning presented in this text places the child at the center. Supporting this vision are the following beliefs:

- *Children construct for themselves the mathematics they come to know.* Therefore, the approach to mathematics learning is an active one, wherein children engage in problem-solving activities that are discovery oriented or open-ended. Chapter 3 describes the importance of teaching problem solving to children, including the problem-solving process and problem-solving strategies. Subsequent chapters reinforce the role that problem solving plays in teaching children to reason and to make mathematical connections.

- *Communication is an important part of the learning process.* Questions embedded in this text's activities are posed to encourage students to reflect on what they are doing in order to clarify ideas for themselves and to share their thoughts with classmates. Also, students are invited to record their work or findings through various modes such as drawings, diagrams, descriptions, and symbols.

- *An active, child-centered approach requires the use of manipulative materials and technology.* Within each chapter, appropriate manipulative materials and technology are identified and numerous activities that incorporate their use are described. Look for the calculator logo that identifies math concepts and strategies that allow for appropriate use of calculators.

- *The teacher's role is to provide children with opportunities to explore mathematics and help them observe and describe patterns and make generalizations about the mathematics topics and relationships they are exploring.* To support teacher development, chapter topics link classroom practice and the NCTM Principles and Standards for 2000, connecting real-world problems, concrete models, language, symbols, and hands-on activities.

We believe the ideas presented in this text support and exemplify the vision of learning and teaching mathematics as encouraged by the *Principles and Standards for School Mathematics,* published by the National Council of Teachers of Mathematics (NCTM) in 2000, which build on NCTM's recommendations for the *Curriculum and Evaluation Standards for School Mathematics* (1989), the *Professional Standards for Teaching Mathematics* (1991), and the *Assessment Standards for School Mathematics* (1995). These documents recommend teaching mathematics from a problem-solving perspective and making communication, reasoning and proof, connections, and representations the primary foci of mathematics learning. These recommendations are highlighted throughout the text in the Principles and Standards Link features, as well as the Classroom Clips, which help readers connect the recommendations of the new standards to Annenberg video segments and the topics in each chapter.

About the Revision

Besides updating all materials with new research, streamlining prose and activities alike, in this edition we have looked closely at the changing needs of middle-school mathematics teachers. You'll find strengthened treatment of middle-school issues, particularly in chapter 14, "Developing Geometric Thinking and Spatial Sense," and chapter 17, "Developing Integers and Algebraic Thinking." We have also chosen a new video, "Polygons and Angles: Discovery," which emphasizes excellent teaching and learning in middle-school classrooms. This video is contextualized throughout chapters in new Video Link features, as well as an entirely new Classroom Clip feature, which integrates video footage, chapter content, and NCTM's Process Standards.

In keeping with our constant effort to integrate appropriate technology into the text and classroom, we have added a new feature to this edition. Technology Links, found in every chapter, highlight and explore specific mathematics-related Internet sites that can be used in the college classroom as well as in elementary and middle-school classrooms.

About the Text Features

We have updated and strengthened the many unique text features aimed at helping readers learn how to teach children mathematics. Readers are encouraged to use all of these features to maximize their own learning.

- **Key Concepts,** at the beginning of each chapter, list the most important topics included in the chapter and serve as an advance organizer for the reader.
- **Focus Questions,** at the beginning of each chapter, include questions based on the key concepts to help focus the reader's attention while studying each chapter. Link to our Companion Website at www.prenhall.com/cathcart to discuss these questions with a global audience by means of our threaded message board.
- **Principles and Standards Links,** throughout each chapter, connect the content of each chapter with the NCTM Curriculum and Evaluation Standards for 2000, the Professional Standards for Teaching Mathematics, and the Assessment Standards.

- **Technology Links,** new in each chapter, look at meaningful website activities for use in the college classroom as well as in elementary and middle-school classrooms. Link to each highlighted site directly from our Companion Website at www.prenhall.com/cathcart.
- **Video Links** throughout chapters connect topics presented in the textbook to videos of outstanding teachers in their own classrooms, including a new video, "Polygons and Angles: Discovery," emphasizing the middle-school mathematics classroom. This feature includes reflection questions to strengthen readers' understanding of each topic and its link to practice.
- **Classroom Clips** are full-color features that highlight outstanding video segments focused on exemplary teachers engaged with children in math classrooms, including a new Classroom Clip highlighting the new middle-school video. Each of these Classroom Clips provides readers with an opportunity to closely consider lessons designed to develop children's understanding of mathematics topics and to consider how each lesson exemplifies the recommendations of the NCTM Process Standards. In addition, these video inserts include ideas for extensions and connections for each math lesson.
- **Literature Links** throughout chapters connect topics presented in the text to children's books. The Literature Links also include ideas for extension activities that readers can use with children to enhance their understanding of the topic.
- **Activities,** prolific throughout each chapter, provide practical applications related to chapter topics. These activities are appropriate for the college classroom as well as the elementary and middle-school classrooms.
- **For Your Journal,** at the end of each chapter, asks readers to respond to specific questions in a math journal to strengthen and help them to reflect on their understanding of chapter topics. Instructors may choose to require students to respond to one or more of these questions as part of a course assignment. Use these questions to create an online journal by linking to the Online Journal module of our Companion Website at www.prenhall.com/cathcart.
- **For Your Portfolio,** at the end of each chapter, describes activities or assignments that readers may complete to help them connect the chapter's key concepts to classroom practice. Instructors may choose to include one or more of these items as course assignments. Compile these pieces for a mathematics teaching portfolio online by clicking on the Online Portfolio module of our Companion Website at www.prenhall.com/cathcart.
- **Links to the Internet,** located at the end of each chapter, lead readers to helpful Internet destinations where they can find valuable resources to

assist their development of teaching strategies. Link to all highlighted websites directly from our Companion Website at www.prenhall.com/cathcart.

- **Blackline Masters,** which can be found in the Appendix, are formatted so they may be copied and used as manipulatives. Readers can handle them to help develop their own understandings of mathematical concepts and then copy them for children in their K–8 classrooms.

About Text Supplements

A **Companion Website** is available for professors and students who adopt this text. It can be accessed via the Internet at www.prenhall.com/cathcart. This truly text-integrated Companion Website is designed to guide readers in their study of the text content and includes access to self-assessments and resources that allow users to link directly to Web destinations identified in Technology Links and Links to the Internet features. Students who use the self-assessments will get immediate feedback and clues for finding correct answers as appropriate. Test results can be e-mailed to course instructors. With the Companion Website, students will also have an opportunity to engage in interactive peer discussions by answering the Focus Questions, which are found at the beginning of each chapter, in the threaded Message Board. In addition, professors who complete the Syllabus Manager feature can make the course syllabus, course assignments, and due dates available to students online.

An **Instructor's Manual** for course instructors includes chapter objectives, strategies for developing major concepts presented in each chapter, transparency masters, and additional projects and discussion questions. The manual is free to adopters of this textbook.

Five videos, free to adopting professors, accompany this text. These text-integrated videos are part of the Annenberg/CPB Math and Science Collection and include the following titles:

The Annenberg/CPB Math and Science Collection

- *The Missing Link (volume 5): Polygons and Angles: Discovery*
- *Whole Number Computation: Teaching Math: A Video Library, K–4; Tape 7*
- *Concepts of Whole Number Operations: Teaching Math: A Video Library, K–4; Tape 4*
- *Geometry and Spatial Sense: Teaching Math: A Video Library, K–4; Tape 8*
- *Fraction Tracks: Teaching Math: A Video Library, 5–8; Tape 1*

Acknowledgments

We appreciate the thoughtful comments and suggestions made by the reviewers for this edition: Lowell Gadberry, Southwestern Oklahoma State University; William Lacefield III, Mercer University; Walter Ryan, Indiana University; and Gertrude R. Toher, Hofstra University. We also appreciate the help given to us by the reviewers of the previous editions: Anna O. Graeber, University of Maryland; Anne Madsen, University of New Nexico; and Ann S. Massey, Indiana University of Pennsylvania. Further, we are grateful for the insights of the reviewers of the Canadian version: Catherine Ebbs, University of Windsor; Douglas Edge, University of Western Ontario; John Grant McLoughlin, Okanagan College; Helen Horsman, University of Saskatchewan; Wilfred L. Innerd, University of Windsor; Werner Liedtke, University of Victoria; Joan McDuff, Queen's University; Howard Riggs, McGill University; Daiyo Sawada, University of Alberta; Thomas Schroeder, State University of New York at Buffalo; Frances M. Butler, Weber State University; Arnold R. Davis, University of Tennessee-Knoxville; Lorel Preston Huhnke, Westminster College; Annette Ricks Leitze, Ball State University; Walter F. Ryan, Indiana University Southeast; Pearl Solomon, St. Thomas Aquinas College; Marilyn E. Strutchens, University of Maryland; and Judith A. Wells, University of Southern Indiana. Their insightful comments became the guidelines used to improve the organization of this text and the applications included.

We would also like to thank Dr. Patricia S. Moyer of George Mason University for her contribution in developing the children's Literature Links, and Dr. Sally Robison for her assistance in revising chapters 14 and 17. We are also grateful to several colleagues at San Diego State University, including Dr. Lisa L. Clement, for her help in developing the section on integrating standards that appears in chapter 1; Gail Moriarty and Dr. Susan Nickerson, for their help in revising chapter 9; and Judy Bippert, for her help in revising chapter 17.

In addition, the suggestions and encouragement received from colleagues and students at San Diego State University, numerous teachers in San Diego City Schools, and the children, teachers, and administrators at Rosa Parks Elementary School were invaluable. Thank you, all.

G. Cathcart
Y. Pothier
J. Vance
N. Bezuk

Brief Contents

Contents

Chapter 6 Developing Understanding of Numeration   100

Chapter 7 Developing Whole-Number Operations: Meaning of Operations   129

**Chapter 8 Developing Whole-
Number Operations: Mastering the
Basic Facts   150**

**Chapter 9 Estimation and
Computational Procedures for Whole
Numbers   166**

CHAPTER 10 Developing Fraction Concepts   203

Chapter 11 Developing Fraction Computation   228

CHAPTER 1

Teaching Mathematics: Influences and Directions

KEY CONCEPTS ▶

✔ **National and state standards**

✔ **National and international assessment**

FOCUS QUESTIONS ▶

When you have finished studying this chapter, you should be able to answer the following questions:

1. What are some of the factors that influence the teaching of mathematics?

2. Why are national and global assessments such as NAEP and TIMSS important to mathematics curriculum development?

3. How might national, state, and local mathematics curriculum standards influence classroom teaching?

"More than ever before, Americans need to think for a living; more than ever before they need to think mathematically."

(Mathematical Sciences Education Board and National Research Council, 1990, p. 3)

Mathematics permeates all facets of our lives. Jennifer organizes her collection of baseball cards into a five-by-eight array and wonders how many cards she has. Marco counts his change to be sure he has received the correct amount after buying his brother a birthday present. Mom mentally calculates 15 percent of the family's restaurant bill and adds that on as gratuity. Elementary-school children gather data on the weather for a week, exchange their data with other schools around the world via telecommunications, and graph this information in order to discuss and write about similarities and differences.

Often the mathematics in real-life situations is not recognized until after one stops and reflects. Children need help in recognizing that mathematics is all around them. They need the right kind of experiences to appreciate the fact that mathematics is a common human activity and that it is important to their present and future well-being.

Teaching mathematics is both challenging and stimulating because significant changes are taking place in mathematics education. New insights, new materials and, of course, children who are growing up in an ever-changing society dictate a different approach to the teaching of mathematics. This chapter is about the various factors that influence the principles, practices, and future direction of mathematics and mathematics instruction. ✔

INFLUENCES ON MATHEMATICS EDUCATION

Many factors and movements have influenced what and how mathematics is taught. It is not important for teachers to be experts on these influences, but it is necessary for teachers to have an awareness of them to better understand the current state of the art and to put future directions into perspective. The following sections address some of the major influences. Although these influences are not exhaustive, they will be discussed in the context of eight broad categories: psychological, professional, technological, language, societal, research, learner, and teacher.

Psychological Influences

Theories about how children learn have ranged from the mental discipline theory prominent in the late nineteenth century to the current constructivist point of view (see Chapter 2). Under the former, children were given many lengthy and often complex problems, particularly computations, because this kind of exercise "strengthened" the mind. The constructivist view maintains that children "construct" their own understanding of mathematical ideas by means of mental activity or through interacting with physical models of the ideas. For example, given a set of blocks that represent our place-value numeration system, children may initially build roads and towers but will, with appropriate suggestions from the teacher, soon begin to structure their play by organizing the blocks by size, resulting in a representation of numbers. The teacher's role is to provide appropriate activities and experiences rather than complex problems.

How children learn mathematics is examined in more depth in Chapter 2. The purpose of introducing it here is to include learning theories as one of the major influences on what and how mathematics is taught.

Professional Influences

Professional organizations have had a significant influence on mathematics in the schools. In the 1970s, the Back-to-the-Basics movement stressed the three Rs—reading, writing, and arithmetic (Morgan & Robinson, 1976). In mathematics, this often meant a heavier emphasis on addition, subtraction, multiplication, and division of whole numbers and fractions and virtual omission of other important topics. The emphasis was on skills needed for survival in a nontechnological age.

In 1977, the National Council of Supervisors of Mathematics (NCSM) published a reaction to the Back-to-the-Basics movement. The council agreed that computational skills were important, but it identified 10 basic skill areas, with problem solving as the principal area. Also in 1977, the National Council of Teachers of Mathematics (NCTM) published a companion statement that included the following:

> In a total mathematics program, students need more than arithmetic skill and understanding. They need to develop geometric intuition as an aid to problem solving. They must be able to interpret data. Without these and many other mathematical understandings, citizens are not mathematically functional. Yes, let us stress basics, but let us stress them in the context of total mathematics instruction. (p. 18)

In 1988, the NCSM updated its 1977 position statement. The new statement, entitled *Essential Mathematics for the 21st Century,* contained 12 components—problem solving, communicating mathematical ideas, mathematical reasoning, applying mathematics to everyday situations, alertness to the reasonableness of results, estimation, appropriate computational skills, algebraic thinking, measurement, geometry, statistics, and probability. In addition to these 12 components, the NCSM paper discussed the importance of the learning climate, technology, and evaluation in the mathematics program.

The NCTM also developed a statement, entitled *An Agenda for Action,* to provide direction for mathematics education in the 1980s. The Agenda contained eight major recommendations, each with numerous subrecommendations. The first recommendation was that "problem solving be the focus of school mathematics in the 1980s" (NCTM, 1980, p. 1). Note that the emphasis from both of these organizations was on problem solving. As a result of these recommendations, curriculum developers included more problem-solving activities in their materials.

Later in the 1980s, the NCTM, in planning for the 1990s, acknowledged that much criticism had been leveled at school mathematics during the 1980s. International studies showed that children in the United States did not fare very well on tests of mathematics proficiency compared with children in some other countries (Lapointe, Mead, & Phillips, 1989; Travers & McKnight, 1984). In an effort to improve this situation, NCTM developed a set of standards for school mathematics, published in 1989, entitled *Curriculum and Evaluation Standards for School Mathematics* (hereafter referred to as the Curriculum Standards). The Curriculum Standards described criteria for a quality mathematics curriculum from kindergarten through the 12th grade, including what children should learn and strategies for teaching the recommended material.

The NCTM recognized that teaching was another important influence on children's learning, but teaching was not addressed in the Curriculum Standards. The NCTM subsequently produced a companion document: *Profes-*

sional Standards for Teaching Mathematics (hereafter referred to as the Professional Standards) (NCTM, 1991). This document outlined six standards for teaching mathematics, eight standards for the evaluation of the teaching of mathematics, six standards for the professional development of teachers of mathematics, and four standards for the support and development of mathematics teachers and teaching.

A belief that "new assessment strategies and practices need to be developed that will enable teachers and others to assess students' performance in a manner that reflects the NCTM's reform vision for school mathematics" (NCTM, 1995, p. 1) prompted the NCTM to develop and publish in 1995 a third set of standards, *Assessment Standards for School Mathematics* (hereafter referred to as the Assessment Standards). This document outlines six mathematics assessment standards and then discusses their use for purposes such as monitoring children's progress, making instructional decisions, evaluating children's achievement, and assessing programs and is discussed in detail in Chapter 4.

In the late 1990s, NCTM convened a group of mathematics education experts to review and revise the 1989 Curriculum Standards. The resulting document, entitled *Principles and Standards for School Mathematics* (NCTM, 2000) was released in April 2000. (Hereafter, this document will be referred to as the Principles and Standards.) This section highlights the contents and vision of the Principles and Standards and emphasizes the implications of the Principles and Standards for classroom teaching.

The Principles and Standards contains a set of principles and content and process standards for prekindergarten through Grade 12. According to the NCTM (2000):

> The Principles describe particular features of high-quality mathematics education. The Standards describe

the mathematical content and processes that students should learn. Together, the Principles and Standards constitute a vision to guide educators as they strive for the continual improvement of mathematics education in classrooms, schools, and educational systems. (p. 11)

The following section presents an overview of each of these elements.

The framework of the Principles and Standards for School Mathematics

The principles. "The principles are statements reflecting basic precepts that are fundamental to a high-quality mathematics education" (NCTM, 2000, p. 6). These principles guide educators in making decisions about teaching and learning and in creating a classroom environment conducive to learning. Table 1-1 lists these principles.

> **TABLE 1-1**

PRINCIPLES FOR SCHOOL MATHEMATICS

The six principles for school mathematics address overarching themes:
- *Equity.* Excellence in mathematics education requires equity—high expectations and strong support for all students.
- *Curriculum.* A curriculum is more than a collection of activities: It must be coherent, focused on important mathematics, and well articulated across the grades.
- *Teaching.* Effective mathematics teaching requires understanding what students know and need to learn and then challenging and supporting them to learn it well.
- *Learning.* Students must learn mathematics with understanding, actively building new knowledge from experience and prior knowledge.
- *Assessment.* Assessment should support the learning of important mathematics and furnish useful information to both teachers and students.
- *Technology.* Technology is essential in teaching and learning mathematics; it influences the mathematics that is taught and enhances students' learning.

Source: From *Principles and Standards for School Mathematics,* 2000, p. 11.

These six principles describe important issues that are woven into all aspects of school mathematics programs. It is important that teachers consider these principles when planning mathematics instruction and designing mathematics learning environments.

The standards.   The Principles and Standards includes 10 standards that describe the mathematical content and processes that students should know and be able to use. These standards include five *content standards,* which describe the mathematics content students should know, and five *process standards,* which describe the mathematical processes students should be able to use in prekindergarten through Grade 12. These standards are listed in Tables 1-2 and 1-3.

The grade bands.   Athough each of the content and process standards applies across all grade levels from prekindergarten through Grade 12, the Principles and Standards also describes in greater detail what students should know and be able to do at different points across the grade continuum. The Principles and Standards discusses four grade-level ranges, called "grade bands," which cluster the grade levels into four grade bands: Prekindergarten through Grade 2, Grades 3 through 5, Grades 6 through 8, and Grades 9 through 12.

According to the Principles and Standards, "even though each of these ten Standards applies to all grades, emphases will vary both within and between the grade bands. For instance, the emphasis on number is greatest in prekindergarten through grade 2, and by grades 9–12, number receives less instructional attention" (NCTM 2000, p. 30).

Table 1-4 compares key features of the Principles and Standards with the 1989 Standards. In particular, please note the differences in the grade bands and the fact that in the Principles and Standards, standards are the same for each grade band, whereas different standards are applied for each grade band in the 1989 Curriculum and Evaluation Standards.

Content standards and expectations in each grade band   Within each grade band, the Principles and Standards describes more specifically what children should know in relation to each content standard. This is referred to as "Expectations." The expectations for each grade band help teachers understand what students are expected to understand within each content standard. Tables 1-5 and 1-6 give examples of content standards and expectations for two different content standards, number and operations, and data analysis and probability, within two different grade bands, Grades 3 through 5 and Grades 6 through 8, respectively.

TABLE 1-2

CONTENT STANDARDS FOR SCHOOL MATHEMATICS

NUMBERS AND OPERATIONS	ALGEBRA	GEOMETRY	MEASUREMENT	DATA ANALYSIS AND PROBABILITY
Instructional programs from prekindergarten through grade 12 should enable all students to—				
• Understand numbers, ways of representing numbers, relationships among numbers, and number systems. • Understand meanings of operations and how they relate to one another. • Compare fluently and make reasonable estimates.	• Understand patterns, relations, and functions. • Represent and analyze mathematical situations and structures using algebraic symbols. • Use mathematical models to represent and understand quantitative relationships.	• Analyze characteristics and properties of two- and three-dimensional geometric shapes and develop mathematical arguments about geometric relationships. • Specify locations and describe spatial relationships using coordinate geometry and other representational systems. • Apply transformations and use symmetry to analyze mathematical situations. • Use visualization, spatial reasoning, and geometric modeling to solve problems.	• Understand measurable attributes of objects and the units, systems, and processes of measurement. • Apply appropriate techniques, tools, and formulas to determine measurements.	• Formulate questions that can be addressed with data and collect, organize, and display relevant data to answer them. • Select and use appropriate statistical methods to analyze data. • Develop and evaluate inferences and predictions that are based on data. • Understand and apply basic concepts of probability.

Source: From *Principles and Standards for School Mathematics,* 2000, pp. 392–400.

TABLE 1-3 ▷

PROCESS STANDARDS FOR SCHOOL MATHEMATICS

PROBLEM SOLVING	REASONING AND PROOF	COMMUNICATION	CONNECTIONS	REPRESENTATION

Instructional programs from prekindergarten through grade 12 should enable all students to—

• Build new mathematical knowledge through problem solving. • Solve problems that arise in mathematics and in other contexts. • Apply and adapt a variety of appropriate strategies to solve problems. • Monitor and reflect on the process of mathematical problem solving.	• Recognize reasoning and proof as fundamental aspects of mathematics. • Make and investigate mathematical conjectures. • Develop and evaluate mathematical arguments and proofs. • Select and use various types of reasoning and methods of proof.	• Organize and consolidate mathematical thinking through communication. • Communicate mathematical thinking coherently and clearly to peers, teachers, and others. • Analyze and evaluate the mathematical thinking and strategies of others. • Use the language of mathematics to express mathematical ideas precisely.	• Recognize and use connections among mathematical ideas. • Understand how mathematical ideas interconnect and build on one another to produce a coherent whole. • Recognize and apply mathematics in contexts outside of mathematics.	• Create and use representations to organize, record, and communicate mathematical ideas. • Select, apply, and translate among mathematical representations to solve problems. • Use representations to model and interpret physical, social, and mathematical phenomena.

Source: From *Principles and Standards for School Mathematics,* 2000, p. 402.

TABLE 1-4 ▷

COMPARISON OF NCTM'S *PRINCIPLES AND STANDARDS FOR SCHOOL MATHEMATICS* (NCTM 2000) WITH NCTM'S *CURRICULUM AND EVALUATION STANDARDS* (1989)

	PSSM 2000	CURRICULUM AND EVALUATION STANDARDS, 1989	
Grade Bands	PreK-2 3–5 6–8 9–12	K-4 5–8 9–12	
Standards in Each Grade Band	10	13	
Standards	Same for all grade-level ranges	Different for each grade-level range	
		Gr. K-4	*Gr. 5–8*
	Number and Operation	Number Sense and Numeration	Number and Number Relationships
		Concepts of Whole-Number Operations	Number Systems and Number Theory
		Whole-Number Computation	Computation and Estimation
		Estimation	
		Fractions and Decimals	
	Algebra	Patterns and Relationships	Patterns and Functions
			Algebra
	Geometry	Geometry and Spatial Sense	Geometry
	Measurement	Measurement	Measurement
	Data Analysis and Probability	Statistics and Probability	Statistics
			Probability
	Problem Solving	Mathematics as Problem Solving	Mathematics as Problem Solving
	Reasoning and Proof	Mathematics as Reasoning	Mathematics as Reasoning
	Communication	Mathematics as Communication	Mathematics as Communication
	Connections	Mathematical Connections	Mathematical Connections
	Representation		

▰▰▰ **TABLE 1-5** ▶

Content Standards for Number and Operations for Grades 3–5

CONTENT STANDARD	STUDENT EXPECTATIONS
Instructional programs from preK–12 should enable all students to—	*In grades 3–5 all students should—*
Understand numbers, ways of representing numbers, relationships among numbers, and number systems	• understand the place-value structure of the base-ten number system and be able to represent and compare whole numbers and decimals; • recognize equivalent representations for the same number and generate them by decomposing and composing numbers; • develop understanding of fractions as parts of unit wholes, as parts of a collection, as locations on number lines, and as divisions of whole numbers; • use models, benchmarks, and equivalent forms to judge the size of fractions; • recognize and generate equivalent forms of commonly used fractions, decimals, and percents; • explore numbers less than 0 by extending the number line and through familiar applications; • describe classes of numbers (e.g., odds, primes, squares, and multiples) according to characteristics such as the nature of their factors.
Understand meanings of operations and how they relate to one another	• understand various meanings of multiplication and division; • understand the effects of multiplying and dividing whole numbers; • identify and use relationships between operations, such as division as the inverse of multiplication, to solve problems; • understand and use properties of operations, such as the distributivity of multiplication over addition.
Compute fluently and make reasonable estimates	• develop fluency with basic number combinations for multiplication and division and use these combinations to mentally compute related problems, such as 30 × 50; • develop fluency in adding, subtracting, multiplying, and dividing whole numbers; • develop and use strategies to estimate the results of whole-number computations and to judge the reasonableness of such results; • develop and use strategies to estimate computations involving fractions and decimals in situations relevant to students' experience; • use visual models, benchmarks, and equivalent forms to add and subtract commonly used fractions and decimals; • select appropriate methods and tools for computing with whole numbers from among mental computation, estimation, calculators, and paper and pencil according to the context and nature of the computation and use the selected method or tools.

Source: From *Principles and Standards for School Mathematics,* 2000, p. 148.

Integrating the content and process standards The Content and Process Standards should not be viewed as discrete elements but rather should be integrated throughout mathematics instruction. Teachers should consider how to link mathematics content and processes by integrating these standards into mathematics lessons and activities.

A sample lesson integrating content standards and process standards in grades preK–2 The following section contains a sample lesson within the number and operations content standard, appropriate for Grade 2 children. Before the lesson is described, the broad goals of the lesson are listed, using the appropriate expectations from the Grades PreK–2 Content Standard, Number and Operations (NCTM, 2000, p. 78), which are listed in Table 1-7. After a brief summary of the lesson, examples of the children's work are provided. The reader will then find a brief description of how each process standard (problem solving, reasoning and proof, communication, connections, and representation) is woven into

this particular lesson. Although every process standard comes into play in some way during the lesson, not every aspect of each process standard is addressed in this lesson.

Sample lesson In this example, second graders will solve problems involving multidigit addition to accomplish the following:

• Use multiple models to develop initial understandings of place value and the base-ten number system.

• Develop a sense of whole numbers and represent and use them in flexible ways, including relating, composing, and decomposing numbers.

• Develop and use strategies for whole-number computations, with a focus on addition and subtraction.

• Develop fluency with basic number combinations for addition and subtraction.

• Use a variety of methods and tools to compute . . . . (NCTM, 2000, p. 78)

TABLE 1-6

CONTENT STANDARDS FOR DATA ANALYSIS AND PROBABILITY FOR GRADES 6–8

CONTENT STANDARD	STUDENT EXPECTATIONS
Instructional programs from preK–12 should enable all students to—	*In grades 6–8 all students should—*
Formulate questions that can be addressed with data and collect, organize, and display relevant data to answer them	• Formulate questions, design studies, and collect data about a characteristic shared by two populations or different with one population. • Select, create, and use appropriate graphical representations of data, including histograms, box plots, and scatterplots.
Select and use appropriate statistical methods to analyze data	• Find, use, and interpret measures of center and spread, including mean and interquartile range. • Discuss and understand the correspondence between data sets and their graphical representations, especially histograms, stem-and-leaf plots, box plots, and scatterplots.
Develop and evaluate inferences and predications that are based on data	• Use observations about differences between two or more samples to make conjectures about the populations from which the samples were taken. • Make conjectures about possible relationships between two characteristics of a sample on the basis of scatterplots of the data and approximate lines to fit. • Use conjectures to formulate new questions and plan new studies to answer them.
Understand and apply basic concepts of probability	• Understand and use appropriate terminology to describe complementary and mutually exclusive events. • Use proportionality and a basic understanding of probability to make and test conjectures about the results of experiments and simulations. • Compute probabilities for simple compound events, using such methods as organized lists, tree diagrams, and area models.

Source: From *Principles and Standards for School Mathematics*, 2000, p. 248.

TABLE 1-7

CONTENT STANDARDS AND EXPECTATIONS: NUMBER AND OPERATIONS, PREK-2

CONTENT STANDARD	EXPECTATIONS
Instructional programs from preK–12 should enable all students to—	*In prekindergarten through Grade 2 all students should—*
Understand numbers, ways of representing numbers, relationships among numbers, and number systems	• count with understanding and recognize "how many" in sets of objects; • use multiple models to develop initial understandings of place value and the base-ten number system; • develop understanding of the relative position and magnitude of whole numbers and of ordinal and cardinal numbers and their connections; • develop a sense of whole numbers and represent and use them in flexible ways, including relating, composing, and decomposing numbers; • connect number words and numerals to the quantities they represent, using various physical models and representations; • understand and represent commonly used fractions, such as $\frac{1}{4}, \frac{1}{3},$ and $\frac{1}{2}$.
Understand meanings of operations and how they relate to one another	• understand various meanings of addition and subtraction of whole numbers and the relationship between the two operations; • understand the effects of adding and subtracting whole numbers; • understand situations that entail multiplication and division, such as equal groupings of objects and sharing equally.
Compute fluently and make reasonable estimates	• develop and use strategies for whole-number computations, with a focus on addition and subtraction; • develop fluency with basic number combinations for addition and subtraction; • use a variety of methods and tools to compute, including objects, mental computation, estimation, paper and pencil, and calculators.

Source: From *Principles and Standards for School Mathematics*, 2000, p. 78.

Children are asked to solve the following problem in two different ways:

Ian has 186 shells in his collection. Over the summer he goes to the beach and collects 149 more shells. How many shells does Ian have now?

The teacher has arranged her classroom so that children have a variety of tools that they may use to solve this problem. Base-ten blocks, paper and pencil, and counting frames (that have 10 metal rods with 10 beads on each rod) are available. Children may select the tool that they are most comfortable working with to solve this problem.

As the teacher moves around the room, she asks the children to explain their approaches to her. Here are a few of their approaches:

Chris writes:

$$
\begin{array}{r}
186 \\
+\ 149 \\
\hline
200 \\
120 \\
+\ 15 \\
\hline
335
\end{array}
$$

He explains: "I added 100 and 100 to get 200; then 80 and 40 is 120, and 6 and 9 is 15. I added 200, 120, and 15 to get 335."

Sarah says:

"149 is only 1 away from 150, so 150 and 100 from the 186 is 250, and 80 more is 330, and 6 more is 336. Then I have to subtract the 1 so it is 335."

Pat uses base-ten blocks to solve the problem. Pat says:

"I took one flat for the 100 in 186 and 1 flat for the 100 in 149. I took 12 longs—8 for the 80 in 186 and 4 for the 40 in 149. I took 15 singles for the 6 in 186 and the 9 in 149. Then I counted like this, '100, 200', then the longs: '210, 220, 230, 240, 250, 260, 270, 280, 290, 300, 310, 320'; then the singles: '321, 322, 323, 324, 325, 326, 327, 328, 329, 330, 331, 332, 333, 334, 335.' So the answer is 335."

A.J. writes:

$$
\begin{array}{r}
11 \\
186 \\
+\ 149 \\
\hline
335
\end{array}
$$

She explains:

"First I added 6 and 9 to get 15. I wrote down the 5 and carried the 1. Then I added 8 and 4 to get 12, plus 1 is 13; I wrote down the 3 and carried the 1 to get 1 and 1 and 1 is 3. So my answer is 335."

How the process standards were used in this lesson   Each process standard was woven into the lesson within the content standard of number and operations. Although every process standard comes into play in some way during the lesson, not every aspect of each process standard is addressed. Table 1-8 describes how this was done in this lesson.

Integrating state and local standards with national math standards   In addition to helping children meet the national standards for mathematics, teachers need to think about helping the children meet state and local standards for mathematics learning. The following section shows how national, state, and local mathematics standards could be linked in two different mathematics activities, one on multiplication facts for Grades 3 through 5 and another on geometry for Grade 2.

Tables 1-9 and 1-10 contain sample lessons showing how national, state, and local standards can be implemented within a lesson.

Technological Influences

Modern school mathematics programs include calculator and computer activities. Many children have access to both calculators and computers at home. Indeed, today's society is technologically very different from that of just a few years ago. Teachers must prepare children to succeed in an electronic environment. The school mathematics curriculum will continue to be influenced by three major developments: the calculator, the computer, and interactive multimedia, including Internet access.

Calculators   In the Agenda for Action (NCTM, 1980), the council recommended that "mathematics take full advantage of the power of calculators and computers at all grade levels" (p. 1). The NCTM followed this recommendation with a published position statement in 1986 on the use of calculators in the mathematics classroom; in 1991, this statement was updated. This statement recommends that all children use calculators to explore and experiment with mathematical ideas, to develop and reinforce skills, to focus on problem-solving processes rather than the associated computation, to perform tedious computations, and to gain access to more advanced mathematical ideas (NCTM, February 1991). There is widespread support from mathematics educators for the use of calculators by children in classrooms (NCTM, 1991; Reys & Reys, 1987). Despite this support

TABLE 1-8 ▷

HOW THE NCTM (2000) PROCESS STANDARDS WERE IMPLEMENTED IN THE SAMPLE LESSON

PROCESS STANDARD	HOW IMPLEMENTED IN SAMPLE LESSON
Problem Solving What kinds of *problem solving* might children be engaged in?	By solving this problem in two different ways, students will • solve problems that arise in mathematics and in other contexts. • apply and adapt a variety of strategies to solve problems. • monitor and reflect on the process of problem solving. (p. 116) By asking the students to solve a problem in two different ways, the teacher challenges the students to consider the variety of strategies that can be used to solve this problem. The teacher can then follow up with questions about the approaches so that the children can reflect on the process of problem solving: Which approach was easier for you to use? Which approach was fastest for you to use? What if the numbers in the problem had been 200 and 350? Which approach would you prefer to use then? Could you pick an approach that you did not use this time and use it next time to solve the next problem? How are the approaches similar? How are they different?
Reasoning and Proof How could children demonstrate their arguments for *reasoning and proof?*	While discussing this problem, students will • make and investigate mathematical conjectures. (p. 122) When the students in the class complete their task of solving the problem in two different ways, the teacher asks the students to share. One student complains that Sarah did the problem wrong, since she started with 149 and not 186. Sarah claimed that it did not matter which number she started with. She would still get the same answer. The teacher asks the students if, when they add two numbers together, they will always get the same answer, no matter which number they begin with. Some agree and others disagree. The teacher asks a student to restate the conjecture while the teacher writes it on the board. The teacher decides that they will discuss and test the conjecture the following day and that this conjecture is something for the students to continue to think about.
Communication How might children *communicate* what they are thinking?	While discussing the various approaches classmates used to solve this problem, students will • communicate their mathematical thinking coherently and clearly to peers, teachers, and others. • analyze and evaluate the mathematical thinking and strategies of others. (p. 128) As stated above, when the students in the class complete their task, the teacher asks the students to share. The teacher prompts students who have difficulty explaining their thinking by asking, "Did you start by adding the hundreds or the ones? You have some interesting writing on your paper. Can you show that to us?" or "Has someone already shared an approach that was the same as yours? No? Can you explain what parts are different?" After several students have shared their approaches, the teacher asks about the relationships among and between the strategies: "Who had strategies that were the same? What made them the same? Who had strategies that were different? How were they different?"
Connections What kinds of *connections* might children make?	In reflecting on their problem-solving processes, students will • recognize and use connections among mathematical ideas. • recognize and apply mathematics in contexts outside of mathematics. (p. 132) When the teacher asks students to discuss the similarities and differences in approaches to solving the problem, she is helping students to recognize similarities and differences among mathematical ideas (for example, that Chris's approach and Pat's approach are similar in that they both begin with the hundreds, but they are different in that Chris next adds the tens (to get 120), while Pat adds one ten at a time to the hundreds (210, 220, 230, etc.). They are both using tens and hundreds to count, but they are counting in different ways. The students also began with a problem that occurs in everyday situations, so the students have an opportunity to recognize and apply mathematics in contexts outside of mathematics.
Representation How would children *represent* what they are thinking?	While creating solutions to this problem, students will • create and use representations to organize, record, and communicate mathematical ideas. • select, apply, and translate among mathematical representations to solve problems. (p. 136) The students in this class used a variety of representations to solve this problem. Chris and A. J. both represented the problem vertically on paper but used different approaches, and thus recorded their thinking in different ways. Pat represented the problem using base-ten blocks, whereas Sarah represented her thinking orally. The teacher encouraged the students to solve the problem in two ways to allow the children to think flexibly about the problem and also to encourage the students to use and make connections among different representations of the problem. For example, Pat's second approach was to write down with symbols what she had done with the base-ten blocks. She wrote: 100 + 100 200 + 10 210 + 10 220 + 10 230 + 10, etc. She was thus making a connection between her work with the base-ten blocks and her work with the symbols.

Source: From *Principles and Standards for School Mathematics,* 2000.

![TABLE 1-9]

SAMPLE LESSON: BASIC MULTIPLICATION FACTS FOR GRADES 3–5

PSSM STANDARD: IN GRADES 3–5 ALL STUDENTS SHOULD—

- develop fluency with basic number combinations for multiplication and division and use these combinations to mentally compute related problems, such as 30 × 50;
- develop fluency in adding, subtracting, multiplying, and dividing whole numbers. (NCTM, 2000, p. 148)

Example: In Grades 3–5, all children should develop fluency with single-digit multiplication facts and their related division facts by Grade 4 and use these facts to efficiently compute related problems (e.g., 30 × 50 is related to 3 × 5, 300 × 5, 15 × 100).

Sample State Standard for Grade 3: Memorize to automaticity the multiplication table for numbers between 1 and 10.

Sample Local School District Standard for Grade 3: Recall multiplication facts up to 10 × 10 and corresponding division facts.

To work toward these standards, children in Grade 3 will engage in the following math activity:

Title: Three in a Row
This activity requires children to work in groups of two to play a game that allows them to practice their multiplication facts.

Materials: Gameboard, two different color markers or game pieces (about 20 of each).

Procedure: One player places one of her game pieces on one number on the Factor Board. The second player places one of his game pieces on one number on the Factor Board, finds the product of the two factors, and places one of his game pieces on that number (product) on the Product Board. Then Player 1 moves her game piece on the Factor Board (without moving Player 2's game piece), finds the product, and covers it on the Product Board with one of her game pieces. Players alternate turns. The first player to get 3 of her or his game pieces in a row (horizontally, vertically, or diagonally) is the winner.

Three in a Row

15	9	27	32	28	36
20	16	5	81	6	14
4	21	48	12	30	3
18	45	8	35	40	1
24	63	42	56	25	64
7	10	54	49	72	2

Product Board

1	2	3	4	5	6	7	8	9

Factor Board

and easy access, calculators are not being optimally used in classrooms. In part, this may be due to parental, perhaps even teacher, fears that children will become dependent on the calculator, which in turn may have a negative effect on learning basic computational procedures and reduce the need to think. Research (e.g., Hembree & Dessart, 1986) has demonstrated that this is not the case; in fact, the opposite seems to be true.

Computers The NCTM published a position statement on technology in learning and teaching mathematics that stated that technology tools are integral to learning and teaching mathematics and recommended that technology should be used to enhance mathematics programs at all levels (NCTM, 1995).

When computers began to appear in schools in the early 1980s, programming was the major activity. Today, however, the computer is used in many other interesting ways. Indeed, the major thrust is to integrate the computer into the curriculum, to use it as a learning tool just as one would use counters, geometric shapes, or a calculator.

Both the quality and quantity of educational software have improved. It is now possible to select high-quality practice programs that are appropriate for the needs of specific students. Further, some software provides assistance or advice to users to help them understand the concepts they are practicing.

Problem-solving and higher-order thinking skills also can be developed using the computer as a tool. Simple ordering, classifying, patterning, and related problems

---

TABLE 1-10 ▶

SAMPLE LESSON: CONNECTING LITERATURE TO MATHEMATICS

PSSM STANDARD: **IN PREKINDERGARTEN THROUGH GRADE 2 ALL STUDENTS SHOULD—**

- recognize, name, build, draw, compare, and sort two- and three-dimensional shapes.
- describe attributes and parts of two- and three-dimensional shapes.
- recognize geometric shapes and structures in the environment and specify their location. (NCTM, 2000, p. 96)

Sample State Standard for Grade 2: Students identify and describe the attributes of common figures in the plane and of common objects in space.

Sample Local School District Standard for Grade 2: The student identifies and describes the elements that compose common figures in the plane and common objects in space.

To work toward these standards, students in Grade 2 will engage in the following math activity:

Title: Geometry Around Us
This activity helps students connect a children's book to geometry in their school environment.

Materials: Tar Beach, math journals, drawing/writing materials.

Procedure: Read *Tar Beach* (Ringgold, 1991). This book is about a girl who lives in New York City who likes to lie on a blanket on the roof of her apartment building at night, looking at the buildings and bridges all around her. She also likes to imagine flying over the city.

  Walk around the school grounds with your class. Discuss the geometric shapes the children see in the buildings and other objects near the school. Go back inside your classroom and have the children record in their math journals what they saw on their trip. Encourage children to draw pictures of what they saw and use mathematical language to name and describe the shapes they observed.

  (Lesson modification: Instead of walking around the school grounds, look around the inside of your classroom and describe the geometric shapes observed in the room.)

---

have been designed for younger students. Millie's Math House (Edmark Corporation, 1993), for example, contains six modules that provide experiences with these processes. Programs involving estimation, guess and test, and other problem-solving heuristics can be used with older children. Some mathematics problems can be solved with the use of computerized spreadsheets.

Simulations are another way the computer can be used to facilitate teaching and learning. Several popular programs exist that simulate the operation of a small business. Children can learn how to control variables to maximize profit (Friel, 1983). At a different level, children might program the computer to simulate the shaking of two dice and the recording of the sum, say 10,000 times. When you do that with real dice (the best way to introduce the concept), you toss the dice only a few times. Yet we know the laws of probability are based on "large" numbers. The computer, therefore, should be able to generate a better estimate.

Further, there are many good educational games (note the adjective *educational*) involving strategy that can be used to develop logical thinking skills. Obviously the computer can be used in many other ways as well, including generating mathematical materials that can be given to children, or having children use a word processor to write about what they have learned in mathematics or to write a report on a famous mathematician whom they have researched. It would also be interesting to develop a database on famous mathematicians or on characteristics of class members (Browning & Channell, 1992).

Interactive multimedia Interactive multimedia is a technology in which text, sound, graphics, photographs, motion pictures, and animation are incorporated into a learning package. Thousands of graphic images, film sequences, and text blocks can be stored on a CD-ROM. They can be randomly and almost instantly accessed by computer control. A child can manipulate mathematical images by responding to questions on a computer screen or by means of the computer mouse. Although this is not a replacement for doing an activity concretely, it can be a powerful learning device at the iconic level. Certainly, the integration of available technology will have a powerful influence on what and how mathematics is taught in the twenty-first century.

The Internet has become a resource for teaching. Lesson plans, classroom activities, and much more can be accessed via the Internet. You might start collecting these resources by visiting the home page of your local school board, university, or state government. The NCTM has many resources on its site at *http://www.nctm.org*. Numerous other excellent sites are available. Some excellent sites include the Eisenhower National Clearinghouse *(http://www.enc.org)* and Teachers' Net *(http://teachers.net)*.

Language Influences

Language and children's levels of language development are other factors that influence the nature of the mathematics program and how it is taught. Language is a part of the thinking process through which problems are solved, relationships are discovered, and ideas are formulated. The "new math" of the 1950s and 1960s emphasized strict use of precise mathematical terms. Admittedly, the language of mathematics is precise, and terms often have very specialized meanings. For example, the expression "fairly small" may be adequate in some settings, but if you were telling mission control how much rocket fuel was stored in and present for launching the shuttle, it is a totally inadequate expression of quantity. However, even in mathematics there is room for children's own language. Their expressions will develop into more precise language as concepts develop.

Currently many children in elementary and middle schools are English language learners whose first language is a language other than English. Teachers must be careful not to confuse limited ability to communicate in English with limited potential for learning mathematics. There are many teaching strategies available, such as sheltered instruction, ESL (English as a Second Language), and SDAIE (Specially Designed Academic Instruction in English) to help children learn English as they learn mathematics. Strategies that many good teachers use to help all children learn mathematics, such as cooperative groups, manipulative materials, and visuals, are especially helpful for English language learners as well.

The language used to convey a mathematical idea has a bearing on the child's understanding of the concept. For example, some children do not understand the term *perimeter*. If you talked about the "distance around" a shape, or if you drew a diagram and asked how much fencing would be needed to enclose the shape, many more children would understand and be able to successfully respond to the question. Likewise, the introduction of terms such as *commutative, associative,* and *distributive* serves no useful purpose if children have not already formed generalizations from repeated experiences illustrating these properties.

Another language-related factor of which you should be aware is children's ability to use mathematics vocabulary without really understanding the concepts. For example, most children can talk about a triangle, but there are many who think that a figure is not a triangle unless it is equilateral, or they might say that the figure on the left (see below) is a triangle. Others might argue that the figure at the right is not a triangle because one side is not horizontal or parallel to the bottom of the page. Children's misconceptions may be due to the visual images presented to them. Are the triangles drawn by the teacher always equilateral in appearance? Teachers must be aware of their own teaching behaviors.

Societal Influences

State government   Each state government is a major determinant of the curriculum in that state, developing curriculum standards or frameworks that guide the teaching of mathematics within the state. Some states also have a statewide textbook adoption process by which a list of textbooks that state funds may be used to purchase is developed. Many states also mandate statewide testing based on these standards. It is essential for teachers to become familiar with the curriculum standards and guidelines in their state.

School districts   Although many states have curriculum standards in place, many school districts develop their own curriculum standards. These local standards usually are based on the state and national standards. Teachers must be aware of the curriculum standards for their school district as well as those for their state.

Lobby groups   Sometimes lobby groups, and even individual parents, can influence curriculum decision makers at the national, state, or local level. For example, educators may form a lobby group in an attempt to influence curriculum on pedagogical grounds. At other times, business or industry might lobby for changes to make mathematics more application-oriented. Lobby groups have been quite effective in promoting change.

Bandwagons   Educators sometimes rally around some new proposal or idea, believing that it will be a remedy for certain problems. Many of these "new" ideas are sound and do result in positive changes; others are just bandwagons, but they do influence schools and the curriculum, at least temporarily. Regrettably, bandwagons often are not recognized as such until after the wheels have fallen off. For example, one curriculum innovation that might be considered a bandwagon was the individualized instruction movement of the 1970s. This movement was based on the idea that children were unique individuals and, as such, learned best independently and individually. In classrooms organized around this philosophy, each child had a learning contract and often spent most of the time working individually, sometimes in workbooks that were self-correcting. Regrettably, this philosophy of learning overlooked the fact that children are also social beings who can and do need to learn from each other as well as alone.

Research Influences

We are sometimes cynical about the ability of educational research to affect the teaching–learning process. Any one piece of research may have limited application or generalizability. However, when taken collectively, research can help us make decisions about what to teach and when and how to teach it.

One good example of research affecting school mathematics programs was William Brownell's research in the 1940s on subtraction algorithms (Brownell, 1947; Brownell & Moser, 1949). Prior to his work, the equal addition algorithm was widely used in North America. After his research, schools gradually switched to the decomposition algorithm, commonly known as the "borrowing" method, which is widely used in this country. Algorithms are discussed in Chapter 9.

It is difficult for a busy teacher to keep up with significant research findings. Strategies that help include reading journals such as *Teaching Children Mathematics* (formerly *The Arithmetic Teacher*) and *Mathematics Teaching in the Middle School* and attending conferences, inservice workshops, and university courses. For example, Suydam (1984) concluded that "lessons using manipulative materials have a higher probability of producing greater mathematics achievement than do lessons in which such materials are not used" (p. 27).

Several books include summaries of research with implications for classroom practice. Teachers may be interested in further investigating these classroom practices as part of their own action research projects. Jensen (1993) and Owens (1993) are examples of very readable books that relate research to classroom practice.

In many respects, the good and creative teacher is a researcher engaged in a variety of "action research" projects. Action research is teachers' ongoing formal evaluation of their own use of teaching strategies, children's activities, classroom organization, resource selection, and other applications of learning theory. We encourage teachers to actively reflect and self-evaluate what they do, what they use, and what happens in the classroom as a result. Such activities contribute to professional and personal growth and to the quality of mathematics instruction.

TIMSS The Third International Mathematics and Science Study (TIMSS) examined the mathematics and science achievement of children at five grade levels in more than 40 countries. TIMSS reported that the mathematics performance of U.S. eighth graders was close to that of other major industrialized nations such as Canada, England, and Germany but ranked well below the average of the 41 countries participating in the TIMSS study (Mullis, 1997; U.S. Department of Education, 1996). The U.S. fourth graders' performance was better, scoring above the international average (U.S. Department of Education, 1997).

NAEP The National Assessment of Educational Progress (NAEP) is a nationwide assessment of mathematics achievement conducted over time. The most recent NAEP study for which data are available was conducted in 1992 (Kenney & Silver, 1997) and is referred to as the Sixth Mathematics Assessment. This assessment was given to a sample of U.S. children nationwide at Grades 4 and 8. The framework for the Sixth Mathematics Assessment evaluated conceptual understanding, procedural understanding, and problem solving across the mathematics content areas of numbers and operations, measurement, geometry, data analysis, statistics and probability, and algebra and functions. This assessment showed that "students continue to maintain or improve their mastery of basic objectives for mathematics education" (Dossey & Mullis, 1997, p. 31). But it was also noted that there still is much to be done to help children nationally to enhance and expand their basic understanding of mathematics concepts.

Learner Influences

There is some evidence that suggests that beginning in late elementary school, some differences in the mathematics performance of boys and girls become noticeable. It is beyond the scope of this book to provide a detailed analysis of gender differences and their possible causes, although interested readers can refer to Meyer and Fennema (1992) for a very readable discussion of this issue. The following list presents observations that teachers should carefully consider.

Some facts
• Girls have lower enrollment rates in advanced Grade 12 and postsecondary mathematics and science courses. This results in limited career choices for women.

• Girls have less confidence in their mathematical competence, even when they have equal ability. Girls (and their parents) are more likely to attribute their success to hard work, whereas boys attribute their success to their own ability.

• Although the gap is narrowing, there are differences in performance at different levels and on different topics. Boys tend to score higher on higher-level thinking tasks, and girls on facts and computation items (Hyde, Fennema, & Lamon, 1990; Meyer, 1989). Male superiority in math seems to increase throughout the grades and as the difficulty level of the material increases.

The causes
• Although boys tend to score higher on spatial visualization tasks, there is no conclusive evidence that genetic factors cause the observed differences.

• The above point notwithstanding, some internal factors, such as affective considerations (motivation, interest, etc.) could be at work.

• Societal and familial expectations and perceptions (i.e., mathematics is a male domain) are thought to be major factors. External factors may also include increased access to technology for boys.

- Differential treatment of boys and girls in the classroom has been documented and may contribute to differences in performance. Teachers tend to interact more with boys than girls (calling on them more often and giving them more criticism and praise) and have higher achievement expectations for boys.

What can teachers do?   Perhaps more than anyone else, it is teachers who can help girls achieve equity in mathematics. Teachers should:

- Increase their interactions with girls on high-cognitive-level mathematics activities, encourage them to engage in independent learning, ensure that they attend to their tasks, and expect them to be successful.
- Place more emphasis on cooperative mathematics activities (which increase girls' achievement) and less emphasis on competitive activities.
- Provide girls with opportunities to work in same-gender groups of children rather than always using mixed-gender groups.

Teacher Influences

The influences previously identified imply that the next decade should be a very exciting time in which to be teaching mathematics in elementary and middle schools. However, we haven't mentioned the most important influence on what mathematics children learn and on how that learning is constructed: an enthusiastic, understanding, and knowledgeable teacher. The assertion that children should construct their own mathematical knowledge is not to suggest that the teacher should sit back and wait for it to happen. Rather, the teacher must actively observe and listen to children as they engage in and talk about their mathematical explorations. The teacher must be skilled in detecting seeds of mathematical concepts and in providing experiences that will enable those seeds to grow into mature understandings.

DIRECTIONS IN MATHEMATICS EDUCATION

What specific changes have occurred as a result of the preceding influences? There are many! Some were identified in the previous sections; others are described later in the chapter.

Looking into the future is difficult. It seems reasonable, however, to predict that problem solving, communication, reasoning and proof, connections within mathematics and between mathematics and other curricular areas, and the use of multiple representations will continue to be emphasized. Further, equity with regard to achievement, the use

of technology, an appropriate role for computation and estimation, and authentic assessment will be implemented. In addition, the issue of parent involvement to enhance children's learning must be considered. The following sections discuss each of these topics.

Problem Solving

Problem solving has always been an important part of a mathematics program. Since the late 1970s, however, it has received increased emphasis and probably will continue to be emphasized. This is in keeping with previously mentioned recommendations from both the NCTM and the NCSM. The increased emphasis on problem solving is evident in modern school texts and government curriculum guides, which now include many good problem-solving activities. This focus on problem solving will continue but will take on a different form as mathematics programs move toward developing mathematics from real-world settings. For example, children may be working on a stamp collection. The problem setting may be how to display the collection, which will probably lead children to explore an array. Multiplication problems arise when the children want to know how many stamps they have displayed in a particular array.

Researchers have been actively trying to document the characteristics of good problem solvers. Likewise, teachers have been experimenting with strategies (often called heuristics) that develop problem-solving skills in children. Problem solving is discussed in more detail in Chapter 3.

Communication

A major factor in shaping mathematics programs and teaching in the next decade concerns mathematics as communication. Children need an opportunity to reflect on and explain or justify their ideas and solutions both

PRINCIPLES AND STANDARDS LINK 1-2
Process Strand: Problem Solving

Instructional programs from prekindergarten through Grade 12 should enable all students to—

- build new mathematical knowledge through problem solving;
- solve problems that arise in mathematics and in other contexts;
- apply and adapt a variety of appropriate strategies to solve problems;
- monitor and reflect on the process of mathematical problem solving. (NCTM, 2000, p. 52)

PRINCIPLES AND STANDARDS LINK 1-3
Process Strand: Communication

Instructional programs from prekindergarten through Grade 12 should enable all students to—

- organize and consolidate their mathematical thinking through communication;
- communicate their mathematical thinking coherently and clearly to peers, teachers, and others;
- analyze and evaluate the mathematical thinking and strategies of others;
- use the language of mathematics to express mathematical ideas precisely. (NCTM, 2000, p. 60)

orally and in writing. There are two aspects to mathematical communication. First, mathematics is a language. Like English, Spanish, or any other language, mathematics has words (symbols) and semantic and syntactical rules; meaning is conveyed through mathematical symbols and their associated rules. A second aspect of mathematical communication involves the use of language within mathematics. This can be a powerful determinant of what is learned and how it is learned.

McKenzie (1990) draws a parallel (and highlights some differences) between reading for meaning and solving a mathematics problem with meaning. Both processes require the use of prior knowledge. Indeed, in both processes, children are continually predicting, sampling, confirming, self-correcting, and reprocessing—further evidence that reading is not an isolated subject to be taught at a particular time of day. Rather, reading for meaning is a process that must permeate all subject areas.

Talking, reading, writing, listening, and representing are important components of communication in mathematics. Children need to engage in all of them. Figure 1-1 suggests a variety of activities for each component that serve to reinforce each component's role in mathematical communication. In addition, asking thought-provoking questions will encourage quality communication. Table 1-11 suggests some categories of questions teachers should ask.

Reasoning and Proof

Mathematics programs often have been criticized for their emphasis on memorization of basic facts, rules, and principles. Today, however, more emphasis is being placed on mathematical reasoning and other higher-order thinking skills such as application, analysis, synthesis, and evaluation. These skills often are included in problem-solving activities. Problems such as the following help children develop reasoning skills: Sarah is younger than Alyssa. She is also older and shorter than Patrick. Alyssa is taller and younger than Juan. Juan is taller than Patrick.

LITERATURE LINK 1-1
Math in Our World
Scieszka, J., & Smith, L. (1995). *Math Curse.* New York: Penguin Books.

Children's literature provides a context through which mathematical concepts, patterns, problem solving, and real-world contexts may be explored. Many of us take the mathematics in the world around us for granted. In *Math Curse,* the main character thinks of everything in life as a math problem.

- Keep a math journal for 1 day, recording all of the mathematical problems you encounter. Be as creative as the narrator in the book and think about ways mathematics may be hidden in typical activities. Create a class book of children's "math curse" experiences.
- Record or bring cut-out examples from magazines, the newspaper, or the Internet of numbers and symbols used in everyday life. Examples might include (1) graphs or other statistics presented in a newspaper, (2) the dollar sign and decimal used in our monetary system, or (3) pictures of repeating or tessellating patterns in various designs. Design a class bulletin board called "Mathematics in the World Around Us."
- Communicate using the vocabulary of mathematical terms and symbols in the book. For example, investigate the Mayan numeral system of counting presented in the story. Discuss why the mathematics teacher in the book is named "Mrs. Fibonnaci."
- Model and solve some of the mathematical puzzles in the book and determine which ones are simply nonsense.
- Investigate the mathematical conversions, tables, measures, and terms illustrated on the end papers of the book.
- Books such as *Math in the Bath (and Other Fun Places Too)* (Atherlay, 1991) for younger children and *Counting on Frank* (Clement, 1994), whose witty narrator will amuse older children, show children how mathematics is a part of their everyday experiences.

Source: Dr. Patricia Moyer, George Mason University.

FIGURE 1-1

COMPONENTS OF MATHEMATICS AS COMMUNICATION

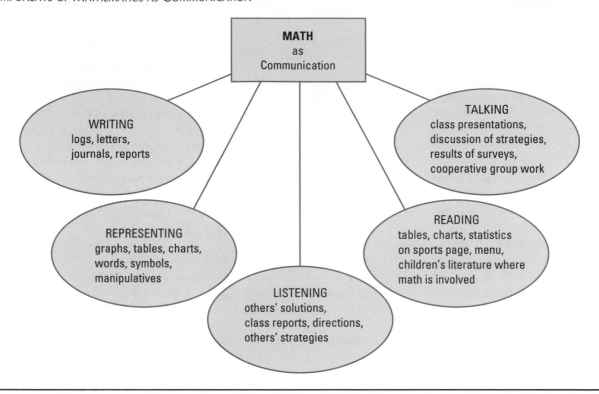

Source: M. Cappo & G. Osterman (1991). Teach students to communicate mathematically. *The Computing Teacher* (now *Learning & Leading with Technology*), 18(5), 34–39 © 1991. International Society for Technology in Education, (800) 336-5191, cust_svc@iste.org, www.iste.org. Reprinted with permission.

1. Arrange the four people by age.
2. Arrange the four people by height.

Connections

In the past, mathematics was often considered a subject unto itself. Frequently, it was broken down internally into many unrelated parts. In the future, however, teachers will find mathematics integrated throughout the curriculum and punctuated by real-world applications.

Integration with other school subjects
When children recognize that mathematics can be used in other subject areas, it becomes more relevant to them. For example, graphing is a skill that children can apply to problems in social studies and science. In art class, geometric concepts such as slides, flips, and turns can be applied to create a variety of interesting designs. And finally, as a language-learning assignment, children can write about the way they solved a problem, how they feel about the mathematics they are doing, or successes or difficulties they experience in understanding mathematics.

TABLE 1-11

QUESTIONS TO STIMULATE COMMUNICATION

CATEGORY	EXAMPLE
Classifying	How are these shapes alike? How are they different?
Hypothesizing	What if . . .? What could be true here?
Specializing	Can you give a specific example of how this works?
Generalizing	Can you see a pattern? Describe it.
Convincing	How do you know you are right?
Analyzing	Is this diagram correct? What is this all about?

 PRINCIPLES AND STANDARDS LINK 1-4
Process Strand: Reasoning and Proof

Instructional programs from prekindergarten through Grade 12 should enable all students to—

• recognize reasoning and proof as fundamental aspects of mathematics;
• make and investigate mathematical conjectures;
• develop and evaluate mathematical arguments and proofs;
• select and use various types of reasoning and methods of proof. (NCTM, 2000, p. 56)

PRINCIPLES AND STANDARDS LINK 1-5
Process Strand: Connections

Instructional programs from prekindergarten through Grade 12 should enable all students to—

- recognize and use connections among mathematical ideas;
- understand how mathematical ideas interconnect and build on one another to produce a coherent whole;
- recognize and apply mathematics in contexts outside of mathematics. (NCTM, 2000, p. 64)

PRINCIPLES AND STANDARDS LINK 1-6
Process Strand: Representation

Instructional programs from prekindergarten through Grade 12 should enable all students to—

- create and use representations to organize, record, and communicate mathematical ideas;
- select, apply, and translate among mathematical representations to solve problems;
- use representations to model and interpret physical, social, and mathematical phenomena. (NCTM, 2000, p. 67)

Integration with real-world settings In the real world, people solve mathematics problems that arise from a particular setting. Pilots use mathematics for navigational problem solving, firefighters apply measurement concepts and processes when they fight fires, interior designers employ mathematics when they order carpeting and wallpaper, and so on. The 1995 NCTM yearbook, *Connecting Mathematics Across the Curriculum,* focuses on mathematics in the real world. Mathematics is holistic in the sense that integrative threads that connect other content areas in the curriculum will be explicitly identified so that children can "see" the connections. Some connections are mentioned in subsequent chapters of this book. One example, a connection between elementary and secondary levels, is illustrated below. A simple number, 7425, familiar to elementary school-aged children, is written in expanded form and, through a series of generalizations, transformed into a polynomial, familiar to secondary school students.

$$7425$$
$$7 \times 1000 + 4 \times 100 + 2 \times 10 + 5$$
$$7 \times x^3 + 4 \times x^2 + 2 \times x + 5$$
$$7x^3 + 4x^2 + 2x + 5$$
$$ax^3 + bx^2 + cx + d$$

Representation of Mathematical Ideas

Much in mathematics is abstract, and making it meaningful to children has been a continuing challenge for teachers. In the past, mathematics was taught at an abstract level, even in elementary school, where children are not yet fully able to make the kinds of abstractions expected for understanding. Because we know now that children learn in different ways, it makes sense for teachers and children to represent mathematical concepts in different ways as well. Considerable emphasis is placed on representing mathematical ideas with concrete materials: Blocks, counters, and many other physical apparatuses

that children can manipulate have been used to embody mathematical ideas. This emphasis will continue, but currently there is a shift to a more multirepresentational approach that includes spoken language, concrete objects, pictures, real-life situations, and written symbols. Observing and making relationships within and among these representations helps children develop understanding (Behr, Lesh, Post, & Silver, 1983; Hiebert, 1990). Principles and Standards Link 1-6 discusses how students should be able to use representations. This topic is discussed in more detail in Chapter 2.

Equity

An achievement gap in mathematics has existed for far too long. In the past, achievement gaps based on gender, race, ethnicity, culture, native language, and socioeconomic status have been noted. The gender gap has begun to narrow in recent years, but other gaps continue to exist. To develop equity in a mathematics program, the NCTM Curriculum Standards include five NCTM goals to apply to all children:

- They learn to VALUE mathematics.
- They become CONFIDENT in their ability to do mathematics.
- They become mathematical PROBLEM SOLVERS.
- They learn to COMMUNICATE mathematically.
- They learn to REASON mathematically.

It is important for all teachers to have high expectations for each child and to work toward ensuring the learning of every child.

Technology

We believe that the use of calculators and other technologies will continue increase. This prediction stems from the following reasons:

- Calculators and other forms of technology continue to be used extensively in the home and office.

- The cost of calculators and other forms of technology continues to decrease while their power and functions continue to increase.
- Curriculum documents increasingly encourage the use of calculators and other forms of technology.
- Some tests currently available allow and even encourage calculator use.

Computation and Estimation

In the past, a heavy emphasis was placed on computation and computational procedures in elementary schools. But according to the Mathematical Sciences Education Board and National Research Council (1989), "Mathematics today involves far more than calculation; clarification of the problem, deduction of consequences, formulation of alternatives, and development of appropriate tools are as much a part of the modern mathematician's craft as are solving equations or providing answers" (p. 5).

The Principles and Standards emphasize the importance of interrelated skills and concepts: Children need not only to be able to compute fluently but also to understand the meanings of operations and make reasonable estimates. The recommendations regarding these skills are listed in Principles and Standards Link 1-7.

Currently, although the need for children to learn computational algorithms is acknowledged, the focus is on less complex calculations. More complex computations (e.g., three-digit multiplier) are more realistically done on a calculator than with paper and pencil. Furthermore, the current emphasis is on algorithmic knowledge growing out of real problems that require a calculator's use, rather than computation for computation's sake. The focus will continue to be on the choices children have. That is, is an estimate sufficient? If not, is mental computation feasible? Can this be done easily with pencil and paper, or should a calculator be used? Figure 1-2, adapted from the Curriculum Standards, reflects this philosophy.

In addition, emphasis is placed on estimation (approximate computation or measure) and mental computation (exact computation without any aids). Estimation and mental computation are being advocated for their utilitarian value and for their contribution to the development of number and operation sense. The renewed emphasis on estimation and mental computation can be traced, at least in part, to the advent of the calculator. The calculator will display a result when keys are pressed, but were the correct keys pressed? Were they pressed in the right sequence? An estimate will tell you whether your answer is reasonable. (Estimation and mental computation are discussed more fully in Chapter 9.)

Assessment

According to the Principles and Standards, "Assessment should support the learning of important mathematics and furnish useful information to both teachers and students" (NCTM, 2000, p. 22). The nature of assessment and strategies for assessing student learning are changing markedly. This topic is discussed in depth in Chapter 4. We mention it here, however, because it is another important area in which significant change is occurring. Assessment must be more than just a score on a test, but it should be an ongoing part of instruction that guides teachers in making instructional decisions. Assessment continues to be an important part of a good mathematics program.

Parent Involvement

Collaboration between teachers and parents is an effective strategy for increasing children's success in mathematics. According to Bezuk, Whitehurst-Payne, and Aydelotte (2000), "collaboration between teachers and parents is critically important to increase student achievement in order to achieve the goal of all students succeeding in mathematics" (p. 148).

There are many ways teachers can involve parents to enhance a child's learning. Some of these strategies include the following:

- Help parents learn more about *what* their child is learning about mathematics and *how* their child is learning mathematics.
- Provide activities parents can do with their children at home to reinforce and extend their children's learning.
- Discuss why mathematics is important for future success, including careers that involve using mathematics.

Suggestions and ideas for activities that can be sent home with children to do with their parents are included in chapters throughout this book.

PRINCIPLES AND STANDARDS LINK 1-7
Content Strand: Number and Operations

Instructional programs from prekindergarten through Grade 12 should enable all students to—

- understand numbers, ways of representing numbers, relationships among numbers, and number systems;
- understand meanings of operations and how they relate to one another;
- compute fluently and make reasonable estimates. (NCTM, 2000, p. 32)

FIGURE 1-2

COMPUTATIONAL DECISION-MAKING PROCESS

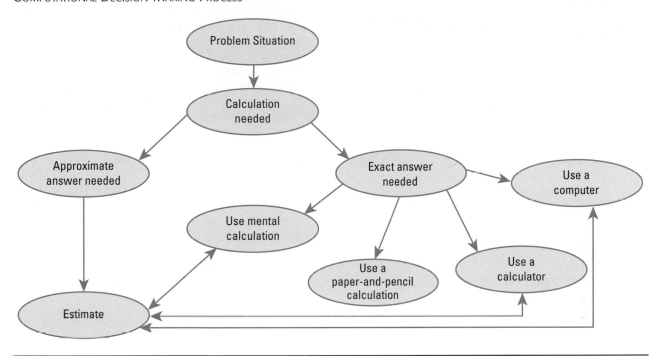

Source: From *Curriculum and Evaluation Standards for School Mathematics,* NCTM, 1989, Reston, VA: NCTM. © 1989 by NCTM.

CONCLUSION

This chapter has described a number of factors that have influenced the course of mathematics education in schools. These factors have changed and will continue to change both the mathematics curriculum and how mathematical ideas are taught.

Sometimes influences pull in opposite directions, making it difficult to maintain a balance. Years ago, Vincent Glennon (1963) argued for a balance in school mathematics among three needs: the needs of the child, the needs of society, and the needs of the subject. He diagrammed it as shown in Figure 1-3.

Glennon's argument for a balance still is valid today. If we overemphasize the computation component of mathematics, for example, we may tend to neglect its application in society and also the needs of the child, resulting in an imbalance.

The suggestions and activities in subsequent chapters of this book will enable you to devise a mathematics program for the children in your classroom that develops mathematical ideas in a nontrivial way, makes applications to society apparent, and carefully considers the needs of the child, making allowances for differences in background, learning style, and motivation to learn mathematics. Throughout the instructional process, the teacher is the most important factor in determining the strength of the mathematics program. Your challenge as a future teacher is to learn as much as you can about how to help children learn mathematics.

For Your Journal

When you have finished studying this chapter, reflect on the following questions in your math journal:

1. Write a mathematics autobiography. Tell about your past study of mathematics and your success in it. Describe your feelings about mathematics at the elementary level and at higher levels. Identify any experiences or mentors you have had in learning

FIGURE 1-3

BALANCE IN SCHOOL MATHEMATICS

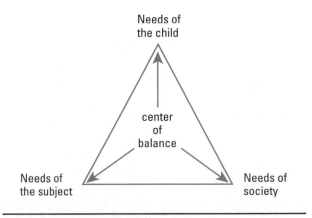

Source: Adapted from "Some Perspectives in Education," by V. J. Glennon, 1963, *Enrichment Mathematics for the Grades, NCTM's 27th Yearbook,* Washington, DC: NCTM. © 1963.

mathematics. (Include factors/persons who were influential in your desire/lack of desire to teach mathematics.)

2. Describe your view of yourself as a future elementary school mathematics teacher. The following prompts may help your thinking: Write about your triumphs and disasters. What do you like about learning math? What do you not like? What is your first (or strongest) memory of learning or doing math? What teacher(s) had a strong impact on your mathematics learning and attitude about mathematics? Describe. Identify an experience that affected your attitude about mathematics. Did your attitude toward math affect your career decision? If so, how? Have you ever been embarrassed, humiliated, or especially proud of your mathematics ability? How do you think your attitude about math will affect your teaching of math?

For Your Portfolio

When you finish studying this chapter, complete the following activities to include in your professional portfolio:

1. Browse through issues of *Teaching Children Mathematics* and *Mathematics Teaching in the Middle School.* Begin collecting articles you find interesting and useful.
2. Interview elementary- or middle-school children. Ask them what they like and don't like about mathematics class. Describe what you as a teacher might do to change any negative attitudes they have.
3. Consult a copy of your state or local mathematics standards. Compare them with the NCTM Principles and Standards.

Resources for Teachers

Children's books
Scieszka, J., & Smith, L. (1995). *Math curse.* New York: Penguin Books.

Books on increasing equity in learning mathematics
Downie, D., Slesnick, T., & Stenmark, J. (1981). *Math for girls and other problem solvers.* Berkeley, CA: Lawrence Hall of Science.
Edwards, C. A. (Ed.) (1999). *Changing the faces of mathematics: Perspectives on Asian Americans and Pacific Islanders.* Reston, VA: National Council of Teachers of Mathematics.
Jacobs, J. E., & Rossi Becker, J. (Eds.) (2000). *Changing the faces of mathematics: Perspectives on gender equity.* Reston, VA: National Council of Teachers of Mathematics.
Krause, M. (1983). *Multicultural mathematics materials.* Reston, VA: National Council of Teachers of Mathematics.

Ortiz-Franco, L., Hernandez, N. G., & De la Cruz, Y. (Eds.) (1999). *Changing the faces of mathematics: Perspectives on Latinos.* Reston, VA: National Council of Teachers of Mathematics.
Secada, W. G. (Ed.) (2000). *Changing the faces of mathematics: Perspectives on multiculturalism and gender equity.* Reston, VA: National Council of Teachers of Mathematics.
Skolnick, J., Langbort, C., & Day, L. (1982). *How to encourage girls in math and science.* Palo Alto, CA: Dale Seymour Publications.
Stenmark, J., Thompson, V., & Cossey, R. (1986). *Family math.* Berkeley: Regents, University of California.
Stenmark, J., Thompson, V., & Cossey, R. (1987). *Mathematica para la familia.* Berkeley: Regents, University of California.
Strutchens, M. E., Johnson, M. L., & Tate, W. F. (Eds.) (2000). *Changing the faces of mathematics: Perspectives on African Americans.* Reston, VA: National Council of Teachers of Mathematics.

Links to the Internet

National Council of Teachers of Mathematics
http://www.nctm.org
Contains information about the NCTM Standards and other publications as well as news releases related to mathematics teaching and learning.

Math Forum
http://mathforum.org/
Contains Student Center, Teachers' Place, Research Division, and a section for parents and other citizens. Also includes Ask Dr. Math, where you can ask questions about K–12 mathematics.

Eisenhower National Clearinghouse
http://www.enc.org
Contains mathematics and science standards, international comparisons such as the TIMSS data, and resources for teachers, including a large set of math and science Internet sites and classroom activities.

Teachers' Net
http://teachers.net
Contains many different types of resources for teachers, including curriculum resources, lesson plans, chatboards, and mailrings.

Millie's Math House
www.superkids.com/aweb/pages/reviews/early1/millies/merge.shtml
Contains a review of Edmark's Millie's Math House.

CHAPTER 2

Learning and Teaching Mathematics

✔ **Behaviorist approach to teaching**

✔ **Constructivist approach to teaching**

✔ **Modes of representation**

✔ **Conceptual and procedural knowledge**

✔ **Communication in the mathematics classroom**

Learning and teaching mathematics—that's what it is all about! The influences and directions discussed in Chapter 1 are important, but only to the extent that they help us understand mathematics education and how children learn mathematics. This chapter will discuss some learning theories and teaching strategies that bring us a little closer to the classroom. ✔

When you have finished studying this chapter, you should be able to answer the following questions:

1. How does the behaviorist approach to teaching differ from the constructivist approach to teaching?

2. What are the five different modes in which a mathematics concept may be represented? Using a mathematics concept of your choice, give an example of each of the modes.

3. Is communication important in the mathematics classroom? Why or why not?

4. How does conceptual knowledge differ from procedural knowledge? Give an example of each of these types of knowledge.

LEARNING STYLES

There are differences in the way children learn best. Some children perform better in a more structured setting, whereas others prefer a less structured environment. An individual's preferred learning style is determined by a host of contextual, personality, and process variables. The important point is that teachers need to be cognizant of the fact that differences in preferred learning style do exist and to provide for them by incorporating a variety of approaches and activities into the mathematics class (Butler, 1988).

LEARNING THEORIES

Theories about how children learn have been classified in various ways (Pa, 1986). These theories have a significant bearing on how mathematics is taught. For example, a predominant theory in the late nineteenth century, *mental discipline,* viewed the mind as a kind of muscle that required a reasonable amount of exercise to keep it properly tuned. In mathematics, lengthy or complex computations were used as a major form of exercise. Instruction stressed ways to perform these computations accurately. More recent theories fall into two general camps: the behaviorist approach and the cognitive or constructivist approaches.

The Behaviorist Approach

During the early part of the twentieth century, curricula and instruction were influenced by behavioral psychology. E. L. Thorndike's stimulus-response (S-R) theory gradually replaced the mental discipline theory. The S-R theory stated that learning occurred when a "bond" was established between some stimulus and a person's response to it. Drill became a major component in the instructional process because the more often a correct response was made to a stimulus, the more established the bond became.

Programmed instruction, often attributed to B. F. Skinner, was one educational outcome of this theory.

In the 1960s Robert Gagné, a *neo-behaviorist,* began to publish some of his research results on intelligence and conditions of learning. Gagné said that for any child, there is a variety of learning situations that can be ordered according to the principle of prerequisite learning. The simplest of these situations is stimulus-response. This is followed in order by simple chaining, verbal sequences, multiple discriminations, concept learning, principle learning and, at the highest level, problem solving (Gagné, 1985).

One of Gagné's major contributions to curriculum development was an emphasis on analyzing the structure of a task or concept to be learned. Gagné focused on prerequisite knowledge. A question frequently asked in a Gagné-type approach is, "What must the child already know or be able to do to learn this new concept or perform this new skill? Figure 2-1 shows one possible hierarchy of tasks for learning addition facts to 18.

The Cognitive/ Constructivist Approach

More recently, mathematics teaching and learning has been influenced by cognitive or constructivist approaches to education. Because we have opted for very broad categories of learning theories in this section, cognitive and constructive theories are discussed together. For the purposes of this text it is adequate to consider constructivism as an extension of cognitivism.

Constructivism consists of two major hypotheses; the first is widely accepted, the second is a more "radical constructivist" position (Goldin, 1990; Lerman, 1989).

1. Knowledge is actively constructed by the individual, not passively received from an outside source.

2. Coming to know is an adaptive process that organizes one's world, not the discovery of some independent, preexisting world outside the mind of the individual.

FIGURE 2-1

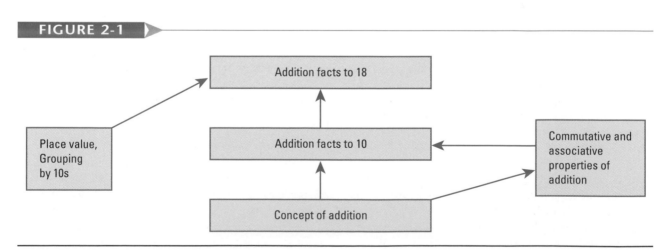

One way to think of the difference between the behaviorist and constructivist views of learning is with respect to the source of knowledge and acquisition of knowledge. The behaviorist view is that the teacher or curriculum designer is the source of knowledge and that person's main task is to transmit this knowledge to the child, who is a passive recipient. A constructivist, on the other hand, believes that the child constructs her or his own knowledge; that is, mathematical knowledge *emerges*. This point of view suggests at least two significant implications for teaching mathematics (Kamii, 1990). We need to focus on children's thinking rather than on their writing correct answers, and we need to encourage children to discuss, even disagree, among themselves rather than concentrate on getting right answers and correcting wrong ones. The teacher's role is to structure appropriate experiences so that the child can actively construct meaning.

It is difficult to describe a classroom or lesson that would reflect a constructivist approach because there would be considerable variation. It seems, however, that a high level of interaction, an emphasis on student autonomy or responsibility, and group work would characterize a constructivist environment. Children would spend much time interacting with materials, representing mathematical ideas and processes in different ways and with different kinds of materials. They would, of course, interact with the teacher, who would encourage, nurture, and provide help, but this would often be in the form of higher-level questions that would encourage children to reflect on what they have done in order to construct meaning. Questions would require children to explain and justify: "Why?", "What does that tell you?", "What can you tell me?", "Why not?", "What do you mean it doesn't work?" (Confrey, 1990). Questions involving classifying, giving examples, generalizing, applying, and other higher-level questions would also be asked frequently.

In a constructivist setting, the teacher is responsible for establishing a learning environment that will spark children's interest and open up areas (topics) of study. This is done by providing appropriate materials, activities, and reinforcement. Learning, however, is ultimately the responsibility of the child. This means that children must have a high level of autonomy in terms of how they interact with the materials and other aspects of the environment. Some children may need supplemental or even different materials and activities than other children.

See Wentworth and Monroe (1995) for another description of a constructivist classroom.

Cooperative learning Group work, although not essential, is very likely a feature of a constructivist learning environment. Small-group *cooperative learning* has been much discussed in current professional literature (Artzt & Newman, 1990a, 1990b; Davidson, 1990a, 1990b; Good, Reys, Grouws, & Mulryan, 1989–90;

Oberholtzer-Sutton, 1992). What is cooperative learning? (Some prefer to use the term *collaborative* rather than *cooperative*.) It is both an organization and a process in which a small group of children (usually three to five in number, heterogeneous in both ability and some personal characteristics) work together to complete a task or project or solve a problem. There are many ways to incorporate cooperative learning into the classroom, but they seem to have four elements in common (Artzt & Newman, 1990a).

> First, the members of a group must perceive that they are part of a team and that they all have a common goal. Second, group members must realize that the problem they are to solve is a group problem and that the success or failure of the group will be shared by all of the members of the group. Third, to accomplish the group's goal, all students must talk with one another—to engage in discussion of all problems. Finally, it must be clear that each member's individual work has a direct effect on the group's success. Teamwork is of utmost importance. (pp. 2–3)

The Curriculum Standards supports the use of small group learning in mathematics. "Small groups provide a forum in which students ask questions, discuss ideas, make mistakes, learn to listen to others' ideas, offer constructive criticism, and summarize their discoveries in writing" (NCTM, 1989, p. 79). Representing, talking, listening, writing, and reading can all be addressed in a cooperative learning setting. It is also an excellent forum for cooperatively and actively exploring a concept with concrete materials.

Davidson (1990b) concludes from research that small group cooperative learning has a positive effect on "academic achievement, self-esteem or self-confidence as a learner, intergroup relations including cross-race friendships, social acceptance of mainstreamed children, and ability to use social skills (if these are taught)" (p. 54).

Many educators and psychologists have influenced the development of constructivism. We will emphasize the work of two: Jean Piaget and Zoltan Dienes.

Jean Piaget The work of Jean Piaget, a Swiss philosopher-epistemologist, has influenced our thinking about how mathematics is learned. Key concepts in Piaget's theory of learning include *schema, adaptation,* and *operations.* A schema is a cognitive structure that one constructs by putting pieces of knowledge together. For example, children develop a "matching" schema and later an "intuitive qualitative correspondence" schema, that is, how one determines whether two sets are numerically equivalent. For example, a "matching" schema refers to children being able to line up two sets of objects to show the one-to-one correspondence between the elements in each set. If the elements match exactly, the sets are

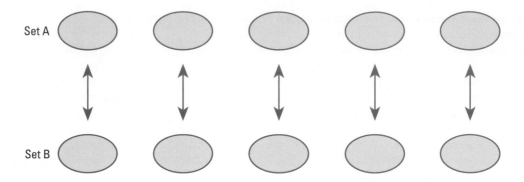

Set A

Set B

numerically equivalent. In the accompanying diagram, each item in Set A is in one-to-one correspondence with an item in Set B, with no items left over, so Sets A and B are the same size.

An "intuitive qualitative correspondence" schema is less procedural. It involves children making an intuitive decision about the relative size of two sets. In the diagram below, a child using the "intuitive qualitative correspondence" schema would determine that Set A seems to have more elements than Set B, without counting or making a one-to-one correspondence.

Schemas are developed by a process of *adaptation,* which can take two forms. *Assimilation* of a schema occurs when one's existing cognitive structure requires little modification to include the new idea. On the other hand, if no relevant schemas exist, new behavior sequences are built up through experimentation, instruction, or both. Piaget calls this process *accommodation.* The mechanism by which a schema is assimilated or accommodated into one's cognitive structure is an *operation,* an internalized action that can modify knowledge. Putting things into a series (for example, arranging sticks from shortest to longest) and constructing a classification (for example, sorting laundry by putting the whites in one pile and the colors in another pile) are examples of operations.

It is the changed mental structures (adaptation) resulting from operations that moves an individual through the developmental stages for which Piaget is so well known: sensorimotor, preoperational, concrete operational, and formal operational. Research suggests that there is considerable variation in the age at which an individual enters a particular stage. The age is affected by many factors, including cultural considerations. Piaget identified four factors that affect how rapidly an individual moves through these stages.

1. *Maturation:* the process of organic growth, a necessary but not a sufficient condition for certain behavior patterns to develop.

2. *Experience:* the physical and psychological experiences an individual has.

3. *Social transmission:* another name for teaching or the imparting of knowledge.

4. *Equilibration:* a process of bringing conflicting "ideas" into balance. It involves the notion of "self-regulation." For example, after a child acknowledges that two pieces of clay are the same size, the child is asked to flatten one and is then asked whether there is the same amount of clay in both pieces or if one has

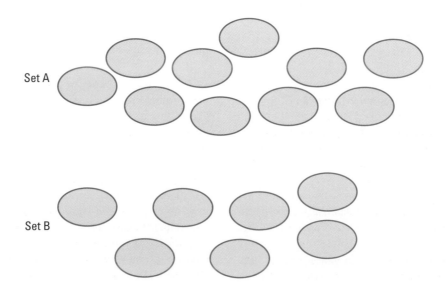

Set A

Set B

more than the other. Because some children are not yet ready to grasp the notion of the conservation of matter, this may cause some disequilibrium in the child's thinking. To convince herself or himself, the child may restore the ball to its original shape and announce that both balls have the same amount of clay. This ability to reverse a transformation leads to a state of equilibrium in which the child knows that the transformation did not change the amount of clay.

Teachers do not have much control over maturation, but they can play a significant role in experience and social transmission and, to some extent, in producing equilibration through the quantity and quality of experiences they provide children.

Implications. Most children in the elementary grades are in what Piaget called the *concrete operations stage.* This means that elementary-school children will learn mathematical concepts by manipulating materials and observing what happens. A teacher must provide the kind of concrete experiences that will facilitate learning. Even for the middle school level, experience and research suggest that children are not yet able to think about many concepts at a formal level and, in fact, still need concrete representations. Visual learners may continue to find such models helpful throughout their educational careers.

Piaget's *conservation* tasks provide us with some ingenious methods for assessing readiness for certain concepts. Conservation involves recognizing that an invariant transformation does not change the property in question. For example, a row of 10 counters still contains 10 counters when spread out or pushed together. "Spreading out" and "pushing together" are invariant transformations with respect to number. (A number conservation task is described in Chapter 5, and several measurement conservation tasks are described in Chapter 15.)

Piaget's work can also provide direction for sequencing the curriculum. For example, children seem to conserve numbers early in the concrete operational stage while mass and volume are not conserved until the end of this stage. These findings suggest that formal measurement of area and volume would appropriately be delayed until intermediate grades.

Piaget's observations on knowledge development suggest that the ideal learning environment is one which allows the elementary- and middle-school child to explore ideas. In mathematics learning, this is most effectively done with the aid of concrete manipulative materials.

Zoltan Dienes Zoltan Dienes developed a theory of mathematics learning that includes the dynamic, perceptual variability, mathematical variability, and constructivity principles.

The *dynamic principle* is a three-phase process. The first is a *preliminary,* or *play* phase, in which activities

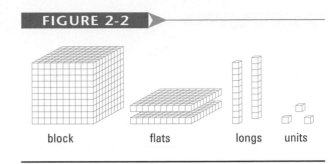

FIGURE 2-2

block   flats   longs   units

are relatively unstructured. The teacher would, however, provide the kinds of materials out of which the structure of a mathematical concept can be developed. For example, children might be given a set of Dienes's Base-Ten Multibase Arithmetic Blocks (MAB), as shown in Figure 2-2. (In subsequent chapters these blocks will be referred to simply as base-ten blocks.) Initially children will build towers, bridges, and other creative objects. Children are very good at making up rules for their play. (You can hear them doing this when you are on playground supervision.) Soon they will start to develop some rules for using the blocks. For example, you have to "use the least number of pieces" when you build a road. This leads to the next phase of the dynamic principle, *structured play* or games. The preceding rule leads to the notion of trading ten short units for one long unit. Children thus become aware of the relationships among the blocks.

The third component of the dynamic principle involves an *explicit representation* of some mathematical concept. For example, children can use their understanding of the relationship among the blocks developed in Phase 2 to represent base ten numbers, say 213, as shown below.

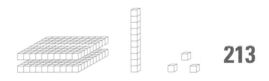

213

Dienes diagrams this process cyclically (Figure 2-3). Actually it is both cyclical and spiral in the sense that the final or more abstract phase can serve as the play stage for a higher-level related concept. For example, the representation of specific numbers can be a play activity in which children represent more than one number and then later, in the more structured phase, combine these to demonstrate addition.

The *perceptual variability principle* (also known as the multiple embodiment principle) says that learning a concept is facilitated when children can "see" the concept in a variety of forms or embodiments. This allows the child to abstract the common or relevant properties of the

FIGURE 2-3

Application of abstraction forms play stage for higher level of a concept

Play

Structuring to form a concept or abstraction

Abstraction

FIGURE 2-4

(a)   (b)

(c)   (d)

concept from various representations. Again, consider the representation of a base-ten number as an example of the perceptual variability principle. Initially children could bundle popsicle sticks, putting groups of 10 together with rubber bands. Later they could use the base-ten blocks to represent, say, 47, as shown at the bottom of the page.

At a more abstract level, 47 could be shown on an abacus. In each case the number represented is the same but each representation is "perceptually" different.

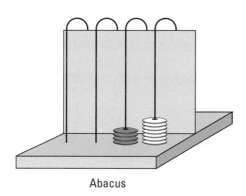

Abacus

Like the perceptual variability principle, the *mathematical variability principle* suggests that children be exposed to a variety of variables so that essential variables become evident by their presence in all examples. The difference is that for mathematical variability, mathematical variables, rather than perceptual variables, are changed.

Again using the base-ten blocks, one could focus on the concept of "grouping" in numeration. What is impor-

tant is the process of grouping, not the number of objects in a group. So a teacher might use a base-three version of the MAB, then a base-five version, and so on.

In teaching the concept of "triangle," a teacher should employ different triangles in different orientations. Many young children will agree that the shape in Figure 2-4(a) is a triangle, but they may not acknowledge that the shape in Figure 2-4(b) is a triangle. Children need many examples of triangles so that they can abstract the essential mathematical variables from the irrelevant ones. Nonexamples of a concept may be included in the mathematical variability principle. However, children need to know that an instance is a nonexample. Using the triangle concept, figures or designs such as those in Figure 2-4(c) and (d) could be identified as nonexamples to help children focus on the relevant mathematical variables.

The *constructivity principle* suggests that children be allowed to build up (construct) their own knowledge from their own experiences. Analysis will come later. Dienes argues that something has to exist before it can be analyzed.

Implications. Dienes's theory, like Piaget's, underlines the importance of an active learning environment in which children are actively involved with a concrete representation of a mathematical concept in order to build up their understanding of the concept. The work of Dienes makes somewhat more explicit the need for teachers to be aware of individual learning rates and styles. One embod-

47 ⇒ 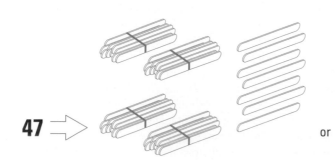   or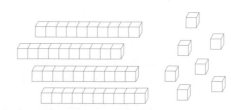

iment of a concept may make sense to one child, but a different embodiment may be needed to help another child understand.

BASIC PRINCIPLES REVIEWED

From the work of Piaget, Dienes, and many others, a number of basic principles can be derived. The following six guidelines, while not exhaustive, are important. For a more exhaustive listing and for more elaboration, the reader should consult a recent text on learning theory.

Begin With Concrete Representation

Children seem to learn best when learning begins with a concrete representation of a mathematical concept. In fact, it is best to provide children with *multiple embodiments* of the concept. To provide multiple embodiments, the use of *manipulative materials* is essential in all mathematics classrooms. This does not mean that concrete manipulatives should be used exclusively. Other forms of representation are also important, including mental images and computer images (Clements & McMillen, 1996).

When building an understanding of the addition algorithm, children should set out bundles of popsicle sticks (or equivalent objects) and manipulate them to represent the process of addition (Figure 2-5). The use of different manipulatives at different times helps children to abstract the essence of the concept and lends variety to the mathematics program.

Manipulatives do not guarantee success. A teacher must take steps to promote success when planning a lesson that includes manipulatives. Ross and Kurtz (1993) suggest that when planning such a lesson, the teacher should be certain that:

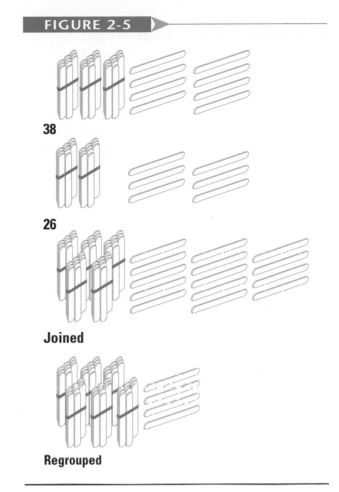

FIGURE 2-5

38

26

Joined

Regrouped

1. manipulatives have been chosen to support the lesson's objectives;
2. significant plans have been made to orient children to the manipulatives and corresponding classroom procedures;
3. the lesson involves the active participation of each child; and
4. the lesson plan includes procedures for evaluation that reflect an emphasis on the development of reasoning skills. (p. 256)

Develop Understanding

Understanding is a term that is often used somewhat synonymously with meaningfulness. Structuring activities and experiences that will enable children to build understanding is the essence of teaching. Beyond the level of straight recall or recognition, children can exhibit understanding through at least four higher-level cognitive processes: application, noting relationships, transformation, and transfer. *Application* involves using concepts in related but somewhat different problems. If children can identify and state *relationships* among concepts, they likely have a meaningful understanding of those

PRINCIPLES AND STANDARDS LINK 2-1
Process Strand: Communication

Instructional programs from prekindergarten through grade 12 should enable all students to—

- organize and consolidate their mathematical thinking through communication;
- communicate their mathematical thinking coherently and clearly to peers, teachers, and others;
- analyze and evaluate the mathematical thinking and strategies of others;
- use the language of mathematics to express mathematical ideas precisely. (NCTM, 2000, p. 60)

concepts. Being able to relate multiplication to addition is one example of this level of understanding.

$$4 \times 5 \quad \rightarrow \quad 5 + 5 + 5 + 5$$

Transformation involves taking a problem or idea in one form and representing it in another form. Restating ideas in other words, constructing a graph, and drawing a diagram to illustrate a concept are examples of transformation. *Transfer* involves using an idea or concept in a context different from that in which it was learned—an extremely important process in a rapidly changing society.

One way to help children develop understanding is for teachers to carefully select the *modes of representation* they use in instruction, or the way in which mathematics concepts are represented (Behr, Lesh, Post, & Silver, 1983). These five modes include real-world situations, manipulative models, pictures, oral language, and written symbols (see Figure 2-6). For example, the concept of five might be represented with five fingers (real-world situation), with five Unifix cubes (manipulative model), with a picture of five flowers (pictures), by saying the word *five* (oral language), and by writing the word *five* or the symbol 5 (written symbols).

Using the preceding example of the concept of five, a teacher might ask a child who has displayed five fingers whether the child could show the same number in another way, such as by drawing a picture of five objects or picking up a group of five blocks. This is called translations. Translations refers to asking children to represent a con-

cept in more than one mode and is indicated by the arrows in Figure 2-6.

Why is this concept important? Research shows that instruction in which children are encouraged to make translations between modes of representation enhances children's understanding. Thus, good teachers ensure that their lessons include a variety of modes of representation and opportunities for children to make translations between modes.

Hiebert (1990) states, "Meaning or understanding in mathematics comes from building or recognizing relationships either *between* representations or *within* representations" (p. 32).

Building relationships *between* representations occurs, for example, when a child listens (spoken language) to a problem, represents and manipulates it with blocks (concrete objects), and then writes a response on paper (written symbols).

Building relationships *within* representations often involves recognizing patterns within the representation. Hiebert (1990) uses the base-ten blocks in a decimal context as an example. In this setting, children can recognize the "pattern of *repeated* partitioning by 10 and the corresponding decrease in the size of the blocks" (p. 33), which could go on forever if the blocks could be cut finely enough.

Reflection enhances understanding or meaningfulness of a concept. Reflection is often needed to observe patterns within a representational system. The teacher or children can encourage reflection by asking appropriate

FIGURE 2-6 ▶

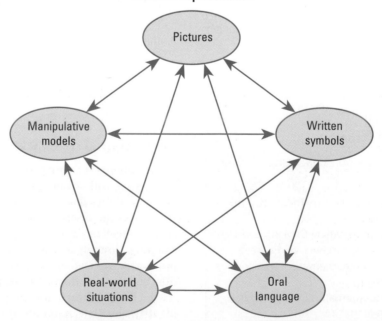

Modes of Representation

LITERATURE LINK 2-1
Learning About Mathematics

Schmandt-Besserat, Denise (1999). *The History of Counting,* New York: Morrow Junior Books.

Children use their own representations as a part of their mathematical development. Yet it is also important that they learn common representations, such as the numerals and number words used in counting and calculating in the base-ten system. In the historically accurate and beautifully illustrated *The History of Counting,* children can investigate the development of this precise and efficient system.

- Encourage children to create their own system of symbols for 1–30 and beyond. Have children describe how they will write very large numbers in their system.
- Demonstrate for children how to count using the ancient system of body counting presented in the text. How might ancient people recall which number is represented by a part of the body?
- Many objects have been used for counting throughout recorded history. Model interesting and efficient record-keeping systems, such as the *quipus* used by people of the Inca empire in Peru. Quipus were made

from colored strings made of dyed cotton or wool. Using 10 as the base, the knots in the cords appeared in the 100s, 10s, and units positions. Children can easily represent these cords with colored string or yarn while reinforcing their understanding of our own system of place value.

- Use paint and Styrofoam cutouts of numerals in different numbers systems (such as Egyptian, Mayan, Babylonian, or Roman) to stamp numbers on cloth.
- Investigate the different ways that time has been recorded using ancients clocks (sundials, water clocks, sand clocks) and calendars (Aztec calendar). Have children collect and analyze information and draw illustrations to accompany their text information. Create a class book on the way time was recorded throughout history and call it *The History of Time.*
- *Mathematics,* by Irving Adler, teaches children about angles, square numbers, Fibonacci numbers, the golden ratio, prime numbers, triangles, polygons, and square roots.

Source: Dr. Patricia Moyer, George Mason University.

questions or by challenging each other's observations. Note again the importance of communication.

Understanding of new concepts is more likely to occur when children understand prerequisite concepts than when they have only a superficial understanding or when they have learned previous skills and concepts by rote. Just as we would not consider building a house without proper footings, so children cannot build mathematical structures without meaningful prerequisite learning. For

example, children who do not have a good understanding of the place-value concept often have considerable difficulty ordering decimal fractions. They often order on the basis of the number of digits (see Chapter 12).

Van de Walle (1994) points out that understanding is demonstrated when connections are formed between procedural knowledge and conceptual knowledge. *Procedural knowledge* is a knowledge of the symbolism used to represent mathematical ideas and the rules and

PRINCIPLES AND STANDARDS LINK 2-2
Process Strand: Representation

Representations can help students organize their thinking. Students' use of representations can help make mathematical ideas more concrete and available for reflection. In the lower grades, for example, children can use representations to provide a record for their teachers and their peers of their efforts to understand mathematics. In the middle grades, they should use representations more to solve problems or to portray, clarify, or extend a mathematical idea. (NCTM, 2000, p. 68)

PRINCIPLES AND STANDARDS LINK 2-3
Process Strand: Communication

Communication is an essential part of mathematics and mathematics education. It is a way of sharing ideas and clarifying understanding. Through communication, ideas become objects of reflection, refinement, discussion, and amendment . . . Students who have opportunities, encouragement, and support for speaking, writing, reading, and listening in mathematics classes reap dual benefits: they communicate to learn mathematics, and they learn to communicate mathematically. (NCTM, 2000, p. 60)

LITERATURE LINK 2-2
Communicating Mathematically

Schwartz, David (1998) *G is for Googol,* Berkeley: Tricycle Press.

A critical mode of representation for children is oral language. Children learn to represent and defend their mathematical ideas through the use of language. *G is for Googol: A Math Alphabet Book* is filled with interesting mathematics vocabulary. The definitions are child friendly while maintaining mathematical accuracy. Mathematics words are given with their meanings, and the diagrams and illustrations support the explanations presented in the text.

- In addition to the mathematical terms give for each letter, other words on each page are presented for children to investigate. For example, on the "P is for probability" page, P is also for palindrome parabola,

parallel, percent, pi, point, polygon, prime number, and Pythagorean theorem. Have the children Investigate and make connections to find the mathematical significance of these additional words.
- Design your own mathematics alphabet book. Select one of the additional words listed in the book and create a child-friendly mathematical definition. Along with the definitions, use drawings, diagrams, and examples that would help children to understand the meaning of the mathematical terms.
- Copy and assemble of the children's definition pages into one large alphabet book so that each child has his or her own copy for reference.

Source: Dr. Patricia Moyer, George Mason University.

procedures used to perform a mathematical task. *Conceptual knowledge* consists of relationships that connect a number of mathematical ideas or concepts. [For example, in Chapter 7 we will see that the concepts of addition and subtraction are related (knowing $6 + 5 = 11$ helps one think about $11 - 5 = 6$).] This conceptual knowledge greatly facilitates acquisition of the procedural knowledge of addition and subtraction computation. An example that nicely illustrates the difference between knowing "how" and knowing "why" involves division of common fractions. Recalling and applying the rule "invert and multiply" is procedural knowledge; being able to explain or justify why it works is conceptual knowledge. Being able to see or make connections between conceptual knowledge and procedural knowledge is what Skemp (1989) calls *relational understanding* (Figure 2-7).

Encourage Communication

Communication plays an important role in children's mathematics learning. It "forces" children to think through a concept, often resulting in more refined under-

standing. Highlighted in the NCTM standards, communicating in mathematics means encouraging children to engage in interactive conversations as they work through mathematical processes. Interactions with other children can help children clarify what they do or do not understand about mathematical concepts or processes. According to Stigler (1988), Japanese teachers spend more time than do most American teachers encouraging students to communicate verbally about mathematics concepts and procedures. It is time for American teachers to capitalize on opportunities to get students talking about mathematics.

Problems and models provide many opportunities for communicating about mathematics. In addition, talking and writing about mathematics helps children solidify their understanding of mathematics.

Communication in the mathematics classroom can take many forms. It can be oral or written. It can be from

FIGURE 2-7 ▶

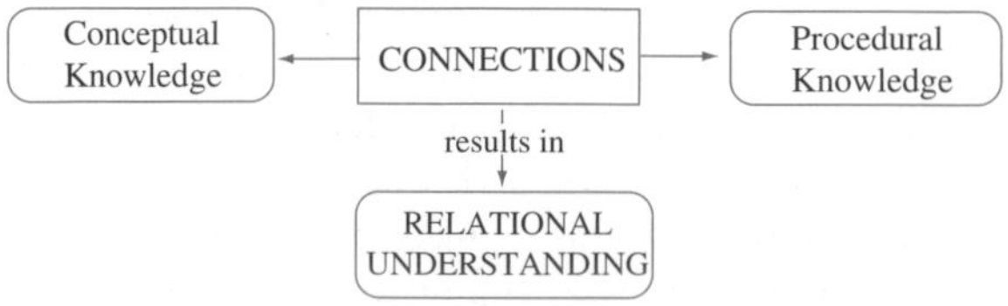

Conceptual Knowledge ← CONNECTIONS → Procedural Knowledge

results in

RELATIONAL UNDERSTANDING

PRINCIPLES AND STANDARDS LINK 2-4
Process Strand: Communication

Students gain insights into their thinking when they present their methods for solving problems, when they justify their reasoning to a classmate or teacher, or when they formulate a question about something that is puzzling to them. Communication can support students' learning of new mathematical concepts as they act out a situation, draw, use objects, give verbal accounts and explanations, use diagrams, write, and use mathematical symbols. (NCTM, 2000, pp. 60–61)

PRINCIPLES AND STANDARDS LINK 2-5
Process Strand: Communication

Writing in mathematics can also help students consolidate their thinking because it requires them to reflect on their work and clarify their thoughts about the ideas developed in the lesson. Later, they may find it helpful to reread the record of their own thoughts. (NCTM, 2000, p. 61)

PRINCIPLES AND STANDARDS LINK 2-6
Process Strand: Connections

Instructional programs from prekindergarten through grade 12 should enable all students to—

- recognize and use connections among mathematical ideas;
- understand how mathematical ideas interconnect and build on one another to produce a coherent whole;
- recognize and apply mathematics in contexts outside of mathematics. (NCTM, 2000, p. 64)

child to child or between a child and the teacher. It can be a report, a story, a word problem for other children to solve, a description of how a child solved a problem, or an entry in a math journal. Keeping a journal is generally associated with the language arts discipline, but a math journal can be used to reinforce a child's understanding of mathematical concepts.

A math journal serves many purposes. It offers an opportunity for children to think about and write about the mathematics concepts they are learning. Further, it provides the teacher with an excellent assessment tool. Journals should be a regular part of mathematics class activities and can be included routinely as part of homework assignments.

Math journal prompts might include the following:

I think the answer is . . .
I solved the problem by . . .
Another way to solve the problem would be . . .
I still have a question about . . .
The thing I liked most was . . .

Communication in the mathematics classroom provides teachers with valuable insights into children's understanding, which helps teachers plan further instructions.

Make Connections

When children build connections between mathematical ideas and other topics, mathematics becomes more meaningful and understanding is enhanced. Using a thematic approach is one way to provide integration because it can address not only basic skills but also more open-ended and higher-level objectives. Individual interests and other individual differences may be more easily accommodated in a thematic unit. The cooperative learning approach lends itself to thematic units.

Thematic units also provide opportunity to connect mathematics to real life through field trips and related activities. For example, children might visit a nearby shopping mall (with permission from the administration) to observe geometric shapes in the mall decor, observe slides, flips, and turns in shop logos, calculate the total cost for each member of their small group to purchase a particular snack at one of the food outlets, and so on.

Even without a thematic approach, however, many opportunities to integrate mathematics with other subjects are encountered daily. For example, an art teacher might reinforce one-to-one correspondence by having a child distribute one paint brush to every child in class. In physical education, children might measure distance and time, count when skipping, and keep track of scores and other statistics in games. Social studies and science offer many opportunities for creating and interpreting graphs. Serendipitous opportunities need to be seized and discussed so that children "see" the connection of mathematics to their in-school and out-of-school experiences.

Connections are not automatic. Teachers must provide experiences in which the connections are "obvious" or at least where they can be made explicit, as described in the previous paragraph. This will encourage children to look for other connections and eventually recognize the pervasive nature of mathematics in the world around them.

Take Time to Motivate Children

Motivation fuels mathematical learning. If children are motivated, they attend to instruction, strive for meaning, and persevere when difficulties arise. Competent teachers, effective instructional models, and thought-provoking activities guide the process, but children must first be motivated to learn mathematics. (Holmes, 1990, p. 101)

Motivation in a child is the child's willingness to give attention, time, energy, and perseverance to learning. It is the willingness to accept the challenge to understand a concept or solve a problem. Motivation also is associated with the belief that one can succeed. Almost all children begin kindergarten with this belief. As the years pass, some lose faith in their ability, especially in mathematics.

Thus, the level of motivation is one of many ways in which children within the classroom differ.

Although motivation is largely internal to each child, there are strategies a teacher can employ to increase motivation. On a general level, individuals become motivated when the concepts they are learning are meaningful and when they experience satisfaction, success, and recognition. Communication and meaningful opportunities for students to engage in mathematics conversations about real-world problems can be very motivating, in addition to enhancing children's understanding of mathematics concepts. Give children meaningful tasks and assignments at which they can be successful, then recognize their achievements.

More specifically, there are differences in what motivates children. So-called academically inclined children are motivated by achievement. Special challenges such as puzzles, nonroutine problems, and strategy games will capture their attention and increase motivation. Other children experience increased motivation when they can see the utilitarian value of what they are learning. Application or real-world types of activities should be designed for these children. This does not imply that certain children are given one type of experience exclusively. All children should experience different types of activities, although some may simply opt for a larger dose of one type than another. Variety in activities helps to enhance motivation.

In the literature, motivation has often been categorized as *extrinsic* (grades, stars, etc.) or *intrinsic* (internal interest and desire to learn). Both types should be considered, although intrinsic motivation seems to be more congruent with the theory that children build their own mathematical understanding.

Attitudes Attitudes are an important part of motivation. Children who feel good about mathematics and their ability to do mathematics will usually be motivated to learn. On the other hand, children who have negative attitudes about mathematics or their ability in mathematics often exhibit disinterest. Given that there is a positive correlation between attitude and achievement in mathematics, it is important for the teacher to provide experiences and the kind of environment that will foster positive attitudes. Minimal stress, emphasis on meaning and understanding rather than memorization, successful experiences, meaningful use of manipulatives, relating mathematics to the real world, and meaningful cooperative group work are some generalized guidelines for fostering the development of positive attitudes regarding mathematics.

It is essential to add that the teacher's attitude toward mathematics also is influential in forming children's attitudes. The teacher needs to be positive and show enthusiasm for and interest in mathematics.

Provide Opportunities for Practice

The belief that mathematics needs to be meaningful and the idea that children construct their own mathematical knowledge do not rule out the need for practice. Practice contributes significantly to making routine procedures automatic. This results in more efficient execution of a procedure, and thus to the expenditure of less mental effort (Hiebert, 1990). Expending as little mental effort as possible on a routine procedure is important because it allows one to give more effort to a more complex task of which the routine is only a part. If a person has to devote too much effort to the routine task, attention to the major task may be lost.

Practice does not have to be dull and boring, though. Games, puzzles, riddles, little surprises, novel algorithms, novel formats, calculators, and computers all are useful ways of providing practice. Of course, this is not to say that worksheets, flash cards, and other traditional means of providing practice should not be used. The difference is in the purpose: thinking versus rote memorization. The following guidelines may be helpful in selecting activities for practice purposes. Teachers must recognize, however, that any one activity may not meet all of the guidelines.

To be effective, practice activities should:

- be based on a well-defined cognitive objective; they should not be "busy work."
- be self-motivating and fun.
- make use of the concept or procedure being reinforced in a new and interesting form.
- be self-checking, that is, children should know when they have done it correctly.
- be adaptable for use with the whole class, a small group, or an individual child.
- provide for extension of knowledge; further exploration of an idea should be stimulated.

Games Children enjoy playing games. Games certainly are self-motivating and fun and, in fact, meet most of the preceding guidelines for practice activities. The public market as well as school supply companies offer many games that might meet specific mathematics objectives. More important, teachers can create or adapt games that are appropriate for the curricular objectives. For example, a teacher might create a template (Figure 2-8) for a bingo-like game. By changing what goes in the cells and the nature of the calling cards, bingo types of games can be created to reinforce many different mathematical ideas and procedures. (If templates are created with a word processor, changes can be made quickly and easily.) Note the use of "I can" in the conventional "Free" space

FIGURE 2-8 ▶

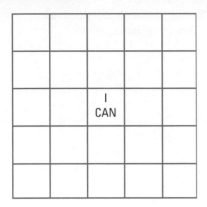

in Figure 2-8. Messages such as this can help to enhance a child's self-concept with respect to mathematics.

Puzzles and riddles Various forms of puzzles and riddles can be used to provide interesting, often self-checking practice. Puzzles can range from simple join-the-dot pictures to complex pattern recognition. Magic squares could also be included in this category. The sample puzzle in Figure 2-9 involves placing numbers from 1 through 14, 3 in each circle, so that the sum in each circle is 21. No number may be used more than once. Note that 3, 6, 7, 10, and 12 have been placed as starters.

Riddles are closely related to puzzles. Many school libraries contain books with riddles of the type "What fish do you see at night?" It takes only a few minutes to turn these into interesting and useful practice exercises. (An example of how this can be done appears in Chapter 6.)

Surprises There are many little "surprises" in mathematics that can be used as warm-up activities at the beginning of a class. For example, a teacher might give the following instructions:

FIGURE 2-9 ▶

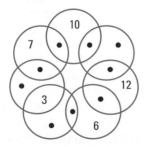

- Write a three-digit number in which the first and third digits are different by at least 2.
- Reverse the digits to create a second number. Subtract the smaller number from the larger.
- Reverse the digits in the difference and add to the difference.
- Did you get 1089?

$$
\begin{array}{r}
591 \\
\underline{195} \\
396 \\
\underline{693} \\
1089
\end{array}
$$

A challenge such as "Do you think this will work for all three-digit numbers" will motivate children to do more of these problems. In the process, they will get a great deal of practice with addition and subtraction—and the teacher doesn't have to photocopy a worksheet. This could also be turned into a problem-solving activity by asking children to explain why this process works.

Novel algorithms An *algorithm* is a routine process used to obtain a certain result. For example, most of us use an algorithm for tying our shoes—an algorithm that we've performed so many times it has become a mindless task. A mathematics algorithm is a process used again and again to find an answer to a mathematics problem. In this country we have standard algorithms for addition, subtraction, multiplication, and division tasks.

Demonstrating a novel (different) algorithm serves two purposes. First, it reinforces the fact that algorithms are human inventions. Second, a novel algorithm can stimulate practice with the conventional algorithm because once children have obtained a result with the new algorithm, they will verify the result by redoing the computation in the conventional way. Again, self-motivating practice is provided without the use of a worksheet. (The *lattice* method of multiplication described in Chapter 9 is one possible alternative algorithm that would serve this purpose.) As an *extension,* a teacher might challenge children to reflect on the algorithm they just completed and try to relate it to the conventional algorithm.

Novel formats Doing the "usual" thing in a different format can also be a means of providing self-motivating practice. For example, if some children are having difficulty with addition and subtraction facts involving 7, the teacher might challenge them to use only the numbers 1, 3, 5, and 7 (in any order) with addition and subtraction to generate consecutive results from say 5 through 14. For example, 14 is the result of $3 + 5 + 7 - 1$. (Restrictions like these may make some results impossible.) Children will try many combinations and in the process they practice the basic facts involving 7. (Several activities such as this are suggested in Chapter 8.) Children could use the calculator for this activity by pretending the 0, 2, 4, 6, 8, and 9 keys are broken.

The calculator as a practice tool   The calculator can be used to provide practice with concepts as simple as counting, for estimation, and for more complex calculations. Even children in the primary grades can use the built-in constant feature (now standard in almost all inexpensive calculators) to verify a counting sequence starting at any number, to count on, to count back, and to skip count. (Chapter 5 elaborates on how this can be done.) Activity 2-1 is an example of a calculator activity providing practice with the concept of numeration.

Personal computers   Personal computers are widely used to provide practice. In the past few years, the quality and quantity of practice courseware has improved markedly. Most allow a considerable number of options to be controlled by the teacher so that a program can be tailored to the individual needs of children. Many programs also keep track of responses so the teacher can analyze student performance later. Children are also given feedback on their responses and a summary at the end. The teacher must carefully review each software program to anticipate any difficulty children might have with data entry, screen displays, etc., and to evaluate the quality of the activity and how it relates to the curriculum. The teacher also needs to know precisely what the program will do so that appropriate options can be set and to decide which children could benefit from inter-

TECHNOLOGY LINK 2-1
Eisenhower National Clearinghouse

This site is packed full of great resources. Check out the Web Links section, including the Digital Dozen, a monthly listing of great instructional websites. This site also includes Professional Resources and Curriculum Resources for teachers, along with updates on education-related news.
Visit http://www.enc.org/ or link from our Companion Website at **www.prenhall.com/cathcart.**

acting with it. Many organizations and school districts provide a list of recommended software that has been carefully evaluated.

THINKING ABOUT TEACHING

Teaching mathematics requires thinking about three things: how children learn, the teaching process, and what to teach. The first has already been discussed; the latter two are the focus of this section.

   The teaching act is a three-phase process: what the teacher does before the lesson, what the teacher does during the lesson, and what the teacher does after the lesson. This is not a totally linear process. Each phase provides input or feedback or both for the others.

Preteaching Activities

Before teaching a lesson, the teacher must be cognizant of the nature of the children, diagnose what the children already know, decide on an appropriate approach that will make the content meaningful, and then plan the instructional sequence and activities in more detail.

Preplanning considerations
Child considerations.   A teacher must consider the child when planning mathematics experiences. Each child is an individual who comes to the classroom with unique needs, interests, attitudes, background, and motivation to learn mathematics.

   Mathematical ideas generally are not learned as the result of one lesson. Teachers need to be patient with the process and with children because the understanding is slower to develop for some children and for some concepts than for others.

   Children's active involvement needs to take many forms: physical as well as mental, verbal as well as written. A teacher should plan for activities that foster, per-

---

ACTIVITY 2-1

PLACE VALUE ON THE CALCULATOR

MATERIALS
Calculators

PROCEDURE
1. Player A announces a number that all other participants enter into their calculator. (For example, Player A selects the number 972.)

2. Player A then announces which digit in the chosen number is to be changed to zero without changing any of the other digits. (For example, Player A wants the 7 in 1972 to be changed to a zero—so the calculator would display the number 902.)

3. All remaining players attempt to change the given digit to zero by doing only one substraction. (The correct answer in this example would be to subtract 70, because 972 − 70 = 902.)

haps at different times, all of these forms of involvement. Because success is a powerful motivator, plan learning activities in which children will be successful. This does not necessarily mean that the activity is to be easy, however. If work is too easy, children lose motivation. Plan activities to be challenging but within the range of a child's ability to complete.

Mathematics anxiety. Mathematics anxiety, also known as math phobia, is a fear of mathematics. There is evidence that mathematics anxiety often starts in elementary school, although the symptoms often are not evident until years later. According to Burns (1998), "the way we've traditionally been taught mathematics has created a recurring cycle of math phobia, generation to generation, that has been difficult to break" (p. x).

Kennedy and Tipps (1991) list five teacher practices that contribute to mathematics anxiety: an emphasis on memorization, an emphasis on speed, an emphasis on doing one's own work, authoritarian teaching, and lack of variety in the teaching-learning process.

So what can teachers do to reduce or prevent math anxiety in children? Martinez and Martinez (1996) suggest that teachers use the following instructional strategies to prevent math anxiety:

- Create an anxiety-free math class, which could include seating children in circles and small groups, with the teacher taking on the role of facilitator of learning.
- Match instruction to children's cognitive levels.
- Plan instruction that connects mathematics to familiar situations in children's everyday lives.
- Incorporate math games and puzzles into instruction.
- Teach math through reading and writing.
- Empower children by using technology and collaborative learning.

Social factors can contribute to an individual's attitude and motivation to learn mathematics. Placing children in nonthreatening cooperative groups can improve their self-concept, raise achievement, and increase motivation for learning. Group work is as important in mathematics as it is in social studies, science, or any other school subject.

Social considerations may also include factors such as the child's home situation and the amount of sleep the previous night. A tense home situation can reduce a child's attentiveness and desire to learn. Furthermore, if an elementary-school child was awake until midnight the night before a test, the child's performance will likely be below expectation.

The teacher significantly influences the social situation within the classroom. Factors such as a child's home situation or sleep patterns, however, cannot be controlled by the teacher. Thus, accountability for learning rests with the parents, the child, and the teacher.

Myths about learning mathematics. According to Ginsburg and Baron (1993), there are five myths about learning mathematics. It is important that all teachers be aware of the fallacy of these myths so that they can plan appropriate instruction.

Myth #1: Some children cannot learn math. There is no reason all children cannot learn math, provided that they have good mathematics instruction. It is a challenge to every teacher to expect that all children will succeed in mathematics and to use a variety of instructional strategies to help them do so.

Myth #2: Boys learn math better than girls. In fact, at the elementary level, there are often few differences in mathematics achievement based on gender. Frequently, differences that do occur begin appearing in middle school and junior high school and seem to be due more to cultural influences. One difference between boys and girls that has been documented, however, is that girls sometimes have slightly weaker spatial visualization ability. This points to the importance of teachers providing opportunities for all children, girls as well as boys, to develop their spatial abilities through hands-on activities in geometry and other topics.

Myth #3: Poor children and children from underrepresented groups cannot learn math. Many success stories point to the fallacy of this myth. The key components of programs that are successful for poor children and children from underrepresented groups include motivation, high expectations, role models, appropriate teaching, and real-world applications.

Myth #4: American children have less mathematical ability than Asian children. Differences in mathematics achievement emerge between American and Asian children after a year or two of schooling. However, these differences seem to be related not to ability but to differences in teaching and in expectations. For example, a common American notion is that "you're either good at math or you're not, and if you're not good at math, there's nothing you can do about it." We must change our expectations to believe that *all* children, given good teaching, can learn mathematics.

Myth #5: Mathematics learning disabilities are common. There are many cases in which children do not seem to learn mathematics. However, as illustrated by the previous myths about learning mathematics, usually this lack of achievement is due not to learning disabilities but to a lack of motivation and appropriate teaching.

Clearly, good math teaching is critical. A teacher who is motivated and knowledgeable can help any child to understand and achieve success in mathematics.

Diagnosing. Mathematics teachers are responsible for learning what mathematics knowledge children have already built and, on this basis, making decisions about current and future mathematical concepts children might be ready to learn. Only when we have learned the nature of the mathematical knowledge children have acquired can we plan appropriate learning activities that will meaningfully expand children's knowledge.

Other preplanning decisions. Other preplanning activities include making decisions about broad goals, what content to include and what to exclude from a unit or lesson, and the nature of the most appropriate activities for children (e.g., hands-on, discussion, computer-based, long-term project).

Planning

The unit. Decisions and observations made in the preplanning stage lead naturally into unit planning. The unit plan generally expands on one curriculum topic and includes lesson plans and teaching strategies for a few days or a few weeks. The unit plan might consist of a series of headings such as:

1. goals
2. prerequisites
3. sequence of new skills to be introduced
4. developmental activities
5. practice activities
6. application of new skills
7. problem solving
8. enrichment activities
9. evaluation of children's learning

Another strategy for developing a unit plan is a *concept map*. A concept map is a schematic organization of your ideas about a particular topic so that relationships among various subtopics are visually displayed (Morine-Dershimer, 1990). A concept map for a unit on multiplication of a two-digit number by a one-digit number has been *started* in Figure 2-10. As you read more about specific instructional strategies for teaching multiplication, you could add to this concept map. Bartels (1995) and Hanselman (1996) describe other uses of concept maps and provide some examples of child-constructed maps.

A teacher will decide what type of format to use for unit planning. The process, rather than the form, is what is important.

Lesson plans. Lesson plans translate the yearly and unit plans into daily activities and experiences for the children. As with unit plans, many special formats have been developed. Some consist of as few as four components—objective, materials, procedures, and evaluation (Morine-Dershimer, 1990)—to much more complex outlines (Orlich et al., 1990). The format will, in part, be determined by such considerations as the preferred teaching style, the nature of the activities, and the topic. Again, it is the process, not the format, that is important.

Box 2-1 contains a simple-format sample lesson plan to develop the commutative property of addition based on the clothes hanger suggestion in Chapter 8.

Process of Teaching

There are many different models or styles of teaching. At a very simplistic level these have sometimes been described as being along a continuum from "pure telling" to

---

FIGURE 2-10

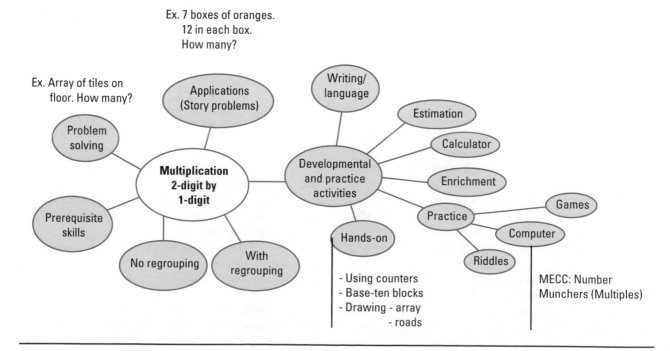

> ### BOX 2-1
>
> ### Sample Lesson Plan Commutative Property of Addition for Grade 1
>
> #### Objectives
>
> - Given concrete materials, children will demonstrate the commutative property of addition with sums less than 10.
> - Given an addition sentence, children will write the commutative form.
>
> #### Materials
>
> - Two clothes hangers with two distinct sets of clothespins clipped onto the bottom wire. For example, one will have 2 pins adjacent to each other, a distinct space, and then 4 pins close together to show sets of 2 and 4. The other hanger will show 4 pins, a space, and then 2 pins.
> - Counters.
>
> #### Procedure
>
> 1. Tell a motivational story about two children who were given money on different days. Trish was given 2 dimes on Saturday and 4 dimes on Sunday. Josh was given 4 dimes on Saturday and 2 on Sunday. Ask, "Who do you think had more dimes? Why?" Allow discussion.
> 2. Show the hanger with the 2–4 arrangement and ask the children to talk about the display. (*2 and 4 is 6.*) Hold the second hanger so that both are visible to the children and elicit discussion about what is the same and what is different about the clothespins.
> 3. Children work in pairs with counters. One child makes two arrangements of two sets (similar to the two hangers), and the other child verifies that when joined, both arrangements have the same number of counters. Change roles. Repeat several times.
> 4. Repeat procedure 3. This time the children record on paper the two arrangements with the results when combined (addition sentences).
>
> #### Closure
>
> Use the hanger with a different arrangement of pins and ask the children to orally give you two addition sentences for the arrangements. Then ask the children
>
> - how they could prove that the two sentences are correct.
> - to articulate what is happening (the "order" property).
> - whether they think the order property holds true for all addition sentences with two numbers.
>
> #### Evaluation
>
> - Could children successfully translate the concrete models to abstract arithmetic sentences?
> - Which children need more help?
>
> #### Extension (if time allows, or as an out-of-class challenge)
>
> Use the numbers 3, 5, and 8. How many *different* addition sentences can you write?
>
> #### Individualized Assessment Task (to be done at a later time)
>
> Show the child a card on which is written 2 + 5 and 5 + 2. Ask the child,
>
> - "Read each of these." (*2 plus 5, 5 plus 2*)
> - "Are they the same or different?" (*different story; same answer*)
> - "Explain how you know they are the same." (*uses counters and switches the two groups*)
> - "If you didn't know the answer and were going to figure it out, which form would you use?" (*5 + 2 is faster because there is less counting on*)

"pure discovery" (Riedesel, 1990). No teacher operates at only one location along this continuum. Teachers normally have a region or range along the continuum in which they feel most "comfortable." Many of the decisions made in the preplanning stage will influence the teaching style for a particular lesson.

Models for teaching mathematics   A teacher with a constructivist theory of learning will likely employ a *developmental* model of teaching in which children ac-

tively engage in inquiry and investigations. Even then there are times when an explanatory approach with the whole class is appropriate.

Riedesel (1990) identifies four aspects in which the "developmental" approach is different from the "telling" approach.

1. The developmental approach emphasizes *active* learning as opposed to waiting for the teacher to explain.

2. The developmental approach builds new knowledge on experience; therefore, it is socially relevant. The explanatory approach tends to build dependence on the teacher or a textbook.

3. Developmental approaches stress children's thinking; therefore, the classroom is child-centered. In an explanatory environment children tend to wait to see what the teacher thinks.

4. The developmental approach emphasizes a "search for relationships and patterns and leads to an understanding of mathematical structure." (p. 12)

A *diagnostic* model places assessing children's current level of mathematical understanding at the core of the teaching process. That knowledge is then used to structure learning activities that will help the child build onto existing mathematical knowledge. A diagnostic model developed by Ashlock, Johnson, Wilson, and Jones (1983) suggested a sequence of five types of lessons arising from a diagnostic core.

1. Initiating—provides experiences with the new concept to be learned.

2. Abstracting—focuses on the attributes of the new concept to develop understanding.

3. Schematizing—focuses on interrelationships between the new concept and previously learned concepts.

4. Consolidating—provides practice to sharpen and clarify the new concept.

5. Transferring—problem-solving activities that show application of the new concept to new settings.

Earlier we referred to the claim of Behr et al. (1983) that meaning in mathematics results from building or recognizing relationships *between* or *within* representations. Building relationships between representations leads to a type of *translation* model for teaching. A teacher might state a problem (spoken language) and ask the children to represent (translate) it using concrete materials. At other times pictures may be used to represent the idea. Later, translations or connections will be made between verbal, concrete, pictorial, and symbolic representations (Sawada, 1985). The translation model may be observed most often in lessons involving the operations. These ideas are summarized in Figure 2-11. The reader should be able to write descriptions in the empty cells.

Children build mathematical knowledge when they explore and experiment with ideas, processes, or data. The *investigative* model focuses on experimentation as well as inquiry. A possible sequence of steps in such a lesson might be as follows:

- Structure a problem or make a statement that stimulates investigation

- Children do something
  —experiment, collect data

- Record or summarize data
  —discuss and decide on appropriate form (table, graph, chart, etc.)

- Analyze or interpret the data
  —look for patterns, relationships, etc.
  —describe the pattern (oral, written, or both)

- Make a generalization or hypothesis
  —test with other data

- Respond to initial problem or statement
  —write a report on the experiment/project

- Extend generalization to other problems, settings, or applications

The preceding steps are not to be interpreted rigidly. They are fluid and flexible and will need to be adapted or modified for different problems and experiments. The emphasis is on exploration, experimentation, interpretation, hypothesizing, and generalizing. The investigative model fits well into a cooperative learning approach.

These models of teaching mathematics are not exclusive. Good teachers adapt a model based on their physical setting, the nature of the children and the children's individual differences, the mathematical topic, and their philosophy of teaching.

Role of communication revisited.   Earlier in this chapter, we stated that communication about mathematics significantly influences the mathematics curriculum and the learning of mathematics.

Communication also is an important factor in daily teaching activities and deserves additional comment here. The Principles and Standards states:

> When students are challenged to think and reason about mathematics and to communicate the results of their thinking to others orally or in writing, they learn to be clear and convincing. Listening to others' explanations gives students opportunities to develop their own understandings. (NCTM, 2000, p. 60)

Why are communication skills important in mathematics? Primarily because they help children clarify their thinking and sharpen their understanding of concepts and procedures. Representing an idea or problem in a different form, talking about a concept or algorithm, listening to explanations by others, writing a definition in our own words, and reading textual material all contribute to an individual's building mathematical understandings.

Reuille-Irons and Irons (1989) state:

> Children's knowledge and excitement about mathematics grow if situations are provided to encourage discussion about their learning. This allows children to extend

FIGURE 2-11 ▶

Teacher Moves

		Concrete	Pictorial	Symbolic	Verbal
Child's Response	Concrete	Teacher shows concrete representation; child manipulates concrete objects	Teacher shows picture; child manipulates concrete objects	Teacher writes; child manipulates concrete objects	Teacher talks; child manipulates concrete objects
	Pictorial	Teacher shows concrete representation; child chooses or draws picture	P⟶P	S⟶P	V⟶P
	Symbolic	Teacher shows concrete representation; child writes symbols	P⟶S	S⟶S	V⟶S
	Verbal	Teacher shows concrete representation; child discusses/talks	P⟶V	S⟶V	V⟶V

their own strategies and build new ones. It is important to plan learning experiences that will foster exploration and investigation. These activities will promote the use of language that can be gradually extended to more sophisticated ideas that might be associated with the important mathematical concepts. (p. 86)

Reuille-Irons and Irons identified four sequential stages in which the development of language in mathematics can occur:

1. *Child's language.* The natural language of the child.
2. *Material language.* This is language that might be associated naturally with a specific representation of a mathematical idea. "Cover up" might be an example

of a material-specific expression if pictures are being used to represent a subtractive situation.

3. *Mathematical language.* This involves using a word or short phrase for the mathematical operation.
8 apples "put with" 2 apples
Start with 3, "add" 5

4. *Symbolic language.* The words or phrases from stage three are now converted to symbols.

Within each stage, Reuille-Irons and Irons recommended language experiences that move from modeling aloud to creating to sharing.

The major purpose of writing in mathematics is that it "forces" one to think through a concept or process, resulting in a honing of one's understanding.

McIntosh (1991) suggests four useful forms of writing. In learning logs, children can reflect on what they are doing and learning. Journals are similar but often less formal and may therefore be more communicative than logs. They may also provide more insight into a child's feelings about mathematics than logs. In expository writing, children explain an idea or process. For example, a child may explain to a new student how she or he does multiplication. Creative writing gives children a chance to use abilities not often a part of school mathematics. Children may write poems about mathematical ideas or stories about concepts, mathematicians, etc. Here are some examples:

- Write a story about 6.
- Write a story about a reflection (flip).
- Write a poem about addition.

If understanding is sharpened through writing, achievement should improve as well. Evans (1984) asked her Grade 5 children to engage in three kinds of writing: explanations, definitions, and troubleshooting (describe an error and tell why it was made). The children made much larger gains in achievement than a control class in which no writing was done other than what was required to answer questions, exercises, and problems. Other writers (Azzolino, 1990; Burton, 1985; Davidson & Pearce, 1988; Fennell & Ammon, 1985; Thompson, 1990) have provided rationales and suggested strategies for incorporating writing into the mathematics class.

Post-Teaching Activities

The teacher's primary responsibilities in the post-teaching phase include the ongoing activities of evaluation and reflection. Evaluation is the process of gathering information and using it to make judgments that in turn are used to make decisions. A teacher should evaluate the lesson and his or her teaching, reflect on the teaching strategies used, and assess learning. (Assessment of children's learning is discussed in Chapter 4.)

Evaluation of teaching   According to NCTM (1991), the goal of evaluating mathematics teaching is to "improve teaching and enhance professional growth" (p. 72). Evaluation should be ongoing and linked to professional development. Teachers should have opportunities to analyze their own teaching and discuss their teaching with colleagues and supervisors. Evaluation should be based on the teacher's goals and expectations for children, the teacher's plans, and evidence of children's learning and understanding.

The NCTM (1991) Professional Teaching Standards lists many components of the evaluation of teaching. In general, the evaluation of teaching should focus on the

teacher's ability to (1) teach concepts, procedures, and connections; (2) promote mathematical problem solving, reasoning, and connections; (3) foster children's mathematical dispositions; (4) assess children's understanding of mathematics; and (5) create a learning environment that promotes the development of each child's mathematical power.

Reflection on teaching   It is critical that teachers spend time reflecting on their instruction (Hart, Schultz, Najee-ullah, & Nash, 1992), including the general approach to teaching and the type of learning activities developed for the children as well as the more overt teaching strategies. Such reflection results in professional growth. Self-evaluation of teaching practices and effectiveness is strongly encouraged in the *Professional Standards*. Specific standards directly related to evaluation of teaching are presented in Box 2-2.

THINKING ABOUT THE CURRICULUM

The mathematics curriculum can be thought about at two levels: first, as the mathematics concepts, procedures, and processes to which the child is exposed; second, especially as it is experienced by the child, as all the activities and tasks the child engages in that are designed to help the child build some mathematical understanding. The beginning teacher is initially more concerned about what to teach; the more experienced teacher is probably more interested in the kinds of activities that help develop the concepts. However, every teacher needs to be concerned with both aspects.

The Mathematics

A teacher needs to know what mathematics knowledge the children have at the start of the school year, what concepts they are expected to learn during the year, and where these concepts will lead. This information may be obtained by assessing children's understanding (see Chapter 4) and by examining the district and state grade-level standards, the textbook and curriculum guide used in the school district, and the end-of-year assessment that children are required to complete.

The teacher must assess what mathematical understandings the children actually possess and then adapt the stated curriculum so that children understand prerequisite skills and concepts before attempting to build new ones.

The Activities

The real curriculum consists of much more than the concepts listed in a mathematics curriculum guide or state or district standards. It is the total of all the mathematics-

BOX 2-2

Creating Mathematical Environments

Does the learning environment foster the development of all children's mathematical power?

Teaching Mathematical Concepts, Procedures, and Connections

Does the teacher have a sound knowledge of the mathematical concepts and have children been given tasks that promote their understanding of those concepts? Has the teacher engaged children in tasks and discussions that will enable them to see and use connections within mathematics and with other disciplines?

Teaching Mathematics as Problem Solving, Reasoning, and Communication

Did the teacher model different aspects of problem solving and engage children in activities and discussions related to a variety of aspects of problem solving? Did the teacher model mathematics as communication, monitor children's mathematical language, and provide opportunities for children to engage in a variety of communication forms? Did the teacher emphasize reasoning processes and provide opportunities for children to reason mathematically?

Promoting Mathematical Disposition

Assessment of a teacher's fostering of children's mathematical dispositions should provide evidence that the teacher—

- models a disposition to do mathematics.
- demonstrates the value of mathematics as a way of thinking and its application in other disciplines and in society.
- promotes children's confidence, flexibility, perseverance, curiosity, and inventiveness in doing mathematics through the use of appropriate tasks and by engaging children in mathematical discourse. (p. 104)

Assessing Children's Understanding of Mathematics

Did the teacher use a variety of appropriate assessment methods? Were these methods congruent with the level and background of the children and with the way in which the concepts were taught? Were the results analyzed for reporting purposes and for modification of future instruction?

---

related experiences a child has, both in and out of school. These experiences include playing counting games at recess, going to the store to purchase something after school, and engaging in the activities designed by the teacher. All such experiences contribute to a child's construction of mathematics knowledge.

When selecting or developing mathematics activities for children, it is important that the teacher keep in mind the standards that the children are expected to meet so that the teacher can clearly write objectives for each lesson and goals for each unit.

CONCLUSION

The importance of meaning or understanding in learning mathematics cannot be overemphasized. The model to the right may help focus the picture. It shows meaning as a function of the child's exploration, often, but not exclusively, with concrete models, construction, and communication—all active, not passive, processes.

Teaching mathematics requires hard work. A teacher's task is to create and help children create for themselves representations of mathematical ideas that will enable the

child to build a significant mathematical knowledge structure. To do this effectively teachers must be:

- cognizant of how children learn mathematics;
- familiar with the mathematics included in the curriculum;

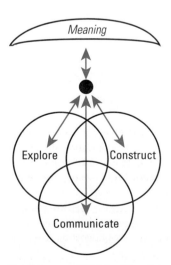

The Process of Making Meaning

- able to design strategies and activities that will help children learn the concepts meaningfully; and
- able to assess the level of development of the concept in children.

A child's attitude toward mathematics must also be assessed and the information used to plan activities that will generate a positive attitude.

For Your Journal

When you have finished studying this chapter, reflect on the following questions in your math journal:

1. Imagine you are an elementary teacher and another teacher in your school asks why you let children choose from a variety of materials when solving problems. How will you respond?
2. Imagine you are an elementary teacher and the parents of one of your students feel that their child is spending too much time talking and writing in math class. How will you respond?
3. Explain the five different modes in which a mathematics concept may be represented and give an example of each for a concept of your choice.

For Your Portfolio

When you have finished studying this chapter, complete the following activities to include in your professional portfolio:

1. Write a lesson plan for a concept of your choice. Include at least two different modes of representation in this lesson and describe the translations that take place during the lesson.
2. Write a lesson plan that develops conceptual knowledge for a concept of your choice.
3. Write a lesson plan that includes several forms of communication.

Resources for Teachers

Books on implementing cooperative learning

Erickson, T. (1989). *Getting it together: Equals.* Berkeley: Regents of the University of California.

Fraser, S. (1982). SPACES: *Solving problems of access to careers in engineering and science.* Palo Alto, CA: Seymour.

Books on preventing math anxiety

Burns, M. (1998). *Math: Facing an American phobia.* Sausalito, CA: Marilyn Burns Education Associates.

Martinez, J., & Martinez, N. (1996). *Math without fear.* Needham Heights, MA: Allyn & Bacon.

Tobias, S. (1978). *Overcoming math anxiety.* Boston: Houghton Mifflin.

Books on using children's literature

Bresser, R. (1995). *Math and literature, Grades 4–6.* Sausalito, CA: Math Solutions.

Burns, M. (1992). *Math and literature, K–3: Book one.* Sausalito, CA: Math Solutions.

California Department of Education. (1993). *Literature for science and mathematics.* Sacramento: California Department of Education.

Kruse, G., & Horning, K. (1991). *Multicultural literature for children and young adults.* Madison: Wisconsin Department of Public Instruction.

Sheffield, S. (1995). *Math and literature, K–3: Book two.* Sausalito, CA: Math Solutions.

Thiessen, D., Matthias, M., & Smith, J. (1998). *The wonderful world of mathematics.* Reston, VA: National Council of Teachers of Mathematics.

Welchman-Tischler, R. (1992). *How to use children's literature to teach mathematics.* Reston, VA: National Council of Teachers of Mathematics.

Links to the Internet

Search engines for lesson plans

http://www.altavista.com

http://www.hotbot.com

http://www.lycos.com

http://www.netscape.com

http://www.yahoo.com

http://www.google.com

Search engines are sites on the Internet where visitors can enter key words and find resources on the Internet. Visit any of the preceding sites and type "math lesson plans." You will receive a list of many sites containing math lesson plans. The following are a few of those sites:

AskERIC Lesson Plans
http://askeric.org/Virtual/Lessons/

Contains more than 1000 lesson plans.

Eisenhower National Clearinghouse
http://www.enc.org/weblinks

Contains links to mathematics lessons and other resources.

ProTeacher
http://www.proteacher.com

Contains lesson plans and education news.

CHAPTER 3

Developing Mathematical Thinking and Problem-Solving Ability

✔ **Types of problems**

✔ **Problem-solving process**

✔ **Solution strategies**

✔ **Selecting problem-solving tasks and materials**

✔ **Clarifying the teacher's role**

✔ **Organizing and implementing problem-solving instruction**

When you have finished studying this chapter, you should be able to answer the following questions:

1. What is a problem?

2. How do the various types of problems differ?

3. What are examples of several different types of problems?

4. What are the four steps involved in the problem-solving process?

5. How do the components of a problem-solving instructional program help teachers plan for instruction?

"A teacher of mathematics has a great opportunity. If he fills his allotted time with drilling his students in routine operations, he kills their interest, hampers their intellectual development, and misuses his opportunity. But if he challenges the curiosity of his students by setting them problems proportionate to their knowledge, and helps them to solve their problems with stimulating questions, he may give them a taste for, and some means of independent thinking."

(Polya, 1957, p. v)

Problem solving is a daily activity for most people. A student considers the most efficient route to the university from a number of alternatives. A parent examines the contents of the cupboard, wondering what to prepare for dinner. A 10-year-old wants to buy an ice cream bar at the local store. She knows that she has several coins in her pocket and recalls that she has at least two quarters. Before approaching the cashier, she wonders whether she has enough money to buy a 75-cent ice cream bar.

The past three decades have witnessed a resurgence of interest in problem solving as an integral part of the mathematics curriculum. Although problem solving has always been a part of mathematics programs, during the 1980s, the National Council of Teachers of Mathematics (NCTM) and other influential groups promoted problem solving as a significant component of mathematics programs. More recently, the NCTM has reiterated the importance of problem solving in mathematics learning by designating problem solving as one of the five process standards for Grades pre K–12 in the Principles and Standards (NCTM, 2000). The Council notes that "problem solving is an integral part of all mathematics learning, and so it should not be an isolated part of the mathematics program" (NCTM, 2000, p. 52). This focus on problem solving may be interpreted as a shift from a concern with algorithms or fixed content toward an emphasis on mathematical thinking and inquiry.

This chapter is about teaching and learning considerations for engaging children in solving problems so that they will develop mathematical thinking and learn mathematics via problem solving. It is also about teaching children how to solve problems. Different strategies that children should learn to enable them to devise solution plans are discussed. Problem examples with some solution processes also are provided. ✔

PRINCIPLES AND STANDARDS LINK 3-1
Process Strand:
Problem Solving

Instructional programs from prekindergarten through grade 12 should enable all students to:

- build new mathematical knowledge through problem solving;
- solve problems that arise in mathematics and in other contexts;
- apply and adapt a variety of appropriate strategies to solve problems;
- monitor and reflect on the process of mathematical problem solving. (NCTM, 2000, p. 52)

 PRINCIPLES AND STANDARDS LINK 3-2
Process Strand:
Problem Solving

Problem solving means engaging in a task for which the solution method is not known in advance. In order to find a solution, students must draw on their knowledge, and through this process, they will often develop new mathematical understandings. (NCTM, 2000, p. 52)

MATHEMATICAL CONSIDERATIONS

The science of mathematics was born from people's efforts to understand their environment. The process of solving environmental problems led to the discovery of mathematical facts, which in turn enabled the resolution of other problems. It is through the process of problem solving that children can experience the power and usefulness of mathematics. When the problems that children are asked to solve are meaningful and interesting, children will wholeheartedly engage in problem-solving activities.

What Is a Problem?

Charles and Lester (1982) define a mathematical problem as a task for which

1. The person confronting it *wants* or *needs* to find a solution.
2. The person has *no readily available procedure* for finding the solution.
3. The person must *make an attempt* to find a solution. (p. 5)

 LITERATURE LINK 3-1
Problem Solving

Anno, Mitsumasa. (1995). ***Anno's Magic Seeds.*** New York: Philomel Books.
Zimelman, Nathan. (1992). ***How the Second Grade Got $8,205.50 to Visit the Statue of Liberty.***
  Morton Grove, Illinois: Albert Whitman & Company.

A good story often places mathematical problems in the context of familiar situations. The problem-solving context is much more convincing when the development of mathematical topics occurs naturally as part of the story, rather than as a context in which mathematics is overlaid on a story where it does not normally arise or is just not appropriate. ***Anno's Magic Seeds*** demonstrates how an interesting story and an interesting mathematics problem can create a wonderful mathematical situation.

- Provide a variety of experiences in which children apply several different problem-solving strategies to make mathematical discoveries. Have children recognize and select different strategies and reason which strategies might work better for certain kinds of problems and why.

- Develop a chart to record the way the number of golden seeds in the story changes. Help children to identify key elements of the mathematical situation, such as what year it is (year 1, 2, 3, etc.) and the number of seeds either eaten or planted.

- Note how this problem is set in a real-world context. The number of seeds follows a mathematical pattern only until some event changes it (for example, Jack gets married and has a child, changing the number of seeds eaten each year, and there is a hurricane that wipes out most of the golden seeds). These real-world occurrences make the mathematics in the story realistic, showing that real-world problems are sometimes "messy."

- ***How the Second Grade Got $8,205.50 to Visit the Statue of Liberty*** is also an example of an interesting problem situation.

Source: Dr. Patricia Moyer, George Mason University.

From this definition, one would conclude that the traditional story problems found at the end of textbook chapters do not qualify as bona fide problems. Generally, there is no evidence that children want to work at this type of problem. Usually, children quickly glance at the problem to note word clues *(altogether, left, times),* then immediately apply some operation to the data to arrive at an answer. Solving this type of problem hardly serves to develop one's mathematical thinking. Thus, other kinds of problems must be included in mathematics programs if children are to develop their thinking processes.

Children must be presented with some interesting and challenging problems so that they will gain experience in analyzing information and in proposing and testing hypotheses. It is essential that they be given the opportunity to develop insights into mathematical relationships.

Types of Problems

Mathematics programs include different types of problems: process problems, translation problems, application problems, and puzzles.

Process problems
Problem 3-1: Air Show
At an air show, 8 skydivers were released from a plane. Each skydiver was connected to each of the other skydivers with a separate piece of ribbon. How many pieces of ribbon were used in the skydiving act?

Problem 3-2: Dividing up the Land
A town has a square piece of land to use as a recreation park. The recreation officer wants to divide the land into as many areas as possible using four straight lines. The areas can be of different sizes. What is the greatest possible number of areas that can be obtained with four straight lines?

Process problems are a type of mathematics problem that requires solution processes other than computational procedures. Such problems are important because of the processes used in solving them.

According to Polya (1949), "to solve a problem is to find a way where no way is known off-hand, to find a way out of a difficulty, to find a way around an obstacle, to attain a desired end, that is not immediately attainable, by appropriate means" (p. 1).

From this definition, it is clear that problem solving involves higher-order thinking. It forces children to think creatively and innovatively to find a new way to solve a problem.

When attempting to solve a process problem, one uses available knowledge and employs certain strategies to devise a solution. When one is engaged in solving a process problem, usually the conditions for a true mathematics problem (according to Charles & Lester, 1982) are met.

Prior to the 1980s, process problems were not found in mathematics textbooks for the elementary grades. At present, process problems form an integral part of mathematics programs, and one can expect that their importance will increase.

 A Solution to the Air Show Problem

Skydiver 1 (S1) is connected to 7 skydivers.
Each skydiver is connected to 7 other skydivers.

$$8 \times 7 = 56$$

But it takes one ribbon to connect S1 to S2 and S2 to S1. Therefore, the total number of ribbons used is 56/2 = 28. Twenty-eight ribbons are needed.

Other strategies that could be used to solve this problem are construct a diagram, model the situation, and solve a simpler problem. These strategies are discussed on pages 50-57. Try them.

Although process problems are regarded as an important component of a mathematics program, there are other types of problems that should not be neglected entirely. These are the kinds of problems that have traditionally been a part of programs, namely translation and application problems.

Translation problems
Problem 3-3: Seating Capacity
A school auditorium can seat 648 people in 18 equal rows. How many seats are there in each row?

Problem 3-4: Jogging Rate
Ryan jogged 2 miles in 15 minutes. At this rate, how long would it take him to jog 26 miles?

TECHNOLOGY LINK 3-1
Brain Teasers

Challenge your students (and yourself) with this website! First, pick a grade-level range (grades 3–4, 5–6, or 7–8). Then choose this week's question or last week's question and solution. These brain teasers can be the focus of a lesson or great enrichment activities! Visit http://www.eduplace.com/math/brain/ or link from our Companion Website at **www.prenhall. com/cathcart.**

Translation problems include the one- and two-step story problems typically found in textbooks. These problems can be a medium for children to develop understanding of the basic operations or to construct their own computational algorithms. Approached in this way, story problems can help children grow in their knowledge of mathematics and enhance mathematical thinking. However, if story problems are presented to children after they have learned how to compute, then the problems are mere practice exercises and they do not help to develop problem-solving ability.

Application problems
Problem 3-5: Electricity Costs

How much does the school board pay for the electricity used in your school in a school year? What is the monthly average cost?

Computation is generally the solution process used to solve application problems. Once the required data have been gathered and a decision has been made about a solution process, a calculator can lessen the time needed to arrive at an answer. Solving applied problems that are of interest to children can enhance their appreciation of mathematics.

Puzzles
Problem 3-6: Nine-Dot Puzzle

Can you join all nine dots using four straight lines without lifting your pencil from the paper?

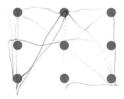

Problem 3-7: Four Congruent Parts

Can you partition the figure in four congruent parts?

Although solving puzzles may not require any mathematical knowledge, puzzles are classified as a type of mathematical problem (Charles & Lester, 1982) and are included in school programs. It is often difficult to identify what strategy to use to solve a given puzzle. Usually, mathematical processes such as visualization, analysis, conjecturing, and testing are involved.

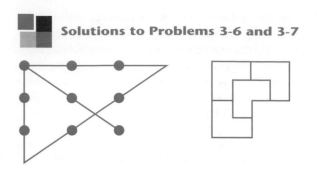

Solutions to Problems 3-6 and 3-7

Ask Children to Write Problems

One way to help children become comfortable with problems and the problem-solving process is to have children write problems. Through such experiences, children develop critical thinking skills, learn to collect and organize data (Fennell & Ammon, 1985), and learn how to express ideas in a clear and succinct manner.

A teacher can collect newspaper clippings, restaurant menus, sale flyers from local businesses, statistics from government departments, etc., and make them available to children to use when writing problems.

Another type of problem-writing activity is to ask children to write a problem for a given mathematical sentence. Some examples are given below.

1. Write a problem that fits the number sentence 46 + 17 = 63.

2. Write a problem that fits the number sentence 35 − 28 = 7 and that asks the question "How many more . . . ?"

3. Write a multiplication story problem for the array.

   . . . .
   . . . .
   . . . .
   . . . .

4. Write a division story problem that asks to solve 138 divided by 6.

5. Write a word problem in which one has to first add, then subtract to answer the question.

> ### PRINCIPLES AND STANDARDS LINK 3-3
> ### Process Strand:
> ### Problem Solving
>
> Posing problems comes naturally to young children: *I wonder how long it would take to count to a million? How many soda cans would it take to fill the school building?* Teachers and parents can foster this inclination by helping students make mathematical problems from their worlds. (NCTM, 2000, p. 53)

The writing process When children are asked to write problems, a teacher may direct them through a process similar to writing stories, that is, there can be a prewriting stage followed by the writing, conferencing, and revising stages. Final stages can be publication and follow-up (Ford, 1990).

The prewriting stage is a time to create or examine a set of data and to think of a story to flesh out the data. When a problem has been written, it should be shared with other children. Conferencing about the problem can assist children in clarifying expressed ideas. When other children cannot understand a problem, the writer must revise it until ideas are clearly expressed. Children may find that in some problems, there are missing data or extraneous information or that the question does not fit the data. Such feedback helps children to revise the problem so that it is comprehensible and acceptable (Ford, 1990).

Children can "publish" their problems on paper to place in a binder or on cards for easy access. Follow-up activities include having a class discuss some problems in order to highlight particular types or having children solve each others' problems. A successful experience of reading and solving a problem written by a classmate may augment a child's interest in learning mathematics.

Posing problems The activity of posing problems is different from that of writing problems as previously described. Problem posing usually refers to the process of changing an existing problem into a new one by modifying the *knowns,* the *unknowns,* or the *restrictions* placed on the answer (Moses, Bjork, & Goldenberg, 1990).

A trusting and supportive relationship between teacher and children will set the stage for both teacher and children to pose interesting problems. Mathematics classes should also be "alive," with children actively participating by questioning, conjecturing, and eagerly testing possibilities for solutions. In such a classroom climate, a teacher can easily encourage children to "study" given problems to see how they might be modified to create new and possibly more interesting and challenging problems. In this way, children become problem posers by generating new problems.

Teachers are encouraged to initiate problem-posing activities with children by:

> . . . modelling the process personally by wondering openly *with* the students, fostering the free exchange of ideas and actively encouraging collaboration among students, honoring students' spontaneous what-ifs and conjectures, and being as interested in *how* students thought about a problem as in *what* they came up with. (Moses, Bjork, & Goldenberg, 1990, p. 86)

Moses, Bjork, and Goldenberg (1990) offer the following four principles for guiding children to engage in posing problems:

1. Have children learn to focus their attention on *known, unknown,* and *restrictions.* Then consider the following questions: What if different things were known and unknown? What if the restrictions were changed?

2. Begin with a comfortable mathematics topic.

3. Encourage children to use ambiguity to create new questions and problems.

4. Teach the idea of domain from the earliest grades, encouraging children to "play the same (mathematical) game with a different set of pieces." (pp. 83–86)

The process of problem posing can contribute considerably to enriching mathematics classes by actively engaging children in constructing mathematics for themselves.

THE PROBLEM-SOLVING PROCESS

Polya's (1957) four phases of problem solving have become the framework often recommended for teaching problem solving:

- understanding the problem;
- devising a plan to solve the problem;
- implementing a solution plan; and
- reflecting on the problem

Understanding the Problem

This first phase of the problem-solving process is important, although some children do not see it as such. Children who do not try to understand the problem look for word clues or quickly decide on an operation to apply to the data. Rather, this first phase of problem solving should be given attention so that children will come to see the need for understanding a problem.

Understanding a problem is more than a matter of reading comprehension. It consists of apprehending the goal being sought, differentiating between required information and extraneous information, and detecting missing information. It also involves checking for assumptions regarding the given conditions.

Provide time for children to familiarize themselves with a problem. Familiarization can happen by rereading the problem in an effort to visualize the situation. Children can be encouraged to "see in their mind the problem situation" and "tell the problem story to themselves." Children can also be asked to tell the problem story to the class in their own words. The intent here is to have children verbalize the problem clearly and succinctly, giving all necessary information to solve the problem. Questions to ask children include the following:

- How would you tell the problem story?
- Can someone describe the problem another way?
- Did _____ give all the important information?
- Is there something that needs to be added to what _____ said?
- Could some information that _____ gave have been left out?
- What will you know when you have solved the problem?

When children understand a problem, they are more likely to accept the problem and devote themselves to finding a solution.

Devising a Plan to Solve the Problem

Allow time for children to reflect on possible solution processes. Children can be invited to share possible solution strategies with one or two classmates. A group of children working together may discuss possible solution strategies. A child would tell the group why she or he thinks a particular strategy is an appropriate one for a given problem. The group may then decide to try a common strategy or have each member try a different strategy.

For a potentially difficult problem, the class as a whole can be invited to discuss solution strategies. This sharing can provide ideas for children who are stumped as to how to begin without removing the challenge to develop a solution process.

Whenever appropriate, encourage children to make an estimate about the quantity, measure, or magnitude of the solution before proceeding to implement a solution plan. The estimate can be revised as they progress through the solution process and recorded as first estimate, second estimate, etc. Making estimates requires that children reflect on what is happening and "think ahead," which can assist them in "seeing" a solution pattern without having to work through all the cases of the problem.

Implementing a Solution Plan

When children have personally decided on a plan, they begin to implement it to find a solution. Children should be allowed and encouraged to use their own ingenuity to develop a solution plan. Figure 3-1 depicts three different tables Grade 5 students constructed to solve the same problem. Children favor the freedom to select and develop solution processes over having to follow uniform procedures.

Children should be encouraged to solve problems in different ways and to discuss the different solution

processes. For example, elementary-school children could solve the Barnyard problem (Figure 3-2) by drawing a picture, through trial and error, and by constructing a table and considering all possibilities. Middle-school children could possibly solve the problem algebraically.

In addition, suggest that children develop their solution process in detail, not erasing "mistakes" or partial solutions. By commenting on the different approaches, teachers can assist children to realize that processes that didn't work can be informative in subsequent problem-solving activities. The analogy can be made to a scientist performing numerous experiments in an effort to discover, for example, a cure for a disease. A scientist does not destroy unsuccessful experimental results but keeps the data to inform further research efforts. Likewise, when children are trying to solve a problem, comparisons can be made with previous attempts to solve a somewhat similar problem. Recorded problem-solving attempts can also serve to provide insights into a child's thinking and assist a teacher in evaluation.

When engaging in problem-solving activities, children should not expect to find a solution to every problem they attempt to solve. The activity of problem solving, that is, the attempt, is more important than the solution.

Reflecting on the Problem

A teacher should advise a child that a solution process should be checked after a solution has been reached or while working through a solution strategy. For example, pausing to reflect on one's approach to solving a problem may lead one to abort a plan and seek another solution strategy.

Upon the completion of a solution, children should be encouraged to *look back* to the problem to see whether the conditions of the problem have been met. Were wrong assumptions made? Has the problem question been answered? Is the answer unique, or are there others?

At this stage, children should also reflect on the solution process and think of other appropriate solution strategies. One might notice how the problem could have been solved, not only by a different approach but also through a more efficient process.

Children should also be encouraged to *look forward* for ways of extending a problem. Asking the question "What if . . . ?" is a good approach to modifying a problem. Changing one aspect of a problem, such as the setting, the conditions, or the data, and then attempting to solve the new problem can lead to insightful learning. It is also worthwhile to ask how the problem is similar to or different from other familiar problems.

Children should "feel right" about their solution before declaring that they have solved the problem. Therefore, this final step in the problem-solving process should not be quickly dismissed but should lead students to be ready to "defend" their solution when called upon to do so.

> **FIGURE 3-1**

Problem:
Josh has 3 pairs of pants, 4 sweaters, and 2 pairs of shoes. How many different pant-sweater-shoes combinations can Josh choose from to wear to school on Monday?

Solution 1 (Paula, Grade 5)

SWEATERS				PANTS			SHOES		SWEATERS				PANTS			SHOES	
O	Y	B	W	B	B	A	B	G	O	Y	B	W	B	B	A	B	G
X				X			X		X				X				X
X					X		X		X					X			X
X						X	X		X						X		X
	X			X			X			X			X				X
	X				X		X			X				X			X
	X					X	X			X					X		X
		X		X			X				X		X				X
		X			X		X				X			X			X
		X				X	X				X				X		X
			X	X			X					X	X				X
			X		X		X					X		X			X
			X			X	X					X			X		X

24 Combinations

Solution 2 (Mark, Grade 5)

P	S	SH	
Jeans	Fluorescent	Reeboks	Vision Streetwear
Joggers	Rockshirt	Reeboks	Vision Streetwear
Acid Washed	White	Vision Streetwear	Reeboks
Jeans	Trappers	Vision Streetwear	Reeboks
Jeans	Rockshirt	Reeboks	Vision Streetwear
Jeans	White	Vision Streetwear	Reeboks
Joggers	Trappers	Reeboks	Vision Streetwear
Joggers	Fluorescent	Vision Streetwear	Reeboks
Joggers	White	Reeboks	Vision Streetwear
Acid Washed	Trappers	Vision Streetwear	Reeboks
Acid Washed	Rockshirt	Reeboks	Vision Streetwear
Acid Washed	Fluorescent	Vision Streetwear	Reeboks

24 combinations

Solution 3 (Carl, Grade 5)

PANTS	SWEATERS	SHOES	NO. OF WAYS
1	1	1	1
1	2	1	2
1	3	1	3
1	4	1	4
1	1	2	5
1	2	2	6
1	3	2	7
1	4	2	8

Think: Since there were 3 pants and each had 8 different ways, you get 24 different ways to dress.

Source: "Writing to Communicate Mathematics," (p. 12), by Y. Pothier, 1992, In Daiyo Sawada (Ed.), *Communication in the mathematics classroom.* Edmonton, AB: Mathematics Council of the Alberta Teacher's Association.

> **FIGURE 3-2**

THE BARNYARD PROBLEM

Jill counted 20 pigs and chickens in the barnyard. Jack counted a total of 54 legs for the 20 animals. How many pigs and chickens were there?

a) Draw a diagram

　　2 legs each. This is 40 legs. Need 14 more. I'll add 2 to 7 animals.
　　Answer: There are 7 pigs and 13 chickens.

b) Trial and error

10 pigs and 10 chickens	$40 + 20 = 60$	Too many legs.
8 pigs and 12 chickens	$32 + 24 = 56$	Still too many.
6 pigs and 14 chickens	$24 + 28 = 52$	Not enough.
7 pigs and 13 chickens	$28 + 26 = 54$	That's it!

Answer: There are 7 pigs and 13 chickens.

c) Consider all possibilities

Pigs	Chickens	Legs	Total	
1	19	4 + 38	42	
2	18	8 + 36	44	
3	17	12 + 34	46	
4	16	16 + 32	48	
5	15	20 + 30	50	Answer: There are 7 pigs
6	14	24 + 28	52	and 13 chickens.
7	13	28 + 26	54	
8	12	32 + 24	56	
9	11	36 + 22	58	

d) Solve algebraically

Let x = the chickens　　　Solve for y　　　　　　Solve for x
Let y = the pigs

$$2x + 4y = 54 \qquad\qquad x + y = 20$$
$$\underline{2x + 2y = 40} \qquad\qquad x + 7 = 20$$
$$x + y = 20 \qquad\qquad 2y = 14 \qquad\qquad x = 20 - 7$$
$$2x + 4y = 54 \qquad\qquad y = 7 \qquad\qquad x = 13$$

Check

$$x + y = 20 \qquad\qquad 2x + 4y = 54 \qquad \text{Answer: There are 7 pigs and}$$
$$13 + 7 = 20 \qquad\qquad 2(13) + 4\,(7) = 54 \qquad \text{13 chickens.}$$
$$26 + 28 = 54$$

PROBLEM-SOLVING STRATEGIES

Learning a number of problem-solving strategies is an asset for problem solving (Suydam, 1984). However, children first should be encouraged to develop their own problem-solving strategies and become facile at using those strategies. This helps them gain confidence in their mathematics ability and enhances their reasoning skills.

After children have developed and mastered their own problem-solving strategies, a teacher can at a given time highlight a particular strategy and lead the children in a class discussion and application of the strategy. In time, children will acquire a repertoire of different strategies to draw upon when faced with a problem. A number of problem-solving strategies are described in this section. Two examples of a problem that can be solved using each strategy are included. Some possible solutions are provided.

Dramatize or Model the Situation and Solution Process

Problem 3-8: The Class Reunion

Twelve people came to celebrate their 10-year high school reunion. Each person shook hands once with all the other persons. How many handshakes were exchanged at the reunion?

PRINCIPLES AND STANDARDS LINK 3-4
Process Strand:
Problem Solving

As with any other component of the mathematical tool kit, strategies must receive instructional attention if students are expected to learn them. In the lower grades, teachers can help children express, categorize, and compare their strategies. Opportunities to use strategies must be embedded naturally in the curriculum across the content areas. By the time students reach the middle grades, they should be skilled at recognizing when various strategies are appropriate to use and should be capable of deciding when and how to use them. (NCTM, 2000, p. 54)

Problem 3-9: Karla's Farewell Party

Karla is moving to another state and her best friend has organized a farewell party for her. The people arrive at the house in the following manner: The first time the doorbell rings, Karla, as the first guest, enters. On each successive ring a group enters that has two more people than the group that entered on the previous ring. How many guests will have arrived after the 12th ring?

Dramatization is a powerful medium to demonstrate understanding of a problem situation and can also lead one to "see" a solution. The Class Reunion and Karla's Farewell Party are examples of problems that children enjoy acting out.

Rather than participate in a dramatization, children may prefer to model the problem situation. For example, children could use objects to represent guests at Karla's party and to keep track of the separate groups arriving at the party.

 Solution to the Class Reunion Problem

In acting out this problem, groups of 12 children could be formed. (The problem could be solved for a smaller group of people to accommodate all the children.)

In a dramatization, each child would shake hands with each of the other people in the group. The realization that there is only one handshake when, for example, Sue shakes hands with Tom and Tom shakes hands with Sue, will assist children in arriving at a solution.

The discussion could be the following:

There are 12 of us. Each one has shaken hands with 11 other persons. That means 12 × 11 or 132 handshakes have taken place. But, there were really only half that number because when two people shake hands, there is

only one handshake and not two. Therefore, when twelve people shake hands with each other, there are 66 handshakes.

Draw a Picture or Diagram

Drawing a picture is a favored strategy of many problem solvers. Some people draw a picture to help them visualize the situation, and when they understand the problem, they use another strategy to solve it.

Young children like to draw and usually enjoy developing a solution process to problems by using pictures. This strategy can be time-consuming, because children may want to draw objects in great detail. In time, they will realize that representational diagrams are all that are required in problem solving.

Problem 3-10: The Cycle Problem

Kyle and Jason watched the children's bicycle and tricycle parade during the summer festival. They agreed to keep count of the number of cycles and the number of wheels as the children's parade passed by. At the end of the parade, Kyle declared he had counted 17 cycles and Jason said he had counted 43 wheels. How many bicycles and tricycles were in the parade?

Problem 3-11: The Barnyard Problem

Jill counted 20 pigs and chickens in the farmyard. Jack counted a total of 54 legs for the 20 animals. How many pigs and chickens were there? (See Figure 3-2.)

 Solution to the Cycle Problem

There were 17 cycles in the parade.

Altogether there were 43 wheels.

Begin by drawing all the cycles with two wheels each.

Seventeen cycles with two wheels each make 34 wheels.

Nine wheels are missing. Draw them on the cycles.

There were 8 bicycles and 9 tricycles in the parade.

If children have solved the Barnyard Problem (see Figure 3-2), they should notice the similarity between the two problems.

Construct a Table or Chart

Constructing a table involves identifying appropriate labels to keep track of pertinent data as one works through a solution process. Some children may be able to set up a table with proper headings but may not be able to systematically list the data to assist them in arriving at a solution. Therefore, provide time for children to practice making organized lists of data. The three solutions in Figure 3-1 show how differently each child organized the data concerning clothing combinations.

Problem 3-12: Clear Pond
Today one blade of grass took root in Clear Pond. Every day the grass population doubles, that is, tomorrow there will be two blades of grass, the next day, four blades, and so on. On the 10th day, how many blades of grass are in the pond? If the capacity of the pond is 1 million blades of grass, on what day will it be filled? Estimate first and then figure it out.

Problem 3-13: The Garden Fence
A gardener has 60 feet of fence to keep animals out of the garden. What is the largest area of garden that this fence will enclose?

 Solution to the Clear Pond Problem

On day one, there is one blade of grass.
Each day, the number doubles.
Setting up a table will help to keep the data organized.
The table headings will be Days and Blades of Grass.
I'll use my calculator to obtain the products.

Days	Blades of Grass
1	1
2	2
3	4
.	.
.	.
.	.
20	524,288
21	1,048,576

Using a calculator, I quickly arrive at day 20 with 524,288 blades of grass. Doubling this amount gives more than a million.
Clear Pond will be filled to capacity on day 21.

Find a Pattern

An efficient way to solve some problems is by recording data in a table and then looking for a pattern.

When children observe data in a table, they should be encouraged to look for a pattern that will enable them to make a prediction about unknown data. Detecting a pattern can abbreviate a solution process considerably.

The Streamer Problem was presented to one combined class of fifth and sixth graders. The children first suggested that acting it out would be a good way to begin. Children were provided with streamers, and they formed groups of six so that they could model a five-sided and then a six-sided room. The children then returned to their desks to record what they had observed and continued to solve the problem.

One sixth grader's work is presented in Figure 3-3. Although Jennifer began by drawing diagrams, she decided that organizing the data in a table would help her find a pattern.

Problem 3-14: The Streamer Problem
Imagine that you have been hired to decorate a room with streamers. The streamers are to be attached at the ceiling in such a way that all opposite corners of the room will be connected. How many streamers are needed to decorate a 10-sided room?

Problem 3-15: The Patio Walk Problem
Suppose you have concrete tiles that measure 2 feet by 1 foot and you wish to use them to construct a patio walk that is 2 feet wide. Three sample patio walks that could be constructed with six blocks are pictured here.

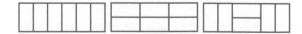

But there are other possibilities. How many different patio walks is it possible to build with eight blocks?

LITERATURE LINK 3-2
Problem Solving

Birch, David. (1988). *The King's Chessboard*. New York: Puffin.

Children need many opportunities to problem solve in meaningful contexts and to practice strategies that make sense of the mathematics in these problem situations. *The King's Chessboard* demonstrates the number pattern of exponential growth. In the story, the king wishes to reward a wise old man who desires no reward from the king. To make a point, the wise old man requests grains of rice according to the number of squares (64) on the king's chessboard. For the first square, 1 grain of rice; the second square, 2 grains of rice; the third square, 4 grains of rice; the fourth square, 8 grains of rice; the fifth square, 16 grains of rice, and so on. With each successive square on the chessboard, the number of grains of rice doubles. Translating the problem in the story into a mathematical sentence is an interesting challenge for children.

- Before children solve the problem posed in the story, have a class discussion eliciting various predictions on how much rice the king will need to give to the wise man.
- Use a representation to record the very large numbers in the story. As children are working, ask them ques-

tions, such as, "Is it possible to use tally marks to keep track of the rice the king gave in the book?" and "Can you think of a way to determine the total number of grains of rice?"

- Write several mathematical sentences to analyze and visualize the problem presented in the story. Share and discuss these mathematical expressions. Encourage the use of calculators.
- While children are working, use questions to help them focus on successful and unsuccessful solution routes. Promote their use of charts, drawings, number tallying, mathematical sentences, and other problem-solving methods that will support their attempts.
- When children are finished, encourage them to share their solution routes and attempts. What methods worked, and what did children do when a method did not work? How did they know they were headed in the wrong direction?
- Create a large chessboard bulletin board display and have children write the number of grains of rice on each square of the chessboard.

Source: Dr. Patricia Moyer, George Mason University.

FIGURE 3-3

THE STREAMER PROBLEM

(Jennifer, Grade 6)

Situation: Decorating a room with streamers. Streamers are needed to connect all opposite corners.

Question: How many streamers are needed to decorate a 10-sided room?

1. -5 streamers
   -walls form a pentagon
   -we made a pentagon

2. -9 streamers
   -walls form a hexagon
   -we made a hexagon with the streamers

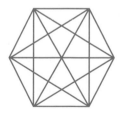

Table:

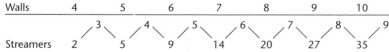

Walls	4	5	6	7	8	9	10
		3	4	5	6	7	8	9
Streamers	2	5	9	14	20	27	35	

I felt proud of myself for having discovered the pattern.

Source: "Writing to Communicate Mathematics," (p. 12), by Y. Pothier, 1992, In Daiyo Sawada (Ed.), *Communication in the mathematics classroom.* Edmonton, AB: Mathematics Council of the Alberta Teachers' Association.

Solve a Simpler Problem

Changing a given problem to a simpler problem can be helpful in visualizing the situation and in determining what procedure to use. Sometimes, beginning with the simplest case and progressing systematically to more difficult cases can yield a pattern that quickly leads to a solution.

Problem 3-16: The Checkerboard Problem

How many squares (of different sizes) are there on an 8-by-8 checkerboard?

Problem 3-17: Connecting Points

A circle has 25 points marked on it. How many straight lines will there be when each of the points is connected to each of the other points on the circle?

 A Solution to the Checkerboard Problem

I'll probably get confused as I count the squares on an 8-by-8 checkerboard, so I'll begin with a smaller board. This should help me find all the squares on an 8-by-8 checkerboard.

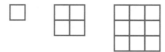

Number of Squares per Size

	1 × 1	2 × 2	3 × 3	4 × 4	. . .	Total
1 × 1	1					1
2 × 2	4	1				5
3 × 3	9	4	1			14
4 × 4	16	9	4	1		30
5 × 5	25	16	9	. . .	. . .	. . .
. . .						

I notice that the number of squares on each different-sized checkerboard is the sum of the square number that is the area of the board and the other smaller square numbers. For example, a 4-by-4 checkerboard has 16 + 9 + 4 + 1 total squares. A 5-by-5 checkerboard has 25 + 16 + 9 + 4 + 1 squares. Therefore, an 8-by-8 checkerboard will have 64 + 49 + 36 + 25 + 16 + 9 + 4 + 1 squares or 204 squares.

Beginning with a simpler case helped me notice a pattern in the table. This enabled me to arrive at the answer quickly.

Guess and Check

For some problems, one first thinks through the problem situation to make a guess and then proceeds to check its accuracy. If the guess is not correct, one uses the knowledge obtained from the guessing-and-checking process to make another more educated guess or change to a different strategy to solve the problem. Although solutions can be obtained through guessing and then checking, the procedure usually is not an efficient one. Use this strategy to solve problems 3-18 and 3-19.

Problem 3-18: Balanced Triangle

Place the digits 1, 2, 3, 4, 5, and 6 in the circles, using each digit only once, so that the 3 numbers on each arm of the triangle add up to 12.

Problem 3-19: Multiples of Five

Find 6 consecutive multiples of 5 that when added make a sum of 345.

 A Solution to the Balanced Triangle

I've made several guesses without any luck.

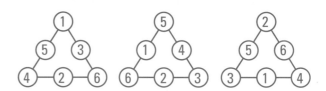

I'll try putting the smallest numbers in the vertices. This doesn't work either. But they all equal 9! I've found one solution!

I'll try the largest numbers in the vertices. Yes, I've found a solution for 12.

An organized list of all the possibilities of sums of 12 is another strategy one could use to solve the problem. The numbers that are used twice go in the vertices.

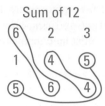

Sum of 12

Working Backwards

In reading the Rock Star Pictures and Apple Orchard problems you will notice that they describe a series of actions or events. Problems of this type are best resolved by beginning at the end state and working backwards until a solution has been reached.

Problem 3-20: Rock Star Pictures
Shane gave one-half of his rock star pictures to Samantha, then gave 6 pictures to Darryl and had 12 left. How many rock star pictures did Shane have before he gave any away?

Problem 3-21: Apple Orchard
The owner hired three watchmen to guard his apple orchard, but a stranger got in and stole some apples. On the way out, the stranger met each watchman, one at a time. To each he gave half of the apples he had then, plus 2 more besides. He escaped with one apple. How many apples did he pick and attempt to steal?

   Elementary-school children find this type of problem difficult to understand and solve. They have to learn that working backwards means not only beginning at the end and working one's way through the steps backwards but also that the operations in the problem must be reversed. One way to have children practice reverse operations is to describe a route from Place *A* to Place *B* and then have them tell how to get from *B* to *A*. They will realize that all the right turns become left turns and vice versa.

   In arithmetic situations, one can ask, What is the opposite of giving away $10? (receiving $10); the opposite of halving 6 (doubling 6); the opposite of 3 times 6 (1/3 of 6). When children understand reverse operations, they can be asked to find solutions to problems that can be solved by working backwards.

 A Solution to the Rock Star Pictures Problem

Shane gave half his pictures to Samantha and 6 to Darryl.

He then had 12 pictures left.

I need to find out how many pictures he had to begin with, so I'll work backwards.

12 pictures. Add the 6 given to Darryl. 18 pictures. Double 18 because half were given to Samantha. 36 pictures.

Shane originally had 36 pictures.

Consider All Possibilities

Problem 3-22: Buying Stamps
Katherine's mother sent her to the post office to purchase some stamps. When Katherine arrived at the post office, she remembered that she was to buy 18 stamps, which her mother had figured out would cost $4.90. Can you help Katherine find out how many 20-cent and 33-cent stamps her mother wants?

Problem 3-23: Police Vehicles
A city's police department has 15 cars and motorcycles. The total number of wheels on the cars and motorcycles is 42. How many police cars does the police department have?

   Some problems involve the consideration of data in different combinations to find a right combination. A strategy used in such instances is to consider all possibilities so that the right combination(s) is (are) found. Making a table and systematically considering all possibilities is an efficient way to resolve such problems.

 A Solution to the Police Vehicles Problem

Information: 15 vehicles. 42 wheels in all.

I'll set up a table and list all the combinations of 15 until I find one that gives 42 wheels.

Motorcycles	Cars	Vehicles	Wheels
15	0	15	30 + 0 = 30
14	1	15	28 + 4 = 32
13	2	15	26 + 8 = 34
12	3	15	24 + 12 = 36

The total goes up by 2.

9	6	15	18 + 24 = 42

There are 9 motorcycles and 6 cars in the police fleet.

Logical Reasoning

Problem 3-24: Partners
Mona, Rita, and Sandra are married to Allan, Fred, and John, but (a) Sandra does not like John, (b) Rita is married to John's brother, and (c) Allan is married to Rita's sister. Who is married to whom?

Problem 3-25: Ranking by Age

Peter is twice as old as Ann will be when Sarah is as old as Peter is now. Can you tell who is the youngest, next youngest, and oldest?

The development of logical reasoning is often stated as a requirement for the successful learning of mathematics. When children state that they solved a problem by thinking it through, they should be encouraged to reflect on how they did it and to discuss the thinking steps they followed. This can assist other children to develop logical thought processes. Problems encountered in everyday life often require logical thinking to arrive at a suitable decision.

 A Solution to the Partners Problem

Setting up a grid will help to organize the information.

	Mona	Rita	Sandra
Allan		x	
John		x	x
Fred			

Because of the information given, I can mark several x's on the chart. By studying the chart, I find that John must be married to Mona, and Rita must be married to Fred. That leaves Sandra and Allan as partners.

Change Your Point of View

Problem 3-26: Planting Tomatoes

Mrs. Andrews planted 10 tomato plants in 5 rows of 4 plants each. How did she do this?

Problem 3-27: Looking for Squares

Find a square with an area of five square units on the grid.

Have you ever met with failure at solving a problem because of the perspective you took in attempting a solution? Often, by taking a certain perspective, we set limits to the considerations of possible solutions. For example, in the nine-dot puzzle (Problem 3-6), many people estab-

lish the perimeter of the square formed by the dots as the boundary for constructing lines. However, to solve the problem, three lines must be extended beyond the dots.

 A Solution to the Planting Problem

Trial and error is the only way that I can see to solve this problem.

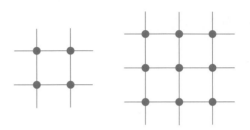

I've tried parallel lines without success.

Oh, what about lines intersecting at vertices?

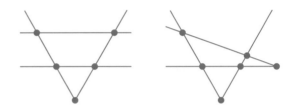

I'm getting only 3 plants per row. But I need another row.

That's it. It looks like a five-pointed star. I can see how 12 plants could be planted in 6 rows of 4 plants each. Can you? What about 19 plants in 9 straight rows with 5 plants in each row?

Write an Open Sentence

Problem 3-28: Fruit Problem

Elaine bought five peaches and three apples. She figures out that she would have to pay 8 cents more if she bought three peaches and five apples. What is the difference between the price of one peach and one apple?

Problem 3-29: Rectangle Size

Find the dimensions of a rectangle whose perimeter is 26 cm and whose area is 36 cm^2.

Some problems presented to elementary-school children can be solved by writing an open sentence and then solving it. For example, the Barnyard problem (see Figure 3-2) can be solved by writing equations and solving first for one variable and then the other. Middle-school children will learn how to write mathematical sentences for word expressions such as "twice as old" ($2x$), "3 times as many plus 6" ($3x + 6$), and then use algebraic skills to solve problems.

 A Solution to the Fruit Problem

p = *peaches*   a = *apples*
$5p + 3a = 3p + 5a + 8$
$2p - 2a = 8$
$p - a = 4$

The difference between the price of a peach and the price of an apple is 4 cents.

PLANNING FOR INSTRUCTION

There are several important components of a problem-solving instructional process (Charles & Lester, 1982): selecting appropriate tasks and materials, identifying sources of problems, clarifying the teacher's role, organizing and implementing instruction, and changing the difficulty of problems. Identifying the essential elements that make up these components can assist teachers in planning effective instruction about problem solving.

Selecting Appropriate Tasks and Materials

Good instruction on problem solving not only uses a variety of problems (Kroll & Miller, 1993) but also considers that problems should:

- Be motivating and culturally relevant;
- Sometimes contain missing, extraneous, or contradictory information;
- Invite the use of calculators, computers, and other technology;
- Engage children in activities that use a variety of problem-solving strategies; and
- Involve children in activities that promote communication about mathematical thinking.

Problems that are motivating and culturally relevant   Children are more interested in solving problems about things they are interested in, problems that are based in realistic, familiar settings, problems that are relevant to their culture, and problems that they or other students have written. It is important to

revise problems to make sure they are motivating and culturally relevant for children.

Problems with missing, extraneous, or contradictory information   Motivating, realistic problems often contain irrelevant or incomplete information and are not well-structured. Because children need practice in solving such problems, instruction should include discussions on organizing the information problems provide and eliminating or ignoring extraneous information.

Problems that encourage the use of calculators, computers, and other technology   Calculator use stimulates children to think more about their approaches to problem solving and permits them to solve more realistic problems.

Activities that require the use of a variety of problem-solving strategies   Children who can use a variety of problem-solving strategies are better able to deal with unfamiliar problem situations. And children who use strategies such as making a diagram or solving a simpler problem are able to more flexibly select another strategy when their first strategy does not work.

Activities that promote communication about mathematical thinking   Children need to be able to explain how they solved a problem. Such explanations are important in refining their own understanding and communicating their understanding to others. Asking children to write word problems, to solve problems written by other children, and to look for errors in the problems or explanations of other children helps to develop their mathematical communication skills.

Sources of Problems

Problems arising from mathematics itself can be about the following:

- Number theory: Are there more prime numbers from 100 to 200 than there are from 1 to 100? How can I find the greatest common factor of three numbers? Sixty-four is both a square number and a cube. What is the next number greater than 64 that has this property?

- Properties of number systems: Is there a multiplicative identity element for fractions? Does the commutative property hold true for integers? For which operations?

- Arithmetic: Is there another algorithm for subtracting whole numbers? How can I subtract $4\frac{4}{5}$ from $6\frac{2}{5}$?

Projects about the school environment can be related to the school store, a school fund-raising project, a paper-conservation endeavor, or other project. Children can gather data from a number of community service organizations, public places, or businesses and use the data to pose and solve problem questions. Here are some examples:

- Airport: Gather data about air traffic, passenger capacity of certain airplanes, baggage capacity, flight schedules, or ticket prices.
- City Park: Obtain data on the number of trees, area for flower beds, types of flowers, or maintenance costs.
- Bridge: Obtain data about daily traffic, income from bridge tolls, maintenance costs.
- Orchard: Gather data on the area of an orchard, the number of fruit trees, average harvest per tree, selling price of fruit, or anticipated profits.
- Public Transportation System: Obtain information on a city's fleet of buses, monthly operating costs, and the daily average number of passengers on a particular route.

Some mathematical problems can be found in math journals or other publications and on the Internet. The "Resources for Teachers" and "Links to the Internet" at the end of the chapter offer some specific examples.

The Teacher's Role

The teacher plays an important role in problem-solving instruction. This role includes sequential activities that identify what a teacher does before children begin to solve a problem, while children are solving a problem, and after children solve the problem.

Before children begin to solve the problem Teachers initiate the lesson by posing a problem to children. Problems can be presented to children orally or in written form. When presented orally, a teacher can employ a story format such as "Suppose you were asked to . . ." or "There once was . . . How would you have solved the problem?" or "What would happen if . . .?" In another format, a teacher can relate the problem orally and write key information on the board. A third way is to have children read the problem. Then, the problem can be written on the board, on an overhead transparency, or on a paper with a copy provided for each child. In the latter case, children can glue the piece of paper on a notebook page or in their math journal and develop a solution plan there. In this way, a record of the problem is kept with the children's work

Before asking children to solve the problem, effective teachers ensure that children understand it. This means asking children to identify what is being asked in the problem, discussing any terms that might be unclear, brainstorming possible solution strategies, and clarifying the task at hand. Finally, a teacher should ask children to devise a plan or select a strategy for solving the problem.

While children are solving the problem While children are working on the problem, the teacher should circulate among them, observing and questioning individuals or children working in groups about the strategies they are using, what they are finding, and what it means. Further, the teacher should ask children questions to help them clarify the direction in which their solution process is taking them. The teacher should provide hints to children who are stuck and encourage children who are finished to solve the problem in a different way or to solve an extension of the problem. The essential goal for the teacher is to consistently ensure that children are answering the question the problem asks.

After children solve the problem   After children are finished working on a problem, the teacher must encourage them to reflect on their solutions and the problem-solving processes they used. Usually this can be done through a whole-class discussion. Most valuable is to emphasize the process as well as the answer and to encourage all children to participate in this discussion. Getting children to communicate their ideas through words and diagrams and with manipulative materials can keep children engaged. It can also assure the teacher of a job well-done if children offer high-level responses.

Organizing and Implementing Instruction

Establishing an effective problem-solving program requires examining factors related to organization and implementation. These factors include providing children with a classroom climate that is conducive to learning, grouping children to facilitate interactive learning, allocating appropriate instructional time, and planning for children's assessments.

Classroom climate A classroom that promotes problem solving is open and supportive, encouraging children to try different solution strategies and endorsing children's efforts. Such a supportive environment encourages children to take risks and to defend their solutions. The teacher should encourage children to persevere in their problem solving and to respect each other's efforts.

Grouping children A classroom that promotes problem solving includes individual, small-group, and whole-class problem-solving experiences. Each of these formats helps children develop distinct and important types of problem-solving skills. Small-group work is particularly useful in that it provides opportunities for all children to interact, discuss, and share solution strategies.

Allocating time A classroom that promotes an adequate allocation of instructional time for problem solving on a regular basis is integral to learning mathematics. Problem solving should be an integral part of mathematics instruction, not an add-on, "Fridays only" topic.

Assessing children's understanding A classroom that promotes problem solving includes assessment of children's understanding, problem-solving skills, and strategy usage. Chapter 4 discusses assessment in greater detail.

Changing the Difficulty of Problems

Remember the discussion at the beginning of this chapter on types of problems? We know much about which problems are easier than others to solve and ways to construct problems to make them easier or harder. For example, the wording of a problem can affect the difficulty level of a problem. Because teachers can control how easy or difficult problems can be and thus meet individual needs, it is a good time to discuss the factors involved in adapting problems. These factors include problem context and problem mechanics or structure.

Problem context The context of a problem is the nonmathematical setting in which it is placed. For example, because of the setting or context of the problem, a problem about two children sharing six cookies is different from a problem about two aliens sharing six mega-blasters. As shown in Box 3-1, different contexts can include abstract (using symbolic or intangible elements), concrete (involving a real situation or objects), factual (describing an actual situation), hypothetical (describing possible situations), and personalized (using the solver's own interests and characteristics in the problem) (Hembree & March, 1993).

Problems involving concrete, factual, or personalized settings are easier for children to solve than are hypothetical or abstract problems.

Problem structure A problem's structure consists of several aspects related to how problem data are presented. These aspects include problem length, readability, whether the problem includes action (e.g., "Tom *gave* Maria 2 more cookies"), the order in which data are presented, the inclusion of extraneous data, and the use of familiar versus unfamiliar terms. The difficulty of each of these aspects is as might be expected. More difficult problems might include any of these factors: longer, more difficult readability, lack of action, presence of extraneous data or information, and unfamiliar terms.

Classroom implications Teachers must be aware of factors that affect problem difficulty, and thus systematically vary those factors to help children become better problem solvers. A common way to sequence problem-solving instruction is to begin with problems involving action and reasonably sized numbers in concrete or personalized settings, later progressing to more complicated problems by varying the factors previously described.

This is not to say, however, that teachers must always pose easy problems. Realistic, real-world problems encountered in everyday situations usually are not clean, tidy, or clearly stated. Children need to learn how to solve such problems. When planning instruction, teachers must find a balance between supporting children's learning and challenging children to solve realistic problems. Teachers must systematically vary problem structure and format to help children learn strategies and develop confidence that will help them solve more complicated problems.

PRINCIPLES AND STANDARDS LINK 3-7
Process Strand: Problem Solving

The teacher's role in choosing worthwhile problems and mathematical tasks is crucial. By analyzing and adapting a problem, anticipating the mathematical ideas that can be brought out by working on the problem, and anticipating students' questions, teachers can decide if particular problems will help to further their mathematical goals for the class . . . Choosing problems wisely, and using and adapting problems from instructional materials, is a difficult part of teaching mathematics. (NCTM, 2000, p. 53)

BOX 3-1

Types of Problem Contexts

Abstract Setting

A certain number is 5 more than 7. What is the number?

Concrete Setting

Matt has 7 baseball cards. Peter has 5 more baseball cards than Matt has. How many baseball cards does Peter have?

In Ms. Garcia's class, there are 7 boys and some girls. There are 5 more girls than boys in the class. How many girls are in Ms. Garcia's class?

Hypothetical Setting

Peter has some baseball cards. If Peter has 5 more baseball cards than Matt has, and Matt has 7 baseball cards, how many baseball cards does Peter have?

Personalized Setting

{Insert Child A's name here} has 7 {insert relevant item here}. {Insert Child B's name here} has 5 more {insert relevant item here} than {Insert Child A's name here} has. How many {insert relevant item here} does {insert Child B's name here} have?

Other Factors Contributing to Children's Difficulties in Problem Solving

From their review of the literature, Kroll and Miller (1993) have identified major factors that contribute to middle-school children's difficulties in problem solving: knowledge, beliefs and affective factors, control, and sociocultural factors. All teachers should address each of these areas during instruction. In particular, the elementary grades should be viewed as a time of "preparation for good problem solving" (Hembree & Marsh, 1993, p. 166).

Knowledge factors Beginning in the elementary grades and throughout the middle-school grades, children should have ample experience in problem solving so that

they can come to recognize structurally similar problems (schema knowledge) and learn varied strategies to solve process problems (strategic knowledge) (Kroll & Miller, 1993). Thus, building prior knowledge required for successful problem solving includes making teachers accountable for developing algorithmic, linguistic, conceptual, and schema and strategic knowledge. As a teacher, you must not only enable children to read problems and compute accurately but also help children come to understand problems so that they can make a wise choice on what operation or strategy to use to develop a solution. Choosing a solution process should emerge from a clear understanding of a problem, rather than be dependent upon word clues or other unreliable strategies.

Beliefs and affective factors Success in problem solving is adversely affected by a lack of confidence in one's own ability to create solutions to problems. Teachers who have a narrow view that there is only one right way to solve a problem can prevent children from experiencing the joy of truly "doing" mathematics.

Control Kroll and Miller (1993) mention the need for children to be able to monitor their own thinking when engaged in problem solving. Research shows that children do not spend sufficient time reflecting on their thinking process or on their approaches to problem solving. Can you understand, then, the need for a teacher to engage children in reflection on their own thinking processes?

PRINCIPLES AND STANDARDS LINK 3-8
Process Strand: Problem Solving

Problem solving is an integral part of all mathematics learning, and so it should not be an isolated part of the mathematics program. . . . The contexts of the problems can vary from familiar experiences involving students' lives or the school day to applications involving the sciences or the world of work. Good problems will integrate multiple topics and will involve significant mathematics. (NCTM, 2000, p. 52)

Sociocultural factors Children's out-of-school experiences are varied; therefore, children develop their own problem-solving strategies. However, children are unable to use their "natural" problem-solving abilities in school mathematics, although such abilities serve them well in out-of-school situations (Kroll & Miller, 1993). As was stated earlier in this chapter, the classroom atmosphere is important in mathematics learning, because it can positively or negatively affect children's achievement. Teachers must keep in mind that they control the environment and context of children's experiences. This is an awesome responsibility but one that separates good instruction from poor student experiences.

A Case to Consider the Children

A problem-solving teaching project with fourth-, fifth-, and sixth-grade children revealed that children valued certain instructional practices when engaged in problem solving (Pothier & Sawada, 1990). Some of the favored characteristics of the teaching-learning situation expressed by the children include time to complete a problem, freedom to choose a solution strategy, receiving personal attention, and an understanding teacher.

- Children need time to work through a problem; they do not want to be rushed to complete a set of problems. When relieved of the pressure to complete work, children feel free to explore solution possibilities.

- Children appreciate the freedom to personally select and develop a solution strategy, rather than follow a uniform procedure. This provides them with the opportunity to transform a problem into something personal, and it becomes an enjoyable task.

- Children appreciate receiving personal attention when engaged in problem solving. This attention can be in the form of a teacher asking questions to direct their thinking, offering hints regarding solution procedures, or merely listening to fellow students talk about what they are doing.

- Children value an understanding teacher. When a trusting relationship is established, children will readily request assistance knowing that, as one child expressed

it, "it's all right if you don't know how to do it." Students will take risks in tackling problems that they might not otherwise attempt, an important component in a mathematics classroom.

A nonthreatening and supportive classroom atmosphere is effective in promoting children's progress in developing their problem-solving abilities.

Benefits of Using a Problem-Solving Approach to Mathematics Instruction

A teacher who decides to approach all mathematics work from a problem-solving point of view has children solve computation problems, work at geometry and measurement activities, and approach number theory investigations from a problem-solving perspective. Process problems that relate to the different mathematics topics are an important part of this kind of program. Children learn problem-solving strategies that enable them to gain insights into mathematical connections and understand that problems are the context for learning concepts and skills, that is, children learn mathematics via problem solving. Such a program promotes children's mathematics understanding and achievement.

Another benefit of a problem-solving approach to mathematics teaching is that it supports children with different learning styles. According to Moser (1992), "an orientation toward problem solving can accommodate individual differences, especially if the philosophy is adopted that there is more than one way to solve most problems" (p. 131). A classroom in which problem solving is the central feature of the mathematics instruction and in which more than one way to solve a problem is not merely tolerated but is valued is an environment that promotes the learning of all children.

CONCLUSION

In this chapter, current thinking about problem solving as an integral part of mathematics programs has been presented. This vision is for children to learn mathematics through problem solving and teachers to teach in a way that allows children to learn how to solve problems. Such a mathematics program should include different types of problems, with more emphasis placed on process problems.

It is not only appropriate but also imperative for teachers to provide instruction in problem-solving strategies to enable children to develop a resource of processes to use when engaged in problem solving. The instructional goal, then, is to ensure that by the end of middle school, children will have developed confidence and some flexibility in using different problem-solving strategies.

PRINCIPLES AND STANDARDS LINK 3-9
Process Strand:
Problem Solving

How can problem solving help students learn mathematics? Good problems give students the chance to solidify and extend what they know and, when well chosen, can stimulate mathematics learning. (NCTM, 2000, p. 52)

For Your Journal

When you have finished studying this chapter, reflect on the following questions in your math journal:

1. Choose three different problems from the chapter and solve them. Describe the solution strategies you used.

2. Imagine you are an elementary-school teacher and one of the children expresses frustration about solving problems, asking you to "just tell me how to do it." How will you respond?

3. Describe how you would establish a classroom environment conducive to problem solving.

For Your Portfolio

When you have finished studying this chapter, complete the following activities to include in your professional portfolio:

1. Begin a collection of process problems.

2. Write a lesson plan for a problem-solving lesson focusing on teaching children to use a solution strategy of your choice. Include the questions you would ask.

3. Visit a classroom and observe the solution strategies used by children. Describe these strategies and the follow-up lessons you might plan if you were the teacher in that classroom.

Resources for Teachers

Books on problem solving

Baroody, A. (1993). *Problem solving, reasoning, and communicating: Helping children think mathematically.* New York: Macmillan.

Charles, R., Lester, F., & O'Daffer, P. (1987). *How to evaluate progress in problem solving.* Reston, VA: National Council of Teachers of Mathematics.

O'Daffer, P. G. (1988). *Problem solving: Tips for teachers.* Reston, VA: National Council of Teachers of Mathematics.

Reys, B. (1982). *Elementary school mathematics: What parents should know about problem solving.* Reston, VA: National Council of Teachers of Mathematics.

Links to the Internet

Problems of the Week

http://www.mathforum.org/elempow/

Contains a weekly "Problem of the Week" as well as a mechanism to submit solutions electronically. Past Problems of the Week and solutions are also available.

Education Place's BrainTeasers

http://www.eduplace.com/math/brain/

Contains math puzzles for Grades 3–8 as well as solution hints.

CHAPTER 4

Assessing Mathematics Understanding

KEY CONCEPTS ▶

✔ NCTM Assessment Standards

✔ Purposes of assessment

✔ Types of assessment

✔ Performance assessment

✔ Portfolio assessment

Assessment in mathematics no longer refers only to a child's score on a test. Instead, assessment involves a more holistic view of each child's understanding, skill, and attitude about mathematics. Assessment communicates to children what we believe is important for them to know and be able to do. It is essential that assessment matches the mathematics curriculum and the instructional strategies in use. This chapter discusses recommendations and methods for assessing children's understanding of mathematics. ✔

FOCUS QUESTIONS ▶

When you have finished studying this chapter, you should be able to answer the following questions:

1. What are the purposes of assessment?

2. What are the different types of assessment and what are the benefits of each type?

3. What are the advantages of using performance assessment? Of using portfolio assessment?

"In order to develop mathematical power in all students, assessment needs to support the continued mathematics learning of each student. This is the central goal of school mathematics."

(NCTM, 1995, p. 6)

THE ASSESSMENT STANDARDS

In 1995 the National Council of Teachers of Mathematics (NCTM) published the *Assessment Standards for School Mathematics.* Completing the trilogy of standards developed by NCTM, these Assessment Standards describe new assessment strategies and practices that "enable teachers and others to assess students' performance in a manner that reflects the NCTM's reform vision for school mathematics" (NCTM, 1995, p. 1). For the purposes of this text, we will refer to the *NCTM Assessment Standards for School Mathematics* as the Assessment Standards.

The Principles and Standards lists assessment as one of its six principles for school mathematics. According to NCTM (2000), "assessment should support the learning of important mathematics and furnish useful information to both teachers and students" (p. 11). The Principles and Standards continues to echo the importance of assessment as stated in the Assessment Standards.

The Assessment Standards describe five shifts that are needed to attain the vision of the Curriculum Standards (see Table 4-1). These shifts clearly characterize the recommended changes in mathematics teaching, learning, and assessment.

PRINCIPLES AND STANDARDS LINK 4-1

Instead of assuming that the purpose of assessment is to rank students on a particular trait, the new approach assumes that high public expectations can be set that every student can strive for and achieve, that different performances can and will meet agreed-on expectations, and that teachers can be fair and consistent judges of diverse student performances. (NCTM, 1995, p. 1)

What is Assessment?

Assessment is "the process of gathering evidence about a student's knowledge of, ability to use, and disposition toward mathematics and of making inferences from that evidence for a variety of purposes" (NCTM, 1995, p. 3).

The Assessment Standards include six standards to guide mathematics assessment and focus on six important areas: mathematics, learning, equity, openness, inferences, and coherence. These six standards set the criteria for determining the quality of mathematics assessments and ultimately the quality of instruction.

The **mathematics standard** states that "assessment should reflect the mathematics that all students need to know and be able to do" (NCTM, 1995, p. 11). This means that teachers must make sure to assess children's understanding of the mathematics concepts and procedures that current recommendations, such as the NCTM Curriculum Standards, say that children should know.

The **learning standard** states that "assessment should enhance mathematics learning" (NCTM, 1995, p. 13), that is, good assessments are those that not only assess children's understanding but also encourage and support further growth in that understanding.

The **equity standard** states that "assessment should promote equity" (NCTM, 1995, p. 15). Equity in this context means that all children are successful in math. Thus, assessments should take into account differences among children to support the learning of all children. This can be done, for example, by permitting different modes of responses to an assessment.

PRINCIPLES AND STANDARDS LINK 4-2

Assessment should be a means of fostering growth toward high expectations. To do otherwise represents a waste of human potential. (NCTM, 1995, p. 1)

> **TABLE 4-1** ▷

RECOMMENDED SHIFTS IN MATHEMATICS INSTRUCTION

A SHIFT IN	TOWARD	AWAY FROM
• Content	• A rich variety of mathematical topics and problem situations	• Just arithmetic
• Learning	• Investigating problems	• Memorizing and repeating
• Teaching	• Questioning and listening	• Telling
• Evaluation	• Evidence from several sources	• A single test judged externally
• Expectation	• Using concepts and procedures to solve problems	• Just mastering isolated concepts and procedures

Source: Adapted from *Assessment Standards for School Mathematics* (pp. 2–3) by National Council of Teachers of Mathematics, 1995, Reston, VA: National Council of Teachers of Mathematics. Copyright 1995 by the National Council of Teachers of Mathematics.

The **openness standard** states that "assessment should be an open process" (NCTM, 1995, p. 17). An open process includes informing the public about the process, involving teaching professionals, and being accepting of review and change.

The **inferences standard** states that "assessment should promote valid inferences about mathematics learning" (NCTM, 1995, p. 19). Valid inferences are those based on relevant evidence, which could include evidence from multiple sources, such as tests, teacher observations, and portfolios.

The **coherence standard** states that "assessment should be a coherent process" (NCTM, 1995, p. 21). Specifically, the assessment process must (1) be complete and sensible, (2) match the purposes for which it is being conducted, and (3) be consistent with curriculum and instruction that have been implemented.

Purposes of Assessment

According to the Curriculum Standards, assessment may be used for several purposes, including diagnosis, instructional feedback, grading, generalized mathematical achievement, and program evaluation. When done well, assessment helps children and parents realize what children have learned and what they still need to learn. It also allows teachers to understand what the children know so they may plan appropriate instruction.

Similarly, the Assessment Standards identify four purposes for assessment: monitoring children's progress, making instructional decisions, evaluating children's achievement, and evaluating programs. A description of each of these purposes follows.

- *Monitoring children's progress* toward learning goals is a continuous process that includes setting high expectations and collecting evidence about children's understanding and progress.
- *Making instructional decisions* refers to teachers using evidence of children's understanding to modify instruction to better meet children's needs and to lead to increased learning.
- *Evaluating children's achievement* must be done at regular intervals and includes collecting evidence, summarizing it, and reporting it. This serves both to inform parents and to ensure that important milestones are attained.
- *Evaluating programs* must be done by collecting evidence about children's learning to ensure that all children are learning.

Each of these four purposes of assessment is an important link in improving teaching and learning. For example, in monitoring a child's progress a teacher can recognize increased growth or a lack of growth on the part of the child. Thus, assessment can affect instructional decision making and lead to improved instruction. Also, because evaluating a child's achievement is a part of effective instruction, assessment records are accumulated to reflect a child's accomplishments or underscore a need for an evaluation to determine the appropriateness of giving special learning support services to the child. Further, evaluating the mathematics program itself can lead to a decision to make program modifications. Each of these assessment purposes provides teachers with information to benefit children's learning. The use of any one of them, however, requires several phases of planning.

Phases of Assessment

There are generally four parts or phases of assessment: planning what kind of assessment tool to use, gathering evidence through its use, interpreting that evidence, and applying the results to measure growth or determine the need for change. These phases are interconnected, although not necessarily sequentially. It often is helpful, however, to keep these phases in mind to aid decision making related to assessment choices.

When planning assessment, think about the purpose of the assessment, the methods you will use to collect and interpret evidence, the criteria you will use to judge performance, and the format you will use to summarize findings. For example, do you intend to use the results of the assessment primarily to decide how to plan tomorrow's math lesson? Or will the results be used to help parents understand their child's strengths and areas needing growth?

When gathering evidence, consider the activities, tasks, and procedures you will use to involve children. For example, might the children choose to respond in different ways, such as by using manipulative materials, drawing a picture, or writing a description, to convey their understanding of a concept?

When interpreting evidence, think about how you will determine comprehension and the criteria you will use to analyze the evidence. For example, how do you hope the children will respond to a question? What other responses are acceptable to demonstrate understanding?

When using results from assessment, consider how the results will be reported, and decide how the results will affect future instructional decisions. For example, will you share the results with parents on written report cards or orally during parent-teacher conferences? How will you use student comprehension to plan instruction for the next lesson or the next unit or to reteach particular concepts?

ASSESSMENT CHOICES

The purpose of the information teachers gather from assessment dictates the nature of its use. For example, generalized mathematics achievement can best be assessed with standardized testing instruments. Standardized testing also is useful to indicate how well the class is doing as a whole and the effectiveness of instruction or instructional programs. Individual diagnosis, however, is better done through a variety of other means, including observation, interviews and oral questioning, performance tasks, and a collection of children's work over time (as in the maintaining of portfolios). Through the use of any of these means a teacher can assess the children's understanding of mathematical concepts, as well as computational ability, problem-solving ability, thinking processes and solution strategies, attitudes, and oral and written communication skills.

Achievement Tests

Tests probably are the first measurement tools that come to mind when considering the evaluation of a child's progress. An achievement test generally falls into one of two categories: standardized or teacher-made.

Standardized tests Most standardized achievement tests are norm-referenced tests because their purpose is to compare a child's level of performance to the performance of a large number of similar children. The norming population usually represents a cross-section of children in a school system, a state, or even a nation. Standardized tests usually are administered on the mandate of a school district or state official and often are given at incremental levels, such as second grade, fourth grade, and so on. Some states and local school districts have expended considerable time, effort, and money to design tests that would be valid for the state or local objectives at different levels. Widely used standardized tests include the Stanford Achievement Test and the Iowa Test of Basic Skills.

Teacher-made tests Teacher-made tests are criterion-referenced tests because they measure knowledge of specific objectives. A chapter test in a textbook often does not reflect all of the objectives a teacher covered, so the teacher may devise a test to assess children's progress in understanding material in the chapter. Teacher-made tests often are given as pretests as well as post-tests. Pretests are important to help a teacher plan instruction based on class needs. In designing a test, the teacher should do the following:

- List all the objectives to be measured.
- List the thought processes children may need to answer test questions.
- Design test items that will match both the objectives to be measured and the critical thinking processes involved.

Further, it is necessary to edit all items carefully to eliminate ambiguity. The teacher should do the following:

- Prepare the test in an attractive and clear format.
- Analyze the results, examining how children responded to each item.

Indeed, it is important that teachers go beyond simply calculating a score to examine each child's response to each item. Use these results to determine instructional needs. For example, if many children made errors on the items that you intended as problem-solving items, you need to provide more experiences with problem-solving and solution strategies.

Diagnostic Tests

Achievement tests usually do not provide the kind of details that allow a teacher to describe strengths or weaknesses of a particular child. A diagnostic test provides such information. Diagnostic tests help teachers understand which parts of a concept children have mastered as well as the topics on which children need more learning experiences.

Although commercial diagnostic tests exist, it is better for teachers to design their own because they interact with the children daily and can use their knowledge of the children to develop appropriate tasks and interpret the responses. Observation and interviews described in the next section are other ways to gather diagnostic data.

Individualizing Assessment

Individual diagnosis of children's understanding of mathematical concepts, computational ability, problem-solving ability, thinking processes and solution strategies, attitudes, and oral and written communication skills are best made through a variety of means. These means include observation, conferences and interviews, performance tasks, collecting children's work over time in portfolios, and self-assessment.

Observation Observation involves systematically examining children's behavior. It is a powerful way to learn more about what children know and are able to do.

Observation is most effective when a teacher concentrates on a few children each day and systematically observes specific aspects, such as solution strategies used, types of problems solved, and level of skill or concept development.

Teachers can record observation data by keeping anecdotal records that include written notes describing children's behaviors. Checklists are another good way to organize data collected via observation. For example, to plan instruction, a teacher might be interested in assessing the counting strategies children use to solve addition problems. The teacher could use a checklist to keep track of which children are using the "counting on from the first addend" strategy and which children are using the "counting on from the larger addend" strategy. The checklist should contain the names of all the children in the class, with columns listing the date on which the teacher observed each child using each strategy and the particular problem on which the strategy was used. Table 4-2 shows part of a sample observation checklist a teacher used to organize these data. Notice that the teacher completed this table over a period of several months. This checklist shows children's progress over time in using the two counting strategies observed.

Conferences and interviews At times a teacher may want to schedule an interview with a child, but most often interviews will occur spontaneously. A planned interview would be more likely to occur when a child does one of the following:

- Reveals a special interest or expertise in a particular topic (the teacher may help the student plan some additional work, culminating with a report or demonstration to the class).
- Demonstrates unusual insight or an unusual algorithm.
- Transfers into the class from another school.
- Demonstrates a particularly negative attitude.

Interviews also may be planned when the teacher wants to assess the level of development of a concept. This could involve asking children to solve an addition word problem or to show three different representations of 3 times 6, for example. Teachers can learn much about the children's mathematical thinking through such interviews.

Spontaneous interviews usually occur as a teacher watches children work. "Tell me how you did that" and "Here is another problem—think aloud as you work it out" are the kinds of questions or statements a teacher might make in these more unstructured interviews. Giving a few words of encouragement may also be classified as a spontaneous interview.

Interviews with parents often reveal information and background that are helpful in understanding their child. For example, previous attitude-forming experiences (positive and negative), experiences that contribute to the child's mathematical knowledge, experiences with computers, and parental attitudes toward mathematics often are useful in helping assess a child's progress or lack of progress. Some schools encourage interviews in which both the child and the parents are present.

Teachers can keep records describing children's understanding of the content standards and their use of the process standards. One effective method to do this is to use an assessment checklist such as that shown in Table 4-3. This checklist lists some of the expectations of a child from the number strand for Grades 3 through 5 of the Principles and Standards as well as the five process standards: problem solving, reasoning and proof, communication, connections, and representation. Teachers could make one copy of this checklist for each child in the class and use the lists to keep track of each child's progress toward using each process while developing the child's understanding of each concept within that strand. Teachers should periodically record children's progress related to these concepts and processes.

Performance Assessment Performance assessment in mathematics involves "presenting students with a mathematical task, project, or investigation, then observing, interviewing, and looking at their products to assess what they actually know and can do" (Stenmark, 1991, p. 13). Performance assessment can include evaluation of children's daily work, observations, conferences, and interviews.

TABLE 4-2

PART OF A SAMPLE OBSERVATION CHECKLIST FOR CHILDREN'S USE OF COUNTING STRATEGIES

	DATE/PROBLEM APPLICATION	
CHILD'S NAME	**COUNTING ON FROM FIRST ADDEND**	**COUNTING ON FROM LARGER ADDEND**
Andrew	10/23 2 + 5 =	1/15 3 + 9 =
Anton	9/22 3 + 4 =	12/2 2 + 9 =
Crystal	10/23 6 + 3 =	11/15 4 + 7 =
Gabriella	1/22 3 + 6 =	
Heather	9/22 3 + 4 =	10/23 3 + 8 =
Juan	9/22 3 + 4 =	11/15 4 + 7 =

PRINCIPLES AND STANDARDS LINK 4-3

To demonstrate real growth in mathematical power, students need to demonstrate their ability to do major pieces of work that are more elaborate and time-consuming than just short exercises, sets of word problems, and chapter tests. Performance tasks, projects, and portfolios are some examples of more complex instructional and assessment activities. (NCTM, 1995, p. 36)

TABLE 4-3

Assessment Checklist Linking Content and Process Standards

Child Expectation: Number Strand	PROBLEM SOLVING: CAN THE CHILD SOLVE PROBLEMS RELATED TO THIS CONCEPT?		REASONING AND PROOF: HOW DOES THE CHILD REASON ABOUT THIS CONCEPT?	
	Developing as expected	Needs development	Developing as expected	Needs development
Understand the place-value structure of the base-ten number system and be able to represent and compare whole numbers and decimals.				
Recognize equivalent representations for the same number and generate them by decomposing and composing numbers.				
Develop understanding of fractions as parts of unit wholes, as parts of a collection, as locations on number lines, and as divisions of whole numbers.				
Use models, benchmarks, and equivalent forms to judge the size of fractions.				
Recognize and generate equivalent forms of commonly used fractions, decimals, and percentages.				
Explore numbers less than 0 by extending the number line and through familiar applications.				
Describe classes of numbers (e.g., odds, primes, squares, multiples) according to characteristics such as the nature of their factors.				

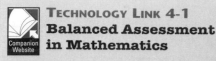

TECHNOLOGY LINK 4-1
Balanced Assessment in Mathematics

This site is a great resource for assessment in mathematics. It includes a searchable library of over 300 assessment tasks. If you find 300 tasks a bit overwhelming, the site also has a listing of a few favorite tasks for each grade-range.
Visit http://balancedassessment.gse.harvard.edu/or link from our Companion Website at **www.prenhall. com/cathcart.**

When engaged in a performance assessment, children demonstrate "their ability to use the skills they have learned and the conceptual understanding they have developed in the context of a real-life application or complex problem" (Collison, 1992). Collison uses the analogy of a driving test to describe processes involved in and characteristics of a mathematical performance assessment.

Performance assessment presents children with an opportunity to demonstrate their understanding rather than just their speed and accuracy. It provides teachers with more detailed information about children's thinking, solution processes, misconceptions, and errors.

COMMUNICATION: CAN THE CHILD COMMUNICATE EFFECTIVELY ABOUT THIS CONCEPT?		CONNECTIONS: CAN THE CHILD MAKE CONNECTIONS RELATED TO THIS CONCEPT?		REPRESENTATION: HOW DOES THE CHILD REPRESENT THE THINKING RELATED TO THIS CONCEPT?	
Developing as expected	*Needs development*	*Developing as expected*	*Needs development*	*Developing as expected*	*Needs development*

Performance assessment can also be a part of daily lessons. For example, at the start of a lesson teachers can ask the children to do a "quick write" of everything they know about the topic of the lesson. For example, during a lesson on fractions, the teacher could ask children to quickly write everything they know about the fraction $\frac{1}{2}$. At the end of the lesson, the teacher asks the children to add anything they'd like to their quick write. Reviewing these writing samples may be helpful in assessing children's understanding. Quick writes provide feedback to the teacher and the child about what the child knows at the beginning of the lesson and what the child learned from the lesson.

Examples of performance tasks. Performance tasks include an elaborate problem-solving activity or an activity as simple as asking a child to set out counters in an array to illustrate a particular multiplication problem. Indeed, concrete materials often are part of the assessment. Performance assessment frequently is done with individuals or small groups. Figures 4-1, 4-2, and 4-3 include examples of performance assessment tasks.

Figure 4-2 contains tasks designed to assess students' understanding of the concept of division (discussed in Chapter 7). Notice there are several types of questions. One question asks students to show how they would use blocks to solve the problem 35 ÷ 5. Another question

FIGURE 4-1 ▶

SAMPLE PERFORMANCE ASSESSMENT TASKS

Fractions: Ask third-grade students who are learning about fractions to show you with manipulatives how they would divide different items, such as 5 candy bars, 10 pencils, or 11 comic books, among 4 students.

Place Value: Have students explain how they would teach a younger sibling to understand the meaning of tens and ones in place value.

Long Division: Give each group of students a different division problem. Ask each group to make a poster to share with the class that explains the methods they used in solving their problem.

Organizing and Displaying Data: Ask a group of students to find and demonstrate the value of *pi* by measuring the diameter and circumference of different circles, expressing the ratios, and finding decimal equivalents on a calculator. Allow the students to choose a way to explain and display their findings.

Data Collection: Your group's task is (1) to identify an interesting question that may be answered by collecting data, (2) to develop a plan for investigating this question, and (3) to prepare an oral report, with overheads or other displays, for the class. Here is a sample question: "How many bicycles are there within two miles of this school?" Your group's planning report is due in three days. Please keep a daily log of your work. Final reports will be due two weeks from today.

Source: Mathematics assessment: Myths, models, good questions, and practical suggestions (pp. 14–15), by J. K. Stenmark (Ed.), 1991, Reston, VA: National Council of Teachers of Mathematics. Copyright 1991 by NCTM.

FIGURE 4-2 ▶

UNDERSTANDING THE CONCEPT OF DIVISION

Do the students understand what division means?

Can the students interpret different representations of division?

For example:

• Partitioning, or sharing—If there are 6 cookies and 2 people, how many will each person get?
• Measuring, or repeated subtraction—If you have 6 cookies and want each person to get 3 cookies, how many people will get cookies?

Take 35 blocks. Use the blocks to show how to do this problem: $35 \div 7 =$

Solve these two problems and explain how they are alike or different:

• If you divide 35 blocks into 7 groups, how many will be in each group?
• If you put 35 blocks into groups of 7, how many groups will there be?

Solve these two problems and explain how they are alike or different:

• José had 6 children at his party. How would he divide 25 cookies among them?
• Jamie wanted each child in the game to have 6 marbles. She had 25 marbles. How many children could be in the game?

Assessment questions:

• Did students distinguish between the two forms of division?
• Were their block arrangements or explanations accurate and explanatory?
• Do they understand how division by grouping and by distributing are alike and different?

Source: Mathematics assessment: A practical handbook for grades 3–5. (p. 9), by J. K. Stenmark and W.S. Bush, 2001, Reston, VA: National Council of Teachers of Mathematics. Copyright 2000 by NCTM.

asks students to explain how two different division problems are alike and different. Other questions ask students to solve story problems involving division. Each question assesses another aspect of students' understanding of the concept of division and provides a teacher with a detailed picture of students' thinking about all aspects of this concept.

Another example is presented in Figure 4-3, this time about the concept of fractions (discussed in Chapter 10). As in the previous example, this task asks students to use models, explain their thinking, and solve story problems centered around important concepts of fractions, including equivalence and comparison.

Materials designed for instruction can be quickly modified for use as a performance assessment by modifying the final question and changing the way it is administered.

The key to an effective performance task is to require children to provide *explanations* rather than *products*. For example, consider a basic activity in which children are asked to use a manipulative material, such as base-ten blocks, to represent a list of numbers. Figure 4-4, which shows possible responses, is an example. This task can easily be modified to focus on children's thinking by asking them to represent one number, say 37, in as many dif-

ferent ways as possible and to explain *why* they are the same. Children who understand that 37 is the same as $27 + 10$, for example, show that they understand equivalent representations and are able to think flexibly about the concept of place value.

What makes a good performance assessment task? According to Stenmark (1991), quality performance assessment tasks include several characteristics: they are *essential* (consistent with the core curriculum), *authentic* (use appropriate mathematics processes), *rich* (have many possibilities), *engaging* (thought-provoking), *active* (children interact with other children), *feasible* (can be done in time available), *equitable* (accessible to children with different learning styles), and *open* (can be solved with more than one solution strategy).

Using rubrics to score performance tasks. Performance tasks give teachers a great deal of information to use in evaluating children's mathematics understanding. Sometimes teachers choose to quantify children's

FIGURE 4-3

UNDERSTANDING THE CONCEPT OF FRACTIONS

Can the students show that a fraction represents equal parts of a whole and that the parts do not have to be congruent?

Here are three small grids. Find three different ways to divide the grids into fourths. Do not divide any of the cells. Color the grids with crayons to show the fractions.

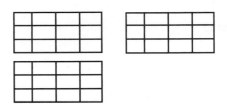

Assessment questions:
• Are the divisions into fourths accurate, with three cells for each fourth?
• Are the arrangements different?
• Did the students understand that the cells used to show one-fourth could be arranged in any manner on the grid, as long as they are identified?

Can they connect the meaning of numerator and denominator to a model or diagram?

Compare 2/3 and 3/2. Which is larger? Use blocks or a drawing to help explain your response.

Jim says that 1/4 is larger than 1/2 because 4 is larger than 2. Is he right? Explain your reasoning and the mathematics you used to find your answer.

Eddie was trying to explain the idea of the numerator and the denominator of a fraction to his brother, so he drew a diagram. Draw a diagram that he might have used, label the parts, and explain what you mean.

Assessment questions:
• Do the students accurately use blocks or diagrams to illustrate numerator and denominator?
• Are the explanations clear and complete?
• Do the explanations show an understanding of the concept? Are they mathematically accurate?

Can the students show that the size of the fractional part depends on the size of the "whole"?

Your friend states that the fractions 2/3 and 5/6 are the same size because both have one "piece" fewer than the whole unit. Is your friend correct? Use words, numbers, and pictures to explain your answer.

What is the same about the two fractional parts and what is different? What fraction is shaded in each of the shapes below?

Assessment questions:
• Can the students explain the relationship of the various fractional parts to the whole unit?
• Can they distinguish between shapes that are identical in size and shape but that represent different parts of the whole?

Can they show an understanding of the relative value of a variety of fractions?

On the number line below, put these fractions in order from the smallest to the largest: 1/4, 2/3, 3/6, 1/5, 3/4.

Explain how you decided where to put each fraction.

Assessment questions:
• Are the fractions placed fairly close to where they should be?
• Do the explanations make sense?
• What suggestions would you make to improve or modify the responses?

Source: Mathematics assessment: A practical handbook for grades 3–5 (p. 11–12), by J.K. Stenmark and W.S. Bush, 2001, Reston, VA: National Council of Teachers of Mathematics.

FIGURE 4-4

CHANGING A LEARNING ACTIVITY TO A PERFORMANCE ASSESSMENT TASK

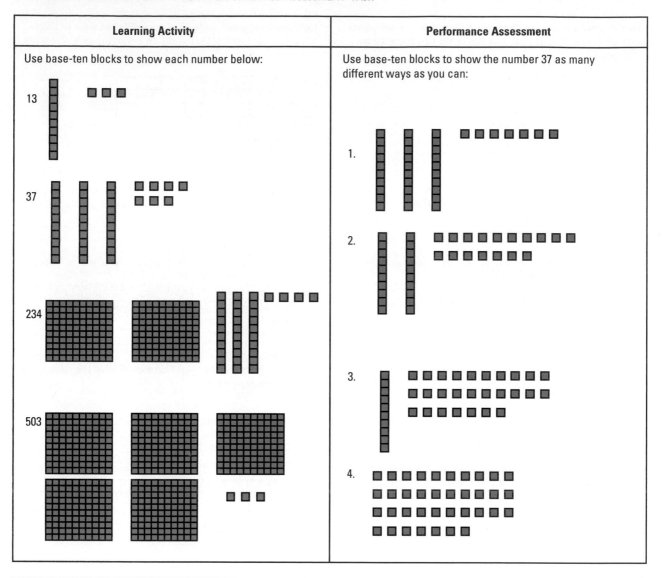

Learning Activity	Performance Assessment
Use base-ten blocks to show each number below:	Use base-ten blocks to show the number 37 as many different ways as you can:

performance on a performance task. One way of doing this is by using a structure or scoring system known as a rubric. A rubric is a scale, often ranging between two and six points, that is used to holistically score a child's work.

Teachers might begin by using a two-point rubric, sorting children's work into two piles based on whether or not the children's work demonstrates understanding. This somewhat crude analysis provides some information about children's performance, but teachers often need more detailed information, and thus move to a three-point scale.

A three-point rubric includes three levels, which might be differentiated as follows:

3 points   demonstrates good understanding of the concept

2 points   demonstrates some understanding of the concept
1 point   demonstrates no understanding of the concept

A four-point rubric allows for more differences to be noted among the children's work. The following is an example of a four-point rubric (California Mathematics Council, 1996):

4 points   fully accomplishes the purpose of the task
3 points   substantially accomplishes the purpose of the task
2 points   partially accomplishes the purpose of the task
1 point   little or no progress toward accomplishing the purpose of the task

Table 4-4 shows a six-point rubric developed by the California Department of Education (Pandey, 1991). This rubric can be used to evaluate a variety of performance tasks with much detail.

Consider the following performance task: Four children want to share three cookies. Show how to share the cookies and explain how you know each person has the same amount. Box 4-1 shows the work of three children who performed this task.

Notice that Andy does not complete the task. He does not seem to realize that each child could get part of a cookie. Using a four-point rubric, the score for his solution would be a "1." He makes little or no progress toward accomplishing the task.

In contrast, Becky makes a good start at solving the problem. She understands that each child will get part of a cookie and cuts each cookie into fourths. But she does not explain how much of a cookie each child gets in all. Using a four-point rubric, the score for her solution would be a "3." She substantially accomplishes the purpose of the task.

Chantal solves the problem completely. She cuts the cookie so that each child gets the same amount, and she uses fraction language to identify the total amount each child receives. Using a four-point rubric, the score for her solution would be a "4." In other words, she fully accomplishes the purpose of the task.

Children can use rubrics to assess their own work and that of other children. One benefit is that children come to understand why their work received the score that it did. But more important, using rubrics helps children recognize that developing an understanding of a concept occurs on different levels. Thus, the children's goal is to try to continue to enhance their understanding of mathematical tasks.

As with all forms of assessment, teachers should keep track of children's rubric scores on performance assessment tasks. Box 4-2 shows a sample record sheet for performance assessment tasks. Note that this record sheet includes children's names, the names of each performance task, and each child's score using a four-point rubric. Teachers also may want to include a space for notes or comments on each child's understanding.

Portfolio assessment   A portfolio is a collection of selected children's work (Crowley, 1993). It provides an opportunity for children to showcase their work and growth in mathematics over a period of time, such as a school year. The use of portfolios promotes children's self-assessment, "encourages students to communicate their understandings of mathematics with a high level of proficiency, and emphasizes the role of the student as the active mathematician and the teacher as the guide" (Lambdin & Walker, 1994, p. 318).

TABLE 4-4

PERFORMANCE STANDARDS FOR CHILDREN'S WORK

LEVEL	STANDARD TO BE ACHIEVED FOR PERFORMANCE AT SPECIFIED LEVEL
6	Fully achieves the purpose of the task while insightfully interpreting, extending beyond the task, or raising provocative questions. Demonstrates an in-depth understanding of concepts and content. Communicates effectively and clearly to various audiences, using dynamic and diverse means.
5	Accomplishes the purposes of the task. Shows clear understanding of concepts. Communicates effectively.
4	Substantially completes purposes of the task. Displays understanding of major concepts, even though some less important ideas may be missing. Communicates successfully.
3	Purpose of the task not fully achieved; needs elaboration; some strategies may be ineffectual or not appropriate; assumptions about the purposes may be flawed. Gaps in conceptual understanding are evident. Limits communication to some important ideas; results may be incomplete or not clearly presented.
2	Important purposes of the task not achieved; work may need redirection; approach to task may lead away from its completion. Presents fragmented understanding of concepts; results may be incomplete or arguments may be weak. Attempts communication.
1	Purposes of the task not accomplished. Shows little evidence of appropriate reasoning. Does not successfully communicate relevant ideas; presents extraneous information.

Source: A sampler of mathematics assessment (p. 30), by T. Pandey, 1991, Sacramento, CA: California Department of Education. Copyright 1991 by the California Department of Education.

BOX 4-1

A Cookie-Sharing Performance Task

Name: _Andy_

"There's not enough cookies for four kids to share."

Name: _Becky_

"Each kid would get one-fourth of each cookie."

Name: _Chantal_

"Each kid would get one-half of a cookie and one-fourth of another cookie. They'd get three-fourths altogether."

Portfolios can provide children, teachers, and parents with much more detail about a child's performance in and understanding of mathematics than a letter grade offers. Further, portfolios are useful for supporting points of discussion in parent-teacher conferences.

What should be included? Portfolios may include a child's daily work, written descriptions of investigations, solved and unsolved problems, excerpts from the child's math journal, group reports, problems that the child wrote, illustrations, photographs of the child's mathematics projects, and videotapes of the child's mathematics presentations or projects.

One method is to have two portfolios: a working portfolio and a permanent portfolio. Children can use the working portfolio over time to collect materials they

BOX 4-2

Sample Teacher's Record Sheet for Performance Assessment Tasks

	RUBRIC SCORE ON PERFORMANCE TASKS (USING 4-POINT SCALE)			
Students	**Cookie Sharing Task**	**Ways to Make 37**		
Andy	1			
Becky	2			
Chantal	4			
Jeff	2			
Juan	3			

might want to keep in their permanent portfolios. At the end of a designated period of time, or as the grading period nears its end, children can reevaluate their work in their working portfolios and decide which entries to move to their permanent portfolios. A child may ask for help in selecting items to move to the permanent portfolio. To ensure that the portfolio reflects a range of work assignments, teachers often specify that children include at least one example of a variety of types of activities, such as journal entries, investigations, nonroutine problems, projects, application problems, and group work.

Further, teachers can require that children write a brief description for each portfolio entry, explaining their selections and what they demonstrate about their understanding. The description should then be attached to the appropriate entry. Some teachers also ask that each child select another child to conduct a written review or peer-evaluation of his or her portfolio, as well as complete a personal review for self-assessment.

Evaluating portfolios. Several criteria may be used for evaluating portfolios. One is to evaluate children's

LITERATURE LINK 4-1
Assessment

Lankford, Mary D. (1998). ***Dominoes Around the World.*** New York: Morrow Junior Books.
Ledwon, Peter, & Mets, Marilyn. (2000). ***Midnight Math.*** New York: Holiday House.
Maisner, Heather. (1996). ***Planet Monster.*** Cambridge, MA: Candlewick Press.

Various children's books assess children's mathematical thinking through games, puzzles, and brief investigations. Children can read and solve the problems posed in the stories individually or with a partner. These books challenge children and provide individualized activities and assessments that do not need teacher guidance.

- ***Dominoes Around the World*** is a collection of domino games and puzzles from around the world. These games are challenging and can be initiated by children with little assistance from the teacher. Mathematics skills and problem-solving strategies are applied during the games.
- ***Midnight Math*** is a collection of 12 brief mathematics games for young children. Children practice basic

skills, such as sorting, addition, subtraction, multiplication, and probability. Many of the games require the use of regular playing cards. Observe children as they work in small groups and record your observations for individual conferences with children or parents.
- ***Planet Monster*** is a self-directed book in which children work through a number puzzle adventure. Basic skills children use in the book include classifying, sorting, counting, telling time, and discriminating shapes. Children can work independently and record their answers, and then do a self-assessment by using the answers that appear at the end of the book.

Source: Dr. Patricia Moyer, George Mason University.

PRINCIPLES AND STANDARDS LINK 4-4

Students learn to share responsibility for the assessment process as they come to understand and make judgments about the quality of their own work. (NCTM, 1995, p. 39)

FIGURE 4-5

characteristics such as problem-solving skills, ability to make mathematical connections, ability to communicate mathematically, and attitudes toward mathematics and self (Crowley, 1993).

Another set of portfolio evaluation criteria (Stenmark, 1991) includes the following:

1. Understands the problem or task.
2. Uses a variety of strategies.
3. Uses models, technology, and other resources.
4. Interprets results.
5. Solves problems in a cooperative group.
6. Relates mathematics to other subjects and the real world.
7. Uses appropriate mathematics language and symbols.
8. Shows evidence of self-assessment and self-correction of work.

Before initiating the use of portfolios, it is wise to determine which criteria are most important and to develop them in a portfolio evaluation plan.

Self-assessment   This technique helps children reflect critically on their own work and reasoning. It also encourages children to take responsibility for their learning and to think independently. This personal assessment may be open-ended or it may include responses to a questionnaire. Likewise, it may be something children write about in their math journals. A sample prompt might be, "Tell me everything you know about multiplication. What else would you like to know about multiplication? Are you good at doing multiplication? Why or why not? Is there anything about multiplication you'd like to do better?"

ASSESSING ATTITUDES TOWARD MATHEMATICS

Success in mathematics often is positively correlated with favorable attitudes toward mathematics. It is important that teachers assess children's attitudes toward mathematics at the beginning of and throughout the school year. There are a number of ways to assess children's feelings toward mathematics. A Likert type of attitude

scale is the most common. In this type of scale the child responds to statements such as "I am happier in mathematics class than in any other class" on a five-point scale labeled in a range from strongly disagree to strongly agree. For children in the primary grades, the statements can be simplified and the choices reduced to three faces, as in Figure 4-5. The happy face is a positive response, the sad face is negative, and the middle face is neutral.

The semantic-differential approach to assessing attitudes consists of devising pairs of opposites, for example, "Easy" and "Hard" (or "Difficult," depending on the level of the children). Children mark a point on a five-point scale to indicate which word most closely represents their feelings. A typical presentation format is shown below:

Easy   Hard

A mark on the left above "Easy" usually is assigned a value of 1, whereas a mark on the right above "Hard" usually is assigned a value of 5, with corresponding values falling in between. The greater the total score, the more positive the attitude toward mathematics.

In addition, sentence completion can be used to assess attitudes. Give children the beginning of a sentence and ask them to complete the sentence. For example,

Mathematics is important because
_____.

Compared with other subjects, mathematics is
_____.

Results are not easily quantifiable but often reveal very important insights into how children feel about mathematics.

Finally, daily routine observations yield important clues about children's attitudes toward mathematics. Half-muttered statements, the level of enthusiasm, the degree of perseverance, and other behaviors are indications of a like or dislike of mathematics.

CONCLUSION

Assessment is an integral part of mathematics teaching and learning, providing information about children's growth and development in conceptual understanding. Many types of assessment are available to teachers; each type plays an important role in evaluating and maximizing children's learning. The type of assessment a teacher chooses to use is dependent on the purpose for the assessment.

For Your Journal

When you have finished studying this chapter, reflect on the following questions in your math journal:

1. Visit an elementary- or middle-school classroom and interview a teacher. How does the teacher assess children's mathematics understanding and achievement? Characterize the assessment according to the types discussed in this chapter.

2. Visit a classroom and ask for samples of the written work of at least two children in mathematics. How would you assess the children's understanding based on that written work?

3. Interview a teacher who uses either performance tasks or portfolios as part of a mathematics assessment plan. How does the teacher employ performance tasks or portfolios in assessing the children?

For Your Portfolio

When you have finished studying this chapter, complete the following activities to include in your professional portfolio:

1. Develop a performance task to assess understanding of a concept of your choice.

2. Analyze a chapter in an elementary mathematics textbook and the corresponding assessment. What would that assessment tell you about children's understanding?

Resources for Teachers

Books on assessment

Bryant, D., & Driscoll, M. (1998). *Exploring classroom assessment in mathematics.* Reston, VA: National Council of Teachers of Mathematics.

Bush, W. S. (Ed.). (2001). *Mathematics assessment: Cases and discussion questions for grades K–5.* Reston, VA: National Council of Teachers of Mathematics.

Bush, W. S., & Leinwand, S. (Eds.). (2000). *Mathematics assessment: A practice handbook for grades 6–8.* Reston, VA: National Council of Teachers of Mathematics.

Lambdin, D. V., Kehle, P. E., & Preston, R. V. (Eds.). (1996). *Emphasis on assessment: Readings from NCTM's school-based journals.* Reston, VA: National Council of Teachers of Mathematics.

Stenmark, J. K. (Ed.). (1991). *Mathematics assessment: Myths, models, good questions, and practical suggestions.* Reston, VA: National Council of Teachers of Mathematics.

Stenmark, J. K., & Bush, W. S. (Eds.). (2001). *Mathematics assessment: A practice handbook for grades 3–5.* Reston, VA: National Council of Teachers of Mathematics.

Links to the Internet

Assessment Resources
http://score.kings.k12.ca.us/assess.html

Contains links to mathematics assessment resources.

Balanced Assessment in Mathematics
http://balancedassessment.gseharvard.edu

Contains sample mathematics assessment tasks for elementary and secondary grades.

Assessment in Mathematics Teaching
http://mathforum.org/mathed/assessment.html

Contains links to publications and presentations about mathematics assessment.

CHAPTER 5

Developing Number Concepts

KEY CONCEPTS ►

✔ **Pre-number activities**

✔ **Types of counting**

✔ **Ways to represent numbers**

✔ **Number relationships**

FOCUS QUESTIONS ►

When you have finished studying this chapter, you should be able to answer the following questions:

1. What types of pre-number activities must children engage in to develop understanding of number concepts?

2. What types of counting abilities are necessary for children to develop?

3. What are several of the ways in which children must be able to represent numbers?

4. What types of number relationships are essential for children to understand?

You have probably observed a child respond to the question "How old are you?" by proudly but shyly holding up the accurate (or inaccurate) number of fingers. You may also have heard a young child respond, "One-two-three-five-ten," when asked to count a set of five objects. Mastering the number names and learning to count are early formal mathematics milestones of children. Such capabilities, however, can be mere mimicking or rote memorization and usually occur before an understanding of numbers is achieved.

This chapter discusses important concepts that relate to the development of number understanding. Numerous and varied experiences are described to demonstrate how to enhance young children's construction of number relationships. ✔

NCTM CONTENT STANDARDS AND EXPECTATIONS ADDRESSED IN THIS CHAPTER

STANDARD	EXPECTATIONS FOR GRADES PRE-K–2	EXPECTATIONS FOR GRADES 3–5
Number and Operations Standard Instructional programs from pre-K–12 should enable all students to—	In prekindergarten through Grade 2 all students students should—(NCTM, 2000, p. 78)	In Grades 3–5 all students should—(NCTM, 2000, p. 148)
Understand numbers, ways of representing numbers, relationships among numbers, and number systems.	• count with understanding and recognize "how many" in sets of objects. • develop understanding of the relative position and magnitude of whole numbers and of ordinal and cardinal numbers and their connections. • develop a sense of whole numbers and represent and use them in flexible ways, including relating, composing, and decomposing numbers. • connect number words and numerals to the quantities they represent, using various physical models and representations.	• understand the place-value structure of the base-ten number system and be able to represent and compare whole numbers and decimals. • recognize equivalent representations for the same number and generate them by decomposing and composing numbers. • describe classes of numbers (e.g., odds, primes, squares, and multiples) according to characteristics such as the nature of their factors.

PRINCIPLES AND STANDARDS LINK 5-1
Content Strand: Number and Operations

In prekindergarten through Grade 2 all students should-

- count with understanding and recognize "how many" sets of objects;
- use multiple models to develop initial understandings of place value and the base-ten number system;
- develop understanding of the relative position and magnitude of whole numbers and of ordinal and cardinal numbers and their connections;
- develop a sense of whole numbers and represent and use them in flexible ways, including relating, composing, and decomposing numbers;
- connect number words and numerals to the quantities they represent, using various physical models and representations;
- understand and represent commonly used fractions, such as $\frac{1}{4}$, $\frac{1}{3}$, and $\frac{1}{2}$ (NCTM, 2000, p. 78)

The Annenberg/CPB Math and Science Collection

VIDEO LINK 5-1
Concepts of Whole Number Operations

Brief Summary: In "Cubes and Containers," Janice Sette-Lund's kindergarteners are sorting Unifix cubes by color and placing them into containers.

1. Near the beginning of this segment, Ms. Sette-Lund asks the children how they might sort the Unifix cubes. What were some of the different ways the children suggested? How did the teacher respond when a child suggested a way that would not work?
2. One group decided they needed more than 10 containers to complete the sorting. Why did they decide this? How did Ms. Sette-Lund handle this situation?

Video Source. Teaching Math: A Video Library, K-4; Tape 4 from The Annenberg/CPB Math and Science Collection.

THE FOUNDATIONS OF NUMBER

Counting activities, comparing sets, and learning the sequence of number names and the numerals to represent one-digit numbers have traditionally formed an important part of kindergarten and Grade 1 mathematics programs, because it is believed that such activities help a child develop an understanding of number concepts.

Other activities that enhance the development of number concepts are classifying, seriating, and patterning (Piaget, 1965). As with counting, by the time children enter kindergarten, they will have had experiences in these processes in their preschool activities, whether through play or through interactions with adults. At school, teachers should plan activities for children so that these processes will eventually extend to number classification, ordering, and patterning.

Understanding numbers resides in the recognition and knowledge of number relationships (Van de Walle, 1994). Knowing the number 5 means more than being able to rationally count a set of 5. It is knowing this number in relationship to other numbers. For example, 5 is 1 less than 6, 5 is 1 more than 4, and 5 is 3 plus 2. Developing number relationships is at the heart of kindergarten and Grade 1 mathematics learning.

Pre-Number Activities

Classification   The process of classifying or sorting a collection of objects involves focusing on an attribute

or characteristic of the objects and subsequently grouping them accordingly. For example, children could sort a collection of books according to the characteristic "stories about animals."

Connecting with science and social studies. Classification is a topic that lends itself nicely to integrating mathematics with other subject areas such as science and social studies.

For science and social studies projects, teachers often take children on outings—trips to the zoo, nature walks, or visits to local establishments such as a grocery store, a department store, a bank, a factory, or a post office. During an outdoor excursion, children can be asked to gather a small collection of objects. Upon return to the classroom, a science lesson might focus on the characteristic "growing" and the objects collected can be classified in

TECHNOLOGY LINK 5-1
Explorer—General Whole Numbers and Numeration

Explorer is a collection of educational resources for K–12 mathematics and science education. Click on "General Whole Numbers and Numeration" to get to a listing of lesson plans and other resources to help children learn about number concepts and numeration. Visit http://explorer.scrtec.org/explorer-db/browse/static/Mathematics/index.html or link from our Companion Website at **www.prenhall.com/cathcart**.

sets of "things that grow" (e.g., leaves, moss, mushrooms, twigs) and "things that do not grow" (e.g., stones, metal, paper). While at a grocery store, children might be asked to observe how food displays are organized (fruits in one section, vegetables in another, meats in another, etc.); at a department store, they could observe the furniture area (bedroom furniture displayed together, living room furniture together in another area, etc.) or how shoes are displayed (children's shoes in one area, women's and men's in other separate areas).

If it is not feasible to go on class field trips, children could be encouraged to notice how objects are classified during family outings or in their home. For example, children can examine kitchen cupboards, clothes closets, linen cupboards, etc., to see how objects are organized. Provide time for the children to report their findings to the class.

Other classification activities. In class, the children themselves can be the objects for classification activities. Attributes that can be considered for classification include wearing glasses and not wearing glasses, wearing something red and wearing something green, wearing a buttoned blouse or shirt and wearing a t-shirt. Depending on the classification category, not all children in a class may be able to participate in a particular activity. The class should discuss this so that children will know why they "do not belong" in either category being classified. Sometimes, all children can participate if two categories are specified as, for example, children wearing footwear with laces and without laces. It is also possible to select more than two classification categories.

Commercial classification sets. A commercial set of Attribute Logic Blocks lends itself to numerous classification activities of varying sophistication. The set consists of plastic blocks in five shapes (triangle, square, rectangle, hexagon, and circle), two different sizes (large and small), two thicknesses (thin, thick), and three colors (yellow, red, and blue) for a total of 60 pieces. The set is structured, that is, there is only one block for every possible combination of values for the attributes. For example, there is only one large, thin, red circle. If purchasing a set of Attribute Logic Blocks is problematic, try making a set from felt. The felt shapes can be placed on flannel- or felt-covered boards for display.

In a lesson observing attributes children may first focus on color. Through maturation and experience, children are able to concentrate on other perceptual characteristics and eventually can classify sets according to abstract attributes such as number.

Class conversation. When all the children have had an opportunity to sort a particular set of materials, a teacher could gather the children on a mat for a class conversation. An opening remark by the teacher might be "Did you notice many differences in the things you've been sorting? Let's see what differences you noticed. Becky, would you begin, please?" As children voice their observations, the teacher could note them on cards to attach to the bulletin board. Sometime during the day or week, each child can affix objects to the bulletin board or gather them into a group under their proper characteristic.

Class conversations can take place following any mathematical activity to provide an opportunity for children to talk about the mathematics they are doing. Such dialogue enhances the development of mathematical understanding (Baker & Baker, 1990).

The following six activities describe classification experiences using unstructured materials, and activities with commercial attribute blocks are described in Activities 5-1 and 5-2.

1. Classifying
   - Ask a small group of children to stand side by side in front of the others.
   - Ask the class, "Can you tell why these girls and boys belong together?" (The teacher decides on an attribute.)

2. Classifying
   - Choose three children who are wearing something blue and one who is not.
   - Ask the class, "Who doesn't belong in this group?" "Why not?"

ACTIVITY 5-1

GUESS WHICH BLOCK I HAVE?

MATERIALS
A set of attribute blocks for each child and the teacher

PROCEDURE
1. Have the children select one block from their set. The teacher does the same without showing the block to the children.

2. A child asks the teacher a question about the chosen block. Example: "Is your block red?" If the teacher's block is not red, the teacher answers, "No, my block is not red." The children who had chosen a red block must change their block for a non-red block.

3. The questioning continues until the teacher's block has been identified. By this time, every child should have in her or his hand a block that is the same as that of the teacher.

4. Have a child identify the block by naming attributes.

   Example: "The block is a large, thin, blue triangle."

5. Repeat procedures with another block. Children could guess the block selected by a child rather than by the teacher.

ACTIVITY 5-2

BUILDING TRAINS

MATERIALS
A set of attribute blocks for each child

PREPARATION
Make an "engine" for each child as pictured below.

(The side of the square measures 8 cm.)

PROCEDURE
1. Direct the children to select a block and place it on their engine.
2. The children are then to select other blocks, in turn, to be the "cars" that the engine has to pull. Each car has to be different from the preceding car in only one way.
3. When the trains are 6 to 8 cars long, children should check each other's train to see whether the rule was followed for each car.

VARIATIONS
Trains can be made with cars that are different in more than one way; in at least two ways.

• Choose someone to replace the child who does belong in this group, based on the chosen attribute.
3. Classifying
   • Provide children with a collection of buttons, seeds, or other objects that have easily distinguishable attributes.
   • Ask them to group the objects in ways they are the same.
   • Have them tell or write about the groupings they made.

Over a period of class days, provide children with lots of opportunities to classify objects, beginning with concrete items and moving to semiconcrete objects such as pictures of objects.

4. Describing properties
   • Have all children stand beside their chairs and ask a child to volunteer to stand where all the children can see her or him.

• Have children, in turn, tell something about the volunteer. Example: "Jeremy has brown hair."
• As the teacher writes "brown hair" on the board, all children who have a different hair color should sit down. Other statements could refer to clothing and jewelry worn or other known facts about the person (e.g., Jeremy takes music lessons).
• Children continue to name properties of the volunteer until the volunteer is the only student left standing.

5. What can we sort?
   • Ask the class to think of some collections they could classify.
   • When a list has been generated, have children, on different days, select one of the collections named and think of ways to classify the collection.
   • Children should record their ideas, which will be used at another time.

6. How can we sort this collection?
   • Using one of the collections identified by the children (previous activity), have them present their ideas about possible ways to sort the objects. If it is feasible to gather a set of the objects, do so for only 1 day, because some children may need to have the objects visible to think of characteristics.
   • The particular set of objects gathered should then be classified.

Seriation *Seriation* is the process of focusing on an attribute and then ordering a set of objects according to that attribute. For example, given a set of crayons, children could be asked to order them according to length. Cuisenaire Rods are a commercial set consisting of ten rods, each of a different color, that can be ordered by length.

Before asking children to order a set of three or more objects, a teacher should have them compare two objects so as to recognize different attributes and learn comparative terms. For example, children should be able to examine two objects and make such statements as the following:

This ruler is longer than that ruler.
This tower is shorter than that tower.
The red paper is larger than the green paper.
The tub of beans is heavier than the tub of macaroni.

When children are able to make these kinds of comparisons, they can be asked to order larger sets according to various attributes.

In seriating or ordering activities, a teacher should vary the number of objects to be ordered, because some children are successful in seriating 7 or fewer items but not with sets of 10 or more. Objects can be ordered, for example, according to mass, shade of color, length, size, height, or thickness.

Objects that can be seriated include the following:

Attribute	Objects to Be Ordered
length	sets of pencils, nails, pieces of rope or yarn
size	mittens, socks, containers, jars
capacity	measuring spoons, jars, boxes
mass	small vials of sugar, flour, rice, beans, etc.
height	children, potted plant seedlings

Teachers can construct sets of objects that vary in length, height, or size according to a fixed ratio such as strips of cardboard, cylinders cut from paper towel rolls, rectangles and other regular shapes, and outlines of houses or other objects. Pairs of objects of different lengths, such as vases and flowers, dolls and hats, or bats and balls, can be constructed and used for double seriation activities. (See Activity 5-3.)

Through classification and seriation activities, a teacher will be able to observe how children's observation skills, logical reasoning ability, and problem-solving strategies are developing.

Patterns The recognition of patterns is a basic skill that enhances the development of mathematics concepts.

ACTIVITY 5-3

DOUBLE SERIATION

MATERIALS
A set of 8 to 12 similar paper balls and bats; each bat differs in length by 1 cm and each ball is proportionally larger

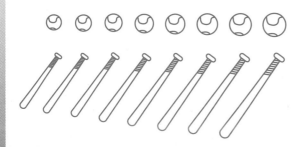

PROCEDURE
1. First, ask children to order the balls from smallest to largest. You may place the smallest and the largest ball in place.
2. Next, ask children to match each bat with the ball to which it belongs. Again, match the first and the last bat.

VARIATION
After children have ordered the balls only, point to one bat from the set and ask children to find the ball to which it belongs.

Prior to recognizing number patterns, children should become familiar with concrete patterns. Varied kinds of patterns such as A B A B A B . . . and A B B A B B . . . can be clapped, tapped, danced, walked, jumped, or otherwise acted out. Patterns can also be sung, read, or recited.

Patterns can be constructed, for example, with colored beads on a string or made with gummed shapes on paper. Other materials include a pegboard and colored pegs, Unifix cubes and multi-link cubes of various colors, and pattern blocks. The following two activities serve as examples.

1. Creating Patterns
   - Provide children with buttons in two colors and a piece of 2-cm grid paper.
   - Invite children to create patterns by placing the buttons on the grid paper.
   - Have children describe the pattern they made.
2. Creating Patterns
   - Provide children with Unifix cubes in two colors.
   - Ask children to construct a pattern by interlocking the cubes a certain way.
   - Have children describe their pattern.

Eventually, children will recognize simple number patterns such as "counting by one," "adding one," or "counting by twos" to generate number series. Upper elementary children will learn that *looking for a number pattern* is a useful problem-solving strategy.

Classification, seriation, and patterning skills can be learned from storybooks. Examples of good storybooks to read to or with a class include *I Was Walking Down the Road* (Barchas, 1975), *Nancy No-size* (Hoffman, 1990), *Have You Seen Birds?* (Oppenheim & Reid, 1986), *I Love Spiders* (Parker, 1988), *Who Said Red?* (Serfoza, 1988), and *Red is Best* (Stinson, 1982).

The next step with patterning is to encourage children to translate patterns from one medium to another. For example, an extension or follow-up task to "Creating Patterns" (#2 above) is as follows: Ask children to represent the pattern they showed with the Unifix cubes in another way—for example, by using another manipulative, such as buttons, or by using letters, such as A and B. Activities of this sort *help children abstract the key features of patterns.*

One-to-one correspondence Prior to developing counting capabilities, children can compare sets by using a one-to-one correspondence strategy. For example, children can be asked to find out whether there are enough books or pencils for each child in a group. Children can be given a set of miniature dolls, a set of cars, small raisin boxes, or other small objects and asked to record in some way (tallies or circles, for example) "how many" objects they have. There should be one tally or mark per object. Children should be aware that the diagram (tallies) shows how many objects there are in the set (see below).

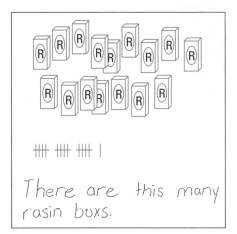

Children need to learn the meaning of comparative terms such as "more than," "fewer than," "the same number as," and "as many as." These terms should be used when comparing sets. As children learn to count objects in sets, they will compare and order sets according to the number of objects in each set. The following activities describe comparison and one-to-one correspondence experiences for children.

1. Comparing Groups
   • Direct children to stand in groups of two, three, and four
   • Ask children to make a statement to compare one group with another. ("This group has one more than that one. This group has one fewer than that one.")

2. Comparing Collections
   • Show children collections of small objects on three plates, each plate with a different number of objects.
   • Ask them to compare the collections.
   • Change the size of the collections and have children compare the sets again.

3. Comparing Collections
   • Place six small objects, all the same, on each of three paper plates and seven objects on another plate.
   • Ask the children, "Which set does not belong?" and "Can you make it belong?"

4. One-to-One Correspondence
   • Provide a child with a set of Valentine's Day cards and envelopes.
   • Ask the child to find out whether there are enough envelopes for the cards.
   • Have the child make a statement about the situation. ("There are more cards than envelopes.")

Other objects to use for one-to-one correspondence include cups and saucers, pencils and paper, books and children, paint jars and brushes.

5. Comparing Pictured Sets
   • Prepare a set of six cards with stickers on them. Each card except one has the same number of stickers on it. One card has one more or one fewer.
   • Ask a child, "Which card is different?", "How is it different?"

Examples

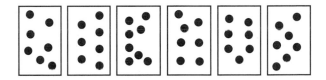

6. Comparing Pictured Sets
   • Show the children a set of six cards with 2, 3, 3, 4, 4, and 5 dots on them.
   • Ask the children, in turn, to select two cards and make a comparative statement: "This card has as many dots as this one"; "This card has more dots than this one"; "This card has one fewer dot than this one."

Classifying according to number.   In one-to-one correspondence activities, close attention should be paid to the comparative language used by children. When children use expressions such as "as many books as children," the expression "as many as" can be used to classify sets. Such sets have the same number. *Number is a property of sets that is independent of attributes such as color, shape, size, and arrangement.* Further, the objects within a set do not have to be uniform.

Conservation of number   The ability to conserve number quantities under varied configurations marks a certain mental maturity. Piaget has identified the age of 6 to 7 years as the time when a child is successful at number conservation tasks, but not all children attain the capability at that age. A teacher should become knowledgeable of children's conservation abilities so that children are not expected to complete number exercises beyond their cognitive level (Marchand, Bye, Harrison, & Schroeder, 1985). For example, a child who cannot yet conserve large numbers will have difficulty making sense of number groupings. Conservation of large numbers can be assessed by having a child count two sets of the same objects, for example, Unifix cubes. One set of, say 32 cubes, is left spread out on the table while the other set is placed in small transparent plastic glasses in groups of 10. The child is subsequently asked to compare the sets.

NUMBER MEANINGS

As children use numbers in their daily lives, they will come to differentiate between three uses of numbers: cardinal, ordinal, and nominal.

Cardinal Use of Numbers

"Cardinal" numbers are used to designate the quantity of a set. The *cardinal* aspect of number is the idea that whenever a set is counted, the last number named is the total number of objects in the set. For example, a child who is asked to count the pieces of chalk on the board ledge and states, after counting to seven, that *there are seven pieces of chalk on the ledge,* is using the cardinal aspect of number.

Ordinal Use of Numbers

"Ordinal" means *order;* ordinal numbers are used to denote the order of an object. In their play, children will often make statements such as the following: "Michelle finished *first*" or "Marc came in *third.*" Other times, children will hear expressions such as "This is the *fifth* time the phone has rung since dinner" or "Christmas is on the 25th day of December." The use of numbers such as first, second, third, etc. is an *ordinal* use of number.

Nominal Use of Numbers

"Nominal" means *name;* nominal numbers are used to name objects. A third use of number is for a *nominal* purpose; that is, numbers are used to identify objects. Numbers are used in a nominal sense, for example, to identify a house on a street, a postal code, a license plate, floors and rooms in large buildings, or a team player.

1. Number Walk
   - Take children on a "number walk" along a city block.
   - Have them look for numerals and jot them down and where they saw them.

PRINCIPLES AND STANDARDS LINK 5-2
Content Strand: Number and Operations

In prekindergarten through Grade 2 all students should-

- develop understanding of the relative position and magnitude of whole numbers and of ordinal and cardinal numbers and their connections . . . (NCTM, 2000, p. 78)

- Back in class, discuss what "numbers" they saw. Ask, "What did the number tell?" (how many; it identified something). "Did you notice a pattern?"
2. Different Uses of Numbers
   - Have children bring to class newspaper or magazine clippings that depict numbers used in a cardinal, an ordinal, and a nominal sense.
   - Discuss the different uses of numbers.
   - The pictures can subsequently be posted on a bulletin board under appropriate headings.

COUNTING

Discrete and Continuous Quantities

As children engage in counting objects in their environment, they will come to realize that counting is not appropriate for some objects. For example, one does not count the amount of water in the bathtub or the amount of cake on a plate. In time, children will be able to discriminate between discrete and continuous quantities.

Discrete objects are those that can be counted to find out "how many" are in the group. For example, one can ask, "How many people are in your family?" "How many books do you own?" *Continuous quantities,* on the other hand, measure "how much." Examples are "How much milk did you drink?" "How long did it take you to clean your room?" Measurements can be of length, area, volume, temperature, mass, or time.

Rote Counting

Rote counting is simply the reciting of the number name sequence in proper order. Some children learn the number sequence to 20 and beyond, even up to 100, without being able to count a set of objects less than 20. Some children who know the number name sequence make counting errors by counting objects in a set more than once or not counting others, that is, they do not establish a one-to-one correspondence between number names and objects.

Rational Counting

According to Gelman and Gallistel (1978), children who are rational counters possess the following capabilities:

- They are able to recite the number-word sequence (i.e., "one, two, three").
- They make a one-to-one correspondence between the items being counted and saying the number (i.e., they say "one" as they touch the first item, say "two" as they touch the second item, etc.)
- They realize that the last number they say represents the total number of objects in the set.

To test the last capability, after a child has counted a set of eight objects, for example, blocks, ask the child to show you eight blocks. Does the child point to the last block counted or to the set of eight blocks?

Children should have ample opportunities to count objects. Sets arranged in linear fashion, such as beads on a string or a row of blocks, are easier to count than a set of objects in scatter formation. Some children may need to be shown how to organize objects when counting to avoid making errors. They can be told to move the objects to the side as each one is counted.

For sets of 20 or more, children can be asked to count the objects twice to see whether they arrive at the same number. If not, a third count should match one of the first two totals.

1. Oral Counting
   - Say to a child, "Count for me."
   - Allow the child to continue counting until several errors are made in the number sequence.
2. Counting Objects
   - Place some Unifix cubes before a child seated at a table.
   - Say, "Count the cubes."
   - Allow the child to continue counting until you notice several errors.

You may want to record what type of errors the child made: Were they number sequence errors? Did the child skip cubes? Did the child count a cube more than once?

3. How many do you see?
   - If there is a window in the classroom that faces a street, have a child count vehicles as they pass by over a period of several minutes.
   - As they look out the window, have children count how many buildings they see; how many trees they see.
   - Ask some children to walk down the hallway and count the doors they see. Then, have children walk down the stairs and count the steps.
   - During recess, ask children to count the windows on one side of the school; count how many cars they see in the parking lot.
4. Counting Objects
   - Place several objects on plates or in boxes, plastic tubs, or jars.
   - Have children count to find out how many objects are in each container.

Children can record their work. ("I counted 12 buttons." "I counted 15 sticks.")

When children know the number-name sequence to at least 20 and can count objects, they can be engaged in more sophisticated counting activities.

Counting All, Counting On

Children use different counting procedures when quantifying sets. For example, suppose a child counts six apples in a basket and then five apples are placed beside the basket and the child is asked to find how many apples there are in all. A child might say "six" then continue to count "seven, eight, nine, ten, eleven" and state that there are 11 apples in all. This is a *counting-on* strategy.

Another possibility is to begin counting at one and recount the 6 apples in the basket and continue counting until 11 has been reached. This latter strategy is called *counting all.*

A teacher should observe how children count sets. For those who always count all the objects, a teacher should demonstrate a counting-on method. See Activity 5-4 for a sample task. Children could use a counting-on and then a counting-all strategy to prove that they produce the same count. Children will eventually see that the counting-on strategy is the quicker way to count. To facilitate this, a teacher might say, "I have six pennies in my hand and these (seven on the table) are left. Count to find how many pennies in all."

When children are able to count on to find the number of objects in given sets, they can be asked to count on from a given number as shown on the cards in Figure 5-1 to find how many in all.

ACTIVITY 5-4

COUNTING ON

MATERIALS
Purse or similar container and approximately 20 pennies or other counters

PROCEDURE
1. Say, "There are seven pennies in the purse. Count to find out how many pennies there are altogether."
2. If the child wants to count the pennies in the purse, allow the child to do so. When the child has counted the 12 pennies, tell the child that another way to count the pennies is to begin at seven and continue to count on.
3. Have the child count several collections as above by first counting all, then counting on.

FIGURE 5-1

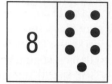 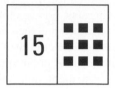 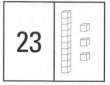

Counting Back

Some children who are proficient counters are unable to *count backward*. An introduction to counting backward can be to ask, "What number is 1 less than 9?" When the child responds, say, "Tell what number is 1 less than 8." Continue in this manner for several more numbers. Then ask the child to write or recite the numbers, counting backward from 9 to 0 thinking of "one less than" the last number named. In time, counting-backward activities should include bridging decades (32, 31, 30, 29, . . .) and eventually centuries (202, 201, 200, 199, . . .).

Skip Counting

Skip counting refers to counting by multiples of a certain number. For example, "skip counting by 5" means to count "5, 10, 15, 20," and so on. Skip counting lays the foundation for understanding the concept of multiplication. It usually is introduced in Grade 1, with children first learning to skip count by 2, 5, and 10.

Skip counting can be taught conceptually by counting groups of objects. For example, skip counting by 2 can be introduced by counting all the feet in the class. All the children could stand in a line, and the teacher could move along the line, pointing to each set of two feet and encouraging the class to skip count together by 2.

Later work on skip counting can also be based on patterns. A Grade 1 child was asked what he could say about the number series 2, 4, 6, 8, . . . He quickly responded, "They're even numbers and it's counting by twos." And what about the numbers 1, 3, 5, 7, . . . ? "They're odd," he

responded. The teacher asked, "This is counting by what?" "By threes. No. I don't know."

In later grades, when children do some skip-counting activities, they should begin counting with different numbers. For example, when counting by 10, have children begin with any single-digit number (e.g., 2, 12, 22, 32, . . .; 6, 16, 26, 36, 46, . . .).

A calculator can assist a child in naming the counting numbers or "skip-counting" sequences. Calculators that have an automatic constant for addition or multiplication are particularly

---

ACTIVITY 5-6

WRITING COUNTING NUMBERS IN REVERSE

MATERIALS
Pencil and paper

PROCEDURE
Write the numerals from 24 to 14

- from 56 to 35
- from 81 to 68
- from 105 to 95

ACTIVITY 5-5

COUNTING BACK

PROCEDURE
Count backward from 22 to 16

- from 33 to 25
- from 62 to 57
- from 112 to 97
- from 152 to 137

ACTIVITY 5-7

COUNTING BY TENS

PROCEDURE
Count by tens. Begin with

10 ___ ___ ___ ___
   ___ ___ ___ ___

3 ___ ___ ___ ___
   ___ ___ ___ ___

8 ___ ___ ___ ___
   ___ ___ ___ ___

12 ___ ___ ___ ___
   ___ ___ ___ ___

> ## ACTIVITY 5-8
> ### COUNTING BY FIVES
>
> **MATERIALS**
> Pencil and paper
>
> **PROCEDURE**
> Write 10 numbers counting by fives.
> Begin with 5; 6; 4; 1.

> ## ACTIVITY 5-9
> ### COUNTING BACKWARD BY TENS AND FIVES
>
> **MATERIALS**
> Pencil and paper
>
> **PROCEDURE**
>
> 1. Write the numbers, counting by tens
>   * from 60 to 10
>   * from 120 to 50
>
> 2. Write the numbers, counting by fives
>   * from 45 to 20
>   * from 110 to 75

>
> ### PRINCIPLES AND STANDARDS LINK 5-3
> ### Content Strand: Number and Operations
>
> Concrete models can help students represent numbers and develop number sense; they can also help bring meaning to students' use of written symbols and can be useful in building place-value concepts. (NCTM, 2000, p. 80)

While children are engaged in counting activities, attention should be given to developing number-related ideas of equality, more than, less than, combining groups, and separating groups. The symbolic form of these operations or relations should be used only to record some meaningful action. The mathematical symbols $=$, $+$, and $-$ are usually introduced in the latter part of Grade 1, and the symbols $<$ and $>$ in Grade 2 or Grade 3.

> ## ACTIVITY 5-10
> ### MAKING SETS
>
> **MATERIALS**
> Nine paper plates and small objects for each child
>
> **PROCEDURE**
> Make sets of all the counting numbers to nine.

useful for this. For calculators with an automatic constant for addition, a key stroke sequence to count by 5 beginning at 4 would be $4 + 5 = = = =$.

Counting backward can also be done on a calculator with the following keystroke sequence for counting by threes beginning with 30: $30 - 3 = = = -$. Some calculators have the constant number registered before the operation sign in the keystroke sequence rather than the number following it. When using a calculator to develop number sequences, children should be encouraged to say the number first, then press the equal key and check the display to see whether they said the right number. This procedure provides instant feedback and children can practice by themselves.

Simple computer programs can be written to "make the computer count." Computer or calculator printouts of number sequences can be helpful to children when studying number patterns.

REPRESENTING NUMBERS

How can the abstract idea of number be modeled so that children will come to know numbers and their properties? An approach has been to use concrete materials and pictures quite extensively in the early grades.

> ## ACTIVITY 5-11
> ### SHOWING NUMBERS ONE TO NINE
>
> **MATERIALS**
> Toothpicks, glue stick, and a piece of cardboard
>
> **PROCEDURE**
> Glue toothpicks on the cardboard to show the numbers from one to nine.

> ## ACTIVITY 5-12
> ### SHOWING NUMBERS TO NINE
>
> **MATERIALS**
> Unifix cubes
>
> **PROCEDURE**
> Use the cubes to construct rods to show numbers to nine.

ACTIVITY 5-13

COUNTING OBJECTS AND WRITING NUMERALS

MATERIALS
A collection of buttons or other small objects (the size of the collection can be 20 to 50 objects.)

PROCEDURE
1. Count the number of objects you have and record the amount in a statement. ("I counted 26 buttons." "There are 32 blocks in the box.")
2. Now recount the amount, checking for accuracy.
3. If the count number is not the same, the collection should be counted a third time.

VARIATION
One child could count a collection and then another child could count the collection. The children then check their count numbers with each other.

ACTIVITY 5-14

COUNTING AND WRITING NUMERALS

MATERIALS
Objects in the room

PROCEDURE
Count three sets of objects in the room and write statements about your findings.

POSSIBLE EXAMPLES
There are 12 books on the top shelf.
There are 26 desks in the room.
There are 30 chairs in the classroom.

VARIATION
The children could count three sets of objects at home and write statements about their findings. For example: There are 10 pairs of shoes in the closet; there are 24 spoons in the drawer; I have 16 books in my room.

Concrete Models

Concrete materials are readily available for use in number development activities. Most primary classrooms are well-equipped with boxes or buckets of small discrete objects for the children to use in counting activities and may include collections of acorns, small pine cones, square ceramic tiles, and buttons. Besides using such materials at their desks, children may be asked to find out how many crayons are in a box, how many books are on a shelf, how many children have brought their lunch, how many rooms are on one floor of the school, etc.

In another counting activity, square tiles can be used to model numbers in geometric patterns. For example, children can be asked to make "number rectangles," as pictured in Activity 5-15. From this activity, the ideas of even and odd numbers can be discussed as well as what happens when one combines two even numbers, two odd numbers, or an even and an odd number.

Square tiles also can be used to model square numbers by constructing squares and the triangular numbers by making staircases.

The base-ten blocks are used by children when they understand grouping, particularly a group of ten. See Figure 5-2 and Blackline Master 1 at the end of the book.

Pictorial and Graphic Representation of Numbers

In general, children enjoy drawing. This capability can be the medium used to record the results of their number-related explorations.

Children can be asked to draw pairs of sets with different numbers of objects and to indicate which set has more objects or which set has the greater number. Provided with graph paper, children can draw the "number rectangles" they constructed with tiles.

Children can attempt to draw pictures of base-ten blocks or be provided with rubber stamps of the blocks. Later, a graphic representation can be made by using a

ACTIVITY 5-15

NUMBER RECTANGLES

MATERIALS
Square tiles

PROCEDURE
1. Show numbers with the tiles in the manner above.
2. Which numbers form rectangles? What can you say about them?
3. Try joining pairs of even and odd numbers. What do you notice?
4. Join two odd numbers. What do you notice?
5. Join two even numbers. What do you notice?

FIGURE 5-2

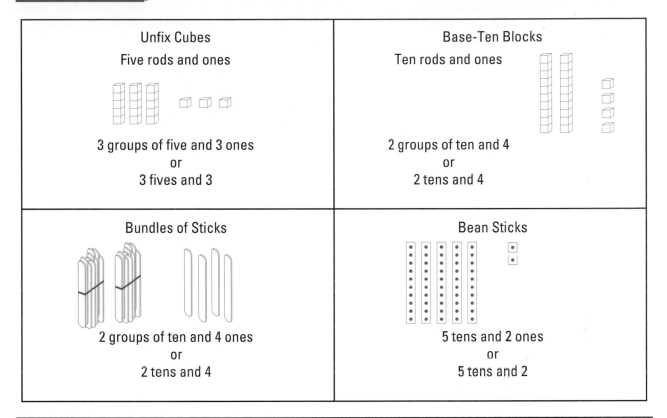

Unfix Cubes	Base-Ten Blocks
Five rods and ones	Ten rods and ones
3 groups of five and 3 ones or 3 fives and 3	2 groups of ten and 4 or 2 tens and 4
Bundles of Sticks	Bean Sticks
2 groups of ten and 4 ones or 2 tens and 4	5 tens and 2 ones or 5 tens and 2

dot for ones, a line for tens, and a square for hundreds, as shown in Figure 5-3.

Symbolic Representation of Numbers

Kindergarten number activities have children counting sets, constructing sets concretely and pictorially, and matching sets with number names and numerals. What is important for children to internalize are number relationships, not how to write numerals or recognize number

FIGURE 5-3

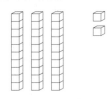

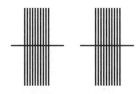

(a) Rubber stamp of base-ten blocks

(b) Graphic representation of base-ten blocks

(c) Graphic representation of stick bundles

symbols. Thus, children should be encouraged to talk about their number work and to record what they do in their own way. Work with number symbols should not appear to be of prime importance and can be delayed for some time.

A teacher can introduce an activity in one of four ways: concretely, pictorially, symbolically, or orally, using number words. Likewise, children can be asked to respond in any of the four ways. An effective teaching or assessment strategy is to present a task in one mode and have the children respond in a different mode (Figure 2-10). Flexibility in transferring from one mode to another is indicative of some understanding. Some materials for number work are shown in Figure 5-4. The following four activities are appropriate for learning to match numerals with number words and quantities.

1. Ordering Numerals
   - Cut out some magazine or newspaper pictures that show a large numeral.
   - Have the children order the pictures according to the numeral on them.
2. Matching Sets With Numerals
   - Prepare a set of numbered garages and a set of cars with dots on them (e.g., one dot on a car, two dots on another).
   - Direct a child to match the cars with the garages.
3. Matching Numerals, Number Names, and Picture Cards
   - Prepare three sets of cards: one with number names, one with numerals, and one with pictures.
   - Have a child match the picture cards with its number name and numeral.

Sample Cards

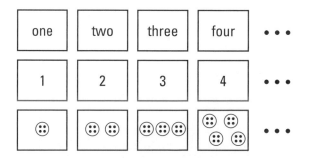

4. Writing Numerals to Match Sets
   - Prepare a set of cards with pictures on them.
   - Ask a child to count the pictures on a card and then write the appropriate numeral on a piece of paper to go with the card.

Numerals

Just as individuals develop their own handwriting style, children also develop their own way of forming numer-

als. For some numerals there is more than one acceptable form (e.g., 4 and ⁴, 2 and ², 9 and ⁹). Teachers usually present young children with one numerical form for each number. However, children will likely see other forms for numerals, such as, for example, on a calculator display. A poster depicting acceptable numerals may help children recognize and write different forms.

Teachers should observe children as they form numerals, either when copying them or when writing them from memory. Devote some time to practice forming numerals so that children can internalize an efficient way of writing each numeral. A recommended stroke sequence is presented here (Baratta-Lorton, 1987).

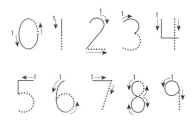

The first stroke (solid line) for each numeral is made in a downward (straight or curved) or horizontal motion. Only the second stroke (dotted line) in the zero, the six, and the eight have an upward motion. Children can practice forming the numerals with their fingers on their desks, in the air, in the sandbox, in shaving cream, or in a water tub; they can write numerals on the board, on individual slates or blackboards, with crayons, and in their notebooks with pencils.

Although children must learn how to form numerals, this activity must not interfere with or take precedence over the development of number sense. When number relationships are being developed, children can use numeral cards or number words to show activity results.

NUMBER RELATIONSHIPS

The development of number sense is an important objective of the K-4 curriculum. Possessing number sense implies in part having well-understood number meanings and having developed multiple relationships among numbers (NCTM, 1989, p. 38). Number relationships cannot be taught directly but must be constructed by children through their own mental activity (Hughes, 1986; Kamii & Joseph, 1988; Van de Walle, 1994). Children need to engage in number explorations so that number relationships can be discovered. Invite them to verbalize number relationships and, when they are capable, to write about them.

Order Relations

Given several sets of varied numerical size, children should be able to order them from smallest to largest.

FIGURE 5-4

Number Cards

| one | two | three | four | five | six | seven | eight | nine |

Numeral Cards

Sets

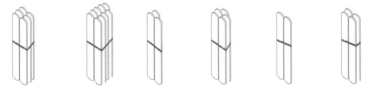

Bundles of sticks

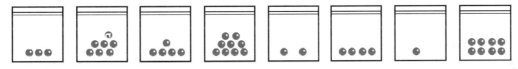

Marbles in bags

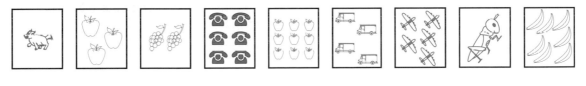

Pictures of sets

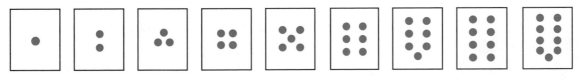

Pattern Dot Cards

Dot Cards

Examples of sets to be ordered are:

- A set of five plates, each with a different number of small objects.
- Vases (paper cups), each with a different number of paper flowers.
- Bags of marbles.
- Boxes of crayons.
- Sets represented on cards as shown in Figure 5-5.
- Discs on vertical rods as shown in Figure 5-6.

More Than, Fewer Than

When children compare sets by counting, number relation questions to ask include: Which set has more? How many more? Which set has fewer? How many fewer? Does this set have as many as that set?

Sets with a small number of objects are easily identified as "more than" or "fewer than" another set. However, the comparative task becomes more challenging when the sets are more than 10 and when the objects are arranged in scatter formation. See Figure 5-7. The strategy used may be one-to-one matching, pattern identification, or counting.

One Greater Than, One Less Than

"One greater" and "one less" relationships can be practiced by showing different sized sets and having children tell the number that is one more than and one less than each set. When numerals are known, they can be written in random order on the board and children can be asked to name the number that is one greater (also, one less) than the numeral they see (Activity 5-16).

Part-Part-Whole Relationships

Children should have experiences in concretely showing numbers in different ways. For example, children could be asked to show six blocks in different ways on a 2-cm square grid. The patterns could be reproduced on a large chart to form the focus of a class discussion. Number

---

FIGURE 5-5

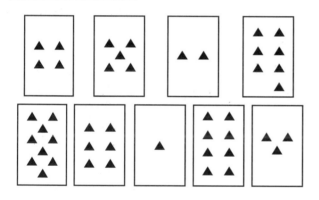

FIGURE 5-7

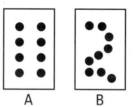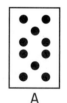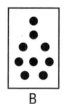

A   B   A   B

Are there more or fewer dots in Set A than in Set B?

FIGURE 5-6

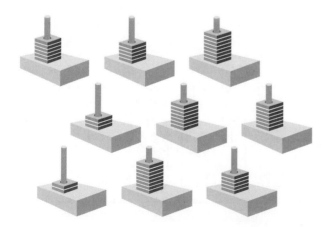

ACTIVITY 5-16

ONE GREATER AND ONE LESS RELATIONSHIPS

PROCEDURE

1. Write numbers on the board. For example:

      6   3   9   5   2   8   4   1   7

2. Have a child read the numbers.

3. Then have the child say the number that is one greater than each number on the board

      (7, 4, 10, . . .).

4. Have the child say the number that is one less than each number on the board (5, 2, 8, . . .).

LITERATURE LINK 5-1
Developing Counting

Anderson, Lena. (2000). *Tea for Ten.* New York: R & S Books.

Anno, M. (1977). *Anno's Counting Book.* New York: Harper Collins.

Anno, M. (1982). *Anno's Counting House.* New York: Philomel Books.

Bang, Molly. (1983). *Ten, Nine, Eight.* New York: Mulberry Books.

Carle, Eric. (1968). *1, 2, 3 To the Zoo.* New York: Trumpet Club.

Charles, Faustin, & Arenson, Roberta. (1996). *A Caribbean Counting Book.* Boston: Houghton Mifflin.

Crews, Donald. (1968, 1986). *Ten Black Dots.* New York: Mulberry Books.

Ernst, Lisa C. (1986). *Up to Ten and Down Again.* New York: Mulberry Books.

Falwell, Cathryn. (1993). *Feast for 10.* New York: Scholastic Press.

Feelings, M. (1971). *Moja Means One: Swahili Counting Book.* New York: Dial Press.

Geisert, Arthur. (1996). *Roman Numerals I to MM.* Boston: Houghton Mifflin (1996)

Hutchins, P. (1982). *1 Hunter.* New York: Greenwillow Books.

Lesser, Carolyn. (1999). *Spots: Counting Creatures from Sky to Sea.* San Diego, CA: Harcourt Brace & Co.

McGrath, Barbara B. (1998). *The Cheerios Counting Book.* New York: Scholastic.

Mora, Pat. (1996). *Uno, Dos, Tres: One, Two, Three.* New York: Clarion Books

Pallotta, Jerry. (1992). *The Icky Bug Counting Book.* New York: Trumpet Club.

Sierra, Judy. (2001). *Counting Crocodiles.* New York: Gulliver Books.

Walsh, E. S. (1991). *Mouse Count.* Orlando, FL: Voyager Books.

Counting is a complex process that requires various and multiple experiences. There are many counting books that illustrate such concepts as number, order, and classification. Using a variety of approaches and books with different features helps children to abstract the essential features of number.

• The most interesting counting books are those that embed counting in a clever story or interesting information. In **Counting Crocodiles,** a resourceful monkey counts crocodiles and in the process is able to walk on the crocodiles' backs to get the bananas he wants on an island across the sea. In the story **Mouse Count,** mice are counted into a jar by a hungry snake. A sock puppet can be used to model the snake in the story, and children can practice counting plastic or felt mice into a large jar to reinforce the concept of one-to-one correspondence.

• Children can practice counting by writing and illustrating their own counting books. Books such as **1 Hunter Ten, Nine, Eight,** and **Ten Black Dots** provide a model for creating and illustrating simple counting books. Other books that explore the numbers from 1 to 10 include **Feast for 10, Up to Ten and Down Again** (beautiful illustrations), **Tea for Ten,** and **1, 2, 3 to the Zoo.** Write large numerals on paper plates, which can be ordered in a line on the floor. As children step on each plate, they can practice counting aloud.

• Some books embed counting in informative science content. For example, **Spots: Counting Creatures from Sky to Sea** counts from 1 to 10 using animals that live in different biomes. **The Icky Bug Counting Book** counts bugs from 0 to 26 (one bug for each letter of the alphabet) and provides information about an interesting variety of bugs.

• **Anno's Counting House** relies on illustrations alone to communicate the basic addition fact combinations for the number 10. Classify the children by sex, clothes, or their possessions. Discuss how the number of children in the houses remains the same even though the children move from house to house. Write number sentences that represent the mathematics in the text.

• Manipulate concrete objects and match these objects with the items on the page of a book to support the development of one-to-one correspondence and conservation of number. Sort and manipulate objects such as Cheerios® using **The Cheerios Counting Book** or linking cubes using **Anno's Counting Book.**

• Many counting books provide children with information about counting in different cultures. In **Roman Numerals I to MM,** children learn to count using Roman numerals; **Uno, Dos, Tres: One, Two, Three** counts from 1 to 10 in English and Spanish, with drawings set in Mexican culture; **A Caribbean Counting Book** contains counting rhymes from the Caribbean; and **Moja Means One** introduces children to the counting numbers from 1 to 10 in Swahili, with beautiful drawings in the text that present information about East African culture.

Source: Dr. Patricia Moyer, George Mason University

patterns can also be shown with pegs on a pegboard (see Figure 5-8).

Finding "two parts" of numbers on a "two-part mat" is another good activity for developing number relationships (see Activity 5-17).

FIGURE 5-8

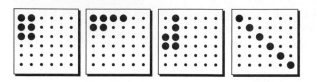

What can you say about six? *(Six is two and two and two. Six is four and two. Six is two and four. Six is six ones.)*

ACTIVITY 5-17

SHOWING TWO PARTS OF SIX

MATERIALS
two-part mat as pictured and six small objects (buttons, chips, or centimeter cubes)

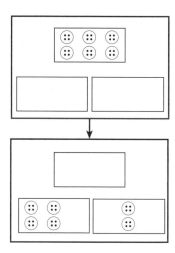

PROCEDURE

1. Direct the children to place the six objects in the rectangle at the top of the mat.

2. Say: Take some of the buttons and place them in one of the rectangles at the bottom of the mat. Now place the remaining buttons in the other rectangle.

3. What can you say about six? Elicit responses such as "Six is four and two." Have children write the statement on a piece of paper.

4. Tell the children to replace the buttons in the top rectangle and to find another two parts of six.

5. Challenge them to find as many two parts of six as they can, recording each one on their paper.

The "family" of combinations for a given number can be easily constructed with Unifix cubes in two colors (Activity 5-18). When children are constructing two parts of numbers, the idea of the combination "zero and a number" may arise. If it has not been done earlier, a discussion on the meaning of the number zero should take place.

Tell children that the number zero tells "how many" when a group or set has no members. For example, ask them, "How many live horses are in the room?" (Zero.) You and the class may decide that when making two parts of numbers, say 6, the combinations "0 and 6" and "6 and 0" are entirely appropriate, as exemplified in Activity 5-18.

As children make concrete representations of numbers, they will begin to use the language of addition and subtraction. Statements to be encouraged include: "six blocks is four blocks and two blocks"; "seven robots is the same as five robots and two robots"; "three keys and four keys are seven keys." Some children have difficulty understanding questions such as "How many are four and

ACTIVITY 5-18

TWO PARTS OF SIX WITH UNIFIX CUBES

MATERIALS
15 Unifix cubes in each of two colors

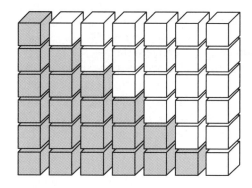

PROCEDURE

1. Ask children to make rods to show two parts of six using cubes in two colors.

2. If children suggest "six and zero" as two parts of six, provide additional cubes so that a rod of each color can be made.

3. Direct children to arrange their rods in a pattern as pictured.

4. Say: "Look at your rods and read the two parts of six in order" (zero and six, one and five, two and four, etc.).

5. Invite children to close their eyes and try to say to themselves the two parts of six. Tell them to open their eyes to look if they get mixed up and to begin again.

LITERATURE LINK 5-2
Developing Number Concepts

Baker, Alan. (1998). *Little Rabbits' First Number Book.* New York: Scholastic.

Fleming, Denise. (1992). *Count!* New York: Scholastic.

Lottridge, Celia B. (1986). *One Watermelon Seed.* Toronto. Oxford University Press.

Sloat, Teri. (1991). *From One to One Hundred.* New York: Dutton Children's Books.

Tildes, Phyllis L. (1995). *Counting on Calico.* New York: Scholastic.

Trinca, Rod, & Argent, Kerry. (1982). *One Woolly Wombat.* New York: Omnibus Books.

Turner, Priscilla (1999). *Among the Odds & Even.* New York: Farrar Straus Giroux.

Walton, R. (1993). *How Many, How Many, How Many.* Cambridge, MA: Candlewick Press.

Wells, Rosemary. (2000). *Emily's First 100 Days of School.* New York: Hyperion Books.

Sorting and classifying helps children to distinguish characteristics of objects and abstract concepts of number. In *Among the Odds & Evens,* X and Y travel to the land of odd and even numbers, where they find some unusual patterns of behavior between these two groups of numbers.

- Sort numbers cards into groups of odds and evens using sorting hoops. Challenge children to formulate a rule that determines whether a number is odd or even.

- Use a hundreds number board to investigate ways to classify numbers, in ways other than odd and even. Some examples might be numbers with zeros, numbers that are doubles (such as 11, 22, and 33), or numbers with a one's place that is a double of the ten's place (such as 12, 24, and 36).

- Investigate whether there are patterns when two odd numbers, two even numbers, or an even and an odd number are added; are subtracted; are multiplied; are divided.

- Sort numbers on a hundreds board to find the prime and composite numbers. Begin by circling the number 2 and then covering all the multiples of 2. Circle the next number that is not covered, which is 3, and then cover all the multiples of 3. Because 4 is covered, the next number that is not covered is 5, so circle 5 and cover all the multiples of 5. Continue until all of the prime and composite numbers have been identified. Ask the children how many of the prime numbers are odd or even. How many of the composite numbers are odd or even? Make a conjecture about why this is so.

- Investigate various counting and classifying number skills by exploring counting books that use the numbers beyond 10. *Emily's First 100 Days of School* counts with Emily from 1 to 100 (Ex: 52 cards in a deck for the number 52). Other books that count beyond 10 include *Counting on Calico* (counts 1 to 20 with a calico cat); *Count!* (counts 1 to 10, then by tens to 50, with colorful illustrations), *Little Rabbits' First Number Book* (counts from 1 to 20); *One Woolly Wombat* (counts from 1 to 14); *From One to One Hundred* (counts 1 to 10, then by tens to 100, with beautiful illustrations); *One Watermelon Seed* (counts 1 to 10, then by tens to 100, and shows things in groups), and *How Many, How Many, How Many* (counts from 1 to 12). To practice writing numerals, children can use a shoebox lid filled with sand or rice and use their fingers to practice drawing the numerals.

Source: Dr. Patricia Moyer, George Mason University

five?" Changing the question to "How many pencils are four pencils and five pencils?" is easier for children to understand (Hughes, 1986). Thus, it is recommended that early work with part-part-whole number relationships should be with and about physical objects.

As children work at constructing parts of numbers (seven is four and three), comparing the whole to its parts (Is eight the same as three and five?), or finding a missing part (Four is one part of six. What is the other part?), observe them to find out whether they have developed the logic of considering the whole and its parts simultaneously. The logic of number addition requires that the parts be considered in relation to each other and that both parts be considered in relation to the whole (the sum). In the absence of these logical ideas, a child solves part-whole problems perceptually (Labinowicz, 1980). A task to assess a child's logical ability to compare a whole and its parts is presented in Activity 5-19 (Labinowicz, 1980, p. 106).

Research has shown that children can complete addition statements such as $1 + 7 = $ _____ symbolically and not be successful at similar problems logically (Labinowicz, 1980). Therefore, it is important that children, particularly in the primary grades, explore concrete representations of numbers so as to construct logical number relationships.

Relationship to 5 and 10 One part-part-whole relationship that is particularly important is the relationship of numbers to 5 and 10. This relationship will be

ACTIVITY 5-19

NUMBER ADDITION LOGICAL TASK

PROCEDURE

Teacher: "I'm going to give you some cookies." (Place eight cookies before the child.) "Today you can have four cookies in the morning and four cookies in the afternoon." (Arrange the cookies in groups of four.)

"Tomorrow you can have one cookie in the morning and seven cookies in the afternoon." (Rearrange the cookies in groups of one and seven.) "Will you have more cookies on one of the days, or will you have the same number on both days?" (Labinowicz, 1980, p. 106).

FIGURE 5-9

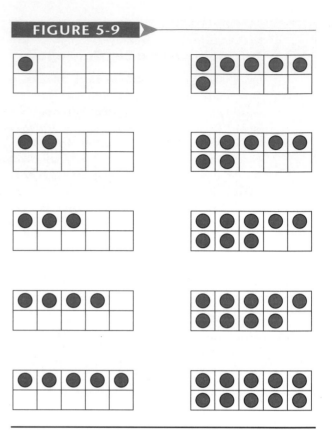

especially useful when children begin learning number facts. For example, if a child knows that 6 is 1 more than 5, that will help the child reason that 6 + 3 must be 1 more than 5 + 3, so if 5 + 3 = 8, then 6 + 3 must be 1 more than 8, or 9.

One way to help children understand the relationship of numbers to 5 and 10 is to use the ten-frame (Wirtz, 1974). The ten-frame consists of a two-by-five array of squares in which dots are placed to represent numbers (see Blackline Master 2). One rule of working with the ten-frame is that the top row of squares must be filled with dots before any dots are placed in the second row. When the top row is filled, there are five dots in the ten-frame. When both rows are filled, there are 10 dots.

Ten-frames can be made on plain white paper or construction paper. Dots to represent the numbers can be bingo chips, buttons, or stick-on dots, which can easily be removed from paper that has been laminated.

It is important to discuss the relationships children observe in a ten-frame. For example, when the number seven is represented in the ten-frame, as in Figure 5-9, the top row is filled and there are two dots in the bottom row. This shows that 7 is 2 more than 5.

Using action language   The formal language of addition and subtraction should be delayed until children are able to perform mental actions on numbers. For example, children may not understand the meaning of "five plus three" or "eight minus five." While working with concrete materials, the language expressing actions is more appropriately used (Skemp, 1989). For example, after an addend has been identified, one could say about the second addend, "I am giving you three more . . . ," "If you put three more . . . ," or "three more arrived . . ."; for subtraction, the expressions "take away four . . . ," "gave away four . . . ," or "four were removed . . ." could be used. In time, children will be able to, for example, parti-

tion a set of nine objects and state, "Nine is six and three" or "five add four is nine."

Number relationships can also be developed through the use of patterned cards. Activities with patterned cards as described below help children learn the combinations of numbers.

1. Two Parts of a Number
   • Prepare patterned cards for a selected number, say, six. Sets of cards as pictured in Figure 5-10 (a)-(d) can be used.
   • Children are told that a set of cards shows two parts of six.
   • Each card is shown, in turn, for a brief moment.
   • Ask: What two parts of six did you see?

2. Two Parts of a Number
   • Prepare a set of patterned number cards for two or three consecutive numbers (e.g., 4, 5, and 6).
   • Show each card, in turn, for a brief moment.
   • Ask: How many objects did you see? What two parts of the number did you see?

Finding the "missing part" of a number helps children learn subtraction facts.

3. Finding the Missing Part
   • Prepare number cards showing a number and one part of the number (Figure 5-10e).

FIGURE 5-10

(a) Cards with bow tie stickers

(b) Dot cards

(c) Dot cards in two colors, rectangular format

(d) Domino cards

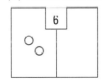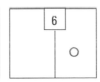

(e) Cards with one part missing

the equal sign. To some, the equal sign means that you "put the answer after it" and operation signs do not belong on the right of an equal sign.

Before the equality or operation symbols are introduced, the language of equality statements should be developed. Thus, when developing the part-part-whole relationships, the children should verbalize and write statements such as the following:

9 is 4 and 5
4 and 5 is the same number as 5 and 4
6 and 3 is the same number as 4 and 5
9 is the same number as 9 and 0
9 is the same number as 9

As children eventually replace the operation and relation words with symbols, it should be easy for them to accept varied forms of equations. Thus, "9 is 4 and 5" can be stated as "9 equals 4 plus 5" and is symbolized as $9 = 4 + 5$. The number sentence "4 and 5 is the same as 5 and 4" can be stated as "4 plus 5 equals 5 plus 4" and is written symbolically as $4 + 5 = 5 + 4$. The focus should be on the correctness of the relationship expressed rather than on the form of the equation. This is different from asking children to "find the answer" to a question such as "What is 4 and 5?" or "4 plus 5 equals what?" Such questions cause children to focus on "the answer" which they record after the "equal sign." There is no opportunity for children to develop an understanding of the meaning of the equality symbol.

A math balance is a good instrument to use in exploring equality statements (Activities 5-20 to 5-22). Children can be asked what they notice on the balance when the numbers are not equal (the *greater* number is *lower*, not higher, on the balance).

- Show a card for a moment and ask children to give the *missing part.*

The number activities just described can be used for a few minutes of mental arithmetic at the beginning of a mathematics period two or three times a week. By the end of Grade 1, children should have learned the basic facts for single-digit numbers.

Bidirectional Relationship of an Equation

Research has shown that children in Grade 3 do not accept as correct equations in the following forms: $6 = 4 + 2$, $4 + 5 = 5 + 4$, $3 + 6 = 6 + 3$, and $5 = 5$ (Labinowicz, 1985). This attests to their narrow understanding of

WORKING WITH A MATH BALANCE

MATERIALS
Math balance

PROCEDURE
1. Place some weight on either side of the math balance to make it balance.

2. Record your work.

EXAMPLES
4 and 2 balance with 1 and 5; 8 balances with 4 and 4; 10 balances with 2 and 2 and 6.

ACTIVITY 5-21

MAKING BALANCING LOADS WITH TEN

MATERIALS
Math balance

PROCEDURE
1. Place a weight on 10 on the left side of the balance.
2. Balance the load by placing weight on two numbers on the right side.
3. How many different balancing loads for 10 can you make?
4. Record your work.

ACTIVITY 5-22

MAKING BALANCING LOADS

MATERIALS
Math balance

PROCEDURE
1. Show 3 plus 4 on the left side of the balance.
2. Now make a balancing load by placing weights on two numbers on the other side.
3. How many different ways can you do this? Record your work.
4. Repeat this activity by placing two other numbers on the left-hand side of the balance.

ESTIMATION

The meaning of the term *estimate* can be developed by referring to the word *about*. Questions such as "About how many apples are in the box?" and "About how many books are on the shelf?" can be used to develop understanding of estimation.

Estimates are approximations rather than exact quantities. Referring to the question, "About how many apples are in the box?", explain to children that, for example, "twelve" is the exact number of apples in the box but that "ten" is a good estimate.

When giving estimates, it is important that "good estimates" be identified. Children should be told that within the range of acceptable estimates, the exact answer is no better than any of the other amounts (NCTM, 1989).

During the first years in school, children should be asked to estimate small quantities and progress to larger amounts as they demonstrate success. Also, ask children to tell how they arrived at their estimates. Estimating strategies should be discussed so that children can learn

PRINCIPLES AND STANDARDS LINK 5-5
Content Strand: Number and Operations

Young students can use number sense to reason with numbers in complex ways. For example, they may estimate the number of cubes they can hold in one hand by referring to the number of cubes that their teacher can hold in one hand. Or if asked whether four plus three is more or less than ten, they may recognize that the sum is less than ten because both numbers are less than five and five plus five makes ten. (NCTM, 2000, p. 80)

ACTIVITY 5-23

FINDING THE SUM OF "DOUBLES"

MATERIALS
Math balance

PROCEDURE
1. Put two weights on hook 4 on the left-hand side.
2. Balance the load by placing a weight on one hook on the other side.
3. Write the number sentence that is represented on the balance.
4. Put two weights on another hook and make a balancing load as before.
5. Do this three more times.
6. Write the number sentences that are represented on the balance.

from each other. Estimation activities with numbers less than 20 are described below.

1. Estimating Quantities
   - Place a collection of 12 objects on a table.
   - With the objects covered, gather the children around the table.
   - Uncover the objects for a moment and then have the children make an estimate of the number of objects displayed.

2. Estimating Quantities
   - Place 12 or 15 objects on an overhead projector.
   - Turn on the machine briefly; then have the children estimate the number of objects that are on the projector.

3. Estimating Quantities
   - Find a large picture with 15 to 20 objects pictured. These could be animals, fruit, cars, or other appropriate objects.

- Show the picture to the children and have them estimate the quantity.
4. How Many Jelly Beans?
   - Fill a small jar with jelly beans.
   - Ask children to estimate how many jelly beans are in the jar.

Other materials for estimating "large" quantities include:

- Unshelled walnuts or peanuts in a clear plastic bag.
- Unifix cubes in a transparent tub.
- Pennies in a jar.

Children can be taught to look for groups of 5 to help them make estimates of quantities over 10. As the quantities are increased, 10 and 20 should be given as important benchmarks in making estimates.

The size of the objects must be taken into consideration when making estimates. Thus, when estimating concrete quantities, estimation interacts with number sense and spatial sense to help children develop an awareness of reasonable results (NCTM, 1989). Specific estimation strategies will be developed when children begin to compute with large numbers.

CONCLUSION

The focus of this chapter has been to present foundational concepts related to the development of number. The principal idea to bear in mind when planning number activities for children is the importance of developing number relationships. This is a significant change from the traditional count, read, and write number program. The activities described are useful in helping children construct number relationships to facilitate mental operations with numbers.

For Your Journal

When you have finished studying this chapter, reflect on the following questions in your math journal:

1. Why is it important for children to be able to represent numbers in more than one way?
2. How might a child's understanding of number help her or him start to develop some beginning mental computation skills?

For Your Portfolio

When you have finished studying this chapter, complete the following activities to include in your professional portfolio:

1. Write a lesson plan to help rote counters become rational counters.
2. Write a lesson plan to introduce the relationship of numbers to 5 and 10.
3. Write a lesson plan in which students are asked to represent numbers in more than one way.

Resources for Teachers

Children's books

Feelings, M. (1972). *Moja means one: Swahili counting book.* New York: Pied Piper Printing.

Giganti, P. (1988). *How many snails? A counting book.* New York: Greenwillow Books.

Jernigan, G. (1988). *One green mesquite tree.* Tucson, AZ: Harbinger House.

Books on number concepts and number sense

Baratta-Lorton, M. (1976). *Mathematics their way.* Menlo Park, CA: Addison-Wesley.

Burton, G. M. (1993). *Number sense and operations: Curriculum Evaluation Standards for School Mathematics Addenda Series Grade K-6.* Reston, VA: National Council of Teachers of Mathematics.

Reys, B. (1991). *Developing number sense: Curriculum Evaluation Standards for School Mathematics Addenda Series Grade 5–8.* Reston, VA: National Council of Teachers of Mathematics.

Richardson, K. (1984). *Developing number concepts using Unifix cubes.* USA: Addison-Wesley Innovative Division.

Richardson, K. (1999). *Developing number concepts, Book 1: Counting, comparing, and patterns.* White Plains, NY: Dale Seymour.

Ward, S. (1995). *Constructing ideas about counting, Grades 3–6.* Mountain View, CA: Creative.

Links to the Internet

Ask Dr. Math (about numbers)

http://www.mathforum.org/dr.math/drmath.elem.html

Contains a list of interesting questions about number concepts and answers given by Dr. Math.

Explorer: General Whole Numbers

http://explorer.scrtec.org/explorer-db/browse/static/Mathematics/index.html

Contains many lessons on and lists of other resources for number concepts.

CHAPTER 6

Developing Understanding of Numeration

✔ **Types and examples of base-ten models**

✔ **Proportional and nonproportional models**

✔ **Grouping by tens**

✔ **Equivalent representations**

FOCUS QUESTIONS ▶

When you have finished studying this chapter, you should be able to answer the following questions:

1. Why is our number system called a "place-value" system?

2. What is an example of a proportional base-ten model? A nonproportional base-ten model? How do these models differ?

3. What are "equivalent representations"?

Which of the following are representations of 25?

XXV	37 − 12
5^2	17 + 8
∩∩|||||	25

They all are! To progress in mathematics, a system for recording quantities is required. A numeration system is a system that enables one to record and thereby communicate one's ideas about number. To comprehend why the numerals 10 and 100 represent numbers ten and one hundred, respectively, and why the two symbols 2 and 5 can be combined to represent twenty-five, one needs to understand the structure of our numeration system.

Children should develop a rich understanding of numbers as they progress through elementary and middle school grades. This rich understanding of numbers should include "what they are; how they are represented with objects, numerals, or on number lines; how they are related to one another; how numbers are embedded in systems that have structures and properties; and how to use numbers and operations to solve problems" (NCTM, 2000, p. 32).

This chapter presents guidelines and activities to help children develop a rich understanding of numbers, focusing on developing number sense and an understanding of our system of numeration. ✔

NCTM CONTENT STANDARDS AND EXPECTATIONS ADDRESSED IN THIS CHAPTER

STANDARD	EXPECTATIONS FOR GRADES PRE-K–2	EXPECTATIONS FOR GRADES 3–5	EXPECTATIONS FOR GRADES 6–8
Number and Operations Standard Instructional programs from pre-K-12 should enable all students to—	In prekindergarten through Grade 2 all students should— (NCTM, 2000, p. 78)	In Grades 3–5 all students should— (NCTM, 2000, p. 148)	In Grades 6–8 all students should—(NCTM, 2000, p. 214)
Understand numbers, ways of representing numbers, relationships among numbers, and number systems.	• use multiple models to develop initial understandings of place value and the base-ten number system.	• understand the place-value structure of the base-ten number system and be able to represent and compare whole numbers and decimals. • recognize equivalent representations for the same number and generate them by decomposing and composing numbers.	• develop an understanding of large numbers and recognize and appropriately use exponential, scientific, and calculator notation.

> **PRINCIPLES AND STANDARDS LINK 6-1**
> **Content Strand: Number and Operations**
>
> Instructional programs from prekindergarten through grade 12 should enable all students to:
>
> - understand numbers, ways of representing numbers, relationships among numbers, and number systems;
> - understand meanings of operations and how they relate to one another;
> - compute fluently and make reasonable estimates. (NCTM, 2000, p. 32)

NUMERATION

Historically, people developed the idea of number before a system of numeration. As symbols were assigned to quantities of one and successive increments of one, people likely became concerned over the potentially large number of different symbols to be created. To limit the number of symbols, rules for using a basic set of symbols were devised. In the case of the Hindu-Arabic numeration system, rules were refined over centuries, until the system we know today was in place. Once a numeration system for recording whole numbers was established, other number systems such as fractions, decimals, and integers were developed to solve particular problems.

Number Systems

A *number system* is characterized by a set (infinite) of elements called numbers, basic operations to perform on those numbers, and some generalizations or principles that hold true for a particular number system. (The operations on whole numbers, fractions, decimals, and integers are the focus of subsequent chapters.)

Numeration Systems

A *numeration system* can be characterized as consisting of a finite set of symbols for certain numbers together with a set of rules governing the use of the symbols. The set of numbers represented by particular symbols is known as the digits of the system. The digits of four different numeration systems are presented in Figure 6-1. Within each system, combinations of the digits represent larger numbers and are interpreted according to established rules.

Historical recordings reveal that different civilizations developed numeration systems to meet their needs. Each system was characterized by its own particular set of symbols and rules. In time, the Western world adapted aspects of a numeration system used by the Hindus and one developed by the Arabs, thus the name *Hindu-Arabic* numeration system.

THE HINDU-ARABIC NUMERATION SYSTEM

An understanding of the Hindu-Arabic numeration system is a prime goal of elementary mathematics programs. Children begin to learn the particular characteristics of the system by constructing numbers concretely in groups of tens and ones and in describing what they have done. For example, a child who says that with 26 buttons she was able to make two groups of 10 and had 6 left will later be able to describe 26 as two tens and six. The Hindu-Arabic numeration system can be described by the following five characteristics: base-ten, positional or place value, multiplicative principle, additive principle, and zero as a placeholder.

Base-Ten

The base of a system is the number of objects used in the grouping process. Our system is a base-ten system; that is, 10 is the number that designates a first grouping. Therefore, there is no special symbol for ten; the largest

FIGURE 6-1

System	Digits of the System
Hindu–Arabic	0, 1, 2, 3, 4, 5, 6, 7, 8, 9
Romans	I, V, X, L, C, D, M
Mayans	•, —
Egyptians	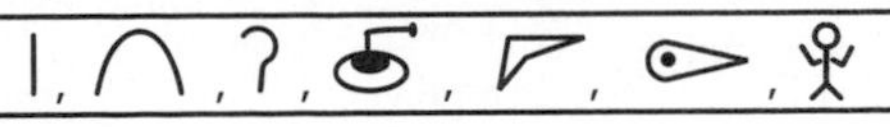

number having a symbol is nine, the number that precedes the grouping size. With zero, there are ten digits in the system. A base-five system would have five symbols: four for the numbers one to four and zero. Knowing this makes it easy to write numbers in different bases.

Positional or Place Value

If the number of digits in a numeration system is limited, it follows that digits will need to be repeated in expressing larger numbers. In a place-value system, a digit takes on a value determined by the place it occupies in a number. The unit digits occupy the place furthest to the right in a multidigit numeral. Because ten is the size of the initial grouping, ten is the value of the place to the immediate left of the "ones" place. Thus, we can say that the second place (to the left) in a numeral is the "tens" place. The numeral 10, therefore, designates "one group of ten and zero ones." One more than nine groups of ten and nine (99) requires a regrouping to show "one group of ten groups of ten" and is represented by the numeral 100. The third place in a numeral, therefore, has the value of "ten groups of ten" or "ten times ten" and is named "hundred." The symbolization system is extended to the left by designating place values for successively larger groups of ten. In a base-five system, places would take on the values of successive groups of five. Figure 6-2 depicts place values for bases ten and five.

To summarize, the *place-value principle* enables one to distinguish between the face value of a digit (e.g., 5 as five) and its value because of its particular position in a numeral (e.g., the digit 5 has the value of fifty in 52 and five hundred in 534).

Multiplicative Principle

Multiplication is employed in determining the value of each digit in a numeral. For example, in the base-ten numeral 333, each 3 has a different quantitative value: the 3 on the left has the value of 3 times one hundred, the 3 in the center has the value of 3 times ten, and the 3 on the right has the value of 3 times one. In a base-five system, each digit in the numeral 333 also has a different value: The 3 furthest to the left has the value of 3 times twenty-five, the 3 in the center has the value of 3 times five, and the 3 furthest to the right has the value of 3 times one.

When children first decode numbers, they are not likely to use the multiplicative term *times*; rather, they talk about "groups." For example, the two in 28 is explained as "two groups of ten" or "two tens."

FIGURE 6-2

BASE-TEN

Places	$base^5$	$base^4$	$base^3$	$base^2$	$base^1$	$base^0$
Base Power	10^5	10^4	10^3	10^2	10^1	10^0
Place Names	hundred thousand	ten thousand	one thousand	hundred	ten	one
Place Value (base-ten)	100 000	10 000	1000	100	10	1

BASE-FIVE

Places		$base^4$	$base^3$	$base^2$	$base^1$	$base^0$
Base Power						
In base-ten numerals		5^4	5^3	5^2	5^1	5^0
In base-five numerals		10^4	10^3	10^2	10^1	10^0
Place Value						
Base-ten names		six hundred twenty-five	one hundred twenty-five	twenty-five	five	one
Base-ten numerals		625	125	25	5	1
Base-five numerals		10 000	1000	100	10	1

Additive Principle

In the Hindu-Arabic system, the additive principle means that numbers are the sum of the products of each digit and its place value in a numeral. For example,

$$765 = (7 \times 100) + (6 \times 10) + (5 \times 1)$$
$$= \quad 700 \quad + \quad 60 \quad + \quad 5$$
$$= \quad 765$$

In numeration systems without a multiplicative principle, the value of a number is determined by the sum of the digits in a numeral. For example, in Roman numeration the number represented by XXVII is determined by adding $10 + 10 + 5 + 1 + 1$ to make 27.

When they have learned the multiplication operation, children can describe numbers as, for example, 36 means "3 times 10 plus 6" or write them in symbolic form as "$(3 \times 10) + 6$."

Zero as a Placeholder

The genius of our numeration system lies in the combined characteristics of place value and a placeholder numeral, that is, a symbol for the number zero.

Although zero is first introduced as a number, children can be asked to do numeration activities that have them specifically think of zero as a placeholder. For example, the teacher says:

- I have 8 hundreds and 3 tens. What's my number? (Children write the number on paper; then one child writes the number on the board. Children check their work.)
- I have 3 hundreds and 6 ones. What's my number?
- I have 1 thousand, 4 tens, and 9 ones. What's my number?
- I have 5 ones and 9 hundreds. What's my number?

A discussion should follow, stimulated by a question such as "Why is a zero needed in each number?"

Each of the characteristics just described comes into play when interpreting a multidigit numeral in Hindu-Arabic numeration. In learning our base-ten system, children should come to realize that the choice of base in a numeration system is arbitrary, as are the number names and symbols we use. Writing numbers in a different base within the structure of our numeration system can help children learn the different characteristics of the system. Also, the structure of the Hindu-Arabic system can be learned via a base other than 10. The popular Chip Trading activities (described in this chapter) encourage this approach.

UNDERSTANDING PLACE VALUE

The foundation for developing place-value concepts lies in *grouping activities*. Thus, first graders should engage in grouping activities and counting activities with sets of objects greater than 9.

PRINCIPLES AND STANDARDS LINK 6-2
Content Strand: Number and Operations

Using concrete materials can help students learn to group and ungroup by tens. For example, such materials can help students express "23" as 23 ones (units), 1 ten and 13 ones, or 2 tens and 3 ones. (NCTM, 2000, p. 81)

Grouping

When children know the numbers zero through nine and can identify and write their respective numerals, they can be engaged in grouping activities. Grouping activities can vary by

- the materials used,
- the size of the groups,
- the number of groups formed, and
- the manner of recording.

Six activities involving grouping that are appropriate for first graders are described below.

1. Making Groups of Airplanes
   - Each child will need a set of centimeter cubes and pieces of black construction paper (about 5 cm by 12 cm). The teacher will need 15 small toy airplanes and pieces of black construction paper.

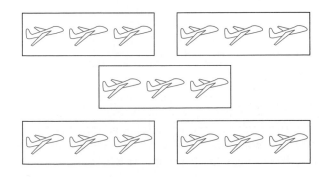

- With the children gathered in an appropriate place in the room, the teacher explains that the airplanes are to be placed on the runways (black paper) with the same number of airplanes on each runway. (The teacher states the size of each group of airplanes.)
- Children should verbalize what they did. For example, "We made groups of three." "There are five groups of three airplanes."
- The above procedures are repeated with another set of airplanes, and different-sized groups are constructed. Again, children should verbalize the groupings.
- Children can then be directed to go to their seats and, pretending the centimeter cubes are airplanes, make groups of four airplanes on each runway. Have the children verbalize what they have done. For example, "I made three groups of four airplanes."
- Children may be asked to draw a picture and then write about what they have done. For example, "I made 6 groups of 4 airplanes."

2. Making Groups of Buttons

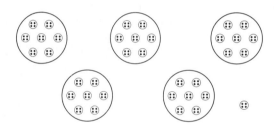

- Each child will need a set of 36 buttons and 10 small plates.
- Direct the children to choose a number and to make groups of that size on each plate.
- Have the children verbalize what they have done. For example, "I made five groups of seven and have one button left."

3. Making Groups of Unifix Cubes
- Each child will need 50 Unifix cubes.

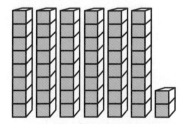

- Direct the children to choose a number and to make towers of that size with the cubes.
- Have the children verbalize what they have done. For example, "I made six towers that are eight blocks high. I have two blocks left."

4. Counting in Groups of Six

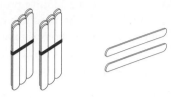

- Have numerous popsicle sticks and elastic bands available.
- Provide each child with 29 sticks and direct them to put the sticks in bundles of 6. After the bundles have been made, have the children count as follows:

One bundle of six,

One bundle of six and one,

One bundle of six and two, . . .

Two bundles of six,

Two bundles of six and one, . . .

- Repeat the above procedure with different-sized bundles.

5. Counting How Many From Groups
- Each child will need approximately 35 small objects to count.

- Say, "Two groups of seven birds and three more birds landed in the school yard. Let's find out how many birds came."
- Have children model the groups with the materials provided, then count to determine the number seventeen.
- Repeat with five groups of 4 birds and 2 birds; three groups of 9 birds and 4 birds; three groups of 10 birds and 3 birds.

6. Making Groups and Recording
- Each child will need a set of small objects (between 30 and 50), pencils and paper, and several small plastic or paper plates. Children need not have the same number of counters.
- Have children first count how many objects they have and then record the number on their paper. A second counting can serve to verify the count.
- Tell the children to decide on a group size and to make as many groups of that size as they can with their materials. Children then record what they have done.
- The children then select another number as a group size and, using the same materials, make as many groups as they can. Recording follows.
- Children could then select a different number of counters and repeat the above steps.

FIGURE 6-3 ▶

Name: _____

I had _____ buttons.

I made _____ groups of _____ buttons and _____ .

I made _____ groups of _____ buttons and _____ .

I made _____ groups of _____ buttons and _____ .

In grouping activities, the group sizes usually are numbers between two and nine, but larger-sized groups can be formed. A first-grade class was given 28 Unifix cubes to place in groups as described in the sixth activity above. Although most children chose to make groups of sizes 2 to 9, several made groups of 10, 15, and 25. Melissa, after having made groups of 6, 2, and 5, decided to make groups of 1 and was surprised to discover upon counting all the groups she had made that she had 28 groups of 1. (She knew she had 28 cubes, but she had to recount them to find out how many groups of 1 there were!) In the same class, Jonathan decided to make groups of zero using the eight plates he had on his desk. His written record of this activity was: "I made 8 groups of 0 and 28 (left)." From this experience, one learns not to be too prescriptive when assigning tasks to children. Left to their own decisions, children will conduct experiments that are meaningful to them.

Communicating Mathematics

In early grouping activities, children can be requested to "tell what you have done." Statements such as "I made four groups of three airplanes" and "I made five groups of four buttons and had two left" should be encouraged. When first recording on paper, a form such as the one in Figure 6-3 can be used. In time, the recording can be in the form of a table as depicted in Figure 6-4. A sample of a child's work is presented in Figure 6-5.

Grouping by Tens

When engaged in making groups of 10, the grouping and recording can progress from "5 groups of ten and 3"

to "1 group of ten and 0." Recording the latter statement in a table similar to that in Figure 6-4 will be an easy link to the numeral 10. Thereafter, when children hear that "when writing numbers, we show groups of ten and ones" they should understand that in 25 there are "2 groups of ten and 5 ones" or "2 tens and 5." Children must come to realize that it is the 1 in 10 that indicates ten and the 0 indicates that it is an even group of ten, whereas the numeral 11 indicates 1 group of ten and 1 more.

Children who have engaged in grouping activities as described above will likely know that when you have 1 group of ten and 9, 1 more will result in 2 groups of ten and is recorded as 20. Thus, the system of numerals could theoretically be developed by children without knowledge of number names. Usually, the reverse is the case. Children learn the sequence of number names and are told that, for example, 15 means "one ten and five ones." This can be confusing to children and the basis for the erroneous symbolization of teen numbers as 101, 102, 103, and so on. This type of error is more commonly made when writing numbers beyond 100 (e.g., 1001 for 101; 1002 for 102), demonstrating a lack of understanding of place value.

An unhurried introduction to grouping experiences can enhance the development of place-value understanding. When children are involved in grouping activities, it is important that they not only construct groups but also describe what they have done before they are given an explanation of two-digit numerals.

Equivalent representations One important component of developing place value understanding is the notion of equivalent representations. *Equivalent*

FIGURE 6-4 ▶

a) Groups of Five	Number Left	b) Number in Group	Ones
		EIGHT	
4	2	5	2

FIGURE 6-5 ▶

I counted 38 squares.
I made seven groups of 5 and had 3 left.
I made nine groups of 4 and had two left.
I made 3 groups of ten and had 8 left.
I made five groups of seven and had 3 left.
I made six groups of six and had 2 left.

Margie, Grade One

LITERATURE LINK 6-1
Equivalent Representations and Grouping Relationships

Dodds, Dayle Ann. (1999). *The Great Divide.* Cambridge, MA: Candlewick Press.
Giganti, P. (1992). *Each Orange Had Eight Slices.* New York: Greenwillow Books.
Long, Lynette. (1996). *Domino Addition.* Watertown, MA: Charlesbridge Publishing.
Tang, Greg. (2001). *The Grapes of Math.* New York: Scholastic.
Schwartz, David M. (1989). *If You Made a Million.* New York: Mulberry Books.
Murphy, Stuart J. (1996). *Too Many Kangaroo Things to Do!* New York: Harper Collins.

The foundations for place value and the whole number operations rely heavily on children's facility with grouping relationships. Being able to group numbers to make 10 (such as 6 and 4, 7 and 3, or 5 and 5) and group tens to make hundreds develops number sense. Activities that focus children on the decomposition of numbers using various equivalent representations support later work with computational procedures and estimation skills. Using both pictorial and symbolic representations of various groupings helps to solidify these understandings.

- In *The Grapes of Math* children are encouraged to use grouping relationships to make counting more efficient. Give children groups of objects (i.e., 24, 50, or 100) in small bags. Ask them to find different ways to group the objects and to represent these groupings. For example, 50 can be represented as 2 groups of 25 or as 5 groups of 10. Record these various representations (using symbols or drawings) on chart paper.
- Systems of money (both coins and dollar bills) represent different ways of grouping monetary amounts. For example there are many different ways to use

coins to make 10¢, 25¢, 50¢ and $1. Use the book *If You Made a Million* to explore the use of different coins to equal sums of money ranging from $1 to $1 million. What could children buy with $1 million?
- *Too Many Kangaroo Things to Do* examines grouping relationships using 10, 20, 30, 40, and 100. Challenge children to write their own "Too Many Things to Do" stories using different grouping relationships that equal 100.
- Other books that explore the ways numbers are grouped for addition, subtraction, multiplication and division include *Domino Addition* (shows fact family combinations that add to get numbers from 1 to 12), *Each Orange Had Eight Slices* (shows objects in groups of groups and reinforces the concept of multiplication as repeated addition), and *The Great Divide* (where 80 participants in a race divide themselves repeatedly until there is only one participant at the finish line). Children can model the operations in these books as they investigate various number combinations and grouping relationships.

representations refers to the fact that a number can be represented in many different ways, all of which are equivalent to the same number but may look different. For example, the number 32 can be represented in a variety of ways using groups of 10: as three groups of 10 and 2 singles, as two groups of 10 and 12 singles, as one group of 10 and 22 singles, and as zero groups of 10 and 32 singles (see Figure 6-6). Children need to understand that each of these representations is equivalent because each represents the number 32. Children who are able to think flexibly and recognize these equivalent groupings will be better able to regroup and rename two-digit numbers, which will assist them later in computation work.

Types of Place Value Materials

As groups of 10 become the dominant grouping activities, children will work with proportional and nonproportional materials to represent numbers. *Proportional materials* should be used first because the representative piece for 10 is actually 10 times the size of the piece that

represents 1 (see Figure 6-7). Examples of proportional materials are:

- prebundled sticks in singles, groups of 10, and groups of 100.
- base-ten blocks in which a "rod" is constructed of 10 "units" and a "square" is made up of 10 rods or 100 units.
- meter, decimeter, and centimeter sticks.

Within the set of proportional models there are variations in the level of abstraction. Counters such as beans or buttons are the most concrete. Ten counters can be put into a cup to represent the number 10. A one-to-one correspondence exists between the material and the number being represented. Craft sticks or connecting cubes such as Unifix cubes are only slightly more abstract in that groups of 10 can be easily formed to create a one-to-ten relationship. The bundles or rods, however, can be taken apart easily for verification. Beansticks or base-ten blocks represent one more step toward abstraction. Here

FIGURE 6-6

EQUIVALENT REPRESENTATIONS OF 32 OBJECTS

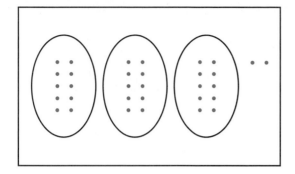

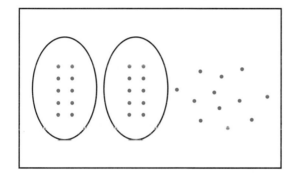

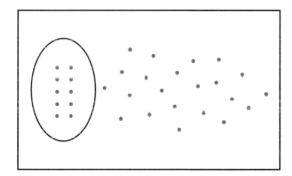

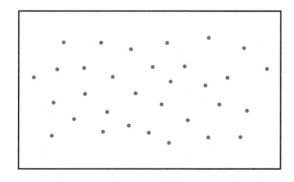

unscored blocks maintain the one-to-ten proportion, but there is no longer visual one-to-one correspondence.

In *nonproportional materials,* the same object is sometimes used to represent ones, tens, and hundreds (see Figure 6-8). Some nonproportional materials are challenging because they necessitate a focus on the position, color, size, or value of objects. For example, when using centimeter cubes on a place-value mat, attention must be on the position of a cube to determine its value rather than on a visible "group of 10" or "group of 100." When using colored chips on a place-value mat (Chip Trading materials), position and color must be considered. Size may have to be considered depending on the materials selected to represent different amounts. When coins (dollars, dimes, and pennies) are used, one must take into consideration the value of each coin. Examples of nonproportional materials are place-value mats and chips, an abacus, pocket charts, and money.

Developing Two-Digit Numbers

When beginning to help children understand the meaning of two-digit numbers, it is preferable to use unstructured materials such as loose craft sticks or interlocking blocks and have the children construct the groupings themselves. At some time in the primary grades, children should have the experience of constructing numbers in this manner even beyond 100. Bundling 10 bundles of 10 sticks or constructing a square with 10 rods of interlocking Unifix cubes will aid children in developing understanding of 100 as 10 tens. The following representative experiences could be used for this purpose:

- Have children use Unifix cubes to show two-digit numbers as, for example, 36, by constructing three rods of ten cubes and six singles.
- Multilink cubes are used in the same manner as Unifix cubes to make groups of 10. For 100, 10 rods are interlocked to make a square.
- Children can place elastic bands around groups of 10 craft sticks and use the bundles and single sticks to show two-digit numbers. For three-digit numbers, 10 bundles of 10 are grouped together.
- Using interlocking Unifix cubes, each child in a class can have the experience of constructing a hundred square to use with rods of ten and singles to show three-digit numbers. (Unifix cubes are readily available in large quantities.)

the groupings are permanent, but verification still is possible through matching or counting because one-to-one correspondence still exists. Unscored base-ten blocks require more abstraction on the part of the child and could serve as a transition to nonproportional materials. The

Although the main focus of the activities is the development of the meaning of two-digit numbers, some children will be interested in knowing how to represent hundreds with the materials. It can be explained that another grouping is made and that this grouping consists of "10 groups of 10."

FIGURE 6-7

EXAMPLES OF PROPORTIONAL BASE-TEN MATERIALS

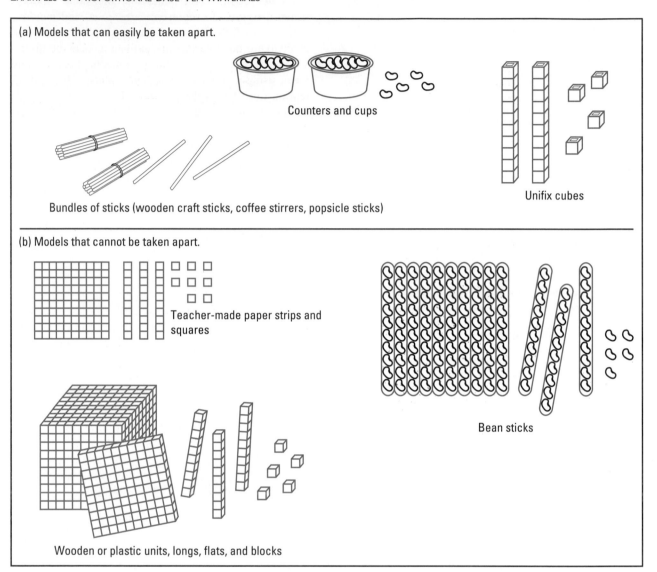

(a) Models that can easily be taken apart.

Counters and cups

Unifix cubes

Bundles of sticks (wooden craft sticks, coffee stirrers, popsicle sticks)

(b) Models that cannot be taken apart.

Teacher-made paper strips and squares

Bean sticks

Wooden or plastic units, longs, flats, and blocks

FIGURE 6-8

EXAMPLES OF NONPROPORTIONAL BASE-TEN MATERIALS

Chip Trading Materials

Green	Blue	Yellow	Red
	◉	◉◉	◉◉◉

Abacus Models

FIGURE 6-9

Meaning of Numbers

Task: Use the popsicle sticks to represent numbers.
        Write how you modeled each number.

Wendy's work.

    52 5 bundles of ten and 2 singles
    47 4 tens and 7 singles
    29 2 groups of ten and 9 ones
    40 4 groups of ten
     7 7 singles and 0 bundles

Note: Wendy used varied expressions in this exercise. It is
wise to encourage students to describe events in different
ways.

As children model numbers with bundles or groups of
10 they have constructed, ask them to describe the numbers. One second grader's work is presented in Figure 6-9.

When it is determined that children know the meaning
of two-digit numbers, that is, they can show, for example,
that 48 means 4 tens and 8 ones, word problems with
two-digit numbers can be solved using proportional
materials.

Introducing Base-Ten Blocks

A teacher could present word problems and ask children
to solve them using the rods of ten and singles they have
constructed with Unifix cubes.

When children can use the materials to solve addition
and subtraction problems with two-digit numbers with
regrouping, the rods and units from the base-ten block set
can be introduced in the following manner:

• The teacher might say, "Someone thought it would be
  good to make rods that do not come apart, like these
  (show rods), to use with singles (show units). Let's see
  how we can represent numbers with these blocks."

MODELING TWO-DIGIT NUMBERS

MATERIALS
Base-ten blocks (rods and units)

PROCEDURE
1. Represent the number 42 with the blocks.

2. Show 42 another way.

3. How many different ways can you show 42 with
   the blocks?

4. Draw a picture or write about what you did.

• Give the children some rods and units and ask them to
  represent 37 (three rods and seven units).

• Ask the children if they can represent the number another way. When someone suggests exchanging a rod
  for 10 units, direct children to do this. Have the children determine that 2 rods and 17 units are also 37.

• The teacher may want the children to exchange another rod to determine that 1 rod and 27 units also represent 37. The next move would be to exchange the last
  rod to obtain all singles. Note that these all are equivalent representations.

After the children have completed an activity similar
to Activity 6-1, the teacher might stimulate discussion by
asking, "What is the simplest way to represent 42 with
the blocks?" (Figure 6-10).

On other occasions, the teacher could show the children numerals and ask the children to use base-ten blocks
to represent each numeral (Activity 6-2).

To solve addition and subtraction problems using the
base-ten blocks, children *exchange* a rod for 10 units
rather than "take apart" a rod, as they did with rods made
from Unifix cubes (Solving addition and subtraction
problems with base-ten blocks is discussed in detail in
Chapter 9.)

Using Place-Value Mats

A caution is offered when using proportional materials
to model numbers a place-value mat. For example,
when using base-ten blocks, if 10 unit blocks are replaced on a place-value mat with a "rod" (10 units) in a
column labeled "tens," then a misleading notion about
place value can develop because the value of a rod in
the tens column is 100. Whenever the expectation is
that children will replace 10 unit blocks with a "rod" to
represent a two-digit number, an organizational mat

FROM NUMERAL CARDS TO BLOCKS

MATERIALS
Base-ten blocks

PROCEDURE
Use the blocks to show each number.

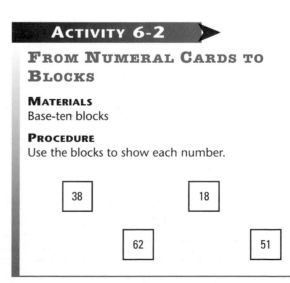

FIGURE 6-10

Modeling 42 with Base-Ten Blocks

(a) □□□□□□□□□□□□□□□□□□□□□
    □□□□□□□□□□□□□□□□□□□□□

(b) ▦▦ □□□□□□□□□ □
    ▦▦ □□□□□□□□□ □

(c) ▦ ▦ □
    ▦ ▦ □

(without column headings) should be used rather than a place-value mat (with headings) (Figure 6-11).

If one is to be consistent with numeral representation, more than nine units should not be placed in any of the columns on a place-value mat. Teachers should note that some commercial abacuses have 9 discs per column whereas some have 10. There are others that have 18 discs per column to show intermediate steps in algorithms.

Changing 10 unit blocks for a tens rod, or 10 sticks for a bundle of 10 sticks, is a concrete representation of numbers. Representing the number 12 on a place-value mat with one chip or a unit cube in the tens column and two

chips or unit cubes in the units column is a more abstract representation of numbers. The introduction of a place-value mat signifies a move from the concrete type of modeling to the semi-abstract type.

Introducing Nonproportional Materials

One way to introduce nonproportional place-value materials to children is to have them play trading games. These can be played with unit blocks from the base-ten

FIGURE 6-11

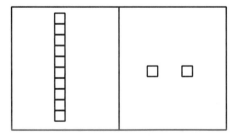

ORGANIZATIONAL MAT

1 rod and 2 units show 12
or
1 ten and 2 are 12

PLACE VALUE MAT

tens	ones
□	□ □

1 ten and 2 are 12

tens	ones
▦	□ □

10 tens and 2 are 102

set, a die, and mats. The procedures for playing with a three-column mat and unit blocks are as follows:

- Children in groups of three or four decide on a number to be the maximum number of blocks allowed in one column, say two (for base three).

- Columns are used from right to left. One block in the column farthest to the right represents one, a block in the second column represents a group of three, and a block in the third column represents a group of "three groups of three," or nine.

- Children toss the die in turn and place in the right-hand column on their mat the number of blocks indicated on the die. Whenever a group of three is obtained, the group is exchanged for a single block in the next column.

- The winner is the first to obtain one block in the left-hand column.

A sample game with two as the maximum number of blocks per column might proceed as follows:

- Jan tosses the die and gets a five. She counts five blocks from the cache, notices a group of three, which she represents on her mat with a block in the second column (two blocks are returned to the cache), and places two blocks on the mat in the first column.

- Timmy tosses the die and gets a six. He counts six blocks, notices two groups of three, and places two blocks in the second column.

GAME

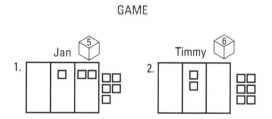

- The game continues until one child has one block in the third column.

Materials from the Chip Trading Kit could also be used. The game procedures are similar to those described above except that color is a factor: yellow chips have a value of one, blue chips represent the group size, green chips represent "groups of groups" or square numbers, and red chips represent the next place value in the particular system chosen, the cubic numbers. A sample game with two players using four (for base-five) as the maximum number of chips allowed per column might proceed as outlined below. The goal is to accumulate two red chips.

- Mike tosses the die and gets a four. He counts four yellow chips and places them on the first column (headed yellow) on his mat.

- Linda tosses the die and gets a six. She counts six yellow chips, notices a group of five, and exchanges them for a blue chip. She completes her move by placing the blue chip in the second column (headed blue) and the remaining yellow chip in the first column.

- Mike tosses again and gets a six. He counts out six yellow chips, notices a group of five, and exchanges them for a blue chip. Then he notices that he has another group of five with the one chip remaining and the four yellow chips on his mat from the first play. He exchanges this set of five for another blue chip, which he places in the second column.

- Linda tosses and gets. . . .

The trading games can be played in a backward manner, that is, beginning with blocks or chips on the mat. When a die is tossed, exchanges are made to "subtract" an amount from that shown on the mat. Figure 6-12 illustrates the beginning of a sample game in which the trading rate is three. Games can be lengthened by changing the starting position. For example, the game can begin with players having one cube in each column on the mat.

Trading games can be extended to include experiences like the following:

- Provide children with 38 counters and a place-value mat with 4 columns.

- Have the children make groups of five, model the number on a place-value mat, and then write the numeral in base five (123). (The procedure should be to count groups of 5, then see if there are *at least* 5 groups of 5, and represent them with one counter in the third column on a mat, then count the remaining groups of 5 and represent them with two counters in the appropriate column on the mat, and lastly the 3.)

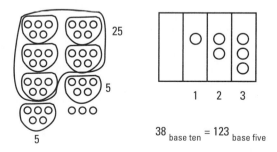

$$38_{\text{base ten}} = 123_{\text{base five}}$$

- Repeat the procedure for other bases.

The ease with which children are able to represent quantities on a place-value mat in different bases will enhance their understanding of base-ten numeration. Using

FIGURE 6-12 ▶

BACKWARD TRADING GAME

MATERIALS:
Unit cubes from base-ten set

PROCEDURE:
Sample game for two. (Trading rate is three.)

1. Starting position for both players.

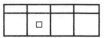

2. Player 1 tosses the die and gets a two. The exchanges are as follows:

3. Player 2 tosses a three. The exchanges are:

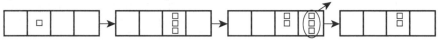

4. Player 1 tosses a five. Exchanges are:

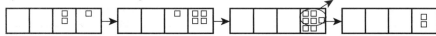

base-five or a smaller base, it is possible for children to carry out regroupings to four and five place values and still be dealing with three-digit numbers.

An abacus is another nonproportional device that is found in many classrooms. Place-value ideas are reinforced when counting on an abacus. The counting process for abacuses with 10 and those with 9 counters per column is different. With an abacus with 10 counters per column, children must exchange one 10 for 10 units and 100 for 10 tens, etc. If the abacus has 9 counters per column, counting proceeds to 9, then as 1 counter in the second column is brought forward for 10, the 9 counters are flipped back; similarly as 100 is counted, the 9 tens and 9 are flipped back.

The relationship between dimes and pennies and between decimeter and centimeter strips also can help children develop an understanding of numeration concepts. Give children some dimes and pennies and ask them to show different amounts with them, such as 46¢, 72¢, and 36¢. Solving problems involving money transactions will provide additional trading experiences. For example:

Jack paid 68¢ for Tom's lunch at school one day. Tom promised to return the money to Jack. What coins will Jack give Tom for change left from a dollar?

Using concrete models and real-world situations helps children deepen their understandings.

Using Hundreds Charts

Hundreds charts are 10×10 charts with numbers written in order. Some hundreds charts contain the numbers 0 through 99; others contain the numbers 1 through 100 (see Figure 6-13 and Blackline Masters 3 and 4 at the end of this book). Teachers should have a large hundreds chart that all children in the classroom can see from their desk. This can be done by enlarging or making an overhead transparency of a hundreds chart. Also, each child or pair of children should have an individual hundreds chart readily accessible.

Hundreds charts help children understand place value and patterns. For example, consider the following activities:

- Put a marker on 37. Put another marker on the number that is 10 more than 37. Now put another marker on the number that is 10 less than 37. What patterns do you notice about those three numbers?

- Put a marker on 21. How would you use the hundreds chart to find a number that is 35 more than 21? (For example, you could count 5 spaces to the right, which is 5 more than 21), and count down 3 rows (which is 30 more).

Activities and questions such as these help children think about numbers as groups of tens and ones.

FIGURE 6-13

HUNDREDS CHARTS

0	1	2	3	4	5	6	7	8	9
10	11	12	13	14	15	16	17	18	19
20	21	22	23	24	25	26	27	28	29
30	31	32	33	34	35	36	37	38	39
40	41	42	43	44	45	46	47	48	49
50	51	52	53	54	55	56	57	58	59
60	61	62	63	64	65	66	67	68	69
70	71	72	73	74	75	76	77	78	79
80	81	82	83	84	85	86	87	88	89
90	91	92	93	94	95	96	97	98	99

1	2	3	4	5	6	7	8	9	10
11	12	13	14	15	16	17	18	19	20
21	22	23	24	25	26	27	28	29	30
31	32	33	34	35	36	37	38	39	40
41	42	43	44	45	46	47	48	49	50
51	52	53	54	55	56	57	58	59	60
61	62	63	64	65	66	67	68	69	70
71	72	73	74	75	76	77	78	79	80
81	82	83	84	85	86	87	88	89	90
91	92	93	94	95	96	97	98	99	100

Assessing Place-Value Knowledge

PRINCIPLES AND STANDARDS LINK 6-3
Content Strand: Number and Operations

Teachers emphasize place value by asking appropriate questions and choosing problems such as finding ten more than or ten less than a number and helping them contrast the answers with the initial number. As a result of regular experiences with problems that develop place-value concepts, second-grade students should be counting into the hundreds, discovering patterns in the numeration system related to place value, and composing (creating through different combinations) and decomposing (breaking apart in different ways) two- and three-digit numbers. (NCTM, 2000, p. 82)

Nonproportional materials can be used to assess place-value understanding in the following ways:

• Given a place-value mat and a single counter placed in the tens column, ask the child to *remove 6*.

• Ask the child to *show 24* on the mat, and then to *add 8*.

• If the children have been playing trading games using different trading values, place two chips in the second

column on an unlabeled place-value mat and ask: "If the trading rate is five, what is the value of the chips on your mat?" A child may wish to "trade backward" to answer the question. Ask similar questions with other trading rates.

Flexibility in figuring out the value of varied representations in different "bases" is evidence of place-value understanding.

Another assessment task is to begin by asking a child to read a numeral as, for example, 36. Next, the child is asked to count that many robots. Observe the child as he or she counts the robots (does the child move the robots? group them in twos, fives, or tens?). Pointing to the "6" in 36, the teacher asks: "Does this part of the 36 have anything to do with how many robots you have?" The question is repeated, this time pointing to the "3" in 36. A child who understands the meaning of 36 will match 6 robots with the "6" and 30 with the "3" (NCTM, 1989, p. 38).

What Research Says About Place-Value Learning

There is evidence that elementary-school children do not understand our numeration system, specifically place value (Kamii & Joseph, 1988; Ross, 1986, 1989; Smith, 1973). One may be surprised at Kamii and Joseph's (1988) findings that third and fourth graders were unable to respond correctly to a tens place-value question. Kamii

FIGURE 6-14

Place Value Task

Show the numeral 16 on a card.

Ask: What does this part (circle the 6 in 16) mean?
Could you show me with the chips what this
part means?

Have the child show (count out) the appropriate number of chips.

Ask: What about this part (circle the one in 16)?
Show me with the chips what this part means.

$$\boxed{16}$$

Source: Adapted from "Teaching Place Value and Double-Column Addition," by C. Kamii and L. Joseph, 1988, *Arithmetic Teacher, 35*, p. 48.

and Joseph report that generally, no first grader gives the expected response that in the numeral 16, "1 means ten," and that only about 33% of third graders and 50% of fourth graders are able to respond appropriately (Figure 6-14). Kamii and Joseph concluded that first-grade children are unlikely to understand place value; rather, they understand 16 as 16 ones, not as 1 ten and 6 ones. These findings corroborate those of Ross (1986, 1989).

Others, however, believe that with carefully planned experiences of counting and grouping by tens and ones, first graders can learn place value to some significant level of performance (Payne, 1988). It is recommended that teachers have first graders engage in grouping activities as foundational experiences for place-value development. Generally, second graders are expected to develop understanding of two-digit numbers and third graders work with numbers greater than 99.

Stages in Place-Value Development

Ross (1989) proposes a five-stage development of place value understanding. At stage 1, children associate two-digit numerals with the quantity they represent. For example, 28 means the whole amount. At stage 2, children can identify the positional names but do not necessarily know what each digit represents. For example, in 54, a child may state that there are 4 ones and 5 tens. This is mere verbal knowledge based on positional labels. At stage 3, children can identify the face value of digits in a numeral as, for example, in 34, the 3 means "3 tens" and the 4 means "4 ones." The value of each digit is not necessarily known, that is, "3 tens" meaning 30. Success in representing numerals with base-ten blocks could merely signify a stage 3 performance. With the Chip Trading materials, a particular color is used to represent tens and another color for ones. Ross describes stage 4 as a transitional stage during which true understanding of place value is constructed. Children progress from unreliable task performance to the point at which they know that the

tens digit represents quantities of 10 units and they can coordinate the part-whole relationships within two-digit numbers. Stage 5 is the level of understanding the structure of our numeration system. The child knows that digits in a two-digit numeral represent a partitioning of the whole quantity into tens and ones and that the number represented is the sum of the parts (Ross, 1989).

Knowledge of place value has great implications for success in computational tasks as will be seen, in part, in Chapter 9. Therefore, care should be taken that children develop a meaningful understanding of numbers.

THREE-DIGIT NUMBERS

When it has been determined that children understand two-digit numbers, the progression to three-digit numbers should be a smooth one. Three-digit numbers can be introduced by an activity such as Activity 6-3. Significant learning occurs as the teacher questions the children during and after the activity. Ask the children about the meaning of each digit in the numeral produced. Explain that when representing numbers, 10 items make a new group. Ten ones are grouped to make a 10 and 10 groups of 10 are grouped to make 100.

TECHNOLOGY LINK 6-1
100th Day of School

Companion Website

This site contains lots of great ideas for 100th Day of School celebrations, related children's books, and reproducible activity sheets to accompany those books. This site will help you plan a great 100th Day Celebration!

Visit http://members.aol.com/a100thday/ or link from our Companion Website at **www.prenhall. com/cathcart.**

ACTIVITY 6-3

THREE-DIGIT NUMBERS

MATERIALS

At least 125 craft sticks for each child

PROCEDURE

1. Make as many groups of 10 as you can.
2. If you have 10 groups of 10, put them together in one pile.
3. Write a numeral to show how many piles of 10 tens, how many groups of 10 and how many ones you have.

Children should be told that 100 also can be represented with a group of 100 singles but that groups of tens make it easier to solve problems using the materials. The language corresponding to groupings of hundreds, tens, and ones should ensue. For example, the teacher could write on the chalkboard (or say) a numeral like 134 and ask the children to model it with bundles of 10 sticks and singles. Have them identify the "hundred," the "thirty," and the "four." Tell them that the 10 groups of 10 for 100 can be bundled together for easy counting.

Discussion after completing the modeling might be focused through questions such as the following:

1. What is the value of the third place in a numeral?
2. How can we describe the value when using bundles of sticks?

(The third place value in a numeral is 10 bundles of 10. One hundred is "1 bundle of 10 bundles of 10," 200 is "2 bundles of 10 bundles of 10," etc.)

The same activity could be done with base-ten blocks. These usually are available in large quantities so that each child in a class can have the experience of putting together 10 rods of 10 to make a 100 square. Three-digit numbers can be modeled using squares, rods of 10, and units. Discussion questions similar to the two above could be used for number work with base-ten blocks.

If children have been constructing different-sized groups, they can be asked to construct, for example, three rods of three, four rods of four, and five rods of five. They will notice that each set can be put together to form a square. Thus, the pattern is, regardless of the group size, singles, rods, and squares. A "game" devised by Skemp (1989) helps children develop mental pictures for numbers and also the language for number relationships. The procedure is described for base-three in Activity 6-4. It is easily adapted for other groupings.

Have children tell what they did. Listen for expressions such as "three rods," "three squares," "three groups

ACTIVITY 6-4

WORKING IN BASE-THREE (AN ACTIVITY FOR 3 OR 4 PLAYERS)

MATERIALS

- 25 interlocking cubes for each child
- 2 dice (red and white) for each group of children
- Game card as pictured

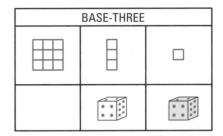

PROCEDURE

1. One child throws the dice and places the red one in the first column and the white one in the second column.
2. Each child makes sets according to the numbers on the dice. When appropriate, they construct rods and squares. Children check their work to see whether they all agree.
3. Procedures are repeated, with children taking turns tossing the dice.

of three," "three threes," and "one three." A class of second graders played the base-ten game. Afterward, children made the following statements about the values:

> *Ten rods have one hundred ones.*
>
> *One square is one hundred.*
>
> *One square has ten rods.*
>
> *Ten squares make one cube.*
>
> *One cube is one thousand.*
>
> *One cube has one hundred rods.*

Number Meanings: Oral Expressions

Children should learn to describe three-digit numbers in several ways. For example, 125 can be described as:

- 125 items is 1 group of 10 groups of 10 plus 2 groups of 10 plus 5.
- 125 is 10 tens plus 2 tens plus 5.

- 125 is 12 tens and 5.
- 125 means 100 plus 20 plus 5.

The number is read "one hundred twenty-five." When focusing on place-value notation, the numeral 100 represents one group of hundred, zero tens, and zero ones. However, children should think of 100 as 10 groups of 10 and as 100 ones.

DEVELOPING NUMBER RELATIONSHIPS

Building on knowledge of single-digit numbers, children are encouraged to develop mental computation strategies with two-digit numbers. Activities 6-5 and 6-6 are appropriate for developing number relationships. Instructions for these activities should be given orally and repeated several times using different number series.

ACTIVITY 6-5

COUNTING ON—BASE-TEN BLOCKS

MATERIALS
Base-ten blocks

PROCEDURE
1. Show 64 with the blocks (6 tens and 4 units)
2. Now show 74.
3. Tell your partner what you did. (*Added another 10*)
4. Now show 86.
5. Tell your partner what you did. (*Added a 10 and 2 units*)

ACTIVITY 6-6

COUNTING ON—CRAFT STICKS

MATERIALS
Craft sticks in bundles of tens and singles

PROCEDURE
1. Show 35 with the sticks.
2. Now add sticks to count up to 67.
3. Record what you did. (*35 + 10 + 10 + 10 + 2 = 67*)
4. Show 28. Count up to 64. Record. (*28 + 10 + 10 + 10 + 2 + 4*)

FIGURE 6-15

Worksheet

Name: _____

Begin with	Count up to
16	35
24	49
61	85
72	91
44	70

Mathematics sentence

16 + 10 + 9 = 35

24 + 10 + 10 + 5 = 49

_____

_____

Note that in the last exercise in Activity 6-6, the child counts from 28 to 60, then to 64. A worksheet could be prepared as presented in Figure 6-15.

A similar activity could be done using a hundred chart for each child and instructions such as the following:

- Begin with 16 and count up to 38. (16, 26, 36, 37, 38)
- Record what you did. (16 + 10 + 10 + 2 = 38)
- Repeat with other numbers.

PRINCIPLES AND STANDARDS LINK 6-4
Content Strand: Number and Operations

It is absolutely essential that students develop a solid understanding of the base-ten numeration system and place-value concepts by the end of grade 2. (NCTM, 2000, p. 81)

Children enjoy counting beyond 100. Give each child an egg carton and 350 to 550 small objects (e.g., buttons, cubes, pieces of straws, match sticks). Have children count the objects by making groups of 10 in each cup (using 10 cups). Instruct children to write about the counting procedures they followed. Two children's sample work is presented in Figure 6-16.

Thinking and Writing About Numbers

One way to find out how children think about numbers is to ask them to respond to number questions in writing.

FIGURE 6-16

Counting Beyond a Hundred

I am counting blocks.
I have ten sets of ten so I have 100.
I have another ten sets of ten so I have 200.
I have 240.
I have another ten sets of ten so I have 300 blocks.
I have another ten sets of ten so I have 400.
I have 460!

Michael, Grade Two

I am counting blocks. Now I have 100.
I got 100 from grouping tens.
Now I have 200. I got 200 from grouping more tens.
I now have 300. I got 300 from still grouping tens.
I have ended at 350. I have grouped all these numbers and got 350.

Jenny, Grade 2

The following are sample questions that are appropriate for second graders.

1. What can you say about the number 25? 45? 90? 100? Write statements about each number.

2. Write the following numerals on the board:

    2, 3, 4, 5, 6, 10, 12, 15, 30

   How many different number sentences can you make?

3. How are these numbers different?

    86 and 806   45 and 450

4. Is the answer more than 100? Write about how you found out.

    25 + 55 + 25   67 + 45   22 + 33 + 44

Some second graders' responses to similar problems as in number 4 are presented below:

88 + 15
   I knew that 90 + 10 = 100, so I took 2 of the 15 and that made 90 on one hand and 13 on the other, so now I just added 13 and it made 103.   —Jill, Grade 2
   35 + 35 + 35
   First I remembered that 3 threes equaled 9. So I knew that three 30s equaled 90, so I added 15, and it left me with 105!   —Annie, Grade 2
   73 + 37
   73 + 37 = 110 because 70 from the 73 and 30 from the 37 = 100 plus 7 and the 3 leftover = 110.
          —Danny, Grade 2

UNDERSTANDING LARGE NUMBERS

> **PRINCIPLES AND STANDARDS LINK 6-5**
> **Content Strand: Number and Operations**
>
> Place-value concepts can be developed and reinforced using calculators. For example, students can observe values displayed on a calculator and focus on which digits are changing. If students add 1 repeatedly on a calculator, they can observe that the units digit changes every time, but the tens digit changes less frequently. Through classroom conversations about such activities and patterns, teachers can help focus students' attention on important place-value ideas. (NCTM, 2000, p. 81)

Number Names

Although children learn the number name sequence fairly early, it is recognized that the words for 11, 12, 13, etc., to 19 are more difficult than the decade names because they do not exhibit a 10 grouping in their names. For the decades, a child can connect the "ty" in each number name to be a derivation from the name ten. The teen numbers would have been advantageously named ty-one, ty-two, etc., or ten-one, ten-two, etc. In this respect, Japanese children, for example, have a head start on English-speaking children. The Japanese system of number names follows a logical development, employing only the names of the digits plus a name for 10 and each successive power of 10. Examining the number names in Table 6-1, one notices how relatively easy it is to progress in naming successive numbers.

TABLE 6-1

JAPANESE NUMBER NAMES

1—ichi	11—juichi	100—hyaku
2—ni	12—juni	101—hyakuichi
3—san	13—jusan	111—hyakujuichi
4—shi	14—jushi	200—nihyaku
5—go	15—jugo	201—nihyakuichi
6—roku	16—juroku	211—nihyakujuichi
7—shichi	17—jushichi	
8—hachi	18—juhachi	1000—sen
9—kyu	19—jukyu	1997—senkyuhyakukyujushichi
10—ju	20—niju	
	21—nijuichi	

FIGURE 6-17

1	2	3					1	2	3	4	5	6		1	2	3	4	5	6	7
4	5	6					7	8	9	10	11	12		8	9	10	11	12	13	14
7	8	9					13	14	15	16	17	18		15	16	17	18	19	20	21
10	11	12					19	20	21	22	23	24		22	23	24	25	26	27	28
13	14	15					25	26	27	28	29	30		29	30	31	32	33	34	35
16	17	..					31	32	33	..	..	..		36	37	..	..	..	..	..

Writing Consecutive Numbers

It is a common practice in school programs to have children write numbers in sequence from 1 to 100. These numbers are often pictured on wall charts or on a hundreds board. Usually, the numbers are recorded in 10 rows of 10. The task can be made somewhat more challenging by providing children with blank charts featuring fewer or more than 10 spaces per row (Figure 6-17).

Elementary-school children should have the experience of writing numbers in sequence beyond 100, as counting by tens or hundreds to 1,000 does not give them a sense of the size of 1,000. Also, when asked to complete a number sequence, children frequently make errors in bridging decades and centuries. A teacher could watch for these difficulties by organizing a group project such as the following:

- Prepare charts for children to write numbers in some organized way. The charts could be strips of poster board with spaces for 50 numbers, or they could be 12 by 12 squares for 144 numbers per chart.

- Children can share the work of writing numbers to 1,000 by each filling in a part of a chart or charts.

- The charts could be displayed on a bulletin board and used in number activities.

Number Periods

When children understand that each position in a numeral has a value that is 10 times as large as the position to its immediate right, they can be introduced to number periods. In multidigit numbers, each group of three digits forms a number period. When children are learning to write numbers to 999, there is no need to talk about number periods.

It is recommended that the thousand, ten thousand, and hundred thousand place-value names be introduced simultaneously because they form one number period. A prominently displayed number periods chart (Figure 6-18) can be the focus for a class discussion. What children need to come to realize is that every number period or group of three digits includes a place value for ones, tens, and hundreds. Therefore, four digits are needed before a new number period is named and a total of seven digits to name yet another number period. Focusing on number periods from the onset of naming thousands would seem to act as a deterrent to falsely naming a five-digit numeral such as 54 623 as 5 million, 4 thousands, etc. It is believed that a number of teaching aids featuring four place values (e.g., a four-column abacus or four-column pocket chart) could unwittingly be a cause of children's errors in reading large numbers. Children using such materials learn the number name sequence one, ten, hundred, thousand without any differentiation of number periods. They also learn that the next new number name after "thousand" is "million." Thus, in reading numbers, some children omit the hundred thousand and ten thousand values. Using place-value materials with three or six place values might alleviate the problem.

When writing numbers, it is the acceptable practice to leave a space (without a comma) between number periods. In a four-digit number, the thousands digit need not be separated from the hundreds digit. Examples: 800 006 070; 34 630 349; 56 458; 2586.

The first two numbers are properly read and written as eight hundred million, six thousand, seventy; thirty-four

FIGURE 6-18

MILLIONS			THOUSANDS			ONES		
hundred	ten	one	hundred	ten	one	hundred	ten	one
	1	4	2	0	5	7	3	6

million, six hundred thirty thousand, three hundred forty-nine. Note that there is no "and" in the numbers; "and" is reserved to indicate a fractional component of a number.

Magnitude of Numbers

Asking children to compare numbers is one way to assess their understanding of numbers. One task is to write a set of six numbers on individual cards and have children order the numbers from least to greatest.

Examples
a. 146   116   106   164   104   140
b. 2105 2015 1520 2520 1250 2555

Ask the child: How can you tell which is larger? A child's response for set (a) could be:

I first look at the digit in the hundred's place. If they are all the same, then I examine the digit in the ten's place; if these are different, I know that the one with the most tens is the greatest number. When two numbers have the same hundreds and tens, then I compare the ones.

It is possible that children could be learning to list sets of names or other words in alphabetical order at the same time as they are learning to order multidigit numbers. Certainly, the similarity should be discussed.

Counting to a Thousand and Beyond

Children should engage in at least a few activities that require them to count objects in the hundreds, thousands, ten thousands, and beyond. This is necessary if they are to develop a sense of the magnitude of large numbers. The following activities are helpful in developing the relative size of numbers.

1. Showing a Thousand
   • Provide children with several cards (2 in. by 4 in.) and some toothpicks.
   • Have them count out 10 toothpicks and glue them close together and centered on the card. (You may wish to place a piece of cellophane tape across the toothpicks to secure them in place.) The class should prepare enough cards to demonstrate at least a thousand.
   • Take 10 cards and attach them to a sufficiently long piece of poster board. Repeat this for each set of 10 cards. Ten strips of poster board can be mounted to a bulletin board or wall with additional strips mounted alongside but separate from the set of a thousand. This is for easy identification of a thousand toothpicks.

   • The toothpicks can be the focus of counting activities.
2. Counting Toothpicks
   • Ask children to count different numbers of toothpicks.

   Example: Count 156 toothpicks.
   Possible response: A child might begin counting at one hundred (while pointing to the first strip of 100 toothpicks), then continue on with "one hundred ten" (pointing to the next group of 10 toothpicks), "one hundred twenty, one hundred thirty, one hundred forty, one hundred fifty, one hundred fifty-one, . . . , one hundred fifty-six."

3. Class Project
   • A class project could be to collect bread bag ties or other small objects.
   • When a sufficiently large amount has been collected, children could count the objects, first forming groups of 10, then groups of 100, then groups of 1000.

Today, numbers in the millions and billions often are heard in media reports; therefore, children must develop some understanding of large numbers. It seems a reasonable expectation to have children at least once in their elementary grades devise a way to represent a million of something. A visual representation of a million dollar signs or other keyboard character can be obtained from a computer printout, although this is not deemed economical to do in terms of computer storage space and time. What may be preferred is to type a page full of dots and photocopy sufficient copies to total a million or part of a million, such as one-quarter or one-half a million. The pages could be mounted on poster board and, following some estimation activity, displayed for some time in the classroom. A teacher may want to organize the "million things" (or part of a million things) by typing 100 characters per piece of paper in a 10-by-10 array. Ten papers of 100 each could then be mounted on a sheet of paper. Thus, the organization of 10, 100, 1000, or 10 000, etc., would be easily recognized.

Another model of one million is to suspend a centimeter cube in a meter cube or skeleton model of a meter cube. It would take a million of the smaller cubes to fill the larger cube.

Hampton-Burnett (1981) suggested the following activity to help children think about the magnitude of a million:

• Ask small groups of children to select an item from nature (a pine needle, blade of grass) or a manufactured one (floor tile, desk, car).

• Describe how to show a million of the item. The children could present the report to their classmates or to another class.

TABLE 6-2

NUMBER PERIOD NAMES

ones	billions	quintillions	octillions
thousands	trillions	sextillions	nonillions
millions	quadrillions	septillions	decillions

Children should be asked to use large numbers in reporting distances, weights, or other scientific information obtained from an encyclopedia or other source. An example is the mass of the earth expressed in kilograms (600 000 000 000 000 000 000 000). For interest's sake, children may want to learn number period names beyond the familiar billion and trillion. The first 12 number period names are presented in Table 6-2.

EXPANDED NOTATION

As children progress in developing an understanding of numbers and numeration they will learn how to write numbers in expanded notation in several ways. In the primary grades, children are expected to write numbers as the sum of two or more parts.

Example

$$63 = 60 + 3$$
$$= 6 \text{ tens} + 3$$

In upper elementary grades, numbers will be written in expanded form using the multiplicative property.

Example

$$785 = (7 \times 100) + (8 \times 10) + 5$$
$$4692 = (4 \times 1000) + (6 \times 100) + (9 \times 10) + 2$$

By Grade 6 or 7, children should be able to use exponential notation.

Example

$$4692 = (4 \times 10 \times 10 \times 10) + (6 \times 10 \times 10) + (9 \times 10) + 2$$
$$= (4 \times 10^3) + (6 \times 10^2) + (9 \times 10^1) + 2$$

ROUNDING NUMBERS

There are occasions when it is practical to give number approximations. For example, when asking what the population of the United States is, you would expect not an exact number but a response such as 200 million, that is, a number rounded to the nearest million. When completing income tax returns, taxpayers are allowed to round

TABLE 6-3

ROUNDING NUMBERS

PLACE VALUE	NUMBER	ROUNDED OFF
Nearest ten	543	540
Nearest hundred	629	600
Nearest ten	748	750
Nearest hundred	748*	700
Nearest hundred	5496	5500

*Note that one does not first round off to tens.

off all amounts reported to the nearest dollar, because it is believed that dollar rounding makes for fewer errors. Rounding skills are used frequently in determining estimates for computation questions.

In elementary schools, rules taught for rounding numbers are as follows: When rounding a number to a specified place value, locate the place value and examine the digit to its immediate right (the key digit). If the key digit has a value of 5 or greater, replace all digits to the right of the place value by zeros and increase the place value digit by one; if the key digit has a value less than 5, replace the digits to the right of the place value by zeros. Table 6-3 shows some examples of rounding off.

Children can learn these rules by modeling numbers to be rounded off with base-ten blocks or by drawing number lines to compare numbers between decades, hundreds, etc.

The models children will construct for Activity 6-7 are shown below. Models for the numbers in Activity 6-8 would be similar. A number line model is used in Activities 6-9 and 6-10.

Note that in the activities described, numbers with a 5 in the determining place value have been omitted. This case merits special attention. When children are successful in rounding off numbers according to the rules described previously, they should be informed that there are instances when another rule governs the process when the key digit is 5. Children could be asked to gather a set of data and then compute the average (see Activity 6-11). Note that in Set B the numbers ending in 5 in Set A have all been rounded up, whereas in Set C the numbers ending in 5 in set A preceded by an even

ACTIVITY 6-7

ROUNDING TO NEAREST TEN— CONCRETE MODEL

MATERIALS
Base-ten blocks

TASK
Round 138 to the nearest ten.

PROCEDURE
1. Show the number with base-ten blocks.
2. What are the two multiples of 10 that are closest to 138?
3. Show these two multiples with the blocks.
4. Examine the three numbers shown. Is 138 closer to 130 or 140?

ACTIVITY 6-8

ROUNDING TO NEAREST HUNDRED—CONCRETE MODEL

MATERIALS
Base-ten blocks

TASK
Round 329 to the nearest hundred.

PROCEDURE
1. Show the number with base-ten blocks.
2. What are the two multiples of 100 that are closest to 329?
3. Model them with the blocks.
4. Examine the three numbers shown. Is 329 closer to 300 or 400?

ACTIVITY 6-9

ROUNDING TO NEAREST TEN— NUMBER LINE MODEL

MATERIALS
An 11-point number line drawn on paper

TASK
Round 673 to the nearest ten.

PROCEDURE
1. What are the two multiples of 10 closest to 673?
2. Label the end points of the number line with these two multiples.
3. Decide where 673 fits on the number line. Mark it on the number line.
4. 673 rounded to the nearest ten is ___.

ACTIVITY 6-10

ROUNDING TO NEAREST HUNDRED—NUMBER LINE MODEL

MATERIALS
An 11-point number line drawn on paper

TASK
Round 4567 to the nearest hundred.

PROCEDURE
1. What are the two multiples of 100 closest to 4567?
2. Label the end points of the number line with these two multiples.
3. Decide where 4567 fits on the number line. Mark it on the number line.
4. 4567 rounded to the nearest hundred is _____.

number have been rounded down, those preceded by an odd number have been rounded up. This rule, known as the computer's rule, avoids the possibility of cumulative errors in rounding off and is employed by scientists, statisticians, and actuaries, among others. Children may notice that when following the computer's rule in rounding off numbers, the retained terminal digit will always be an even number. Children could be asked to determine which rounding-off rule their calculator is programmed to use.

ACTIVITY 6-11

EFFECTS OF ROUNDING

MATERIALS
Data collected

PROCEDURE
1. Study the following sets of numbers for which the average has been calculated:

	Set A	Set B	Set C
	243	240	240
	247	250	250
	245	250	240
	235	240	240
	236	240	240
	231	230	230
	225	230	220
	255	260	260
Average:	239.63	242.5	240

2. Which average is closer to the exact average of Set A? Why?

ESTIMATING

Good number sense enables one to estimate quantities. Rounding numbers is one way to estimate totals or products. (This estimating strategy along with others is discussed in Chapter 9.)

There are times when one needs to estimate a quantity "at a glance." For example, an approximation of the number of people in attendance at a rally or sports event may be required. Children who have developed good number sense both in physical representations and in understanding number compositions (additive and multiplicative) will feel competent in providing a sensible estimate of the group size.

What strategies could be employed in making such estimates? In a large gathering, one could note a "group of ten" or a "group of twenty" and quickly determine ten or five such groups for the physical size of a "group of hundred." From this number, a look around the arena or other area will enable one to determine "at a glance" an approximate number for the gathering. Whole student body or multiple class gatherings can be occasions when children can practice estimating quantities in the tens and hundreds. Teachers can use different occasions to have children make estimates. Examples include the following:

- Holiday concert: About how many parents attended the concert?

- Class visit to a museum: About how many samples are in the rock collection? About how many butterflies are in the display?

- Class visit to the public library: About how many science fiction books are there in the children's section? About how many adventure books?

Children can be asked to estimate the number of small objects in a jar or clear plastic bag. A child estimating the

---

LITERATURE LINK 6-2
Numeration, Place Value, and Large Numbers

Anno, Masaichiro & Anno, Mitsumasa. (1983). *Anno's Mysterious Multiplying Jar.* New York: Philomel.
Murphy, Stuart J. (1997). *Betcha.* New York: Harper Trophy.
Schwartz, David. (1985). *How Much Is a Million?* New York: Lothrop, Lee, and Shepard.

Two important skills of numeration are working with large numbers and learning to make reasonable estimates. Using and exploring various number benchmarks and practicing with mental computations support children's understanding of and facility with the base-10 number system.

- *How Much Is a Million?* explores very large numbers such as million, billion, and trillion. Use the author's calculations in the back of the book to determine distance, time, area, and volume needed for a very large number selected by each child. For example, if a child selects the number 275,000, the child should explain and illustrate this number using a length measurement, such as "275,000 inches would be long enough to cover. . . ," and do the same with time, area, and volume measurements.

- Challenge children to visualize very large numbers. Ask them questions such as "What will the date be in 1 million minutes?" "Have you lived 1 million seconds?", "How long will it take to spend 1 million dollars if you spend 25 dollars a day, 50 dollars a day?", and "How much area would 1 million 1-inch color tiles cover?"

- Other number systems are often based on various ways of grouping numbers by fives, tens, and twenties. Investigate how very large numbers were written in numerals such as Roman, Mayan, Egyptian, and Babylonian. Perform basic addition and subtraction operations using these numerals.

- Connect numerical relationships such as exponential growth and factorial numbers using books such as *Anno's Mysterious Multiplying Jar.* The concept of factorials is introduced through pictures and illustrations showing how factorials can be applied to everyday situations. Children can explore the use of factorials by computing things that come in groups.

- Estimation is an important skill in developing number sense and is one of the most commonly used daily mathematical skills. In *Betcha*, the main character shows strategies for making reasonable estimates by grouping things into arrays (length and width) and by their volume (length, width, and height). Teachers can fill a large jar with different items for estimation. Students can estimate the items in the jar (for example, cotton balls, toothpicks, jellybeans, lima beans, marbles). Children's estimates can be recorded on a weekly chart, and children can analyze their strategies for estimating different objects.

Source: Dr. Patricia Moyer, George Mason University.

number of jelly beans in a cylindrical jar might think the following:

There are about 20 jelly beans in 1 layer and 12 layers altogether. Twenty times 10 is 200 and 2 times 20 is 40, so I estimate that there are about 240 jelly beans in the jar.

Another estimating activity is to scatter a number of centimeter cubes (25 to 35) on an overhead projector and then turn on the projector for a brief moment. Have children tell about how many blocks they saw pictured on the screen. Other small objects could be placed on a table, and children could be directed to look at the objects for a few seconds and then to make an estimate about the number. Children should be encouraged to see "groups of five" or "groups of ten" to help them make quick approximations about the number of objects there are in all. To discourage random guessing, after an estimate has been made, ask, "How did you figure out the amount?" Other children can learn estimating strategies from hearing children's descriptions.

CONSOLIDATING NUMBER SKILLS

Children who have engaged in the kinds of activities described in this chapter accompanied with frequent oral and written expressions of their work should eventually develop an understanding of our numeration system together with number sense. To consolidate these ideas, additional experiences may be necessary. Some activities are suggested below.

1. Numeral Cards
   - Write each of the digits 1 to 9 on three cards (27 cards in all).
   - Shuffle the cards.
   - Have a child draw six cards and write the numbers drawn in any order on a chart (Figure 6-19). Zeros are then written in the empty places.

- Have the child read the number.
- Fewer or more number cards can be drawn, and the chart can be extended to other number periods.

2. Pocket Chart
   - A place-value pocket chart showing three or more number periods can be placed on the board ledge.

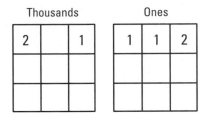

- In turn, children put digits on the chart and ask classmates to read the numbers aloud. The aim should be to represent "tricky" numbers to challenge their classmates.

3. Colored Chips
   - Direct children to represent the number 111 on a four-column mat with colored chips (1 yellow, 1 red, and 1 blue).
   - Ask them to show the number using only two colors.
   - Have them record the two parts of 111 (see diagram).

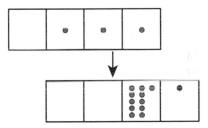

- The task can be repeated with different three-digit numbers.
- With four-digit numbers, have the children represent a number using two or three different colors.
- A base other than 10 can be used for this activity.

FIGURE 6-19

BILLIONS			MILLIONS			THOUSANDS			ONES		
hundred	ten	one	hundred	ten	one	hundred	ten	one	hundred	ten	one
				9	1	0	0	4	6	3	4
			4	5	0	2	1	9	0	3	0
	1	4	0	0	2	0	0	0	2	1	8

4. Calculator
- Direct children to enter a six-digit number on their calculator and ask them to "wipe out" a specified digit.

    Example: Enter 345 876. Wipe out the digit 8.

- Children can keep a record of their work as shown below (Reys, Shydam, & Lindquist, et al., 1984, p. 79).

Enter	Wipe out	Keys pressed	Display
345876	8	−800	345076

5. Die

(A set of number cards 0 to 9 could be used in place of a die.)
- Players try to create the largest possible multidigit number using the digits generated by repeatedly tossing a die or drawing a card from a set of cards 0 to 9.
- As each digit is revealed, players must write it in one of the place-value positions and cannot later change a position.

    Example: <u>5</u> <u>4</u> <u>3</u> <u>6</u> <u>2</u>

- The player making the greatest number is the winner.

6. Counting in a Foreign Language
- Have children write numbers in sequence in French, Spanish, or another language, assuming the number names are logically developed. For example, in English, a logical development would be: ten, ten-one, ten-two, . . . , ten-nine, two tens, two tens-one, etc.
- French and Spanish number names are provided below.

	French	Spanish
1	un	uno
2	deux	dos
3	trois	tres
4	quatre	cuatro
5	cinq	cinco
6	six	seix
7	sept	siete
8	huit	ocho
9	neuf	nueve
10	dix	diez
100	cent	cien

7. Calendar Activity
- Have children make a calendar writing the numbers in a base other than 10.
- Children can be challenged to devise their own number symbols.

OTHER NUMERATION SYSTEMS

Upper elementary and junior high children can be invited to study ancient numeration systems with a view to developing a better understanding and appreciation of our own system. Ideas for such activities are suggested in Activities 6-12 to 6-15. Some information is provided on several numeration systems that could be shared with children as an introduction to further study.

As an extension, children in groups of four or five could invent their own numeration system. When completed, their "very own" numeration system can be

ACTIVITY 6-12

STUDYING ANCIENT NUMERATION SYSTEMS

1. Select an ancient numeration system (e.g., the Babylonian, Egyptian, Mayan, Roman) and conduct a study of the system to learn its symbols and the particular rules for using the symbols to represent numbers.

2. Write some large numbers as you think the people would have done.

3. Try to perform the operations of addition and subtraction with the numerals.

4. Try to construct an addition and a multiplication basic fact table for the system.

5. Write about the advantages and disadvantages of the numeration system.

ACTIVITY 6-13

MAYAN NUMERALS

MATERIALS
Paper and pencil

PROCEDURE
1. Write the numerals for the numbers 20 to 50 in Mayan symbolization.

2. At which number would the Mayans require a third place value? Write that number in Mayan symbols.

ACTIVITY 6-14

WRITING ROMAN NUMERALS

MATERIALS
Paper and pencil

PROCEDURE
1. Write the current year in Roman numerals.
2. Write the year of your birth in Roman numerals.
3. Write in Roman numerals the year that you anticipate seeing on your high school diploma.
4. Write in Roman numerals the year that your school was built.

ACTIVITY 6-15

COMPARISON OF NUMERATION SYSTEMS

MATERIALS
Paper and pencil

PROCEDURE
1. Write the Mayan numeral for 1 million.
2. Write the Roman numeral for 1 million.
3. Write the Egyptian numeral for 2 million.
4. Which numeral was easiest to write? Why?

shared with classmates or other classes in the school. Provide the following suggestions or hints:

* Invent a numeration system with the same characteristics as the Hindu-Arabic system.
* Begin by choosing a base, then create the symbols for the system, giving each single-digit number a name.
* In naming multidigit numbers, try to employ logic so that successively larger numbers can be easily named.

Babylonian Numeration

The Babylonian cuneiform method of recording quantities is among the oldest numeral systems in existence. Although the symbols were mere wedge-shaped imprints on

clay tablets, the rules for using those templates to represent numbers were rather complicated. The Babylonians developed (approximately 5000 years ago) a sexidecimal (base-60) place-value system with numbers less than 60 represented in base-ten. The place values and accompanying symbols are shown in Figure 6-20a. Because the Babylonians had no symbol for zero, their numerals are difficult to interpret, as can be seen in Figure 6-20b.

Egyptian Numeration

The Egyptian method of recording quantities can be said to be based on 10 with a symbol for 1, 10, and each successive power of 10. For their number symbols, the Egyptians used a distinct hieroglyphic or picture for each

FIGURE 6-20

BABYLONIAN CUNEIFORMS

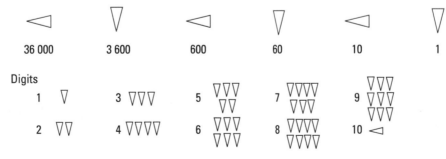

(a) Babylonian symbols

| 36 000 | 3 600 | 600 | 60 | 10 | 1 |

Digits
1, 2, 3, 4, 5, 6, 7, 8, 9, 10

(b) Examples of Numerals

→ 10 + 10 + 3

→ 600 + 600 + 60 + 60 + 60

→ 2 × 36 000 + 3 × 3600

Source: "Mayan arithmetic," by J. K. Bidwell, 1967, *Mathematics Teacher,* 60(7), p. 234.

FIGURE 6-21

EGYPTIAN HIEROGLYPHICS

(a)

1 000 000	100 000	10 000	1000	100	10
astonished man	tadpole	pointing finger or bent line	lotus flower	coiled rope or scroll	heel bone

(b) Numerals 1 to 9

1 I   2 II   3 III   4 IIII   5 III
                                    II

6 III   7 IIII   8 IIII   9 III
   III   III   IIII   III
                                   III

(c) 231 ----→ ??I∩∩∩ or ∩∩∩??I or I??∩∩∩

(d) 10 234 ----→ ⌐??∩∩∩\IIII

power of 10 (Cowle, 1970) (Figure 6-21a), whereas their numerals from 1 to 9 consisted of simple strokes arranged at most in groups of 4 horizontally (Figure 6-21b). An additive rule and the absence of place value rendered the system impractical because symbols had to be repeated the required number of times and could be written in a different order to represent the same number (Figure 6-21c). There was no symbol for 0; therefore, a particular symbol was omitted in a numeral when that multiple of 10 was not part of a number (Figure 6-21d).

Mayan Numeration

The Mayans of Central America (before 1000 BC) developed a numeration system in base-20 complete with place value and a symbol for zero. They were a "barefoot people," and their probable early use of fingers and toes to indicate quantity may have influenced their choice of 20 for a number base. Place-value notation was in top-to-bottom manner, with the ones in the lower place and each place value separated by a space (Figure 6-22a). The digits of the system are presented in Figure 6-22b (Bidwell, 1967, p. 764).

FIGURE 6-22

MAYAN NUMERATION AND NUMERALS

MAYAN NUMERATION

(a)

·· / = / ··	$(12 \times 20) + 7$	
		· / —· 6×20^3
		— 5×20^2
		⊙ 0×20
		···· 4

MAYAN NUMERALS

(b)

0 ⊙	5 —	10 =	15 ≡
1 •	6 •̲	11 •̳	16 •̳
2 ••	7 ••̲	12 ••̳	17 ••̳
3 •••	8 •••̲	13 •••̳	18 •••̳
4 ••••	9 ••••̲	14 ••••̳	19 ••••̳

Base 20 system

TABLE 6-4 ▶

PLACE-VALUE NAMES FOR MAYAN COUNTING SYSTEM

hablat	20^7
alau	20^6
kinchil	20^5
cabal	20^4
pic	20^3
bak	20^2
kal	20^1
hun	1

The Mayans used only three symbols to represent all numbers: a dot, a bar, and a symbol for zero. The simplicity of the numerals and a vertical place-value scheme facilitated the representation of large numbers. The Mayan number names for each place value are presented in Table 6-4 (Bidwell, 1967, p. 764).

Roman Numeration

Although Western Europe and most of Asia chose to merge the numeration systems of the Hindus and Arabs over that of the Romans, Roman numerals were not completely shunned. This is evidenced by their use today on timepieces, tombstones, preface pages and section headings of books, cornerstones of buildings and bridges, degree certificates, and various commemorative events. Because of its continued use, the Roman system is generally included in current mathematics programs.

Similar to the Egyptians, the Romans created a distinct symbol for one, ten, hundred, and thousand. In addition, they created a symbol for numbers that are half of the powers of 10 symbolized, that is, 5, 50, and 500. Figure 6-23 shows the seven basic Roman numerals and their Hindu-Arabic equivalents.

Chiefly a repetitive and additive system, the advantage over the Egyptian system lies in the simplicity of the symbols and in a subtractive element that reduces the number of digits in a numeral.

The use of position to designate whether a number was to be added or subtracted may have been a historical first step in establishing a system based on digit po-

sition in a numeral. Examples of the use of position to determine the value of a digit are the numerals for four and six:

$$\text{IV means } 5 - 1 \rightarrow 4 \quad \text{VI means } 5 + 1 \rightarrow 6$$

Only the symbols I, X, and C are used to indicate subtraction to represent certain numbers: I may be subtracted only from V or X; X may be subtracted from L or C; and C may be subtracted from D or M. Multiples of 10 beyond 1000 are symbolized by placing a line over any of the symbols and designates 1000 as a multiplier. Thus, $\overline{X}$ means 10 000 and $\overline{\overline{X}}$ symbolizes 10 000 000.

CONCLUSION

This chapter has discussed the structural characteristics of our numeration system together with instructional considerations for developing number meanings and relationships.

A good understanding of numeration is a prerequisite for mental computation and computational estimation with whole numbers. Place-value tasks of renaming and regrouping numbers underlie algorithmic procedures for computation. Therefore, children's understanding of numbers and numeration should be assessed before proceeding to the development of computational procedures.

For Your Journal

When you have finished studying this chapter, reflect on the following questions in your math journal:

1. How is our number system different from those of the Babylonians, Egyptians, Mayans, and Romans?

2. What does it mean to show equivalent representations of a number? Explain what 4 equivalent representations of 56 would include. Why is it important that children understand the concept of equivalent representations?

3. Imagine that you are a first-grade teacher. You want to begin instruction to help the children understand place value. How might you assess what the children already know? What would you include in that assessment?

For Your Portfolio

When you have finished studying this chapter, complete the following activities to include in your professional portfolio:

1. Write a lesson plan to help children understand the concept of grouping tens. Make sure to describe the type of base-ten model you would use.

FIGURE 6-23 ▶

	NUMERALS						
Hindu-Arabic	1	5	10	50	100	500	1000
Roman	1	V	X	L	C	D	M

2. Write a lesson plan to help children understand the concept of equivalent representations.

Resources for Teachers

Children's books

Friedman, A. (1995). *The king's commissioners.* New York: Scholastic.

Schwartz, D. (1985). *How much is a million?* New York: Scholastic.

Schwartz, D. (1989). *If you made a million.* New York: Lothrop, Lee & Shepard Books.

Zimelman, N. (1992). *How the second grade got $8,205.50 to visit the Statue of Liberty.* Morton Grove, IL: Whitman.

Books on numeration

Brodie, J. (1995). *Constructing ideas about large numbers.* Mountain View, CA: Creative.

Burns, M. (1994). *Math by all means: Place value, Grade 2.* Sausalito, CA: Math Solutions.

Reak, C., Stewart, K., & Walker, K. (1995). *20 thinking questions for base-10 blocks Grades 3–6.* Mountain View, CA: Creative.

Reak, C., Stewart, K., & Walker, K. (1995). *20 thinking questions for base-10 blocks Grades 6–8.* Mountain View, CA: Creative.

Richardson, K. (1999). *Developing number concepts: Place value, multiplication, and division.* White Plains, NY: Seymour.

Links to the Internet

Ask Dr. Math (place value)

http://www.mathforum.org/dr.math/tocs/placevalue.elem.html

Contains a list of interesting questions about place value and answers given by Dr. Math.

100th Day of School Web sites

http://members.aol.com/a100thday/

http://www.angelfire.com/ma/1stGrade/page100.html

http://www.siec.k12.in.us/~west/proj/100th/

These websites contain ideas for ways to celebrate the 100th day of school.

CHAPTER 7

Developing Whole-Number Operations: Meaning of Operations

KEY CONCEPTS ▶

✔ **Types of word problems for each operation**

✔ **Addition and subtraction: Join, Separate, Part-part-whole, Compare**

✔ **Multiplication and division: Equal groups (repeated addition, Partitive division, Measurement division), area and arrays, Multiplicative comparison, and Combinations**

✔ **Using objects to model problem situations**

FOCUS QUESTIONS ▶

When you have finished studying this chapter, you should be able to do the following:

1. Write a word problem for each type of addition, subtraction, multiplication, and division problem.

2. Know how each word problem from question 1 could be modeled with objects. For each type of word problem, draw a picture to illustrate a model.

3. Explain the difference between partitive and measurement division. How might a child use counters to show $6 \div 2$ for each interpretation of division?

The NCTM Principles and Standards emphasize the importance of children understanding the meaning of operations, stating that "understanding the fundamental operations of addition, subtraction, multiplication, and division is central to knowing mathematics" (NCTM, 1989, p. 41).

PRINCIPLES AND STANDARDS LINK 7-1
Content Strand: Number and Operations

During the primary grades, students should encounter a variety of meanings for addition and subtraction of whole numbers. . . . Multiplication and division can begin to have meaning for students in prekindergarten through grade 2 as they solve problems that arise in their environment, such as how to share a bag of raisins fairly among four people. In grades 3–5, helping students develop meaning for whole-number multiplication and division should become a central focus. (NCTM, 2000, p. 34)

NCTM CONTENT STANDARDS AND EXPECTATIONS ADDRESSED IN THIS CHAPTER

STANDARD	EXPECTATIONS FOR GRADES PRE-K–2	EXPECTATIONS FOR GRADES 3–5
Number and Operations Standard Instructional program from pre-K–12 should enable all students to—	In prekindergarten through Grade 2 all students should—(NCTM, 2000, p. 78)	In Grades 3–5 all students should— (NCTM, 2000,p. 148)
Understand meanings of operations and how they relate to one another	• understand various meanings of addition and subtraction of whole numbers and the relationship between the two operations. • understand the effects of adding and subtracting whole numbers. • understand situations that entail multiplication and division, such as equal groupings of objects and sharing equally.	• understand various meanings of multiplication and division • understand the effects of multiplying and dividing whole numbers. • identify and use relationships between operations, such as division as the inverse of multiplication, to solve problems.

This document goes on to list four key aspects of "developing operation sense," or understanding the operations:

✔ recognizing real-world settings for each operation;

✔ developing an awareness of models and properties of each operation;

✔ recognizing relationships among the operations; and

✔ understanding the effects of an operation.

Understanding the mathematical operations and their related computational procedures requires that the concepts of the operations be grasped, the basic facts be learned, and computational procedures be developed. This chapter discusses understanding the concepts of the operations. (Learning facts and developing computational procedures are examined in subsequent chapters.) ✔

INTRODUCE OPERATIONS WITH WORD PROBLEMS

Children begin to construct meaning for mathematical operations before they enter school. Informal, real-life experiences such as sharing cookies or combining collections of cards or marbles help children construct knowledge of mathematical operations. Because these experiences can be translated into word problems and because they are more meaningful to children than symbolic expressions, early instruction on operations should introduce children to addition, subtraction, multiplication, and division by having children solve word problems. Learning about operations should be based on developing meaning and understanding by beginning with real-world settings or problems.

A Model for Beginning With Word Problems

Young children develop an understanding of operations by solving a variety of word problems. If those problems come from real-world experiences, children can see more personal relevance, which enables them to more easily analyze the problem and its component parts. Real-world problems can come from everyday classroom opportunities such as routine opening activities, classroom events,

 PRINCIPLES AND STANDARDS LINK 7-2
Content Strand: Number and Operations

In developing the meaning of operations, teachers should ensure that students repeatedly encounter situations in which the same numbers appear in different contexts. (NCTM, 2000, p. 83)

 PRINCIPLES AND STANDARDS LINK 7-3
Content Strand: Number and Operations

As students in the early grades work with complex tasks in a variety of contexts, they also build an understanding of operations on numbers. Appropriate contexts can arise through student-initiated activities, [through] teacher-created stories, and in many other ways. (NCTM, 2000, p. 83)

or even examples from children's literature. In addition, children can help make decisions about sharing and distributing classroom supplies, especially when many-to-one groupings need to be made, which are meaningful contexts for multiplication and division (Kouba & Franklin, 1993). For example, if 10 children get 5 minutes each to use the computer, how much time will be needed? Teachers can take advantage of these familiar experiences to pose problems and discuss operations. Such rich, familiar contexts in which mathematical operations are introduced naturally not only help children recognize personal relevance and math connections but also help them judge the reasonableness of their answers.

After introducing a real-world problem, a teacher should then represent or translate it into some model (see Figure 7-1). Initially, this model should be a concrete

FIGURE 7-1

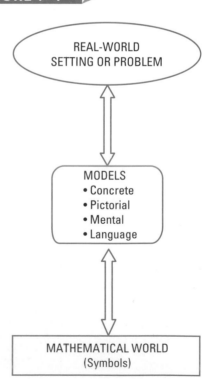

representation of the setting; later, the teacher can introduce iconic (pictorial) representations. Mental modes and children's natural language skills also can play key roles here in developing conceptual understanding.

Teachers should make different materials available to children to use in modeling problems. They also should encourage children to be creative in their representations of problem situations, whether concretely or pictorially. Further, they should provide ample opportunities for children to discuss and interpret situations presented concretely and pictorially. Once children are able to interpret different types of problems and identify and model the operation needed to solve each one, they can write number sentences to represent solution processes. It is important to remember, however, that children must have an extensive number of experiences with meaningful problem solving before they are introduced to symbolic expressions.

It is important to note that meanings develop over time and, while they are being developed, there should not be any pressure on children to memorize basic facts. In fact, understanding the meaning of the operations is a critical component of mastering the basic facts. Likewise, working with word problems should be the basis of children's early experiences with operations and must not be delayed until children "know their facts." The most important consideration is for children to connect their real-life experiences and language with the mathematical language and symbolism associated with each operation (Trafton & Zawojewski, 1990).

It also is important to mention now that the "key word" strategy—common translations in word problems of key words such as "*is* means *equal*" and "*of* means *times*"—is purposeless. In fact, teaching children to look for "key words" to solve word problems is ineffective and detrimental (Sowder, 1988). A much better use of instructional time is to help children develop understanding of the meaning of operations.

Encoding and Decoding Word Problems

Once children understand the meaning of a variety of problem situations, they should be asked to both *encode* and *decode* their number sentences. In other words, not only should children translate a real-life setting into a model or mathematics sentence (encoding), but they should also, given a model or mathematics sentence, be able to write a word problem that illustrates that situation. Children should be encouraged to describe and justify their translation. This process is represented in Figure 7-1 by the double-headed arrows which suggest that the translation process goes both ways. For example, a teacher might give children the following problem to solve:

Tom had 7 cookies and gave 3 to Matt. How many cookies does Tom have left?

The teacher might ask the children to solve the problem using counters or by drawing a picture and to write a number sentence that matches the problem situation. On another occasion, the teacher might give children a number sentence and ask them to write a word problem that illustrates that number sentence.

Different parts of this generalized, conceptual model, depicted in Figure 7-1, are emphasized at different stages in the three-component process thus mentioned. When developing the concept or meaning of operations, it is most effective for children to focus on the real-world setting, the model for the setting, and the translation of one to the other. Mathematical symbols are not totally ignored but are used only incidentally.

In summary, research suggests that exposure to a wide range of word problems from the beginning of the school experience significantly improves children's mathematics performance (Stigler, Fuson, Ham, & Kim, 1986).

Having children engage in solving word problems before they learn the basic facts enables them to focus on the nature of the problem and to model it to find an unknown answer (Burns, 1991).

UNDERSTANDING ADDITION AND SUBTRACTION

Researchers have identified four types of addition and subtraction problems: Join, Separate, Part-part-whole, and Compare (Carpenter & Moser, 1982). Join and Separate problems involve action. Part-part-whole and Compare problems do not involve action but are identified by the relationships of the quantities in the problems. Research shows that this classification system matches the way children think about these problems (Fennema, Carpenter, Levi, Franke, & Empson, 1997).

Types of Addition and Subtraction Word Problems

The four addition and subtraction problems types—Join, Separate, Part-part-whole, and Compare—are distinguished by the presence or absence of action and the types of relationships involved. The basic structure of each of these problem types is illustrated in Figure 7-2.

Examples of each problem type   In each of the addition and subtraction problem types, two quantities are given and one is unknown. The examples in Figures 7-3 through 7-7 use the fact family 4, 7, and 11 to illustrate each problem type.

Join problems.   In a *Join problem,* elements are being added or joined to a set. The three quantities involved are

FIGURE 7-2

THE STRUCTURE OF THE FOUR ADDITION AND SUBTRACTION PROBLEM TYPES

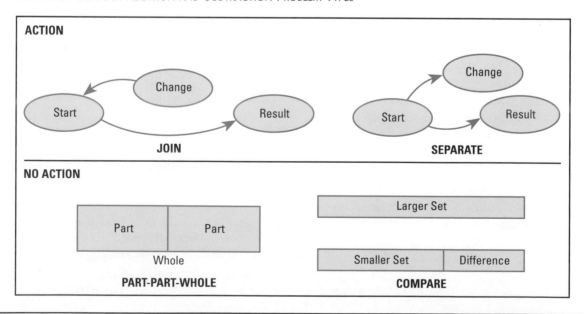

BOX 7-1

A Join Problem Written by a Student

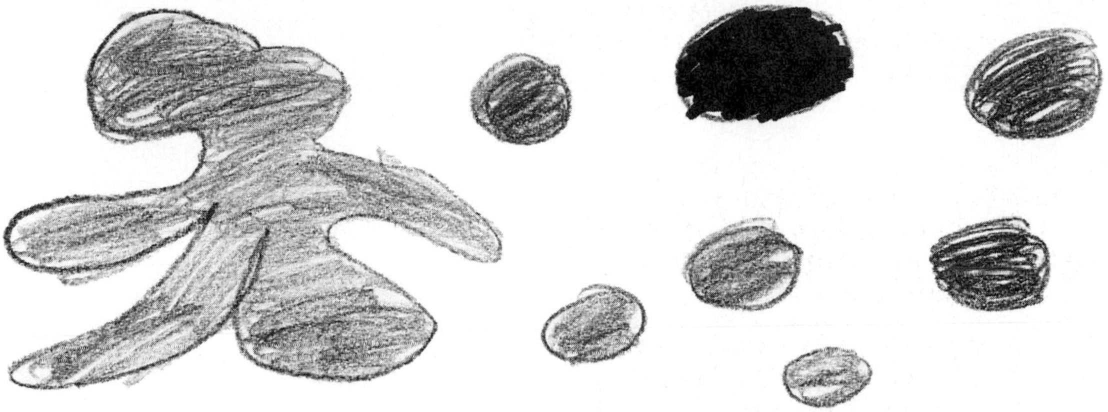

There were 5 ghost and

3 came How meny in all?

5 + 3 = 8

Martha

the starting amount, the change amount, and the resulting amount. Figure 7-3 contains examples illustrating these three types of Join problems. Box 7-1 shows a sample of a second grader's work. Notice that the child wrote a Join problem, drew a picture illustrating the problem situation, and wrote a corresponding number sentence.

Separate problems. In a *Separate problem,* elements are being removed from a set. As in Join problems, the three quantities involved are the starting amount, the change amount, and the resulting amount. Figure 7-4 shows examples of these three types of Separate problems. Box 7-2 shows a sample of a second grader's work.

FIGURE 7-3

EXAMPLES OF JOIN PROBLEMS WITH DIFFERENT UNKNOWN QUANTITIES

TYPE	EXAMPLE	RELATED NUMBER SENTENCE
Join Result Unknown	Peter had 4 cookies. Erika gave him 7 more cookies. How many cookies does Peter have now?	4 + 7 = [ ]
Join Change Unknown	Peter had 4 cookies. Erika gave him some more cookies. Now Peter has 11 cookies. How many cookies did Erika give him?	4 + [ ] = 11
Join Start Unknown	Peter had some cookies. Erika gave him 7 more cookies. Now Peter has 11 cookies. How many cookies did Peter have to start with?	[ ] + 7 = 11

BOX 7-2

A Separate Problem Written by a Student

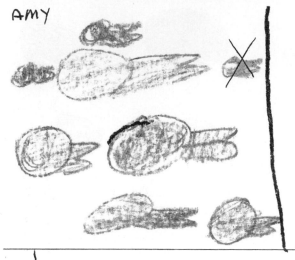

AMY

There were 8 orange fish and
1 fish swam away
How many are left?
8 – 1 = 7

FIGURE 7-4

EXAMPLES OF SEPARATE PROBLEMS

TYPE	EXAMPLE	RELATED NUMBER SENTENCE
Separate Result Unknown	Peter had 11 cookies. He gave 7 cookies to Erika. How many cookies does Peter have now?	11 − 7 = [ ]
Separate Change Unknown	Peter had 11 cookies. He gave some cookies to Erika. Now Peter has 4 cookies. How many cookies did Peter give to Erika?	11 − [ ] = 4
Separate Start Unknown	Peter had some cookies. He gave 7 cookies to Erika. Now Peter has 4 cookies. How many cookies did Peter have to start with?	[ ] − 7 = 4

BOX 7-3

A Part-Part-Whole Problem Written by a Student

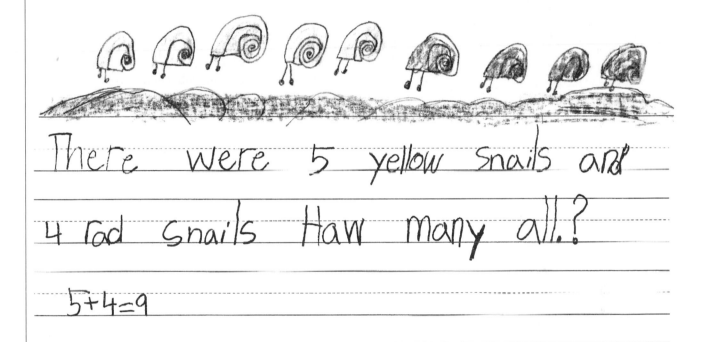

There were 5 yellow snails and 4 rad snails Haw many all.?

5+4=9

This child wrote and illustrated a Separate problem and wrote a corresponding number sentence. Notice that this child showed that one fish swam away by crossing it out in the picture.

Part-part-whole problems. In *Part-part-whole problems* there is no action. Instead, these problems focus on the relationship between a set and its two subsets. The three quantities involved are the two parts and the whole. Unlike Join and Separate problems, there is no change over time. Figure 7-5 contains examples of the two types of Part-part-whole problems. Box 7-3 shows a sample of a second grader's work. This child wrote and illustrated a Part-part-whole problem. Notice how the use of two different colors of snails clearly shows the two parts of the problem.

FIGURE 7-5

EXAMPLES OF PART-PART-WHOLE PROBLEMS

TYPE	EXAMPLE
Part-part-whole Whole Unknown	Peter has some cookies, Four are chocolate chip cookies and 7 are peanut butter cookies. How many cookies does Peter have?
Part-part-whole Part Unknown	Peter has 11 cookies. Four are chocolate chip cookies and the rest are peanut butter cookies. How many peanut butter cookies does Peter have?

FIGURE 7-6 ▶

EXAMPLES OF COMPARE PROBLEMS

TYPE	EXAMPLE
Compare Difference Unknown	Peter has 11 cookies and Erika has 7 cookies. How many more cookies does Peter have than Erika?
Compare Larger Unknown	Erika has 7 cookies. Peter has 4 more cookies than Erika. How many cookies does Peter have?
Compare Smaller Unknown	Peter has 11 cookies. Peter has 4 more cookies than Erika. How many cookies does Erika have?

Compare problems. There is no action in *Compare problems*. Instead, they involve comparisons between two different sets. The three quantities involved are the two wholes and the difference. Figure 7-6 contains examples of these three types of Compare problems.

These four addition and subtraction word problem types result in 11 different kinds of addition and subtraction problems. Figure 7-7 presents these 11 types in one grid in order to better examine their similarities and differences.

Using Models to Solve Addition and Subtraction Problems

Direct modeling Addition and subtraction problems can be modeled with many different types of materials, including real-world objects (such as pencils) and manipulative materials (such as poker chips). The term direct modeling refers to the process of children using concrete materials to exactly represent the problem as it is written. For example, consider the following Join problem:

Joyce had 3 pencils. Scott gave her 5 more pencils. How many pencils does Joyce have now?

This problem can be solved by having two children (representing Joyce and Scott) directly model or act out the problem by having one child display three pencils and another child give her five more pencils. The children then can count the number of pencils in the joined sets of pencils now held by Joyce.

Have the children use pencils and other classroom materials to create other problems to solve. Ask the children to solve those problems and discuss their solutions.

It usually is easier for children to solve a problem by modeling it with the actual objects referred to in the problem, as done in the previous example. Ask the children to solve the problem and discuss its solution. Then, after solving a number of problems using the actual objects in the problem for direct modeling, begin to use counters. You should be aware, however, that using a manipulative material such as poker chips to model a problem about pencils is somewhat more abstract and will be a bit more difficult for children to successfully solve.

Problems involving action, such as Join and Separate, are easiest for children to solve by direct modeling. Part-part-whole and Compare problems are more difficult to model. Delay introducing these types of problems until

FIGURE 7-7 ▶

ELEVEN ADDITION AND SUBTRACTION PROBLEM TYPES

Join	*Result Unknown* Peter had 4 cookies. Erika gave him 7 more cookies. How many cookies does Peter have now?	*Change Unknown* Peter had 4 cookies. Erika gave him some more cookies. Now Peter has 11 cookies. How many cookies did Erika give him?	*Start Unknown* Peter had some cookies. Erika gave him 7 more cookies. Now Peter has 11 cookies. How many cookies did Peter have to start with?
Separate	*Result Unknown* Peter had 11 cookies. He gave 7 cookies to Erika. How many cookies does Peter have now?	*Change Unknown* Peter had 11 cookies. He gave some cookies to Erika. Now Peter has 4 cookies. How many cookies did Peter give to Erika?	*Start Unknown* Peter had some cookies. He gave 7 cookies to Erika. Now Peter has 4 cookies. How many cookies did Peter have to start with?
Part-Part-Whole	*Whole Unknown* Peter has some cookies. Four are chocolate chip cookies and 7 are peanut butter cookies. How many cookies does Peter have?	*Part Unknown* Peter has 11 cookies. Four are chocolate chip cookies and the rest are peanut butter cookies. How many peanut butter cookies does Peter have?	
Compare	*Difference Unknown* Peter has 11 cookies and Erika has 7 cookies. How many more cookies does Peter have than Erika?	*Larger Unknown* Erika has 7 cookies. Peter has 4 more cookies than Erika. How many cookies does Peter have?	*Smaller Unknown* Peter has 11 cookies. Peter has 4 more cookies than Erika. How many cookies does Erika have?

children can successfully use direct modeling to solve Join and Separate problems.

Note that diagrams such as in Figure 7-8 sometimes can cause confusion. For example, when asked how many trucks are in set C, a young child may respond that there are none. Some young children do not understand class inclusion, that is, that set A and set B are contained in set C. These children may say that all the trucks are in sets A and B, so there are none in set C. This is one reason why concrete objects should be used first in developing problem-solving skills. When children physically join two sets, the initial sets lose their identity, although they can be reconstructed, and the difficulty sometimes associated with the diagram in Figure 7-8 does not occur.

Modeling separate problems. Separate problems are fairly easy for children to model. To do so, remove a subset, the subtrahend, from an original set (the total number or minuend), and observe the difference (cardinal number of the remaining subset). Consider the following problem:

> *Megan had 6 cookies (the minuend). She gave 2 (the subtrahend) to her brother. How many cookies does Megan have left (the difference)?*

Using counters, children could set out six, physically remove two, then count the four remaining counters. Using a pictorial model, children might place an X through the two cookies given away.

Pictorial models of subtraction are more difficult to use and at times can be confusing. A typical textbook picture to illustrate $3 - 1$ would show three objects, with one of the objects crossed out. Some children write $2 - 1$ because they see groups of two and one.

A better approach would be to show or have children draw a "before" and "after" picture as in Figure 7-9. The pictures show that there were three flowers, one is being "taken away," and the remaining set has two members.

When moving to a more abstract pictorial model, the set being taken away might be circled with an arrow, implying it is being removed. Children can easily learn to identify the original set and each subset in such diagrams.

FIGURE 7-8

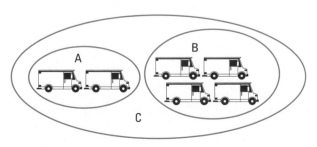

FIGURE 7-9

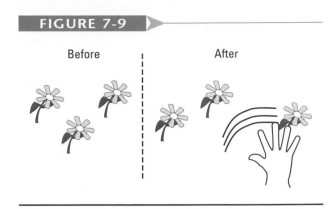

Before   After

Page (1994) has created a set of sequenced lessons intended to develop an understanding of subtraction as take-away. Integral to these lessons is a chart similar to the one in Figure 7-10 on which children record their subtraction stories.

Modeling Part-part-whole and Compare problems. Part-part-whole and Compare problems necessitate matching two sets through a one-to-one correspondence and noting the number of objects in one set that are

---

PRINCIPLES AND STANDARDS LINK 7-8
Content Strand: Number and Operations

An understanding of addition and subtraction can be generated when young students solve "joining" and take-away problems by directly modeling the situation or by using counting strategies, such as counting on or counting back (Carpenter & Moser 1984). Students develop further understandings of addition when they solve missing-addend problems that arise from stories or real situations. Further understandings of subtraction are conveyed by situations in which two collections need to be made equal or one collection needs to be made a desired size. (NCTM, 2000, p. 83)

FIGURE 7-10

SUBTRACTION RECORDING SHEET

	Start With	Take Away	Have Left
1			
2			
3			
4			
5			

FIGURE 7-11

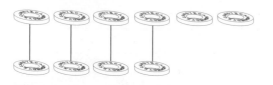

unmatched. The real-life setting for this approach to subtraction usually focuses on "how many more" or "how many fewer" there are in one group than another. Figure 7-11 is a pictorial model for the following problem:

> *Manuel had 6 candies and Keisha had 4 candies. How many more candies did Manuel have than Keisha?*

Concretely, children could set out sets of six and four candies or counters to represent candies, place one from one set beside or on top of another from the other set and note the number of unmatched candies.

The "how many more (fewer)" setting could be illustrated with the following problem:

> *Heather has 6¢. A sticker at the flea market costs 15¢. How much more money does Heather need to be able to buy the sticker?*

A child might verbalize "six and how much more makes fifteen?" This language is suggestive of addition,

but computationally the problem requires subtraction to solve. The 6¢ is removed from the 15¢ to find out how much money remains to be saved.

Using measurement models   Another way to model addition and subtraction problems is by using measurement models. In this approach lengths, rather than discrete, countable objects, are used to represent the quantities in the problem. Unifix cubes, Cuisenaire rods, and a number line are appropriate and effective ways to communicate different quantities.

Unifix cubes can be used individually, but because they interlock, they also can be used as "towers" or "trains" to indicate length. To represent addition, two towers can be constructed separately and then joined. Plastic "boats" or trays that come with the Unifix cubes hold lengths of 1 through 10 cubes. These trays can help children associate a number with a length. Figure 7-12 illustrates using measurement models to solve $3 + 6 = 9$.

Cuisenaire rods are color-coded. The unit rod is white, and each of the rods 2 through 10 is a different color. The red rod (2) and the light green rod (3) are joined in the illustration below. The combined length is five unit rods, which is equivalent to the yellow rod.

red light green

yellow

📖 **LITERATURE LINK 7-1**
Meaning of Multiplication

Friedman, Aileen. (1994). *The King's Commissioners.* New York: Scholastic.
Neuschwander, Cindy (1998). *Amanda Bean's Amazing Dream.* New York: Scholastic.

By using different representations of mathematics concepts, we provide children with many opportunities to develop intuitive, computational, and conceptual knowledge. Although children can solve mathematical exercises, they may have difficulty expressing their work using mathematical symbols. Many children's books provide a contextualized problem that children can translate into a symbolic equation.

- *The King's Commissioners* shows children several ways of skip counting (by twos, fives, and tens), a foundational skill for learning multiplication, division, and place value. Investigate and make a list of things that are counted by twos, fives, and tens. Practice skip counting by other numbers (such as threes or fours) using a hundreds board. Select a number between 50

and 100 and represent the number in groups of twos, fives, and tens just like the characters in the story.

- *Amanda Bean's Amazing Dream* encourages children's transition from counting to skip counting to multiplication as Amanda learns how important it can be to know her multiplication facts. Model arrays of the groups of objects in the story by using graph paper or concrete objects. Write multiplication sentences that will help Amanda solve the mathematical problems she encounters in the story.

- Use other books that count things in groups, such as *Reese's Pieces Count by Fives* (Palotta, 2000), which uses candy to count by fives to 100, and *M & M's Counting Book* (McGrath, 1994), which uses candy to count 1 to 12 and explores factors of 12.

Source: Dr. Patricia Moyer, George Mason University

FIGURE 7-12

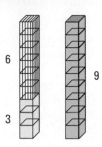

This represents the addition sentence 2 + 3 = 5. A measurement model such as this one is useful for representing a real-world problem.

Addition and subtraction also can be modeled on the number line, which is a semiconcrete device. Children can hop grasshoppers or kangaroos along the number line, making it more concrete. The addition sentence 2 + 7 = 9 is modeled as a hop of 2 followed by a hop of 7 along the number line. Similarly, Separate problems also can be solved using the number line model. For example, to solve the problem 6 − 2 − n, a child could begin at 6, take a hop backward of 2, and note the resulting position on the line.

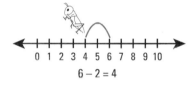

6 − 2 = 4

Teachers should note that the number line is a more difficult model for children to understand and should not be the first device used to model an operation. For example, children sometimes want to start at "1" instead of "0" and confuse spaces with points on the line. However, after children's experiences with other models, the number line should be introduced because it is handy and concise and a common model for representing integers and the

FIGURE 7-13

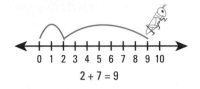

2 + 7 = 9

operations with integers (Chapter 17). Further, sometimes a more abstract model such as a number line may be used to assess children's ability to transfer from the concrete to a more symbolic representation.

Offer children frequent opportunities to translate a measurement model into a real-life problem. For example, given the model in Figure 7-13, a group of children might talk about some settings and decide on the following: To get to school Henry walks 2 blocks north and then 7 blocks west. How many blocks does Henry walk to school?

Writing Number Sentences for Addition and Subtraction

Once children have had many experiences modeling and talking about real-life problems, the teacher should encourage them to write mathematical symbols for problems. Figure 7-14 illustrates this three-step process. Activity 7-1 suggests that the process should also go in the opposite direction, that is, from symbolic expression to expression using a model.

Although it is important that children explore addition and subtraction word problems of each type, a teacher must be flexible in accepting the number sentence form in which children write a problem. Ask a child to explain why he or she wrote $a + n = b$ rather than $b − a = n$. Accept the child's explanation if it makes sense. Children's flexibility in selecting alternative number sentences to represent a problem seems to be related to the size of the numbers (Carey, 1991).

FIGURE 7-14

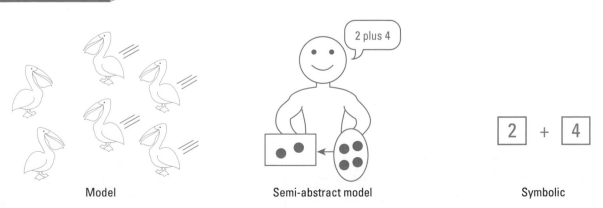

Model   Semi-abstract model   Symbolic

2 plus 4

2 + 4

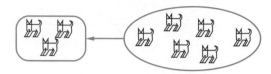

ACTIVITY 7-1

WRITING A PROBLEM

MATERIALS
The diagram below

PROCEDURE

1. In your group, discuss some problems that match the picture.

2. Decide on two problems. Write them in your notebook.

The Annenberg/CPB Math and Science Collection

VIDEO LINK 7-1
Concepts of Whole Number Operations

Brief Summary: In "Domino Math," teacher Alma Wright's first and second graders use dominoes to find various combinations of numbers equal to a given sum.

1. How did this lesson help develop children's understanding of addition?

2. How are dominoes different from flash cards? How are they similar?

3. What aspects of the lesson provide for children's individual differences?

4. What modes of representation did the teacher and children use?

5. What follow-up lessons might help the children extend their understandings?

Video Source. Teaching Math: A Video Library, K–4; Tape 4 from The Annenberg/CPB Math and Science Collection.

UNDERSTANDING MULTIPLICATION AND DIVISION

Multiplication and division problems are fundamentally different from addition and subtraction problems, owing to the different types of quantities represented in multiplication and division problems. For example, consider the differences between these problems:

Problem 1: Peter has 2 cookies. Tammy gave him 3 more cookies. How many cookies does Peter have now?

Problem 2: Peter has 2 bags with 3 cookies in each bag. How many cookies does Peter have?

How are these problems the same, and how are they different? Both problems contain the numbers 2 and 3 and are about cookies. In fact, the questions in each problem are almost identical ("How many cookies does Peter have (now)?"). But look more closely: What do the "2" and the "3" *mean* in each problem? In Problem 1, both numbers and the answer represent a number of cookies. But in Problem 2, each number means something different: The "3" represents the number of cookies in each bag, whereas the "2" stands for the number of bags, and the answer (6) represents the total number of cookies in both bags. This is an example of why multiplication and division are harder for children to understand than addition and subtraction problems: There are more factors for children to pay attention to when solving multiplication and division problems.

Another difference between multiplication and division as compared to addition and subtraction is the type of counting children are asked to do. In addition and subtraction, children use counting by ones to find the result. But in multiplication and division, children are counting by groups, sometimes called "skip counting," to find the result. This transition is significant and more difficult for children.

The following sections will describe ways teachers can help children understand multiplication and division. Multiplication will be discussed first, followed by division, and ending with a section describing relationships between the operations.

Types of Multiplication Word Problems

Researchers have identified several different types of multiplication and division problems (Greer, 1992). These include Equal groups, Area and Array, Multiplicative comparison, and Combination problems. The instruction that teachers give to children must help them connect the different ways of describing multiplication

---

PRINCIPLES AND STANDARDS LINK 7-9
Content Strand: Number and Operations

In grades 3-5, students should focus on the meanings of, and relationship between, multiplication and division. (NCTM, 2000, p. 150)

LITERATURE LINK 7-2
Meaning of Division

Hutchins, Pat. (1986). *The Doorbell Rang.* New York: Morrow.

A challenging mathematical investigation set in the context of an interesting story provides the perfect setting for using a children's book to investigate mathematics. *The Doorbell Rang* engages children in the common situation of fair sharing, which is a foundational concept for learning division. The story shows that real-world problems sometimes have multiple solutions and are not typically static, such as those problems children frequently see in their textbooks.

• Connect the story with mathematics by writing addition number sentences that show the number of people arriving at the house each time the doorbell rings. Write division number sentences that show the sharing of the cookies throughout the story.

• Manipulate counters to represent the cookies in the story and investigate various ways to group the 12 cookies. Explore ways to group other numbers of cookies, such as 16 cookies, 24 cookies, or 60 cookies.

• Partition a large piece of construction paper into eight sections and use it as storyboard. Show number sentences and pictorial representations of the mathematics in the book. This is an important exercise because children often have difficulty translating problems into number sentences and other representations.

• Make a reasonable estimate of the number of cookies on Grandma's tray at the end of the story. Write a number sentence and an illustration to show various ways to divide these cookies. Discuss what to do if the number of cookies does not divide evenly.

Source: Dr. Patricia Moyer, George Mason University.

and division to the interpretations and representations that make sense to them (Kouba & Franklin, 1993). Teachers should encourage children to explain relationships and situations in their own words and then help them link their own less formal language with the more formal mathematical language. The following sections will discuss each interpretation and describe ways to support children in developing understanding of these operations.

Examples of each problem type   The four types of multiplication problems (Equal groups, Area and Array, Multiplicative comparison, and Combination problems) are shown in Figure 7-15.

Equal groups problems involve making a certain number of equal-sized groups. The three numbers in the problem represent the number of groups, the size of the groups, and the total number of objects. Equal groups problems generally are the most familiar type of multiplication problems. In Equal groups problems, the multiplication sign can be interpreted as "groups of." For example, the problem 2×3 means "2 groups of 3" or "2 copies of 3" using the equal groups interpretation of multiplication.

Area and Array problems involve finding the area of a rectangular region or finding the total number of objects in a rectangular array (or arrangement). The area of a rectangle can be found by covering the region with unit

FIGURE 7-15

MULTIPLICATION PROBLEM TYPES

PROBLEM TYPE	EXAMPLE PROBLEM	RELATED NUMBER SENTENCE
Equal Groups	Maria has 2 bags of oranges. There are 3 oranges in each bag. How many oranges does Maria have altogether?	$2 \times 3 = 6$
Area and Array	Maria's parents have some orange trees planted behind their house. There are 2 rows of orange trees with 3 trees in each row. How many orange trees are planted behind Maria's house?	$2 \times 3 = 6$
Multiplicative Comparison	Maria has 3 oranges. Tony has 2 times as many oranges as Maria does. How many oranges does Tony have?	$2 \times 3 = 6$
Combination	How many different outfits can be made with 2 blouses and 3 pairs of slacks?	$2 \times 3 = 6$

squares and counting them or by multiplying the length by the width; both methods yield the area in square units. In contrast, arrays are rectangular arrangements of discrete, countable objects, such as desks arranged in rows in a classroom.

Multiplicative comparison problems involve comparing two quantities multiplicatively. In other words, these problems describe *how many times as much* one quantity is as compared to another quantity. These situations also can be thought of as *stretching* the original quantity by a certain factor.

Combination problems, also known as Cartesian products, involve different combinations that can be made from sets of objects, such as the number of outfits that can be made from two shirts and three pairs of pants. This type of problem is the most difficult type of multiplication and division problem to model.

The importance of language in understanding multiplication word problems.   Many of the difficulties children have with multiplication relate to the clarity and familiarity of the language used. For example, a child might understand "give each child four cookies" but not understand "give four cookies per child."

Initially, children could be encouraged to use "groups of" to indicate joining of a number of equal groups. They would use language such as, "I have three groups of five—that's fifteen." The meanings of other expressions such as "three fives," "three times five," and "three of these fives" should be developed before the symbolic expression "3 × 5 = 15" is expected to be used. Likewise, 3 × 5 should not be read as "3 multiplied by 5," because in this example, 3 is the multiplier and indicates the number of groups.

Be sure to pay particular attention to the meaning of each quantity. Notice that the multiplication problem 2 × 3 = 6 can be interpreted as "2 groups of 3 objects" or 3 + 3. This is different from 3 × 2 = 6, which means "3 groups of 2 objects" or 2 + 2 + 2 = 6. Even though the total number of objects is the same in both problems, the problems have different meanings. Until they understand the commutative property, verbalizing that 2 × 3 is the same as 3 × 2 will confuse many children. For young children, three groups of two objects is fundamentally different from two groups of three objects. Children think in concrete terms: Two children who each get three pieces of candy are luckier than three children who each get two pieces of candy (Anghileri & Johnson, 1992). The fact that the total amount of candy is the same may not be important to the child who is thinking about the lucky children who each got three pieces of candy!

Types of Division Word Problems

Each of the four types of multiplication problems may be expressed as a division problem. In addition, there are two different types of equal groups division problems. The following sections will discuss each interpretation and describe ways to support children in developing understanding of these operations.

Examples of each problem type   There are four types of division problems: Equal groups (Partitive and Measurement division), Area and Array, Multiplicative comparison, and Combination problems, which are shown in Figure 7-16.

Equal groups problems involve splitting a larger group into several smaller groups. The three numbers in the problem represent the number of groups, the size of the groups, and the total number of objects. There are two different types of Equal groups division problems: Partitive and Measurement division.

In *Partitive* division problems, the total number of objects is *partitioned* into a specified number of groups. In

---

FIGURE 7-16 ▷

DIVISION PROBLEM TYPES

PROBLEM TYPE	EXAMPLE PROBLEM	RELATED NUMBER SENTENCE
Equal groups: Partitive Division	Maria has 6 oranges. She put the oranges into 2 bags with the same number of oranges in each bag. How many oranges are in each bag?	6 ÷ 2 = 3
Equal Groups: Measurement Division	Maria has 6 oranges. She put 2 oranges into each bag. How many bags of oranges did she use?	6 ÷ 2 = 3
Area and Array	Maria's parents are going to plant 6 orange trees behind their house. They want to plant the trees in 2 equal rows. How many orange trees should they plant in each row?	6 ÷ 2 = 3
Multiplicative Comparison	Tony has 6 oranges, which is 2 times as many oranges as Maria has. How many oranges does Maria have?	6 ÷ 2 = 3
Combination	How many pairs of slacks are needed to make 6 different outfits by using 2 blouses?	6 ÷ 2 = 3

the Partitive division example in Figure 7-16, 6 oranges are split, or partitioned, into *2 equal groups.* Partitive division is also referred to as "fair sharing."

In contrast, in *Measurement* division problems, the total number of objects is *measured out* into groups of a certain size. In the Measurement division example in Figure 7-16, 6 oranges are split into *groups of 2 oranges.* Measurement division is also referred to as "repeated subtraction."

Here's another way to look at the distinction between these two types of division: When you know the number of groups (or *parts*) to make, the problem is known as a Partitive division problem. And when you know the size of the groups *to be measured out,* the problem is known as a Measurement division problem. These distinctions will help you remember the names.

Area and Array problems for division involve finding one of the dimensions of a rectangular region or of a rectangular array (or arrangement), when the total area or total number of objects in the arrangement is given.

The following interpretations of division appear much less often, but are included here for the sake of completeness.

Multiplicative comparison problems for division involve comparing two quantities multiplicatively. But in the case of division, the multiplicative relationship, in other words, *how many times as much* one quantity is as compared to another quantity is known, as is one the quantities being compared. The task is to find the second quantity being compared. These situations also can be thought of as *shrinking* the original quantity by a certain factor. See Figure 7-16 for an example problem.

Combination problems, also known as Cartesian products, involve different combinations that can be made from sets of objects, such as the number of outfits that can be made from 2 shirts and 3 pairs of pants. In the case of division combination problems, the total number of combinations is known, as is the number of one of the elements being combined. The task is to find the number of the second elements being combined. See Figure 7-16 for an example problem.

The importance of language in understanding division word problems.   As in multiplication, the clarity and familiarity of the language used in division problems is very important. Children experience division situations throughout their everyday lives—but they may not recognize that when they're sharing food with other family members, they're doing division. A challenge for teachers is to help children connect these understandings with more formal mathematical representations of these situations.

One way to help children make these connections is to use familiar language when first modeling division situations, and then build on these understandings when introducing more formal language. The terms "shared by" and "equal groups" make sense to children and should be used in early experiences. Similarly, the phrase "divided by" is more formal and its use should be delayed until children are successful at solving problems using less formal language. Then teachers can help children understand the connections between this informal and formal terminology.

LITERATURE LINK 7-3
Meaning of Division

Pinczes, Elinor. (1995). *One Hundred Hungry Ants.* New York: Houghton Mifflin.

Assertions that children's inability to solve word problems results from their inability to read or to compute effectively simply are not true. The difficulty is that children do not know how to choose the correct operation or sequence of operations to solve the problem. *One Hundred Hungry Ants* explores various ways of grouping 100 ants who are on their way to a picnic and provides an opportunity for children to connect a problem presented in words with appropriate calculations.

- Explore the factors of 100 presented in the book. Use 1-inch color tiles or other blocks to group the number 100 into various arrays. The length and the width of each array represent the factor of 100.
- Use 1-inch color tiles to explore other numbers of ants (for example, 60, 75, or 90) and create arrays to determine the factors of these numbers. If each child

uses a different number, these can be recorded on large pieces of chart paper for an analysis of patterns.

- Connect the rectangular arrays the ants formed in the story to division by writing the number sentences that represents the regroupings of the ants.
- Predict what might have happened if the littlest ant in the story had suggested that the ants form 3 lines, 6 lines, or 8 lines. Encourage children to use different presentations to explain their thinking.
- Ask children to select their own number of ants. Have each child use pictorial representations and number sentences on a large piece of paper to show various ways to divide their "imaginary ants."
- Challenge children to create their own stories in which the characters must use division to solve a real-life problem.

Source: Dr. Patricia Moyer, George Mason University.

Division with remainders. If children are solving division problems set in meaningful real-world settings, they will encounter some problems that don't have a whole number as the solution. For example, when sharing 5 cookies among 2 people, each person will get 2 cookies and there will be one left over. Teachers should take advantage of this opportunity for a rich discussion about what to do with the cookie that's left over. Frequently, even young children will suggest that they split the remaining cookie into smaller parts. In this problem, each person will get 2 cookies.

This type of problem is an excellent introduction to other types of division problems (those whose solution is not a whole number) and to a discussion about what to do with "leftovers" when dividing.

Such discussions about realistic problems can be extended to include situations in which it may be appropriate to continue to divide what's left into fractional parts, when the leftovers might just be set aside, and when it may be appropriate to make unequal groups (for example, when 9 children need to ride in 2 cars, it would not be appropriate to cut a child in half or to leave one home, but rather to put 4 children in one car and 5 in the other).

Avoiding misconceptions and dead-ends. There are two common misconceptions about multiplication and division: that "multiplication makes bigger" and "division makes smaller." For example, students will sometimes *incorrectly* generalize that when you multiply, the answer is *bigger than* the two factors, whereas when you divide, the answer is *smaller than* the starting amount (the dividend). These generalizations *are correct for whole number multiplication and division.* However, they are *incorrect* when considering multiplication and division of fractions and decimals. It's important for teachers to be aware of these misconceptions in order to address them and not to reinforce or accept them when they come up in class discussions.

In addition, there is an instructional "dead-end" that teachers should try to avoid: that division means only fair shares (or partitive division). Teachers make many instructional decisions. These decisions sometimes are even harder to make when faced with the large amount of content to be covered in what never seems to be enough class time. It is tempting for teachers to consider omitting some of the interpretations of operations discussed in this chapter. In particular, teachers will sometimes want to teach only one interpretation of division, partitive division, which often is the meaning of division that is most familiar to them. But teachers who do not help their students understand both meanings of equal-groups division (partitive and measurement division) are leading their students into an instructional dead-end. This dead-end may not show up until students are introduced to division of fractions, but students who see division only as fair

sharing will have more difficulty understanding division of fractions. Consider the following problems:

Problem 1: Peter has 6 cookies. He wants to give 2 cookies to each of his friends. How many friends will get cookies? (measurement division—whole number divisor)

Problem 2: Peter has 6 cookies. He wants to give $\frac{1}{2}$ of a cookie to each of his friends. How many friends will get cookies? (measurement division—fraction divisor)

Problem 3: Peter has 6 cookies. He wants to put the cookies into 2 bags with the same number of cookies in each bag. How many cookies will be in each bag? (partitive division—whole number divisor)

Problem 4: Peter has 6 cookies. He wants to put the cookies into $\frac{1}{2}$ of a bag with the same number of cookies in each bag. How many cookies will be in each bag? (partitive division—fraction divisor)

Problems 1 and 2 are both measurement division—and both are reasonable problems, as is Problem 3, which is partitive division. But what about Problem 4? It is a situation that is harder to visualize.

Problem 4 illustrates the "dead-end"—partitive division situations with fraction divisors are harder to understand; measurement division situations with fractions make more sense to most children. But what if a teacher has decided not to cover the measurement division interpretation with whole numbers? That teacher's students will be at a disadvantage when learning division of fractions. Division of fractions will be discussed in more detail in Chapter 11; it is mentioned here only to encourage teachers to make sure that students understand both partitive and measurement division in order to avoid a dead-end in future learning.

Using Models to Solve Multiplication and Division Problems

As in addition and subtraction, many different models can be used to illustrate relationships posed in multiplication and division problems. The following section describes some of these models.

PRINCIPLES AND STANDARDS LINK 7-10
Content Strand: Number and Operations

By creating and working with representations (such as diagrams or concrete objects) of multiplication and division situations, students can gain a sense of the relationships among the operations. (NCTM, 2000, p. 34)

FIGURE 7-17

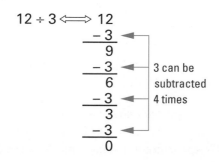

FIGURE 7-19

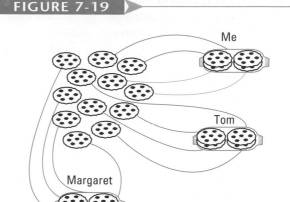

$12 \div 3 = \square$

Modeling equal groups and multiplicative comparison problems Equal groups problems, such as in the following example, can be modeled using a set model.

Maisha and Peter decided to sell cookies in packages of 3 at their school's bake sale. Mrs. Walsh bought 6 packages. How many cookies did Mrs. Walsh buy?

A set model is illustrated in Figure 7-17, in which six groups of three are assembled. Activities could include the children placing an equal number of cookies or counters on a specified number of plates or putting an equal number of marbles in bags. The mathematics sentence for the representation is $6 \times 3 = n$.

Similarly, Measurement division and Partitive division problems can be modeled using a set model. Generally, children are introduced to division using a subtractive, or measurement, setting. They are to find the number of groups. The repeated subtraction process for the following problem is symbolically represented in Figure 7-18.

Janice has 12 cookies. She wants to put 3 cookies into each bag. How many bags does she need?

In a partitioning setting, the total number and the number of equal groups are known. The child is to determine the number in each group. For example:

A father is making lunches for his 3 children. He wants to use 12 cookies and each child is to be served the same number of cookies. How many cookies will each child get?

Children can find the solution by acting out a sharing or "dealing out" process (Figure 7-19). At its most basic level, a child might say "one for me, one for Tom, one for Margaret, one for me, one for Tom, one for Margaret. . . ." Later, children will realize that they can share two or more at a time, thereby making the process more efficient.

FIGURE 7-18

$12 \div 3 \Longleftrightarrow$

$$
\begin{array}{r}
12 \\
-\ 3 \\
\hline
9 \\
-\ 3 \\
\hline
6 \\
-\ 3 \\
\hline
3 \\
-\ 3 \\
\hline
0
\end{array}
$$

3 can be subtracted 4 times

PRINCIPLES AND STANDARDS LINK 7-11
Content Strand: Number and Operations

In grades 3-5, students should focus on the meanings of, and relationship between, multiplication and division. It is important that students understand what each number in a multiplication or division expression represents. For example, in multiplication, unlike addition, the factors in the problem can refer to different units. If students are solving the problem 29×4 to find out how many legs there are on 29 cats, 29 is the number of cats (or number of groups), 4 is the number of legs on each cat (or number of items in each group), and 116 is the total number of legs on all the cats. Modeling multiplication problems with pictures, diagrams, or concrete materials helps students learn what the factors and their product represent in various contexts. (NCTM, 2000, p. 150)

Modeling area and array problems Area and Array problems can be modeled using a row-by-column representation. Consider the following problem:

Maisha and Peter decided to sell cookies in rows of 3 at their school's bake sale. They put 6 rows of 3 cookies each on one tray. How many cookies were on that tray?

The preceding problem would be represented by the array shown. By convention the rows represent the number of groups and the columns represent the number in each group. The array pictured here is a 6-by-3 array, or 6 rows of 3. Encouraging children to construct an array to represent a problem according to convention facilitates group work, class discussion, and assessment.

A teaching aid that helps children model Area and Array problems is the 10-by-10 multiplication array (Blackline Master 5, see Appendix). This array consists of 10 rows of circles with 10 circles in each row. Children use pieces of paper or index cards to frame the circles corresponding to the problem they are solving (and to cover the extra circles not needed for that problem). For example, for the bake sale problem above, with 6 rows of cookies and 3 cookies in each row, children would lay their index cards on the 10-by-10 array so that only a 6-by-3 array of circles was visible. They could then count the number of circles in the 6-by-3 array to find the answer to the problem. The multiplication array saves time by eliminating the need to actually arrange the counters into 6 rows of 3. Note, however, that the multiplication array should be introduced only *after* children are able to construct arrays of counters themselves.

Modeling combination problems Although Combination problems are the least used of the four approaches, they can be very helpful in building the concept of multiplication—particularly multiplication with zero. Consider the following example:

Lindsay has a choice of 6 flavors of ice cream and 3 different toppings. How many different kinds of ice cream sundaes could Lindsay have?

Some children have difficulty matching each topping to one flavor and then repeating that for each of the flavors. The use of a six-by-three chart (similar to an array)

facilitates understanding this approach (Kouba & Franklin, 1993).

Consider how the preceding problem about ice cream sundaes would change if there were *zero* flavors of ice cream and 3 toppings. In this situation, no sundaes could be made, illustrating that $0 \times 3 = 0$.

Other models for multiplication
A measurement interpretation. The number line can be used to represent a measurement approach to multiplication. On the number line, equal groups are represented by equal "hops" along the line. As shown, the bake sale problem would be represented by six hops or moves, each three units in length.

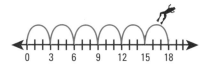

The "crossroads" or network model. A more abstract model is to have the children think of crossroads. The ice cream sundae problem could be represented with six roads (lines) running horizontally and three running vertically as shown. The points of intersection represent the product.

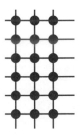

This representation of multiplication is effective in demonstrating multiplication with zero:

0×3 is represented with 0 horizontal lines and 3 vertical lines.

3×0 is represented with 3 horizontal lines and 0 vertical lines.

**The Annenberg/CPB
Math and Science Collection**

Classroom Clips:
Amazing Equations

Previewing the Video

One of the daily activities for teacher Flo Pearson's first and second graders is to gather at the classroom calendar and write "Amazing Equations." These are story problems that have answers equal to the day's date. On the morning of April 20, for example, children write problems that have an answer of 20.

At the beginning of the lesson, Ms. Pearson has the children sit together on the rug in front of an easel. She asks children to think of and share amazing equations that equal 20. As the children state their problems, Ms. Pearson records the problems modeling the appropriate use of mathematical symbols on a large sheet of blank paper clipped to the easel.

Matthew's Amazing Equation

Matthew:	"I was at the store and bought 17 pieces of candy. Two more pieces of candy that my uncle gave to me. I need one more and I got it from my big sister Katy."
Ms Pearson:	"Okay, so we put it all together."
Matthew:	"I got 20."
Ms. Pearson:	"What sign do we need for this one, Fanicia?"
Fanicia:	"A plus."
Ms. Pearson:	"Read math equations. Colanthia?"
Colanthia:	"17 pieces of candy plus 2 more equals plus 1 more equals 20."

$$\begin{array}{r} 17 \\ 2 \\ +\ 1 \\ \hline 20 \end{array}$$

Nate's Amazing Equation

Ms. Pearson:	"Does anyone have a subtraction problem?"
Nate:	"I had 21 dinosaurs chasing Ms. Pearson."
Ms. Pearson:	"Are you going to get me out of this one?"
Nate:	"Maybe, maybe not."
Ms. Pearson:	"Are they friendly?"
Nate:	"Sort of. But they want dinner."
Ms. Pearson:	"I think I have a problem on my hands!"
Nate:	"Then 1 went away to Charlie's house. And then I had 20 altogether."
Ms. Pearson:	"So you left me in quite a jam, didn't you? So what kind of problem do we have?"
Nate:	"A take-away."
Ms. Pearson:	"So we've got to put our take-away sign in here."

$$21 - 1 = 20$$

Process Standard: **Problem Solving**

This lesson is centered around children writing and solving story problems. By allowing the children to create and solve their own problems, encouraging the children's creativity and naturally inquisitive minds, Ms. Pearson helps them to explore the process of problem solving.

Notice Ms. Pearson's interaction with the children. **How does her lesson help children develop conceptual understanding of addition and subtraction? How does she help children build new mathematical knowledge through problem solving? What types of problems did the children write? (Be specific—use the terminology from the textbook, such as "separate result unknown" problem.)**

Focus on Standards

Children can learn to compute accurately and efficiently through regular experience with meaningful procedures. They benefit from instruction that blends procedural fluency and conceptual understanding. (NCTM, 2000, p. 87)

Process Standard: **Representation**

Ms. Pearson wraps up the whole-group part of the lesson by reviewing how to write the equations with symbols, and then asking, "Is there more than one way to get to 20? (Children: "Yes!") All right, let's see how many more ways we can find today."

Working in groups of 3, children write story problems with 20 as the answer. Some children use manipulatives to model the story as they write it. Ms. Pearson circulates around the room, asking questions and providing assistance as needed. Ms. Pearson encourages students to develop an oral story first and then write down what happened in that story.

> "No matter what the activity, whether it's math or whatever curriculum you're dealing with, I try to provide opportunities for children to speak through it, draw through it, feel through it, talk through it, whatever, so they have the opportunity to learn it in whatever way they need to learn it."
>
> — F. Pearson

At the end of the class time, Ms. Pearson reconvenes the class as a whole group on the rug to share their Amazing Equations. She asks one child from each group to read their story and another to read the corresponding equation.

Erin:	"10 candles on a cake for my little brother's birthday plus 10 more candles equals 20."
Vi:	"10 plus 10 more equals 20."

Colanthia:	"I am on the tot lot playing with my friends and we had fun. We is swinging and sliding."
Cam:	"19 plus 1 more is 20."

Matt:	"Me and Pat and Rommel and Ms. Pearson we each found 5 bikes and when we (I didn't get to finish the rest)."
Ms. Pearson:	"So we each had 5 bikes and how many did we end up with? (20). Did you write the equation?"
Matt:	"5 plus 5 plus 5 plus 5 equals 20."

Nate:	"We had 19 books and Chris gave us 1 at the library and then we had 20 books."
Shea:	"19 plus 1 equals 20."

Ms. Pearson encourages children to use different ways to represent problems. With this lesson her class is learning to translate oral representations to symbol representations of math problems. **What are some difficulties children in her class seem to have with different representations? How might a teacher help children overcome those difficulties?**

Focus on Standards

Watch as the children in Ms. Pearson's class work with different representations. How do they:

- create and use representations to organize, record, and communicate mathematical ideas?
- select, apply, and translate among mathematical representations to solve problems?

"I try to provide as many opportunities as possible to allow children to speak to one another. But I also recognize that children learn in many different ways. Where one child needs to verbalize it, the other child needs to put it in their hands—they need to touch it, they need to feel it."
— F. Pearson

Process Standard: **Communication**

Ms. Pearson encourages children to communicate mathematically by helping them to develop oral language related to mathematics and by fostering collaboration among the children. **What were you able to learn about children's understanding by watching and listening to them solve these problems? What lessons might the teacher do next with this class? Describe some follow-up activities to this lesson that also emphasize communication.**

"I work with Amazing Equations to develop oral language with the children, to lay in the language of math."
— F. Pearson

Focus on Standards

Watch the way Ms. Pearson guides the class through the lesson and notice how she helps the children to:

- communicate mathematical thinking coherently and clearly.
- use the language of mathematics to express mathematical ideas precisely.

"I have been modeling the writing of the equations. I will make a quick note on the board and use the equations on the board and I will be careful to lay in both directions of writing equations and saying the terms as I write them."
— F. Pearson

5 Butterflies met 2
Butterflies How many in all?
5 + 2 = 7

Riley

Proof of an understanding of whole number operations is Riley Wolfington's story for September 7th.

Process Standard:
Reasoning and Proof

To emphasize mathematical reasoning and proof with the children, Ms. Pearson frequently asks her students to describe their solution strategies. **How does she encourage children to extend their reasoning? To use different solution strategies?**

Focus on Standards

Notice the way Ms. Pearson introduces the concepts of reasoning and proof to her second graders by asking them to:

- make and investigate mathematical conjectures.

Process Standard:
Connections

Ms. Pearson helps her children connect mathematics to their lives and to interesting situations by encouraging them to write rich, creative problems and helping them to understand the connections between addition and subtraction problem situations.

Focus on Standards

How else could Ms. Pearson:

- help children to recognize and apply mathematics in contexts outside of mathematics or outside of the classroom environment?

How could this lesson be expanded to help children understand how mathematical ideas interconnect and build on one another to produce a coherent whole?

For other connection ideas, including lesson plans and games for helping children understand addition and subtraction, please visit Chapter 7 of our website at **www.prenhall.com/cathcart**

Try This!
What Does a Design Worth 20 Look Like?

Materials: Pattern blocks, paper, pencils, and crayons for each person.

Task: Use pattern blocks to make a design that is worth exactly 20 points. Use the following set of values for each block:

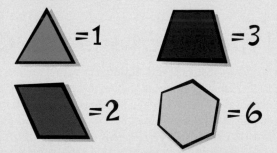

Write a number sentence showing the value of your design. Trace and color your design. Explain how you know your design is worth 20 points.

Follow-up questions:
- How many blocks did you use to create your design? Did anyone create a design worth 20 points with more blocks? With fewer blocks?

- Would you need more blue blocks or yellow blocks to make a design worth 20? Explain.

Clearly, there are no intersections, so the product is 0 in both cases.

How would you use the crossroads model to illustrate the sundaes problem if there were three kinds of toppings and no ice cream left? Use the model again to show the situation in which any number of ice cream flavors but no toppings are available.

Children should have the freedom to adapt these ideas or invent their own. The important consideration is that children build a sound understanding of the different situations that require multiplication as a solution process.

An instructional sequence for modeling multiplication and division Kouba and Franklin (1993) use the problem "If 8 plates hold 4 cookies each, how many cookies are on all the plates?" to illustrate a sequential development in understanding multiplication:

> *Level 1: A child sets out 8 plates, puts 4 cookies (or objects) on each plate, and counts the total number.*
>
> *Level 2: A child makes 8 groups of 4 without using separate objects for plates.*
>
> *Level 3: A child makes one group of 4 and recounts it 8 times, keeping track of how many groups have been counted by using fingers or another memory device.*

"More advanced levels of representation include counting by fours; counting on when they cannot recall the next multiple, for instance, 4, 8, . . . , 9, 10, 11, 12, and so on; adding fours; and using such derived facts as 'Four groups of 4 are 16 and 16 plus 16 is 32.'" (Kouba & Franklin, pp. 575–576)

ANOTHER WORD ABOUT NOTATION AND CHILDREN'S LANGUAGE

Children have a natural way of talking about the action involved in the operations. Capturing this natural language and using it in the classroom can help children in understanding whole number operations. Do not rush into using symbolic notation. Instead, make a slow, gradual transition from natural language to symbolic language.

Listen to the language children use as they talk about problems. They will use phrases such as "ran away" and "joined in" as they describe real-life actions. You also will hear language like "and 3 more," "start with 7 and cross out 4," "3 bags with 2 each," and "12 to be shared by 4." Encourage children to write statements about the problems they are doing and to write number sentences using words rather than mathematics symbols.

To capture this natural language, write key terms or phrases on cards such as those shown in Figure 7-20. The

FIGURE 7-20

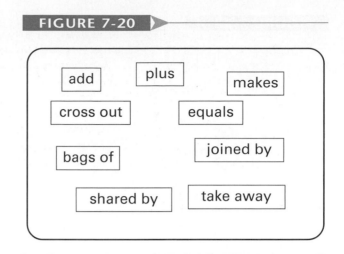

cards created for a specific class will vary with the language used by the children in the class. Also prepare numeral cards with the numbers encountered in the basic facts. Encourage the children to create sentences for problems and for concrete or pictorial models of the operations by using the cards as in Figure 7-21.

Using number and language cards in the classroom can help make the transition from horizontal to vertical notation more natural. Sentences such as those shown in Figure 7-21 can be arranged in vertical format. Initially, the sentences might be formed as a simple 90-degree rotation of the horizontal sentence (Figure 7-22). Later, the format can be altered to conform more closely to conventional notation. See Figure 7-23.

Over a period of time, introduce the conventional symbols for the different action words. Also introduce the "−" symbol for words such as "makes" and "leaves." Write these conventional symbols on cards as well and have children use them to generate sentences for problems and models in the same way they did with the natural language cards.

FIGURE 7-21

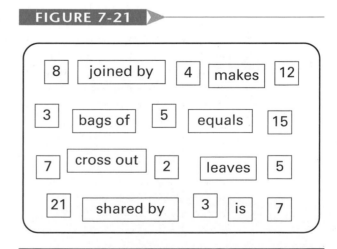

FIGURE 7-22

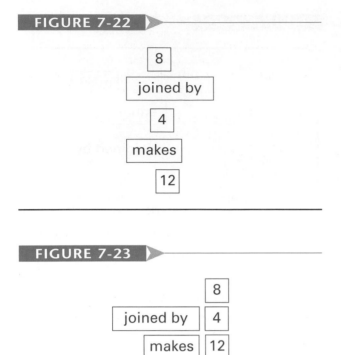

FIGURE 7-23

Children should understand that the "=" sign means "is the same number as" or "is another name for." Having children write several expressions equivalent to a given expression should facilitate this understanding. For example, give children 5 + 7 = [   ] and ask them to write at least three true expressions (not just one number) in the blank. They may respond with:

$$5 + 7 = 6 + 6 \qquad 5 + 7 = 10 + 2$$
$$5 + 7 = 24 \div 2 \qquad 5 + 7 = 15 - 3$$

Vertical notation could be developed in the same way as it was with the word cards. The arrangement in Figure 7-24 seems to be a natural first step in the transition. The fact that this form is not used in elementary school textbooks does not mean that a teacher could not use it effec-

FIGURE 7-24

9
6
=
3

tively as a transition. The reason the "=" symbol is not used in the vertical format is that this format suggests that a standard answer is wanted. The solid line separating the answer from the components of the operation is more appropriate for this more limited response expectation.

Notice that the notation for division is particularly confusing to children. There are three common symbolic representations for division: $6 \div 2$, $2\overline{)6}$, and 6/2 or $\frac{6}{2}$. The latter format usually is delayed until children are studying fractions. The first usually is read as "6 divided by 2" and the second as "2 goes into 6," although it should also be read as "6 divided by 2." The second representation is the most common, but also it is the only symbolic representation that should not be read from left to right, as "2 goes into 6." It is important to help children connect the phrase "6 divided by 2" to each of the symbolic forms above.

CONCLUSION

It is critical that children build a sound understanding of whole number operations. Therefore, children should be allowed time to manipulate and assimilate their ideas. Solving word problems of many different types is necessary for children to develop this "operation sense." To rush on to "more advanced" work is a mistake that often comes back to haunt children and teachers.

For Your Journal

When you have finished studying this chapter, reflect on the following questions in your math journal:

1. Imagine that you are a first-grade teacher. You want to begin instruction to help your students understand addition and subtraction. What will you do? What problems will you ask students to solve? What materials will you use? What teaching strategies will you employ?

2. Imagine that you are a classroom teacher. A colleague asks why you are spending so much instructional time having children solve word problems rather than drilling them on basic facts. How will you respond?

For Your Portfolio

When you have finished studying this chapter, complete the following activities to include in your professional portfolio:

1. Write a lesson plan to help introduce children to the Join type of addition problems.

2. Write a lesson plan to help introduce children to the Equal groups type of multiplication and division problems.

3. Write a lesson plan to help children understand division by 0.

Resources for Teachers

Children's books

Anno, M., & Anno, M. (1983). *Anno's mysterious multiplying jar.* New York: Philomel.

Giganti, P. (1992). *Each orange had eight slices: A counting book.* New York: Greenwillow Books.

Hutchins, P. (1986). *The doorbell rang.* New York: Greenwillow Books.

Mahy, M. (1987). *17 kings and 42 elephants.* New York: Dial Books for Young Readers.

Mathews, L. (1978). *Bunches and bunches of bunnies.* New York: Scholastic.

Neuschwander, C. (1998). *Amanda Bean's amazing dream.* New York: Scholastic.

Pinczes, E. (1993). *One hundred hungry ants.* Boston: Houghton Mifflin.

Pinczes, E. (1995). *A remainder of one.* New York: Houghton Mifflin.

Books on whole number operations

Brodie, J. (1995). *Constructing ideas about multiplication and division, Grades 3–6.* Mountain View, CA: Creative.

Burns, M. (1991). *Math by all means: Multiplication, Grade 3.* Sausalito, CA: Math Solutions.

Creative Publications. (1994). *The Maharajas' tasks: Investigating division.* Mountain View, CA: Creative.

Ohanian, S., & Burns, M. (1995). *Math by all means: Division, Grades 3–4.* Sausalito, CA: Math Solutions.

Richardson, K. (1999). *Developing number concepts, Book 2: Addition and subtraction.* White Plains, NY: Seymour.

Richardson, K. (1999). *Developing number concepts, Book 3: Place value, multiplication and division.* White Plains, NY: Seymour.

Ward, S. (1995). *Constructing ideas about number combinations.* Mountain View, CA: Creative.

Links to the Internet

ProTeacher: Addition and Subtraction

http://www.proteacher.com/100011.shtml

Contains links to lessons to help children understand and practice addition and subtraction.

ProTeacher: Multiplication and Division

http://www.proteacher.com/100012.shtml

Contains links to lessons to help children understand and practice multiplication and division.

Explorer: Whole Numbers

http://explorer.scrtec.org/explorer/explorer-db/browse/static/Mathematics/

Contains many lessons on whole number operations.

CHAPTER 8

Developing Whole-Number Operations: Mastering the Basic Facts

KEY CONCEPTS ▶

✔ **Basic facts**

✔ **Three-step approach to fact mastery**

✔ **Thinking strategies**

✔ **Fact families**

✔ **Consolidating activities**

FOCUS QUESTIONS ▶

When you have finished studying this chapter, you should be able to answer the following questions:

1. What are the three components of instruction on basic facts?

2. For each whole number operation, what are some thinking strategies that children can employ? Describe several thinking strategies for each operation.

3. What is the role of consolidating activities for drill and practice? Describe several of these activities.

4. How are games useful in promoting the immediate recall of basic facts?

NCTM CONTENT STANDARDS AND EXPECTATIONS ADDRESSED IN THIS CHAPTER

STANDARD	EXPECTATIONS FOR GRADES PRE-K–2	EXPECTATIONS FOR GRADES 3–5	EXPECTATIONS FOR GRADES 6–8
Number and Operations Standard Instructional programs from pre-K–12 should enable all students to—	In prekindergarten through Grade 2 all students should— (NCTM, 2000, p. 78)	In Grades 3–5 all students should—(NCTM, 2000, p. 148)	In Grades 6–8 all students should—(NCTM, 2000, p. 214)
Understand meanings of operations and how they relate to one another		• identify and use relationships between operations, such as division as the inverse of multiplication, to solve problems. • understand and use properties of operations, such as the distributivity of multiplication over addition.	• understand and use the inverse relationships of addition and subtraction, multiplication and division, and squaring and finding square roots to simplify computations and solve problems.
Compute fluently and make reasonable estimates	• develop fluency with basic number combinations for addition and subtraction.	• develop fluency with basic number combinations for multiplication and division and use these combinations to mentally compute related problems, such as 30 3 50.	

WHAT ARE BASIC FACTS?

The basic facts for addition and multiplication involve all combinations of single-digit addends and factors. For example, $7 + 9 = 16$ is an addition basic fact, because the two addends, 7 and 9, both are single-digit numbers. Because there are 10 digits, there are 100 combinations for both addition and multiplication.

The basic facts for subtraction are the inverses of the addition facts. Using the example from the previous paragraph, the addition problem $7 + 9 = 16$ may be transformed into two subtraction basic facts: $16 - 7 = 9$ and $16 - 9 = 7$. Consequently, there are 100 basic facts for subtraction.

Similarly, the basic facts for division are the inverses of the multiplication facts. For example, the multiplication fact $3 \times 8 = 24$ may be transformed into two division basic facts: $24 \div 3 = 8$ and $24 \div 8 = 3$. There are 90 basic facts for division because there are no facts with zero as a divisor. Thus, there are a total of 390 basic facts.

These are basic facts:	These are *not* basic facts:
$3 + 9 = 12$	$4 + 11 = 15$
$14 - 8 = 6$	$19 - 9 = 10$
$7 \times 4 = 28$	$5 - 10 = 50$
$6 \times 0 = 0$	$46 \div 9 = 5\,R1$
$48 \div 6 = 8$	$15 \div 0 =$ undefined
$0 \div 5 = 0$	$20 \div 10 = 2$

Can you determine why each of the number sentences in the second column above is *not* a basic fact? Recall that basic facts consist of addends or factors that are between 0 and 9, inclusive, and the corresponding subtraction and division facts.

In the process of developing number relationships and the meaning of the operations, some basic facts will have been learned already. In fact, many children come to school knowing a number of basic facts. For example,

many kindergartens can state that "one and one is two." But for children to learn all 390 basic facts, teachers must do more than have them endlessly repeat basic facts with the hope that children will memorize them.

The NCTM (2000) affirms the importance of children's developing proficiency with basic facts and algorithms but cautions against overemphasizing the memorization of facts before understanding is developed, or to the exclusion of other important topics.

In learning the basic facts, children focus less on real-life problems and more on the relationship between models and the symbolic representation of the facts. Children need many opportunities to discuss and to physically translate from model to symbol and vice versa before they can be expected to operate solely at the symbolic level. The approach described in the following section facilitates the learning of basic facts.

A THREE-STEP APPROACH TO FACT MASTERY

Many beginning teachers believe all they need to do is have children practice, practice, practice to automatically memorize the basic facts. Practice is important, but it is not effective if other understandings and skills are not already in place.

One very effective method for helping children learn basic facts is the three-step approach (Rathmell, 1978). The three-step approach includes understanding the meaning of the operations, using thinking strategies to retrieve facts, and using consolidating activities for drill and practice. This approach is the best way to help children recall the basic math facts.

Step 1: Understanding the Meaning of the Operations

As described in Chapter 7, children must understand the meaning of each operation. This understanding lays the foundation for further use of these operations and the development of operation sense. Children who understand the meaning of operations are then able to use thinking strategies to relate the facts they've already learned to new facts.

Step 2: Using Thinking Strategies to Retrieve Facts

Thinking strategies are mental strategies that can be used to relate known facts to unknown facts. For example, if children know that $2 + 2 = 4$, the "one more than" thinking strategy would help them determine that the sum of $2 + 3$ must be one more than the sum of $2 + 2$, or 5.

Thinking strategies help children find the answer to basic facts problems without using concrete materials by "providing structure for organizing facts so that recall is easier" (Rathmell, 1978, p. 18). Although many children will "invent" one or more of these thinking strategies on their own (Thornton, 1978), explicit teaching on the use and selection of thinking strategies is necessary. A variety of detailed thinking strategies for each operation follows.

Step 3: Consolidating Activities for Drill and Practice

Consolidating activities provide children with opportunities to practice facts they are learning so as to memorize them. Drill and practice are most effective after children have learned efficient thinking strategies for recalling those basic facts.

ADDITION AND SUBTRACTION FACTS

The 100 addition facts often are summarized in an addition table as shown in Figure 8-1. To find the sum of 4 and 6, locate the first addend, 4, in the left-hand column, and the other addend, 6, along the top row, or vice versa. The cell in the body of the table that represents the intersection of this row and column contains the sum, 10.

FIGURE 8-1

+	0	1	2	3	4	5	6	7	8	9
0	0	1	2	3	4	5	6	7	8	9
1	1	2	3	4	5	6	7	8	9	10
2	2	3	4	5	6	7	8	9	10	11
3	3	4	5	6	7	8	9	10	11	12
4	4	5	6	7	8	9	10	11	12	13
5	5	6	7	8	9	10	11	12	13	14
6	6	7	8	9	10	11	12	13	14	15
7	7	8	9	10	11	12	13	14	15	16
8	8	9	10	11	12	13	14	15	16	17
9	9	10	11	12	13	14	15	16	17	18

The 100 subtraction facts can be derived from the addition table as illustrated in Figure 8-1. Locate the minuend (10) opposite the subtrahend (4) in the left-hand column. Read the difference (6) in the top index row.

Obviously, the whole table is not given to children initially, because it contains facts they may not have had an opportunity to learn. Children normally develop the table during the first and second grades.

All of the joining, separating, and comparing activities described in Chapter 7 can be used to help children learn the basic facts. These activities should now be extended to include more symbolic representation of the facts. Using Cuisenaire rods, activities such as those in Activity 8-1 emphasize the model-symbol interaction. Interlocking Unifix cubes could be used equally as well for this activity.

Thinking Strategies for Addition and Subtraction

Rathmell (1978) described several important thinking strategies that children use when learning addition and subtraction basic facts: counting on, counting back, one more or one less than a known fact, and compensation. For children to use thinking strategies flexibly, they need many experiences using such strategies. Teachers should develop one of the strategies, then provide daily opportunities for children to use and verbalize the strategy for several days before introducing another strategy.

Counting on   The counting-on strategy involves starting with the larger addend, counting on the number of the second addend, and noting the ending result. With $2 + 5$, the child would start with 5 and count forward two times, saying "six, seven." Although counting on is a somewhat "natural" strategy for children, they need specific guidance in starting with the larger addend. Children have a tendency to start with 2 and count on 5

ACTIVITY 8-1

NUMBER SENTENCES FOR TRAINS

MATERIALS
Cuisenaire rods

PROCEDURE
1. Write number sentences for these trains. Write the sum.

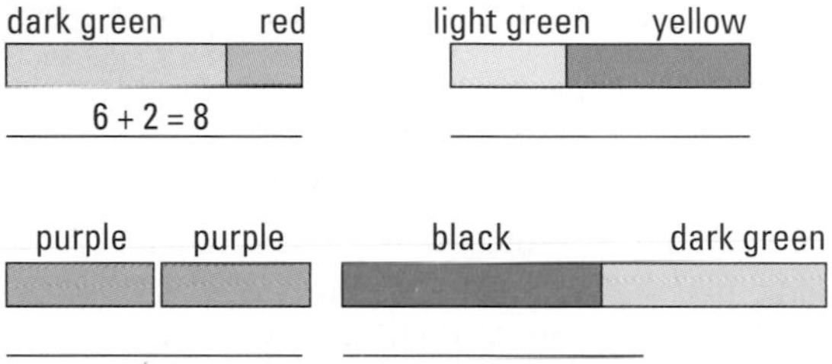

dark green	red
6 + 2 = 8	

light green	yellow
_____	

purple	purple
_____	

black	dark green
_____	

2. Make a train for each of the sentences below. Write the sum.

$$8 + 5 = \square \qquad 4 + 0 = \square$$
$$9 + 1 = \square \qquad 5 + 7 = \square$$

more numbers. This is much more difficult than starting with 5 and counting on 2. An understanding of the commutative property will help with this process. Counting on is most effective when one of the addends is relatively small.

Experiences with counting on could be set up with dice or cards as suggested by Activity 8-2. Cards with

PRINCIPLES AND STANDARDS LINK 8-4
Content Strand: Number and Operations

Teachers should also encourage students to share the strategies they develop in class discussions. Students can develop and refine strategies as they hear other students' descriptions of their thinking about number combinations. For example, a student might compute 8 + 7 by counting on from 8: ". . . , 9, 10, 11, 12, 13, 14, 15." But during a class discussion of solutions for this problem, she might hear another student's strategy, in which he uses knowledge about 10; namely, 8 and 2 make 10, and 5 more is 15. She may then be able to adapt and apply this strategy later when she computes 28 + 7 by saying, "28 and 2 make 30, and 5 more is 35." (NCTM, 2000, p. 84)

ACTIVITY 8-2

COUNTING ON

MATERIALS
Two dice for each pair of children

PROCEDURE
1. Work with a partner.
2. One person rolls two dice. Beginning with the larger number, count on by the number of dots on the other dice.
3. The other partner writes an addition sentence.
4. Change roles and play the game several more times.

larger dots (or another design) may be easier for some children to work with than regular dice.

Counting on in subtraction   Counting on also is a useful strategy in subtraction. It is best used in situations in which the difference is small. Children would begin with the subtrahend and count on to the minuend, noting the number added through counting. For example, to find the answer to 10 − 7, a child would start at 7 and count forward to 10, saying "eight, nine, ten." The answer is the total number of counts forward—in this example, three.

The number line and the calendar are helpful devices for counting on in subtraction. For example, a child might wonder on Thursday how many days it has been since Monday (9 − 6 on the calendar in Figure 8-2). Counting on from 6 would give the answer, 3.

Mrs. Weill's Hill (Weill, 1978) is an example of a counting-on strategy that is effective with children with learning disabilities (see Figure 8-3). It works with minuends greater than 10. For example, consider the problem 16 − 7. Have the children draw a curve (hill) and underneath place the minuend (16) near the top, the subtrahend (7) near the bottom and the number 10 between them. The children should determine how many steps (count on) from the subtrahend to 10, write that number above the hill as shown and then do the same using 10 and the minuend. Now add the two numbers above the curve to get the difference of 9.

FIGURE 8-2

Sun	Mon	Tue	Wed	Thur	Fri	Sat
			1	2	3	4
5	6	7	8	9	10	11

FIGURE 8-3

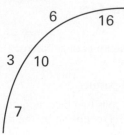

FIGURE 8-4

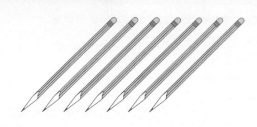

How many pencils?   (7)
I am going to subtract 2.
I count backward as I do it to find out how many are left.   (7, 6, 5)

Counting back   Counting back is a useful strategy for learning the subtraction facts. This involves counting backward from the minuend by the subtrahend amount. For example, to find the answer to $10 - 2$, a child would start at 10 and count backward two times, saying "nine, eight."

Counting backward is not as easy for children as counting forward. To use this strategy, children need to have experiences with counting backward outside of the context of subtraction. Counting backward on the hundreds chart, the calendar, orally, or by writing the numbers in order from some starting point, say, 18, would be helpful.

With this background, children can then apply the skill to subtraction. Show the children a set of objects and ask them to count backward to tell how many are left when, say, 2 are subtracted. Figure 8-4 presents a sample interaction. This strategy is useful when the subtrahend is small.

Another difficulty children encounter with the counting-back strategy is that they also have to count forward to keep track of the number of steps. This can become confusing. Baroody (1984) found that both the number line and a classroom clock are effective aids to help children count backward in subtraction.

One more or one less than a known fact
Recognizing an unknown fact to be one more or one less than a known fact is helpful, especially with the harder facts. For example, if children know a "doubles fact"

such as $4 + 4 = 8$, they can use this knowledge to find the sum of $5 + 4$, that is, they might think "4 plus 4 is 8, and 5 plus 4 is one more, which is 9."

Similarly, if children know that $4 + 4 = 8$, they can use this strategy to reason that $4 + 3$ must be one less than 8, or 7.

The one more or one less strategy can be demonstrated through activities such as the following:

Show two groups of 6 objects.

Ask, "How much is 6 plus 6?"

Add one more to one of the groups.

"Now there are 6 plus 7. How many altogether?"

If necessary, say "One more than 12."

Verify that there are 13 objects.

"6 + 6 is 12, so 6 + 7 is one more, or 13."

Compensation   The compensation strategy involves increasing one addend while decreasing the other by the same amount. This can be used for any combination but is especially useful where the sum is greater than 10. For example, $8 + 5$ has the same sum as $10 + 3$. Children can imagine taking 2 away from the 5 (which becomes 3) and giving it to the 8 (which becomes 10), so $8 + 5$ is the same as $10 + 3$, which is 13. These two changes compensate for each other.

The compensation strategy is most useful when it is used with 10, because it is very easy to add a number to 10. Most young children will be able to relate to this because of their experiences with numeration activities. They have already learned, for example, that 17 is one group of 10 and 7 and, conversely, a group of 10 and 7 is 17. In small groups, have the children work on exercises such as the one in Activity 8-3. Encourage the children to talk about the process (that is, what they do in this activity). Later, pencil-and-paper exercises such as the one shown in Activity 8-4 can help children focus on the compensation strategy.

PRINCIPLES AND STANDARDS LINK 8-5
Content Strand: Number and Operations

Teachers can help students increase their understanding and skill in single-digit addition and subtraction by providing tasks that (a) help them develop the relationships within subtraction and addition combinations and (b) elicit counting on for addition and counting up for subtraction and unknown-addend situations. (NCTM, 2000, p. 84)

ACTIVITY 8-3

COMPENSATION

MATERIALS
Counters

PROCEDURE
With your counters, show these groups:

Change it into a problem with 10. Draw your new groups.

8 and **4**

10 + □ = □

So: 8 + 4 = □

Another type of activity that helps children learn the basic facts involves making all possible combinations of a sum. Using chips with a different color on each side, children take a given number of chips (18 or fewer), shake them, spill them out, and record the two addends determined by the colors showing.

Using thinking strategies to organize instruction Instruction on mastering the basic facts often is organized around the size of the number combinations. Instruction frequently begins with facts with sums up to 5 (e.g., 1 + 2 = 3; 2 + 3 = 5). However, research has shown that the size of the numbers is not the only issue to be considered in planning instruction (Baroody, 1984; Moser, 1992).

Instruction that is organized around thinking strategies has been shown to be very effective in promoting mastery of basic facts. For example, doubles facts and their corresponding subtraction facts, such as 6 + 6 = 12 and 12 − 6 = 6, are the easiest to learn, as are the facts with 0 (e.g., 6 + 0 = 6 and 8 − 0 = 8) and the facts with 1 (e.g., 6 + 1 = 7 and 8 − 1 = 7). Combinations to make 10 (e.g., 3 + 7 = 10 and 10 − 3 = 7) and "one more than doubles" facts (e.g., 6 + 7 = 13 and 13 − 7 = 6) also are among the easier facts for children to learn.

Mathematical Properties of Addition and Subtraction

Understanding the commutative and associative properties of whole numbers and the zero property of addition contributes significantly to children's understanding of the operations and their ability to master the basic facts. The distributive property is discussed in the multiplication section of this chapter. An understanding of these properties usually is developed as children model problems. Memorizing the actual words or names of the properties is not critical; what is important is that children recognize the properties and are able to use them when working with the operations.

Commutative property Mathematically, the commutative property states that for all numbers a and b in the system of whole numbers, $a + b = b + a$ and $a \times b = b \times a$. The child might say, "I know that 7 and 8 is 15 so 8 plus 7 must be 15," or "Since 3 times 7 is 21, 7 times 3 must be 21," or more generally, "I can add or multiply the numbers in any order."

Understanding the commutative property reduces the cognitive stress involved in learning the basic facts. Some experts argue that applying the commutative property reduces the number of facts to be learned from 100 to 55 for each of addition and multiplication. This is true in theory, but a child who learns 3 + 4 still will model 4 + 3. It is only after working through a number of problems that the child will recognize that both sums are the same and will thus construct an understanding of the commutative property.

There are many activities for helping children build an understanding of the commutative property. One strategy that works well is to clip clothespins on a hanger and arrange the clothespins in two distinct sets (Figure 8-5). Ask the children to write the mathematics sentence (3 + 5 = 8) for the set. Now rotate the hanger 180° horizontally. Ask the children to write the sentence for the set (5 + 3 = 8). After several examples of this type, ask the children if they notice anything common in all the examples. Guide them to articulate the commutative property for addition of whole numbers.

ACTIVITY 8-4

WHICH IS EASIER?

PROCEDURE
Draw a ring around the easier problem in each pair.

10 + 5 = □   9 + 5 = □   9 + 8 = □

9 + 6 = □   10 + 4 = □   10 + 7 = □

FIGURE 8-5

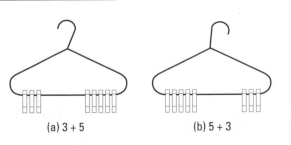

(a) 3 + 5   (b) 5 + 3

When learning a concept, children should also encounter nonexamples of the concept. Nonmathematical examples of commutativity and operations in which commutativity does not hold true should be discussed. Activity 8-5 suggests one approach to doing this.

Through activities, children should come to understand that the commutative property does not hold for either subtraction or division, that is, $6 - 2$ is not equal to $2 - 6$, nor is $24 \div 6$ equal to $6 \div 24$.

A clear understanding of where the commutative property can be applied may help reduce the tendency of some children to always subtract the smaller number from the larger and to make other common computational errors.

Associative property   Because both addition and multiplication are binary operations, only two numbers can be joined at a time. The associative property enables one to join more than two sets in sequence.

Mathematically, the associative property states that for all numbers *a, b,* and *c* in the system of whole numbers, $(a + b) + c = a + (b + c)$ and $(a \times b) \times c = a \times (b \times c)$. Children's language might include a statement such as, "When adding or multiplying three or more numbers, I can group them any way I like." Children may combine the commutative and associative properties and simply say, "It doesn't matter in what order I add or multiply numbers."

The associative property is useful in allowing the combination of "easy numbers" first. Figure 8-6 illustrates two ways in which this can be done. The "doubles" basic facts are easier for many children than some of the other facts. "Near doubles" can be changed into doubles with the use of the associative property as shown in Figure 8-6(a). In Figure 8-6(b), the associative property is used to combine pairs of numbers that are easy to work with.

Addition property of zero   The addition property of zero is also referred to as the identity element for addition. Mathematically, the addition property of zero

FIGURE 8-6

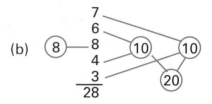

(a) $6 + 7 = 6 + (6 + 1)$
$= (6 + 6) + 1$
$= 12 + 1$
$= 13$

states that for any whole number *a, a* + 0 = *a*. Children might use less formal language, such as "Zero added to any number gives you the same number (or doesn't change the answer)".

An understanding of the addition property of zero helps children learn the 19 addition facts involving zero. When children are solving addition problems, sometimes they will encounter a set of zero elements joined to a set with a non-zero number of objects. These experiences will help them build an understanding of the addition property of zero. For example, consider the following problem:

> Juan had 0 cookies and his mother gave him 4 cookies. How many cookies did he have then?

This is a very simple situation that children can quickly solve. Teachers can use problems such as this to help children make the generalization that zero added to any number or any number added to zero results in that number. This is what the addition property of zero means.

Fact Families for Addition and Subtraction

The relationship between addition and subtraction allows the basic facts to be organized into "families." Except for the "doubles" (e.g., $4 + 4$), each family consists of four related facts as illustrated for 3, 5, and 8 in Figure 8-7. Organizing facts into families helps children learn them. More particularly, when they know the addition facts, children can more easily recall the related subtraction facts. The 10 family (or, in other words, sums that equal 10) is particularly important.

To help children learn fact families, construct a set of cards with a variety of pictorial models similar to the stars in Figure 8-7. Have the children form small groups, draw a card, then discuss and write the family of related facts. This activity could easily be converted into a game format.

ACTIVITY 8-5

COMMUTATIVE AND NONCOMMUTATIVE EXAMPLES

PROCEDURE

1. Discuss the truthfulness of these statements. Is the result the same?
   - Put on right shoe *followed by* left shoe = put on left shoe *followed by* right shoe
   - Put on socks *followed by* shoes = put on shoes *followed by* socks

2. Write other examples of commutativity and non-commutativity.

FIGURE 8-7

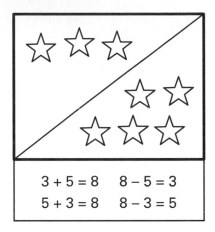

$$3 + 5 = 8 \qquad 8 - 5 = 3$$
$$5 + 3 = 8 \qquad 8 - 3 = 5$$

In programs incorporating the fact families organization, addition and subtraction are taught together. The addition facts for a family normally are learned first, followed by the subtraction facts. Children should work with addition facts from several families together, then focus on the corresponding subtraction facts.

MULTIPLICATION AND DIVISION FACTS

The multiplication facts can be summarized in a table format, as shown in Figure 8-8. For example, the basic fact $4 \times 6 = 24$ is found by first locating the two factors, 4 and 6. The product, 24, is found in the cell defined by the intersection of these two factors as shown by the arrows. The two related division facts, $24 \div 4 = 6$ and $24 \div 6 = 4$, also are shown in this figure, with the divisor and quotient (4 and 6) found on the outside of the table and the dividend (24) found in the cell that is the

FIGURE 8-8

X	0	1	2	3	4	5	6	7	8	9
0	0	0	0	0	0	0	0	0	0	0
1	0	1	2	3	4	5	6	7	8	9
2	0	2	4	6	8	10	12	14	16	18
3	0	3	6	9	12	15	18	21	24	27
4	0	4	8	12	16	20	24	28	32	36
5	0	5	10	15	20	25	30	35	40	45
6	0	6	12	18	24	30	36	42	48	54
7	0	7	14	21	28	35	42	49	56	63
8	0	8	16	24	32	40	48	56	64	72
9	0	9	18	27	36	45	54	63	72	81

intersection of those two numbers. As in addition and subtraction, this table illustrates the interrelationship between multiplication and division.

Figure 8-8 is a summary table and is not intended for children to use in its entirety—at least not until all the facts have been introduced. Children could be asked to complete such a table as they work on learning different facts.

Thinking Strategies for Multiplication and Division

Rathmell (1978) described several thinking strategies that children use when learning multiplication and division basic facts: repeated addition, skip counting, splitting the product into known parts, facts of five, and patterns.

Repeated addition   Using repeated addition, children might say three groups of five is "five plus five plus five." In this example, a child would "repeatedly add" 5 three times.

Skip counting   Skip counting involves counting by the second factor the number of times indicated by the first factor. For example, 3×5 could be found by skip counting in the following way: "5, 10, 15." This method builds on the meaning of multiplication, because counting by five three times corresponds with counting three groups of five. Children use counting by fives to generate the entire "fives" multiplication table.

Skip counting also can be done with a calculator. To skip count by five on most inexpensive nonscientific calculators, the child would enter the following keystrokes: $5 + - = \ldots$

Splitting the product into known parts This strategy actually includes two strategies: *one-more-set* and *twice-as-much as a known fact*.

One-more-set strategy.   The one-more-set (or group) strategy is very useful, especially for learning the facts in sequence. Each fact in turn can be used to help learn the next fact for either factor. Given the model in Figure 8-9, the child would verbalize along these lines: "I know that 5 threes is 15, and 1 more group of 3 is 18, so 6×3 must be 18."

To help children learn this strategy, show them 3 groups of 7 objects and ask them to tell (write) a number sentence for the display. Then show one more group of 7 and ask, "If 3 sevens is 21, what will one more group, or 4 sevens be?" This type of activity should take just a few minutes each day. It can be efficiently executed if the teacher prepares a series of folded cards similar to the one shown in Figure 8-10. Some of these cards also could be used for the next strategy (twice-as-much) as well, and a few may be used with the facts-of-five strategy.

FIGURE 8-9

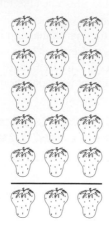

FIGURE 8-10

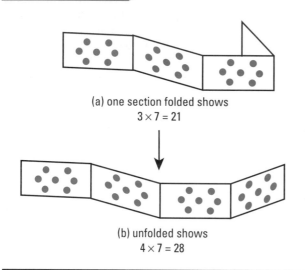

(a) one section folded shows
$3 \times 7 = 21$

(b) unfolded shows
$4 \times 7 = 28$

Twice-as-much strategy. When at least one of the factors is even, the product may be split into two equal parts. This is referred to as the twice-as-much strategy. The model in Figure 8-11 suggests a thought process such as "2 sixes is 12, 4 sixes is twice as much, that is, 24."

FIGURE 8-11

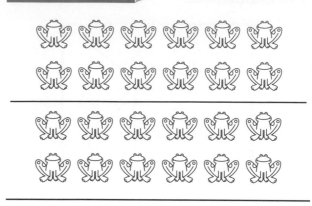

Show the children arrays that already are split in half and ask them to write (or orally state) a number sentence for each half and then for the total. Also give the children arrays of 4, 6, and 8, and ask them to split each array in half and write number sentences for each part and the total.

Facts-of-five   Another strategy, facts-of-five, is useful for the "larger" facts. One of the factors must be greater than 5, because this strategy involves breaking one of the factors into a group of 5 and another group. It is assumed that the children already know the facts with 5. Figure 8-12 illustrates this strategy with 7×6.

Using this strategy, a child would reason, "I know that 5 sixes is 30 and 2 sixes is 12, so 7 sixes must be $30 + 12$, or 42." This strategy is easier to use when the non-partitioned factor is 6 or 8, because 5×6 and 5×8 are multiples of 10, an easy addend. Otherwise, the first product

FIGURE 8-12

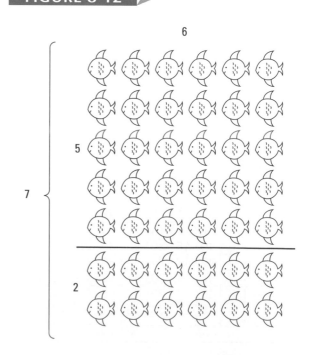

FIGURE 8-13

0	0	0	0	0	0	0	0	0	0
0	1	2	3	4	5	6	7	8	9
0	2	4	6	8	10	12	14	16	18
0	3	6	9	12	15	18	21	24	27
0	4	8	12	16	20	24	28	32	36
0	5	10	15	20	25	30	35	40	45
0	6	12	18	24	30	36	42	48	54
0	7	14	21	28	35	42	49	56	63
0	8	16	24	32	40	48	56	64	72
0	9	18	27	36	45	54	63	72	81

FIGURE 8-14

$$0 \times 9 = 0$$
$$1 \times 9 = 9$$
$$2 \times 9 = 18$$
$$3 \times 9 = 27$$
$$4 \times 9 = 36$$
$$5 \times 9 = 45$$
$$6 \times 9 = 54$$
$$7 \times 9 = 63$$
$$8 \times 9 = 72$$
$$9 \times 9 = 81$$

has a 5 in the ones position. If one of the factors is less than 6, the child would likely use another strategy.

Activities to teach the facts-of-five strategy could be similar to the ideas suggested for the twice-as-much strategy. This time, the children would break the array into a 5-by-n array and an x-by-n array, where x is the difference between the factor being partitioned and 5.

Pattern A pattern strategy can be used for many of the facts, but it is most helpful and most often used with the facts involving 9. Expecting children to see patterns is one situation in which the multiplication table could be used prior to the introduction of all the facts. On the multiplication table, children can shade all the multiples for each fact set. For example, by shading in all the multiples of 5, children will observe that all the multiples of 5 end in either a 0 or a 5.

To help children look for patterns, give them several copies of the multiplication table and ask them to shade in multiples for different factors. Multiples of 3 and 9 are shaded in Figure 8-13. Referring to one set of multiples, direct the children to describe a pattern. Then ask them to find and describe another pattern in the table.

Exploring patterns on the multiplication table for the factor 9 shown in Figure 8-14, children will make all or some of the following observations:

The sum of the digits for each product, other than zero, always is 9.
The tens digit increases sequentially from 1 to 8.
Where there is a tens digit, it is always one less than the non-nine factor.
Except for the zero fact, the units digits decrease by one from 9 to 1.

Another strategy for working with facts of 9 is illustrated in Activity 8-6.

ACTIVITY 8-6

FINGER MULTIPLICATION

PROCEDURE

1. Hold both hands in front of you with the palms facing away from you.

2. To show 2×9, begin counting at the left. Bend the second finger. The finger to the left represents the tens and the fingers to the right of the bent finger represent the ones.

3. Use the finger method to show other multiplication facts of 9.

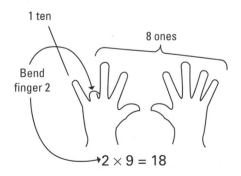

Mathematical Properties of Multiplication

An understanding of mathematical properties contributes to operation sense. In the addition and subtraction section of this chapter, the commutative and associative properties and the identity element for both addition and multiplication were defined and illustrated for addition. This section illustrates these concepts for multiplication and discusses the multiplication property of one and the distributive property of multiplication over addition.

Commutative property   The commutative property of multiplication can be exemplified by gluing or drawing an array of objects on a card. See Figure 8-15(a). Ask the children to write the mathematics sentence for the array ($4 \times 6 = 24$). Now rotate the card 90° as shown in Figure 8-15(b). Have the children write a sentence for the new arrangement ($6 \times 4 = 24$). Repeat the procedure with several other cards. Ask the children to talk about the different situations, discussing how they are different and what is common to each. Rotating an array on a pegboard or a rectangular region marked off on a geoboard would provide additional illustrations of the same concept.

Associative property   Children will find the associative property useful in situations that give rise to fairly large computations such as $26 \times 5 \times 2$. They will recognize that if they combine 5 and 2 first, the problem becomes very easy compared with trying to do 26×5 first.

A three-dimensional model may help children visualize the associative property. Consider the following, for example: $3 \times 2 \times 4 = n$. Ask the children, "Will it make a difference if we multiply 3×2 first or 2×4 first?"

FIGURE 8-15

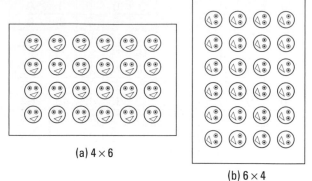

(a) 4×6

(b) 6×4

Beginning first with 3×2, have the children use interlocking cubes to build a 3-by-2 array, which shows 3×2, and then build 3 more arrays to show 4 times (3×2) (using the commutative property). Have the children count the total number of cubes used. The product is 24 [see Figure 8-16(a)].

Next, have the children construct a 2×4 array and then 2 more to show 3 times (2×4). The product still is 24 [see Figure 8-16(b)]. Ask the children to compare the final models.

Distributive property of multiplication over addition   Mathematically, the distributive law for multiplication states that for any a, b, and c in the system of whole numbers, $a \times (b + c) = (a \times b) + (a \times c)$ or $a(b + c) = ab + ac$. Also, $(a + b) \times c = (a \times c) + (b \times c)$ or $(a + b)c = ac + bc$. Children will use language such as "6 times 3 plus 2 is the same as 6 times 3 plus 6 times 2." Alternatively, they might say, "3 plus 2 times 6 is the same as 3 times 6 plus 2 times 6."

FIGURE 8-16

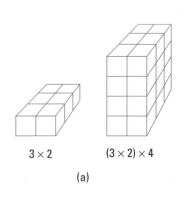

3×2 $(3 \times 2) \times 4$

(a)

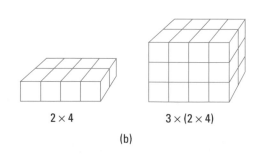

2×4 $3 \times (2 \times 4)$

(b)

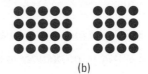

ACTIVITY 8-7

DISTRIBUTIVE PROPERTY FROM ARRAYS

MATERIALS
Counters

PROCEDURES
1. Write a mathematics sentence for this array.

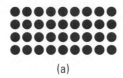

(a)

2. Write two mathematics sentences, one for each array.

(b)

3. What do you notice about the sentence for array (a) and the two sentences for (b)?

4. Use counters and set out of 4-by-9 array. How many different ways can you separate it into two parts?

5. For each way, complete a sentence, such as $4 \times 9 = (4 \times \underline{\ }) + (4 \times \underline{\ })$.

Using the distributive property makes learning some of the more difficult basic facts easier. Consider the following, for example: 8×7 can be thought of as $8 \times (5 + 2)$. Note that 8×5 and 8×2 are easier facts. The products, 40 and 16, can now be added to obtain the product.

In another example, 6×9 can be thought of as $(5 + 1) \times 9$. Note that 5×9 and 1×9 are easier facts. The products, 45 and 9, can be added to obtain the product.

An array of counters is used in Activity 8-7 to help children construct a meaningful understanding of the distributive property. Note also the problem-solving component. Later, children can use this strategy to model the multiplication of a teen number. If the example was 4×13, children would discover among other groupings that $4 \times 13 = (4 \times 10) + (4 \times 3)$. In Chapter 7 this idea is incorporated into the vertical multiplication algorithm.

The multiplication property of one   The multiplication property of one, also known as the identity element for multiplication, refers to the fact that multiplying by one does not change a number. Mathematically, the multiplication property of one states that for any whole number a, $a \times 1 = a$. Children might use less formal language such as "any number multiplied by one gives you the same number."

The multiplication property of one helps children learn the 19 multiplication facts that have 1 as one of the factors. Children can model problems that have 1 as one of the factors by making one set of the given size, or making one jump of the given length along a number line, or forming an array with one row or one column. Such modeling helps children understand the multiplication property of one.

The role of zero in multiplication   For any a in the system of whole numbers, $0 \times a = 0$, or $a \times 0 = 0$. Children will likely say "any number multiplied by zero is zero" and "zero multiplied by any number is zero." This is because zero groups of any number of objects is zero, as is any number of groups of zero objects.

In Chapter 7 the crossroads model was suggested as a good model to help children think about $0 \times n$ and $n \times 0$. It is easy for children to see that there are zero intersections when there are zero roads in one direction. Other models for multiplication can be used, but some element of deduction has to be included. For example, the array cannot be used to picture multiplication with zero, but children could be asked to find the pattern in the following examples and then deduce that $0 \times 3 = 0$.

4 rows of 3 is 12
3 rows of 3 is 9
2 rows of 3 is 6
1 row of 3 is 3
0 rows of 3 is 0

Real-life experiences involving multiplication by zero may seem a bit contrived; for example, "Walter put zero marbles in each of four bags. How many marbles did he use?" Ask the children to make up some of their own examples. Word problems involving multiplication of zero may seem a bit funny to children, but they will help children understand that zero sets of anything or any number of zero sets still is nothing.

A note on division by zero   Division by zero is one of the more confusing issues in mathematics for many adults. Making sense of this concept depends on linking it to concepts that learners already understand. Children can generalize the fact that division by zero is undefined through observing patterns and relationships such as the following:

$3 \div 0 = n$ $3 = 0 \times n$ *(no number makes this true)*

$2 \div 0 = n$ $2 = 0 \times n$ *(no number makes this true)*

$0 \div 0 = n$ $0 = 0 \times n$ *(any number makes this true)*

$6 \div 2 = n$ $6 - 2 - 2 - 2 = 0$ *(remove 3 twos to get 0)*

$6 \div 0 = n$ $6 - 0 - 0 - 0 \ldots$ *(never get to 0 by subtracting zeros)*

These generalizations may be visualized through some semi-contrived problems such as this measurement situation (Watson, 1991):

> The ball park is 10 blocks from your home. If you walked 2 blocks each minute, how many minutes would it take to get to the park? If you walked one block per minute, how long would it take? If you walked zero blocks each minute, how long would it take?

Fact Families for Multiplication and Division

As with addition and subtraction, the multiplication and division facts can be organized into number sentence families. Such organization facilitates learning of the facts. With the exceptions noted below, families have four members. The crossroads diagram (Figure 8-17) can be used to derive the four facts listed below the diagram.

For the "square" facts, there are only two members in the family. The family of facts relating 4, 4, and 16 consists of $4 \times 4 = 16$ and $16 \div 4 = 4$. When one of the factors is 0, there are only 3 members in the family. For

FIGURE 8-17 ▶

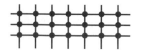

- $3 \times 7 = 21$
- $7 \times 3 = 21$
- $21 \div 7 = 3$
- $21 \div 3 = 7$

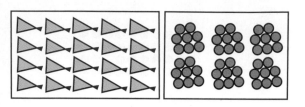

ACTIVITY 8-8

FACT FAMILIES

PROCEDURE

1. For each picture below, write all the multiplication and division sentences that you can.

2. For each sentence, write 7 mroe related sentences (use the same numbers).

$$3 \times 6 = 18 \qquad 35 = 5 \times 7$$

3. Draw a picture to show each family in part 2.

example, for 0, 3, 0, the family comprises $0 \times 3 = 0$, $3 \times 0 = 0$, and $0 \div 3 = 0$.

When a number sentence contains an unknown to be solved for, there are actually 24 forms the sentence could take for any fact family. This applies to the addition and subtraction families as well. For 3, 7, and 21, some forms include the following:

$3 \times 7 = n$	$7 \times 3 = n$
$21 \div 3 = n$	$21 \div 7 = n$
$n \times 7 = 21$	$n \times 3 = 21$
$21 \div n = 7$	$21 \div n = 3$
$21 = 3 \times n$	$21 = 7 \times n$
$7 = n \div 3$	$3 = n \div 7$

The remaining 12 forms are left for the reader to complete. Discussing bidirectional relationships of an equality sentence (sentences in lines 5 and 6 compared with lines 1, 2, 3, and 4 above) will help children build a better understanding of mathematics sentences, number relationships, and the operations.

Children need time and experiences to make the concept of fact families a part of their thinking. Activities similar to Activity 8-8 may facilitate the process. For the first part of the activity, the teacher may elect to construct arrays or groups on the overhead projector and have the children write sentences on paper.

CONSOLIDATING ACTIVITIES FOR DRILL AND PRACTICE

During the process of developing meanings for the operations and learning basic facts, take time periodically to provide consolidation activities. These are intended primarily to improve speed and accuracy, but they also can sharpen understanding and provide another means of assessment for the teacher.

Effective consolidating activities have the following features:

- Activities are short and interesting.
- Activities are organized around sets of facts based on thinking strategies and fact families.
- Activities are self-checking.
- Activities include an approximately equal mix of facts children have and have not yet mastered.
- Children should understand the goals toward which they are working and understand their progress toward those goals. Children should have individual charts showing their goals and progress. There *should not* be a class chart showing individual children's progress or lack thereof. Such charts cause great anxiety to many children, which *reduces*, rather than enhances, their progress.

Effective consolidation of concepts and facts can occur through a variety of brief activities at the beginning of class. Some examples include the following:

Write a set of single-digit numbers on the chalkboard in random order. Beside them write a rule such as "add 4."

    ADD 4: 3   6   4   9   2   7

Ask specific children to use the rule on each number. Listen for cases in which a child hesitates.

TECHNOLOGY LINK 8-1
A+ Math

This website is primarily a resource for children. It includes lots of fun games, such as Matho, Concentration, and Hidden Picture, and puzzles to help children learn basic math facts. It also contains a section on electronic flash cards, including a flash card creator.

Visit http://www.aplusmath.com/ or link from our Companion Website at **www.prenhall.com/ cathcart.**

Prepare a set of cards with a single-digit number on each. Say, "Let's think about the number 15." Show a card and have children tell the other part of 15. For example, if you showed the card with 6 on it, children should respond with 9.

Display an expression such as 7 + 8 on the overhead projector. Have the children give you the sum and then tell how they know. For example, a child might respond, "15, because I know 7 + 7 is 14, so 7 + 8 is one more." [This type of exercise enables the children (and the teacher) to focus on strategies, reasoning, and patterns (Feinberg, 1990) rather than only on the answer.]

In Chapter 2, several categories of activities were suggested for consolidating or practice activities. Sample activities from some of the categories are described below to illustrate that these activities do not have to be boring or routine.

Games

Games are a motivational and fun way for children to both develop and maintain mastery of basic facts. To play a bingo-type game, children could be given a copy of the template from Figure 8-18 and asked to randomly fill in the cells with numbers. For addition and subtraction facts, they should use only the numbers 0 through 18. Five of these numbers can be repeated to complete the 24 cells. The teacher or a child calls out basic addition and subtraction facts that can be generated from flash cards or randomly by a computer. Otherwise, the game is played similarly to bingo.

FIGURE 8-18

		I CAN		

The Annenberg/CPB Math and Science Collection

VIDEO LINK 8-1
Concepts of Whole Number Operations

Brief Summary: In "Domino Math," teacher Alma Wright's first and second graders use dominoes to find various combinations of numbers equal to a given sum.

1. How could this lesson be modified to provide practice with basic facts?
2. What properties and thinking strategies did the children in this video use?

Video Source. Teaching Math: A Video Library, K–4; Tape 4 from The Annenberg/CPB Math and Science Collection.

The same strategy works for multiplication, except that the numbers on the cards should be randomly chosen from the set of possible products. There are 37 acceptable numbers to choose from. This time there need be no repeats.

Another popular game for practicing basic facts is the *24 Game* (Suntex International). The object of the game is to make 24 using all four numbers on a card by adding, subtracting, multiplying, or dividing. For example, one card contains the numbers 1, 5, 7, and 8. One possible solution for this card is the following number sentence: $(8 - 5) \times (1 + 7) = 24$. Several versions of the game are available as well that include addition and subtraction only, factors and multiples, fractions, and exponents.

Puzzles and Riddles

The sample riddle from Chapter 2—What fish do you see at night?—can be made into a practice exercise. Because the teacher knows the answer—starfish—the teacher can assign numerical values to each of the letters in the answer, then make up a question that has that answer. Figure 8-19 is a sample riddle sheet that could be given to children for consolidating division facts. Note that a few extra questions are inserted so that children will be less likely to try to simply rearrange the letters into a sensible word. Some children might prefer to create their own riddle practice activities.

Novel Formats

Using formats different from what children have seen is another way to provide interesting consolidation. Create an array of numbers. Figure 8-20 is one example. Ask the children to circle as many pairs as they can of adjacent numbers—which have a specified difference—in a column, row, or diagonal. Two differences of four, for example, have been circled in Figure 8-20.

Computer Software

Computer software needs to be carefully evaluated by the teacher to be sure it provides the kind of practice children need and that it does so in a pedagogically sound way. *Math Blaster* (Davidson and Associates) is a popular, fast-moving, arcade type of game that provides practice with the basic facts for all four operations. The teacher can control the level of difficulty and the teacher or children can generate their own problem sets. The objective is to launch a rocket corresponding to the correct answer to a problem that appears at the top of the screen. The game can be played at five speeds to encourage both accuracy and quick recall.

Millie's Math House (Edmark) has some interesting activities at the conceptual level that younger children would enjoy. Likewise, *KidsMath* (Great Wave Software) and *Treasure MathStorm* (The Learning Company) could be used with older children. Parts of these programs provide practice with basic facts in a game setting. Many other programs also contain good practice activities. See "Links to the Internet" at the end of this chapter for URLs of these programs and others.

FIGURE 8-19 ▶

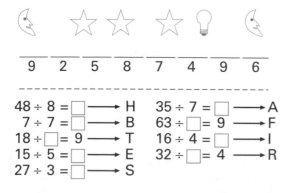

WHAT FISH DO YOU SEE AT NIGHT?

9 2 5 8 7 4 9 6

48 ÷ 8 = ☐ ⟶ H   35 ÷ 7 = ☐ ⟶ A
7 ÷ 7 = ☐ ⟶ B   63 ÷ ☐ = 9 ⟶ F
18 ÷ ☐ = 9 ⟶ T   16 ÷ 4 = ☐ ⟶ I
15 ÷ 5 = ☐ ⟶ E   32 ÷ ☐ = 4 ⟶ R
27 ÷ 3 = ☐ ⟶ S

FIGURE 8-20 ▶

12	15	11	16
8	4	3	7
9	7	13	10
3	5	9	6

CONCLUSION

This chapter described a three-step approach to mastery of basic facts. This approach includes understanding the meaning of the operations, using thinking strategies to retrieve facts, and using consolidating activities for drill and practice. It is critical that children memorize the basic facts but this memorization must be based on an understanding of the operations and thinking strategies. Rushing memorization before this understanding is developed is a mistake that often comes back to haunt children and teachers.

For Your Journal

When you have finished studying this chapter, reflect on the following questions in your math journal:

1. Imagine that you are a fifth-grade teacher. You discover at the beginning of the school year that many of the children have not mastered the basic facts. What will you do? What materials will you use? What teaching strategies will you employ?

2. Imagine you are a classroom teacher. The parents of one of the children in your class are concerned about your use of class time to teach thinking strategies and would prefer their child to have much more practice with flash cards. How will you respond?

For Your Portfolio

When you have finished studying this chapter, complete the following activities to include in your professional portfolio:

1. Design a nonbingo type of game that could be used to practice some of the basic facts.

2. Using (a) manipulative activities, (b) calculator explorations, or (c) both, write a lesson plan to help children understand the concept that division by zero is undefined.

3. Write a lesson plan to help children master one thinking strategy.

Resources for Teachers

Books on basic facts

Barson, A. (1992). *Mathematics games for fun and practice.* Menlo Park, CA: Addison-Wesley.

Childs, L., & Choate, L. (1998). *Nimble with numbers: Grades 3 and 4.* White Plains, NY: Seymour.

Childs, L., & Choate, L. (1998). *Nimble with numbers: Grades 4 and 5.* White Plains, NY: Seymour.

Childs, L., & Choate, L. (1999). *Nimble with numbers: Grades 5 and 6.* White Plains, NY: Seymour.

Childs, L., Choate, L., & Jenkins, K. (1999). *Nimble with numbers: Grades 1 and 2.* White Plains, NY: Seymour.

Childs, L., Choate, L., & Wickett, M. (1998). *Nimble with numbers: Grades 2 and 3.* White Plains, NY: Seymour.

Childs, L., Hill, P., & Choate, L. (1999). *Nimble with numbers: Grades 6 and 7.* White Plains, NY: Seymour.

Links to the Internet

A+ Math

http://www.aplusmath.com/

Contains many different practice activities for operations, including games and electronic flash cards.

FunBrain

http://www.funbrain.com/kidscenter.html

Contains several games to practice operations.

Math Blaster

http://www.knowledgeadventure.com/blaster/

Math software to practice basic facts.

CHAPTER 9

Estimation and Computational Procedures for Whole Numbers

FOCUS QUESTIONS ▶

When you have finished studying this chapter, you should be able to answer the following questions:

1. How is mental computation different from computational estimation? Give an example of each.

2. How do algorithms differ for different operations? Give an example of two algorithms for each operation.

3. Why is it important to link mental computation and computational estimation with paper-and-pencil computation and the use of calculators?

What is *computation?* A common but somewhat narrow view of computation is that it is a sequence of steps for producing an answer in standard form. These step-by-step procedures are commonly referred to as *algorithms.* This chapter will develop the standard algorithms, but first, three points need to be emphasized. ✔

NCTM CONTENT STANDARDS AND EXPECTATIONS ADDRESSED IN THIS CHAPTER

STANDARD	EXPECTATIONS FOR GRADES PRE-K–2	EXPECTATIONS FOR GRADES 3–5
Number and Operations Standard Instructional programs from pre-K–12 should enable all students to—	In prekindergarten through Grade 2 all students should—(NCTM, 2000, p. 78)	In Grades 3–5 all students should—(NCTM, 2000, p. 148)
Compute fluently and make reasonable estimates	• develop and use strategies for whole-number computations, with a focus on addition and subtraction. • use a variety of methods and tools to compute, including objects, mental computation, estimation, paper and pencil, and calculators.	• develop fluency with basic number combinations for multiplication and division and use these combinations to mentally compute related problems, such as 30×50. • develop fluency in adding, subtracting, multiplying, and dividing whole numbers. • develop and use strategies to estimate the results of whole-number computations and to judge the reasonableness of such results. • select appropriate methods and tools for computing with whole numbers from among mental computation, estimation, calculators, and paper and pencil according to the context and nature of the computation and use the selected method or tools.

PRINCIPLES AND STANDARDS LINK 9-1
Content Strand: Number and Operations

Instructional programs from prekindergarten through grade 12 should enable all students to—

- understand numbers, ways of representing numbers, relationships among numbers, and number systems;
- understand meanings of operations and how they relate to one another;
- compute fluently and make reasonable estimates. (NCTM, 2000, p. 32)

First, computation is much broader than using just the standard paper-and-pencil algorithms. It also includes estimation, mental computation, and the use of a calculator. Many times all that is needed is an estimate. Strategies for estimating an answer to a computational problem can be quite different from the standard paper-and-pencil procedures. Sometimes an exact answer may be more efficiently calculated using mental procedures than by using either a calculator or paper and pencil. Estimation and mental computation often make better use of good number sense and place-value concepts that are explicitly employed when using a paper-and-pencil algorithm.

The second point for emphasis is that children can and should be allowed to create and use their own algorithms. The following shows a child's procedure for subtracting (Cochran, Barson, & Davis, 1970):

$$
\begin{array}{r}
64 \\
-28 \\
\hline
-4 \\
40 \\
\hline
36
\end{array}
$$

Other interesting child-created computational procedures have been documented (Bidwell, 1991; Hamic, 1986; Harel & Behr, 1991; Madell, 1985).

Third, there is no *one* correct algorithm. Just as we can alter our normal routine for getting ready for work in the morning, so variations in computational procedures can be made. There are many algorithms that are efficient and meaningful. Also, different computational algorithms are used in different parts of the world, even by different cultures within the same country. For this reason, and because of the mobile nature of our society, teachers should be familiar with some of the more common alternative algorithms.

Children should explore different algorithms for several reasons:

- Alternative algorithms may help children develop more flexible mathematical thinking and "number sense."
- Alternative algorithms may serve reinforcement, enrichment, and remedial objectives.
- Alternative algorithms provide variety in the mathematics class.
- Awareness of different algorithms demonstrates the fact that algorithms are inventions and can change. This needs to be communicated to children so that they will not develop a belief that there is only one way to perform a mathematical computation.

The National Council of Teachers of Mathematics (NCTM) emphasizes the importance of *computational fluency,* that is, "having efficient and accurate methods for computing" (NCTM, 2000, p. 152). Computational fluency includes children being able to flexibly choose computational methods, understand these methods, explain these methods, and produce answers accurately and efficiently. According to the NCTM, by the end of fifth grade, children should be computing fluently with whole numbers. This chapter explains how teachers can help children attain this goal.

PRINCIPLES AND STANDARDS LINK 9-2
Content Strand: Number and Operations

Developing fluency requires a balance and connection between conceptual understanding and computational proficiency. On the one hand, computational methods that are over-practiced without understanding are often forgotten or remembered incorrectly. On the other hand, understanding without fluency can inhibit the problem-solving process. (NCTM, 2000, p. 35)

TECHNOLOGY LINK 9-1
Ask Dr. Math

Companion Website

Ask Dr. Math is a collection of questions and answers about elementary school mathematics. For example, would you like to know why the lattice multiplication algorithm works? Click on *Multiplication* and then on *Lattice Multiplication Explained* for the scoop.
Visit http://www.mathforum.org/dr.math/drmath.elem.html or link from our Companion Website at **www.prenhall.com/cathcart.**

ESTIMATION AND MENTAL COMPUTATION

Estimation and mental computation play such a pervasive role in out-of-school settings that children must have a wide variety of experiences with the skills. Over 80% of out-of-school problem-solving situations involve mental computation and estimation (Reys & Reys, 1986). These processes are often used together but involve quite different ideas (Atweh, 1982). Mental arithmetic involves computing an *exact answer* without the aid of paper and pencil, calculators, or any other device. Estimation has to do with the precision of an answer. Estimation may also employ mental computation, but the end result is an approximate answer rather than an exact answer.

In practice, estimation and mental computation should not be taught in isolation but should be incorporated into the teaching of paper-and-pencil computation and other topics. For example, if children are solving the following problem, the first question they might ask is, "*About* how many more children attend Rosa Parks School?"

There are 826 children enrolled at Rosa Parks Elementary School and 589 children enrolled at Kennedy Elementary School. How many more children are enrolled at Rosa Parks than at Kennedy?

Teachers help children understand the importance of estimation and mental computation through their questioning, for example, by not just asking for exact answers but also asking for estimates, as in the example above.

Estimation and mental computation skills should be developed along with paper-and-pencil computation because they help children spot unreasonable results. They also contribute to an understanding of the paper-and-pencil procedures and provide a fertile source for computational creativity on the part of children.

Mental Computation

Mental computation has had a turbulent history with respect to curricular emphasis. Around the turn of the 20th century, mental computation was advocated as a form of mental discipline. As this theory fell into disfavor, the emphasis on mental computation waned. The recent renewal of interest is based on the way in which mental computation can both enhance an understanding of numeration, number properties, and operations and promote problem solving and flexible thinking (Reys, 1985; Reys & Reys, 1990).

If children are encouraged to compute mentally, they will develop their own strategies and, in the process, develop good number sense. Good number sense helps students use strategies effectively. Children should be asked, on occasion, to explain to the teacher or to the class how they did the computation.

It is important for children to learn to solve problems such as 80 + 60 through mental computation. Children can talk about this as 6 *tens* joined to 8 *tens,* which makes 14 *tens.* From their numeration experiences, they will recognize this as 140.

In addition, mental computation often is employed even when a calculator is being used. For example, when adding 350, 785, 256, and 150, individuals with good number sense will mentally combine 350 and 150 and enter 500 into the calculator before entering the other numbers (Sowder, 1990).

Estimation

Researchers have begun to investigate a variety of factors related to computational estimation. Reys (1986) describes five strategies for computational estimation: front-end, rounding, clustering, compatible numbers, and special numbers. Each of these can be used to some extent by children in the elementary grades, whereas older children can apply them with greater sophistication. Each strategy will be described in greater detail later in this chapter.

- **Front-end strategy.** The *front-end* strategy focuses on the left-most or highest place-value digits. For example, children using this strategy would estimate the sum of 267 + 521 by adding the front-end digits, 2 and 5, estimating 700 for the sum.
- **Rounding strategy.** *Rounding* is a familiar strategy to most adults. Children using the rounding strategy to estimate the problem above would round 267 to 300 and 521 to 500 and find the sum, 800.
- **Clustering strategy.** The *clustering* strategy is used when a set of numbers are close to each other in value.
- **Compatible numbers strategy.** When using the *compatible numbers* strategy, children adjust the numbers so that they are easier to work with. For example, using compatible numbers in division involves altering the divisor, the dividend, or both so that they are easy to work with mentally.

PRINCIPLES AND STANDARDS LINK 9-3
Content Strand: Number and Operations

Part of being able to compute fluently means making smart choices about which tools to use and when. Students should have experiences that help them learn to choose among mental computation, paper-and-pencil strategies, estimation, and calculator use. (NCTM, 2000, p. 36)

PRINCIPLES AND STANDARDS LINK 9-4
Content Strand: Number and Operations

Estimation serves as an important companion to computation. It provides a tool for judging the reasonableness of calculator, mental, and paper-and-pencil computations. (NCTM, 2000, p. 155)

- **Special numbers strategy.** The *special numbers strategy* involves looking for numbers that are close to "special" values that are easy to work with, such as one-half or powers of ten.

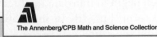

VIDEO LINK 9-1
Whole Number Computation

Brief Summary: In "This Small House," teacher Bobbie Bateson's second and third graders each have only $1.00 to spend to decorate homes they built out of milk cartons.

1. What different methods did students use to calculate the total amount of money they spent?
2. How could the teacher use this activity as an assessment tool?

Video Source. Teaching Math: A Video Library, K–4; Tape 7 from The Annenberg/CPB Math and Science Collection.

PAPER-AND-PENCIL COMPUTATION

How are U.S. children doing on paper-and-pencil computation? The sixth National Assessment of Educational Progress (NAEP) assessment noted fairly strong performance of 4th, 8th, and 12th graders on whole-number computation in symbolic and word problems (Kouba, Zawojewski, & Struchens, 1997). Children did best on one-step problems. For example, on a problem involving adding 2 three-digit numbers with regrouping, 88% of the 4th graders and 93% of the 8th and 12th graders were able to choose the correct sum. However, only 53% of the fourth graders and 84% of the eighth graders were able to find the solution to $503 - 207$. Similar trends were noted for multiplication and division.

Results on the NAEP show difficulties with regrouping in subtraction, with interpreting the meaning of remainders in division, on multistep multiplication and division problems, and in children's ability to justify and explain their work. These findings point to the need for a continued emphasis on teaching for meaning and on communication in the mathematics classroom.

An Instructional Philosophy

It is important for children to know how to compute using paper and pencil. However, once children can complete with understanding and reasonable skill exercises such as those shown below, nothing new is learned by working with larger numbers or by doing many exercises.

$$
\begin{array}{cccc}
327 & 3207 & 347 & 18\overline{)1096} \\
809 & -489 & \times 26 & \\
86 & & &
\end{array}
$$

Computational procedures will continue to be an essential component of the elementary school program, but

the many hours children currently spend doing long, complex calculations are essentially wasted. Some of the time saved by not having children do tedious paper-and-pencil computation should be added to the time spent developing an understanding of the operations and computational procedures through concrete manipulations and simple examples such as those above. Time also needs to be allocated for children to explain and write about the procedures they use.

Usiskin (1998) lists several reasons for having algorithms as well as the dangers that are inherent in all algorithms. Reasons for having algorithms include: (1) power, (2) reliability, (3) accuracy, and (4) speed. Dangers include: (1) blind acceptance of results, (2) overzealous application of algorithms, (3) a belief that algorithms train the mind, and (4) helplessness if the technology for the algorithm is not available. Usiskin notes that both paper-and-pencil algorithms and calculator or computer algorithms require the user to have some equipment.

The instructional model developed in Chapter 7 emphasized connecting the real world and the world of mathematical symbols when learning computational procedures, that is, computation should emerge from the need to solve some problem.

If children have had adequate experiences with concrete and pictorial models when solving simple computational problems, they will understand the concept of the operations and can focus on meaningful procedures to find answers to problems with larger numbers. Our recommended approach is to allow children ample time and opportunity to develop computational procedures for themselves. Initially, problems should be solved with manipulatives. Children should then be encouraged to record, *in their own way,* the processes they used. Children's *verbal description* of the processes provides them with a connection between the concrete and symbolic procedures (Sawada, 1985; Stanic & McKillip, 1989).

Children can then begin to translate their recording into a more symbolic form, but still in their own way. Over time, the symbolic recording can become more concise, eventually resulting (for most children) in the standard algorithm. As we emphasized earlier, this process may differ in different countries or regions of a country.

Prerequisites

Before children can be expected to develop paper-and-pencil computational procedures, they should demonstrate a conceptual understanding of the operations by recognizing different contexts that require the operations to resolve a problem (NCTM, 1989).

Knowledge of *some* basic facts is required before children begin computation with larger numbers. Strategies for knowing the basic facts continue to be developed and practiced as children work at solving problems with larger numbers. Second graders, for example, usually do not know all the basic facts for addition and subtraction, but they can still solve some two-digit problems. The final objective, however, for learning paper-and-pencil procedures is to be able to use them efficiently without the use of models. Achievement of this objective does require a mastery of the basic facts.

Children need to have a good understanding of the place-value numeration system, because each algorithm is based on principles of the numeration system. In particular, children need to be able to group ones into tens, tens into hundreds, and so on; and they need to be able to break hundreds into tens, tens into ones, and so on.

An understanding of some mathematical properties of whole numbers learned during the concepts and basic facts stages of instruction can help children with computational procedures. In particular, the *commutative law* and the *distributive property* of multiplication over addition can facilitate computation. For example, the exercise shown in Figure 9-1(a) would be easier to work out if the commutative law was applied as in Figure 9-1(b).

Understanding the distributive property also is prerequisite to efficient algorithm development. An exercise such as 8×37 can be reorganized mentally, or on paper, to $(8 \times 30) + (8 \times 7)$ or $8(30 + 7)$. The extension fact, 8×30, is relatively easy to determine mentally and 8×7 is a known basic fact. The product, then, is the sum of 240 and 56. Notice that expanded notation is included in the use of the distributive property ($37 = 30 + 7$).

Estimation may also be considered a prerequisite. What is prerequisite is an *attitude* of estimation. Children should approach computation with an attitude that estimation is a legitimate mathematical tool.

Important Considerations When Teaching Computational Procedures

The remainder of the chapter will focus on computation for each of the four operations. For each operation, the following components will be described:

- Posing story problems set in real-world contexts: Problems are more meaningful and children are better able to determine the reasonableness of their solutions when instruction begins with problems that are based in familiar, real-world contexts.
- Using models for computation: Concrete models, such as base-ten blocks, help children visualize problems.
- Using estimation and mental computation: These processes help children determine the reasonableness of their solutions.
- Developing bridging algorithm(s) to connect problems, models, estimation, and symbols: Several bridging algorithms are available to help children connect their existing understandings.
- Developing the traditional algorithm: The traditional algorithm can be developed meaningfully through the use of language and models.
- Examining children's work: Teachers can learn a great deal about children's understandings by examining their work. This analysis helps teachers assess students' learning and plan instruction.
- Determining the reasonableness of solutions: Many approaches, including estimation and checking answers, are important final steps in solving computation problems.

Issues related to language and place value will be woven throughout each section. Each of these topics is an important component of instruction aimed at helping all students develop computational fluency.

A note about models for computation   The first work with computation should be with *proportional* materials such as the base-ten blocks. *Nonproportional* materials should be used only when children can easily solve problems with proportional materials. If children can transfer the execution of a computation from proportional to nonproportional materials, then they probably have good understanding of the process. Once children have explored both types of materials, they will freely

---

FIGURE 9-1 ▶

$$
\begin{array}{cc}
40 & 27 \\
\times\ 27 & \times\ 40 \\
\hline
\text{(a)} & \text{(b)}
\end{array}
$$

move back and forth from proportional to nonproportional materials. Chapter 6 discusses proportional and nonproportional materials in greater detail.

A note about language   As indicated in Chapter 7, children should continue to use their own, less formal language to describe computational processes. During work with computation, the teacher should use mathematical language associated with each operation so that children will develop more technical language. Children should be allowed to use informal language for some time while they are learning precise mathematical terminology.

In addition, place-value language can help children make sense of computation. For example, in the problem $38 + 59$, when adding the digits in the tens column, it is preferable to say "30 plus 50 equals 80" rather than "3 plus 5 equals 8," which ignores the place value of the 3 and the 5.

A note about the role of calculators in computation   Checking computation can be done on the calculator. However, this is a *poor* use of time and of the calculator. The calculator should be used in a more substantive way to help children think about the algorithms, develop estimation skills, and solve computational problems. Activity 9-1 involves finding patterns related to multiplication. Activity 9-2 could be used to help children think about the multiplication and division algorithms, and Activity 9-3 suggests one way the calculator could be used to enhance estimation skills.

A note about children's thinking   Teachers can learn a great deal by examining children's work. Also, in the process of doing paper-and-pencil computation, children will sometimes make errors. But rather than merely being random mistakes, many errors are systematic and may reveal children's misunderstandings or limited understandings of computational algorithms.

Ashlock (2002) notes that errors can be helpful in the process of learning if they are used to analyze patterns of errors. Error-pattern analysis gives teachers information to use to modify instruction to meet children's needs.

According to Ashlock, "we need to examine each student's paper diagnostically—looking for patterns, hypothesizing possible causes, and verifying our ideas. As we learn about each student we will find that a student's paper is sometimes a problem or puzzle to be solved" (2002, p. 13). Children's errors often are a result of overgeneralizing or making generalizations based on limited data. Children's thinking and examples of children's common error patterns are discussed throughout this chapter for each operation, along with suggestions for helping children who make such errors.

ACTIVITY 9-1

PATTERNS

MATERIALS
Calculator

PROCEDURE
1. Choose some two-digit numbers. Use your calculator to multiply each by 99. Record and compare the results. When you think you see a pattern or a relationship, use it to predict some other results. Write a statement describing your pattern.

2. Choose only 2 three-digit numbers. Multiply each by 999. Record and examine the results. Predict the results of multiplying 2 other three-digit numbers by 999.

Write statements that tell how this pattern is

- The same as the one for two-digit numbers × 99.
- Different from the two-digit × 99 pattern.

ACTIVITY 9-2

MISSING NUMBERS

MATERIALS
A calculator

PROCEDURE
1. Estimate first, then use your calculator to help you find the missing numbers.

$$6\overline{)\square\square\square}^{\,65\ R2} \qquad 7\overline{)2\square3}^{\,\square\square} \qquad \square\square\,\overline{)3819}^{\,109\ R4}$$

2. Use only 5, 7, 8, and 9 to make
   - The largest possible product.

$$\begin{array}{r} \square\square\square \\ \times\ \ \square \\ \hline \end{array}$$

   - The smallest possible product.

$$\begin{array}{r} \square\square\square \\ \times\ \ \square \\ \hline \end{array}$$

3. Find the missing numbers. All four partial products are shown.

$$\begin{array}{r} \square 5 \\ \times\ \ 3\square \\ \hline \square\square \\ 100 \\ 1\square 0 \\ \hline \square\square\square\square \\ \square\square\square\square \end{array}$$

ACTIVITY 9-3

ESTIMATION

MATERIALS
Calculator

PROCEDURE
Play with a partner. Each player needs a calculator.

1. Agree on a target number. Circle it.

76	1111	410	309
107	2345	731	
96	296		

2. Enter any number into your calculator.

3. Press the × key.

4. Within 5 seconds enter another number that you think will give you a product close to the target number. Then press the = key.

   Example: Target = 107
   Entered: 38 ×
   then 3 =
   Display shows 114

5. The person closest to the target number wins the round.

6. Play 10 rounds.

Repeat the procedure using the ÷ key.

ADDITION

Posing Story Problems Set in Real-World

In the past it was common to introduce the addition algorithm with computation that did not require children to regroup. If one begins with realistic problems, some will require renaming, others will not. If children have been doing computation in which no regrouping is involved and then encounter a problem for which regrouping is needed (or vice versa), they will notice the difference, grapple with it, and resolve it with proper guidance from the teacher.

It is important that instruction begins with asking children to solve problems situated in real-world settings. This will help children make sense of the computation and be better able to judge the reasonableness of results. When solving addition problems, terms such as *joined to* are meaningful to children. (See Chapter 7 for more on realistic problems for addition.)

For example, teachers could begin instruction by posing a problem such as the following:

On the last Grade 3 field trip there were 28 children on one bus and 34 children on the other bus. How many children went on the field trip?

The following section describes how to use models to solve this problem.

Using Models for Computation

If necessary, suggest that children use the base-ten blocks to solve the problem above. They will likely first group the tens as shown in Figure 9-2, then combine the ones. Finally, they will trade 10 ones for 1 ten to get 6 tens and 2 ones, that is, children naturally want to group the larger pieces first (Lee, 1991). This left-to-right process is discussed later in this chapter.

Using the blocks (no recording), children can easily extend this process to include numbers in the hundreds, provided they have had relevant numeration experiences. In fact, children gain satisfaction from working with larger numbers. They should do this not just for the sake of working with larger numbers but because of a need to solve some relevant real-life problem. This is a good setting in which to encourage estimation. Children could use their previous experience with extension facts and say, "There are at least 20 plus 30, or 50, children on the field trip."

A transition to the recording phase could be made by giving children an organizational mat described in Chapter 6 on which they could do their manipulations. Children may need some initial guidance in how to use each space. The second column in Figure 9-3 illustrates how

FIGURE 9-2

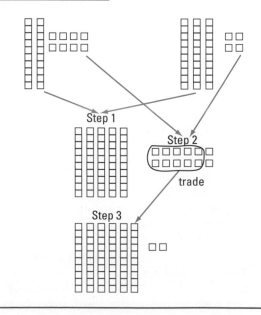

FIGURE 9-3

Problem/Steps	Concrete Representation	Symbolic Representation
28 on first bus. 34 on second bus. How many in all?	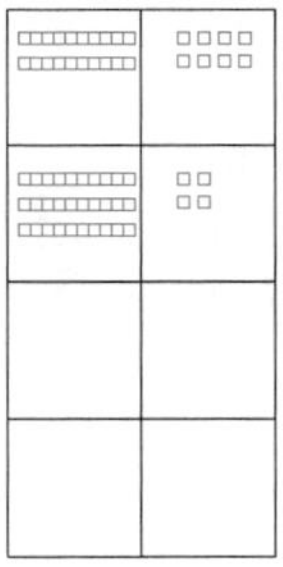	2 8 + 3 4
Join the tens and record.	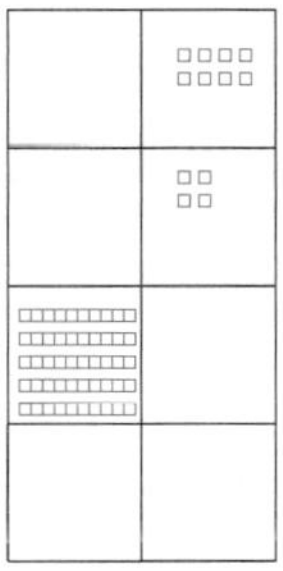	2 8 + 3 4 5 0
Join the ones, trade, and record.	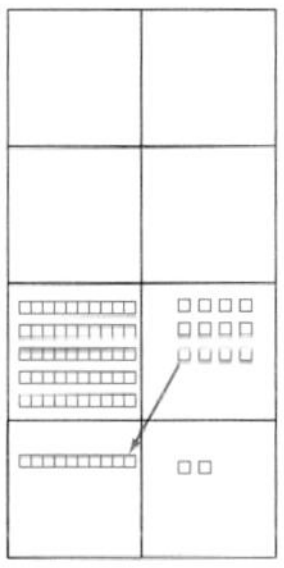	2 8 + 3 4 5 0 1 2
Join the tens, join the ones, and record.	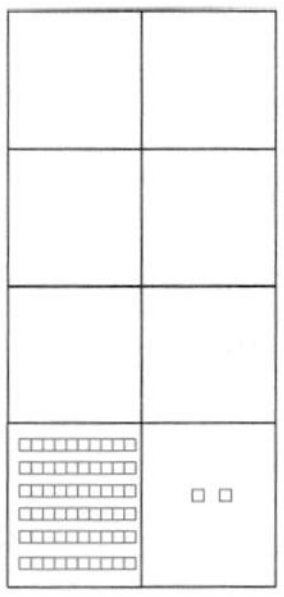	2 8 + 3 4 5 0 1 2 6 2

this mat might be used for the field trip problem. At this stage, children would do only the steps illustrated in the second column.

Place-value language   Encourage children to use place-value language as they describe their manipulations. For example, "2 tens and 3 tens make 5 tens" and "8 ones plus 4 ones is 12 ones." This will help them to focus on the value of the digits and prepare them for multiplication and division computation in which the use of place-value language is more critical.

Developing Bridging Algorithm(s) to Connect Problems, Models, Estimation, and Symbols

Once children feel confident using the base-ten blocks to add two numbers, the next step is to begin keeping a record of what was done. This recording will go through a series of refinements and culminate in a concise and efficient symbolic procedure.

Children might begin by using a mat for doing the manipulations with the blocks and a sheet of paper for recording. To avoid skipping steps in the recording, children could work in pairs: one recording, the other manipulating. Figure 9-4 illustrates each step in the process and the corresponding record. Note that the series is based on the assumption that children naturally work from left to right (Lee, 1991). This method is referred to as the *partial sums algorithm* because children record each partial sum individually before combining the partial sums to find the sum. Figure 9-4 shows two addition problems solved using this algorithm.

Some educators recommend that once recording begins, children should be told to work right-to-left. This adds an additional component to an already big and important step. Allow children to be as natural as possible and match paper-and-pencil work as closely as possible to the steps used in the concrete mode. Working right-to-left may not alter the notation used in the last row of Figure 9-4, only some of the intermediate steps.

Furthermore, other activities such as working with money, where people almost always group the largest denomination first and proceed to the smallest denomina-

tion (Lee, 1991), reinforce left-to-right procedures. In fact, the only reason to add right-to-left is when several multidigit numbers need to be added. Even then the left-to-right procedure works well, but the recording can become a little "messy." Keep in mind that these computations should be done on a calculator.

Using Estimation and Mental Computation

As children are solving problems, the teacher should ask questions to help the children connect the meaning of the problem with the solutions they are obtaining. For example, in the field trip problem, a teacher could ask questions such as "Will the answer be more than or less than 100? Why?" and "What will the answer be *close to* (60)?"

Strategies for mental computation   Mental computation often is done by looking for *compatible* (or "friendly") *numbers*. The following examples indicate two ways in which children might mentally add $16 + 11 + 24 + 35$.

$16 + 11 + 24 + 35$	$16 + 11 + 24 + 35$
$40 + 35 = 75$	$35 + 35 = 70$
$75 + 11 = 86$	$70 + 16 = 86$

Strategies for computational estimation
Using the front-end strategy for addition.   The *front-end* strategy is probably the easiest for younger children to use. This strategy can be introduced when children know some basic facts and the meaning of larger numbers. This strategy focuses on the left-most or highest place-value digits. At the most basic level, children would estimate the sum of $267 + 521$ by adding the front-end digits, 2 and 5, estimating 700 for the sum. Later, children will look at the remaining digits and adjust their estimate by thinking "67 and 21 is nearly one more hundred so I'll estimate 800."

For elementary- and middle-school children, the front-end estimation strategy has one of its most relevant applications in money settings.

Brad wants to buy some school supplies. The items he has picked out cost $1.29, $3.59, and $1.99. About how much will Brad spend?

Because children naturally want to group the dollars first, the front-end strategy is a natural one to use in this setting. Some children will look only at the dollar amounts and estimate about $5. Others will adjust this step because they recognize that $0.99 is almost another dollar and $0.29 + $0.59 is also close to another dollar. They would estimate $5 + $1 + $1 or $7.

FIGURE 9-4

28	367
+34	+ 85
50	300
12	140
62	12
	452

Children will soon recognize that the front-end strategy with whole numbers always results in an estimate that is *less than or equal to* the actual product. This level of estimation is adequate for most purposes for most elementary-school children. Older children will be able to add a second level front-end adjustment to their original estimate.

Using the rounding strategy for addition. *Rounding* is a skill that is often introduced in the third or fourth grade, usually in the context of numeration. Computing mentally or using paper and pencil with rounded numbers is another frequently used estimation strategy. In the previous example of 267 + 521, children might round to the nearest hundred. Their estimate of the sum, then, would be 300 + 500, or 800. In the money problem, children could round to the nearest whole dollar. Their estimate would then be $1 + $4 + $2 or $7. Older children, recognizing whether rounding results in an overestimate or an underestimate, may make an adjustment similar to that used in the front-end approach.

Rounding can be concretized by using a number line; marking multiples of 10, 100, or whatever place-value position one wants to round to; and having children note which of two adjacent multiples a given number is closest to. Bohan, Shawaker, and Bohan (1994) also suggest using stacks of chips for the same purpose.

Using the clustering strategy for addition.   The *clustering* strategy is used when a set of numbers are close to each other in value.

Juan surveyed each room in his school. He prepared this table for his group. About how many children are in Juan's school?

Room 1	29	Room 5	28
Room 2	32	Room 6	29
Room 3	30	Room 7	31
Room 4	34	Room 8	27

With guidance, children can observe that all the numbers are close to 30, so a good estimate would be 8 × 30, or 240. Children who have worked with the concept of "average" will recognize that 30 is an estimate of the average number of children in each room.

Using the compatible numbers strategy for addition.   When using the *compatible numbers* strategy, children adjust the numbers so that they are easier to work with. A form of the compatible numbers strategy can be used in addition when there are multiple addends, as in the following example.

Six children kept a record of how many minutes of television they watched on Monday. Altogether, about how many minutes did the children watch television?

Heather	25	Trevor	60
Roberta	44	Gwen	57
Sam	35	Michael	80

Given the preceding addition exercise, children could use the compatible numbers strategy to look for groups of 100. They would estimate that together the children watched about 300 minutes of television.

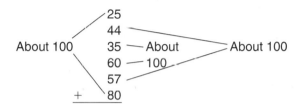

Developing the Traditional Algorithm

Teachers can help children connect the partial sums algorithm to the traditional (or compact) algorithm for addition. For example, consider the partial sums algorithm as shown on the next page. After solving the field trip problem using the partial sums algorithm, the teacher could discuss with children the meaning of the 12, and ask if they can think of any other way to record the 12. If no children suggest the idea of recording the one ten above the first addend (28), the teacher could demonstrate and explain (see the figure below). It is very important to discuss with the children the meaning of the one that was regrouped and written above the first addend, so that this method becomes a meaningful procedure.

H	T	O
	2	8
	3	4
	1	2
	5	0
	6	2

H	T	O
	¹2	8
	3	4
	5	2

Expanded notation is another type of transitional step. Children might compute the answer to the field trip problem like this:

$$2 \text{ tens and } 8 \text{ ones}$$
$$\underline{3 \text{ tens and } 4 \text{ ones}}$$
$$5 \text{ tens and } 12 \text{ ones}$$
$$6 \text{ tens and } 2 \text{ ones}$$
$$62$$

Whatever approach is encouraged, it is important to remember that children will shorten the steps on their own. Some children need more transitional steps than others, and some need to spend a longer time at some steps than other children. Allow children to discover their own shortcuts. Do not rush them into using the standard algorithm.

When children feel competent in working through computations using two-digit numbers, they should be invited to solve problems with larger numbers. The organizational mat could be extended to four columns (thousands through units).

It is the number and type of regroupings more than the magnitude of the numbers that the teacher needs to consider when planning instruction. The three problems below are cognitively all the same and could be worked on at the same time. In practice, however, we would not normally expect 2nd graders to do the last two problems, despite the fact that they have learned all the skills they need to know to solve them.

$$\begin{array}{ccc} 32 & 564 & 8704 \\ \underline{+47} & \underline{+231} & \underline{+1263} \end{array}$$

Problems with two and three regroupings are more difficult for children. Again, the importance of adequate preparation in the form of concrete numeration experiences and addition in a concrete mode must be stressed. Such experiences will minimize the difficulty children will have with multiple regroupings.

Activity 9-4 will stimulate discussion and provide experience with estimation, addition computation, and the calculator. Children should work in a group or with a partner.

Examining Student Work

Boxes 9-1 and 9-2 contain samples of children's work in practicing adding whole numbers. Look closely at the work and try to determine the errors the children are making. Why might they be making these errors? If you were their teacher, what might you do to help them?

Description of addition error pattern 1   In Box 9-1, Mike is not regrouping. When he gets a sum greater than 9, he simply records it in the answer rather than regrouping.

How a teacher might help.   The teacher could strengthen Mike's understanding of place value by using a manipulative material for place value, such as base-ten blocks or bundles of 10 sticks and individual sticks. Emphasize the process of regrouping when there are more than 9 ones. The game "Race to a Flat," discussed in Chapter 6, could help Mike understand the process of regrouping.

Description of addition error pattern 2   In Box 9-2, Dorothy is adding the second addend to both the digit in the ones column and the digit in the tens column of the first addend. This error commonly appears after children have learned multiplication with one-digit multipliers, such as 23×4.

How a teacher might help.   Encourage Dorothy to estimate the result of each problem. For example, in

ACTIVITY 9-4 ▶

CALCULATOR GAME (ADDITION)

MATERIALS
Calculator for each student

PROCEDURE
1. One person writes four numbers on paper for all others to see.
2. Without the others seeing, add three of the numbers on your calculator.
3. Write the sum on paper for the others to see.
4. The others decide, by estimation, which one of the four numbers was not used and then check their guesses on their calculators.
5. Take turns doing the activity several more times.

BOX 9-1

Addition Error Pattern 1

Name _Mike_

A. 74
 +56
 1210

B. 35
 +92
 127

C. 67
 +18
 715

D. 56
 +97
 1413

Source: Error Patterns in Computation 8/e by Ashlock, ©2002, p. 100. Reprinted by permission of Pearson Education, Inc., Upper Saddle River, NJ.

BOX 9-2

Addition Error Pattern 2

Name _Dorothy_

A. 75
 + 8
 163

B. 67
 + 4
 111

C. 84
 + 9
 183

D. 59
 + 6
 125

Source: Error Patterns in Computation 8/e by Ashlock, ©2002, p. 102. Reprinted by permission of Pearson Education, Inc., Upper Saddle River, NJ.

problems A through D, the number being added is less than 10, so the sum should be about 10 more than the first addend. Her answers are much larger.

Determining the Reasonableness of Solutions

After children finish solving problems, the teacher should ask questions to help children evaluate the reasonableness of the solutions they found. For example, in the field trip problem, a teacher could ask questions such as "Does it make sense that the answer is less than 100? Why?" and "What would you say to another child who said the answer was 512? Is that right or wrong? How do you know?" Such questioning is very important to help

children understand the importance of judging the reasonableness of the solutions after solving any problem.

SUBTRACTION

Posing Story Problems Set in Real-World Contexts

As for addition, it has been common practice to introduce the subtraction algorithm with computation that did not require children to regroup. Also as for addition, beginning with realistic problems exposes children to subtraction with regrouping in a realistic context, which will help them make sense of the situations.

In subtraction, children can use other terms for regrouping and renaming, such as *trade, group, break apart, break a ten,* and *make a group.* Also, children should be able to use the terms *subtract, subtraction,* and *difference* meaningfully in a sentence. (See Chapter 7 for more on realistic problems for subtraction.)

For example, teachers could begin instruction by posing a problem such as the following:

The clerk in the doughnut shop counted 63 doughnuts on the shelf. A family bought 24 doughnuts. How many doughnuts were left?

The following section describes how to use models to solve this problem.

Using Models for Computation

To solve the problem above, children may want to set out blocks to represent 24 as well as 63. This would be done if the comparison interpretation of subtraction was being used, but not for the take-away approach. The teacher may need to review the notion of subtraction as take-away, namely, that there is a known number of objects (63) and that a specified number (24) is to be removed from this group.

The organizational mat should be modified for subtraction as shown in Figure 9-5. It also provides a transition to the recording phase. In the unstructured activities phase, children would simply manipulate the blocks in the spaces provided on the mat, as illustrated in the second column in Figure 9-5. Children would start with 63 displayed in the first row, then would separate 24 and put them in the second row (regrouping as necessary), resulting in 39 blocks remaining to be moved to the bottom row.

As children become successful with this process, teachers can ask them to be more systematic, beginning by first taking away the 4 ones, moving the remaining ones to the bottom row, before working with the tens place. This procedure more closely mirrors the symbolic algorithm.

When children use only the base-ten blocks without recording, they experience very little difficulty extending the above process to three-digit numbers provided they have had relevant trading experiences involving hundreds. Of course, these larger numbers need to come from some real-life problem that must be solved.

Using Estimation and Mental Computation

Encouraging children to estimate an answer will help them verify and feel good about their concrete solution. Children might say, "My answer should be about 40 because I know that 60 minus 20 is 40" (extension fact).

Using the front-end strategy Given a real-life setting that involved subtracting 254 from 725, younger children could estimate the result by subtracting the front-end digits (7 − 2), to get 500. Middle-school children can make adjustments to get a closer estimate. They might reason that another 54 to be subtracted makes the answer closer to 450. Others with good number sense might also consider the additional 25 and decide that 475 is a closer estimate.

Other activities such as those suggested by Activities 9-5 and 9-6 could be structured to provide experience with estimation and mental computation.

Developing Bridging Algorithm(s) to Connect Problems, Models, Estimation, and Symbols

The development of a paper-and-pencil subtraction algorithm should follow as closely as possible the method used by children when they subtract with base-ten blocks. The strategy recommended for addition could be used here also, that is, use an organizational mat and a sheet of paper, with one child manipulating the blocks with the other child records on the paper. Children then change roles. Figure 9-5 illustrates steps a child might use to solve the doughnut problem and the corresponding record.

The process of regrouping shown in Figure 9-5 warrants comment. Notice that, after regrouping, the 10 ones

---

ACTIVITY 9-5

HOW MANY DIGITS?

PROCEDURE
Tell how many digits are in the answer.

$$609 - 538$$
$$1215 - 347$$
$$13\,325 - 4467$$

ACTIVITY 9-6

DIFFERENCE OF 50

PROCEDURE
1. In 1 minute, find as many pairs of numbers as you can from this list whose difference is 50.

32	9	97	36	62	37	76	58
64	81	14	39
82	69	93	71	19	85	22
86	25	121	24	47

**The Annenberg/CPB
Math and Science Collection**

Classroom Clips:
Choose a Method

Previewing the Video

Not unlike when teaching reading, Mary Holden often divides her math class into three groups. While one group independently solves problems on computers, another works on math games and puzzles. That allows Ms. Holden a chance to work with a third small group and talk about real-world applications to problem solving. She asks the children to choose several different methods to solve the same problems.

She begins by having children build structures using base-ten blocks. They then estimate the structure's value, based on price values assigned to each type of block.

Ms. Holden records children's estimates in a chart (see below) on the chalkboard and asks children to explain the reasons for their estimates. Then Ms. Holden has children use a different method to determine the exact value of each building, which she also records in the chart. The children then compare their estimates with the actual value of each building.

Child's Name	Estimated Value of Their Building	Actual Value of Their Building
Nataya	$2.73	$3.58
Aubrey	$3.47	$4.20
Andy	$3.48	$4.01

As a group, they decide their estimates are close enough to the actual values to be reasonable. Then Ms. Holden asks, "As a group, would you say we are under-estimators or over-estimators?" The children overwhelmingly agree that they are under-estimators. Ms. Holden recommends that "Sometimes you need to know that about yourself so the next time you estimate you know to aim a slight bit higher."

"We used money just to make it seem real and to come up with some real-world applications. I really don't think that isolated lessons with some printed-out problems is probably good learning. Learning within the context of the situation is the best."

— M. Holden

Follow along with this lesson to see what math process standards might be covered...

> "I try to set up a classroom or learning situation where children are experts and they're teaching others. And sometimes it has to happen under real intense guidance on my part, but that's what it's all about."
>
> — M. Holden

Process Standard:
Problem Solving

Notice the problems Ms. Holden asks her children to solve. Most of the problems are set in real-world situations that are familiar and interesting to the children.

A Problem from the Video: Ms. Holden asks one child to model 23¢ with base-ten blocks. Then she asks, "What if you had 5 times that much? How would you show that?" She asks the group to tell the child who is working with the base-ten blocks what to do.

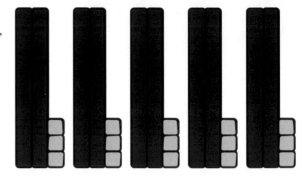

The group instructs the child to make 5 different piles with 23¢ in each pile, as shown at the right.

How could we figure that out using mental math? Ms. Holden asks the children, "What coin is 23¢ close to?" (a quarter), and then asks them to mentally calculate what 5 quarters are worth ($1.25). The children then decide that their 5 groups of base-ten blocks are close to $1.25, so their answer to 5 x 23¢ is probably correct.

- What do these children's solution strategies tell you about their understanding?
- How might a teacher use children's descriptions of their solution strategies as assessment information to plan follow-up lessons?
- How did Ms. Holden encourage the children to consider a variety of computational methods?
- What techniques were used to construct meaning and develop number sense?

Focus on Standards

Notice the way Ms. Holden addresses problem solving in this lesson to enable students to:

- solve problems that arise in mathematics and in other contexts.
- apply and adapt a variety of appropriate strategies to solve problems.
- monitor and reflect on the process of mathematical problem solving.

Process Standard: Representation

Ms. Holden encourages students to use different ways to represent problems and to think about problems in different ways. **How do you think different materials, such as base-ten blocks, enhance children's understanding? Why do you think Ms. Holden relates money to the value of the blocks?**

Slushies for Sale!

Problem: Slushies are on sale today for 29¢. You're going to buy one for everyone who sits at your table (4 children sit at each table). How much did you spend?

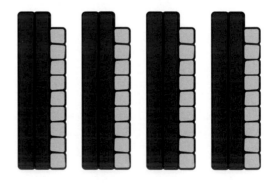

How some students solved this problem:

- **Aubrey** used base-ten blocks and made 4 groups of 29¢, as shown to the right.
- **Tara** got an answer of 33¢ using a calculator. Then she solved the problem again and got $1.16.
- **Trible** said, "I'm totally off, I know that." He got $2.48.

- **Letisha** got 47¢ using mental math.
- **Ms. Holden** says, "Let's think that through. Let me give you a little trick for the 29. 29 is hard to work with, isn't it? If you think in your mind, 4 times 29, that's hard to do, isn't it? What's 29 close to? (30) So 4 times 30 is $1.20."
- **Kyle** joins in: "Then you take away a penny away for each one, and you get $1.16."
- **Ben** solved the problem in another way: "You can use the tens first and when you're done you count up the ones." Ms. Holden models making 4 groups of 20, which is 80, and then 4 times 9 is 36, so 80 plus 36 is "eleventy-six," or $1.16.

The children chuckle about the word "eleventy-six" and Ben says, "I messed up, sorta." Ms. Holden smiles and says, "I can see how your mind worked when you were thinking that up, and thanks for sharing."

Focus on Standards

Review the slushies problem Ms. Holden gives her class.
How does she encourage children to use different representations to:

- create and use representations to organize, record, and communicate mathematical ideas?
- select, apply, and translate among mathematical representations to solve problems?

Process Standard: **Communication**

Ms. Holden asks children which method they prefer: mental math, base-ten blocks, paper and pencil, or calculator.

> **Jared:** Pencil and paper
> **Brenna:** Calculator
> **Gianna:** Calculator
> **Trible** says, "I think it would depend. If it's a harder question, it would have to be calculator, but if it's an easier one, it would be a lot easier for mental math."
> **Keli** says, "I think it would be mental math, because you can round everything off to something."
> **Riley** says, "I think it would be mental math, because when you go into a store, when you buy a few things that are the same, you're going to expect about the price if you add it all up. Most of the time you'll get a reasonable answer, maybe it will be a little more, when they ring it up."

Ms. Holden asks, "Can we say that there's any method that's the best method? (children say "no") No. Does it depend on what you're doing?" (children say "yes")

What do you see as the benefits and disadvantages (or limitations) of having students describe their solution strategies?

Focus on Standards

Notice the way Ms. Holden addresses communication in this lesson to enable students to:

- organize and consolidate their mathematical thinking through communication.
- communicate their mathematical thinking coherently and clearly to peers, teachers, and others.
- analyze and evaluate the mathematical thinking and strategies of others.
- use the language of mathematics to express mathematical ideas precisely.

> "I think the best kind of math communication and the best kind of math writing come from feeling safe to express that in front of other people and to express 'wrong turns' and how, when somebody makes a 'wrong turn' in their thinking, that we can correct them again, but it's safe to say that out loud in front of a group of peers and their teacher so we can get that corrected."
>
> — M. Holden

Try This!

Change for a Dollar

Materials: Dice, Price List, paper, pencils, and calculators (optional) for each person.

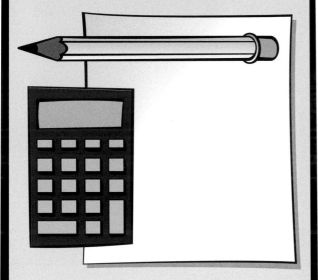

PRICE LIST			
Pencils	20¢	Poster board	95¢
Pens	45¢	Index cards	10¢
Erasers	25¢	Spiral notebook	$1.00
Markers	50¢	Notebook paper	5¢/sheet

- Roll dice and form a money sum with that roll (a roll of six and four could become $.64 or $.46).
- Players purchase something from the classroom store, or choose to save that amount of money, keeping track on their paper, to combine with another roll before purchasing something from the list.
- The first player to buy every item on the list wins.

Extension: Have students write shopping lists and estimate the amount needed to purchase everything on their list, then calculate the exact amount necessary.

Process Standard: Reasoning and Proof

Ms. Holden frequently asks her students to describe and reflect on their solution strategies. Think of some examples from the video of good reasoning and of reasoning that is incomplete or flawed. **How did Ms. Holden reinforce the notion of "reasonable" when examining a solution?**

Focus on Standards

Reasoning mathematically is a habit of mind, and like all habits, it must be developed through consistent use in many contexts. (NCTM, 2000, p. 56)

How does Ms. Holden address reasoning in this lesson to enable students to:

- recognize reasoning and proof as fundamental aspects of mathematics?
- select and use various types of reasoning and methods of proof?

Process Standard: Connections

Focus on Standards

How could Ms. Holden address connections in this lesson to enable students to:

- recognize and apply mathematics in contexts outside of mathematics?

How could this lesson be extended to help children understand how mathematical ideas interconnect and build on one another to produce a coherent whole?

For other connection ideas, including a unit idea for practicing computation while planning a driving vacation, including calculating travel time and determining costs of travel-related expenses, please visit Chapter 9 of our website at **www.prenhall.com/cathcart**

FIGURE 9-5 ▶

Problem/Steps	Concrete Representation	Symbolic Representation
63 doughnuts		H T O 6 3 -
Sold 24 doughnuts. Need to trade 1 ten for 10 ones. Then take away 4 ones and 2 tens. (move 24 to second row).		H T O ⁵6̷ ¹³3̷ - 2 4
Move remaining blocks to bottom row. Record.		H T O ⁵6̷ ¹³3̷ - 2 4 3 9

were joined to the 3 ones in the first row rather than in a regrouping space, as was done in addition. Why? In the concrete mode, the 10 ones were joined to the group of 3 ones, making 13 ones. Putting all 13 ones in the same cell on the mat better illustrates an intermediate step of the regrouping process. After regrouping 6 tens and 3 ones into 5 tens and 13 ones, children can then take-away 4 ones to solve the problem. This process also provides a concrete representation for the symbolic regrouping shown in the column on the right in Figure 9-5.

Developing the Traditional Algorithm

After children have had some experiences with the translation suggested by Figure 9-5 and can explain the steps in the subtraction procedure, they will begin to make refinements, which become more symbolic, shorter, and more efficient. The sequence of refinements illustrated in Figure 9-6 is one possibility. Many variations on these may be developed. For example, Young (1984) describes a transitional step based on covering all numbers not

FIGURE 9-6 ▶

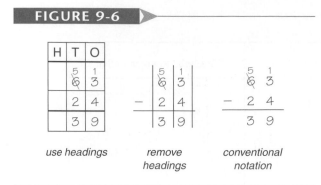

use headings   remove   conventional
                    headings   notation

needed in a specific step of the algorithm. Expanded notation is encouraged by some teachers as a transitional step. The notation shown below illustrates one way the doughnut problem might be recorded and solved using expanded notation.

$$6 \text{ tens} + 3 \text{ ones} \rightarrow 5 \text{ tens} + 13 \text{ ones}$$
$$\underline{-2 \text{ tens} + 4 \text{ ones}} \qquad \underline{-2 \text{ tens} + 4 \text{ ones}}$$

$$5 \text{ tens} + 13 \text{ ones} \rightarrow 39$$
$$\underline{-2 \text{ tens} + 4 \text{ ones}}$$
$$3 \text{ tens} + 9 \text{ ones}$$

Because the need to do a particular computation arises from the need to solve some real-life problem, the magnitude of numbers that children need to deal with will vary. As the number of required regroupings increases, so does the difficulty level. A teacher, therefore, may want to structure or filter problems so that children can experience success and not become frustrated with problems that they are unable to solve.

The number of regroupings needed provides a guideline. When subtracting up to a three-digit number from a three-digit number, there can be no regrouping or any one of four possible regrouping situations (Figure 9-7): tens to ones, hundreds to tens, hundreds to ones, and tens to ones and hundreds to tens.

After children have used proportional materials such as the base-ten blocks, the abacus could be used to reinforce the trading process with larger numbers. Figure 9-8 illustrates steps a child might take to compute 1495 − 637 on the abacus proceeding in the traditional right-to-left sequence.

FIGURE 9-7 ▶

376	246	325	305	355
− 51	− 29	− 172	− 109	− 186
no regroupings	tens to ones	hundreds to tens (via tens)	hundreds to ones	tens to ones and hundreds to tens

Special cases: zeros in the minuend   Occasionally children encounter problems with one or more zeros in the minuend. The computational procedures involved need careful development. With a three-digit minuend, there are three cases to consider.

Case 1: Zero in the ones place.   Sometimes children want to begin reading the problem below as "5 minus 0." Their grouping and regrouping numeration experiences should enable them to rename 60 as 5 tens and 10 ones.

$$760 \longrightarrow \overset{5\,1}{7\cancel{6}0}$$
$$\underline{-\,345} \qquad \underline{-\,345}$$

Case 2: Zero in the tens place.   One example involves only one regrouping, from hundreds to tens, as required, for example, in 406 − 242. Using the base-ten blocks, children will quickly understand that 4 hundreds can be renamed as 3 hundreds plus 10 tens (Figure 9-9). An appropriate paper-and-pencil recording might look like the one on the right in Figure 9-9.

A second example in which regrouping also is needed in the ones position is more difficult. Consider the problem 403 − 246. There are two approaches children might take. Most children will regroup the 4 hundreds as 3 hundreds and 10 tens (first example) and then rename the 10 tens as 9 tens and 13 ones as shown below. This parallels what would be done using base-ten blocks.

$$403 \qquad \overset{3\;\;9}{4\cancel{0}\cancel{3}}$$
$$\underline{-\,246} \qquad \underline{-\,246}$$

At the symbolic level, children with good insight into numeration might recognize that the 40 tens can be renamed as 39 tens and 10 ones. Children's recording may look like this example.

$$\overset{3\,9}{4\cancel{0}3}$$
$$\underline{-\,246}$$

Case 3: Zeros in both the tens and ones places.   This is the most difficult case. Children should have many experiences using concrete simulations before they move to paper-and-pencil recording. Figure 9-10 illustrates the steps with the problem 400 − 245.

The same steps are shown symbolically below. Children may include some transitional steps if they need

$$\overset{3\,1}{4\cancel{0}0} \qquad \overset{3\;\;9}{4\cancel{0}\cancel{0}}$$
$$\underline{-\,245} \qquad \underline{-\,245}$$

FIGURE 9-8

$$1495 - 637 = 858$$

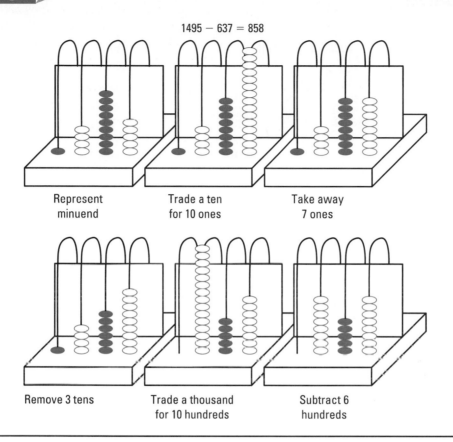

Represent
minuend

Trade a ten
for 10 ones

Take away
7 ones

Remove 3 tens

Trade a thousand
for 10 hundreds

Subtract 6
hundreds

FIGURE 9-9

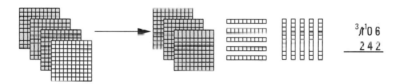

them. As indicated earlier, some children may combine the two renaming steps, that is, they will think of the 40 tens as 39 tens and 10 ones and record it as the second example in Case 2 (zero in the tens place). Children with good number sense sometimes mentally compute the answer to this type of problem by saying, "From 245 to 250 is 5, 50 more to 300 is 55, another hundred to 400 is 155."

Algorithms based on the comparison interpretation of subtraction The comparison interpretation of subtraction, discussed in Chapter 7, requires different modeling. So far in this chapter, we've focused on the "take-away" interpretation of subtraction. Matching techniques can be used to model comparison situations. This can be done with larger numbers, but it becomes more cumbersome. Figure 9-11 illustrates the comparison suggested by the following problem.

FIGURE 9-10

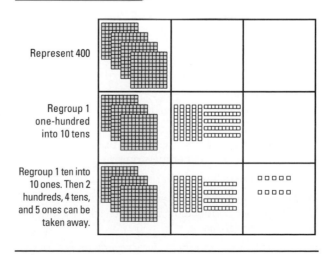

Represent 400

Regroup 1
one-hundred
into 10 tens

Regroup 1 ten into
10 ones. Then 2
hundreds, 4 tens,
and 5 ones can be
taken away.

FIGURE 9-11

364 — 198 = 166

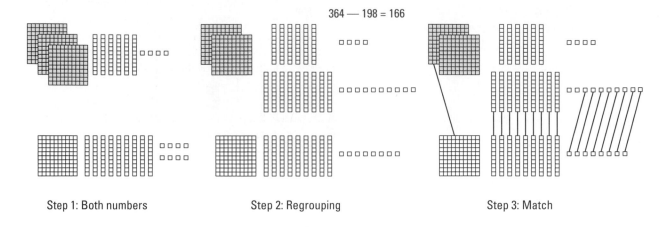

Step 1: Both numbers   Step 2: Regrouping   Step 3: Match

There are 364 children in Roseview Elementary School and 198 in Brooklyn Park Elementary School. How many more children go to Roseview than Brooklyn Park?

The difference, 166, is the number represented by the blocks in the upper row not matched to a block in the lower row. The on-paper algorithm is identical to the take-away setting.

Activity 9-7 parallels Activity 9-4 but involves subtraction. Children should work in a group or with a partner and discuss reasons for their choice of number.

Equal additions algorithm   This algorithm was taught in North America until the mid-1900s (Brownell, 1947; Brownell & Moser, 1949). Thereafter its use declined and the decomposition method prevailed. The equal additions algorithm, also known as the "same change" al-

gorithm, is taught in some new curricula and in some other countries, so teachers should be aware of it and understand how it works. When taught meaningfully, both the equal additions and the decomposition algorithms are effective. The two methods are compared in Figure 9-12.

Using the equal additions method, a child might reason: "I can't subtract 8 from 6, so I will add 10 ones. Since I added 10 to the top number (346), I must add 10 to the bottom number (178). I will increase the 7 tens to 8 tens. 8 from 16 is 8. Now I can't subtract 8 tens from 4 tens so I'll add 10 tens to the top number (346) and 10 tens in the form of one hundred to the bottom number (178). 8 tens from 14 tens is 6 tens and 2 hundreds from 3 hundreds leaves 1 hundred."

Note that this method is based on a compensation property. What is added to one number (the minuend) must be added to the other number (the subtrahend) to keep the difference the same. This algorithm, then, is based more on the properties and structure of the number system, whereas the decomposition algorithm is based more on the structure of the numeration system. Children can easily be convinced of the validity of the compensation property through an exercise like the one in Activity 9-8.

Mental computation in subtraction   A form of the *equal-additions* algorithm is sometimes used to subtract mentally. Given the problem, 725 — 294, if 6 is added to each number, the subtraction becomes easy:

CALCULATOR GAME (SUBTRACTION)

MATERIALS
Calculator for each student

PROCEDURE
1. One person writes three numbers on paper for all others to see.
2. Without the others seeing, find the difference between two of the numbers on your calculator.
3. Write the difference on paper for the others to see.
4. The others decide, by estimation, which two numbers were subtracted and then check their guesses on their calculator.
5. Take turns doing the activity several more times.

FIGURE 9-12

Decomposition	Equal additions
2 3 1	1 1
3 4 6	3 4 6
− 1 7 8	− 2 ₁ 8 7 8
1 6 8	1 6 8

$731 - 300 = 431$. Instead of adding 10, as in the equal-additions algorithm, any convenient number can be used. Children could be taught this strategy, which then could be reinforced occasionally with brief mental exercises.

ACTIVITY 9-8

COMPENSATION INVESTIGATION

PROCEDURE

1. Find the difference.

8	9	10	8	18	28	18	19	20
-3	-4	-5	-3	-13	-23	-13	-14	-15

2. Write a sentence about what you notice.

Examining Student Work

Boxes 9-3 and 9-4 contain samples of children's work in practicing subtraction of whole numbers. Look closely at the work and try to determine the errors the children are making. Why might they be making these errors? If you were their teacher, what might you do to help them?

Description of subtraction error pattern 1
In Box 9-3, Cheryl is subtracting the smaller number from the larger number instead of subtracting the subtrahend (bottom number) from the minuend (top number). Note that example A ($32 - 16$) is correct, perhaps because it is a double and Cheryl knows that answer. Cheryl may be applying a rule she has heard that you "always subtract the little number from the big one" (Ashlock, 2002, p. 110). She may not understand place value and regrouping.

BOX 9-3

Subtraction Error Pattern 1

Name _____Cheryl_____

A.	32	B.	245	C.	524	D.	135
	-16		-137		-298		-67
	16		112		374		132

Source: Error Patterns in Computation 8/e by Ashlock, ©2002, p. 103. Reprinted by permission of Pearson Education, Inc., Upper Saddle River, NJ.

BOX 9-4

Subtraction Error Pattern 2

Name _____George_____

A.	1⁸9⁷7	B.	1⁶7⁷6	C.	3⁷8⁷4
	-43		-23		-59
	1414		1413		325

Source: Error Patterns in Computation 8/e by Ashlock, ©2002, p. 104. Reprinted by permission of Pearson Education, Inc., Upper Saddle River, NJ.

How a teacher might help. The teacher could strengthen Cheryl's understanding of place value and regrouping by using a manipulative material for place value, such as base-ten blocks or bundles of sticks. Emphasize the process of regrouping when the digit in the subtrahend is greater than the digit in the minuend. Make sure to stress that it is possible to take a larger number away from a smaller number if the number can be regrouped.

Description of subtraction error pattern 2 In Box 9-4, George always regroups, even when not needed, such as in problem B, where George regroups to change 6 − 3 to 16 − 3 and records the answer of 13 below. He needs help in determining when regrouping is needed.

How a teacher might help. Reinforce George's understanding of regrouping by modeling these problems with manipulative materials and discussing whether regrouping is needed. Encourage George to verbalize a rule he uses for determining when to regroup.

Determining the Reasonableness of Solutions

It is often more difficult for children to determine the reasonableness of their solutions to subtraction problems than for addition problems. Thus, it becomes even more important for teachers to help children by asking questions; for example, for the doughnuts problem, a teacher could ask "Why is your answer less than (or greater than) 100? Why does this make sense?"

MULTIPLICATION

Posing Story Problems Set in Real-World Contexts

Several interpretations of multiplication were discussed in Chapter 7. All of them help children build a concept for multiplication. When it comes to developing a multiplication algorithm, the array representation is probably the most effective, because it enables one to easily represent large numbers, which will be described below.

Children's first multiplication computations should arise from real-life problems involving one-digit multi-pliers. A problem such as the following could serve as a context for exploring multiplication:

The principal bought 3 cases of sodas for the second-grade party. Each case had 24 cans. How many cans were purchased?

Using Models for Computation

Children can set out a rectangular array using as few base-ten pieces as possible, as shown in Figure 9-13(a) and note that the answer is 60 (3 × 20) plus 12 (3 × 4) or 72. They will recognize from previous experiences that 3 × 20 is 3 groups of 2 tens and the result is 6 tens. To this end, encourage children to verbalize in different ways what they have done and encourage the use of *place-value language* illustrated below using the blocks as a model. The following sequence of activities suggests a possible approach.

1. Ask the children to construct a 2-by-6 rectangle using as few base-ten blocks as possible. (See Figure 9-13[b]). They will be able to do this by using only unit cubes. Encourage children to use place-value language, such as "2 ones times 6 ones equals 12 ones."

2. Have the children construct a 2-by-60 rectangle using as few pieces as possible. (See Figure 9-13[c]). They should be able to say, "2 ones times 6 tens equals 12 tens." From these kinds of experiences, children will be able to generalize the following:
   • 3 × 10 is 3 tens, or 30.
   • 3 × 20 is 3 × 2 tens, which makes 6 tens, or 60.

It is important to allow children ample time to solve numerous problems concretely while recording, *in their own way,* what they did. In the process, encourage them to describe their work using the place-value language.

Once children feel comfortable with place-value language, they could then record products and regroup them in a place-value chart as shown below.

H	T	O		H	T	O
		6			6	0
×		2		×		2
		12			12	0
	1	2		1	2	0

FIGURE 9-13 ▶

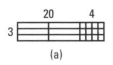

(a)

(b)

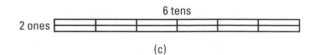

(c)

A note about language for multiplication
In the case of multiplication computation, there are a greater number of terms that children *may* eventually learn. In a problem requiring the computation, $27 \times 42 = n$, the *multiplicand* (42) is the number in each group and the *multiplier* (27) is the number of groups. These are often referred to simply as *factors*. In typical classroom interaction, the terms *multiplicand* and *multiplier* are not used extensively. Children should be allowed to use informal language for some time, rather than be expected to memorize "proper" terminology.

Using Estimation and Mental Computation

Encouraging children to estimate an answer will help them verify their concrete solution. For example, for the problem above, children might say, "My answer should be about 60, because I know that 3 times 20 is 60." Teachers can also ask questions such as "What if another child said that the answer was 600? Is that correct? Why or why not?"

Strategies for mental computation in multiplication Before children can become proficient with mental computation, they must master multiplication by powers of 10, that is, they need to be able to mentally compute exercises such as 6×10, 6×100, 6×1000, and 36×100.

Next, children should be able to use multiples of powers of 10, that is, they should be able to mentally compute exercises such as 6×30, 6×400, and 14×2000. In the last two examples, children could think: $6 \times 4 = 24$, so $6 \times 400 = 2400$; $14 \times 2 = 28$, so $14 \times 2000 = 28\,000$.

The *front-end strategy* for multiplication involves multiplying the left-most digit in each factor and using zeros in all other positions. A front-end estimate of the product of 6 and 43 would be 6×40, or 240. When both numbers have 2 or more digits, the number of zeros in the estimate becomes more critical. Children need good place-value understanding and good facility with the place-value language to become good estimators. For example, the front-end estimate of 76×93 is 7×9 or 63, but 63 what? Because we are multiplying tens by tens, the result is hundreds, so the estimate will be 6300. Writing (or thinking) 70×90 will help children make the association between "hundreds" and the two zeros in the factors.

In *front-end estimation*, problems such as 50×70 must be solved. The ability to mentally compute exercises such as this facilitates estimation. A good grasp of place-value language will help children recognize that 50×70 is 35 hundreds because tens multiplied by tens are hundreds.

Upper elementary- and middle-school children working with larger numbers will encounter a small problem with computations such as 7000×30, or 21 ten thousands, which normally is thought of as 210 000. Children will need some experiences with this dual form to become proficient at mental computation. These experiences should be included in the development of computational procedures.

Rounding is a useful strategy in multiplication. On occasion, rounding actually becomes front-end estimation. For example, in 6×43, 43 is rounded to 40, which gives the same factors used with the front-end method.

One of the most useful strategies for computing a multiplication exercise mentally is to employ the *distributive property*. For example, 5×76 can be computed as $(5 \times 70) + (5 \times 6)$. Note that it is best to multiply the tens first to get 350, then add the 30 ones to get 380. This is an illustration of the front-end approach with a second-level adjustment.

A type of *substitution* is particularly useful in mental computation when one factor ends in 7, 8, or 9. For example, 6×48 can be thought of as $(6 \times 50) - (6 \times 2)$, or $300 - 12$.

The *special numbers* strategy, also known as *landmark numbers*, involves looking for numbers that are close to "special" values or "landmarks" that are easy to work with. This strategy overlaps with the rounding and compatible numbers strategies. Special numbers could be powers of 10. If working with fractions or decimals, special numbers might be ½ or 1. Percentages such as 10% could also be considered a special number.

> *Monica was visiting another state. She discovered the sales tax was 9.4%. About how much would this add to the cost of a T-shirt that sold for $19.95?*

In solving this problem, children would reason that 9.4% is close to 10%, $19.95 is close to $20, and estimate 10% of $20, or about $2.

Developing Bridging Algorithm(s) to Connect Problems, Models, Estimation, and Symbols

After solving the problem above by making a rectangular array of base-ten blocks and noting that the solution is 72, children should be encouraged to examine the array and look for patterns. Notice that the array is made up of two parts: a 3-by-4 array of unit cubes, and a 3-by-20 array of longs. These two parts of the array are parts of the product, or *partial products*. Children should record each of the partial products, as shown in Figure 9-14. Also note the language shown in that figure, which uses place value language to help children make sense of their results. For example, 3 ones times 4 ones is 12 ones, and 3 ones times 2 tens is 6 tens. Making these connections among concrete representation, place-value language, and symbols

FIGURE 9-14

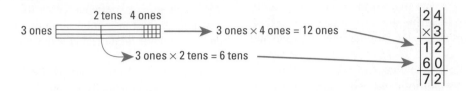

helps children make sense of computation. Children should have many experiences making these three-way connections before moving to the traditional algorithm.

Activity 9-9 will help children with the connections suggested in Figure 9-14. A set of problem cards with problems similar to the one about the principal and the soft drinks at the beginning of this section will need to be prepared in advance.

Two-digit multiplier Problems with two-digit multipliers, such as 25 × 67, are more complicated. For example, consider the following problem:

There were 25 rows of cars in the parking lot at the shopping mall. There were 67 cars in each row. How many cars were there in all?

It is important that teachers do not rush to present these problems. Be sure children can solve problems with one-digit multipliers and can explain the meaning and the procedure before introducing problems with two-digit multipliers. Two required extensions to children's place-value language are described and illustrated below when the multiplicand is also a two-digit number.

1. "2 tens times 7 ones equals 14 tens." (This is the commutative form of the "ones × tens = tens" concept learned with one-digit multipliers.)

$$\begin{array}{r} 67 \\ \uparrow \\ \times\ 25 \\ \hline \end{array}$$

2. "2 tens times 6 tens equals 12 hundreds."

$$\begin{array}{r} 67 \\ \uparrow \\ \times\ 25 \\ \hline \end{array}$$

Children should have many opportunities to use the above place-value language in the context of base-ten blocks before doing any recording. To help children with the "tens × tens = hundreds" concept, have them set out several arrays with the blocks showing multiplication with multiples of 10, as shown. When children are encouraged to talk about their array, expressions such as "2 tens times 6 tens makes 12 hundreds" will develop.

ACTIVITY 9-9

PROBLEM CARDS

MATERIALS
A set of problem cards; base-ten blocks

PROCEDURE
Work in groups of three.

1. Choose a problem card.
2. One person uses the blocks to show the problem.
3. Another describes the partial products shown by the blocks. Use language such as "4 ones times 2 tens equals 8 tens."
4. The third person records the problem and its solution in written form.
5. Change roles and do another problem.

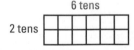

This type of array can now be extended to represent a problem such as 25 × 67 (similar to Figure 9-15). Children should have many experiences representing this type of problem with base-ten blocks, recording their work in their own way. Children could then transfer their individual method of recording to a place-value chart much like the one suggested for one-digit multipliers. The arrows and boldface print in Figure 9-16 show the two new partial products from 25 × 67.

Again, children need to see the connections between the concrete, place-value language, and the paper-and-

FIGURE 9-15

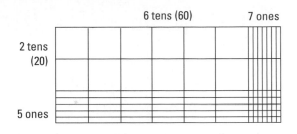

FIGURE 9-16

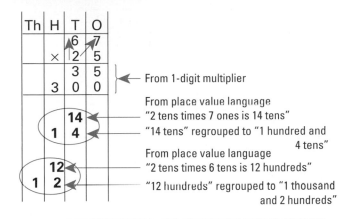

pencil algorithm. This connection is shown in Figure 9-17, which is more readily interpreted if one considers the dimensions of the base-ten pieces rather than the area. For example, the rod consists of 10 units (area) and has dimensions 1 × 10. One dimension of an array composed of a rod and a flat would be 11 (10 from the flat plus 1 from the rod), or 1 ten and 1 unit.

Note that the written record can be recorded left-to-right or right-to-left, the only difference being the order of the partial products. Some children might record their work in horizontal form prior to the vertical format: (5 × 7) + (5 × 60) + (20 × 7) × (20 × 60).

Developing the Traditional Algorithm

After children have had adequate experiences representing multiplication problems using the base-ten blocks and writing a corresponding algorithm for the representation, they will begin to shorten the algorithm. Normally only one partial product is recorded for each digit in the multiplier. The teacher can encourage children to "compress" the partial products by asking questions such as, "Try to find a shorter way to record a multiplication with two partial products."

For the first sample problem in this section, 3 × 24, the final step in the progression toward the traditional algorithm is to record the final product in one line. The dif-

ference is that rather than recording the 12 obtained when 3 ones are multiplied by 4 ones as a partial product, the 12 ones are regrouped into 2 ones, which is recorded below, while the 1 ten is written above the multiplicand and added to the number of tens obtained when the 2 tens are multiplied by the 3 ones. By placing the two methods of recording side by side, as illustrated in Figure 9-18, children will be able to connect the two and see that the 1 ten in each case (see the arrow) is the same. The connection and transition might be facilitated if children are allowed to use either format. Examples similar to those shown in Figure 9-19 could be used for a class discussion. A child could be asked to tell how the procedures are different or similar. Children should also be asked to explain the meaning of the "small" 3 and "small" 2 and to identify their corresponding number in the left-hand chart.

For two-digit multipliers, using the 25 × 67 example above, children could begin the transition by focusing only on the 5 and treating the problem as 5 × 67. They could then focus on the 2 tens as the multiplier. Because tens × ones = tens, the first digit in the second partial product will be placed in the tens position. There are 14 tens (2 tens × 7 ones), so the 4 tens will be recorded and

FIGURE 9-17

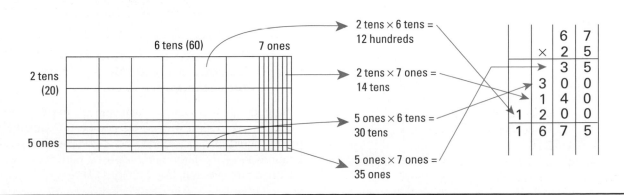

FIGURE 9-18

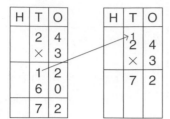

FIGURE 9-19

H	T	O
	3	6
×		6
	3	6
1	8	0
2	1	6

H	T	O
	³3	6
×		6
2	1	6

2	7	3
×		3
2	1	0
6	0	
8	1	

²2	7	3
×		3
8	1	

FIGURE 9-20

Step 1

Th	H	T	O
	³	6	7	5
	×	2	5
	3	3	5

Step 2

Th	H	T	O
	¹		6	7
	×	2	5
1	3	4	

Combined

Th	H	T	O
	¹	³	6	7	5
	×	2	5
	3	3	5
1	3	4	
1	6	7	5

the remaining 10 tens will be regrouped and recorded as 1 hundred in the hundreds column, as shown in Figure 9-16. These shorter steps are illustrated in Figure 9-20.

The connection between the long form (four partial products) and the shortened form (two partial products) should be apparent to children. To ensure this, the teacher might present both forms side-by-side, as shown in Figure 9-21, and ask children to explain the similarities and differences. Children may draw arrows as in Figure 9-21 to show the connection between the two forms.

Three- and more digit multipliers Children who are confident with two-digit multipliers should be able to move to three-digit multipliers on their own if they need to. The main extension is in the use of the place-value language developed for one- and two-digit multipliers. Although calculators will normally be used

to solve multiplication problems with large numbers, children could be invited to "prove" they know how to multiply large numbers by writing a few examples in horizontal form using the distributive property and in vertical form.

Other algorithms We have advocated exposing children to different computational procedures because it helps them understand that any algorithm is simply a series of steps that will solve a computational problem and that no one algorithm has any kind of "special" power. Experience with different algorithms also promotes reasoning and flexible thinking.

Lattice. Some programs introduce the lattice method of multiplication as enrichment or to add some variety. One drawback of this method, however, is that it is difficult to attach meaning to it or to connect place value un-

FIGURE 9-21

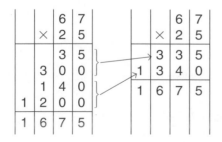

FIGURE 9-22

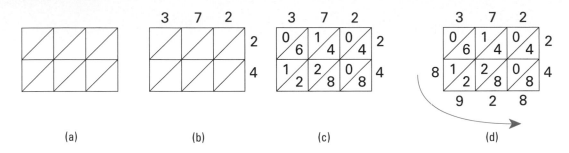

(a) (b) (c) (d)

derstandings to it and, therefore it should not be a mainstay of a unit on *multiplication*. The procedure works like this:

- Prepare an $n \times m$ grid of squares or rectangles with diagonals through each, as shown in Figure 9-22(a). The n and m represent the number of digits in the two factors.
- Write the digits from the two factors above and to the right, as shown in Figure 9-22(b).
- In each rectangle, enter the product of the corresponding digits from the two factors. [see Figure 9-22(c)]. Enter the tens digit in the upper left portion of the rectangle and the ones digit in the lower right. If the product is a single digit, enter 0 in the upper left section.
- Beginning at the lower right, add all the digits in each diagonal. When the sum is a two-digit number, regroup to the next diagonal in the normal way.
- The product is the sequence of digits obtained in the previous step, reading from upper left to lower right, as indicated by the arrow in Figure 9-22(d).

A historical computing device, *Napier's rods* (sometimes called *Napier's bones*), is related to the lattice method of multiplication. The reader is invited to read elsewhere about the nature and operation of Napier's rods.

Connections Many concepts run like threads through the mathematics curriculum from early elementary school through high school and beyond. For example, when high school students expand $(a + b)(c + d)$ as $ac + ad + bc + bd$, they are actually doing the same thing they did in elementary school when they identified and listed the four partial products in an exercise such as 27×35. In fact, they may well use a diagram similar to the representation with base-ten blocks (Figure 9-23).

The expansion of $(a + b)^2 = a^2 + 2ab + b^2$ is just a special case of the above.

Examining Student Work

Boxes 9-5 and 9-6 contain samples of children's work in practicing multiplying whole numbers. Look closely at the work and try to understand children's thinking and understand any errors the children are making. Why might they be making these errors? If you were their teacher, what might you do to help them?

Description of multiplication error pattern 1 In Box 9-5, when multiplying by tens, Bob reuses the number regrouped (recorded about the tens column) when multiplying by ones.

How a teacher might help. Use the partial product algorithm and compare the answer Bob gets when using that algorithm with his original answer. Relate the partial products algorithm to the compact algorithm (that Bob uses). Assist Bob in describing the differences and generalizing how to correct his errors.

Description of multiplication error pattern 2 In Box 9-6, Joe adds the number regrouped (recorded about the tens column) before multiplying the digit in the tens column, rather than multiplying first and then adding on the number regrouped. This error could be carried over from how Joe was taught to add; perhaps Joe was taught that "the first thing you do is to add the number you carry" (Ashlock, 2002, p. 131).

FIGURE 9-23

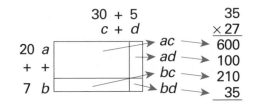

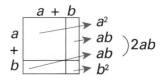

BOX 9-5

Multiplication Error Pattern 1

Name _____Bob_____

A. $\overset{2}{4}6$
× 24
184
102
1204

B. $\overset{1}{7}6$
× 32
152
228
2432

C. $\overset{5}{4}8$
× 57
336
250
2836

Source: Error Patterns in Computation 8/e by Ashlock, ©2002, p. 125. Reprinted by permission of Pearson Education, Inc., Upper Saddle River, NJ.

BOX 9-6

Multiplication Error Pattern 2

Name _____Joe_____

A. $\overset{2}{2}7$
× 4
168

B. $\overset{2}{3}4$
× 6
304

C. $\overset{3}{4}5$
× 7
495

Source: Error Patterns in Computation 8/e by Ashlock, ©2002, p. 125. Reprinted by permission of Pearson Education, Inc., Upper Saddle River, NJ.

How a teacher might help Use the partial product algorithm or build an array with base-ten blocks to solve the problem. Compare the answers obtained in each way. Assist Joe in describing the correct sequence for dealing with the number regrouped.

Determining the Reasonableness of Solutions for Multiplication

It is often even more difficult for children to determine the reasonableness of their solutions to multiplication problems than for addition or subtraction problems. This difficulty is often a result of children not fully understanding place value and its relationship to multiplica-

tion. For example, children sometimes have difficulty determining the result to 3 × 70, even though they know that 3 × 7 is 21. It is important for teachers to frequently ask questions such as "How is 3 × 70 different from 3 × 7? How is it similar to 3 × 7?" Other questions that are helpful to ask include (for the problem 3 × 74) "What will the answer be *close to?*" and "Another child said the answer was 2112. Is this reasonable? Why or why not?"

DIVISION

Although the process of division is a "natural" part of children's experiences, computational procedures have proved to be difficult for children to learn for several reasons. Probably the most significant is that not only do children need to know the division basic facts but also they need to be able to multiply and subtract efficiently.

A great deal of time is spent in elementary and middle school trying to help children master the division algorithm. This is unjustifiable given that adults will reach for a calculator when a long-division computation is needed.

Instruction on division computation should emphasize one-digit divisors so that children can develop an understanding of the steps involved. Some experience with two-digit divisors also is necessary, particularly to help children develop skill in estimating partial quotients. Extending this to a four-digit dividend can provide all the experience needed to become proficient with paper-and-pencil division computation. Beyond that, virtually all adults reach for a calculator, so why shouldn't children? There are times when division with larger numbers is required to solve a problem and a calculator may not be available. These "large computations," however, should not be the focus of instruction.

Posing Story Problems Set in Real-World Contexts

Instruction should begin with a real life problem. For example:

Five children agreed to share equally all the apples they collected on Halloween. They collected 67 apples. How many apples did each child get?

Notice that the above problem results in a remainder. Sharing situations in which there is no remainder are rare, and they can be treated as a special case of the general algorithm.

The problem with the same numbers can be posed using an area and array interpretation, as below:

A teacher wanted to arrange 67 chairs into 5 rows. How many chairs will be in each row?

Using Models for Computation

Children can use base-ten blocks to find the solution to the apples problem, as shown in Figure 9-24. Notice that the blocks are split evenly among the five groups.

The chairs problem also can be solved using base-ten blocks. In this interpretation, however, it makes more sense to model the problem as an array, as shown in Figure 9-25. Notice that in division problems using the area and array interpretation, the area (67) is known and the number of rows (5) are known, and the task is to find the length of the rows). In both interpretations, make sure children understand the meaning of each of the numbers in the problem, and how those numbers connect with the base-ten blocks. As with the other operations, making

these connections among concrete representation, place-value language, and symbols helps children make sense of computation. Children should have many experiences making these three-way connections before moving to the traditional algorithm.

A note about language for division As in multiplication, there are many terms related to division that children *may* eventually learn. In a division setting, the total number to be "divided up" (shared) is the *dividend,* the number in each group is the *divisor,* and the resulting number of groups is the *quotient.* (Some problems require the divisor and quotient to exchange meanings.) The number of objects, if any, that cannot be shared equally is referred to as the *remainder.* Children often call these the "leftovers."

Using Estimation and Mental Computation

Mental computation with division problems is probably best achieved by thinking of division as the inverse of multiplication, that is, using a basic fact example, $48 \div 6$, children can think, "What times 6 is 48?" This works particularly well when the dividend is a number such as 18 000 and the divisor is a single digit. For example, $18\,000 \div 6$ is 3000 because 6×3 is 18, so 6×3000 is 18 000.

Where the divisor is also a multiple of 10, there are two main approaches children could use to compute mentally. First, children are commonly taught to mentally divide each number by 10. In this case, $240 \div 40$ becomes $24 \div 4$, $2400 \div 40$ is $240 \div 4$, and so on. These examples are now equivalent to the examples in the preceding paragraph. The second way is to consider only the non-zero digits and then determine the place value of the quotient afterward. For $18\,000 \div 60$, think: "$6 \times$ what is 18? $6 \times 3 = 18$. The 3 must be hundreds because tens (60) $\times$ hundreds (300) is thousands (18 000). The quotient is 300." For the most part, computations more complex than these should be done by elementary- and middle-school children using paper-and-pencil algorithms or calculators rather than mentally.

Developing Bridging Algorithm to Connect Problems, Models, Estimation, and Symbols

Learning the paper-and-pencil algorithm is essentially learning a means of recording what is done concretely. Using place-value language and the base-ten blocks is a natural and efficient way to do this.

The first step is to introduce children to a "different" way of writing $67 \div 5$, as shown here.

$$5)\overline{67}$$

FIGURE 9-24

PROBLEM/STEPS	CONCRETE REPRESENTATION	SYMBOLIC REPRESENTATION		
		LADDER ALGORITHM	PYRAMID ALGORITHM	TRADITIONAL ALGORITHM
67 apples shared among 5 children. How many does each child get?	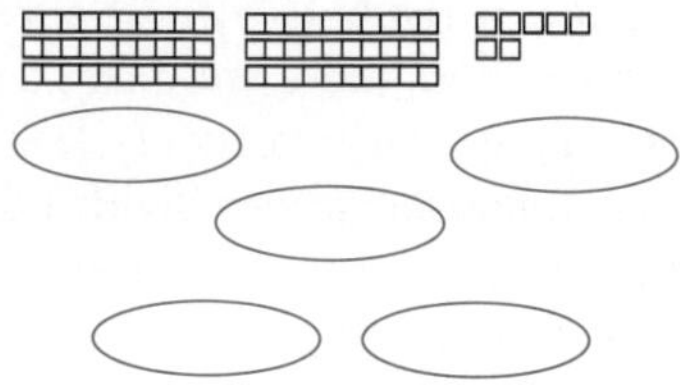 *(concrete drawing)*	$5\overline{)67}$	$5\overline{)67}$	$5\overline{)67}$
Distribute tens.	*(concrete drawing)*	$5\overline{)67}$ -50 ∣ 10 17	10 $5\overline{)67}$ -50 17	1 $5\overline{)67}$ -50 17
Regroup tens to ones. Distribute ones.	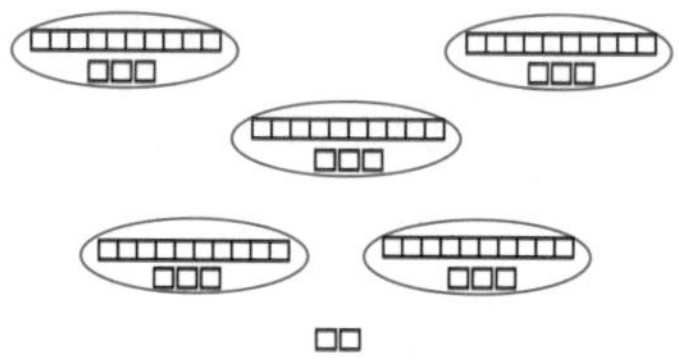 *(concrete drawing)*	$5\overline{)67}$ -50 ∣ 10 17 -15 ∣ 3 2	3 10 $5\overline{)67}$ -50 17 -15 2	13 $5\overline{)67}$ -50 17 -15 2
Result: Each child gets 13 apples. There are 2 apples left over.	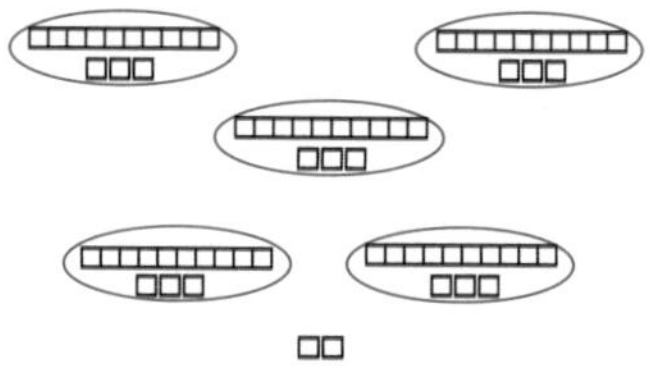 *(concrete drawing)*	13r2 $5\overline{)67}$ -50 ∣ 10 17 -15 ∣ 3 2 ∣ 13	13r2 3 10 $5\overline{)67}$ -50 17 -15 2	13r2 $5\overline{)67}$ -50 17 -15 2

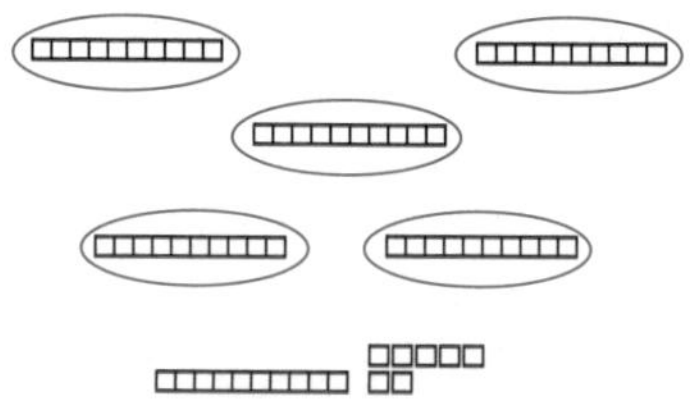

FIGURE 9-25

PROBLEM/STEPS	CONCRETE REPRESENTATION
67 chairs arranged into 5 rows. How many in each row?	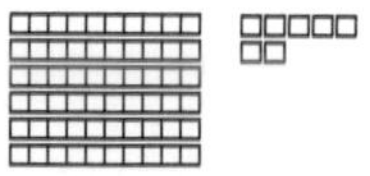 *(concrete drawing)*
Arrange tens into 5 rows.	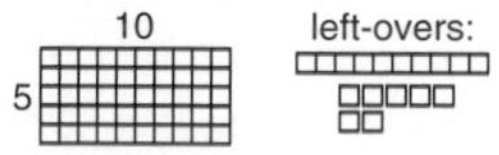 *(concrete drawing: 10, left-overs)*
Regroup ten to ones. Arrange ones into 5 rows	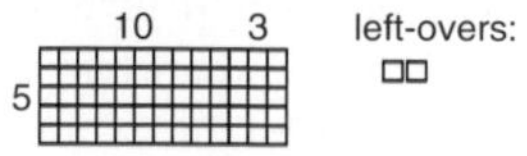 *(concrete drawing: 10, 3, left-overs)*
Result: There are 13 chairs in each row, with 2 chairs left over	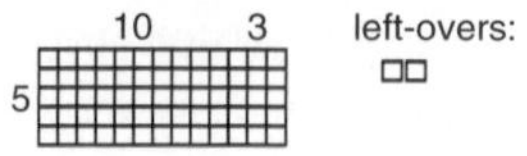 *(concrete drawing: 10, 3, left-overs)*

When solving division questions such as 67 divided by 5, the phrase "5 goes into 67" should *not* be used (it has no meaning). Rather, language that is appropriate for the context should be used such as "67 apples to be shared among 5 people" or "5 groups to share 67 apples." In a measurement context, expressions such as "67 apples to be separated into groups of 5" might be used. In an area or array context, a phrase such as "67 chairs arranged into 5 rows" could be used.

Figure 9-24 illustrates two different ways the sharing and place-value language could be translated into a paper-and-pencil recording process. These algorithms are known as the *ladder* or *repeated subtraction* algorithm, and the *pyramid* or *partial quotients* algorithm. Notice that in the ladder method, the number in each group is recorded *down the right side* of the problem, and then added and transferred above the dividend. Similarly, in the pyramid method, the number in each group is recorded *above* the divisor, then added to form the quotient. The usefulness of these algorithms will become more apparent in the following section, where we consider three-digit dividends. It is important, however, to begin using these algorithms with two-digit divisors for consistency.

Three-digit dividend   Problems with three-digit dividends are a bit more complicated. Consider the following problem:

Six children agreed to share 739 baseball cards. How many baseball cards did each child get?

The reader should set out the base-ten blocks and manipulate them in step with the sequence in Figure 9-26, in which 739 things shared among 6 children is illustrated.

After solving the problem using base-ten blocks, start again, this time recording the result of each step, using the ladder algorithm and the pyramid algorithm. Think about what each number means in each algorithm.

For example, what does the 100 mean in the ladder algorithm? It means that we put 100 into each group (or, using the context of the problem, that each child got 100 baseball cards). Now consider the 100 in the pyramid algorithm—it means the same thing but is written in a different location. Finally, consider the 100 (or the 1 in the hundreds place) in the traditional algorithm. It also means the same thing—but it is a little more abstract, because rather than it being written as 100, it is written as 1 in the hundreds place. This distinction is often overlooked or misunderstood by children, so it is important that teachers call attention to it through discussion.

Children need to work through many problems involving one-digit divisors and two- and three-digit dividends. Teachers should not rush into introducing division with two-digit divisors until children can clearly verbalize and model what they are doing as they solve one-digit divisor problems using paper and pencil.

Developing the Traditional Algorithm

After children have had adequate experiences representing division problems using the base-ten blocks and using either the ladder algorithm or the pyramid algorithm for the representation, they will begin to shorten the algorithm. In the traditional algorithm, only a one-digit partial quotient is recorded for each digit in the dividend. The teacher can encourage children to "compress" the partial quotients by asking questions such as "Try to find a shorter way to record a division problem." The following section describes this in greater detail.

For the first sample problem in this section, $67 \div 5$, the final step in the progression toward the traditional algorithm is to record the quotient on one line above the

dividend, as shown in the far right column in Figure 9-24. Making sense of the traditional algorithm depends on children having a strong understanding of place value as well as the teacher using language and asking questions that emphasize place value.

The difference between the traditional algorithm for division and the ladder and pyramid algorithms is a great emphasis on place value. For example, rather than recording the 10 obtained when 67 is split into 5 groups, in the traditional algorithm this would be recorded as 1 group of ten by writing a 1 above the 6 tens in the divisor. By placing the three algorithms side-by-side, as illustrated in Figure 9-24, children will be able to connect the algorithms and see that the 1 ten in each case is the same. The connection and transition will be facilitated if children are allowed to use either format.

Similarly, for problems with three-digit divisors, such as $739 \div 6$, rather than recording the 100 obtained when 739 is split into 6 groups, in the traditional algorithm this would be recorded as 1 group of one hundred by writing a 1 above the 7 hundreds in the divisor. By placing the three algorithms side-by-side, as illustrated in Figure 9-26, children will be able to connect the algorithms and see that the 1 ten in each case is the same. The connection and transition will be facilitated if children are allowed to use either format.

Making sense of remainders   All of the examples in this section involved remainders. It is customary to report remainders in one of two ways, as shown below. In the first case, the remainder is simply reported as a remainder. In the second example, the remainder is reported as a fraction of the divisor and is an integral part of the quotient.

$$
\begin{array}{r} 1\,0\,4\text{ R}1 \\ 6\overline{)6\,2\,5} \end{array}
\qquad
\begin{array}{r} 1\,0\,4\tfrac{1}{6} \\ 6\overline{)6\,2\,5} \end{array}
$$

Either of the above is an acceptable response if the computation is strictly a symbolic process. When the computation arises from a real-life context, the remainder must be interpreted in the context of the problem and handled in a way that is appropriate to that context. Consider the following four cases.

Case 1: Part of the answer.

I have a 29-inch length of ribbon from which I want to make five award ribbons of equal length. How long will each ribbon be?

Here the answer, 5 R4, does not make sense because there is no need to have wasted material. In this case, the answer 5 inches makes more sense. The "remainder" is part of the answer.

FIGURE 9-26

PROBLEM/STEPS	CONCRETE REPRESENTATION	SYMBOLIC REPRESENTATION		
		LADDER ALGORITHM	**PYRAMID ALGORITHM**	**TRADITIONAL ALGORITHM**
739 baseball cards shared among 6 children. How many cards does each child get?	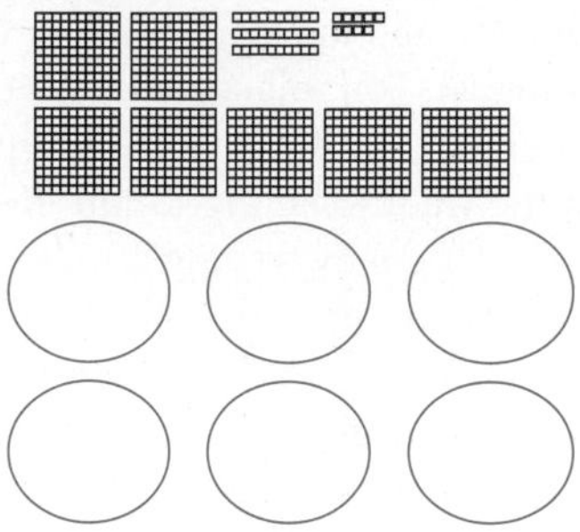	$6\overline{)739}$	$6\overline{)739}$	$6\overline{)739}$
Distribute hundreds into 6 groups.	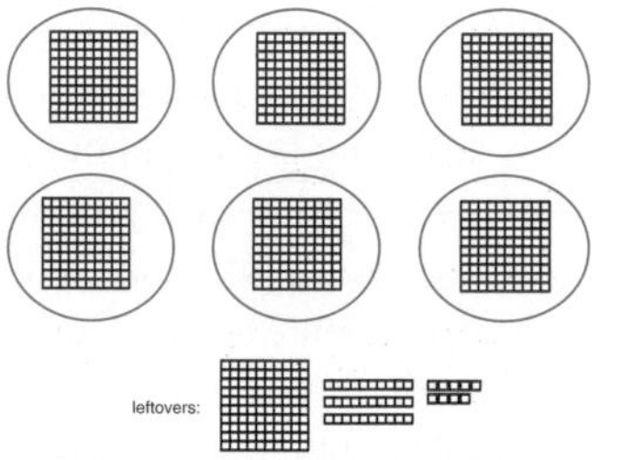 leftovers:	$\begin{array}{r} 6\overline{)739} \\ -600 \ \ \lfloor 100 \\ \hline 139 \end{array}$	$\begin{array}{r} 100 \\ 6\overline{)739} \\ -600 \\ \hline 139 \end{array}$	$\begin{array}{r} 1 \\ 6\overline{)739} \\ -600 \\ \hline 139 \end{array}$
Regroup hundred into tens. Distribute tens into 6 groups.	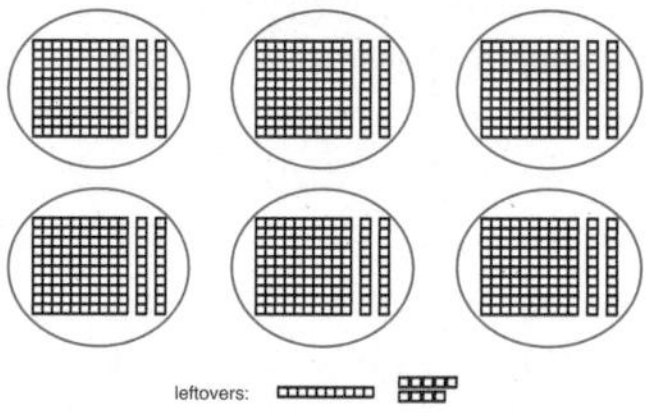 leftovers:	$\begin{array}{r} 6\overline{)739} \\ -600 \ \ 100 \\ \hline 139 \\ -120 \ \ 20 \\ \hline 19 \end{array}$	$\begin{array}{r} 20 \\ 100 \\ 6\overline{)739} \\ -600 \\ \hline 139 \\ -120 \\ \hline 19 \end{array}$	$\begin{array}{r} 12 \\ 6\overline{)739} \\ -600 \\ \hline 139 \\ -120 \\ \hline 19 \end{array}$
Regroup ten into ones. Distribute ones into 6 groups	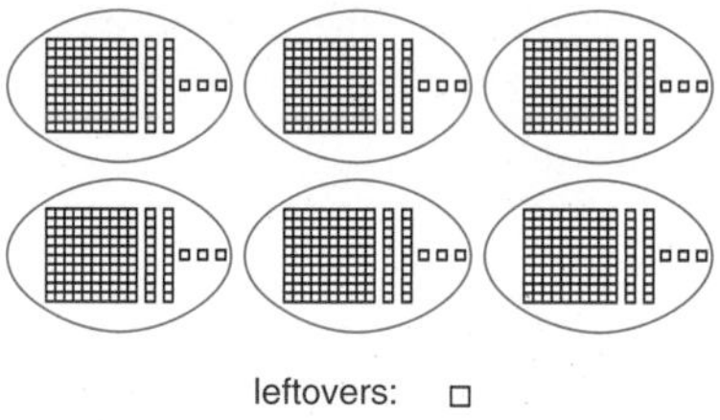 leftovers: □	$\begin{array}{r} 6\overline{)739} \\ -600 \ \ 100 \\ \hline 139 \\ -120 \ \ 20 \\ \hline 19 \\ -18 \ \ 3 \\ \hline 1 \end{array}$	$\begin{array}{r} 3 \\ 20 \\ 100 \\ 6\overline{)739} \\ -600 \\ \hline 139 \\ -120 \\ \hline 19 \\ -18 \\ \hline 1 \end{array}$	$\begin{array}{r} 123 \\ 6\overline{)739} \\ -600 \\ \hline 139 \\ -120 \\ \hline 19 \\ -18 \\ \hline 1 \end{array}$
Result: Each child gets 123 cards. There is 1 card left.	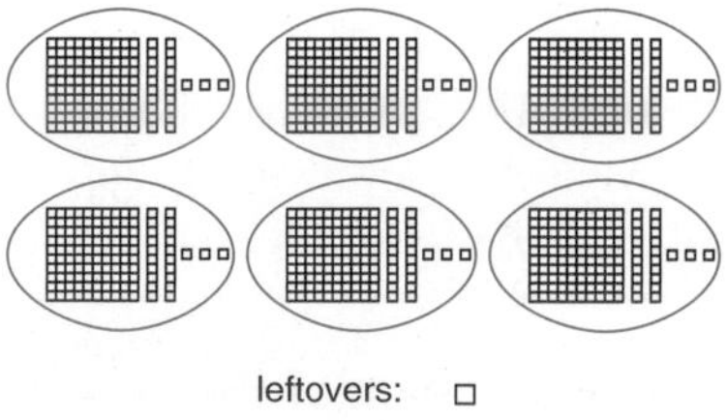 leftovers: □	$\begin{array}{r} 123r1 \\ 6\overline{)739} \\ -600 \ \ 100 \\ \hline 139 \\ -120 \ \ 20 \\ \hline 19 \\ -18 \ \ 3 \\ \hline 1 \ \ 123 \end{array}$	$\begin{array}{r} 123r1 \\ 3 \\ 20 \\ 100 \\ 6\overline{)739} \\ -600 \\ \hline 139 \\ -120 \\ \hline 19 \\ -18 \\ \hline 1 \end{array}$	$\begin{array}{r} 123r1 \\ 6\overline{)739} \\ -600 \\ \hline 139 \\ -120 \\ \hline 19 \\ -18 \\ \hline 1 \end{array}$

Case 2: Include remainders.

Seven parents have volunteered to drive Mrs. Clemenson's class on their field trip to the zoo. There are 31 people going on the trip, including the parents. How many people will be in each car?

Neither 4 R3 nor 4 makes any sense in this case. What would actually happen is that 4 cars would take 4 people and 3 cars would have 5 people. No one will be left behind. Again, there really is no remainder. The "remainder" has to be included by evenly distributing it among as many groups as necessary.

Case 3: Round up.

A grocery store sells spaghetti sauce at 2 jars for $1.39. How much would a customer pay for one jar?

Again, neither 69 R1 nor 69 makes any sense. The quotient would be rounded up, and the customer would pay 70¢ for one jar.

Case 4: Ignore remainder.

Thirty seven children try out for three teams. If 11 players are allowed on each team, how many teams can be formed?

Clearly, neither 3 R4 nor 3 is an appropriate answer. Four children cannot be included on a team. They can be scorekeepers, timers, or equipment managers but have to be "ignored" as part of the teams.

Two-digit divisors The role of estimation becomes much more significant when children need to use a divisor with two (or more) digits. Consider a computation such as $493 \div 62$. Children can take several approaches to estimating the quotient.

1. *Rounding.* By rounding the divisor to the nearest 10, a logical estimate is 8 because 8×60 is 480. However, $8 \times 62 = 496$, which is larger than the dividend.

2. *Ignore the last digit in both the divisor and the dividend.* This results in the exercise, $49 \div 6$. Again, 8 is a reasonable, but too high, estimate.

3. *Round the divisor up to the nearest 10.* The above example would be thought of as $493 \div 70$. Because 7×70 is 490, a reasonable estimate is 7, which works well. However, if the problem had been $503 \div 62$, the estimate would still be 7 because $7 \times 70 = 490$ and $8 \times 70 = 560$, which exceeds the dividend. However, 7 is too small in this case.

4. *Round the divisor up and round the dividend down to the nearest compatible number.* This produces the most conservative estimate, often too low. Using the previous example, the quotient estimate would be based on $420 \div 70$. In this case, 6 is the best estimate, but it is too small. We shall return to this problem shortly.

LITERATURE LINK 9-1
Addition, Subtraction, Multiplication, Division, Estimation, and Computational Procedures

Pinczes, Elinor. (1995). *A Remainder of One.* New York: Houghton Mifflin.

Developing the language of mathematics, including both the words that children use to communicate orally and the written symbol system, is essential for mathematical understanding yet it lags behind the performance of mathematical computations. Using children's books with authentic problem situations helps children see that learning computation solves a real-life purpose. *A Remainder of One* is the story of a squadron of 25 bugs who try unsuccessfully to divide evenly for a parade. After several attempts, the squadron finds that five rows of five is the solution to their mathematical dilemma.

• Create groups or arrays using snap cubes or centimeter cubes to model the formations of the 25th squadron in the story.

• Represent numbers other than 25. Determine which of those numbers divide evenly and which of them have remainders.

• Have children select a number between 26 and 50 and divide their number by 2, 3, 4, and 5. Write number sentences showing each of these division sentences and illustrate the division of their own bug squadron on large sheets of construction paper. Look for patterns, such as those numbers that always have a remainder or those that never have a remainder.

• Determine the different factors of numbers by using color tiles or graph paper to group different numbers into arrays. Identify numbers that have several factors and those that have only two factors. Make a chart of these numbers and identify them as "prime" and "composite" numbers.

Source: Dr. Patricia Moyer, George Mason University.

The language corresponding to the steps in the algorithm is essentially the same as for the one-digit divisor. A sample of the language associated with each step in computing 493 ÷ 62 is described in Figure 9-27.

Employing the compatible number strategy along with rounding up the divisor will produce conservative estimates as long as the compatible number is less than the dividend. In fact, many times an estimate that is too small will occur with this combined strategy. This is a problem meant more for adults than for children who are familiar with this phenomenon in real life. For example, a child may share some sweets with other members of a group by giving each person two sweets. More can still be equally shared, so another round of sharing takes place.

The same process can be used with the division algorithm. The only question is how to record successive sharing of the same place-value pieces. If a child had used 420 as the compatible number for the dividend, the first estimate of the quotient would be 6. Figure 9-28 shows how the paper-and-pencil record might be kept.

The final result of the algorithm must be recorded in either form (a) or form (b) in Figure 9-29.

Examining Student Work

Boxes 9-7 and 9-8 contain samples of children's work in practicing dividing whole numbers. Look closely at the work and try to determine what the children understand

---

FIGURE 9-27 ▶

CONNECTING PLACE-VALUE LANGUAGE AND SYMBOLIC RECORD FOR TWO-DIGIT DIVISORS

LANGUAGE	RECORD
I cannot share 4 hundreds among 62 groups. I cannot share 49 tens among 62 groups, but I can share 493 ones among 62 groups.	62)493
I will estimate how many ones I can share by rounding the 62 groups to 70.	Think 70 → 62)493
What number is compatible with 70 that I can use for the dividend? 490	Think 70 → 62)493 ← Think 490 70)490
7 × 70 is 490 so I can distribute 7 ones to each group. Recording the 7 in the ones position since I am distributing ones.	7 62)493
How many ones were distributed to the 62 groups? 7 × 62 = 434.	7 62)493 434
How many ones are left? 59. Can I distribute any more ones? No. There is a remainder of 59.	7 62)493 434 59

FIGURE 9-28 ▶

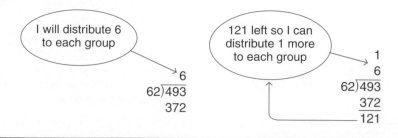

BOX 9-7

BOX 9-7

Division Error Pattern 1

Name _____Gail_____

A.
$$
\begin{array}{r}
44 \\
2\overline{)88} \\
8 \\
\hline
8 \\
8 \\
\end{array}
$$

B.
$$
\begin{array}{r}
14 \\
4\overline{)164} \\
16 \\
\hline
4 \\
4 \\
\end{array}
$$

C.
$$
\begin{array}{r}
67 \\
3\overline{)228} \\
21 \\
\hline
18 \\
18 \\
\end{array}
$$

D.
$$
\begin{array}{r}
39 \\
5\overline{)465} \\
45 \\
\hline
15 \\
15 \\
\end{array}
$$

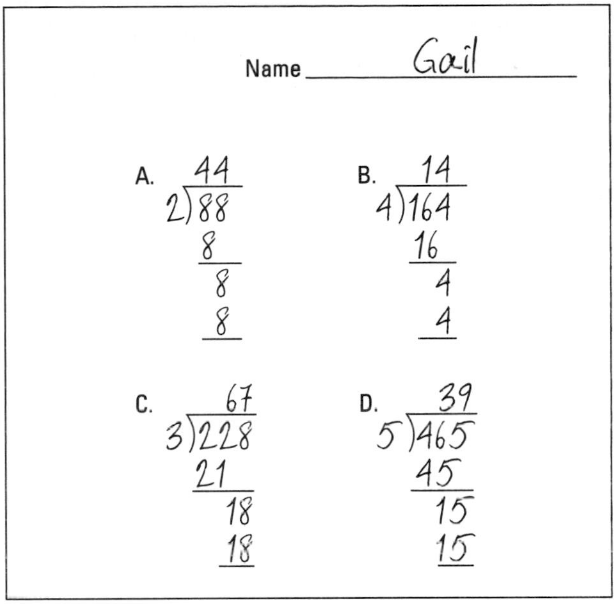

Source: Error Patterns in Computation 8/e by Ashlock, ©2002, p. 128. Reprinted by permission of Pearson Education, Inc., Upper Saddle River, NJ.

about division and analyze the errors the children are making. Why might they be making these errors? If you were their teacher, what might you do to help them?

Description of division error pattern 1 In Box 9-7, Gail records the quotient (answer) from right to left. She may be overgeneralizing procedures that she uses in addition, subtraction, and multiplication, where the ones digit of the answer is usually recorded first.

How a teacher might help. Emphasize estimating the quotient for each problem. For example, in Problem B,

164 ÷ 4 should be about 40, and in Problem D, 465 ÷ 5 should be about 90. Encourage Gail to compare these estimates with her answers. Discuss with Gail the correct placement of digits in the quotient.

Description of division error pattern 2 In Box 9-8, John does not record a zero in the quotient. He may be bringing down one digit at a time and not recording a zero when he cannot divide, or he may be bringing down groups of two digits at a time from the dividend.

How a teacher might help Use the pyramid algorithm to help John understand the role of place value in the answer to a division problem. Also, encourage John to estimate each result before beginning a division problem.

Determining the Reasonableness of Solutions

It is critically important for children to think about the reasonableness of their solutions to division problems. As with other operations, teachers' questioning can help children focus on reasonableness. For example, consider the problem 804 ÷ 2. The 0 in the dividend will often cause difficulties for children; a common incorrect answer to this problem is 42. It is important for teachers to

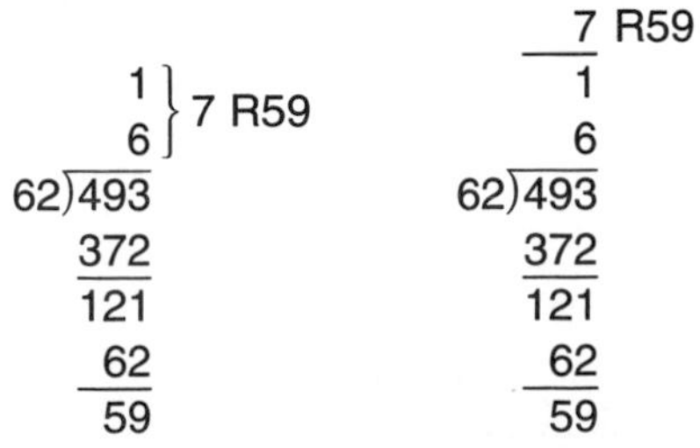

FIGURE 9-29

(a)
$$
\begin{array}{r}
\left.\begin{array}{r} 1 \\ 6 \end{array}\right\} 7 \text{ R59} \\
62\overline{)493} \\
372 \\
\hline
121 \\
62 \\
\hline
59 \\
\end{array}
$$

(b)
$$
\begin{array}{r}
7 \text{ R59} \\
1 \\
6 \\
62\overline{)493} \\
372 \\
\hline
121 \\
62 \\
\hline
59 \\
\end{array}
$$

BOX 9-8

Division Error Pattern 2

Name _____John_____

A.
$$7\overline{)456}\ \ \ ^{65}R1$$
42
36
35
1

B.
$$6\overline{)5426}\ \ \ ^{94}R2$$
54
26
24
2

C.
$$8\overline{)4860}\ \ \ ^{67}R4$$
48
60
56
4

D.
$$8\overline{)4035}\ \ \ ^{54}R3$$
40
35
32
3

Source: Error Patterns in Computation 8/e by Ashlock, ©2002, p. 129. Reprinted by permission of Pearson Education, Inc., Upper Saddle River, NJ.

frequently ask questions such as "If 804 things are shared by 2 children, *about how many* will each child get?" Other questions that are helpful to ask include "What will the answer be *close to?*" and "Another child said the answer was 42. Is this reasonable? Why or why not?"

CONSOLIDATION AND ENRICHMENT

Once children have developed computational procedures, they need many activities that will help to consolidate their understanding and to develop proficiency in terms of accuracy and speed. In addition, enrichment activities can be motivating to children. Doing straightforward computations is all right once in a while, but a teacher needs to have a large repertoire of ideas and activities for practice purposes. The following categories are only examples of the different types of activities a teacher might use.

Puzzles

Puzzles provide an interesting and novel way for children to practice computation (Neufeld, 1991). Children will receive a great deal of practice with addition and subtrac-

tion as they attempt to complete the puzzle in Activity 9-10. How do they get practice with subtraction?

In the puzzle in Figure 9-30, children are to trace a path from the upper left cell to the lower right cell by joining cells that contain a number divisible by 7. Cells may be joined vertically, horizontally, or diagonally.

Games

Many games are useful for consolidation purposes. Games where winning is based on mental strategy rather than on chance should be used. Activity 9-11 is one example.

Some variations on Activity 9-11 could include the following:

- Use worksheets with 3 three-digit numbers, 3 two-digit numbers, etc.
- Go for the lowest sum.
- Use subtraction. (Use one less digit in the subtrahend than in the minuend to reduce the possibility of negative numbers.)
- Use multiplication or division.
- Will your strategy be different if balls are *not* replaced?

ACTIVITY 9-10

HONEYCOMB SUM

MATERIALS

PROCEDURE

1. Make each column sum to 38. You can use only the numbers 1 through 19. Use each number only once.

2. Can you do it a different way?

Activity 9-12 encourages children to apply some "number-sense thinking" about possible combinations while providing some practice with the algorithms involving small numbers. Many of the combinations will not involve division because division will not produce a whole number. Nevertheless, children will need to consider division and make a mental decision as to whether the number will divide evenly.

FIGURE 9-30

START ↓

				7 AS A DIVISOR			
7	1005	634	904	1111	156	63	427
238	268	928	56	1215	297	5123	5
494	84	1015	96	140	307	77	7963
47	2047	82	5326	217	3131	9876	357
721	6055	214	63	3333	384	197	4242
128	9	4014	546	753	2114	595	1584
539	4021	535	246	2499	872	287	59
749	587	2121	8642	37	3977	861	4536

FINISH

ACTIVITY 9-11

GREATEST SUM

MATERIALS
- 10 Ping-Pong balls with numerals 0, 1, 2, . . . 9. (Cards could be used, but they tend to stick together, reducing randomness.)
- Worksheet as below. (Several grids can be placed on one page to facilitate multiple games.)

PROCEDURE

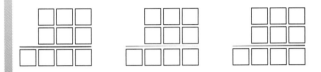

1. Select a leader to draw balls. (If this is a whole-class activity, the teacher may act as leader.)

2. The leader draws a ball and announces the number on it. All players write this number in one of the addend boxes on the worksheet. Once a number has been placed, it cannot be moved or changed.

3. Replace the ball and shake the bag.

4. Repeat steps 2 and 3 until all addend boxes are filled.

5. Compute the sum.

6. The winners are all those with the greatest sum.

ACTIVITY 9-12

ALL-OPS

MATERIALS
- 3 dice: 1 regular (numbers 1–6)
            1 with numbers 7–12
            1 with numbers 13–18
- Game board for each player

OBJECT
To be the first to place 5 markers in a row, column, or diagonal.

PROCEDURE

1. One player shakes all 3 dice.

2. All players then use the 3 numbers showing and any combination of the 4 operations to try to produce a number on their card.

3. Each player must have one other player verify his or her work.

4. Players take turns rolling the dice.

Two of the dice must be specially prepared, as will a variety of game boards. Numbers from 1 to 1296 can be used randomly to create the game boards. How can 1 be achieved? How can 1296 be achieved? A sample game board is shown in Figure 9-31.

Like all bingo-type cards, the card in Figure 9-31 will not contain responses for some rolls of the dice. If a combination cannot be found in a reasonable time, play goes to the next player. Does the card in Figure 9-31 have a response for a roll of 5, 9, or 17?

Riddles

Riddles are another motivating way for children to practice computation. The solution to a riddle similar to the one suggested in Chapter 8 could be developed with larger numbers to provide addition and subtraction computation practice. Once you have found (or created) a riddle, it is not difficult to construct exercises such as those shown in Activity 9-13 and Figure 9-32. Knowing the answer to a riddle, the teacher can simply create the kind of questions the class or small group of children need practice with and then associate each letter with the answer to a computation. The difficulty level can be changed to suit the level of the class. The exercises could also be altered to include decimals or common fractions.

Computer Software

Research suggests that the use of the computer does enhance computational performance (Cathcart, 1990, 1991). Computer software is one more ingredient in a teacher's repertoire of ideas to provide variety in practice activities. Many excellent software programs are available to practice computation.

FIGURE 9-31

ALL-OPS

4	88	19	38	89
1024	55	76	106	8
60	3	I Can	111	635
149	91	384	9	63
904	210	788	500	1296

ACTIVITY 9-13

WHY DOES A HUMMINGBIRD HUM?

PROCEDURE

1. Do each computation, then use the code to find the matching letter. The first one is done as an example.

CODE

37 – W	122 – C	232 – H
54 – N	123 – O	241 – K
73 – M	154 – R	259 – E
78 – T	162 – D	287 – S
83 – I	163 – L	341 – A

$36 + 47 = \underline{83} \ \underline{1}$ $386 - 145 = \underline{} \ \underline{}$

$143 - 65 = \underline{} \ \underline{}$ $618 - 564 = \underline{} \ \underline{}$

$64 + 98 = \underline{} \ \underline{}$ $66 + 9 + 48 = \underline{} \ \underline{}$

$12 + 69 + 42 = \underline{} \ \underline{}$ $100 - 63 = \underline{} \ \underline{}$

$345 - 86 = \underline{} \ \underline{}$ $155 - 77 = \underline{} \ \underline{}$

$402 - 115 = \underline{} \ \underline{}$ $155 + 77 = \underline{} \ \underline{}$

$92 - 38 = \underline{} \ \underline{}$ $167 + 92 = \underline{} \ \underline{}$

$97 + 26 = \underline{} \ \underline{}$ $108 - 71 = \underline{} \ \underline{}$

$212 - 134 = \underline{} \ \underline{}$ $254 - 131 = \underline{} \ \underline{}$

$88 + 66 = \underline{} \ \underline{}$

$115 + 47 = \underline{} \ \underline{}$

$136 + 295 - 144 = \underline{} \ \underline{}$

Other Algorithms

The Russian Peasant algorithm can be presented in the form of a story. Provide the following background to the story.

A certain Russian peasant (fictional, of course), who had attended school only occasionally, was in charge of a cabbage farm for the Russian czar. He could add well, double a number, and divide by 2 but had no idea what to do with remainders, so he ignored them. He had no formal knowledge of fractions. He had an intuitive idea that somehow multiplication (doubling) was the opposite of dividing by 2. He could also recognize odd and even numbers.

Early one spring this Russian peasant was pacing off his field to determine how many cabbage plants he needed for transplanting. Just as he finished, the overseer came riding up on his big white horse and demanded, "How many cabbage plants do you need this spring?"

"We-l-l-l sir, I'm not sure. I know I have room for 25 rows and I can put 36 in each row."

"How many is that!" demanded the overseer.

FIGURE 9-32

How does a monster count to 20?

$4\overline{)136}$ → S $5\overline{)1600}$ → A

$8\overline{)280}$ → G $7\overline{)2975}$ → C

$9\overline{)5319}$ → N $6\overline{)144}$ → F

$6\overline{)1458}$ → T $7\overline{)105}$ → O

$9\overline{)801}$ → L $5\overline{)65}$ → E

$3\overline{)396}$ → I $8\overline{)3064}$ → R

15	591	132	243	34		
24	132	591	35	13	383	34

"I-I-I-I'm-m-m not sure, sir."

"I'm going down the road to see the next farmer. If you don't know how many plants you need by the time I get back, I'll have your head."

The poor peasant sat down to see whether he could figure out how many cabbage plants he needed.

He wrote: **25   36**

"Well, I could double the 36. That would give me 72. No, I need a lot more than that. Since I doubled 36, maybe I'd better halve 25.   ~~**12**~~   ~~**72**~~

Let's see, that is 12." (Keep in mind he didn't know what to do with remainders.)

"Perhaps I should do that again."   **6**   ~~**144**~~
(He continued this process   **3**   **288**
until he got to 1 on the   **1**   **576**
left-hand side.)

"U-m-m-m, I'm sure I need more than 576 plants. Oh, yes, that astrologer friend of mine told me that numbers associated with even numbers are unlucky."

"I'll strike out the 12 and 6 rows. I can't see that helps me.   **25   36**

I wonder what would   **12   72**
happen if I added this side   **6   144**
[pointing to the right-hand   **3   288**
column]?" He adds 36 288,   **1   576**
and 576 to get 900.   **900**
Just then overseer comes riding back on his big white horse.

Ask the children to do an example on their own and to tell how they know their answer is correct. To determine the correctness of the answer, children will likely use a conventional algorithm, thus practicing multiplication with it. If they are challenged with the query, "I wonder whether there are any numbers for which the Russian Peasant method doesn't work?", they will receive considerable self-motivating and self-checking practice.

Philipp (1996) describes the benefits of teachers talking with children and their families about the algorithms they use to solve problems. Many people, especially those who learned mathematics in another country, use different algorithms from those customarily taught in this country. According to Philipp, this "legitimizes the mathematics learning of either the child or a member of the child's family but also presents an opportunity to honor this learning in both the child's eyes and, depending on what is done with the information, in [*sic*] the eyes of all the students in the class" (p. 129).

CONCLUSION

Solving a problem involving computation can be done in a number of ways, and children should be encouraged to develop their own computational procedures. This takes some time, but it is time well spent.

In developing computational procedures, try to capture as many serendipitous events as possible to provide a meaningful context. Choose events that are current, involve the children, and have some bearing on their lives.

In general, children will proceed through several phases as they learn computational procedures. They should begin by finding the answer to a real-world problem through the manipulation of base-ten blocks or other concrete material. Children should then be encouraged to record in their own way the process they used to find the answer. Over time, this recording will become more symbolic and concise, but still it is done in the child's own way. Later, children can be guided into recording in the most concise form (standard algorithm). Even here there can be variation because algorithms are not universally common.

Throughout the process of developing computational procedures, children should be encouraged to use estimation and mental computation. This helps children learn computational strategies and develops number sense. Estimation and mental computation can also provide a check on the accuracy of paper-and-pencil or calculator computation. As such they become a part of the looking-back phase of problem solving. Calculators should be available to help children solve problems, particularly with larger numbers.

Children also need practice to become proficient with computational procedures. The key is to employ a *variety* of interesting activities for practice.

For Your Journal

When you have finished studying this chapter, reflect on the following questions in your math journal:

1. Estimate each sum and describe the thinking processes you use.

$$
\begin{array}{rr}
258 & 4921 \\
819 & 2121 \\
234 & 866 \\
560 & \underline{7295} \\
\underline{602} &
\end{array}
$$

2. For each list of exercises below, describe the error pattern, complete the remaining problems using the error pattern, and describe a remediation plan for each type of error.

I.
$$
\begin{array}{ccccc}
347 & 468 & 516 & 739 & 604 \\
-189 & -342 & -209 & -485 & -368 \\
\hline
242 & 126 & 313 & &
\end{array}
$$

II.
$$
\begin{array}{ccccc}
28 & 394 & 476 & 366 & 37 \\
36 & +242 & +708 & +547 & 21 \\
\underline{+21} & \overline{5136} & \overline{11714} & & \underline{+55} \\
715 & & & &
\end{array}
$$

3. Visit elementary classrooms and talk with children about the algorithms they or members of their families use to solve problems. Describe these algorithms and compare them with the traditional algorithm taught in this country.

For Your Portfolio

When you have finished studying this chapter, complete the following activities to include in your professional portfolio:

1. Visit elementary classrooms and make copies (with the teacher's permission) of children's written work using algorithms to solve problems. Identify the errors made and any patterns in those errors. Discuss what you might do if you were their teacher to enhance the children's understanding.

2. Write a lesson to help children connect meaning to symbols for an algorithm of your choice.

Resources for Teachers

Books About Algorithms

Ashlock, R. B. (2002). *Error patterns in computation (8th ed.).* Upper Saddle River, NJ: Merill/Prentice Hall.

Morrow, L. J., & Kenney, M. J. (Eds.). (1998). *The teaching and learning of algorithms in school mathematics.* Reston, VA: National Council of Teachers of Mathematics.

Links to the Internet

Ask Dr. Math

http://www.mathforum.org/dr.math/drmath.elem.html

Contains numerous resources for computation, including alternate algorithms such as lattice multiplication.

CHAPTER 10

Developing Fraction Concepts

KEY CONCEPTS

✔ **Fraction concepts**

✔ **Comparison and ordering**

✔ **Fraction number sense**

✔ **Equivalence**

What are fractions, and what should children know about them? As with many other mathematics topics, traditionally there has been a rush to introduce abstract symbols before children understand the underlying concepts. This chapter explains what fractions are and what children need to learn about them. ✔

FOCUS QUESTIONS

When you have finished studying this chapter, you should be able to answer the following questions:

1. What should children understand about fractions?

2. What three models can be used in teaching the part-whole interpretation of fractions? What teaching considerations are involved? Give an example of each.

3. What strategies can teachers use to help children understand how to compare fractions?

4. Why is it important to help children understand the equivalence of fractions?

NCTM CONTENT STANDARDS AND EXPECTATIONS ADDRESSED IN THIS CHAPTER

STANDARD	EXPECTATIONS FOR GRADES PRE-K–2	EXPECTATIONS FOR GRADES 3–5	EXPECTATIONS FOR GRADES 6–8
Number and Operations Standard Instructional programs from pre-K–12 should enable all students to—	In prekindergarten through Grade 2 all students should— (NCTM, 2000, p. 78)	In Grades 3–5 all students should— (NCTM, 2000, p. 148)	In Grades 6–8 all students should—(NCTM, 2000, p. 214)
Understand numbers, ways of representing numbers, relationships among numbers, and number systems	• understand and represent commonly used fractions, such as $\frac{1}{4}$, $\frac{1}{3}$, and $\frac{1}{2}$.	• develop understanding of fractions as parts of unit wholes, as parts of a collection, as locations on number lines, and as divisions of whole numbers. • use models, benchmarks, and equivalent forms to judge the size of fractions. • recognize and generate equivalent forms of commonly used fractions, decimals, and percents.	• work flexibly with fractions, decimals, and percents to solve problems. • compare and order fractions, decimals, and percents efficiently and find their approximate locations on a number line.

WHAT ARE FRACTIONS?

The term *rational number* is rarely used in elementary classes. This is because fractional and decimal numbers are emphasized, whereas other interpretations of rational numbers such as ratio, rate and percent usually are not studied in depth at that level. In this chapter, the focus is on fractions. (Decimals, integers, and other interpretations of rational numbers are addressed in subsequent chapters.)

The fractions studied in elementary school are rational numbers that express the indicated quotient $\left(\frac{a}{b}\right)$ of one whole number a by a counting number b (nonzero number). In algebra, the definition is broadened and fractions are defined as the indicated quotient of an algebraic expression divided by another. From this definition, one can see that numbers such as $\frac{\pi}{5}$ and $-\frac{4}{5}$ also are fractions.

The term *fraction* is derived from a Latin word meaning "to break." From this literal meaning, it is assumed that an early concept of fractions was a broken whole or something "less than a whole." One can find ample support for using this primitive interpretation when introducing fractions to children.

In "parts of a whole" the metaphor used is fractions as things rather than as numbers. One-fifth of a pizza is a certain-sized piece of pizza, not necessarily a number that answers the question "how much?" The idea of fractional parts representing numbers emerges over time. Having children respond to the question "How much?" or "What is the share?" in instances of sharing a whole can lead to their thinking about fractions as numbers.

PRINCIPLES AND STANDARDS LINK 10-1
Process Strand: Problem Solving

Beyond understanding whole numbers, young children can be encouraged to understand and represent commonly used fractions in context, such as $\frac{1}{2}$ of a cookie or $\frac{1}{8}$ of a pizza, and to see fractions as part of a unit whole or of a collection. Teachers should help students develop an understanding of fractions as division of numbers. (NCTM, 2000, p. 33)

PRINCIPLES AND STANDARDS LINK 10-2
Content Strand: Number and Operations

And in the middle grades, in part as a basis for their work with proportionality, students need to solidify their understanding of fractions as numbers. (NCTM, 2000, p. 33)

What Do Children Know About Fractions?

What do we know of the fraction understanding of children in the United States? The sixth National Assessment of Educational Progress (NAEP) noted that most 4th-, 8th-, and 12th-grade children tested were able to correctly choose pictorial representations for simple fractions, but they had more difficulty representing equivalent fractions (Kouba, Zawojewski, & Struchens, 1997). Only about two-thirds of the eighth graders tested were able to correctly choose a picture showing an equivalent fraction or choose an equivalent fraction for a given picture.

NAEP results also showed that children had difficulty comparing fractions in items such as the following:

José ate $\frac{1}{2}$ of a pizza. Ella ate $\frac{1}{2}$ of a pizza. Jose said that he ate more pizza than Ella, but Ella said they both ate the same amount. Use words and pictures to show that José could be right. (Dossey, Mullis, & Jones, 1993)

Over half of the fourth graders did not answer this item correctly, and only about one-fourth of the children gave satisfactory responses to this question. Some children felt that José could not be right, since "one-half is always equal to one-half." Children who answered correctly were able to recognize that José's whole pizza might have been larger than Ella's, which would mean that José's statement was correct. Items such as this point to the importance of teachers' helping children understand fraction concepts.

Hiebert and Behr (1988) recommended that increased attention be devoted to developing the meaning of fraction symbols, developing concepts such as order and equivalence that are important in fostering a sense of the relative size of fractions, and helping children connect their intuitive understandings and strategies to more general, formal methods.

According to Bezuk and Bieck (1993), "instruction [is crucial] to strengthen students' understandings before progressing to operations on fractions, rather than assuming that students already understand these topics" (p. 119).

Mack (1990) noted that children often possess informal, real-world knowledge about fractions that they are able to use to understand fraction symbols and procedures. Teachers should help children connect their real-world experiences with fractions to classroom work with fractions to strengthen children's understanding.

What Should Children Understand About Fractions?

Children must understand several aspects about fraction concepts and relationships before beginning fraction computation. The prerequisite topics include understanding fraction concepts, comparing fractions and developing

PRINCIPLES AND STANDARDS LINK 10-3
Content Strand: Number and Operations

Representing numbers with various physical materials should be a major part of mathematics instruction in the elementary school grades. By the middle grades, students should understand that numbers can be represented in various ways, so that they see that $\frac{1}{4}$, 25%, and 0.25 are all different names for the same number. (NCTM, 2000, p. 33)

number sense about fractions, and recognizing equivalence. These topics are discussed in detail in this chapter.

DEVELOPING FRACTION CONCEPTS AND NUMBER SENSE

Number Sense With Fractions

Number sense with fractions develops over a long period of time; therefore, elementary- and middle-school teachers need to focus on this topic. A first goal is for children to develop conceptual understanding of fractions as numbers. Then there are various abilities that children must acquire to work effectively with fractions:

1. The ability to represent numbers using words, models, diagrams, and symbols and make connections among various representations.
2. The ability to give other names for numbers and justify the procedures used to generate the equivalent forms.
3. The ability to describe the relative magnitude of numbers by comparing them to common benchmarks, giving simple estimates, ordering a set of numbers, and finding a number between two numbers.

Guidelines for developing these abilities together with conceptual understanding are included in this chapter.

PRINCIPLES AND STANDARDS LINK 10-4
Content Strand: Number and Operations

Students' understanding and ability to reason will grow as they represent fractions and decimals with physical materials and on number lines and as they learn to generate equivalent representations of fractions and decimals. (NCTM, 2000, p. 33)

Assessing fraction number sense When assessing fraction number sense, teachers can ask children to model fractions concretely, pictorially, and symbolically. At times, teachers may present a task in one mode and have children respond in another mode. Vance (1990) suggests the following tasks for assessing fraction number sense:

Task 1   *Represent six-tenths with the fraction circles.*
         Can you show six-tenths on a number line?

Task 2   *Can you read this number? (Show $\frac{2}{5}$ on a card.)*
         Can you draw a picture to show what it means?
         Explain what the 2 and the 5 mean.

Task 3   *If the following diagram shows $\frac{3}{5}$ of a set, draw the whole set.*

         Could another set be used? Explain.

Task 4   *If this length is four-tenths, draw length one.*
         _____
         If this part is three-tenths, draw the whole.
         _____

Task 5   *Can you give this fraction another name?*
         $\frac{3}{5}$
         Another name?

Writing is a powerful way to assess children's understandings (NCTM, 1989). Teachers are encouraged to ask children to write about the mathematics they are doing. For example, children's responses to a simple direction such as "Write about what you did" or "Write about what you learned" can reveal much about a child's fraction understandings. Two examples of children's responses to the invitation to write a story about one-half or one-third are presented in Figure 10-1.

Developing the meaning of half Children come to school knowing the term *half* as they have used it in their sharing experiences. However, this does not mean that they know the fractional term *half* in its precise meaning, that is, half is one of two equal parts. Several activities to help develop the concept of half are described below. The first involves sets rather than a region model. It is included here because of its focus on half.

1. Sharing for two
   • Set the context by relating a story such as: "Jane and Jill are sisters and they frequently have things to share. They each are to get half of the things."

FIGURE 10-1 ▶

One Half

One day I went to the "It Store" and I bought 14 scratch 'n' sniff stickers. The next day I went to my friend's house and we traded stickers. We traded and I gave her 7 stickers, or half of the stickers.

(The 14 stickers were drawn with 7 crossed out.)

P.S. Half means you have two equal parts and you take one away. Then you have half.

Jack, Grade 3

Half

My mommy got a pizza for me and my brother. My mommy cut it in eight pieces.

I had 2 pieces and my brother 2 pieces of pizza. All together, we ate half the pizza.

Beth, Grade 3

- Ask the children to tell how the sisters will share

  6 pieces of gum
  10 baseball cards
  12 dimes
  8 barrettes

- Encourage the children to verbalize. Listen for expressions like "They shared the gum and they each got the same amount. So they each got half the gum."

2. Cutting in half
   - Obtain a knife and two oranges, two apples, two soft cookies, or two other objects suitable for cutting.
   - Explain that you are going to cut each orange in two parts.
   - Cut one orange into two parts, as equal as possible, then ask, "How have I cut this orange? What can you say about the pieces?"
   - Cut the other orange into two obviously unequal parts, then ask, "How have I cut this orange? What can you say about the pieces?"
   - Encourage the children to verbalize. Some expressions could include the following:

   This orange is cut in two parts that are the same size. The parts are equal.

   The orange is cut in half. Each piece is one-half the orange. The other orange is not cut in half because

the pieces are not the same size. The pieces are not equal.

In the preceding verbalization, note the dual expressions "same size" and "equal." For some time, both should be used to develop and consolidate the meaning of the term equal.

3. Partitioning a square in half
   - You will need a large colored square cut from heavy paper, art foam, or other suitable material and several narrow strips of white poster board to demonstrate "cutting" lines. The strips should be at least as long as the diagonal of the square.
   - Set the context by asking the children to pretend that one day their mother baked a small square cake for them to share with a friend.
   - Ask the children to explore the possibilities of "cutting the cake" in two parts that are the same amount. The white strips are to be used to show cuts on the cake.
   - Ask the children to indicate or record the cuts they think produce parts that show the same amount. The recording can be done in one of two ways: Provide children with squares drawn on a piece of paper and have them draw the cutting line, or provide a square for the children to trace on paper and then have them mark the partitioning line.

For the purpose of a class discussion, the teacher could draw a series of squares on a transparency. Children in turn can show one way to cut the cake in two parts that are the same amount. Each type of cut is discussed. Ask questions such as "Does this cut show two parts that are the same amount?" "How can you tell?" "How much cake will each of you get?"

The teacher can explain the meaning of half as follows and then have the children verbalize the various expressions.

Cutting in half means that we show two parts that are the same amount. The parts are the same size. When a figure has been cut in half, each part is half the shape, a half, or one-half.

The last expression should be encouraged because it helps name other fractions such as two-halves, three-halves, etc.

This activity can be extended by repeating it using a rectangle, an equilateral triangle, a regular pentagon, a hexagon, or an octagon, as suggested in Activity 10-1. Have children record their partitionings on paper and then discuss the conclusions they have reached.

Activity 10-2 can be used to assess a child's mental development level as well as to help children develop the concept of "half." Some children in Grades 5 and 6 are unable to reason that if the figures are the same size (congruent) and the parts within each are the same size, then all the parts are the same amount or have the same area. The activity should be used after children have had expe-

ACTIVITY 10-1

PARTITIONING FIGURES IN HALF

MATERIALS
Several of each of the following figures for each child; small sticks to show cutting lines

PROCEDURE
1. Use sticks to divide each figure in half.
2. Can some of the figures be divided in two ways? In more than two ways?

riences in partitioning squares, rectangles, triangles, and pentagons.

Fraction Names

When the fraction names are first learned, that is, halves, thirds, fourths, etc., children might confuse these with ordinal numbers. Thus, comparisons between, for example, *second* and *half, third* and *thirds, fourth* and *fourths,* etc., should be made to help clarify the differences. An activity similar to Activity 10-3 may be worthwhile.

In early fraction work, the fraction words should be used without the symbols. Children can record findings

ACTIVITY 10-3

MEANING OF NUMBER TERMS

MATERIALS
Paper and pencil

PROCEDURE
Draw a picture to show what each of the following terms means to you.

| two | second | half |
| five | fifth | fifths |

such as "one-sixth of the pie has been eaten" or "one-half and one-fourth is the same as three-fourths." This manner of recording makes children focus on "what objects are being considered" and not merely on "how many." In time, recording work with fractions can be abbreviated to "1 half + 1 fourth = 3 fourths." Formal symbolization should be required only when children demonstrate an understanding of fractions through problem-solving activities.

Teachers should not assume that children who use fractional terms properly in some context have an understanding of fractions. Children who use fraction terms such as *half* and *quarter* frequently use them in a narrow sense and sometimes erroneously. "Split the cookie in half in three pieces" and "Break it in half in four pieces" are common verbalizations by young children. It is recommended that teachers provide opportunities for children to use familiar fractional terms to determine what meaning each child affixes to them. For example, a child may use the term *half* when referring to an action as in "halve it" or "cut it in half," not to name a part. Another

ACTIVITY 10-2

DETERMINING WHETHER PARTS ARE THE SAME SIZE

MATERIALS
Pairs of partitioned figures as shown

PROCEDURE
1. A child is shown the partitioned figures in pairs as in the diagram.

2. Look at these two figures. Are parts (a) and (b) the same size? [or, Do parts (a) and (b) show the same amount?]. Explain how you know.

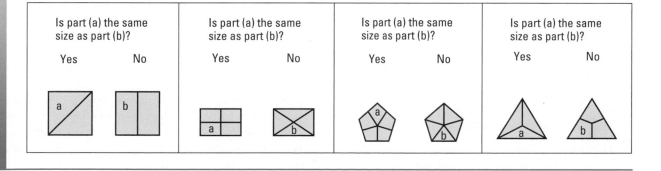

child may use the term *half* to name parts when a whole is divided in two, three, or more parts. Frequently, the parts need not be the same size to be labeled "half." This knowledge is important before moving on to further work with fractions.

Fraction symbols should be introduced only when children understand the meaning of the terms *one-half, one-third, one-fourth,* etc. Peck and Jencks (1981) present an interesting way of developing an understanding of fraction symbols with young children. They have children first read $\frac{1}{3}$ as "share among 3," then $\frac{2}{3}$ as "share among 3, cover 2." This process causes children to think of the denominator first, then the numerator, implying that the language "two-thirds" is "backward" to the thinking process. It is interesting to note that in Chinese, fractions are read by naming the denominator first. This might be an advantage in learning fractions.

Fraction symbolism   Fraction symbols should be introduced when children can use fractions in problem situations involving regions and parts of a set and in measurement. Fraction symbols should be written with a horizontal bar, although a slanted bar often is used on keyboards and calculators.

There is no reason children should learn the terms *numerator* and *denominator* when fraction symbols are introduced. Referring to the "top number" and "bottom number" in a fraction symbol would be an understandable designation for children.

Comparisons can be made to connect each number in the fraction symbol with the fraction language that children have been using. For example, have children count fraction circles. As they count, write the fraction words on the board, as in the second column below.

	one-sixth	1 sixth	$\frac{1}{6}$
	two-sixths	2 sixths	$\frac{2}{6}$
	three-sixths	3 sixths	$\frac{3}{6}$
	four-sixths	4 sixths	$\frac{4}{6}$
	five-sixths	5 sixths	$\frac{5}{6}$
	six-sixths	6 sixths	$\frac{6}{6}$

Ask the children, "What is a short form we have been using when writing fraction?" Then write the third column on the board. Finally, write the last column, explaining that there is a still shorter form in which to write fractions.

The teacher should facilitate discussion by matching the "two" and both "2s" in the same row and asking what each represents. Repeat with the "sixths" and "6." Ask, "Why was the term *sixth* repeated when you counted? Why were the counting numbers used?"

For children who understand fraction parts, the following explanation of the fraction symbol should be adequate:

In fractions, the top number counts the parts and the bottom number tells what sized parts are being counted.

To consolidate the idea, have children count eighths and record the fractions in pictorial, written, and symbolic forms. Subsequently, children can be told that they can use any of the fraction forms whenever they are recording their work. In time, only the fraction symbols will be used.

Different units   The meaning of fractions is developed by considering different units. Units generally are represented by continuous (regions) and discrete (a set of distinct objects) quantities. A unit also can be:

- Continuous but divisible (e.g., a chocolate bar cut into squares to be shared among three siblings).
- A discrete set with divisible elements (e.g., six cookies to be shared among four children).
- A discrete set with separate subsets (e.g., 5 boxes of candy, 12 candies per box to be shared among 4 people).

For certain problems, a unit may also consist of part of a whole or more than one whole. These are not simple concepts for young children. See Figure 10-2.

PRINCIPLES AND STANDARDS LINK 10-5
Content Strand: Number and Operations

In addition to work with whole numbers, young students should also have some experience with simple fractions through connections to everyday situations and meaningful problems, starting with the common fractions expressed in the language they bring to the classroom, such as "half." At this level, it is more important for students to recognize when things are divided into equal parts than to focus on fraction notation. (NCTM, 2000, p. 82)

FIGURE 10-2

(a) A continuous quantity.

These regions are considered continuous quantities. The parts are measured rather than counted.

(b) Sets of discrete objects as the unit.

 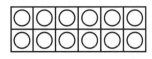

These are sets of discrete objects, that is, one can count the objects in each set.

(c) The unit is a continuous quantity that has been divided.

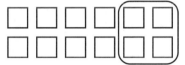

A Hershey bar cut up. Gerry's share is these 4 pieces, or one-third of the bar.

(d) The unit is a discrete set with the elements divisible.

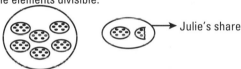

Four children share 6 cookies. What is each child's share? Julie's share is one and one-half cookies.

(e) The unit is a discrete set with divisible subsets.

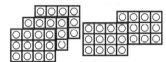 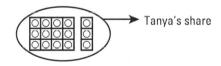

A set of 5 boxes of candy with 12 candies per box, to be shared among 4 friends. How much does each person get? Tanya's share is one and one-fourth boxes of candies.

(f) Part of a whole as a unit.

What portion is one-half of the remaining pie? Three-fourths of the pie is the unit. One-half of three-fourths is three-eighths.

(g) The unit is more than a whole.

The shaded parts show how much pizza Paul has eaten. Paul has eaten one and one-fourth mini pizzas.

Different Interpretations of Fractions

Fractions can be interpreted in several ways. Kieren (1980) identifies four meanings: part-whole, quotient, ratio, and operator (multiplicative aspect). The part-whole interpretation is the one emphasized in elementary mathematics programs. However, one should not conclude that young children are unable to understand other interpretations. The other three interpretations of fractions are discussed at the end of this section.

Part-whole interpretations The part-whole meaning of fractions comprises different units. It can be:

- A region (an object to be shared or an area to be divided).
- A set of objects.
- A unit of linear measure.

Teaching considerations about each type are presented in the following subsections.

Region model. There is substantial agreement that the region model of fractions should be learned before the model of "parts of a set" (Hollis, 1984; Payne, 1984; Skypek, 1984). Traditionally, regular geometric regions have been judged to be good fraction models because any unit fraction can be readily represented. It is suggested that children be allowed to experiment with partitioning different figures or regions rather than work solely with prepartitioned figures. Without the personal experience of partitioning figures into equal parts, children are unable to use the model in problem-solving activities (Kieren, Nelson, & Smith, 1985; Pothier & Sawada, 1984).

Equality of parts. Children often are satisfied that parts "look the same size" when modeling fractions. For example, a regular pentagon or a heart shape partitioned by a horizontal "half cut" is often declared to be shared equally (see Figure 10-3). Therefore, in early fraction work, children should be required to construct parts that are congruent, that is, the same size and shape.

At a later time, children will come to see (in area measurement) that noncongruent parts of regions can be equal. For example, consider a set of tangrams, illustrated in Figure 10-4. Notice that there are three different tan-

FIGURE 10-4

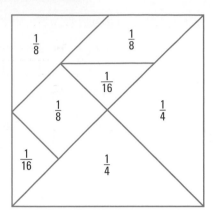

gram shapes that represent one-eighth of the whole tangram square. These three shapes are not congruent, but they each cover one-eighth of the area of the whole tangram square, so they each are one-eighth of the tangram. This example provides another opportunity to discuss with children that fractions do not have to be congruent to be the same part of the whole.

Children's judgments about the equality of parts in a few situations are presented in Figure 10-5.

Pothier and Sawada (1990) recommend that teachers provide children with opportunities to practice partitioning physical objects into equal-sized parts rather than just draw lines on the outlines of shapes. Teachers can do this by positioning coffee stirrers on top of uncut circles or rectangles and asking children to place the stirrers to show where the whole should be cut to make thirds, for example.

Parts drawn on cut-out figures can be tested for congruency by folding or by dividing, cutting, and then su-

FIGURE 10-3

FIGURE 10-5

Statements to explain why children think the parts they have produced are the same size (equal).

Barry (7 years)

"All the same size. Not the same shape."

Ryan (7 years)

"This part looks smaller but it's just the same size because like I split it in half this way and I split it in half this way."

Joshua (7 years)

"I think I could do four!" He partitions the triangle. "It looks bigger but it isn't bigger . . . Cause it's thinner here and thicker here."

ACTIVITY 10-4

GIVEN A PART, DRAW THE WHOLE

MATERIALS
Figures drawn on paper

PROCEDURE

1. If this is one-fifth of a chocolate bar, what size is the whole bar?

2. This is three-fourths of a cake. Draw the whole cake.

3. This is three-eighths of a cheese block. Draw the whole block.

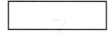

perimposing the parts. Older children can measure the angles and sides of the parts produced. Activity 10-4 provides children with an opportunity to explore the iteration of equal parts. The following two teacher-directed activities aim to develop the concept of equality of parts in fractions:

1. Developing the Concept of Equality of Parts in Fractions
   - Materials: Figures drawn on paper to represent giant cookies: a heart, an equilateral triangle, a regular pentagon.
   - Provide children with at least two heart-shaped cookies and direct them to show how a cookie could be shared equally between two friends.
   - Focusing on a vertical cut, ask, "How can you prove each person gets the same amount?" (or, "How can you prove the pieces are equal?") Suggest that children fold one part over the other to see whether the parts are equal.
   - Ask, "Can you cut the cookie a different way so that each person gets the same amount?"
   - Focusing on a horizontal cut, ask, "Would each person get the same amount now?" Have children cut the shape on the fold line and superimpose the two parts.

- Ask, "How are you sure the parts are equal? Why?"
- Say, "When we're sure the parts are equal, we can say that each part is one-half of the cookie."
- Repeat the procedures with a triangle, a pentagon, and other figures.

2. Equality of Parts: One-fourth
   - Materials: A square, a triangle, a parallelogram, a pentagon, a heart, and other figures.
   - Say: "Let's try two cuts on different figures to find out whether they produce equal parts."
   - In each case ask, "Can the parts be called one-fourth of the figure? Why or why not?"

The following story could be used to assess children's understanding of equality in fractions:

A boy named Don told me that a heart-shaped cake cut into 4 parts like this [demonstrate a vertical and a horizontal halving line] makes parts equal because "this stick is in the middle of this one." What would you say to Don?

Children's responses can reveal whether they are focusing on the partitioning techniques or on the parts produced when assessing equality of parts.

A teacher who plans partitioning activities for children will learn which fractional parts are easy and which are difficult for children to attain on a circle, square, or other regular geometric figure. Children should be allowed to discover for themselves, for example, how to attain thirds and fifths on a circle or fifths on a pentagon. In time, children should be able to partition a region to model unit fractions with even and odd denominators.

The activity of partitioning figures should be repeated at different times during the year and at different grade levels, because further partitioning experiences will lead to more discoveries. The following questions could be the focus of class discussions:

- On what figures is it easy to attain thirds? fourths? fifths? sixths? eighths? tenths?
- What partitioning techniques work best on a particular figure?

Successful partitioning of regions requires capabilities such as the following:

1. An awareness of some geometric properties of figures, such as numbers of sides and vertices, the diagonals, midpoints of sides, and the center point of the figure.

2. Knowledge of possible operations on figures, for example, dividing sides into equal segments, constructing points in the interior of a figure, and attaining differently shaped parts within a given figure.

FIGURE 10-6

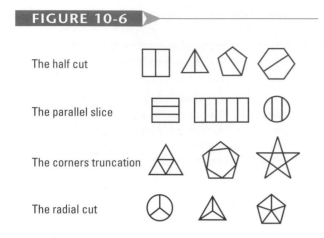

The half cut

The parallel slice

The corners truncation

The radial cut

ACTIVITY 10-5

FRACTIONAL PARTS OF A WHOLE

MATERIALS
Fraction Factory Pieces

PROCEDURE
1. Find how many
   • thirds are in a whole
   • fifths are in a whole
   • tenths are in a whole
   • twelfths are in a whole
2. Do you notice a pattern?
3. Write a statement about what you have found.

3. Partitioning techniques such as the half cut using different orientations, the parallel slice, the corners truncation, and the radial cut, as shown in Figure 10-6.

These capabilities emerge slowly over time and provide children with one model for fractional numbers.

One excellent model for representing fractions is fraction circles. These are available commercially as sets of plastic circles partitioned into different numbers of equal-sized pieces. Sets of fraction circles also can be made economically from paper; draw circles on white paper and then duplicate each different denominator onto different colors of paper, which children can cut out (see Blackline Masters 6, 7, and 8 in the Appendix). Laminating the paper before cutting will help retain the shape of the pieces and extend their usefulness.

Fraction circles are the model that perhaps is most familiar to children, but this is a difficult model for children to construct on their own. Using premade sets provides children with a convenient, easy-to-understand model for fractions.

The commercial set of Fraction Factory Pieces is another example of the region model. The set is made of colored plastic rectangular pieces representing a whole and its fractional parts ($\frac{1}{2}$, $\frac{1}{3}$, $\frac{1}{4}$, $\frac{1}{5}$, $\frac{1}{6}$, $\frac{1}{8}$, $\frac{1}{10}$, and $\frac{1}{12}$), as shown in Figure 10-7. Exploratory activities can be planned for children using the materials as in Activity 10-5.

Part-of-a-set model.   The difficulty of the *part-of-a-set model* for fractions resides in naming the result of partitioning rather than in the action itself. For example, children can easily share 20 candies among four friends but when asked *what* part of the candies each one gets, "five" is apt to be the reply. Children must learn that the question "how many" warrants a whole-number answer (5), whereas the questions "how much" and "what part" have fraction number answers ($\frac{1}{5}$).

When working with sets, children find it easier to identify, for example, one-tenth of a set of 10 than to find one-fifth of 10 objects. Students appear to think of "fifth" as "five." Thus, when finding one-fifth of 10, they partition the set in two groups of five rather than in five groups of two. The idea to learn is that, for example, when talking about fifths, the whole is partitioned into five parts. The number of objects in each fifth depends upon the size of the set (see Figure 10-8). Activities 10-6 to 10-12 should be helpful in developing this important idea.

From Activity 10-6, children should observe that because *thirds* is the fraction part, the set is *always* divided into *three parts*.

For Activity 10-7, children should draw pictures of what they have done and write statements such as:

Twelve buttons are one-half of 24 buttons.

One-fourth of 24 buttons is 6.

Children might respond to Activity 10-8 with a construction and statements such as:

Here are 12 discs.

I can make four groups of three.

Therefore, three is one-fourth of 12.

FIGURE 10-7

FIGURE 10-8

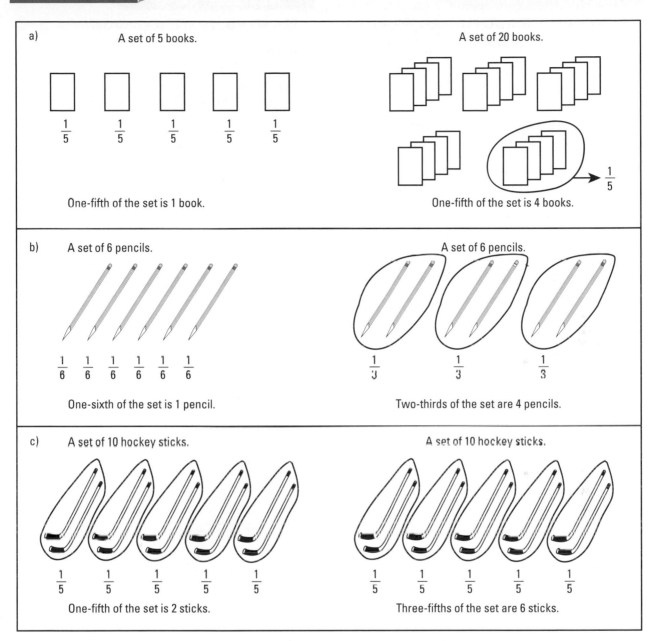

a)   A set of 5 books.   A set of 20 books.

One-fifth of the set is 1 book.   One-fifth of the set is 4 books.

b)   A set of 6 pencils.   A set of 6 pencils.

One-sixth of the set is 1 pencil.   Two-thirds of the set are 4 pencils.

c)   A set of 10 hockey sticks.   A set of 10 hockey sticks.

One-fifth of the set is 2 sticks.   Three-fifths of the set are 6 sticks.

Two children's solutions to the problem in Activity 10-10 are presented below:

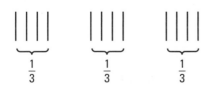

The library bought 12 nonfiction books. I know this because if 4 books are $\frac{1}{3}$, then $\frac{3}{3}$ is 12 books.

Janice, Grade 6

12 nonfiction books were bought. If 4 computer books are one-third of all the nonfiction books, I need two more thirds.

A third = 4 so 3 × 4 = 12.

□ = 1 book

$\frac{1}{3}$ $\frac{1}{3}$ $\frac{1}{3}$

Mark, Grade 6

ACTIVITY 10-6

FINDING A FRACTIONAL PART OF A SET: PICTORIAL

MATERIALS

1. 🐝🐝🐝🐝🐝🐝🐝🐝🐝
2. 🐝🐝🐝🐝🐝🐝🐝🐝🐝🐝🐝🐝
3. 🐝🐝🐝
4. 🐝🐝🐝🐝🐝🐝
5. 🐝🐝🐝🐝🐝🐝🐝🐝🐝🐝🐝🐝
6. 🐝🐝🐝🐝🐝🐝🐝🐝🐝🐝🐝🐝 🐝🐝🐝🐝🐝🐝 🐝🐝🐝🐝🐝🐝

PROCEDURE

1. Show two-thirds of each of the sets shown above.
2. Write a statement about each set.

ACTIVITY 10-7

FINDING A FRACTIONAL PART OF A SET: CONCRETE

MATERIALS

A set of 24 buttons for each child and 8 small plates or "mats"

PROCEDURE

Place buttons on the plates to show:

1. One-half of 24 (use 2 plates).
2. One-fourth of 24 (use 4 plates).
3. One-sixth of 24 (use 6 plates).
4. One-eighth of 24 (use 8 plates).

ACTIVITY 10-8

NAMING THE FRACTIONS

MATERIALS

A set of 20 discs or other small objects

PROCEDURE

Use the discs (or other objects) to answer the following:

1. What part of 12 is 3?
2. What part of 6 is 2?
3. What part of 20 is 4?
4. What part of 20 is 5?

ACTIVITY 10-9

FINDING A PART OF A SET

PROCEDURE

1. Solve the following problem. Draw a picture to show how you arrived at an answer.

Three-fifths of the 10 books on the shelf are mysteries. How many are mystery books?

ACTIVITY 10-10

FINDING THE WHOLE SET: FIXED TOTAL

PROCEDURE

1. Solve the following problem. Draw a diagram to show how you arrived at an answer.

The school library has acquired some new books. The four books about computers are one-third of the nonfiction books. How many nonfiction books were bought?

A child might respond to the problem in Activity 10-11 in the following way:

Because I have to find $\frac{3}{8}$ and $\frac{1}{6}$ of a set, I'll choose 24 as the number of bows in the bag because 8 and 6 are factors of 24, so it's easy to find eighths and sixths of 24.

$$\frac{3}{8} \text{ of } 24 \text{ is } 9 \qquad \frac{1}{6} \text{ of } 24 \text{ is } 4$$

$$\frac{1}{8} \qquad\qquad\qquad \frac{1}{6}$$

9 and 4 = 13. Therefore, 11 bows were white.

$\frac{11}{24}$ *of the bows were white.*

If Ellen had bought a bag of 48 bows, she would have 22 white bows.

Measurement model. The measurement model can be exemplified using tape, ribbon, or other appropriate material. Children can be asked, for example, to find fractional parts of a given strip of paper. Number lines are another example of the measurement model for fractions.

ACTIVITY 10-11

FINDING THE WHOLE SET: VARIABLE TOTAL

PROCEDURE

1. Solve the following problem. Show how you arrived at an answer.

Ellen purchased a bag of bows to put on Christmas presents. She found that three-eighths of the bows were red and one-sixth were green. How many (the remaining bows) were white? What fraction of the total number of bows were white?

ACTIVITY 10-12

DRAW THE WHOLE SET

PROCEDURE

Draw pictures to help you answer the following questions.

1. Kevin has a collection of model airplanes. Three-tenths of his collection is three airplanes. How many airplanes does Kevin have in his collection?

2. Sharon enjoys taking pictures. She has taken 9 pictures, which is one-fourth of the pictures she can take with that roll of film. How many pictures can Sharon take with that roll of film?

3. Tanya has a paper route. Having delivered 12 papers means that she has one-third of the papers left to deliver. How many papers does Sharon deliver each day?

Folding is one way to find fractional parts of strips of paper. Activity 10-13 could be used for this purpose.

One conclusion children should come to as a result of doing Activity 10-13 is that when comparing two unit fractions, the one with the smaller denominator is the larger fraction.

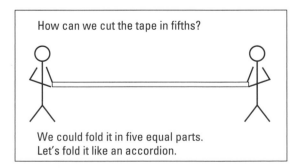

How can we cut the tape in fifths?

We could fold it in five equal parts. Let's fold it like an accordion.

Fraction Bars and *Cuisenaire rods* are two commercial sets of materials that can be used by children to help them discover fraction concepts using the measurement model. Fraction Bars are a set of plasticized paper strips,

ACTIVITY 10-13

FOLDING STRIPS TO FIND FRACTIONAL PARTS

MATERIALS
A set of paper strips about 30 inches long for each child

PROCEDURE

1. Fold the strips to find the following fractions:

$$\frac{1}{2}, \frac{1}{4}, \frac{1}{3}, \frac{1}{5}, \frac{1}{6}, \frac{1}{8}, \frac{1}{10}$$

2. Use your set of fractions strips to compare the following pairs of fractions:
   (a) one-half of fractions
   (b) one-third and one-fourth
   (c) one-fourth and one-fifth
   (d) one-fifth and one-sixth

What conclusion do you reach?

6 inches long, partitioned to show twelfths (13 bars), tenths (11 bars), sixths (7 bars), fifths (6 bars), fourths (5 bars), thirds (4 bars), and halves (3 bars) (see Blackline Master 9 in the Appendix). The 13 bars for twelfths are pictured in Figure 10-9.

Cuisenaire rods are a set of three-dimensional colored plastic or wooden rods of proportional lengths from 1 cm to 10 cm.

Books describing activities accompany both sets of materials. Activities 10-14 to 10-18 present sample activities.

FIGURE 10-9

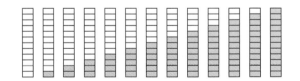

ACTIVITY 10-14

COMPARING FRACTIONS—A

MATERIALS
Fraction Bars

PROCEDURE

1. Use Fraction Bars to compare the following:
   (a) 1 part out of 3 and 1 part out of 4
   (b) 5 parts out of 6 and 3 parts out of 4
   (c) 1 part out of 2 and 5 parts out of 12

ACTIVITY 10-15

COMPARING FRACTIONS—B

MATERIALS
Fraction Bars

PROCEDURE
1. Find Fraction Bars that have a greater shaded amount than a blue bar with 3 parts shaded.

2. Find Fraction Bars that have less shading than a red bar with 1 part shaded.

ACTIVITY 10-16

COMPARING FRACTIONS—C

MATERIALS
Cuisenaire rods

PROCEDURE
1. Select the orange rod as the unit. Write fractional names for three other rods in terms of your unit.

2. Choose a different rod as the unit and do the same task.

ACTIVITY 10-17

FRACTIONS ON A NUMBER LINE

MATERIALS
Number lines

PROCEDURE
1. Draw three number lines the same length.

2. Divide one line in eighths, one in tenths, and one in twelfths.

3. Use your number lines to order the following sets of fractions

$$\frac{1}{3} \quad \frac{5}{8} \quad \frac{3}{5} \qquad \frac{9}{12} \quad \frac{6}{10} \quad \frac{5}{8}$$

$$\frac{4}{8} \quad \frac{3}{10} \quad \frac{5}{12} \qquad \frac{7}{8} \quad \frac{11}{12} \quad \frac{9}{10}$$

ACTIVITY 10-18

GIVEN A PART, FIND THE WHOLE

PROCEDURE
1. A part of a line is drawn. Draw the whole line.

one-third of a line _____

one-fifth of a line _____

two-sixths of a line _____

three-tenths of a line _____

A number line is frequently employed when using a measurement model. In this case, it is the distance from zero that is being named rather than points (Figure 10-10).

Area model.   The area model is based on the idea that fractional parts may have the same area but might not necessarily be congruent. Consider rectangles A–D below. Each rectangle is divided into four parts. But are the parts fourths? Most children would agree that Rectangles A, B, and C are divided in fourths, but they may disagree about Rectangle D, because two of the parts are shaped differently than the other two parts.

How might children determine whether the four parts in Rectangle D are the same size? One way is to cut one of the triangular pieces as indicated below and rearrange it to form a small rectangle—which will be exactly the same size and shape as the two small rectangular pieces.

FIGURE 10-10

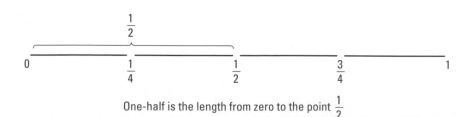

Measurement Model

One-half is the length from zero to the point $\frac{1}{2}$

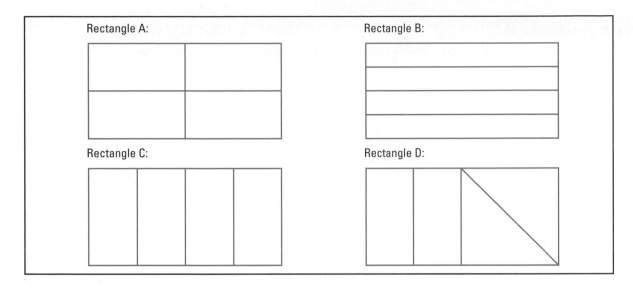

This shows that all four pieces have the same area, so Rectangle D *is* divided into fourths.

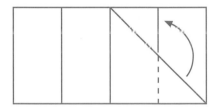

Other examples of shapes that have been cut into fractional parts using the area model are shown below. How

might you verify that each part has the same area as other parts within the whole?

Geoboards can be used to represent the area model. A geoboard is a square that has several pegs, usually a 5-by-5 arrangement, on which rubber bands can be stretched to outline shapes. Children can be asked to show how a geoboard can be split into fractional parts, such as halves, fourths, or eighths. Figure 10-11 shows several ways in which a geoboard could be split into halves. Note that some of the halves are congruent, but others aren't. It is important for children to understand that shapes that are not congruent can still cover the same fractional part of a whole.

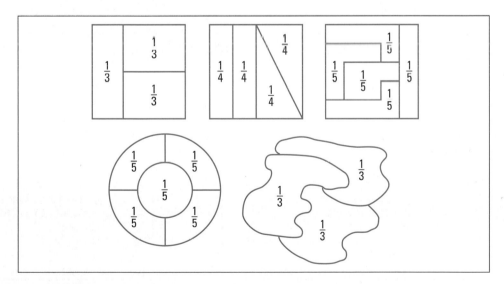

Other interpretations of fractions   In addition to the part-whole interpretation of fractions, described in the preceding pages, there are three other interpretations of fractions: ratio, quotient, and operator (see Figure 10-12).

Ratio interpretation of fractions.   The ratio interpretation of fractions is based on the idea that a fraction

can represent a ratio between two quantities. For example, if a set of marbles contains 10 red and 14 blue marbles, the ratio of red to blue marbles in that set can be represented by the fraction $\frac{5}{7}$. Note that the denominator of this fraction, 7, has a different meaning than in the part-whole interpretation of fractions. In the ratio interpretation, the 5 and 7 represent different quantities; in this

FIGURE 10-11

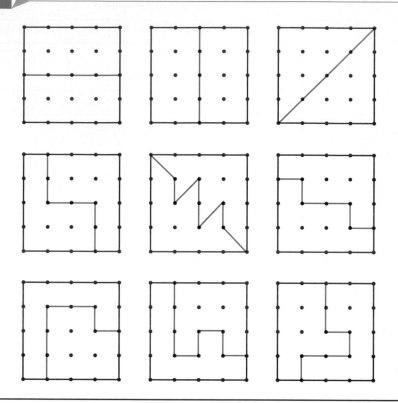

FIGURE 10-12

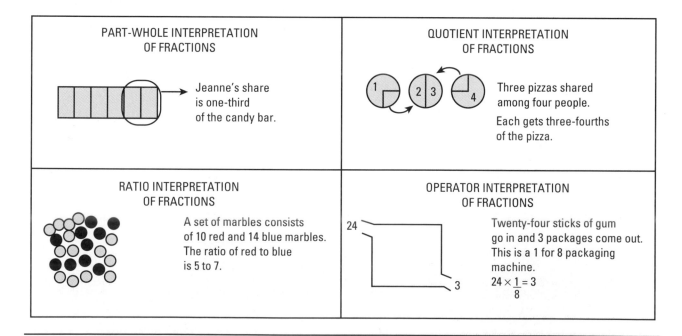

case, the number of red and blue marbles. In the part-whole interpretation, the denominator represents the total number of elements (or parts) in the whole. This difference is sometimes confusing to children and makes this interpretation more difficult than the part-whole interpretation.

Quotient interpretation of fractions. The quotient interpretation of fractions is based on the idea that a fraction can express a division or sharing. For example, if three pizzas are shared by four people, each person gets $\frac{3}{4}$ of a pizza. In this interpretation, $\frac{3}{4}$ expresses 3 wholes split into 4 equal groups. This interpretation also is more difficult for children to understand than the part-whole interpretation of fractions.

Operator interpretation of fractions.   The operator interpretation of fractions is based on the idea that a fraction can express an operation. For example, a machine that takes in 24 sticks of gum and produces 3 packs of gum represents an $\frac{8}{1}$ operator, because every 8 sticks of gum come out of the machine as 1 pack. This is perhaps the most difficult and least common interpretation of fractions.

DEVELOPING COMPARISON AND ORDERING OF FRACTIONS

Another important fraction topic is comparison and ordering. This refers to a child's ability to judge the relative size of two or more fractions and to arrange two or more fractions in order based on their size.

Comparing and Ordering Fractions

Students need opportunities to *compare* and *order* fractions. Fractions should be compared by representing them concretely and pictorially before using an algorithm (Figure 10-13).

Experiences in comparing fractions at the concrete and pictorial levels will help children develop an intuitive sense of the numeric value of fractions. Formal symbolic work can then proceed (see Activities 10-19 to 10-21).

Children could be asked to compare a set of fractions with the same denominator, with the same numerator, and with different numerators and denominators to help them develop fraction number sense (see examples below). Then, they could model the fractions to verify their work as pictured in Figure 10-14.

Examples:

$$\frac{3}{12}, \frac{6}{12}, \frac{2}{12}, \frac{9}{12}, \frac{12}{12}, \frac{4}{12}.$$

$$\frac{2}{7}, \frac{2}{3}, \frac{2}{9}, \frac{2}{5}, \frac{2}{10}, \frac{2}{15}.$$

$$\frac{2}{3}, \frac{3}{4}, \frac{4}{5}, \frac{5}{6}, \frac{6}{7}, \frac{7}{8}.$$

$$\frac{5}{6}, \frac{3}{8}, \frac{2}{3}, \frac{1}{4}, \frac{1}{6}, \frac{3}{5}.$$

Activities 10-22 to 10-24 also help children develop a sense of fraction size.

FIGURE 10-13 ▶

Which is the largest fraction:
2 fourths, 4 tenths, or 4 sixths?

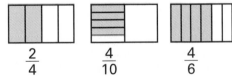

$$\frac{2}{4} \qquad \frac{4}{10} \qquad \frac{4}{6}$$

4 sixths is the largest.

Order the fractions from smallest to largest:
1 half, 2 thirds, 5 sixths, 3 fourths, 5 eighths.

$$\frac{1}{2} \quad \frac{5}{8} \quad \frac{2}{3} \quad \frac{3}{4} \quad \frac{5}{6}$$

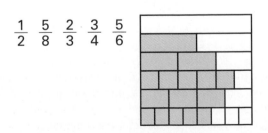

ACTIVITY 10-19 ▶

COMPARING FRACTIONS

PROCEDURE
1. Which is greater? $\frac{4}{5}$ or $\frac{2}{3}$
2. How do you know?
3. Use materials or draw a picture to show that you are right.

ACTIVITY 10-20 ▶

ORDERING FRACTIONS

PROCEDURE
1. Order the fractions from smallest to largest.

$$\frac{1}{3} \qquad \frac{3}{8} \qquad \frac{5}{16} \qquad \frac{1}{2} \qquad \frac{5}{12}$$

2. Write how you know.

ACTIVITY 10-21 ▶

SYMBOLIC FRACTIONS

PROCEDURE
1. Which is smaller?

$$\frac{2}{5} \text{ or } \frac{2}{10} \qquad \frac{3}{5} \text{ or } \frac{4}{7}$$

2. Draw a picture to show that you are right.

FIGURE 10-14

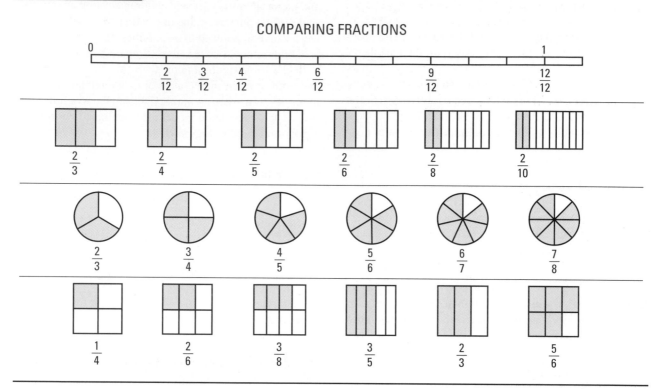

COMPARING FRACTIONS

ACTIVITY 10-22

VARIATIONS ON A THEME

PROCEDURE

1. Write fractions that get closer and closer to 1, staying above 1.
2. Write fraction that get closer to 1 by alternating above and below 1.

ACTIVITY 10-23

GETTING CLOSE TO $\frac{3}{4}$

Given set A = $\{\frac{1}{2}, \frac{1}{3}, \frac{1}{4}, \frac{1}{5}, \frac{1}{6}, \frac{1}{7}, \ldots\}$, get close (and closer) to $\frac{3}{4}$ using three numbers from the set and the operation of addition.

ACTIVITY 10-24

TARGET NUMBER IS $1\frac{1}{2}$

Given set B = $\{\frac{1}{2}, \frac{1}{3}, \frac{1}{4}, \frac{2}{4}, \frac{3}{4}, \frac{1}{5}, \frac{2}{5}, \frac{3}{5}, \frac{4}{5}\}$, try to construct $1\frac{1}{2}$.

For variation in Activity 10-23, more than one operation can be used or four or more numbers can be used from the given set.

Variations in Activity 10-24 could include:

- Change the target number.
- Use as few or as many numbers from set B as you can.
- Numbers may (or may not) be used more than once.

When comparing fractions at the symbolic level, the power of the notion of equivalent fractions is recognized. Common denominators are found for the given fractions and then the numerators are compared.

A child's work for Activity 10-19 might look like this:

$\frac{4}{5}$ is greater than $\frac{2}{3}$

Using a calculator to compare fractions The *Math Explorer* calculator can assist children in comparing and ordering fractions. The process is as described in the previous section by first renaming the fractions to be compared so they will have a common denominator.

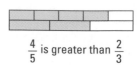

PRINCIPLES AND STANDARDS LINK 10-6
Content Strand: Number and Operations

In grades 3 through 5, students can learn to compare fractions to familiar benchmarks such as $\frac{1}{2}$ (NCTM, 2000, p. 52).

Relative Size of Fractions

In learning the relative size of fractions, children should first compare fractions concretely and pictorially. Comparisons are made relative to certain benchmark numbers such as one, one-half, and zero. Activities 10-25 through 10-32 provide examples.

 ACTIVITY 10-28

FRACTIONS THAT ADD UP TO ALMOST ONE (SYMBOLIC)

PROCEDURE

1. Use the numbers 1, 2, 3, 4, 5, 6, 8, 10 to make two fractions that add up to almost one.

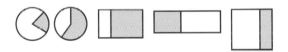

EXAMPLE:
Three-fourths and one-sixth makes almost one.

2. Can you make other fraction pairs that add up to almost one?

ACTIVITY 10-25

RELATIVE SIZE OF FRACTIONS (PICTORIAL: REGION)

PROCEDURE

1. About what size is the shaded part in each figure?

ACTIVITY 10-29

WHAT MAKES ALMOST ONE-HALF? (CONCRETE: MEASUREMENT)

PROCEDURE

1. Use Fraction Bars to group two fractions that make almost one half.

2. Can you find other pairs?

ACTIVITY 10-26

WHAT MAKES ALMOST ONE? (CONCRETE: REGION)

PROCEDURE

1. Use fraction pie pieces to help you find two different fractions that make almost one.

2. Can you find another pair of fractions that make almost one?

ACTIVITY 10-30

WHAT MAKES ALMOST ONE-HALF? (CONCRETE: REGION)

PROCEDURE

1. Use Fraction Factory pieces to help you find pairs of fractions that make almost one-half.

ACTIVITY 10-27

WHAT MAKES JUST OVER ONE? (CONCRETE: MEASUREMENT)

PROCEDURE

1. Use Fraction Bars to help you group two different fractions to make just over one. Can you find other pairs of fractions that make just over one?

ACTIVITY 10-31

WHAT MAKES ALMOST ONE-HALF? (SYMBOLIC)

PROCEDURE

1. Using the numbers 1, 3, 4, 5, 8, 10, write pairs of fractions that make almost one-half.

ACTIVITY 10-32

FRACTIONS THAT ARE ABOUT ZERO, ONE-HALF, OR ONE

PROCEDURE

1. Which of these fractions are close to zero, one-half, or one?

$\frac{12}{20}$	$\frac{1}{50}$	$\frac{2}{10}$	$\frac{8}{9}$	$\frac{3}{5}$
$\frac{6}{7}$	$\frac{1}{25}$	$\frac{15}{32}$	$\frac{4}{14}$	$\frac{6}{15}$
$\frac{99}{100}$	$\frac{15}{16}$	$\frac{4}{9}$	$\frac{2}{100}$	$\frac{11}{23}$

Improper Fractions and Mixed Numbers

An interpretation of fraction as numbers less than one probably led to a distinction between such fractions and those representing numbers greater than one. The terms *proper fraction and improper fraction* have been assigned, respectively, to the two kinds of fractions (Figure 10-15).

It is not an easy task for young children to represent improper fractions concretely or diagrammatically. For example, the shaded portion in Figure 10-16 often is labeled $\frac{4}{6}$ rather than $\frac{4}{3}$.

FIGURE 10-15

PROPER FRACTIONS

$$\frac{1}{2}, \frac{2}{3}, \frac{4}{5} \cdots$$

For every $\frac{a}{b}$, a < b

IMPROPER FRACTIONS

$$\frac{3}{2}, \frac{4}{3}, \frac{5}{4}, \frac{5}{5} \cdots$$

For every $\frac{a}{b}$, a > b or a = b

FIGURE 10-16

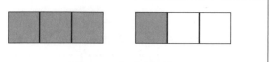

What part is shaded?
$\frac{4}{3}$, or $1\frac{1}{3}$, is shaded.

Any fraction that is greater than one can be written as an improper fraction or as a *mixed number*. A mixed number is a way of expressing a number greater than one as a whole number and a fraction. Addition is implied in a mixed number even though the + symbol is not written.

Example: $3\frac{2}{5}$ $\rightarrow$ $3 + \frac{2}{5}$

The process of changing a mixed number to an improper fraction can be demonstrated as follows:

Example: Change $\frac{18}{5}$ to a mixed number.
Recall: $1 = \frac{5}{5}$
Think: $18 = 5 + 5 + 5 + 3$

Therefore, $\frac{18}{5}$ can be written as $\frac{5}{5} + \frac{5}{5} + \frac{5}{5} + \frac{3}{5}$
which $= 1 + 1 + 1 + \frac{3}{5}$
$= 3 + \frac{3}{5}$ or $3\frac{3}{5}$

In repeatedly working through this process, children may see that what is essentially being done is dividing 18 by 5 to obtain the quotient $3\frac{3}{5}$. From this analysis emerges the *quotient* interpretation of fractions, that is, $\frac{18}{5}$ is the same as 18 divided by 5.

The process of changing a mixed number to an improper fraction is similar to the process of checking a division exercise.

Example: $14 \div 3 = 4$ R2 or $4\frac{2}{3}$
Check: $(3 \times 4) + 2 = 14$

The mixed number (quotient) $4\frac{2}{3}$ has been changed to an improper fraction by multiplying the two factors (divisor and quotient) and adding the remainder to obtain the product 14 (dividend).

Using the Math Explorer calculator
Converting improper fractions to mixed numbers can be performed on the Math Explorer calculator by using the $\boxed{\text{Ab/c}}$ key.

Example: Change $\frac{8}{5}$ to a mixed number
Enter 8 $\boxed{/}$ 5 $\boxed{\text{Ab/c}}$ Display 1 u 3/5
(The *u* separates the whole number from a fraction.)

UNDERSTANDING EQUIVALENT FRACTIONS

Another important fraction topic is equivalent fractions, a concept that refers to the notion that different fractions can represent the same amount. For example, $\frac{1}{2}$ and $\frac{2}{4}$ are different fractions that represent the same amount; however, to many children these are two completely different

TECHNOLOGY LINK 10-1
Fresh Baked Fractions

Practice identifying equivalent fractions on this site! First, set your own difficulty level (easy, medium, hard, or super brain). Then examine a group of four fractions, and decide which fraction is not equal to the other three. Each correct answer provides you with a piece of pie. If you earn 24 pieces of pie, you can put your name on the list of master pie bakers!
Visit http://www.funbrain.com/fract/ or link from our Companion Website at **www.prenhall.com/ cathcart.**

fractions. Many children believe that $\frac{2}{4}$ must be more, because the numbers are larger. Indeed, understanding equivalent fractions is another important prerequisite to fraction computation and helps children evaluate the reasonableness of answers.

Equivalent Fractions

When dealing with fractions, the notion that every number can be expressed in different ways is critical. When assigning different names for a specified fraction, we say that we are writing *equivalent fractions.*

Children should understand unit fractions and composite fractions before they are introduced to equivalent fractions. For example, children should be able to readily compare fractions such as $\frac{1}{4}$ and $\frac{1}{6}$; $\frac{7}{10}$ and $\frac{5}{10}$; $\frac{2}{4}$ and $\frac{2}{8}$.

Bezuk and Bieck (1993) recommend that teachers discuss the meaning of the word *equivalent* ("equal value") and also discuss how equivalent fractions are both alike and different. They also recommend that teachers help children generalize from their experiences with manipulatives the symbolic algorithm for finding equivalent fractions.

PRINCIPLES AND STANDARDS LINK 10-7
Content Strand: Number and Operations

During grades 3–5, students should build their understanding of fractions as parts of a whole and as division. They will need to see and explore a variety of models of fractions, focusing primarily on familiar fractions such as halves, thirds, fourths, fifths, sixths, eighths, and tenths. By using an area model in which part of a region is shaded, students can see how fractions are related to a unit whole, compare fractional parts of a whole, and find equivalent fractions. (NCTM, 2000, p. 149)

PRINCIPLES AND STANDARDS LINK 10-8
Content Strand: Number and Operations

Through a variety of activities, [children] should understand that a fraction such as $\frac{1}{2}$ is equivalent to $\frac{5}{10}$ and that it has a decimal representation (0.5). (NCTM, 2000, p. 149)

Although the idea of equivalent fractions can be introduced early to children, mastery of the concept should not be expected until upper elementary grades or later (Driscoll, 1984).

Children can engage in activities with fraction circles, Fraction Factory pieces, or Fraction Bars to discover for themselves that fractions such as one-half and two-fourths name the same amount. They can fold paper strips or rectangles to discover equivalent fractions. Several activities that are designed to help children understand equivalent fractions are presented in this section (see Activities 10-33 to 10-35).

1. Equivalent Fractions
   - Provide each child with narrow strips of paper.
   - Ask children to fold one strip of paper into two equal pieces. Have them identify the fractional parts and label the midpoint as $\frac{1}{2}$ and the endpoint as $\frac{2}{2}$.

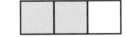
ACTIVITY 10-33

EQUIVALENT FRACTIONS

PROCEDURE
1. What part of the bar is shaded?

2. Divide each part of the bar in half. What part is shaded now? Write an equivalent fraction.

3. Divide each part of these bars in half. Write equivalent fractions for the shaded parts.

ACTIVITY 10-34

WRITING EQUIVALENT FRACTIONS

MATERIALS

A sheet of paper on which three rectangles have been drawn

PROCEDURE

1. Draw thirds on the first rectangle.

2. Draw sixths on the second rectangle.

3. Draw twelfths on the third rectangle.

4. Write equality statements about what you observe in your figures.

EXAMPLE:

2 thirds = 4 sixths.

ACTIVITY 10-35

FINDING EQUIVALENT FRACTIONS

MATERIALS

A set of 12 chips, 4 of one color and 8 of another color

PROCEDURE

1. Use the set of chips to show the fractions: 2 sixths, 1 third, 4 twelfths.

2. Draw a picture to show how you grouped the chips to show each fraction.

3. What can you say about each fraction?

Note that the $\frac{1}{2}$ is the distance from the beginning point to the center and the $\frac{2}{2}$ is the distance from the beginning point to the end.

• Have children fold a second strip of paper in fourths, open it up, and name the four parts on the foldlines and the end points as $\frac{1}{4}, \frac{2}{4}, \frac{3}{4}, \frac{4}{4}$.

• Direct children to fold a third strip of paper in eighths and label each part produced in eighths. The strips should be labeled as in the following diagram.

		$\frac{1}{2}$			$\frac{2}{2}$
	$\frac{1}{4}$	$\frac{2}{4}$		$\frac{3}{4}$	$\frac{4}{4}$
$\frac{1}{8}$	$\frac{2}{8}$	$\frac{3}{8}$	$\frac{4}{8}$	$\frac{5}{8}$	$\frac{6}{8}$	$\frac{7}{8}$	$\frac{8}{8}$

• Ask children to find equal lengths on the strips that have been labeled differently. The idea that frac-

tional lengths can be named differently or that fractions can have more than one name should be highlighted in the discussion. Equality statements could be written on the board.

Examples: $\frac{1}{2}$ and $\frac{2}{4}$ are the same length. $\frac{2}{2}, \frac{4}{4}$, and $\frac{8}{8}$ all indicate the same length.

2. Finding Equivalent Fractions

• Have children use Fraction Bars to find equal lengths with different names.

Examples:

Orange and blue bars

9 twelfths is the same length as 3 fourths

Green and red bars

1 half equals 3 sixths

3. Finding Equivalent Fractions

• Provide Fraction Factory pieces for each group of children.

• Direct children to select the black rectangle.

• Ask them to use other pieces to cover half of the black rectangle in at least two different ways.

• Have them cover other fractional parts of the rectangle in at least two different ways.

• Have children write equality statements about what they have done.

• Have children read aloud what they have written.

• The statements could be displayed on a bulletin board under the caption: Fractions Have More Than One Name.

4. Equivalent Fractions

• Provide a set of buttons in two colors for each child.

• Have children arrange 12 buttons, 6 of each color, in a two-row array.

• Ask, "What part of the buttons are (say) white?" (one-half)

• Ask, "Can you group the buttons another way so that you can give a different fraction name to the group of white buttons?"

• Have children repeat the last step.

Possible solutions include the following:

• Provide children with 24 buttons, 12 of each color. Ask the students to find equivalent fractions for one-half; for two-thirds.

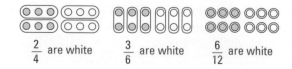

$\frac{2}{4}$ are white $\frac{3}{6}$ are white $\frac{6}{12}$ are white

- Given an appropriate number of buttons, the process can be repeated for any unit or composite fraction.

5. Renaming Fractions (adapted from Jensen & O'Neil, 1982)
   - For this activity, each group of children will need egg cartons separated into 2, 4, 6, 8, and 12 "cups" and small objects to represent eggs.
   - Have the children choose a 4-cup tray and place 2 eggs in it. Ask: "What part of the tray is filled?" (elicit $\frac{1}{2}$; $\frac{2}{4}$)
   - Continue in this manner, using in turn, a 6-, an 8-, and a 12-cup tray. Each time, have children indicate in several ways what part of the tray is filled. (12-cup tray, 6 eggs: $\frac{1}{2}$, $\frac{2}{4}$, $\frac{3}{6}$, $\frac{6}{12}$).
   - Have children record their work on paper.
   - Ask, "What conclusions do you reach about the fractions you have written?"

Renaming and Simplifying Fractions

The idea that each fraction number can be represented in different numeric form is an important one for children to learn. (Example: $\frac{1}{2} = \frac{2}{4} = \frac{3}{6} = \frac{4}{8} \ldots$)

Some children may detect the pattern and articulate a rule for easily *renaming a fraction* (writing equivalent fractions), such as multiplying each part of the fraction numeral by the same number. What may not be readily evident to children is that the multiplicative identity element, one, is being used in a different form, that is, as $\frac{2}{2}$, $\frac{3}{3}$, $\frac{4}{4}$, etc. Middle-school children should comprehend the following reasoning.

Any number that multiplies 1 or is multiplied by 1 equals 1.

Examples: $6 \times 1 = 6$ $\frac{1}{2} \times 1 = \frac{1}{2}$
$\quad\quad\quad\quad\quad 1 \times 45 = 45$ $1 \times \frac{2}{5} = \frac{2}{5}$

Represent "1" as $\frac{2}{2}$, $\frac{3}{3}$, $\frac{4}{4}$, etc.

If $\frac{1}{2} \times 1 = \frac{1}{2}$ If $\frac{1}{2} \times 1 = \frac{1}{2}$
and $\frac{1}{2} \times \frac{2}{2} = \frac{2}{4}$ and $\frac{1}{2} \times \frac{3}{3} = \frac{3}{6}$
Then, $\frac{1}{2} = \frac{2}{4}$ Then, $\frac{1}{2} = \frac{3}{6}$

Facility in renaming fractions is of utmost importance when comparing fractions and as a preparation for computation.

Simplifying fractions is the process of renaming a fraction through division. The fraction is divided by the multiplicative identity element represented in fraction form. The choice of representation for the identity element depends on the fraction being simplified, that is, a divisor common to each term of the fraction numeral must be used.

Examples:

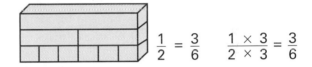

The algorithmic work of renaming fractions should be accompanied for some time by concrete (Figure 10-17) or pictorial (Figure 10-18) representations of the process.

Renaming and simplifying fractions using a calculator   After children understand the process of renaming and simplifying

---

> **FIGURE 10-17**

Using Cuisenaire Rods

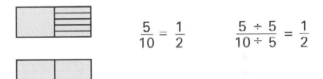

Using Fraction Factory Pieces

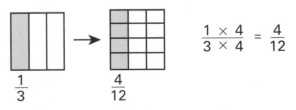

> **FIGURE 10-18**

Renaming Fractions

Simplifying Fractions

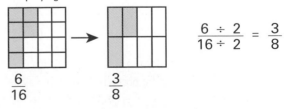

LITERATURE LINK 10-1
Fraction Concepts

Matthews, Louise. (1995). *Gator Pie.* Littleton, MA: Sundance.
Murphy, Stuart J. (1986). *Give Me Half.* New York: Harper Collins.

Children begin school with basic understandings of many mathematics concepts. Fraction terms like *half* referring to "half of a cookie" or *quarter after* to "quarter after five" when telling time may already be a part of their informal mathematical knowledge. In the story *Gator Pie,* two alligators, Alvin and Alice, find a delicious-looking pie near the swamp. They plan to share the pie equally in two halves, but other alligators come along, and they are forced to think about cutting the pie into thirds, fourths, and eventually hundredths. In the end, Alvin comes up with a clever solution.

- On several pages of the book, fractions are written in words and pictorial models of a circular region are shown. Practice writing the words and the numerals and drawing various pictures models for some common fractions.
- Use paper plates as circular region model of the pie in the story. Attempt to do what Alice did and cut the pie into 100 equal pieces by drawing lines on the paper plates to indicate the slices.
- Investigate "halves" using other region models such as squares, rectangles, triangles, and pentagons cut from construction paper. Fold each shape to create two equal halves.

- Introduce concepts and terms such as *partitioning* and *congruence* by investigating construction paper cutouts of different shapes. Use a ruler to measure and cut these region models into thirds, fourths, fifths, sixths, and so on. By cutting the pieces of construction paper apart, children can place each piece on top of others to compare to be sure all pieces are the same shape and size.
- Use manipulatives such as fraction circles (or fraction pies) to identify common fractions in a circular region model. Introduce children to representations of fractions in numbers, words, pictorial models, and concrete models.
- Books such as *Give Me Half!* help children to understand beginning concepts of "half." Examine a paper cutout of a half-circle, a half-square, and half of a group of 6 counters (3 counters). Discuss why all of these representations are called "half" when it is empirically obvious that they do not look the same. Talk about what "half" means so that children have the opportunity to abstract this concept through various representations.

Source: Dr. Patricia Moyer, George Mason University.

---

fractions, they can be allowed to use a calculator with that capability to assist them in problem solving. In renaming fractions with the Math Explorer calculator, the procedure is as follows:

Example:
Write an equivalent fraction for $\frac{3}{8}$.

Enter 3 $\boxed{/}$ 8 $\boxed{\times}$ 2 $\boxed{/}$ 2 $\boxed{=}$ Display: 6/16

The fact that the multiplicative identity is employed (1 written as 2/2 in this case) in renaming fractions will be emphasized when using a calculator. A child who merely multiplies a fraction by a whole number factor will note that the denominator has not changed.

Example:
Simplifying a fraction can be performed in two ways:

Enter: 2 $\boxed{/}$ 16 $\boxed{\times}$ 2 $\boxed{=}$ Display: 4/16

(1) the calculator can choose the common factor, or
(2) the child can do so.

Example: Simplify $\frac{4}{24}$

Enter 4 $\boxed{/}$ 24 $\boxed{\text{Simp}}$

The calculator displays $\boxed{\text{Simp}}$ N/D → n/d in the left corner, indicating that the fraction can be simplified. The two ways to proceed to simplify the fraction are:

1. Calculator chooses the common factor

   Enter = to get 2/12

   The calculator reduces the fraction to the next simpler term. If N/D → n/d still is displayed, that means that the fraction can be simplified further. Pressing the $\boxed{\text{Simp}}$ and the $\boxed{=}$ keys again simplifies the fraction to the next simpler term.

   To find out which factor the calculator used, enter the $\boxed{\text{x} \frown \text{y}}$ key and the factor will be displayed.

Enter the $\boxed{x\text{—}y}$ *key again to display the simpler fraction.*

2. Child chooses the common factor:

Enter 2 (a common factor of 4 and 24)

Enter $\boxed{=}$ *to obtain 2/12*

To reduce the fraction further, press 2 (a common factor of 2 and 12) and $\boxed{=}$ *to obtain the simplest fraction 1/16. If a number is entered that is not a common factor of the two fraction terms, the calculator will simply display the fraction again.*

Example: 4/24 Enter $\boxed{\text{Simp}}$ *5* $\boxed{=}$ *Display is 4/24*

CONCLUSION

Fractions are an important part of the mathematics curriculum. Understanding fraction concepts, comparison, ordering, number sense, and equivalence lays the foundation for later work with fraction computation and prepares children for using mathematics in their everyday lives.

For Your Journal

When you have finished studying this chapter, reflect on the following questions in your math journal:

1. Think back on your own experiences learning about fractions. Describe how you were taught about the topics in this chapter and discuss your understandings of these topics. Will the way you were taught have any effect on how you will teach these topics to children?

2. Draw a diagram to illustrate the equivalence of $\frac{1}{2}$ and $\frac{3}{6}$ and explain why these fractions are equivalent.

3. Informally interview one or two intermediate-grade children to assess their understanding of fraction concepts, comparison, and equivalence. Describe their understandings.

For Your Portfolio

When you have finished studying this chapter, complete the following activities to include in your professional portfolio:

1. Write a lesson to help children understand comparison of fractions, using the benchmarks of 0, $\frac{1}{2}$, and 1.

2. Write a lesson to help children understand the concept of equivalence using manipulative materials and making connections to symbols.

Resources for Teachers

Children's books

Mathews, L. (1979). *Gator pie.* Littleton, MA: Sundance.
Murphy, Stuart J. (1996). *Give me half.* New York: Harper Collins.

Books on fractions

Brodie, J. (1995). *Constructing ideas about fractions, Grades 3–6.* Mountain View, CA: Creative.
Corwin, R., Russell, S., & Tierney, C. (1990). *Seeing fractions: A unit for the upper elementary grades.* Sacramento: California Department of Education.
Cramer, K., Behr, M., Post, T., & Lesh, R. (1997a). *Rational Number Project: Fraction lessons for the middle grades level 1.* Dubuque, IA: Kendall/Hunt.
Cramer, K., Behr, M., Post, T., & Lesh, R. (1997b). *Rational Number Project: Fraction lessons for the middle grades level 2.* Dubuque, IA: Kendall/Hunt.
Curcio, F. R., & Bezuk, N. S. (1994). *Understanding rational numbers and proportions: Curriculum and Evaluation Standards for School Mathematics Addenda Series Grade 5–8.* Reston, VA: National Council of Teachers of Mathematics.
Lappan, G., Fitzgerald, W., Winter, M., & Phillips, E. (1986). *Middle Grades Mathematics Project: Similarity and equivalent fractions.* Menlo Park, CA: Addison-Wesley.
Ward, S. (1995). *Constructing ideas about fractions, decimals, and percents.* Mountain View, CA: Creative.

Links to the Internet

Ask Dr. Math (Fractions and Decimals)

http://www.mathforum.org/dr.math/tocs/fractions.elem.html

Contains a list of interesting questions about fractions and decimals and Dr. Math's answers.

ProTeacher: Fractions and Decimals

http://www.proteacher.com/100014.shtml

Contains lesson plans on fractions and decimals.

Explorer: Fractions

http://explorer.scrtec.org/explorer/explorer-db/browse/static/Mathematics/browse/f34.html

Contains many lessons on fractions and lists of other resources.

Who Wants Pizza?

http://math.rice.edu/~lanius/fractions/index.html

Contains many lessons on fractions and lists of other resources.

Fresh-Baked Fractions

http://www.funbrain.com/fract/

Contains games on finding equivalent fractions.

CHAPTER 11

Developing Fraction Computation

✔ **Prerequisites for operations on fractions**

✔ **Operation sense**

✔ **Meaning of each operation on fractions**

✔ **Modeling operations on fractions**

When you have finished studying this chapter, you should be able to answer the following questions:

1. What are the prerequisites for operations on fractions?

2. What does it mean to help children develop operation sense?

3. What does each operation on fractions mean? Discuss a real-world situation that exemplifies each operation on fractions.

4. What models help children understand operations on fractions?

NCTM CONTENT STANDARDS AND EXPECTATIONS ADDRESSED IN THIS CHAPTER

STANDARD	EXPECTATION FOR GRADES 3–5	EXPECTATIONS FOR GRADES 6–8
Number and Operations Standard Instructional programs from pre-K–12 should enable all students to—	In Grades 3–5 all students should— (NCTM, 2000, p. 148)	In Grades 6–8 all students should—(NCTM, 2000, p. 214)
Understand numbers, ways of representing numbers, relationships among numbers, and number systems		• work flexibly with fractions, decimals, and percents to solve problems.
Understand meanings of operations and how they relate to one another		• understand the meaning and effects of arithmetic operations with fractions, decimals, and integers. • use the associative and commutative properties of addition and multiplication and the distributive property of multiplication over addition to simplify computations with integers, fractions, and decimals.
Compute fluently and make reasonable estimates	• develop and use strategies to estimate computations involving fractions and decimals in situations relevant to students' experience. • use visual models, benchmarks, and equivalent forms to add and subtract commonly used fractions and decimals. • select appropriate methods and tools for computing with whole numbers from among mental computation, estimation, calculators, and paper and pencil according to the context and nature of the computation and use the selected method or tools.	• select appropriate methods and tools for computing with fractions and decimals from among mental computation, estimation, calculators or computers, and paper and pencil, depending on the situation, and apply the selected methods. • develop and analyze algorithms for computing with fractions, decimals, and integers and develop fluency in their use. • develop and use strategies to estimate the results of rational-number computations and judge the reasonableness of the results.

Fraction computation is arguably the mathematics topic with which most adults have had the *least* success and the *most* bad memories! The traditional curricular emphasis on mastering algorithms for adding, subtracting, multiplying, and dividing fractions without first developing understanding lead to this frustration and lack of achievement.

One reason for the difficulty many children have with fraction computation is that children often are expected to compute with fraction symbols before they have developed a good understanding of fractions and related concepts. The temptation to have children progress quickly to working symbolically with fraction computation may arise from the thinking that because the children already know how to add, subtract, multiply, and divide whole numbers, it follows that they are ready to use these operations to compute with fractions.

Often this is not the case. Most children have great difficulty linking what they already know about operations on whole numbers with operations on fractions. Teachers must help children make these connections by carefully designing instruction to link these concepts. If these connections are not made, children will not be able to predict what a reasonable answer might be or make sense of the process, forcing them to memorize meaningless procedures. Too often, the result is frustration and lack of learning.

Some suggest that operations on fractions should be relegated to calculators, maintaining that calculators have eliminated the need for any instruction on fraction computation. It is true that the availability and power of calculators certainly reduces the level of paper-and-pencil mastery of fraction computation that children must achieve. But the availability of technology also increases the importance of children's developing operation sense, which refers to an understanding of the meaning of operations, as well as the need for the ability to determine the reasonableness of solutions.

PRINCIPLES AND STANDARDS LINK 11-2
Content Strand: Number and Operations

The development of rational-number concepts is a major goal for grades 3–5, which should lead to informal methods for calculating with fractions. For example, a problem such as $\frac{1}{4} + \frac{1}{2}$ should be solved mentally with ease because students can picture $\frac{1}{2}$ and $\frac{1}{4}$ or can use decomposition strategies, such as $\frac{1}{4} + \frac{1}{2} = \frac{1}{4} + (\frac{1}{4} + \frac{1}{4})$ . . . By grades 6–8, students should become fluent in computing with rational numbers in fraction and decimal form. (NCTM, 2000, p. 35)

Teachers must carefully consider what children need to know concerning fraction computation. There are *four goals of instruction* regarding fraction computation:

1. Children need to recognize situations that involve operations on fractions.

2. Children need to find the answer to fraction computation problems by using models.

3. Children need to estimate the answer and understand the reasonableness of results to fraction computation problems.

4. Children need to find an exact answer to fraction computation problems.

Notice that finding an exact answer is only one goal of instruction. The other three goals are equally important and will help children be successful in finding exact answers. This chapter presents ways to help children attain these four goals.

PRINCIPLES AND STANDARDS LINK 11-3
Content Strand: Number and Operations

As students acquire conceptual grounding related to rational numbers, they should begin to solve problems using strategies they develop or adapt from their whole-number work. At these grades, the emphasis should not be on developing general procedures to solve all decimal and fraction problems. Rather, students should generate solutions that are based on number sense and properties of the operations and that use a variety of models or representations. (NCTM, 2000, p. 154)

Prerequisites for Fraction Computation

What must children understand *before* beginning work on fraction computation? There are two prerequisites for fraction computation:

1. Understanding of fraction concepts, comparison, and equivalence.
2. Understanding of the meaning of operations on whole numbers.

Attempts to teach children to perform fraction computation prior to their attainment of these prerequisites will result in frustration for both the child and the teacher. Children will be forced to mindlessly memorize procedures rather than understand what they are doing and why. Instead of rushing toward algorithms, teachers should spend time helping children master the prerequisites, which will enable them to perform fraction computation with a greater degree of understanding and success.

INTRODUCING COMPUTATION

Developmental Activities

As children work through introductory fraction activities, they progress from thinking of fractions as "parts of things" to operating with them as numbers, each with a precise location on the number line.

Throughout developmental activities, children should have opportunities to construct concrete representations of fraction quantities and, from the representations, to record their findings on paper. Using concrete models to assist in problem solving should be looked upon as the norm in elementary classrooms. Therefore, appropriate manipulative materials should be available to children for as long as they find them helpful.

TECHNOLOGY LINK 11-1
ProTeacher: Fractions and Decimals

This ProTeacher site is a collection of interesting mathematics lesson plans for fractions, decimals, and percents. For example, the "Cooking Up Fractions" activity provides practice multiplying and dividing fractions to change recipes to triple a batch of cookies. Visit http://www.proteacher.com/100014.shtml or link from our Companion Website at **www.prenhall.com/cathcart.**

Although regular figures such as triangles, rectangles, pentagons, hexagons, octagons, and decagons are good models to show fractional parts, the circular shape is more versatile because any unit fraction can easily be represented (Figure 11-1). Also, the circles can be used to model fraction computation.

Introductory computation activities should have children work with fractions in different contexts because a narrow view of what fractions are (e.g., fractions are parts of a whole) is thought to be a reason for the generally unsatisfactory performance in fraction work (Hope & Owens, 1987). The part-whole, measurement, and part-of-a-set interpretations should be embodied in different problem-solving situations. In time, the quotient, operator (multiplicative aspect), and ratio interpretations will also be explored (Kieren, 1976).

FIGURE 11-1

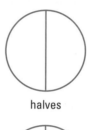
halves    sevenths

thirds   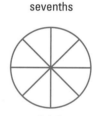 eighths

fourths    ninths

fifths    tenths

 sixths    twelfths   fifteenths

Allow adequate time for the algorithmic computation processes to emerge from children's active explorations with concrete and pictorial representations.

About Algorithms

The complexity of the algorithms for computing with whole numbers can be said to depend on the numbers used in the computation. For example, in subtraction, children find it difficult to subtract numbers with zeros, such as 4002 − 307. In multiplication, it is easier to find the product with a one-digit multiplier than with a two-digit multiplier; in division, single-digit divisors are easier than two-digit divisors when working through the long division algorithm, and zeros in the quotient add to the complexity. Because of these difficulties for children, the algorithms for computing with whole numbers generally are developed in stages over several grade levels.

The algorithms for computing with fractions are simple when compared with whole-number computation algorithms. Because of the simplicity of these algorithmic rules, children may readily learn them so that they can compute with fractions. However, when procedures are not understood, some children become confused about which rule to use in a particular computation situation. They do not recall which fraction to invert or when common denominators are needed.

The goal is to have children learn to compute with fractions in a meaningful way. Therefore, children's first computations with fractions should be with concrete and pictorial models.

Connecting Operations on Whole Numbers With Operations on Fractions

There are several different interpretations of operations on whole numbers, as discussed in Chapter 7. Several of those interpretations work well for helping children un-

derstand operations on fractions, but a few are a bit confusing. Figure 11-2 shows examples of word problems using whole numbers and word problems using fractions for many of the different interpretations of the operations. These interpretations are discussed in more detail throughout this chapter.

Properties

Learning to compute with fractions at the middle-school level will include "testing" whether fractions possess the same properties as whole numbers. Through explorations, children will conclude that the commutative and associative properties hold for addition and multiplication; that multiplication is distributive over addition; and that the

---

FIGURE 11-2

WORD PROBLEMS FOR FRACTIONS

Addition

Tom ate $\frac{1}{2}$ of an apple pie yesterday and $\frac{1}{4}$ of an apple pie today. How much pie did Tom eat altogether? (Join)

Number sentence: $\frac{1}{2} + \frac{1}{4} = $ _____

Subtraction

Alberto has $\frac{3}{4}$ of a chocolate chip cookie and Juana has $\frac{1}{4}$ of a cookie. How much more does Alberto have? (Comparison)

Number sentence: $\frac{3}{4} - \frac{1}{4} = $ _____

Alberto has $\frac{3}{4}$ of a chocolate chip cookie. He ate $\frac{1}{4}$ of a whole cookie. How much cookie does Alberto have left? (Separate)

Number sentence: $\frac{3}{4} - \frac{1}{4} = $ _____

Multiplication

There is $\frac{2}{3}$ of a chocolate pie in the refrigerator. Peter ate $\frac{1}{2}$ of it. What part of the whole pie did Peter eat? (Area and Array)

Number sentence: $\frac{1}{2} \times \frac{2}{3} = $ _____

Shawntrice had 4 bags of cookies, with $\frac{1}{2}$ of a cookie in each bag. How many cookies did Shawntrice have? (Repeated addition)

Number sentence: $4 \times \frac{1}{2} = $ _____

Division

Steve has 4 cups of sugar. He needs $\frac{2}{3}$ of a cup of sugar to make one batch of his favorite cookies. How many batches of cookies can Steve make? (Measurement/repeated subtraction)

Number sentence: $4 \div \frac{2}{3} = $ _____

Steve has 4 cups of sugar. That is enough to bake $\frac{2}{3}$ of a batch of his favorite cookies. How much sugar will he need to make 1 batch of cookies? (Partitive/fair sharing*)

Number sentence: $4 \div \frac{2}{3} = $ _____

*Notice that partitive division/fair sharing is NOT very easy to understand with fractions!

closure property holds true for addition, multiplication, and division. The new property from whole-number computation is the closure property for division, that is, any fractional number can be divided by any fractional number except zero to obtain a quotient within the system.

ADDITION AND SUBTRACTION OF FRACTIONS

The concepts of addition and subtraction of fractions are the same as for addition and subtraction of whole numbers. Children will know that for problems wherein two fraction addends are given, the operation required to solve the problem is addition; likewise, when a fraction addend and a fraction or whole number sum is given, the operation of subtraction will provide the missing addend. As with whole numbers, addition fraction problems can be join problems, and subtraction problems can be separate or comparison problems.

Developing Addition Procedures

Children in Grades 3 and 4 enjoy finding addition sentences when working with concrete materials such as Fraction Bars, Fraction Factory pieces, and fraction circles (Figure 11-3). After constructing a number of "simple" examples, they can progress to find more compli-

cated ones, such as fractions with unlike denominators and some with more than two addends.

The addition sentences provided by the children could be classified as "easy" ones and "complicated" or "tricky" ones. Picking up on a child's example involving unlike denominators, a teacher could ask, "How did you figure that out? Could you write those fractions a different way?"

Example: $\frac{1}{4} + \frac{2}{3} = \frac{11}{12}$

Possible thinking:

I found that 1 fourth is the same as 3 twelfths and that 2 thirds is the same as 8 twelfths. So we can write

1 fourth	$\rightarrow$	3 twelfths
+ 2 thirds	$\rightarrow$	8 twelfths
		11 twelfths or

$$\frac{3}{12} + \frac{8}{12} = \frac{11}{12}$$

Activities 11-1 to 11-6 have children construct addition sentences using Fraction Bars. The activities could be repeated to advantage using a different set of materials such as fraction pies, fraction squares, or a set of objects. Other addition problems could be embedded in familiar contexts such as parts of a dozen eggs (12 as lowest common denominator [LCD]), parts of a day (24 as LCD), or parts of an hour or minute (60 as LCD). More structured tasks are described in Activities 11-7 to 11-10.

ACTIVITY 11-1

FRACTION ADDITION SENTENCES

MATERIALS
Fraction Bars

PROCEDURE
1. Use the Fraction Bars to help you add different fractions.
2. Record the addition sentences you make.

ACTIVITY 11-2

FINDING A SUM OF 1

MATERIALS
Fraction Bars

PROCEDURE
1. Use the Fraction Bars to help you find two fractions that equal 1.
2. How many different pairs of fraction addends can you find to equal 1?

ACTIVITY 11-3

FINDING A SUM OF 1 WITH MORE THAN TWO ADDENDS

MATERIALS
Fraction Bars

PROCEDURE
1. Use the Fraction Bars to help you write addition sentences that add up to 1 using more than two fraction addends.

   Example: 1 fourth + 1 third + 1 sixth + 3 twelfths is the same as 1 bar (or equals 1).

ACTIVITY 11-4

FINDING A MISSING ADDEND

PROCEDURE
1. Can you find out which fraction goes in the blank space to make a true statement?

   2 thirds + —————— = 11 twelfths

   1 fifth + —————— = 3 tenths

FIGURE 11-3

Modeling Addition of Fractions

Part of a Whole

Fraction Bars

$$\frac{1}{3} + \frac{1}{4} = \frac{7}{12}$$

Fraction Factory Pieces

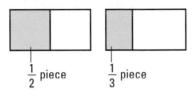

$$\frac{1}{2} \text{ piece} \qquad \frac{1}{3} \text{ piece}$$

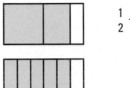

$$\frac{1}{2} + \frac{1}{3} = \frac{5}{6}$$

Fraction Circles

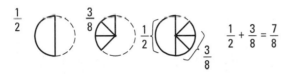

$$\frac{1}{2} + \frac{3}{8} = \frac{7}{8}$$

Fraction Rods

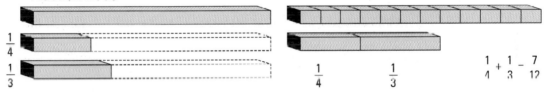

$$\frac{1}{4} \qquad \frac{1}{3} \qquad \frac{1}{4} + \frac{1}{3} = \frac{7}{12}$$

Part of a Set

How much is $\frac{1}{3} + \frac{3}{4}$?

Thirds and fourths can be modeled with a set of 12.

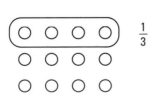

$$\frac{1}{3}$$

$\frac{1}{3}$ is the same as $\frac{4}{12}$

$$\frac{3}{4}$$

$\frac{3}{4}$ is the same as $\frac{9}{12}$

$$\frac{1}{3} + \frac{3}{4} = \frac{4}{12} + \frac{9}{12} = \frac{13}{12}$$
$$= 1\frac{1}{12}$$

ACTIVITY 11-5

ADDING FRACTIONS

MATERIALS
Fractions Bars

PROCEDURE
1. Use Fractions Bars to help you add $\frac{1}{2} + \frac{1}{5}$.
2. Do some other examples.

ACTIVITY 11-6

FINDING PARTICULAR SUMS

PROCEDURE
1. Write addition sentences with a sum of 15 sixteenths.
2. Write addition sentences using different-sized fractions with 11 twelfths as the sum.

ACTIVITY 11-7

ADDING FRACTIONS

PROCEDURE
1. Use fraction families (equivalent fractions) to add $\frac{3}{4} + \frac{1}{5}$.
2. Do some other addition problems.

Possible solution:

3 fourths	→	15 twentieths
1 fifth	→	4 twentieths
		19 twentieths, or $\frac{19}{20}$

ACTIVITY 11-8

FINDING THE LOWEST COMMON DENOMINATOR

PROCEDURE
1. Find the lowest common denominator to help you find the sum of $\frac{2}{5} + \frac{1}{6}$.
2. Do some other examples.

Possible solution:

2 fifths	→	12 thirtieths
1 sixth	→	5 thirtieths
		17 thirtieths

ACTIVITY 11-9

FRACTION ADDITION

MATERIALS
Fraction Bars

PROCEDURE
Do any of these fraction pairs add up to 1?
Use Fraction Bars to help you find the answer.

$$\frac{1}{6} + \frac{10}{12} = \qquad \frac{3}{4} + \frac{3}{12} = \qquad \frac{2}{3} + \frac{2}{6} =$$

ACTIVITY 11-10

FRACTION ADDITION

Write fraction addition statements with sums less than 1.
Write fraction addition statements with sums greater than 1 but less than 2.

Following several sessions of constructing addition equations (Activities 11-1 to 11-6), children could collect and organize different addition statements on a chart or bulletin board. The display could be the focus of a class discussion with the intention of having children verbalize how they know the sentences are true.

Addition algorithms Addition of fractions should not be problematic for children if fraction concepts are well understood, that is, if children can talk and write about fraction numbers, compare and estimate fractional quantities, and readily verify their work with concrete or pictorial representations.

Adding unlike fractions. Computing unlike fractions should evoke an automatic move to rewrite the fractions as same-sized denominators before proceeding with addition. The special characteristic of equivalent fractions enables one to add any set of fractions by first rewriting each fraction so that all fractions in the expression have same-sized denominators before proceeding with addition.

Children should be encouraged to formulate computation rules. Children's procedural descriptions might be like the following:

Examples:
$\frac{1}{5} + \frac{3}{5} = $ —— *I'm adding fifths, so I find how many fifths in all.*

$\frac{2}{3} + \frac{1}{2} = $ —— *I have 2 thirds and 1 half, so I change the fractions so they are the same-sized parts, then I add the number of parts in each group.*

The inclination to merely add across numerators and denominators should be offset by having children verbalize and explain the meaning of composite fractions.

Examples:

$\frac{3}{10}$ means 3 parts, each 1 tenth in size.

$\frac{3}{10} = $ 1 tenth + 1 tenth + 1 tenth, or 3 × 1 tenth

$\frac{3}{10} - \frac{1}{10} + \frac{1}{10} + \frac{1}{10}$, or 3 × $\frac{1}{10}$

Addition: 3 tenths
            +   5 tenths
            _____
                          8 tenths

Therefore, $\frac{3}{10} + \frac{5}{10} = \frac{8}{10}$ (not $\frac{8}{20}$)

Finding common denominators. Addition of unlike fractions involves finding a common denominator of the fraction addends. There are several ways to find common denominators of two or more fractions.

1. The common denominator of two fractions can be found using Fraction Bars (see Figure 11-4).

$$\frac{1}{4} + \frac{2}{3} = ?$$

$$\frac{1}{4} + \frac{2}{3} - \frac{3}{12} + \frac{8}{12} = \frac{11}{12}$$

2. At the symbolic level, common denominators can be found by first listing successive multiples of the given denominators and then identifying a common multiple. Usually, one selects the lowest common multiple (LCM) so that the sum will be in simplest form.

Example:

$$\frac{1}{4} + \frac{2}{3}$$

Denominators	Multiples
4	4, 8, (12) 16, 20, ...
3	3, 6, 9, (12) 15, 18, ...

The lowest common multiple of 4 and 3 is 12.

Therefore, $\frac{1}{4} + \frac{2}{3} = \frac{3}{12} + \frac{18}{12} = \frac{11}{12}$

3. Common denominators can be found by listing equivalent fractions until a common denominator is found.

Example:

$$\frac{1}{4} + \frac{2}{3}$$

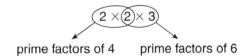

The fractions $\frac{3}{12}$ and $\frac{8}{12}$ have a common denominator, thus, $\frac{1}{4} + \frac{2}{3} = \frac{3}{12} + \frac{8}{12} = \frac{11}{12}$.

4. The lowest common denominator of two or more fractions can also be identified by finding the prime factors of the denominators and computing the product of the maximum set of unique prime factors.

Example:

$$\frac{1}{4} + \frac{1}{6}$$

Denominators	Prime factors
4	2 × 2
6	2 × 3

The maximum set of unique prime factors is 2 × 2 × 3, that is, the prime factors of 4 are in the set and the prime factors of 6 are in the set.

Product: 2 × 2 × 3 = 12

The LCD of 4 and 6 is 12.

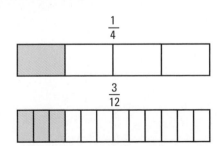

FIGURE 11-4

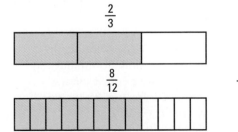

Children should be allowed to use the method they prefer to find a common denominator of a set of fractions.

When working with Fraction Bars or other materials, children may record addition sentences as follows:

Examples:

$$\frac{1}{2} + \frac{1}{4} = (\frac{1}{4} + \frac{1}{4}) + \frac{1}{4} = \frac{3}{4}$$
$$\text{or } \frac{2}{4} + \frac{1}{4} = \frac{3}{4}$$

$$\frac{1}{6} + \frac{1}{2} = \frac{1}{6} + (\frac{1}{6} + \frac{1}{6} + \frac{1}{6}) = \frac{4}{6}$$
$$\text{or } \frac{1}{6} + \frac{3}{6} = \frac{4}{6}, \text{ or } \frac{2}{3}$$

Developing an addition algorithm. Algorithms for adding unlike fractions require finding a common denominator for the fraction addends. If the lowest common denominator is desired, one of the methods described in the preceding section can be employed.

Example:
$\frac{3}{4} + \frac{5}{6}$

The multiples of 4 are 4, 8, 12, 16, . . .
The multiples of 6 are 6, 12, 18, . . .
Twelve is the least common multiple of 4 and 6, and therefore is the lowest common denominator for renaming the fractions $\frac{3}{4}$ and $\frac{5}{6}$.

$\frac{3}{4} = \frac{?}{12}$　Because 4 was multiplied by 3 to obtain 12, the numerator 3 must also be multiplied by 3 to obtain the number of twelfths $\frac{3}{4}$ equals.

$\frac{5}{6} = \frac{?}{12}$　Similarly, 5 must be multiplied by 2 to obtain the number of twelfths $\frac{5}{6}$ equals.

$\frac{3}{4} + \frac{5}{6} = \frac{9}{12} + \frac{10}{12} = \frac{19}{12}, \text{ or } 1\frac{7}{12}$

In algorithmic form, this process demonstrates that each fraction is essentially being multiplied by one, the multiplication property of one.

$$\frac{3}{3} = 1 \quad \frac{2}{2} = 1$$

$$\frac{3}{4} + \frac{5}{6} = \frac{3 \times 3}{4 \times 3} + \frac{5 \times 2}{6 \times 2} = \frac{9}{12} + \frac{10}{12} = \frac{19}{12}$$

When adding fractions, it is not necessary to find the lowest common denominator. An algorithm for finding a common denominator consists of writing equivalent fractions by multiplying each term of a fraction by the denominator of the other fraction. The like fractions can then be added. The algorithm results in a common denominator but not necessarily the lowest.

Example:

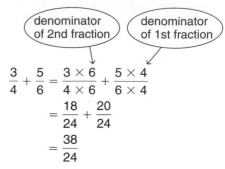

$$\frac{3}{4} + \frac{5}{6} = \frac{3 \times 6}{4 \times 6} + \frac{5 \times 4}{6 \times 4}$$
$$= \frac{18}{24} + \frac{20}{24}$$
$$= \frac{38}{24}$$

The procedure can be abbreviated to

$$\frac{3}{4} + \frac{5}{6} = \frac{(3 \times 6) + (5 \times 4)}{4 \times 6} = \frac{18 + 20}{24} = \frac{38}{24}$$

This leads to the generalization:

$$\frac{a}{b} + \frac{c}{d} = \frac{ad + bc}{bd}$$

Addition of mixed numbers. Addition of mixed numbers can be approached from the perspective of adding whole numbers because, in both instances, the numbers are indicated sums.

Example:

$$76 = \quad 7 \text{ tens} + 6 \text{ ones}$$
$$+ 61 = \quad 6 \text{ tens} + 1 \text{ one}$$
$$= 13 \text{ tens} + 7 \text{ ones} \text{ or } 137$$

Example:

$$3\frac{1}{5} = 3 + \frac{1}{5}$$
$$+ 2\frac{2}{5} = 2 + \frac{2}{5}$$
$$5 + \frac{3}{5} \quad \text{or} \quad 5\frac{3}{5}$$

Just as some whole-number addition problems require regrouping, so do some fraction addition problems.

Example:

$$47 \quad 40 + 7$$
$$+ 25 \rightarrow 20 + 5$$
$$72 \quad 60 + 12 = 60 + 10 + 2 = 72$$

Example:

$$3\frac{1}{5} = 3 + \frac{8}{40}$$
$$+ 1\frac{7}{8} = 1 + \frac{35}{40}$$
$$4 + \frac{43}{40}$$
$$= 4 + \frac{43}{40}$$
$$= 4 + \frac{40}{40} + \frac{3}{40}$$
$$= 4 + 1 + \frac{3}{40}$$
$$= 5\frac{3}{40}$$

Developing Subtraction Procedures

The procedures for developing subtraction of fractions parallel those for addition. It would seem, therefore, that children who are competent with fraction addition would be equally successful with subtraction. However, there are reports that indicate that children make more errors in subtracting fractions involving renaming than in whole-number subtraction with renaming; also, subtraction seems to be the most difficult of the four basic operations with fractions.

Early subtraction activities   First subtraction activities should have children writing subtraction statements from their work with manipulative materials. Children could be asked to write fraction subtraction stories (Activity 11-11) to demonstrate understanding of fractions and the subtraction operation.

LITERATURE LINK 11-1
Fraction Computation

Adler, David. (1996). *Fraction Fun*. New York: Holiday House.

Leedy, Loreen. (1994) *Fraction Action*. New York: Holiday House.

Understanding fractions is difficult for children because children are often introduced to symbols and operations without a strong conceptual foundation. Children need many opportunities to construct meaning in the context of concrete and pictorial models and allow abstract ideas to emerge from these experiences. Key ideas in learning about factors, such as partitioning and equivalence, can be found in books like *Fraction Fun* and *Fraction Action*. The authors show various representations of common fractions, both region and set models, fair sharing, fractions and money, and pictorial ways to represent fractions using paper plates, graph paper, and other models.

- Identify real-world models of fractions such as sharing a pizza, using a recipe, or dividing candy equally Realistic problem-solving contexts in which children try to make sense out of a fraction problem prior to learning the mathematical procedures help children to abstract fraction ideas.
- Draw pictorial models to solve fraction problems and try to determine a reasonable answer prior to using formal operations.
- Use pattern blocks to name fractions, find equivalent fractions, and add and subtract fractions. The fraction amounts that can be identified with the blocks are dependent upon determining what represents "one whole."

- Draw halves, fourths, and eighths on paper plates and compare these circular region models. Use a scissors to cut a radius in each paper along one of the fraction lines. Combine two plates to add and subtract fractions. (For example, to add $\frac{1}{4}$ and $\frac{4}{8}$, combine the fourths plate with the eighths plate.)
- Use geoboards to show various ways to make "one half" or "one-third" using the area model of fractions. The parts must be the same size (or area) but they do not have to be the same shape.
- Use a set of 24 two-color counters. Break the group of counters into halves, thirds, fourths, sixths, and eighths by grouping the counters and flipping the correct number. Challenge children to flip the counters to show $\frac{3}{8}$ in red or $\frac{2}{3}$ in yellow. Children need many experiences working with set models of fractions to abstract this concept.
- Other books, such as *The Hershey's Milk Chocolate Fraction Book* (Palotta, 1999), use a manipulative (a Hershey bar) to explore parts of a whole, equivalent fractions, simple addition of fractions, lowest terms, subtraction, and improper fractions. Use a real candy bar or a construction paper copy to model operations in the book and explore further operations with "twelfths."

Source: Dr. Patricia Moyer, George Mason University

After children have had experiences in writing subtraction sentences from their work with concrete materials, they can be asked to do specific subtraction problems. Activities 11-12 to 11-15 have children modeling subtraction sentences to find the missing addend. Each activity should be followed with a class dialogue.

ACTIVITY 11-12 ▶

SUBTRACTING FRACTIONS (CONCRETE)

MATERIALS
Fraction circle pieces

PROCEDURE
1. Use fraction circle pieces to find

$$\frac{5}{8} - \frac{1}{4} = ? \qquad \frac{3}{4} - \frac{1}{2} = ?$$

Solve other examples.

ACTIVITY 11-13 ▶

FINDING THE MISSING ADDEND (CONCRETE)

MATERIALS
Fraction Bars

PROCEDURE
1. Use Fraction Bars to find the missing number.

$$\frac{3}{4} - \text{\_\_\_\_} = \frac{5}{8} \qquad \frac{4}{5} - \text{\_\_\_\_} = \frac{7}{15}$$

Solve other examples.

ACTIVITY 11-14 ▶

SUBTRACTING FRACTIONS

Write as many subtraction statements as you can with a difference of $\frac{1}{8}$; $\frac{1}{10}$; $\frac{1}{12}$.

ACTIVITY 11-15 ▶

ADDING AND SUBTRACTING FRACTIONS

Draw rectangles to help you find sums and differences of fractions.

Renaming fractions The process of writing equivalent fractions is sometimes called "renaming fractions." In fraction subtraction, another renaming process is introduced that parallels renaming in whole-number subtraction. For example, when subtracting 28 from 175, the 7 tens and 5 ones are renamed as 6 tens and 15 ones before the subtraction is carried out. Similarly, renaming is required in some fraction subtractions.

Example:
$5\frac{3}{8} - 2\frac{7}{8}$
Although the subtrahend ($2\frac{7}{8}$) is less than the minuend ($5\frac{3}{8}$), the fraction part of the subtrahend is greater than the corresponding part of the minuend. Renaming the minuend facilitates the operation. The process can be

$$5\frac{3}{8} = 4 + \frac{8}{8} + \frac{3}{8} = 4\frac{11}{8}$$
$$\underline{-2\frac{7}{8} = \qquad 2 + \frac{7}{8} = 2\frac{7}{8}}$$
$$2\frac{4}{8} = 2\frac{1}{2}$$

Take care that children do not erroneously show the procedures as $5\frac{3}{8} = 4\frac{13}{8}$.

In whole-number subtraction, it is a "ten" that is added to the ones column; in fraction subtraction, it is a "one" that is added to the fraction part of the addend. The "one" is expressed with the same denominator as the fraction addend.

Symbolic fraction algorithm The procedures for the development of a meaningful subtraction algorithm parallel those for an addition algorithm. A subtraction algorithm that is commonly presented in textbooks is

$$\frac{3}{4} - \frac{1}{6} = ?$$

$$\frac{3 \times 6}{4 \times 6} - \frac{1 \times 4}{6 \times 4} = \frac{18}{24} - \frac{4}{24} = \frac{14}{24} = \frac{7}{12}$$

In the example, the common denominator is found by multiplying each term of a fraction by the denominator of the other fraction. We have seen that this procedure does not always produce the lowest common denominator.

The procedure can be abbreviated as follows:

$$\frac{(3 \times 6) - (1 \times 4)}{4 \times 6} = \frac{18 - 4}{24} = \frac{14}{24} = \frac{7}{12}$$

This leads to the generalized algorithm for subtraction:

$$\frac{a}{b} - \frac{c}{d} = \frac{ad - bc}{bd}$$

MULTIPLICATION AND DIVISION OF FRACTIONS

General Considerations

In developing the operations of multiplication and division with fractions, ideas can be drawn from the operations with whole numbers. For example, multiplication can be interpreted as repeated addition, whereas division can be presented as repeated subtraction.

Two common misunderstandings related to multiplication and division of fractions are that "multiplication makes bigger" and "division makes smaller" as discussed in Chapter 7. This means that many children expect the product to be greater than both factors in multiplication of fractions problems as it is in multiplication of whole numbers. Similarly, children expect the quotient to be smaller than the divisor and the dividend in division of fractions problems as it is in division of whole numbers. For example, many children expect that $6 \div \frac{1}{2}$ is 3, because they believe the answer to a division problem is smaller than the numbers in the problem. But this generalization is true only for whole-number division. According to Bezuk and Bieck (1993), a goal of instruction should be "to enable students to determine the reasonableness of the results of operations on fractions" (p. 131). Instruction must lead children to recognize that these generalizations are incorrect and help them make sense of answers to fraction computation problems.

PRINCIPLES AND STANDARDS LINK 11-5
Content Strand: Number and Operations

Students should also develop and adapt procedures for mental calculation and computational estimation with fractions, decimals, and integers. . . . Because these methods often require flexibility in moving from one representation to another, they are useful in deepening students' understanding of rational numbers and helping them think flexibly about these numbers. (NCTM, 2000, p. 220)

PRINCIPLES AND STANDARDS LINK 11-6
Content Strand: Number and Operations

In grades 6–8, students should acquire computational fluency—the ability to compute efficiently and accurately—with fractions, decimals, and integers. (NCTM, 2000, p. 219)

There is the potential risk for learning how to multiply and divide fractions by rote because the algorithmic rules are simple. For multiplication, the colloquial rule is "multiply top numbers and then bottom numbers" and for division it is "change the sign and invert the second fraction." Children who learn to compute with fractions in this way often have to wait years before the mystery of fraction computation is revealed and understanding emerges.

Developing Fraction Multiplication

When children are learning to solve fraction multiplication problems, they should be asked to use concrete materials or draw diagrams and to write some kind of symbolic record of the solution process. This could be a word description, mathematical symbols, or a combination of both. Examples of diagrams and possible solution records are presented in the activities and problems that follow.

There are several different types of fraction multiplication problems:

- Multiplying a fraction by a whole number
- Multiplying a whole number by a fraction
- Multiplying a fraction by a fraction
- Multiplying mixed numbers.

Each type is discussed below.

Multiplying a fraction by a whole number
Probably the easiest multiplication situation for children to interpret is to multiply a fraction by a whole number. This type of problem can be related to whole-number multiplication.

Examples:

- 3×4 means 3 groups with 4 objects in each group or 3 groups of 4 objects, which is 12 objects.

$$
\begin{array}{ccc}
\circ\circ & \circ\circ & \circ\circ \\
\circ\circ & \circ\circ & \circ\circ
\end{array}
\qquad 3 \times 4 = 12
$$

- $3 \times \frac{4}{5}$ means 3 groups of 4 fifths, or 12 fifths.

Bags of caramels, 5 candies in each bag

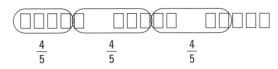

$$\frac{4}{5} \qquad \frac{4}{5} \qquad \frac{4}{5}$$

12 fifths in all, or 2 and $\frac{2}{5}$ bags.

Algorithm: $3 \times \dfrac{4}{5} = \dfrac{3 \times 4}{5} = \dfrac{12}{5}$ or $2\frac{2}{5}$

• $3 \times \frac{5}{6}$ means 3 times 5 sixths

Chocolate Bar

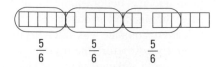

$$\frac{5}{6} \qquad \frac{5}{6} \qquad \frac{5}{6}$$

15 sixths in all, or 2 bars and $\frac{1}{2}$ of another bar.

Algorithm: $3 \times \frac{5}{6} = \frac{3 \times 5}{6} = \frac{15}{6} = 2\frac{3}{6} = 2\frac{1}{2}$

Activity 11-16 and Problem 1 should assist children in understanding why the value of the product is between the whole-number factor and the fraction factor. When the whole number is one, the product equals the fraction factor.

A possible solution to Activity 11-16 is shown in Figure 11-5.

Problem 1 is a simple problem that can be solved in several ways. Four possible solutions are presented.

Problem 1

The remaining Ritz crackers in a box were all broken and Carl's mother gave him 7 half crackers. Carl receives the equivalent of how many crackers?

Possible solution strategies:

1. A child could use real crackers or paper circles cut in half, then assemble them to make whole crackers/circles. The product could then be easily determined.

ACTIVITY 11-16

MULTIPLICATION: TIMES AS MUCH

MATERIALS
Fraction circles to represent pizzas

PROCEDURE
1. Take one-third of a pizza.
2. Now take twice as much pizza. How much is 2 times $\frac{1}{3}$?
3. Make your share 3 times as large as two-thirds. How much pizza is this? How much is 3 times $\frac{2}{3}$?
4. How much pizza is a share 4 times as large as two-thirds?
5. Write multiplication sentences for your findings.

---

2. A child could reason:

Two halves make one. With 7 halves, Carl has 3 whole crackers with an extra half. So, Carl's mother gave him the same amount as 3 and $\frac{1}{2}$ crackers.

3. Repeated addition can be employed to solve the problem.

$$\frac{1}{2} + \frac{1}{2} + \frac{1}{2} + \frac{1}{2} + \frac{1}{2} + \frac{1}{2} + \frac{1}{2} = \frac{7}{2} \text{ or } 3\frac{1}{2}$$

$$1 + 1 + 1 + \frac{1}{2} = 3\frac{1}{2}$$

FIGURE 11-5

A Solution to Activity 11-16

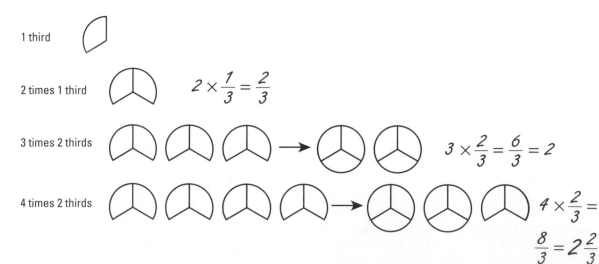

4. The problem can be solved multiplicatively.

$$7 \times \frac{1}{2} = \frac{7 \times 1}{2} = \frac{7}{2} \text{ or } 3\frac{1}{2}$$

Multiplying a whole number by a fraction

Problems 2, 3, and 4 are about taking a fractional part of a set. After solving a number of similar problems, children should come to realize that taking a fractional part of something implies multiplication. Thus, "$\frac{3}{4}$ of 8" means 8 multiplied by $\frac{3}{4}$ or $\frac{3}{4} \times 8$. The statements "$\frac{3}{4}$ times 8" and "$\frac{3}{4}$ of 8" both are appropriate for the expression $\frac{3}{4} \times 8$. In situations in which the multiplier is not a whole number, the multiplication symbol is more frequently read as "of" rather than "times."

Problem 2

Kim has a collection of 15 books. One-third of them are science fiction. How many books are science fiction?

In this situation, the multiplier is a fraction and the multiplicand is a whole number. Because the commutative property holds true for fraction multiplication, it is expected that the product will be between the whole-number factor and the fraction.

Repeated addition is not an appropriate solution strategy for Problem 2, but setting up an array is.

Possible solution strategy:

Tiles, representing books, can be set up in one row of 15 or in three rows of 5.

□□□□□ $\frac{1}{3}$

□□□□□ $\frac{1}{3}$

□□□□□ $\frac{1}{3}$

There are 3 thirds in the whole set.

One-third of 15 is 5 books.

$$\frac{1}{3} \times 15 = 5$$

Kim has 5 science fiction books.

$$\text{Algorithm: } \frac{1}{3} \times 15 = \frac{1 \times 15}{3} = \frac{15}{3} = 5$$

Problem 3

Two-fifths of the 20 baseball cards Andy has are of New York Yankees. How many Yankees cards does Andy own?

A child's thinking and subsequent record of the solution process might be as follows:

The problem question is, What is two-fifths of 20?

One-fifth means one of five equal parts.

Two-fifths means two of five equal parts.

First, I'll find out what is one-fifth of 20.

Twenty divided by 5 is 4.

Therefore, one-fifth of 20 is 4.

$\frac{1}{5}$ *of 20 is 4* $\frac{2}{5}$ *of 20 is 8*

Andy has 8 baseball cards of the Yankees.

$$\text{Algorithm: } \frac{2}{5} \times 20 = \frac{2 \times 20}{5} = \frac{40}{5} = 8$$

Based on the child's reasoning that the problem can be solved by dividing 20 by 5, the following step in the algorithm can be discussed: $\frac{1}{5} \times 20 = \frac{1 \times 20}{5} = \frac{20}{5} = 4$

Problem 4

Monique had 8 candies and she ate $\frac{3}{4}$ of them during recess. How many candies does she have left?

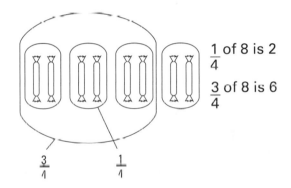

$\frac{1}{4}$ of 8 is 2

$\frac{3}{4}$ of 8 is 6

$\frac{3}{4}$ $\frac{1}{4}$

Solution process:

Monique ate 6 candies and has 2 candies left.

$$\text{Algorithm: } \frac{3}{4} \times 8 = \frac{3 \times 8}{5} = \frac{24}{4} = 6$$

The idea that whole numbers can be expressed in fraction form can be discussed and another step in the development of the algorithm can follow.

$$8 = \frac{8}{1}$$

Therefore, in the problem above, one can write

$$\frac{3}{4} \times 8 = \frac{3}{4} \times \frac{8}{1} = \frac{3}{4} \times \frac{8}{1} = \frac{24}{4} = 6$$

Multiplying a fraction by a fraction
When two proper fractions are multiplied, the product is smaller than either factor. This result may not match the children's expectations for multiplication. Therefore, care

should be taken to provide realistic problem situations so that children will realize why fraction multiplication works this way.

Constructing an array is an appropriate strategy to help solve a problem when both factors are fractions. Consider the situations in Problems 5 to 7.

Problem 5

How much is $\frac{1}{2}$ of $\frac{1}{3}$ of a candy bar?

Possible solution process:

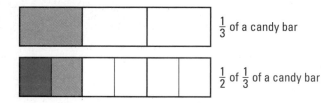

$\frac{1}{3}$ of a candy bar

$\frac{1}{2}$ of $\frac{1}{3}$ of a candy bar

Therefore, one-half of one-third is one-sixth.

Algorithm: $\frac{1}{2} \times \frac{1}{3} = \frac{1 \times 1}{2 \times 3} = \frac{1}{6}$ or $\frac{1}{2} \times \frac{1}{3} = \frac{1}{6}$

Problem 6

When Jane's friend arrived for a visit, Jane had just finished eating one-fourth of 8 chocolate-coated raisins. Jane and her friend each ate one-half of the remaining raisins. What part of the 8 raisins did Jane's friend eat?

Possible solution process:

The problem question is: $\frac{1}{2}$ of $\frac{3}{4} = ?$

The raisins can be arranged in a rectangular array.

Jane had eaten $\frac{1}{4}$ or 2 raisins.

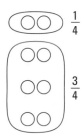

$\frac{1}{4}$

$\frac{3}{4}$

Six raisins are $\frac{3}{4}$ of the set of 8 raisins.

If one thinks of the 6 raisins, one can say $\frac{1}{2}$ of 6 is 3.

But if one thinks of $\frac{3}{4}$ of a whole set, the question to ask is,

What is $\frac{1}{2}$ of $\frac{3}{4}$? or $\frac{1}{2} \times \frac{3}{4} = ?$

Three raisins are 3 eighths of the whole set of raisins.

Algorithm: $\frac{1}{2} \times \frac{3}{4} = \frac{1 \times 3}{2 \times 4} = \frac{3}{8}$

Jane's friend ate three raisins, which is three-eighths of the whole set of raisins.

When multiplying two fractions, the process involves taking a *part of a part* but the product is a part of the original unit. This operational trait of the changing unit can be problematic for children; therefore, it is important to provide clear examples. Having children talk about their problem-solving process is an effective way to find out how they are thinking about fractions. Figure 11-6 shows how to model fraction multiplication with rectangles.

Problem 7

How many eggs is $\frac{1}{4}$ of $\frac{2}{3}$ of a dozen eggs?

Possible solution process:

Two-thirds of a dozen eggs is 8 eggs.

One-fourth of 8 eggs is 2 eggs.

Therefore, one-fourth of two-thirds is two-twelfths.

Algorithm: $\frac{1}{4} \times \frac{2}{3} = \frac{1 \times 2}{4 \times 3} = \frac{2}{12}$ or $\frac{1}{4} \times \frac{2}{3} = \frac{2}{12}$

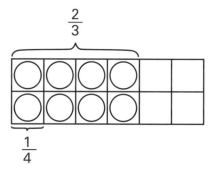

Problems 2, 3, and 4 all exemplify multiplying a whole number by a fraction. Problem 2 is solved concretely with the answer derived from the array. In Problems 3 and 4, principles used in the multiplication algorithm are highlighted:

- A whole number can be written in fraction form $20 = \frac{20}{1}$
- Division is involved
  $\frac{20}{5}$ means 20 divided by 5
- Numerators are multiplied
  $\frac{1}{5} \times 20 = \frac{20}{5}$

**The Annenberg/CPB
Math and Science Collection**

Classroom Clips:
Fraction Tracks

Previewing the Video

Hilory Paster's fifth graders are playing a cooperative
game for two players in which students draw fraction
cards from a deck and move markers on their
gameboards' "Fraction Tracks." The object of the game is
to get all six markers from zero to one by moving them the
distance specified on the card drawn. Children are
encouraged to rename the fraction drawn to a sum of
equivalent fractions, allowing them to advance on more than
one track at a time.

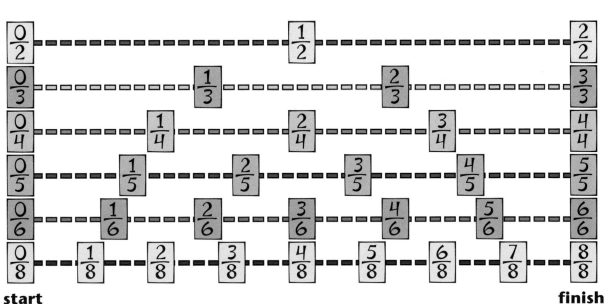

start　　　　　　　　　　　　　　　　　　　　　　**finish**

INTEGRATING STANDARDS, TECHNOLOGY, AND TEACHING

Follow along with this lesson to see what math process standards might be covered...

Process Standard:
Problem Solving

Notice the way Ms. Paster uses the game directions to encourage the children to use a variety of problem-solving strategies and uses questioning to encourage problem solving. **What are some of the questions she asks?**

Focus on Standards

How does Ms. Paster address problem solving in this lesson to enable students to:

- build new mathematical knowledge?
- apply and adapt a variety of appropriate strategies?
- monitor and reflect on their processes of mathematical problem solving?

Process Standard: **Representation**

Ms. Paster believes that an opportunity to explore fractions with concrete manipulatives helps some children to more fully understand the math. **How do you think materials, such as fraction pieces, enhance children's understanding?**

Focus on Standards

How does Ms. Paster address aspects of representation in this lesson to encourage students to:

- organize, record, and communicate mathematical ideas?
- select, apply, and translate among mathematical representations to solve problems?
- model and interpret physical, social, and mathematical phenomena?

Fraction pieces help to provide concrete examples of equivalent fractions for students.

Standards 2000 Process Strand: Communication   Communication is an essential part of mathematics and mathematics education. It is a way of sharing ideas and clarifying understanding. Through communication, ideas become objects of reflection, refinement, discussion, and amendment....Students who have opportunities, encouragement, and support for speaking, writing, reading, and listening in mathematics classes reap dual benefits: they communicate to learn mathematics, and they learn to communicate mathematically. (NCTM, 2000, p. 60)

Process Standard: **Communication**

Hilory Paster identifies several benefits children receive when they work together. She believes children come to a truer understanding of the math when they:

- share their problem-solving strategies.
- expand upon their ideas using their own language and examples.
- question and challenge each other in new ways.

What do you see as the pros and cons of using cooperative games in the classroom?

Focus on Standards

Listen to the children in Ms. Paster's class as they communicate with one another for examples of meaningful exchanges that

- organize and consolidate mathematical thinking.
- communicate mathematical thinking coherently and clearly to peers, teachers, and others.
- analyze and evaluate the mathematical thinking and strategies of others.

"Showing their thinking to each other helps them to negotiate the moves they want to make."
— *Hilory Paster*

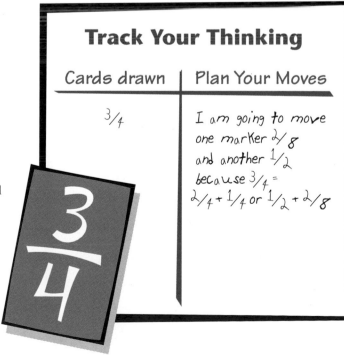

Track Your Thinking

Cards drawn	Plan Your Moves
3/4	I am going to move one marker 2/8 and another 1/2 because 3/4 = 2/4 + 1/4 or 1/2 + 2/8

$$\frac{3}{4}$$

Process Standard: **Reasoning and Proof**

Communication and reasoning and proof blend in this lesson, as you may find they often do in the mathematics classroom. Ms. Paster uses rephrasing not only to emphasize the children's communication of the math, but also as the vehicle the children use to reason through and prove their understanding. She believes that, through rephrasing, children are much more in tune with the lesson.

Ms. Paster uses rephrasing as an assessment of the children's understanding. **What other types of assessment might you use for this lesson?**

Focus on Standards

How does Ms. Paster address aspects of reasoning and proof in this lesson to encourage children to

- make and investigate mathematical conjectures?
- develop and evaluate mathematical arguments and proofs?

Try This!

To build up to equivalent fractions.

"The Fractionator"

- 2 players, 4 dice, counters
- Divide the counters in half
- Each player rolls two dice at the same time. To form fractions, put the lower numbers on the top and higher numbers on the bottom.

   = $\frac{3}{5}$

- The player with the lower fraction gives the other player a counter.
- What if the fractions are equal? Each player leaves one die on the table, as is, and rolls the other die. Combine the new roll with the old die to form a new fraction. The higher fraction wins three counters.
- Players roll until a winner has all the counters.

Try This! activity from: *Ready, Set, Roll: Number Cube Games* by Lorraine Hopping Egan. Published by Scholastic Professional Books, a division of Scholastic, Inc. Copyright ©1998 by Lorraine Hopping Egan. Reprinted by permission.

Process Standard: **Connections**

How could this lesson be extended to help children understand how mathematical ideas interconnect and build on one another to produce a coherent whole?

For other connection ideas, including an equivalent fraction lesson for third- and fourth-grade children, and a lesson idea for working with seventh and eighth graders on fractions, equivalent fractions, and decimals, please visit Chapter 11 of our website at **www.prenhall.com/cathcart**

FIGURE 11-6

Fraction Multiplication

$\frac{1}{5} \times \frac{1}{2}$ Draw two congruent rectangles and show each fraction.

Then draw a third rectangle congruent to the others and shade $\frac{1}{5}$ and $\frac{1}{2}$ of the rectangle as shown below.

$\frac{1}{10}$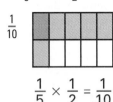

The part where the shading intersects shows $\frac{1}{5}$ of $\frac{1}{2}$.

$\frac{1}{5}$ of $\frac{1}{2}$ is $\frac{1}{10}$.

$$\frac{1}{5} \times \frac{1}{2} = \frac{1}{10}$$

$\frac{1}{2} \times \frac{3}{4}$ Draw two congruent rectangles. Show $\frac{1}{2}$ on one rectangle and $\frac{3}{4}$ on the other rectangle as shown.

Draw another rectangle, congruent to the others and show eighths as pictured.

Shade in $\frac{1}{2}$ of the rectangle, then $\frac{3}{4}$.

The part where the shading intersects shows $\frac{1}{2}$ of $\frac{3}{4}$.

$$\frac{1}{2} \times \frac{3}{4} = \frac{3}{8}$$ The twice-shaded part is $\frac{3}{8}$ of the figure.

In problems 5, 6, and 7, both factors are fractions. Concrete or pictorial solutions to similar problems can lead children to formulate the algorithmic rule: multiply numerators together and denominators together.

As children solve problems, some of their "algorithms" could be written on the board or on an overhead transparency to provide the focus for a class dialogue. Reflecting on their problem-solving processes and discussing them with classmates can lead to insights about related procedures and to a refinement of the procedures. Thus, children can develop an algorithm for multiplying fractions that will be meaningful to them.

Multiplying mixed numbers Whole-number multiplication can be used to exemplify the process of multiplying mixed numbers. Use of the distributive property is evident in the following two examples.

Example 1

$$\begin{aligned}
23 \times 45 &= (20 + 3) \times (40 + 5) \\
&= (20 \times 40) + (20 \times 5) + \\
&\quad (3 \times 40) + (3 \times 5) \\
&= 800 + 100 + 120 + 15 \\
&= 1035
\end{aligned}$$

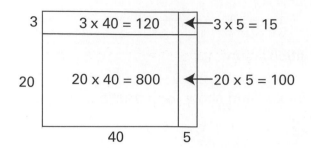

Partial products are 800, 100, 120, and 15. Adding them gives 1035.

Example 2

$$3\frac{2}{5} \times 4\frac{1}{3} = \left(3 + \frac{2}{5}\right) \times \left(4 + \frac{1}{3}\right)$$

$$= (3 \times 4) + \left(3 \times \frac{1}{3}\right) + \left(\frac{2}{5} \times 4\right) + \left(\frac{2}{5} \times \frac{1}{3}\right)$$

$$= 12 + \frac{3}{3} + \frac{8}{5} + \frac{2}{15}$$

$$= 12 + 1 + 1\frac{3}{5} + \frac{2}{15}$$

$$= 14 + \frac{9}{15} + \frac{2}{15}$$

$$= 14\frac{11}{15}$$

The sum of the partial product is $12 + 1 + \frac{8}{5} + \frac{2}{15} = 13\frac{26}{15} = 14\frac{11}{15}$

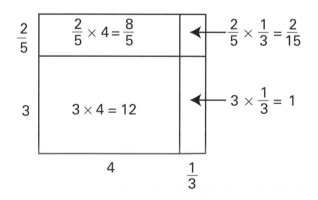

Another way to approach multiplication of mixed numbers is to change each mixed number to an improper fraction and then multiply the two fractions.

Example 3

Understanding that $3 = \frac{15}{5}$ and $4 = \frac{12}{3}$, the child might write:

$$3\frac{2}{5} \times 4\frac{1}{3} = \left(\frac{15}{5} + \frac{2}{5}\right) \times \left(\frac{12}{3} + \frac{1}{3}\right)$$

$$= \frac{17}{5} \times \frac{13}{3}$$

$$= \frac{221}{15}$$

$$= 14\frac{11}{15}$$

Other considerations

Simplifying.   When children begin to work symbolically with fraction multiplication, they are encouraged to simplify the factors before proceeding to multiply. Simplifying should be thought of as a process of renaming or exchange and not cancellation (Example 1). Thinking of simplifying as cancellation can lead to errors in computation. For example, if children are told to "cancel like factors" as in Example 2 below, they may go on to erroneously cancel common digits as in Example 3.

Example 1

$\frac{2}{6} \times \frac{3}{8} =$

Thinking process:

Rename $\frac{2}{6}$ as $\frac{1}{3}$, then simplify

$\frac{2}{6} \times \frac{3}{8} = \frac{1}{3} \times \frac{3}{8} = \frac{3}{3 \times 8} = \frac{3}{3} \times \frac{1}{8} = \frac{1}{8}$

or

$\frac{2}{6} \times \frac{3}{8} = \frac{2 \times 3}{6 \times 8} = \frac{6}{6 \times 8} = \frac{1}{8}$

Example 2

$\frac{2}{6} \times \frac{3}{8} =$

$\frac{2}{6} \times \frac{3}{8} = \frac{\cancel{2}}{\cancel{2} \times \cancel{3}} \times \frac{\cancel{3}}{2 \times 4} = \frac{1}{8}$

Example 3

(Incorrect procedure)

$$\frac{2\cancel{3}}{\cancel{3}5} = \frac{2}{5}$$

There are a few cases when indeed the like digits can be cancelled and the resulting fraction will be a correct simplification. Examples: $\frac{16}{64} = \frac{1}{4}$ and $\frac{26}{65} = \frac{2}{5}$.

An investigation to find other fractions for which this procedure holds true should lead to the realization that the procedure works only for a very small number of cases. Therefore, the procedure should be thought to be generally incorrect.

Reciprocals.   Like whole numbers, fractions have a reciprocal or multiplicative inverse (except a fraction with a numerator of 0). The definition of multiplication can be used to demonstrate to children that the product of a fraction and its multiplicative inverse equals one.

Example:

Is there a factor that, when multiplied by $\frac{3}{4}$, will give the product 1?

$\frac{3}{4} \times n = 1$

The reciprocal of $\frac{3}{4}$ is $\frac{4}{3}$.

$\frac{3}{4} \times \frac{4}{3} = \frac{3 \times 4}{4 \times 3} = \frac{12}{12} = 1$

In general terms, $\frac{a}{b} \times \frac{b}{a} = 1$.

This procedure is helpful in understanding the fraction division algorithm.

Developing Fraction Division

As discussed in Chapter 7, there are two types of division problems: measurement and partitive. Likewise, fraction division problems can be of the two types. A teacher would be wise to review with children both problem types before introducing fraction division problems to ensure that children understand the problems and that they will therefore be able to concentrate on the division process. Problems 8 and 9 below are examples of measurement division problems; Problem 10 is a partitive division problem.

Division problems involving fraction divisors and whole number dividends are easiest and should be presented first. Both even and uneven division should be modeled. Division problems with fraction and whole number divisors are exemplified below.

Whole number divided by a fraction:
Even division
Problem 8

Randy has 6 sticks of gum. He wants to break each in half-sized pieces. How many pieces will he get?

Possible solution process:

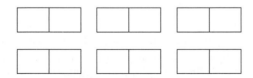

$6 \div \frac{1}{2} = 12$

Whole number divided by a fraction:
Uneven division
Problem 9

Jane is responsible for wrapping small packages for the local fall fair. She is cutting a roll of ribbon in $\frac{3}{4}$-yard lengths to make bows for the packages. How many pieces of ribbon $\frac{3}{4}$ yard long will she get from 5 yards of ribbon?

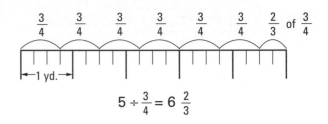

$$5 \div \frac{3}{4} = 6\,\frac{2}{3}$$

Possible solution process:

Jane will get 6 pieces of ribbon $\frac{3}{4}$ yard long. She will have $\frac{2}{3}$ of another piece.

Fraction divisor and whole number dividend
Problem 10

For her birthday, Molly received a box of chocolates with 32 chocolates in it. After her family had some, Molly calculated that $\frac{3}{4}$ of the chocolates remained. One day, she shared the remaining chocolates equally among herself and five friends. What part of the box of chocolates did each friend receive?

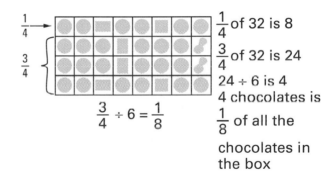

Possible solution process:

Each friend received $\frac{1}{8}$ of the chocolates, or 4 chocolates $(\frac{1}{8} = \frac{4}{32})$.

Fraction divisor and dividend When children are able to concretely represent problems with a whole number divisor or dividend, they can be asked to solve problems that have fraction divisors and dividends. Quotients may be whole numbers or fractions. Problem 11 is an example with a whole number quotient.

Problem 11

Max has $\frac{1}{2}$ quart of lemonade. He wants to pour $\frac{1}{6}$ quart into small glasses. How many servings of lemonade will Max have?

Possible solution process:

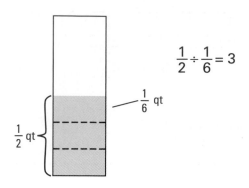

$$\frac{1}{2} \div \frac{1}{6} = 3$$

Max will have 3 servings of lemonade.

Mixed number dividend
Problem 12

Mrs. Hanson bought $2\frac{1}{2}$ yards of magnetic tape to use in displaying a set of geometric figures on the classroom metallic board. She wants to cut each yard into 12 equal pieces, that is, each piece is to be $\frac{1}{12}$ yard long. How many pieces $\frac{1}{12}$ yard long can Mrs. Hanson get?

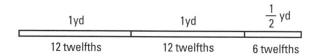

Possible solution strategy:

12 pieces $\frac{1}{12}$ yard long in 1 yard

24 pieces in two yards

6 pieces in $\frac{1}{2}$ yard

Therefore, Mrs. Hanson can get 30 pieces of tape.

Problems with composite fractions for both divisor and dividend are more challenging to represent pictorially, and children's work deserves careful supervision. Examples are shown in Figure 11-7 using a rectangular model.

Developing a symbolic division algorithm

In the preceding sections, several problems were presented with concrete or diagrammatic solution processes. As children demonstrate the ability to solve division problems, encourage them to record their work in mathematical sentences. At appropriate times, class discussions can serve to draw children's attention to patterns or relationships in their solution procedures. A class could produce answers to sets of problems similar to the different types exemplified in Problems 8 to 12. Subsequently, the equations could be listed on the board to be examined by the class. Observations should be verbalized and discussed. The following activities illustrate this strategy.

FIGURE 11-7

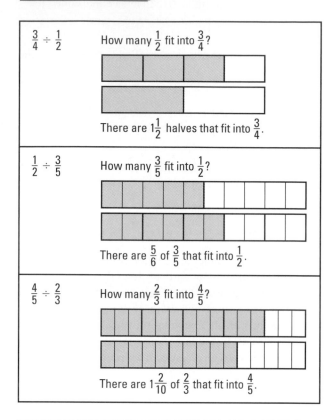

1. Provide each pair of children with a fraction division question similar to $6 \div \frac{1}{2}$ to solve by drawing a diagram. The pairs of children check each other's work.

Examples:

$6 \div \frac{1}{2} =$ $\quad 5 \div \frac{1}{2} =$ $\quad 3 \div \frac{1}{3} =$

$6 \div \frac{1}{5} =$ $\quad 4 \div \frac{1}{3} =$ $\quad 5 \div \frac{1}{4} =$

- When all pairs have completed the work, write the equations on the board.
- Invite children to examine the equations and write about their observations.
- Ask children to share their observations. [The whole number (dividend) and the denominator of the divisor are multiplied.]
- Ask children to write a multiplication equation for each division equation.

2. Follow the procedures above but use a different set of questions.

Examples:

$5 \div \frac{3}{4} = \frac{20}{3}$ $\qquad 3 \div \frac{2}{3} = \frac{9}{2}$ $\qquad 4 \div \frac{2}{3} = \frac{12}{2}$

Question: How can you obtain $6\frac{2}{3}$ from $5 \div \frac{3}{4}$ See Figure 11-8. Observation: Multiply the dividend and the denominator of the divisor, then divide this number by the numerator of the divisor.

FIGURE 11-8

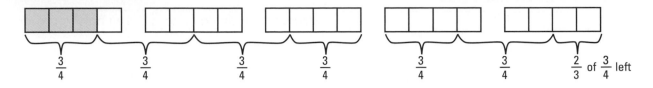

$$\frac{3}{4} \qquad \frac{3}{4} \qquad \frac{3}{4} \qquad \frac{3}{4} \qquad \frac{3}{4} \qquad \frac{3}{4} \qquad \frac{2}{3} \text{ of } \frac{3}{4} \text{ left}$$

$$5 \div \frac{3}{4} = 6\frac{2}{3}$$

The rule may be verbalized: Change the question to a multiplication and invert the divisor, and then multiply the two numbers.

Algorithm: $5 \div \frac{3}{4} = 5 \times \frac{4}{3} = \frac{20}{3} = 6\frac{2}{3}$

Children can subsequently test whether this procedure works whenever fractions are divided.

An algorithm that provides a meaningful explanation of the "invert and multiply rule" is to change the divisor to one using reciprocals and the multiplicative identity element.

Example:

$\frac{2}{3} \div \frac{4}{5} =$

Expressed as a complex fraction, the procedure is

$$\frac{\frac{2}{3}}{\frac{4}{5}} = \frac{\frac{2}{3} \times \frac{5}{4}}{\frac{4}{5} \times \frac{5}{4}} = \frac{\frac{2}{3} \times \frac{5}{4}}{1} = \frac{2}{3} \times \frac{5}{4}$$

→ This is equal to one, the multiplicative identity element.

Throughout the development of computation algorithms, teachers should keep in mind that the aim in fraction computation is conceptual understanding of the operations and not memorization of algorithmic procedures. The fractions used in problems should be those that can be visualized concretely or pictorially and are likely to be met in everyday situations (NCTM, 1989).

COMPUTING FRACTIONS WITH A CALCULATOR

Calculators that display fractions, as, for example, the Texas Instruments Math Explorer, can be used to advantage by children to help develop computational competence. Systematic

explorations can be made to discover patterns and relationships.

Examples:

- Find $\frac{1}{2}$ of these fractions: $\frac{2}{3}, \frac{4}{5}, \frac{5}{6}, \ldots$
- Find $\frac{1}{3}$ of these fractions: $\frac{2}{5}, \frac{2}{6}, \frac{2}{7}, \frac{2}{8}, \ldots$
- Divide these fractions by 2: $\frac{1}{2}, \frac{1}{3}, \frac{1}{4}, \frac{1}{5}, \ldots$
- Divide these fractions by 2: $\frac{2}{8}, \frac{3}{8}, \frac{4}{8}, \frac{5}{8}, \ldots$

Ask children to compare answers to finding $\frac{1}{2}$ of a number with dividing that number by 2.

Children can be invited to draw diagrams or model the problems they solve with a calculator. When using the Math Explorer to add and subtract fractions, the calculator displays the answer with the lowest common denominator.

Example:

2 $\boxed{/}$ 3 $\boxed{+}$ 5 $\boxed{/}$ 8 = Display: 31/24

To convert the improper fraction $\frac{31}{24}$ to a mixed number, follow the procedure:

31/24 $\boxed{\text{Ab/c}}$ = Display: 1 u 7/24 (1 unit and 7/24)

In multiplying fractions, the calculator displays the product of the numerators and that of the denominators. In division, the calculator uses the invert and multiply rule. To simplify the answers in multiplication and division, the function $\boxed{\text{Simp}}$ used.

Example:

			Display		Display
5 $\boxed{/}$ 8 $\boxed{\times}$ 2 $\boxed{/}$ 3 =		10/24	$\boxed{\text{Simp}}$	5/12
4 $\boxed{/}$ 7 $\boxed{\div}$ 2 $\boxed{/}$ 3 =		12/14	$\boxed{\text{Simp}}$	6/7

MENTAL ARITHMETIC AND ESTIMATION

A judicious amount of mental arithmetic and estimation exercises should accompany fraction computation and problem-solving activities. Sets of exercises such as the following examples can easily be developed for brief practice sessions.

Example 1: Mental arithmetic

Problem	Possible thinking processes
$5\frac{3}{4} + 3\frac{1}{2}$	$\rightarrow$ $8, 9, 9\frac{1}{4}$
$7 - 2\frac{1}{3}$	$\rightarrow$ $5, 4\frac{2}{3}$
$\frac{1}{7} \times 280$	$\rightarrow$ $\frac{280}{7} = 40$
$8 \div \frac{1}{3}$	$\rightarrow$ $8 \times 3 = 24$

Example 2: Estimation

Problem	Possible thinking processes
$\frac{3}{5} + \frac{9}{10} + \frac{1}{23}$	$\rightarrow$ $\frac{1}{2} + 1 + 0 \rightarrow 1\frac{1}{2}$
$6\frac{1}{8} - 2\frac{4}{7}$	$\rightarrow$ $4, 3\frac{1}{2}$
$1\frac{1}{2} - \times 5\frac{6}{7}$	$\rightarrow$ $1\frac{1}{2} \times 6$ $\rightarrow 6 + 3 = 9$
$6\frac{1}{5} \div \frac{1}{2}$	$\rightarrow$ $6 \div \frac{1}{2}$ $\rightarrow 12$
$\frac{2}{3} \div \frac{7}{8}$	$\rightarrow$ divisor is close to 1, quotient is greater than $\frac{2}{3}$ but less than 1

ASSESSING FRACTION KNOWLEDGE

Fraction knowledge can be assessed by asking children to respond in writing to questions or to develop detailed solution processes to problems. Some questions and problems are presented in Figures 11-9 to 11-11; Figure 11-10 and 11-11 also show examples of responses received from children.

FIGURE 11-9 ▶

Assessment Questions

1. Is this correct? $\frac{1}{2} + \frac{1}{8} = 1$ Tell how you know.

2. Is this correct? $\frac{5}{6} - \frac{2}{3} = 1$ Tell how you know.

3. Which quotient is the greatest? Explain how you know.

   8 divided by 1   8 divided by $\frac{1}{2}$ 8 divided by $\frac{1}{4}$

4. Which quotient is the least? Explain how you know.

   The number of threes in 24. The number of thirds in 24. The number of twos in 24.

FIGURE 11-10 ▶

Question: Is $\frac{10}{16}$ equal to $\frac{5}{8}$? Tell how you know.

Martha's response:

$\frac{10}{16}$ *is equal to* $\frac{5}{8}$ *. One way I know this is by looking at the* $\frac{5}{8}$ *and the* $\frac{10}{16}$ *. As you can see, with* $\frac{5}{8}$ *all you are doing is doubling the 5 and the 8 to get* $\frac{10}{16}$ *and you can see they are equal.*

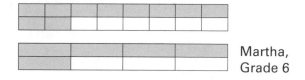

Martha, Grade 6

Martha's response (Figure 11-10) of ". . . all you are doing is doubling the 5 and the 8 [$\frac{5}{8}$]" without the accompanying diagram might lead one to think that she is merely reciting a rule. However, her drawing serves to verify (probably to herself as much as to the teacher) that indeed the answer to the question is yes. Ajay (Figure 11-11) shows that he understands the fraction addition algorithm; also, his mathematical language is commendable.

CONCLUSION

In this chapter mathematical ideas about fractions have been presented. Teaching considerations have been offered together with a number of activities to help children develop conceptual understanding and number sense about fraction computation. An important point is to make extensive use of concrete materials to model fractions and computational work with fractions and to connect operations on fractions with operations on whole numbers. Work with concrete and pictorial models should extend throughout the elementary grades and possibly well into the middle grades, particularly if computation activities are delayed until then.

For Your Journal

When you have finished studying this chapter, reflect on the following questions in your math journal:

1. For each operation, write a word problem and draw a picture showing how to solve the problem using a model.

2. How can a teacher help children understand fraction computation?

3. What does it mean for a person to have "operation sense"?

FIGURE 11-11

Problem:

Samantha and Jennifer have ordered a large pizza. Samantha is able to eat one-third of the pizza and Jennifer eats two-fifths of the pizza. How much of the pizza was not eaten?

Ajay's response:

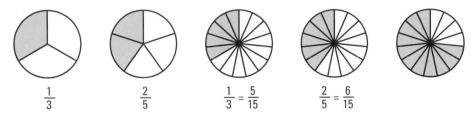

$$\frac{1}{3} \qquad \frac{2}{5} \qquad \frac{1}{3} = \frac{5}{15} \qquad \frac{2}{5} = \frac{6}{15}$$

In this problem, I figured it would be easier to relate the fifths and thirds to the lowest common denominator, fifteenths. I found that one-third is equal to five-fifteenths and two-fifths is equivalent to six-fifteenths. Six-fifteenths plus five-fifteenths is eleven-fifteenths. Therefore, four-fifteenths is left.

Ajay, Grade 6

For Your Portfolio

When you have finished studying this chapter, complete the following activities to include in your professional portfolio:

1. Visit a fifth- or sixth-grade classroom. Informally interview several children about their understanding of fraction operations. Write a summary of their understandings and ideas about the instructional activities you might plan to enhance their understanding.

2. Write a lesson to introduce a fraction operation of your choice. Pay particular attention to the real-world situations and models used in the lesson.

Resources for Teachers

Books on fraction computation

Berman, B., & Friederwitzer, F. (1988). *Activities for fraction circles plus.* USA: Seymour.

Brodie, J. (1995). *Constructing ideas about fractions, Grades 3–6.* Mountain View, CA: Creative.

Charles, L., & Roper, A. (1990). *Activities for fraction circles plus.* Mountain View, CA: Creative.

Corwin, R., Russell, S., & Tierney, C. (1990). *Seeing fractions: A unit for the upper elementary grades.* Sacramento: California Department of Education.

Walker, K., Reak, C., & Stewart, K. (1995a). *20 thinking questions for fraction circles, Grades 3–6.* Mountain View, CA: Creative.

Walker, K., Reak, C., & Stewart, K. (1995b). *20 thinking questions for fraction circles, Grades 6–8.* Mountain View, CA: Creative.

Ward, S. (1995). *Constructing ideas about fractions, decimals, and percents.* Mountain View, CA: Creative.

Links to the Internet

Ask Dr. Math (fractions and decimals)

http://www.mathforum.org/dr.math/tocs/fractions. elem.html

Contains a list of interesting questions on fractions and decimals and Dr. Math's answers.

ProTeacher: Fractions and Decimals

http://www.proteacher.com/100014.shtml

Contains lesson plans on fractions and decimals.

Explorer: Fractions

http://explorer.scrtec.org/explorer/explorer-db/browse/static/Mathematics/browse/f38.html

http://explorer.scrtec.org/explorer/explorer-db/browse/static/Mathematics/browse/f39.html

Contains many lessons on fractions and lists of other resources.

CHAPTER 12

Developing Decimal Concepts and Computation

"Because decimal fractions look similar to the familiar whole numbers, it seems reasonable to predict that children . . . might understand them without much difficulty. However, appearance is deceiving. The research on learning decimal fractions agrees on one point: There is a lack of conceptual understanding."

(Owens & Super, 1993, p. 137)

FOCUS QUESTIONS ▶

When you have finished studying this chapter, you should be able to answer the following questions:

1. How can you use models to help children understand decimals and operations on decimals?

2. How are decimals related to whole numbers and fractions?

3. What does each operation on decimals mean? Give a real-world situation that exemplifies each operation on decimals.

What do we know of U.S. children's understanding of decimal concepts and computation? The sixth National Assessment of Educational Progress (NAEP) assessment noted that most fourth, eighth, and twelfth graders tested had fairly weak understanding of these topics. Only about half of the eighth graders tested were able to correctly identify the fraction closest to 0.52 (Kouba, Zawojewski, & Struchens, 1997).

Similarly, the results to the following item were disappointing: George buys two calculators that cost $3.29 each. If there is no tax, how much change will he receive from a $10 bill? Only 21% of the fourth graders were able to correctly answer this question.

NCTM CONTENT STANDARDS AND EXPECTATIONS ADDRESSED IN THIS CHAPTER

STANDARD	EXPECTATIONS FOR GRADES 3–5	EXPECTATIONS FOR GRADES 6–8
Number and Operations Standard Instructional programs from pre-K–12 should enable all students to—	In Grades 3–5 all students should—(NCTM, 2000 p. 148)	In Grades 6–8 all students should—(NCTM, 2000, p. 214)
Understand numbers, ways of representing numbers, relationships among numbers, and number systems	• understand the place-value structure of the base-ten number system and be able to represent and compare whole numbers and decimals. • recognize and generate equivalent forms of commonly used fractions, decimals, and percents.	• work flexibly with fractions, decimals, and percents to solve problems. • compare and order fractions, decimals, and percents efficiently and find their approximate locations on a number line.

STANDARD	EXPECTATIONS FOR GRADES 3–5	EXPECTATIONS FOR GRADES 6–8
Number and Operations Standard Instructional programs from pre-K–12 should enable all students to—	In Grades 3–5 all students should—(NCTM, 2000 p. 148)	In Grades 6–8 all students should—(NCTM, 2000, p. 214)
Understand meanings of operations and how they relate to one another		• understand the meaning and effects of arithmetic operations with fractions, decimals, and integers. • use the associative and commutative properties of addition and multiplication and the distributive property of multiplication over addition to simplify computations with integers, fractions, and decimals.
Compute fluently and make reasonable estimates	• develop and use strategies to estimate computations involving fractions and decimals in situations relevant to students' experience. • use visual models, benchmarks, and equivalent forms to add and subtract commonly used fractions and decimals. • select appropriate methods and tools for computing with whole numbers from among mental computation, estimation, calculators, and paper and pencil according to the context and nature of the computation and use the selected method or tools.	• select appropriate methods and tools for computing with fractions and decimals from among mental computation, estimation, calculators or computers, and paper and pencil, depending on the situation, and apply the selected methods. • develop and analyze algorithms for computing with fractions, decimals, and integers and develop fluency in their use. • develop and use strategies to estimate the results of rational-number computations and judge the reasonableness of the results.

PRINCIPLES AND STANDARDS LINK 12-1
Content Strand: Number and Operations

In grades 3–5 all students should—

• understand the place-value structure of the base-ten number system and be able to represent and compare whole numbers and decimals; . . .
• recognize and generate equivalent forms of commonly used fractions, decimals, and percents; . . . (NCTM, 2000, p. 148)

PRINCIPLES AND STANDARDS LINK 12-2
Content Strand: Number and Operations

In grades 6–8 all students should—

• work flexibly with fractions, decimals, and percents to solve problems;
• compare and order fractions, decimals, and percents efficiently and find their approximate locations on a number line; . . .
• understand the meaning and effects of arithmetic operations with fractions, decimals, and integers; . . .
• select appropriate methods and tools for computing with fractions and decimals from among mental computation, estimation, calculators or computers, and paper and pencil, depending on the situation, and apply the selected methods;
• develop and analyze algorithms for computing with fractions, decimals, and integers and develop fluency in their use;
• develop and use strategies to estimate the results of rational-number computations and judge the reasonableness of the results; . . . (NCTM, 2000, p. 214)

Research on children's learning of decimals consistently shows a lack of understanding of the concepts related to decimals, which leads to difficulty in determining the reasonableness of answers. Hiebert and Wearne (1986) found that children often lack "a link between their conceptual knowledge (of decimals) and a notion that written answers should be reasonable" (p. 220).

There are two different approaches to helping children learn decimals: building on place-value knowledge and building on fraction knowledge. Although it is tempting to assume (or hope) that children will easily connect what they know about place value to decimals, this can result in fairly low-level performance and a lack of understanding, particularly if concepts are taught procedurally. The place-value approach encourages children to build on their knowledge of place value, for example, by "lining up" the places when adding and subtracting decimals. But this approach has limitations, especially regarding multiplication and division of decimals, in which children do not need to "line up" the decimal points. Instruction that merely focuses on "moving the decimal point" is difficult for children to understand, resulting in a lack of ability to estimate and determine the reasonableness of solutions.

The second approach to helping children learn decimals is to connect understanding of decimals with children's existing fraction understanding. This approach helps children develop conceptual knowledge of decimals as well as an understanding of the meaning of operations on decimals. For example, when multiplying 0.3×0.7, why will there be two decimal places in the answer? The traditional procedural response to this is "because you count the number of decimal places in both factors." But *why* is this true? Because 0.3 can be written as $\frac{3}{10}$ (see below) and 0.7 can be written as $\frac{7}{10}$, and $\frac{3}{10} \times \frac{7}{10}$ means we're finding 3 tenths of 7 tenths, which is $\frac{21}{100}$, which can be written as 0.21 (which has two decimal places). This sort of connection must be made if children are to understand, rather than merely memorize procedures, which too often are quickly forgotten.

$$0.3 \times 0.7 = \underline{\hspace{1cm}}$$
$$0.3 = \frac{3}{10}$$
$$0.7 = \frac{7}{10}$$
$$\frac{3}{10} \times \frac{7}{10} = \frac{21}{100} = 0.21$$
$$\text{So } 0.3 \times 0.7 = 0.21$$

This chapter presents an integrated approach to instruction on decimals, connecting place-value understanding and fraction understanding to help children develop a strong foundation in decimal concepts and operations. ✔

INSTRUCTIONAL CONSIDERATIONS

Connections to Familiar Concepts

In introducing decimal numeration to children, it is important to make connections to familiar concepts. Decimals are closely related to *whole numbers* in that the

TECHNOLOGY LINK 12-1
Real World Math:
Math Travels

Integrate decimals and geography with this site! While planning a vacation trip around the United States, children use decimal concepts for many purposes, including measuring distances, calculating travel time, and determining costs of all travel-related expenses. This site also discusses standards children are working toward while participating in these activities.

Visit http://www.realworldmath.com/ or link from our Companion Website at **www.prenhall.com/ cathcart.**

characteristics of whole-number numeration apply to decimals. Also, the computation algorithms are basically the same for whole numbers and decimals. However, to understand decimals quantitatively, one must develop *fractional number* concepts. Ordinarily, fraction concepts are developed before decimals are introduced; in this sequence, students draw upon their knowledge of fractions. For example, the decimal number 0.2 can also be expressed as the fraction $\frac{2}{10}$.

Whole-number connection Learning to read and interpret whole numbers involves learning the characteristics of our numeration system. These characteristics were presented in Chapter 6. It may be worthwhile to review the characteristics when children begin to work with decimals. Then, investigations to find out whether the characteristics also describe decimal numbers can be part of the development of decimal number concepts.

Place value. An understanding of the place-value system for whole numbers is a prerequisite for reading and interpreting decimals. When learning whole-number

PRINCIPLES AND STANDARDS LINK 12-3
Content Strand: Number and Operations

In grades 6–8, students should deepen their understanding of fractions, decimals, percents, and integers, and they should become proficient in using them to solve problems. By solving problems that require multiplicative comparisons (e.g., "How many times as many?" or "How many per?"), students will gain extensive experience with ratios, rates, and percents, which helps form a solid foundation for their understanding of, and facility with, proportionality. (NCTM, 2000, p. 215) place value, children group numbers in 10 and multiples of 10. They learn that for whole numbers, the value of a place is *ten times* the value of the place to its immediate right. Another way to state this relationship is to say that the value of a place in a numeral is *one-tenth* the value of the place to its immediate left. This latter relationship is important in interpreting decimal numbers. The value of the place to the right of the tens is one-tenth of 10, or 1; the value of the place to the right of the ones is one-tenth of 1 or one-tenth. Kieren (1984) cautions that acting out fractional regrouping may not be easy for children. He states that "we should not assume that the grouping-ungrouping action that allows one to go from ones to tens to hundreds will also allow one to go from ones to tenths to hundredths; dividing up is simply different from un-grouping" (p. 3). Allow children time to explore such re-groupings concretely.

Whole numbers. Compare the value of each 1 in the numeral 115. What is the relationship of the leftmost 1 and the 1 on its right? Modeling the number 115 with bundled sticks and singles shows that the value of the leftmost 1 is 10 times the value of the 1 on its right.

115

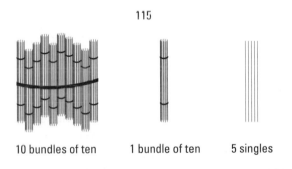

| 10 bundles of ten | 1 bundle of ten | 5 singles |

The middle digit, or the 1 to the immediate left of the 5, can be represented by one bundle of 10 sticks. It has the value of 10. To show the value of the leftmost 1, group together 10 groups of 10 sticks. Its value is hundred, or 10 times 10. Its value is *10 times* the value of the 1 on its right.

One can also ask, What is the relationship of the 1 on the immediate left of the 5 to the leftmost 1? Modeling the numbers shows that the 1 next to the 5 is *one-tenth* the value of the 1 on its left.

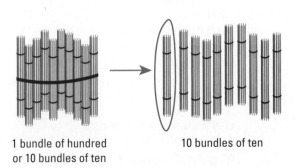

1 bundle of hundred
or 10 bundles of ten   10 bundles of ten

The leftmost 1 has the value of hundred. To show the value of the 1 on its right, take a large bundle (10 groups of ten) and separate it into 10 bundles of ten. One small bundle (a group of 10 sticks) shows the value of the 1 to the left of the 5. Its value is *one-tenth* the value of the left-most 1.

Children who understand and can verbalize the "ten times" and the "one-tenth" relationships between adjacent digits in whole numbers are ready to interpret decimal numeration.

Decimal numbers. Consider 21.1 as an example. The 1 before the decimal point has the value of 1. It can be represented with a square.

The value of the 1 on the right of the decimal point can be represented by dividing a square (1) in 10 parts.

21.1

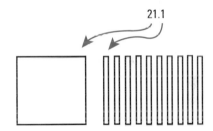

The value of the 1 on the right of the decimal point is *one-tenth* the value of the 1 to the left of the decimal point. This maintains the place-value relationship established above.

As a second example, consider the number 2.11. Using a square to represent 1 unit (as above), the process of subdividing can be extended a step further to demonstrate the value of the rightmost 1 in the number 2.11 (see drawing on next page).

The rightmost 1 has a value of *one-hundredth*. It is one-tenth the value of the 1 on its left. One-hundredth is one-tenth of one-tenth.

The familiar whole-number place-value chart can be extended to include decimal places as in Figure 12-1. Notice that the chart is symmetric about the ones place and not the decimal point.

Middle-school children may appreciate the patterns inherent in the symbolic representation of place values as in Figure 12-2.

FIGURE 12-1 ▷

THOUSANDS	HUNDREDS	TENS	ONES	TENTHS	HUNDREDTHS	THOUSANDTHS
2	3	6	4.	1	2	7

FIGURE 12-2 ▷

10^3	10^2	10^1	10^0	10^{-1}	10^{-2}	10^{-3}
1000	100	10	1	$\frac{1}{10}$	$\frac{1}{100}$	$\frac{1}{1000}$
7	8	2	3	5	4	5

2.11

The following two exercises will help children develop meaning of decimal numbers by connecting them to whole numbers.

1. Begin by asking children to respond to the following questions:
   - How many hundreds in 66 600? (six hundred sixty-six)
   - How many tens in 6660? (six hundred sixty-six)
   - How many ones in 666? (six hundred sixty-six)
   Next, continue the pattern using decimals.
   - How many tenths in 66.6? (six hundred sixty-six)
   - How many hundredths in 6.66? (six hundred sixty-six)
   - How many thousandths in 0.666? (six hundred sixty-six)

2. Have children read and write numbers in the following manner:
   - 444 000   four hundred forty-four thousands
   - 44 400   four hundred forty-four hundreds
   - 4440   four hundred forty-four tens
   - 444   four hundred forty-four ones

Then, continue the pattern using decimals.
- 44.4   four hundred forty-four tenths
- 4.44   four hundred forty-four hundredths
- 0.444   four hundred forty-four thousandths

Reading numbers as described in the second exercise helps to reinforce the fact that no matter where the decimal point is, each digit is 10 times as much as the digit on its right and one-tenth of the digit on its left.

The different reading sequences should also be noticed:

- Whole numbers reading sequence: thousands, hundreds, tens, ones

- Decimal reading sequence: tenths, hundredths, thousandths

Additive quality   To develop the idea that decimals, like whole numbers, are additive, have children first show different ways to write specified whole numbers, then decimal numbers. For example:

Whole numbers

$$45 = 40 + 5$$

$$643 = 600 + 40 + 3$$
   or 6 hundreds + 4 tens + 3 ones
$$= 500 + 140 + 3$$
   or 5 hundreds + 14 tens + 3 ones
$$= 600 + 30 + 13$$
   or 6 hundreds + 3 tens + 13 ones

Decimal numbers

$$0.45 = 0.4 + 0.05$$
   or 4 tenths + 5 hundredths
$$= 0.40 + 0.05$$
   or 40 hundredths + 5 hundredths

$$6.43 = 6 + 0.4 + 0.03$$
$$\text{or } 6 + 4 \text{ tenths} + 3 \text{ hundredths}$$
$$= 5 + 1.4 + 0.03$$
$$\text{or } 5 + 14 \text{ tenths} + 3 \text{ hundredths}$$
$$= 6 + 0.3 + 0.13$$
$$\text{or } 6 + 3 \text{ tenths} + 13 \text{ hundredths}$$

Multiplicative quality The multiplicative aspect of decimal numbers can be highlighted when children learn to write decimals in expanded notation. For example:

$$452.69 \rightarrow (4 \times 100) + (5 \times 10) + (2 \times 1) +$$
$$(6 \times 0.1) + (9 \times 0.01)$$
$$\rightarrow (4 \times 100) + (5 \times 10) + (2 \times 1) +$$
$$(6 \times \tfrac{1}{10}) + (9 \times \tfrac{1}{100})$$

Fraction number connection Pause a moment and order the following fractions from least to greatest:

$$\frac{5}{100} \quad \frac{5}{1000} \quad \frac{51}{100} \quad \frac{501}{100\,000} \quad \frac{5}{1000} \quad \frac{150}{1000} \quad \frac{1005}{100\,000}$$

How does this task compare to that of ordering decimals? Many children find ordering fractions when the denominators are powers of 10 easier than ordering decimals. Why is this so? One reason may be that it is easier to visualize the size of a fraction such as $\frac{51}{100}$ (51 parts of 100 parts) than it is to concretize "point five one" (0.51).

The common practice of reading decimals by naming the digits rather than expressing them properly as decimal fractions thwarts the ability to view decimals as fractional numbers. The number 0.51 should be read as "fifty-one hundredths" rather than "point five one," to emphasize its value, and will be discussed in the following section.

Another factor that can contribute to the difficulty in determining the value of a decimal number is the lack of concrete and semiconcrete experiences that children have when working with decimal numbers. In the past, some mathematics programs have not encouraged extensive modeling of either decimals or fractions. In practice, it is believed that modeling decimals has occurred even less than modeling fractions, particularly as parts of a whole.

PRINCIPLES AND STANDARDS LINK 12-4
Content Strand: Number and Operations

Students can develop a deep understanding of rational numbers through experiences with a variety of models, such as fraction strips, number lines, 10 × 10 grids, area models, and objects. These models offer students concrete representations of abstract ideas and support students' meaningful use of representations and their flexible movement among them to solve problems. (NCTM, 2000, p. 215)

Children who understand fractions prior to studying decimals should be able to make connections between the two systems of representing rational numbers.

Example: $8.45 \rightarrow 8 \text{ and } 0.4 + 0.05$
$$\text{or } 8 \text{ and } 0.45$$
$$\rightarrow 8 \text{ and } \tfrac{4}{10} + \tfrac{5}{100}$$
$$\text{or } 8 \text{ and } \tfrac{45}{100} \rightarrow 8\tfrac{45}{100}$$

Reading and Writing Decimals

In elementary classrooms, one frequently hears children reading decimals as, for example, "two decimal six" or "two point six" (for 2.6). Some teachers accept this (some textbooks recommend it!) and children go on to say things like "3 point 4 plus 5 point 2 equals 7 point 6." On the lips of adults, statements like these do not upset us. However, if children use such expressions when learning the meaning of decimal numbers, it is possible they may not readily develop understanding of the quantitative value of decimal numbers. The practice is tantamount to reading whole numbers by naming the digits that form a number as, for example, reading 647 as "six four seven." The expression "six hundred forty-seven" conveys some understanding of the value of each digit in the numeral. The same is true when reading decimals. Children should be required to state the quantitative value of digits when they read a decimal numeral.

Examples: 4.5 Read as "four and five-tenths."
0.35 Read as "zero and thirty-five hundredths" or "thirty-five hundredths."

Decimal point In fraction form, it is easy to distinguish between the whole number and the fraction part (e.g., $4\frac{5}{10}$). With decimal numeration, the denominator is not visible; therefore, a sign is needed to denote when a fraction part of a number is indicated. The sign is the decimal point and is read "and" when reading decimal numbers. As stated in Chapter 6, it is not proper to use "and" when reading whole numbers.

Example: 100, 101, 102, . . .
Not correct:
"one hundred, one hundred *and* one, one hundred *and* two, . . ."
Correct:
"one hundred, one hundred one, one hundred two, . . ."

Decimal names Take care to pronounce the decimal terms distinctly (possibly slightly exaggerating the "th" and "ths" endings) so that children will be able to discriminate between them and whole-number terminology.

Example: ten and tenth; tens and tenths
hundred and hundredth; hundreds
and hundredths
thousand and thousandth, . . .

In early work with decimals, it is recommended that decimal numerals be written on the board or a chart for reference (a teacher can point to the parts) when communicating decimal numbers orally. This will aid children in matching the "th" and "ths" endings with the numeric place-value terms and to distinguish them from whole-number place-value terms.

Decimal notation   Decimal notation has changed over the years and even today it is not uniform throughout the world. In the United States, a point is used and is placed immediately after (to the right of) the ones digit; people in some European countries use a comma in the same position. This is the reason the use of a comma to separate number periods has been discontinued (see Chapter 6 for the proper way to record numbers).

Example: English   French
0.05   0,05
245.63   245,63

This symbolization transfers to monetary values.

Example: $4.95   4,95$
$56.08   56,08$
$0.05   0,05$

When reading a number, the decimal point is read as "and."

Example: 6.5 or 6,5
Read as: six *and* five-tenths
$1.49 or 1,49$
Read as: one dollar *and* forty-nine cents

If children read decimals properly, writing decimals will be a simple exercise. Reading decimals properly also enhances children's ability to readily identify denominators, which enables them to think of decimals as fractional numbers.

Children may more easily visualize a fraction in concrete terms than a decimal. For example, it is easier to visualize $\frac{3}{4}$ of something than 0.75. Thinking about decimals as fractions (rather than manipulating digits) helps to develop decimal number sense. Teaching ideas for developing decimal number sense through concrete and semiconcrete models are provided in the next section of this chapter.

The following activities provide practice in reading and writing decimal numbers:

1. Reading and writing decimals
   • Provide a calculator for each child and a calculator for use on an overhead projector.
   • Dictate the decimal number, *seven and fifty-five hundredths.*
   • Ask children to enter the number in their calculators.
   • Then display the number on an overhead projector calculator (or on a transparency if a calculator is not available) for the children to self-check.
   • Repeat the procedure with other numbers:
     three and four-hundredths
     sixty and sixteen-thousandths
     two hundred three and five-hundredths

2. Reading decimal numbers
   • Display a decimal numeral on an overhead projector calculator or write it on the board. Example: 4.65
   • Ask a child to read the number.
   • Repeat with other numerals:
     40.08   0.095   0.002   306.36   500.05

3. Writing decimal numbers
   • Write several decimal numerals on the board. Examples: 0.405   60.05   300.003
   • Have children write the numbers in words.

DEVELOPING DECIMAL NUMBER SENSE

It is important to devote time to developing the meaning of decimal numbers through concrete and semiconcrete models. Several examples are described here together with suggestions for activities.

Base-Ten Blocks

Children will have used base-ten blocks when learning to interpret whole numbers and their operations. These materials also can be used to represent decimal numbers provided children are able to understand that different blocks can be selected to represent the unit.

 PRINCIPLES AND STANDARDS LINK 12-5
Content Strand: Number and Operations

Students in these grades [Grades 3–5] should use models and other strategies to represent and study decimal numbers. (NCTM, 2000, p. 149)

A "tens" block as the unit   A first activity could be to select a tens block (called a "rod" or a "long") to represent the unit. Questions such as the following can be asked:

- If this piece represents (or is worth) one, what is the value of this piece (small cube)?
- What is the value of 2 of these small cubes? 3 small cubes? . . . 10 small cubes?

Change the questioning to:

- If this piece (a rod) is one, show me one-tenth; three-tenths; nine-tenths.

A "hundreds" block as the unit   Take a "hundreds" block (called a "square" or a "flat"). Say:

- Now let's say that this square block is one or one whole. Can you find a block that is one-tenth of this square block?
- Can you show two-tenths of this square block with the blocks? three-tenths? . . . ten-tenths?

Change the questioning to:

- I have five rods (tens) here. What part of the square are they?
- I have one small cube in my hand. Can you tell what part of the square this small cube is? Why do you call it that?

A "thousands" block (large cube) as the unit   Children can be invited to write relation statements about the various blocks when a thousands block is designated as the unit. They can be challenged to write as many different relationships as they can. Two other activities with base-ten blocks follow:

1. A square as the unit
   - Designate a square as the unit.
   - Write the numeral 2.5 on the board (or display it on an overhead projector calculator or transparency).
   - Have children model the number with the blocks. Children can check each other's work.
   - Ask a child to tell what number has been modeled.
   - Repeat with other numerals such as:
     1.6   0.2   0.12   0.06   0.56
2. Choose a unit
   - Tell children to select a block as the unit and then to represent a number with the blocks. Have them record what they have done.

   Possible sample work:

   I chose the square as one. I made the number 2.25. This is how I made the number.

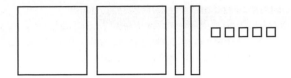

I chose the large cube as one. I made the number 0.036. This is how I made the number.

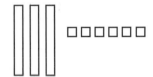

Decimal Squares

The commercial kit Decimal Squares consists of colored paper squares 1 dm^2 or 1 sq. dm partitioned in tenths (red), hundredths (green), and thousandths (yellow). The 10 tenths squares are shaded to represent 0.1, 0.2, . . . , 1.0. The hundredths and thousandths squares are shaded to represent multiples of five and ten fractional parts. Children can use the squares to compare decimal fractions (Activities 12-1 to 12-3) and for simple addition and subtraction. Teachers can construct a similar model using decimal grids (see Blackline Master 10 in the Appendix), which can be used to represent one whole, tenths, and hundredths.

Measurement Sticks

Measurement is one real-world application of decimal number knowledge. It is not necessary for children to

ACTIVITY 12-1

COMPARING DECIMAL FRACTIONS: TENTHS AND HUNDREDTHS

MATERIALS
A set of Decimal Squares (red and green) for each child

PROCEDURE
1. Select a red square. Now find a green square with the same amount shaded. Write a statement about the two amounts.
   Example: *Eight-tenths and eighty-hundredths are the same amount.*

2. Find other pairs of decimal squares that show the same amount shaded and write a statement about the pairs of decimal fractions.

ACTIVITY 12-2

COMPARING DECIMAL FRACTIONS: TENTHS AND THOUSANDTHS

MATERIALS

A set of Decimal Squares (red and yellow) for each child

PROCEDURE

1. Select a red square. Then find a yellow square with the same amount shaded. Write a statement about the two decimal fractions.

2. Find other pairs of decimal squares with the same amount shaded and write statements about the pairs of decimal fractions.

ACTIVITY 12-3

COMPARING DECIMAL FRACTIONS: INEQUALITIES

MATERIALS

A set of Decimal Squares for each child

PROCEDURE

1. Select two decimal square cards. After examining them, write a statement about the two decimal fractions represented.

   Examples:

   Three-hundredths is less than one-tenth.

   0.03 is less than 0.1

   Four-hundredths is greater than twenty-five-thousandths.

   0.04 is greater than 0.025

2. Compare other pairs of decimal fractions and write statements in words and in symbolic form.

know the different basic unit prefixes to read measurements as part of a unit of measure.

Children can be provided with noncalibrated meter, decimeter, and centimeter sticks. (The decimeter and centimeter pieces can be cut from stiff cardboard.) Children should be able to articulate the relationships among the linear pieces.

The following activities require additional teacher direction.

1. Modeling linear measurements
   - You will need a meter stick, 10 decimeter sticks, 10 centimeter sticks, and a collection of ribbon pieces.
   - Relate a scenario such as the following:

     While cleaning a closet one day, you find a box of pieces of ribbon. You decide to measure them and label each length.

   - Provide children in small groups with several ribbon lengths and a set of measurement sticks. Direct them to measure each piece of ribbon with the materials, then write the length to the nearest hundredth of a meter on a piece of paper and affix it to the ribbon. Example: 1.24 m.

2. Decimal measurements
   - First model some lengths with meter, decimeter, and centimeter sticks.
   - Give pairs of children a written direction as follows: Draw a line with chalk on the classroom floor that is 1.2 meters long.
   - Have children tell the length in two ways. For example:

     The length is 1 and 2 tenths meters.
     The length is 1 and 20 hundredths meters.

A metric chart could be constructed and displayed on a bulletin board and subsequently used to read different lengths (or weights or capacities) using decimal numbers. The chart may depict metric names and matching place value names or symbols (Figure 12-3).

Graph Paper

Graph paper marked in 10-cm squares is useful for showing different decimal fractions. The paper can be centimeter or millimeter graph paper (see Blackline Master 15 in the Appendix). Children can be asked to shade parts of the squares to show different decimal fractions, to compare decimal fractions, or to show addition and subtraction of decimal fractions.

1. Modeling decimal fractions pictorially (hundredths)
   - Provide children with several pieces of centimeter graph paper marked in 10-cm squares.
   - Direct children to show decimal fractions on the pieces of graph paper by coloring or shading.

FIGURE 12-3

KILOMETER	HECTOMETER	DEKAMETER	METER	DECIMETER	CENTIMETER	MILLIMETER
1000	100	10	1	0.1	0.01	0.001

Examples: 0.4, 0.45, 0.5, 0.05, 0.25

2. Modeling decimal fractions pictorially (thousandths)
   • Provide children with millimeter graph paper marked in 10-cm squares.
   • Direct children to show decimal fractions on the graph paper by coloring or shading.

Examples: 0.35, 0.08, 0.075, 0.009, 0.016

Working with millimeter graph paper will communicate to children how relatively small the third place value in a decimal fraction really is. Another way to get children to realize the relative sizes of decimal fraction place values is to have them partition a centimeter hundred square in thousandths and then in ten-thousandths. Procedures for this exercise are described below.

1. Provide children with a 10-cm square piece of centimeter graph paper.
2. Direct them to shade in the amount of 0.57142 by first shading in 5 tenths, next 7 hundredths, then 1 thousandth, then 4 ten-thousandths, and finally 2 hundred-thousandths. Children will soon realize that it is difficult to designate the area for ten-thousandths.
3. Discussion: What did you learn from this exercise?

Number line A number line is a good model to demonstrate the density property of decimals. Provide children with number lines drawn on paper and have them write several numbers between 0 and the given number. For example:

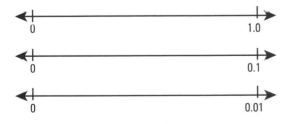

PRINCIPLES AND STANDARDS LINK 12-6
Content Strand: Number and Operations

At the heart of flexibility in working with rational numbers is a solid understanding of different representations for fractions, decimals, and percents. In grades 3-5, students should have learned to generate and recognize equivalent forms of fractions, decimals, and percents, at least in some simple cases. In the middle grades, students should build on and extend this experience to become facile in using fractions, decimals, and percents meaningfully. (NCTM, 2000, p. 215)

This kind of exercise, can help children realize that it is always possible to name decimal numbers between any two given numbers.

A number line also can be used to write decimal numbers in specified increments such as 0.1, 0.5, or 0.01. This type of activity helps children count from one place value to another larger one, as from hundredths to tenths. This is not a trivial task for children because of the whole-number influence. With whole numbers, when counting up, one goes from tens to hundreds; with decimals, one goes from hundredths to tenths.

Give children appropriate number lines drawn on paper. Ask them to:

• Begin with 0.8, count by tenths.
• Begin with 7.5, count by 5 tenths.
• Begin with 0.56, count by tenths.

Two examples of children's counting errors are

12.08, 12.09, 13.00
20.97, 20.98, 20.99, 30.00

Activities 12-4 through 12-6 contain additional number line activities.

Money

Some teachers use coins to model decimal computation. Recording amounts in dollars and cents does involve decimal fractions, but care must be taken that children see the connection between the coins and the fractional part of a decimal number. For example, children do not readily relate $2.25 to 2 dollars and 25 hundredths of a dollar or a dime to one-tenth of a dollar. If money is used as a model for decimals, children need to think of dimes and pennies as fractional parts of a dollar.

ACTIVITY 12-4

LABELING POINTS ON A NUMBER LINE

Write numbers for A, B, and C on each line.

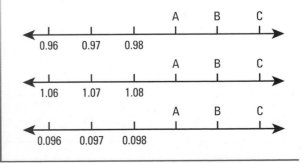

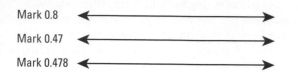

ACTIVITY 12-5

MARKING PRECEDING AND SUBSEQUENT POINTS

Mark the indicated numbers on the number line. Then mark two preceding and two following numbers.

Mark 0.8 ⟵—————————⟶

Mark 0.47 ⟵—————————⟶

Mark 0.478 ⟵—————————⟶

ACTIVITY 12-6

COUNTING

Write 15 numerals for each,

- Counting by 0.02. Begin with 1.
- Counting by 0.1. Begin with 0.95.
- Counting by 0.05. Begin with 0.05.
- Counting by 0.01. Begin with 0.197.

Examples: 5 pennies = 5 hundredths of a dollar
3 dimes = 3 tenths of a dollar

Provide children with pennies, dimes, and a dollar coin (play money is fine). Ask them to first display the following sets of coins and then to write the decimal number that they represent.

- 1 dollar, 4 dimes (1.40 or 1.4)
- 3 dimes, 5 pennies (0.35)
- 15 pennies (0.15)
- 2 dimes, 12 pennies (0.32)

ACTIVITY 12-7

RECORDING PRICES

Sara and her brother Bill have set up a lemonade stand at the beach. They want to make a sign to indicate the price of large, medium, and small glasses of lemonade. What are two ways Sara and Bill can show the prices?

Large glass: ninety-five cents

Medium glass: seventy-five cents

Small glass: fifty cents

It is not uncommon to find in commercial advertisements an incorrect use of decimal notation when recording costs. For example, the price of an item may be indicated as .25¢. The assumption is that .25¢ means the same as $0.25 when in fact it means 25 hundredths of a cent, that is, less than one cent! Activity 12-7 can help children practice recording money properly.

The expected answer to Activity 12-7 would be $0.95 or 95¢, $0.75 or 75¢ , and $0.50 or 50¢.

Other Materials to Model Decimals

Most base-ten models can be used to represent decimal numbers. For example, children may like to work with pocket charts or a vertical abacus. If such materials are used, the ones place should be indicated in some manner on the materials (Figure 12-4).

EQUIVALENT DECIMALS

Usually, more attention is given to equivalent fractions than to equivalent decimals in mathematics programs. Equivalent fractions are necessary for fraction computa-

FIGURE 12-4

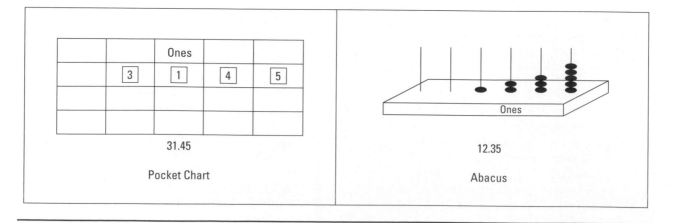

	Ones		
3	1	4	5

31.45

Pocket Chart

12.35

Abacus

tion, whereas one can work through decimal computations without thinking of equivalent decimals. Nonetheless, equivalent decimals help children understand decimal computation.

If the process of naming equivalent decimals is connected to that of writing equivalent fractions, there is nothing new to learn. The fact that each decimal fraction can be written differently will not be surprising to children.

Example: $\frac{4}{10} = \frac{40}{100} = \frac{400}{1000}$

The fraction $\frac{4}{10}$ was multiplied by "one" in the form of $\frac{10}{10}$ and $\frac{100}{100}$, respectively. In a decimal numeral, the process is the same although the denominator is not visible.

Example: $0.4 = 0.40 = 0.400$

These numerals are read as 4 tenths = 40 hundredths = 400 thousandths. This is similar to the equivalent fractions above.

A concrete "proof" of the equivalency could be demonstrated by using base-ten blocks and comparing, for example, 4 tenths (4 rods) and 40 hundredths (40 ones) on a square unit (a hundreds flat) (Figure 12-5).

Children who have had experiences in modeling decimal fractions and in recording amounts in different ways (e.g., 5 tenths or 50 hundredths, 0.5 or 0.50) should develop a sense of the size of decimal numbers. In particular, they should be able to compare tenths and hundredths and to rename one decimal fraction to an equivalent form. They will have a mental referent for the process. The generalization that adding zeros to decimal fractions produces numbers of equivalent value is not difficult to conceptualize.

ORDERING AND COMPARING DECIMALS

Children who have developed decimal number sense will be able to order decimals. Children who do not understand decimals sometimes use erroneous thinking strategies when ordering decimals. One line of thinking is that "longer is greater" as, for example, 0.65 is less than 0.0345 because "65" is shorter than "345." Another false

method of comparison is that "shorter is greater" as, for example, *0.3 is greater than 0.41 because tenths are greater than hundredths* (Vance, 1986b). It is wise for a teacher to ask children to tell how they arrive at solutions in order to learn their thinking processes.

Children can be taught to compare decimals by focusing, in turn, on each place-value position beginning from the left and moving to the right until a comparison can be made. This is similar to the process of comparing whole numbers.

Examples:
1. 1.52 and 1.48

   Comparison: ones place—same digit;

   tenths place—5 tenths and 4 tenths.

   Therefore, 1.52 > 1.48

2. 0.0156 and 0.85

   Comparison: 0 tenths and 8 tenths or

   1 hundredth and 85 hundredths

   Therefore, 0.0156 < 0.85

3. 0.314 and 0.28

   Comparison: 31 hundredths and 28 hundredths

   Therefore, 0.314 > 0.28

Another method used to order decimals is to write equivalent decimal fractions.

Example:
Order the following decimals from least to greatest.

   1.06   0.36   0.06   0.0306   0.0063

Changing all the numbers to the same-sized decimal fraction, one obtains

   1.0600   0.3600   0.0600   0.0306   0.0063

It is now easy to list the numbers in order of size. Activities 12-8 and 12-9 provide practice in constructing and ordering decimals.

COMPUTATION

Understanding computation with decimals requires an understanding of place value, decimal concepts, and computation of fractions. Investing time in developing that understanding before beginning decimal computation will pay off in enhanced understanding and increased achievement for children.

Children who have developed an understanding of decimal concepts and place value will have no difficulty adding and subtracting decimals. For multiplication and division, there is a need to practice the operations with 10 and multiples of 10 as a factor. The ability to mentally

FIGURE 12-5

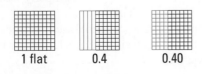

1 flat   0.4   0.40

ACTIVITY 12-8

CONSTRUCTING AND ORDERING DECIMALS

MATERIALS
Four small cards for each child with the numerals 0, 1, 2, and a decimal point written on the cards

PROCEDURE
1. Use the cards to show as many different decimal numbers as you can.

   Examples: 0.12   1.02

   Discuss with the class whether numerals such as 012. or .120 are allowed.

2. Record each number as you make it.

3. When you are sure you cannot make any more numbers, order all your numbers from least to greatest.

ACTIVITY 12-9

ORDERING DECIMALS

MATERIALS
Five small cards for each student with the numerals 0, 1, 2, 3, and a decimal point written on the cards

PROCEDURE
1. Use the cards to show at least five decimals that are less than one.

   Write each numeral as you make it.

   Order your decimals from least to greatest.

2. Use your cards to show at least five decimals that are more than one-tenth.

   Write each numeral as you make it.

   Order your decimals from greatest to least.

multiply and divide by 10, 100, etc., greatly facilitates the operations of multiplication and division, particularly in ascertaining the reasonableness of an answer.

Children who have a sense of the quantitative value of decimal numbers can be expected to compute with greater accuracy than when computation is done by applying meaningless rules.

Addition and Subtraction

Addition and subtraction of decimals should be related to addition and subtraction of whole numbers and of fractions. As discussed in Chapters 7 and 11, solving word problems set in familiar, real-world situations helps chil-

dren understand operations and judge the reasonableness of answers. An easy-to-understand interpretation of addition is the "join" interpretation, in which two quantities are combined. The "separate" and "comparison" interpretations of subtraction, in which two quantities are separated or compared, also are easy to understand.

Addition and subtraction of decimals should be introduced by posing problems based on "join" and "separate" situations involving quantities measured in decimal units, such as lengths of ribbon, pounds of food, and money. Figure 12-6 contains sample word problems for addition and subtraction of decimals and compares them with similar problems involving fractions. Notice the similarities between the problem contexts.

Addition questions can be represented on 10-cm graph paper squares. Children can shade in a set of addends and subsequently "read" the number shaded.

The children have measured the mass of some paperback storybooks in the classroom. The four books that Therese and Monica weighed had a mass of 0.25 kg, 0.3 kg, 0.17 kg, and 0.09 kg. What is the mass of the four books? Show the shadings on graph paper.

0.25
0.3
0.17
<u>0.09</u>

 OR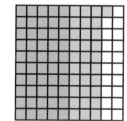

The mass of the books is 0.81 kg.

If children are required to add several sets of numbers by shading the amounts, they probably will find that it helps to shade in the tenths first, then to add the hundredths and shade them in as tenths plus hundredths, as in the right-hand grid above. For example, for the numbers listed above, a child would first shade in 1, 2, and 3 tenths to make 6 tenths; next, the child would shade in 2 tenths plus 1 hundredth for a total of 0.81 shaded. This procedure causes one to think of the value of each digit and should help children learn how to properly write ragged decimals in vertical columns.

When adding ragged decimals, children can be encouraged to write equivalent decimal fractions by adding zeros as required.

FIGURE 12-6

	WORD PROBLEM WITH FRACTIONS	NUMBER SENTENCE	WORD PROBLEM WITH DECIMALS	NUMBER SENTENCE
Addition (Join)	Tom ate $\frac{1}{2}$ of an apple pie yesterday and $\frac{1}{4}$ of an apple pie today. How much pie did Tom eat altogether?	$\frac{1}{2} + \frac{1}{4}$ = _____	Tom ate 0.25 pound of turkey and 0.10 pound of cheese. How much food did Tom eat altogether?	0.25 + 0.10 = _____
Subtraction (Separate)	Alberto has $\frac{3}{4}$ of a cookie. He ate $\frac{1}{4}$ of a whole cookie. How much cookie does Alberto have left?	$\frac{3}{4} - \frac{1}{4}$ = _____	Maria had 0.37 meter of ribbon. She used 0.25 meter to make a bow. How much ribbon does Maria have left?	0.37 − 0.25 = _____
Subtraction (Comparison)	Alberto has $\frac{3}{4}$ of a cookie and Juana has $\frac{1}{4}$ of a cookie. How much more does Alberto have?	$\frac{3}{4} - \frac{1}{4}$ = _____	Maria has 0.37 meter of red ribbon and 0.25 meter of blue ribbon. How much more red ribbon does she have than blue ribbon?	0.37 − 0.25 = _____

Example:

Given: 0.4 + 0.078 + 0.1056 + 0.23

Change to: 0.4000 + 0.0780 + 0.1056 + 0.2300

This method can be thought of as adding the numerators of same-sized decimal fractions.

In subtraction, when the subtrahend is expressed in tenths and the minuend is in hundredths or thousandths, it is a common practice to rename the decimal fractions to the same-sized fractions (all hundredths or thousandths, etc.) by adding zeros to facilitate using the standard algorithm.

Two alpine skiers finished a race with the following time scores: 13.50 seconds and 12.96 seconds. What is the time difference of their scores?

Solution process:

Subtract: 13.50 − 12.97

The subtraction algorithm is the same as with whole numbers.

Addition and subtraction questions with mixed decimals can be modeled using base-ten blocks. A concrete demonstration of regrouping is easily carried out with these materials (Figure 12-7).

Other concrete and semiconcrete material used to add and subtract whole numbers can be used to add and subtract decimals provided there is a way of showing place values smaller than the ones place.

Regrouping in addition and subtraction can also be carried out with dollar and dime coins. However, these are visually nonproportional materials, and therefore should not be the first materials used.

Multiplication

As with addition and subtraction, multiplication and division of decimals should be related to those operations on whole numbers and on fractions. The interpretations of multiplication and division of decimals that are easiest to understand are repeated addition, Area and Array multi-

FIGURE 12-7

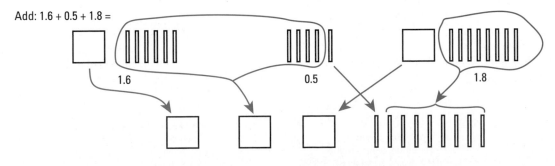

ADDING MIXED DECIMALS WITH BASE-TEN BLOCKS

Add: 1.6 + 0.5 + 1.8 =

1.6   0.5   1.8

1.6 + 0.5 + 1.8 = 3.9

plication, and Measurement division (repeated subtraction). Recall that repeated addition problems involve repeatedly adding quantities that are the same size, whereas area and array problems involve finding the area of a rectangular region. Measurement division, also known as repeated subtraction, involves measuring out groups of a certain size from a whole. Figure 12-8 contains sample word problems for multiplication and division of decimals and compares them with similar problems involving fractions. Notice the similarities between the problem contexts.

Multiplication of decimals should be introduced with simple problems involving tenths and gradually progress to smaller decimal fractions.

The following is a suggested sequence for multiplication of decimals:

1. tenths by a whole number $4 \times 0.2; 3 \times 0.4$
2. hundredths by a whole number 3×0.05
3. tenths by tenths 0.4×0.6
4. hundredths by tenths $0.3 \times 0.04; 0.4 \times 0.15$
5. hundredths by hundredths $0.05 \times 0.09; 0.04 \times 0.56; 0.12 \times 0.23$

Multiplication questions such as the first two can be represented concretely with base-ten blocks using a square (hundreds block) as the unit.

Example: $4 \times 0.2 = 0.8$

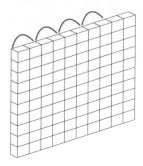

Read: 4 times two-tenths = eight-tenths

Example: $3 \times 0.4 = 1.2$
Read: 3 times four-tenths = twelve-tenths

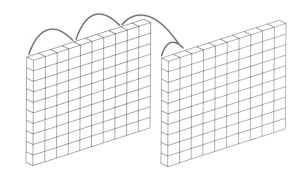

Similarly, hundredths multiplied by a whole number can be represented with base-ten blocks.

FIGURE 12-8

	WORD PROBLEM WITH FRACTIONS	NUMBER SENTENCE	WORD PROBLEM WITH DECIMALS	NUMBER SENTENCE
Multiplication (Repeated Addition)	Shawntrice had 4 bags of cookies, with $\frac{1}{2}$ of a cookie in each bag. How many cookies did Shawntrice have?	$4 \times \frac{1}{2} =$ _____	Shawntrice had 4 bags of sliced cheese, with 0.75 pound of cheese in each bag. How much cheese did Shawntrice have?	4×0.75 = _____
Multiplication (Area and Array)	There is $\frac{2}{3}$ of a chocolate pie in the refrigerator. Peter ate $\frac{1}{2}$ of it. What part of the whole pie did Peter eat?	$\frac{1}{2} \times \frac{2}{3} =$ _____	Peter has a garden that is 2.5 meters long and 1.5 meters wide. What is the area of Peter's garden?	2.5×1.5 = _____
Division (Measurement— Repeated Subtraction)	Steve has 4 cups of sugar. He needs $\frac{2}{3}$ of a cup of sugar to make one batch of his favorite cookies. How many batches of cookies can Steve make?	$4 \div \frac{2}{3} =$ _____	Steve has \$4.00. He wants to buy several candy bars that cost \$0.65 each. How many candy bars can Steve buy?	$4.00 \div 0.65$ = _____

FIGURE 12-9

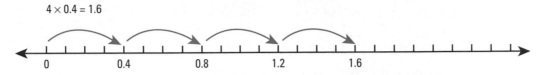

MULTIPLYING DECIMALS

$4 \times 0.4 = 1.6$

Example: $5 \times 0.05 = 0.25$

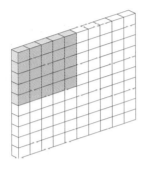

Read: 5 times five-hundredths = 25 hundredths

Multiplication of a decimal number by a whole number can also be pictured on a number line as in Figure 12-9.

When multiplying tenths by tenths, it is helpful to interpret the question as, for example, four tenths of three tenths. A representation of this problem with base-ten blocks through a teacher-guided lesson could be as follows:

• Designate a square (hundreds block) as the unit.

• Ask the children to show three-tenths in two ways using the blocks.

a.

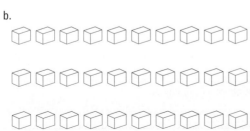

b.

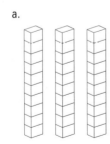

• Ask, "Which arrangement allows four-tenths of three-tenths to be removed?" (The thirty-hundredths should be chosen.)

• Ask the children to identify four-tenths of three-tenths.

• Ask, "How can we state what number this is?" (twelve-hundredths)

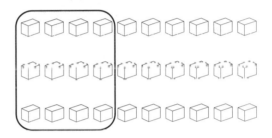

The process can be shown pictorially on a 10-cm square piece of graph paper (Figure 12-10).

A commercial set of Decimal Squares made of colored acetate is available for use on an overhead projector. Decimal multiplication can be represented by overlaying two squares as in shading grid paper. The region where the shaded parts overlap represents the product (Figure 12-11).

FIGURE 12-10

A PICTORIAL REPRESENTATION OF MULTIPLICATION

$0.4 \times 0.3 = 0.12$

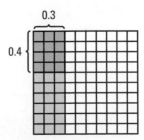

The product is the part of the unit that is shaded twice

FIGURE 12-11

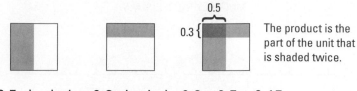

0.5 shaded   0.3 shaded $0.3 \times 0.5 = 0.15$

The product is the part of the unit that is shaded twice.

Multiplying decimals by powers and multiples of 10 is an important skill to develop. Progressing from concrete representations to paper-and-pencil work to mental calculations, children should develop a rule for the placement of the decimal point in products when multiplying by a power of 10 (Figure 12-12).

A place-value chart can be used to justify the rule for multiplying by 10 (by 100, and by 1000).

Example:

Hundreds	Tens	Ones	Tenths	Hundredths
		3	2	5
	3	2	5	
3	2	5		

Because the value of each position is 10 times that of the position to its right, multiplying by 10 "moves" each digit one place to the left. This is equivalent to "moving" the decimal point one place to the right.

Example: $3.25 \times 10 = 32.5$
$32.5 \times 10 = 325.$

A number of concrete experiences followed by written statements will assist children in generalizing a rule for locating the decimal point in products. The concrete modeling can proceed in a systematic way so that children notice patterns that will help them develop rules (see Figure 12-13). The following are examples of lists that children can write as they multiply decimals concretely or pictorially.

4×1 tenth = 4 tenths	$4 \times 0.1 = 0.4$
4×2 tenths = 8 tenths	$4 \times 0.2 = 0.8$
4×3 tenths = 12 tenths	$4 \times 0.3 = 1.2$
4×4 tenths = 16 tenths	$4 \times 0.4 = 1.6$
4×5 tenths = 20 tenths	$4 \times 0.5 = 2.0$

4 tenths $\times$ 1 tenth = 4 hundredths
$0.4 \times 0.1 = 0.04$
4 tenths $\times$ 2 tenths = 8 hundredths
$0.4 \times 0.2 = 0.08$
4 tenths $\times$ 3 tenths = 12 hundredths
$0.4 \times 0.3 = 0.12$
4 tenths $\times$ 4 tenths = 16 hundredths
$0.4 \times 0.4 = 0.16$
4 tenths $\times$ 5 tenths = 20 hundredths
$0.4 \times 0.5 = 0.20$

Patterns can be generated with a calculator when studying multiplication with decimals. The following are examples:

Enter:	Display:
$5 \times 0.1 =$	0.5
$0.5 \times 0.1 =$	0.05
$0.05 \times 0.1 =$	0.005
$0.005 \times 0.1 =$	0.0005

If the calculator has a multiplicative constant, one needs only to press "=" after the first multiplication to generate the products listed above.

FIGURE 12-12

MULTIPLYING WITH POWERS OF 10

$10 \times 0.3 = 3$ $100 \times 1.85 = 185$

$100 \times 0.6 = 60$ $400 \times 0.28 = 112$

Rule: Move the decimal point the same number of places to the right of its original position as there are zeros in the multiple-of-10 multiplier.

FIGURE 12-13

| | DECIMAL PLACES | | | |
PROBLEM	*First Factor*	*Second Factor*	PRODUCT	DECIMAL PLACES IN PRODUCT
3 × 0.2	0	1	0.6	1
3.1 × 4.71	1	2	14.601	3
0.3 × 5.2	1	1	1.56	2
0.25 × 0.11	2	2	0.0275	4

Example: 5×0.1 [=] [=] [=] [=]

Children could use a calculator to complete a table as in Figure 12-13, and then look for a pattern to help them articulate a rule for placing the decimal point in products.

One needs to be selective about the numbers chosen for such an exercise because for some numbers it appears that the rule does not work.

Problem: $0.24 \times 39.5 = ?$

According to the rule, there should be three decimal places in the product. However, a calculator response is 9.48. Children need to be aware of how their calculator displays numbers. In this case, the calculator drops final zeros after a decimal point.

Middle-school children may appreciate the following explanation of why the number of places to the right of the decimal point in each factor is summed up and used to place the decimal point in the product.

Example:

$2.36 \times 3.4 = 8.024 \qquad 2.36 = \frac{236}{100} \qquad 3.4 = \frac{34}{10}$

$\frac{236 \times 34}{10^2 \times 10^1} = \frac{8024}{10^3} = \frac{8024}{1000} = 8.024$

Division

Children who know a division algorithm for whole numbers should be able to divide with decimals.

Early division problems should involve whole number divisors.

Example: $5\overline{)25.75} \qquad 12\overline{)292.2}$

Using the principle that adding zeros does not change the value of the decimal, the second problem could easily be carried out to an even division. Division with decimal number divisors could be introduced with a problem and dialogue similar to that presented in Figure 12-14.

Problems involving decimal fraction divisors in the hundredths and mixed decimal numbers should be presented to children to discuss and solve. The following generalization should eventually be articulated: Multiplying both the divisor and the dividend by the same multiple of 10 does not affect the answer. The connection to equivalent decimals should be made as well (also to equivalent fractions, if appropriate at the time).

Example: $0.62\overline{)744}$ is like $\dfrac{744}{0.62}$

Writing equivalent fractions, we have

$$\frac{774}{0.62} \qquad \frac{7440}{6.2} \qquad \frac{74400}{62}$$

Decimal form: $0.62\overline{)744} \quad 6.2\overline{)7440} \quad 62\overline{)74400}$

Although a decimal division problem is commonly rewritten so that the divisor is a whole number, some children may wish to change both divisor and dividend to whole numbers before dividing.

Example: $0.36\overline{)2.695}$

$$\frac{2.695 \times 1000}{0.36 \times 1000} \rightarrow \frac{2695}{360} \rightarrow 360\overline{)2695}$$

Decimal form: $0.36 \times 1000 = 360$
$2.695 \times 1000 = 2695$

Therefore, $0.36\overline{)2.695} \rightarrow 360\overline{)2695}$

If children come to use the expression "move the decimal point *n* places to the right in the two numbers" when

FIGURE 12-14

Problem: Sheilagh has bought 12 m of ribbon to make bows to decorate flower pots. It takes 0.8 m of ribbon to make one bow. Sheilagh wants to figure out how many bows can be made with the length of ribbon she has.

Sheilagh first writes the problem question as

$$0.8\overline{)12}$$

Then she thinks: There are 10 tenths in 1 m
therefore 12 m = 120 tenths.

Using this knowledge, she rewrites the question as 120 tenths divided by 8 tenths

$$8\overline{)120}$$

Sheilagh then divides and finds that 12 m of ribbon can make 15 bows.

Questions to ask:
- What do you think of Sheilagh's work?
- Why is it proper to change the division question as Sheilagh did?
- Could Sheilagh have written a different division question and still have arrived at the answer?

---

dividing decimals, a teacher should question them to find out whether they understand why that "works."

Some children make errors in division situations that require zeros in the dividend. A good way to have children represent such division questions is to use money. Educational 1000-, 100-, and 10-dollar bills, and 1-dollar coins, dimes, and pennies can be distributed to groups of children to have them solve division problems by sharing amounts of money among different-sized groups of people. The situation of winning a lottery can provide a context for dividing up large amounts. By working through a problem such as $7387.20 to be shared among 24 people using "play" money, children will see the necessity of including a 0 in the dividend.

Estimating With Decimals

In their daily lives, children probably will estimate with decimals more frequently than they will calculate exact answers. It is therefore important that they learn estimation skills.

What are some of the techniques that facilitate estimation with decimal numbers? First of all, children must be able to read and write multidigit decimal numbers and understand place value of decimal fractions. They must also be able to order and compare decimals, and they must be able to round decimals (Vance, 1986a).

Children should have practice rounding decimal numbers. Two strategies to use are using the leading digit and using the rounded leading digit in a number.

Examples:

	Number	Rounded
Leading digit	365.75	300
	0.0463	0.04
Rounded leading digit	365.75	400
	0.0463	0.05

Estimates for sums and differences of decimal numbers can be obtained by using either the leading-digit or the rounded-leading-digit strategy. Children should recognize which strategies will give estimates that are more than or less than the actual numbers. This knowledge will enable them to decide when to use which strategy. Have them consider situations such as the following and decide which strategy they would use.

- You want to be certain that you have sufficient cash to pay for groceries.
- You know the amount the family pays for electricity per month and you want an estimate of the yearly cost.
- You have measurements to the nearest meter of the distance run by an athlete in a certain time during practice sessions. You want an approximation of the average distance the athlete runs in that time span.

In multiplication questions, the leading-digit strategy can produce significantly lower estimates than the actual product.

Example:

$$485 \times 0.23$$

leading digit	400×0.2	$\rightarrow$	80
rounding	500×0.2	$\rightarrow$	100
actual	485×0.23	$\rightarrow$	111.55

It appears that the rounded-digit strategy gives an estimate that is closer to the actual product than the leading-digit strategy. When rounding digits, one can round both factors up or round one factor up and the other factor down.

Example:

783×0.26	$\rightarrow$	800×0.3	$\rightarrow$	240
or	$\rightarrow$	800×0.2	$\rightarrow$	160
or	$\rightarrow$	700×0.3	$\rightarrow$	210
	actual		$\rightarrow$	203.64

In this case, the closest estimate is 210.

In division, when estimating quotients, it is a common practice to round both numbers in the same direction (up or down).

Example:

$0.28\overline{)675.94}$	$\rightarrow$	$0.3\overline{)700}$	$\rightarrow$	2333.30
	or	$0.2\overline{)600}$	$\rightarrow$	3000.0
	actual		$\rightarrow$	2414.07

In this case, the best estimate is the first one. If one used compatible numbers (evenly divisible), the division question would become $0.3\overline{)690}$, to arrive at an estimate of 2300.

WRITING FRACTIONS AS DECIMALS

Decimal number sense is enhanced by studying decimals in relationship to fractions. Exploring the decimal forms of different fractions in a systematic way is an opportunity to discover patterns and relationships.

Examples:

1. $\frac{3}{10} = 0.3$ $\quad \frac{3}{100} = 0.03$ $\quad \frac{3}{1000} = 0.003$

   $\frac{45}{10} = 4.5$ $\quad \frac{45}{100} = 0.45$ $\quad \frac{45}{1000} = 0.045$

2. Change the denominator to a power of ten

   $\frac{2}{5} = \frac{4}{10} = 0.4$

   $\frac{3}{20} = \frac{15}{100} = 0.15$

   $\frac{1}{8} = \frac{125}{1000} = 0.125$

3. Divide

   $\frac{3}{8} = 88\overline{)3.000}$

Using the Math Explorer Calculator

The Math Explorer calculator has the function $\boxed{\text{F} \rightleftarrows \text{D}}$ to change fractions to decimals or decimals to fractions in one step.

Example: To change $\frac{1}{3}$ to a decimal enter

$\frac{1}{3} \boxed{\text{F} \rightleftarrows \text{D}}$ Display: 0.3333333

Some fraction sequences that children could write as decimals are presented in Activity 12-10.

After they complete the activity, have children examine the sets of decimals for patterns. Discuss these patterns as a class.

When changing decimals to fractions, the Math Explorer calculator works only with terminating decimals.

Terminating and Repeating Decimals

When changing fractions to decimals by division, children will notice that some divide evenly and others do not. In the case of even division, the decimals produced are said to be *terminating decimals*. In uneven division, the decimals produced are called *repeating decimals*. It is possible to tell whether a fraction will result in a terminating or repeating decimal by finding the prime factors of its denominator. Fractions whose denominators have 2

ACTIVITY 12-10

WRITING FRACTIONS AS DECIMALS

MATERIALS
Calculator

PROCEDURE
Use a calculator to change several of the following fraction sequences to decimals. Look for patterns. Write the decimals.

1. $\frac{1}{2}, \frac{1}{3}, \frac{1}{4}, \frac{1}{5}, \frac{1}{6}, \frac{1}{7}, \frac{1}{8}, \frac{1}{9}$.

2. $\frac{1}{3}, \frac{2}{3}, \frac{1}{4}, \frac{2}{4}, \frac{3}{4}, \frac{1}{5}, \frac{2}{5}, \frac{3}{5}, \frac{4}{5}$.

3. All the proper fractions with 7 as denominator.

4. $\frac{1}{13}, \frac{1}{17}, \frac{1}{19}, \frac{1}{23}, \frac{1}{29}, \frac{1}{37}$.

5. $\frac{1}{9}, \frac{2}{9}, \frac{3}{9}, \frac{4}{9}, \frac{5}{9}, \frac{6}{9}, \frac{7}{9}, \frac{8}{9}$.

6. $\frac{1}{11}, \frac{2}{11}, \frac{3}{11}, \frac{4}{11}, \frac{5}{11}, \ldots$

or 5 as their prime factors will be terminating decimals; fractions with denominators that have other prime factors (not 2 or 5) will be repeating decimals.

In a repeating decimal, the group of digits that repeat is known as the *repetend*. The repetend is indicated by a bar over the repeating digits.

Example:

$\frac{2}{3}$	0.666666 . . .	$0.\overline{6}$
$\frac{1}{12}$	0.0833333 . . .	$0.08\overline{3}$
$\frac{1}{7}$	0.142857142857 . . .	$0.\overline{142857}$

SCIENTIFIC NOTATION

Middle-school children will learn to express numbers in a special notation called *scientific notation*. Scientific notation reduces the number of digits to record in a numeral by expressing numbers as the product of two factors; the first factor is a number greater than or equal to 1 and less than 10 and the second factor is a power of 10.

- The United States produces approximately 42 000 000 tons of garbage every year. This amount expressed in scientific notation is 4.2×10^7

- The diameter of an electron is 0.00 000 000 000 056 354 cm, or 5.6354×10^{-13}.

Although scientific notation generally is used when dealing with very large or very small numbers, any number can be expressed in that notation. Study the following examples to find out what happens to the decimal point when a number is greater than 1 and when a number is greater than 0 but smaller than 1.

6	→	6×10^0
386.5	→	3.865×10^2
0.2006	→	2.006×10^{-1}
0.00007	→	7×10^{-5}

In 386.5, the four digits are called significant digits because they appear when the number is expressed in scientific notation; in 0.0007, the 7 is significant because it alone appears in scientific notation. It is possible to compute numbers written in scientific notation using the laws of exponents.

CONCLUSION

The focus of this chapter has been the development of understanding of decimals. The main goal of instruction is to develop understanding of decimals in order to operate intelligently and effectively with them. Children should come to view decimals as an extension of place-value numeration and as another way to symbolize fractions. Activities have been presented to help children develop a good sense of decimals so that together with fractions, they enable children to use these rational numbers to solve problems.

For Your Journal

When you have finished studying this chapter, reflect on the following questions in your math journal:

1. What concepts about decimals should children understand? Draw pictures showing how to use a model to illustrate each concept.

2. Write a word problem for each operation and draw a picture showing how to solve the problem using a model.

3. How can a teacher help children understand decimals and decimal computation?

For Your Portfolio

When you have finished studying this chapter, complete the following activities to include in your professional portfolio:

1. Write a lesson to help children understand a decimal concept of your choice.

2. Write a lesson to introduce decimal computation (for an operation of your choice) by linking this topic to fraction computation.

3. Visit an intermediate-grade classroom and informally interview several children to assess their understanding of decimal concepts and computation. Write a short paper describing their understanding and discuss what you would do next if you were their classroom teacher.

Resources for Teachers

Books on decimals
Bennett, A. (1982). *Decimal squares: Step-by-step teacher's guide.* USA: Scott Resources.
Creative Publications. (1994). *Beyond Activities Project Mathematics replacement curriculum: Getting to the point! Investigating decimals.* Mountain View, CA: Author.

Links to the Internet

Real World Math
http://www.realworldmath.com/

Contains an integrated simulation of travel for Grades 3–8 in which children apply the concepts of measurement, multiplication, division, decimals, and time by planning vacations across given states.

Explorer: Decimals
http://explorer.scrtec.org/explorer-db/browse/static/Mathematics/index.html

Contains links to lessons and activities involving decimals.

CHAPTER 13

Understanding Ratio, Proportion, and Percent

KEY CONCEPTS

✔ **Ratio**

✔ **Rate**

✔ **Proportion**

✔ **Unit rate**

✔ **Percent**

FOCUS QUESTIONS

When you have finished studying this chapter, you should be able to answer the following questions:

1. How do ratios, rates, unit rates, proportions, and percents differ from one another?

2. What are some real-world settings in which ratio, rate, unit rate, proportion, and percent are used?

3. What models can be used to help children understand percents?

SPEED 55 LIMIT

Other than familiar signs such as the one shown, real-world examples involving the ratio concept include the following:

✔ Two candy bars for 97¢.

✔ The map scale is 1:1 000 000.

✔ Sales tax is 7%.

NCTM CONTENT STANDARDS AND EXPECTATIONS ADDRESSED IN THIS CHAPTER

STANDARD	EXPECTATIONS FOR GRADES 3–5	EXPECTATIONS FOR GRADES 6–8
Number and Operations Standard Instructional programs from pre-K–12 should enable all students to—	In Grades 3–5 all students should— (NCTM, 2000, p. 148)	In Grades 6–8 all students should—(NCTM, 2000, p. 214)
Understand numbers, ways of representing numbers, relationships among numbers, and number systems	• recognize and generate equivalent forms of commonly used fractions, decimals, and percents.	• work flexibly with fractions, decimals, and percents to solve problems. • compare and order fractions, decimals, and percents efficiently and find their approximate locations on a number line. • develop meaning for percents greater than 100 and less than 1. • understand and use ratios and proportions to represent quantitative relationships.
Compute fluently and make reasonable estimates		• develop, analyze, and explain methods for solving problems involving proportions, such as scaling and finding equivalent ratios.

Ratio, proportion, and percent are important topics in the mathematics program in the middle-school grades. Meaningful instruction builds on and extends understanding of fractions and decimals and emphasizes problem solving and applications in real-world situations. This chapter describes and illustrates the key concepts for these topics, points out potential sources of difficulty, and suggests teaching strategies and problem settings for use in the classroom. ✔

RATIO AND RATE

A *ratio* is a comparison of two numbers or quantities. As illustrated in the examples presented at the beginning of this chapter, the ratio concept arises in many practical and scientific situations and in several different mathematical contexts. When the measuring units describing two quantities being compared are different, the ratio is called a *rate*. Many everyday examples involve speed (Lisa ran 100 m in 12 sec) or price (12 ears of corn for $2.50). When the second term is 1, the rate is referred to as the *unit rate*. Thus, typing 40 words per minute and earning $5.50 per hour are unit rates.

PRINCIPLES AND STANDARDS LINK 13-1
Content Strand: Number and Operations

In grades 6–8 all students should—

- work flexibly with fractions, decimals, and percents to solve problems; . . .
- understand and use ratios and proportions to represent quantitative relationships. . . . (NCTM, 2000, p. 214)

PRINCIPLES AND STANDARDS LINK 13-2
Content Strand: Number and Operations

Attention to developing flexibility in working with rational numbers contributes to students' understanding of, and facility with, proportionality. Facility with proportionality involves much more than setting two ratios equal and solving for a missing term. It involves recognizing quantities that are related proportionally and using numbers, tables, graphs, and equations to think about the quantities and their relationship. Proportionality is an important integrative thread that connects many of the mathematics topics studied in grades 6–8. (NCTM, 2000, p. 216)

In the early grades, children learn about comparison subtraction situations. In intermediate grades, ratio is introduced as another way of comparing two quantities. For example, given 6 balls and 3 bats, we could say that there are 3 more balls than bats, but we also note that there are twice as many balls as bats or that there are 2 balls for every bat. The idea of ratio involves *multiplicative* rather than additive comparisons.

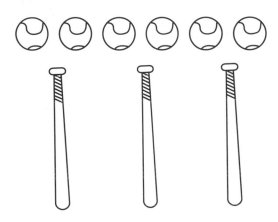

There has been a disappointingly low level of understanding about ratio and proportions among children in the United States (Cramer, Post, & Currier, 1993; Hoffer & Hoffer, 1992). The sixth National Assessment of Educational Progress (NAEP) assessment also noted a low level of success by 4th, 8th, and 12th graders (Kouba, Zawojewski, & Struchens, 1997). Most children incorrectly solved ratio problems by performing a one-step operation. For example, consider the following problem given to fourth graders.

A package of birdseed costs $2.58 for 2 pounds. A package of sunflower seeds costs $3.72 for 3 pounds. What is the difference in the cost per pound?

Most fourth graders chose an answer of $1.14, which is the difference between the two costs listed in the problem, neither of which is the cost *per pound*. Only 8% of the fourth graders answered this problem with the correct answer of $0.05, which is the difference between the cost per pound of birdseed ($1.29) and the cost per pound of sunflower seeds ($1.24). These results indicate a need for increased emphasis on understanding and reasonableness in instruction about ratios and rates.

Language and Notation

To introduce the language and notation, the teacher might refer to a picture or a sketch of 3 pelicans and 2 frogs. The children are told that the *ratio* of pelicans to frogs in this picture is 3 to 2 and that this can be written $3:2$ or $\frac{3}{2}$. They can then be asked to state and write the ratio of frogs to pelicans $(2:3)$ and the ratio of pelicans to animals (3 : 5). Note that this last ratio is a *part-to-whole comparison,* whereas the other two are *part-to-part comparisons.* The two numbers in a ratio are referred to as the *first term* and the *second term.*

Ratio and Rational Number

Number and ratio are different concepts, but the word "*rati*onal" and the use of the fraction symbol for a ratio suggest that there are overlapping elements. Because a fraction represents a part-to-whole relationship, fractions are types of ratios. In the previous example, the ratio of pelicans to animals is 3 to 5 and three-fifths of the animals are pelicans. The two ideas are essentially the same and both are represented by the symbol $\frac{3}{5}$. However, 2 frogs to 3 pelicans is a part-to-part comparison and, in this situation, the ratio 2 to 3 is quite different from the fraction $\frac{2}{3}$. We note further in this example that although the ratios 2 to 3 and 3 to 2 can both be used to express the relationship between the numbers of pelicans and frogs, the fractions $\frac{2}{3}$ and $\frac{3}{2}$ name different rational numbers.

Children should also understand that combining ratios is not the same as adding fractions. To illustrate, suppose there are 2 boys and 3 girls in one group and 3 boys and 4 girls in another group. If the two groups joined, the ratio of boys to girls would be 5 to 7. However, the sum of the numbers $\frac{2}{3}$ and $\frac{3}{4}$ is definitely not $\frac{5}{7}$! Similarly, whereas the ratio of boys to children could be expressed as $\frac{5}{12}$, it would be incorrect to write $\frac{2}{5} + \frac{3}{7} = \frac{5}{12}$. Arithmetic operations such as addition are performed on numbers, not on ratios.

PROPORTION

Aaron reasons: "If 3 oranges cost 60¢, then 6 oranges would cost $1.20 and 1 orange would cost 20¢" (see diagram at bottom of page).

A *proportion* is a statement that two ratios are equal. Finding unit rates and making scale drawings are examples of proportion problems.

Proportional Reasoning

The ability to understand ratios is one aspect of *proportional reasoning,* which is considered to be an indicator of a shift from concrete to formal operational levels of thought. Proportional reasoning involves both qualitative and quantitative thinking and concerns prediction and multiple comparisons (Lesh, Post, & Behr, 1989).

Ratio is a difficult concept because it involves a relationship between two quantities. At first children tend to focus on only one of the parts of a ratio. Quintero (1987) found that many 9-year-olds will predict that 6 tablespoons of white sugar mixed with 8 tablespoons of brown sugar would be lighter in color than 4 tablespoons of white sugar mixed with 3 tablespoons of brown sugar, because 6 is larger than 4.

Considerable research has been conducted to investigate children's thinking as they solve proportion problems. A version of one widely used task, "Mr. Short and Mr. Tall" (Karplus, Karplus, & Wollman, 1974), is described in Figure 13-1. On items such as this, many children use an incorrect addition strategy, focusing on the difference between the numbers, rather than on their

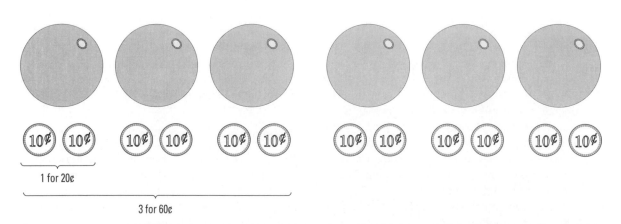

1 for 20¢

3 for 60¢

6 for $1.20

FIGURE 13-1

Mr. Short (shown) is 4 buttons high.

Mr. Tall (not shown) is 6 buttons high.

Use paper clips to measure Mr. Short (6).

How many paper clips high will Mr. Tall be?

ratio. Thus, they will say 8 paper clips are needed, because there are 2 more buttons. Even children who have been taught ratio and proportion will sometimes use this method, particularly if the ratio involved is not a simple one such as 1 : 2.

On easy proportion questions, some children will consistently use repeated addition rather than multiplication. Consider the following problem:

Snakes are fed according to their length. If the 5-inch-long snake is fed 2 cubes of food, how many cubes of food should the 10-inch and 15-inch snakes be fed?

A common solution is to add 2 cubes of food for the 10-inch snake and 2 more for the 15-inch snake, rather than multiplying 2 times 2 and 3 times 2 (Hart, 1989). Children who use addition rather than multiplication have difficulty solving proportions involving more complex relationships.

Equal Ratios

Introductory experiences for equal ratios include activities involving number patterns and repeated addition. For example, children in the early grades could be asked to make a table showing the relationship between the number of horses and the number of legs. The children might use toy animals to make sketches in solving the problem.

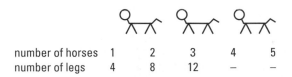

number of horses	1	2	3	4	5
number of legs	4	8	12	–	–

It is important that older children see the multiplicative relationship in the number pairs. They should be able to use multiplication directly to determine how many legs 9 horses have and use division to figure out the number of horses that corresponds to 28 legs. Frequent group oral questions such as "If a video costs 4 dollars to rent, how much would it cost to rent 7 videos?" and "If 3 child movie tickets cost 15 dollars, how much would one ticket cost?" should be asked.

As children examine the horses and legs table on this page, they note that if 1 horse has 4 legs, then 2 horses have 8 legs, and so on. The teacher states that the ratios 1 to 4 and 2 to 8 are *equal* and writes:

$$1 : 4 = 2 : 8 \text{ or } \frac{1}{4} = \frac{2}{8}$$

Children should be encouraged to discover and verbalize the procedure for generating equal ratios: multiply both terms by the same (counting) number. They should also explore what happens when the same number is added to both terms and conclude that the resulting ratios are usually not equal. For example:

$$\frac{1}{4} \neq \frac{(1 + 2)}{(4 + 2)}$$

Children will likely see the connection with the rule for writing equivalent fractions. The use of the same notation for ratios and fractions could be discussed in this context. Finding a lower-terms ratio is accomplished by dividing both terms by the same number; the connection to the procedure for simplifying fractions is immediate. This idea is applied in finding a unit rate as in the following problem.

Brian types 100 words in 4 minutes. How many words is that per minute?

Since $\frac{100}{4} = \frac{25}{1}$*, the unit rate is 25 words per minute*

In Activity 13-1, children write equal ratios suggested by a diagram.

Introductory questions that require children to find a missing term in a pair of equal ratios should involve only whole number multiplication, as in the following problem.

MARBLE RATIOS

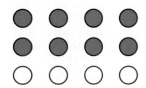

- What is the ratio of blue marbles to white marbles in the picture? Can you write the ratio in more than one way?
- Now write the ratio of blue marbles to marbles in as many ways as you can.

If the ratio of children to adults is 17 to 2 and there are 6 adults, how many children are there?

If we let n represent the number of children,

$$\frac{17}{2} = \frac{n}{6}$$

Since 6 = 2 × 3, n = 17 × 3 = 51. There are 51 children.

Comparing Ratios

Which mixture will be lighter in color—3 parts white sugar to 5 parts brown sugar or 2 parts white sugar to 3 parts brown sugar? Questions such as this can be used to motivate the idea of renaming the two ratios so that they have the same second term. So to compare $\frac{3}{5}$ and $\frac{2}{3}$, we might look at $\frac{9}{15}$ and $\frac{10}{15}$. We conclude that the ratio of white to brown sugar is greater in the second mixture. The second mixture will be slightly lighter in color, although this might be difficult to discern visually.

This is, of course, the same procedure as that learned for comparing two fractions. A common second term or denominator is a common multiple of the two second terms or denominators. In some cases, it is easiest to use the least common multiple. For example, to compare $\frac{3}{4}$ and $\frac{5}{8}$, we would likely consider $\frac{6}{8}$ and $\frac{5}{8}$, and for $\frac{3}{4}$ and $\frac{5}{6}$ we might write $\frac{9}{12}$ and $\frac{10}{12}$. However, children should appreciate that any common multiple of the two second terms will work and that a particularly easy one to find is the product of the two numbers. Thus, $\frac{3}{4}$ and $\frac{5}{6}$ could also be compared as $\frac{18}{24}$ and $\frac{20}{24}$, where 24 is the product of 4 and 6.

In a basketball game Amy made 3 of 5 free throws and Diane made 4 of 7 attempts. Which performance was better?

We write equal ratios with 5 × 7 as the second term.

$$\frac{3}{5} \qquad\qquad \frac{4}{7}$$

$$\frac{3 \times 7}{5 \times 7} \qquad \frac{5 \times 4}{5 \times 7}$$

$$\frac{21}{35} \qquad\qquad \frac{20}{35}$$

Amy's shooting was slightly better than Diane's.

Number sense reasoning, which is similar to that used in comparing fractions, can also be used to compare ratios. For example, the relations $\frac{4}{7} > \frac{4}{9}$, $\frac{5}{6} < \frac{6}{7}$, and $\frac{3}{5} > \frac{4}{9}$ are true whether the symbols apply to fractions or to ratios. Although these relations can be verified by computing equal ratios, children should be challenged to use quantitative explanations. A child might think about the preceding relations as follows: 4 hits out of 7 times at bat is better than 4 hits out of 9; if I have made 5 of 6 free throws during a game and make my next one, I will be 6 for 7; 3 out of 5 is more than half, whereas 4 out of 9 is less than half.

Cross Products

Given several pairs of equal ratios such as $\frac{3}{6} = \frac{5}{10}$, children can be challenged to find a relationship among the four terms. They should be able to discover that the *cross products* are equal: $3 \times 10 = 6 \times 5$.

Children should also be able to explain why this relationship holds. Comparing $\frac{3}{6}$ and $\frac{5}{10}$ by finding equal ratios with 60 as the second term, we multiply both terms of the first ratio by 10 and both terms of the second ratio by 6, giving 3×10 and 6×5, respectively, as the first terms. Thus, computing cross products provides a simple test for determining whether two ratios (or fractions) are equal. We can tell, for example, that $\frac{2}{3} \neq \frac{3}{4}$ because $2 \times 4 \neq 3 \times 3$.

In addition, if three of the four terms in a proportion are given, the fourth can be calculated directly using the cross product relationship. This method is particularly useful where noninteger ratios are involved.

If 3 pounds of apples cost $4.00, how many pounds could you get for $6.00?

$4 \times n = 3 \times 6 = 18$; n = 18 ÷ 4 = 4.5. You would get 4.5 pounds.

Note that instead of considering the pounds-to-dollar ratios, we could have written the proportion $\frac{3}{n} = \frac{4}{6}$, which relates the pound-to-pound ratio and the dollar-to-dollar ratio. Two other proportions that model this situation and lead to the same computations are created by interchanging the first and second terms: $\frac{4}{3} = \frac{6}{n}$ and $\frac{n}{3} = \frac{6}{4}$.

PRINCIPLES AND STANDARDS LINK 13-3
Content Strand: Number and Operations

Instruction in solving proportions should include methods that have a strong intuitive basis. The so-called cross-multiplication method can be developed meaningfully if it arises naturally in students' work, but it can also have unfortunate side effects when students do not adequately understand when the method is appropriate to use. Other approaches to solving proportions are often more intuitive and also quite powerful. (NCTM, 2000, p. 220)

A more direct way to solve the first proportion above is to reason that because 6 is 1.5 times 4, $n = 3 \times 1.5 = 4.5$. But in most real-life situations the numbers are large or "messy" and the cross product method, using a calculator to perform the multiplication and division, is the most efficient procedure. In the previous example, the apples would more likely be priced at 3 pounds for $3.95 rather than $4.00.

The majority of proportion problems in the intermediate grades should have solutions that do not require the use of cross products. Although the cross product algorithm is a powerful tool, children should appreciate that many problems can be solved in more than one way and be encouraged to look for alternative solutions. See Activity 13-2 and the soup problem that follows.

A recipe for soup for 8 people calls for 6 onions. How many onions should be used in preparing soup for 12 people?

$\frac{8}{6} = \frac{12}{n}$

Then $8n = 6 \times 12 = 72$ and $n = 9$.

Therefore, 9 onions are needed.

There are several things that might be discussed by a class after examining this solution. First, the proportion $\frac{8}{6} = \frac{12}{n}$ can be solved without using cross products. One way is to note that $\frac{8}{6} = \frac{4}{3}$ and consider $\frac{4}{3} = \frac{12}{n}$. Because $12 = 4 \times 3$, $n = 3 \times 3$. Second, we could have also considered the ratios, 8 people to 12 people and 6 onions to n onions, and written the proportion $\frac{8}{12} = \frac{6}{n}$. Two other proportions describing the same situation are $\frac{6}{8} = \frac{n}{12}$ and $\frac{12}{8} = \frac{n}{6}$. In all three cases the numerical ratio can be simplified. Finally, we could reason that because there are 4

more people and 4 is half of 8, you would make a recipe and a half. Therefore, you would need 6 plus 3 onions.

Scale Drawings

Reading maps and floor plans, enlarging or reducing pictures, and finding corresponding dimensions of similar geometric figures all involve the idea of a *scale*. A scale drawing is a smaller or larger representation of an object. The scale is the ratio of a dimension in the drawing to the corresponding dimension of the actual object. Three sample problems and solutions follow.

Below is a scale drawing of a bee. Find the bee's actual length.

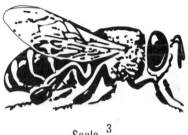

Scale $\frac{3}{1}$

The length of the bee in the scale drawing is about 48 mm. Therefore the bee's length is one-third of 48 mm, which is about 16 mm. The related proportion is $\frac{3}{1} = \frac{48}{n}$.

The scale on a city street map reads:

1 in. = 3 miles

1 : 3

Find the distance between two schools 7 inches apart on the map.

7 inches represents 7×3 miles $= 21$ miles. So the schools are about 21 miles apart. The related proportion is $\frac{1}{3} = \frac{7}{n}$.

In the following diagram, the second triangle is an enlargement of the first. Find the scale ratio of the enlargement and compute the length of the longest side of the larger triangle.

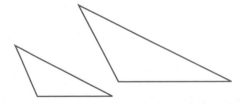

Using a ruler, we find that the bases of the triangles measure 2 cm and 3 cm. Therefore, the scale ratio for the

ACTIVITY 13-2

TRAVEL ON

Solve the following problem in at least two different ways.

A car travels 212 km in 4 hours. At this rate of speed, how far would it travel in 7 hours?

PRINCIPLES AND STANDARDS LINK 13-4
Content Strand: Number and Operations

As different ways to think about proportions are considered and discussed, teachers should help students recognize when and how various ways of reasoning about proportions might be appropriate to solve problems. (NCTM, 2000, p. 220)

BUYING POTATOES

An 8-kg sack of potatoes costs $2.49, whereas a 25-kg sack sells for $6.99.

- Determine which is the better buy in at least two different ways.
- Discuss your conclusion.

enlargement is 3:2 (or 150%). Measuring the longest side of the smaller triangle, we find that its length is 3 cm. We can compute the length of the corresponding side of the enlarged triangle using a proportion, and then compare the answer with the measured length.

$$\frac{2}{3} = \frac{3}{n}$$

The length is 4.5 cm.

Comparison Shopping

Determining which size of package gives the most product for the money is another type of problem involving ratios that can be solved in several ways. The data in the following example were taken from the bread counter in a major supermarket.

A 16-ounce loaf of bread costs $1.99, and a 24-ounce loaf costs $2.49. Which loaf of bread is the better buy?

The unit price is the cost of 1 ounce of bread. The unit price of the smaller loaf is $1.99/16 = $0.12 per ounce, and the unit price of the larger loaf is $2.49/24 = $0.10 per ounce. Because the larger loaf has a lower unit price, it is the better buy.

This solution involves complex calculations that would usually be done using a calculator. A shopper in a store might use mental arithmetic to solve this problem as follows: The 16-ounce loaf is 1 pound and the 24-ounce loaf is $1\frac{1}{2}$ pounds. One-and-a-half of the smaller loaves would cost $1.99 plus half of $1.99, which is about $2 + $1 = $3. The larger loaf costs only $2.49, which is less than $3, so the larger loaf is the better buy.

The class should discuss why the largest size package does not always have the lowest unit price and also why the lowest unit price might not always represent the "best buy" (see Activity 13-3).

PERCENT

Percents are used in many everyday situations. Unfortunately, they are also frequently misused. For example, a store advertises prices reduced by 100% (rather than

50%), an interest rate of .13% is offered (rather than 13%), and a newspaper reports murders up by 200% (correct, but a little misleading, since they went from 1 to 3).

What do we know of U.S. children's understanding of percents? The sixth National Assessment of Educational Progress (NAEP) noted a low level of performance by 8th and 12th graders, whose average total correct ranged between 33% and 40% on questions involving percent (Kouba et al., 1997). A particular concern was the high number of children giving unreasonable answers. For example, children were asked to find the total cost of a used car bought for $5375 plus 15% tax. Twenty-five percent of the 8th graders and 20% of the 12th graders selected an answer of $806, which is the correct amount of tax but not the correct *total cost* of the car. As with ratio and proportion, these disappointing results point to a need for increased emphasis on understanding and reasonableness in instruction about percents.

Meaning and Notation

The term percent means "parts per hundred." A *percent* is a part-to-whole ratio that has 100 as its second term. For example, seven percent means seven parts per hundred, which is written 7;100, or $\frac{7}{100}$. We introduce the notation 7%, noting the connection between the percent symbol and the numeral 100.

> 7 per hundred
> 7 percent
> 7:100
> 7%

A 7% tax on a $100 item is $7. The $100 is referred to as the *base*, 7% is the *rate*, and $7 is the *percentage*. Because percents are part-to-whole ratios, they can also be thought of as fractions with denominators of 100. Expressed as common or decimal fractions, percents can be treated as numbers and used in arithmetic computations.

Number Sense

Introductory activities should help children form visual images and develop a quantitative feel for numbers expressed as percents. An effective pictorial model is a 10-by-10 grid that children shade to represent various percents (Figure 13-2). Corresponding activities at the concrete level involve placing small cubes on the flat of the base-ten materials.

Special emphasis should be placed on 1%, 50%, and 100%. Other important benchmarks are 10% and 25%. Children naturally come to associate these ratios with their corresponding common fractions. Percents less than 1 (such as $\frac{1}{2}$%) and percents greater than 100 (such as 150%) can also be represented using the grid model (Figure 13-3).

FIGURE 13-2

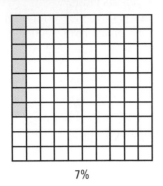 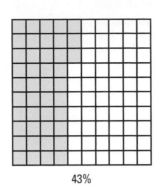 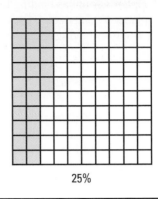

7%   43%   25%

The following activities, which use an unmarked rectangle, can help children develop estimation skills with percents.

1. Shade about 50%, 10%, 75%, 2%, 97%, 35%.

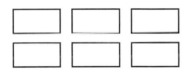

2. About what percent has been shaded in each rectangle?

Fraction and Decimal Equivalents

A key idea in mathematics is that numbers can be represented in many ways. A rational number can be expressed as a fraction, a decimal, or a percent. As children show percents on a 10-by-10 grid and reflect on the language they use to describe their representations, the fraction and decimal names for the numbers will become apparent. For example, because 9% means 9 out of 100, it is nine-hundredths, which is written $\frac{9}{100}$ in fraction notation and 0.09 in decimal notation.

9%   nine-hundredths $\frac{9}{100}$ 0.09

Further, $150\% = \frac{150}{100} = 1.5 = \frac{3}{2} = 1\frac{1}{2}$

Decimals as percents   Writing a decimal as a percent involves finding an equivalent decimal in hundredths. For example,

three-tenths = thirty-hundredths = thirty percent

0.3 = 0.30 = 30%

Generalizing from examples such as 17 hundredths = 17 percent (0.17 = 17%), children find that to change a decimal to a percent, one multiplies by 100, which means "moving" the decimal point two places to the right. Thus, 0.135 = 13.5% and 9.1 = 910%. To express a percent as a decimal, the opposite rule is employed: divide by 100. Thus, 6.9% = 0.069.

FIGURE 13-3

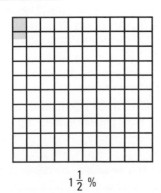 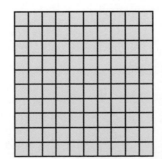 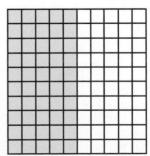

$1\frac{1}{2}$ %   150%

Fractions as percents Children can be challenged to apply their understanding to find ways of writing a fraction as a percent. A basic method is to find an equivalent fraction having a denominator of 100. For example,

$$\frac{2}{5} = \frac{40}{100} = 40\%$$

Another procedure is to first write the fraction in decimal form and then multiply this number by 100. Children recall that one way of accomplishing the first step is to divide the numerator by the denominator: $2 \div 5 = 0.4 = 40\%$. Multiplying the numerator by 100 before dividing by the denominator would give the same answer: $200 \div 5 = 40$, which means 40%.

$$
\begin{array}{r}
0.4 \\
5)\overline{2.0} \\
\underline{2.0} \\
0
\end{array}
\qquad
\begin{array}{r}
40 \\
5)\overline{200} \\
\underline{20} \\
00
\end{array}
$$

In most cases the computation would be carried out with the aid of a calculator. To express $\frac{3}{8}$ as a percent, press $3 \div 8 =$ and mentally multiply the answer 0.375 by 100. Alternatively, pressing $300 \div 8 =$ gives 37.5. Children can later be shown that on most simple calculators, pressing $3 \div 8\%$ gives 37.5 directly.

Some fractions have repeating decimal representations. When children attempt to shade $\frac{1}{3}$ of 100 squares, they find they shade 33 whole squares and a third of one square. Thus, $\frac{1}{3} = 33\frac{1}{3}\%$. Rounding to the nearest whole number, we say that $\frac{1}{3}$ is about 33%. Calculators should be used to help find approximate percent equivalents for fractions with repeating decimal representations. For example,

$$\frac{5}{12} = 0.41666 \ldots, \text{ which child rounds to 42\%.}$$

Percents as fractions Expressing a percent as a fraction with a denominator of 100 is accomplished by applying the definition of percent: $67\% = \frac{67}{100}$. In some cases, the resulting fraction can be written in simpler form:

$$8\% = \frac{8}{100} = \frac{2}{25}$$

$$87.5\% = \frac{87.5}{100} = \frac{875}{1000} = \frac{7}{8}$$

The Math Explorer calculator (Texas Instruments) is programmed to carry out these computations.

Keystrokes	Display
87.5%	0.875
F⇄D	875/1000
Simp =	175/200
Simp =	35/40
Simp =	7/8

There are several computer programs that deal with equivalent percents, decimals, and fractions. Activity 13-4 describes a card game, Math Rummy (Brown,

ACTIVITY 13-4

MATH RUMMY

MATERIALS
Deck of 52 cards comprising 13 numbers in 4 equivalent forms.

PROCEDURE
Two, three, or four players can play. The object of the game is to lay all your cards down.

1. Begin by dealing seven cards to each player. The remainder of the pack is placed face down on the table. The top card is then placed face up next to the pack to begin the discard pile.

2. The first player may either draw the top card from the face down pile or pick up the top card on the discard pile. The player must then discard a card, and the play goes to the next player.

3. When one player has accumulated three cards of equivalent value, these are laid face up on the table. The player who has the fourth equivalent value for the set lays that card face up on the table in front of himself or herself. The player next to the one who laid down the three equivalent cards continues the play.

4. When the pack is gone, the discard pile is turned over and becomes the pack.

5. The first player to lay down all his or her cards wins that hand. Each player receives 5 points for every card laid down and −5 points for every card still held.

6. The game is over when one player has 100 points.

1973), which provides practice in recognizing fraction, decimal, and percent names of common numbers. To prepare a deck of 52 cards, make a list of 13 numbers, each of which has four equivalent forms. For example: $20\% = \frac{20}{100} = \frac{1}{5} = 0.2$.

Finding the Percent of a Number

Computing sales tax, discount, commission, and interest are examples of everyday situations involving finding a percent of a number. To help children understand that the operation involved is multiplication, a problem such as the following might be presented:

In our class of 28 children, 50% went skiing during winter break. How many of our class members went skiing?

Children know that 50% is one-half and that one-half *of* 28 is expressed by $\frac{1}{2} \times 28$. The general procedure then is to express the percent in either fraction or decimal form and multiply by the other given number.

Early examples should involve percents that have simple fraction or decimal equivalents (such as 50%, 25%, 10%, 200%), together with numbers chosen so that the computation can be carried out using mental arithmetic procedures for multiplying a whole number by a unit fraction or power of 10.

$$50\% \text{ of } 28 = \frac{1}{2} \times 28 = \frac{28}{2} = 14$$

$$25\% \text{ of } 80 = \frac{1}{4} \times 80 = \frac{80}{4} = 20$$

$$10\% \text{ of } 70 = \frac{1}{10} \times 70 = \frac{70}{10} = 7$$

$$100\% \text{ of } 63 = 63$$

$$200\% \text{ of } 45 = 2 \times 45 = 90$$

$$30\% \text{ of } 80 = 0.3 \times 80 = 24$$

$$10\% \text{ of } 235 = 0.1 \times 235 = 23.5$$

$$1\% \text{ of } 469 = 0.01 \times 469 = 4.69$$

Because most real-life computations will be carried out using a calculator, children need to learn to estimate answers and judge the reasonableness of results. This requires a good sense of number and the ability to do mental arithmetic with rounded or "special" numbers. Examples such as the following should be discussed and practiced.

49% of 85	about $\frac{1}{2}$ of 84
102% of 543	a little more than 543
31% of 68	about $\frac{1}{3}$ of 69 or 0.3×70
9.5% of 752	a little less than 75
36% of 851	about 0.4×800

To estimate a 6% sales tax on a purchase of $135.97, the shopper might think: 10% is about $14; 6% would be a bit more than half or about $8. With a calculator: $135.97 \times 0.06 =$ gives 8.1582; the tax is $8.16. Later, children learn that they can use the percent key rather than the decimal form of the percent: $135.97 \times 6\%$ gives 8.1582 directly.

The following activity is described by Vance (1982). Seventh graders working in pairs were given department store catalogs (and calculators) and told that they had $400 to purchase clothing. They were to assume a 20% discount on prices listed and 6% sales tax. The children began by identifying several items they wanted to buy. They would then find the total cost, compute the discount and the sale price, and finally compute the tax and find the total cost. After comparing this figure with $400, they would add or delete items and repeat the process. The problem soon became that of finding the maximum list price that would lead to a final cost of not more than $400 after the discount and tax were considered. Several interesting alternative procedures and hypotheses were generated and evaluated by the various groups as they worked toward a solution.

1. Could you simply subtract 14% (20% − 6%) from the list price to get the final cost price? (No)
2. Do you get the same final answer if you first add the tax and then subtract the discount (on the list plus the tax), rather than doing it the other way? (Surprisingly, yes)
3. Can you compute the sale price in one step? (Yes, multiply by 0.8)
4. Given the sale price, can you compute the final cost in one step? (Yes, multiply by 1.06)

Given the last two results, some groups wrote the following equation:

final cost = list price $\times$ 0.8 $\times$ 1.06 = list price $\times$ .848

They were then able to compute the maximum list price directly:

$$\$400 \div 0.848 = \$471.70.$$

Several children came close to this figure by repeatedly using the guess and check method.

Finding the Percent

The Owls soccer team won 13 of 20 games played last season. What percent of its games did the team win?

Finding what percent one number is of another amounts to expressing the corresponding fraction as a percent. Thus, $\frac{13}{20} = \frac{65}{100} = 65\%$. As previously discussed, this can be done on a calculator by dividing 13 by 20 and (mentally) multiplying by 100, by dividing 1300 by 20, or by pressing 13 ÷ 20%. Before children are shown this last calculator procedure, they need to have many experiences computing easy examples and estimating answers to more difficult questions. Consider the following sample questions and solutions:

$$\frac{3}{5} = \frac{60}{100} = 65\%$$

$\frac{4}{7}$ is close to half, so it is just over 50%

$\frac{23}{70}$ is about $\frac{1}{3}$, so it is about 33%

$\frac{8}{9}$ is almost 1, so it is a little less than 100%

$\frac{3}{478}$ is small—under 1%

Other Procedures for Solving Percent Problems

In the previous two sections, instructional strategies for finding the percentage and the rate were presented. For both types of problems, the solutions follow directly from the meaning of percent. Three other approaches to solving percent problems are now considered: the proportion method, the equation method, and the unitary analysis method.

The proportion method The statement 30% of 70 = 21 can be written as a proportion:

$$\frac{30}{100} = \frac{21}{70}$$

Therefore, given two of the three numbers 30, 21, and 70, we can compute the third using cross products. To find 30% of 70, we let n represent the percentage and solve the proportion $\frac{30}{100} = \frac{n}{70}$. To find what percent 21 is of 70, we let n represent the rate and solve the proportion $\frac{n}{100} = \frac{21}{70}$.

Although this can be a meaningful and very powerful method, it should not be introduced until children have

learned to find a percent of a number and what percent one number is of another, as previously discussed. Writing a proportion is an excellent way of solving problems in which the base is to be found.

Of the sixth-grade children in a school, 21 usually walk to school. This represents 30% of the sixth-grade children.

How many sixth graders are there?

$\frac{30}{100} = \frac{21}{n}$

$30n = 2100$

$n = 70$

There are 70 sixth graders.

To help children see the structure of a proportion problem and estimate the answer, Dewar (1984) suggests having them complete a comparison scale. The steps for the previous example are shown in Figure 13-4. From the two scales it seems reasonable that because 30 is just less than a third of 100, n should be a bit more than 3 times 21.

The equation method The statement 30% of 70 = 21 is represented by the equation 30% × 70 = 21. Given two of these three numbers, the third can be computed by inspection or using inverse operations. To find what percent 21 is of 70, we solve for the variable n in the equation $n \times 70 = 21$. Because $n = 0.3$, the rate is 30%.

If the base is unknown, we solve for n in the equation $0.3 \times n = 21$. Neither this method nor rules such as "to find the base divide the number by the percent" should be formally taught to elementary-school chil-

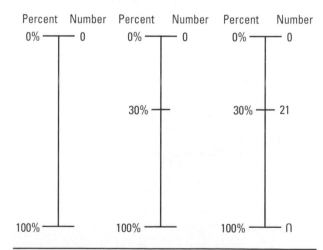

FIGURE 13-4

Percent	Number	Percent	Number	Percent	Number
0%	0	0%	0	0%	0
		30%		30%	21
100%		100%		100%	n

Source: "Another look at the teaching of percent," by A.M. Dewar, 1984, Arithmetic Teacher, 31 (71, p. 49).

TECHNOLOGY LINK 13-1
Fibonacci Numbers and the Golden Section

Have you heard about the Fibonacci numbers or the Golden Section and wondered what they were? Then this site is for you. It explains all about Fibonacci numbers and the Golden Section. This site also includes connections to nature and puzzles based on these concepts.
Visit http://www.mcs.surrey.ac.uk/personal/r.knott/fibonacci/fib.html or link from our Companion Website at **www.prenhall.com/cathcart.**

dren. These learners should, however, be encouraged to use their understanding of percent and the "guess and check" strategy to find answers to questions such as the following:

> 50% of ____ = 32
>
> 6 is 10% of ——
>
> 78 is 120% of a number. What do you know about the number?

The unitary analysis method   The unitary analysis or unit method was once popular in schools in the United States. It is presented here because it illustrates logical reasoning and mental computation strategies. Examples for each of the three types of percent problems follow:

> Find 5% of 700.
>
> 1% of 700 is 7.
> Therefore 5% of 700 is 5 × 7 = 35.
>
> What percent is 2 of 5?
>
> 5 is 100% of the total.
> Therefore 1 is 20% of the total. (100% ÷ 5)
> And 2 is 2 × 20% = 40% of the total.
>
> 60 is 20% of what number?
>
> 20% of the number is 60.
>
> Therefore 1% of the number is 3. (60 ÷ 20)
> And 100% of the number is 300.

The numbers in these examples are easy to work with. In many problems, however, the intermediate steps involve cumbersome fractions or decimals. For this reason, the method generally is not taught formally today.

ASSESSMENT AND INSTRUCTION

Assessing Proportional Reasoning

An important aspect of proportional reasoning is the ability to discriminate between proportional and nonproportional situations. Cramer, Post, and Currier (1993) reported that most of the preservice teachers in a mathematics methods course wrote a proportion to solve the following problem:

> *Sue and Julie were running equally fast around a track. Julie started first. When she had run 9 laps, Sue had run 3 laps. When Julie completed 15 laps, how many laps had Sue run?*

In addition to missing-value problems, such as the "Mr. Short and Mr. Tall" task, and numerical comparison problems, such as predicting the relative strength of orange juice given different mixtures of concentrate and water, qualitative prediction or comparison situations such as the following can be used to assess proportional reasoning.

> *If today Eric ran fewer laps in more time than he did yesterday, was his speed faster, slower, the same, or can't you say for sure?*
>
> *If Lisa ran more laps than Craig and she ran for less time, who was the faster runner—Lisa, Craig, they ran the same speed, or can't you say for sure?*

Everyday Life Problem Settings

Newspaper and magazine articles, as well as radio and television reports, are continuing sources of up-to-date information on topics of interest to young people, such as sports, entertainment, and environmental concerns. Such data can be used in concept and skill development activities related to ratio and percent. For example, children could write various part-to-part and part-to-whole ratios based on the number of medals won by a country at the recent Olympic Games: Winter—2 gold, 3 silver, and 2 bronze; Summer—6 gold, 5 silver, and 7 bronze, for example.

Children who collect sports cards or follow professional teams might be asked to explain what certain statistics mean and how they are computed:

- a hitter's batting average of .317
- a pitcher's earned run average of 2.85
- a team's powerplay percentage of 21%
- a quarterback's passing percentage of 62%
- a player's 3-point shooting percentage of 46%

Children could be encouraged to keep various statistics on games in a sport in which they participate or are spectators. Problems or class projects based on data from printed sources could then be generated and solved by class members.

Another source of information is data collected in surveys conducted by children. For example, the number of people who prefer certain soft drinks, watch certain TV shows, or recycle paper can be reported and compared in ratio or percent form. Activities such as these have obvious connections to topics and concepts in the data analysis strand, which focuses on collecting, representing, and interpreting quantitative information (see Chapter 16).

CONCLUSION

In this chapter, procedures for developing the concepts of ratio, proportion, and percent have been described. Suggestions for effective instruction have emphasized higher-level reasoning, number sense, and real-world applications. Children should rely on conceptual understanding rather than mechanical rules when solving problems, and they should know that problems can be solved in many different ways. Mental computation and estimation skills need to be developed for these topics. Calculators should be used for complex computations.

For Your Journal

When you have finished studying this chapter, reflect on the following questions in your math journal:

1. Why do children have low levels of achievement on ratio, proportion, and percent problems? What might a classroom teacher do to help strengthen children's understandings of these topics?
2. Imagine you are an intermediate-grade or middle-school teacher. The parents of one of the children are concerned that you have not yet taught their child the "cross-multiply-and-divide" method for solving proportions. What would you say to them?
3. Solve the following problem using at least two different methods. Reflect on each method. Which method do you prefer, and why?

   6 is 40% of what number?

For Your Portfolio

When you have finished studying this chapter, complete the following activities to include in your professional portfolio:

1. Visit an intermediate-grade or middle-school classroom and informally interview several children. Have them solve and describe their solution methods for a few ratio, proportion, and percent problems. Write a short description of their solution strategies and their understandings of these kinds of problems. If you were their teacher, what would you plan for their next lessons about these topics?
2. Write a lesson plan to help children understand the meaning of ratio and proportion by linking them to their everyday lives.
3. Write a lesson plan to help children understand and use unit rates to solve proportion problems.
4. Write a lesson plan to help children understand percents by using a model.

Resources for Teachers

Books on ratio and proportion

Curcio, F. R., & Bezuk, N. S. (1994). *Understanding rational numbers and proportions: Curriculum and Evaluation Standards for School Mathematics Addenda Series, Grades 5–8.* Reston, VA: National Council of Teachers of Mathematics.

Links to the Internet

Fibonacci Numbers and the Golden Section
http://www.mcs.surrey.ac.uk/Personal/R.Knott/ Fibonacci/fib.html

Contains information about Fibonacci numbers and the Golden Section (or ratio), including how they appear in nature and how to calculate them.

Math Forum
http://mathforum.org/dr.math/tocs/fraction.middle.html

Contains answers to frequently asked questions about percents.

◀ CHAPTER 14 ▶

Developing Geometric Thinking and Spatial Sense

With Contributions by Dr. Sally A. Robison

KEY CONCEPTS ▶

✔ van Hiele levels of geometric thought

✔ Developing spatial sense

FOCUS QUESTIONS ▶

When you have finished studying this chapter, you should be able to answer the following questions:

1. How might a teacher use the van Hiele levels of geometric thought in planning instruction?
2. How might a teacher help children develop spatial sense?
3. What concepts should be taught to encourage children to develop geometric thinking and spatial sense?
4. How does a teacher encourage students to investigate, describe, and recognize geometric shapes and properties of geometric shapes?

NCTM CONTENT STANDARDS AND EXPECTATIONS ADDRESSED IN THIS CHAPTER

STANDARD	EXPECTATIONS FOR GRADES PRE K–2	EXPECTATIONS FOR GRADES 3–5	EXPECTATIONS FOR GRADES 6–8
Geometry Standard Instructional programs from pre-K–12 should enable all students to—	In prekindergarten through Grade 2 all students should— (NCTM, 2000, p. 96)	In Grades 3–5 all students should— (NCTM, 2000, p. 164)	In Grades 6–8 all students should—(NCTM, 2000, p. 232)
Analyze characteristics and properties of two- and three-dimensional geometric shapes and develop mathematical arguments about geometric relationships	• create mental images of geometric shapes using spatial visualization. • recognize and represent shapes from different perspectives. • relate ideas in geometry to ideas in number and measurement. • recognize geometric shapes and structures in the environment and specify their location.	• investigate, describe, and reason about the results of subdividing, combining, and transforming shapes. • explore congruence and similarity. • make and test conjectures about geometric properties and develop logical arguments to justify conclusions.	• precisely describe, classify, and understand relationships among types of two- and three-dimensional objects (e.g., angles, triangles, quadrilaterals, cylinders, cones) using their defining properties. • understand relationships among the angles, side lengths, perimeters, areas, and volumes of similar objects. • create and critique inductive and deductive arguments concerning geometric ideas and relationships, such as congruence, similarity, and the Pythagorean relationship.

STANDARD	EXPECTATIONS FOR GRADES PRE-K–2	EXPECTATIONS FOR GRADES 3–5	EXPECTATIONS FOR GRADES 6–8
Geometry Standard (*continued*) Instructional programs from pre-K–12 should enable all students to—	In prekindergarten through Grade 2 all students should— (NCTM, 2000, p. 96)	In Grades 3–5 all students should— (NCTM, 2000, p. 164)	In Grades 6–8 all students should—(NCTM, 2000, p. 232)
specify locations and describe spatial relationships using coordinate geometry and other representational systems	• describe, name, and interpret relative positions in space and apply ideas about relative position. • describe, name, and interpret direction and distance in navigating space and apply ideas about direction and distance. • find and name locations with simple relationships such as "near to" and in coordinate systems such as maps.	• describe location and movement using common language and geometric vocabulary. • make and use coordinate systems to specify locations and to describe paths. • find the distance between points along horizontal and vertical lines of a coordinate system.	• use coordinate geometry to represent and examine the properties of geometric shapes. • use coordinate geometry to examine special geometric shapes, such as regular polygons or those with pairs of parallel or perpendicular sides.
apply transformations and use symmetry to analyze mathematical situations	• recognize and apply slides, flips, and turns. • recognize and create shapes that have symmetry.	• predict and describe the results of sliding, flipping, and turning two-dimensional shapes. • describe a motion or a series of motions that will show that two shapes are congruent. • identify and describe line and rotational symmetry in two- and three-dimensional shapes and designs.	• describe sizes, positions, and orientations of shapes under informal transformations such as flips, turns, slides, and scaling. • examine the congruence, similarity, and line or rotational symmetry of objects using transformations.
use visualization, spatial reasoning, and geometric modeling to solve problems	• create mental images of geometric shapes using spatial memory and spatial visualization. • recognize and represent shapes from different perspectives. • relate ideas in geometry to ideas in number and measurement. • recognize geometric shapes and structures in the environment and specify their location.	• build and draw geometric objects. • create and describe mental images of objects, patterns, and paths. • identify and build a three-dimensional object from two-dimensional representations of that object. • identify and build a two-dimensional representation of a three-dimensional object. • use geometric models to solve problems in other areas of mathematics, such as number and measurement. • recognize geometric ideas and relationships and apply them to other disciplines and to problems that arise in the classroom or in everyday life.	• draw geometric objects with specified properties, such as side lengths or angle measures. • use two-dimensional representations of three-dimensional objects to visualize and solve problems such as those involving surface area and volume. • use visual tools such as networks to represent and solve problems. • use geometric models to represent and explain numerical and algebraic relationships. • recognize and apply geometric ideas and relationships in areas outside the mathematics classroom, such as art, science, and everyday life.

he study of geometry at the elementary level is an opportunity to connect mathematics to the environment. Children can learn to interpret and describe their physical environments through geometric modeling and spatial reasoning. The study of geometry can also provide important tools in problem solving (NCTM, 2000). The mode of study should be informal, with the gradual implementation of more systematic and rigorous study as the child's age and experience level increases.

The ideas presented in this chapter are about "getting to know" objects in the world so that eventually such objects can be measured and quantified. Working with concrete objects leads to intuitive discoveries of geometric properties and relationships.

The geometry component of the mathematics program at the elementary level includes, in part, the study of two-dimensional and three-dimensional shapes and objects. As their understanding develops, children are able to recognize different shapes and figures, name and describe them, deduce their properties, and eventually express relationships both within and between shapes and figures. The study of geometry also is about developing spatial sense, that is, the ability to build and manipulate mental representations of two- and three-dimensional objects and perceive them accurately from different perspectives (NCTM, 2000).

What do we know of U.S. children's understanding of geometry and spatial sense? The sixth National Assessment of Educational Progress (NAEP) noted that fourth graders were able to identify properties of simple geometric figures but had more difficulty with more complex figures and with producing more extensive written explanations (Struchens & Blume, 1997). As with other topics, teachers must give children many opportunities to experience a variety of geometric concepts with hands-on materials and to encourage children to communicate about those concepts. ✔

PRINCIPLES AND STANDARDS LINK 14-1
Content Strand: Geometry

Instructional programs from prekindergarten through 12 should enable all students to—

- analyze characteristics and properties of two- and three-dimensional geometric shapes and develop mathematical arguments about geometric relationships;
- specify locations and describe spatial relationships using coordinate geometry and other representational systems;
- apply transformations and use symmetry to analyze mathematical situations;
- use visualization, spatial reasoning, and geometric modeling to solve problems. (NCTM, 2000, p. 41).

DEVELOPMENT OF GEOMETRIC THINKING

Why Teach Geometry?

Students typically enjoy the topics found in a geometry unit, because they can relate so much of what they explore to the real world. Learning geometric properties and shapes helps them make sense of their environment as they become more capable of describing their world. As a result, they find the subject naturally interesting and, therefore, more motivating. Geometry is a foundational subject to many other areas of mathematics, such as algebraic thinking through patterns and problem-solving activities involving area and perimeter of geometric shapes. As students work on the geometric topics through the use of models and hands-on activities, they discover examples and nonexamples, grow in spatial abilities, learn to apply geometric concepts, terminology and formulas, and gain in what NCTM refers to as mathematical power: problem solving, communication, reasoning, representing, and connections.

The van Hiele Levels of Geometric Thought

The work of two Dutch educators, Dina van Hiele-Geldof and Pierre van Hiele (pronounced "van HEEley"), has influenced the teaching of geometry. The van Hieles were concerned about the difficulties their students were having with geometry (Geddes & Fortunato, 1993), so they conducted research aimed at understanding children's levels of geometric thinking to determine the kinds of instruction that could best help children. The van Hieles observed five levels of geometric thinking, listed in Table 14-1 (Crowley, 1987). Each level describes how children think about geometric concepts.

Children at the visualization level think about shapes in terms of what they resemble. For example, a child at this level might describe a triangle as a "mountain." The child, however, might not recognize the same triangle after it is rotated 180°, saying, "It's not a triangle because it doesn't look like a triangle. A triangle can't stand upside down." Children at this level are able to sort shapes into groups that look alike based on their perceptions. They can sort, identify, match, and describe objects in a limited capacity. They need examples and nonexamples of the geometric shapes to help them formulate their perceptions of the shapes. Students should be encouraged to construct and draw shapes as well as practice in putting shapes together to form figures they recognize followed by practice in taking them apart.

Children at the analysis level think in terms of properties. They understand that all shapes in a group such as parallelograms have the same properties, and they can describe those properties. For example, they are able to

TABLE 14-1

VAN HIELE LEVELS OF GEOMETRIC THINKING

LEVEL	DESCRIPTION
0—Visualization	Children recognize shapes by their global, holistic appearance.
1—Analysis	Children observe the component parts of figures (e.g., a parallelogram has opposite sides that are parallel) but are unable to explain the relationships between properties within a shape or among shapes.
2—Informal deduction	Children deduce properties of figures and express interrelationships both within and between figures.
3—Formal deduction	Children create formal deductive proofs.
4—Rigor	Children rigorously compare different axiomatic systems.

describe a parallelogram as having four sides, with opposite sides parallel, with opposite sides congruent, and with opposite angles congruent. However, they don't see any relationships between any of the properties. Because they don't realize that some properties imply others, children's thinking at this level will list every property of a shape that they can think of. Students should be encouraged to solve problems involving geometric shapes, to use models that help them explore the properties of shapes, and to classify figures based on certain properties, such as all shapes that have right angles.

Children at the informal deduction level not only think about properties of shapes but are also able to notice relationships within and between figures. It is at this level of thinking that children are first able to understand inclusion relationships, using words such as all, some, and none; for example, "All dogs are animals, but not all (only some) animals are dogs." Or, to give a mathematical example, "All squares are rectangles, but not all rectangles are squares." Converse statements involving if-then conditions, such as "If this shape is a rectangle, then it has 4 right angles" versus the converse "If this shape has 4 right angles, then it is a rectangle," should be explored for validity. It is also at this level that children are first able to formulate meaningful definitions. Definitions acquired prior to this level will generally be memorized without real understanding. Students working at this level should make property lists of shapes, discuss necessary and sufficient conditions required to make a shape, use descriptive language leading to meaningful definitions, and learn to identify a class of shapes based on certain properties. At this level, children are also able to make and follow informal deductive arguments. Making and testing hypotheses about the shapes, such as "Do the

diagonals of all parallelograms bisect each other?" will lead to generalizations and counterexamples.

Children at the formal deduction level think about relationships between properties of shapes and also understand relationships between axioms, definitions, theorems, corollaries, and postulates. They understand how to construct a formal proof, understand why proof is needed, and learn to argue meaningfully. For successful completion, the typical high school geometry course requires geometric understanding at the formal deduction level.

Children at the rigor level can think in terms of abstract mathematical systems. They can work with a variety of axiomatic systems that do not require the need for parallel lines to remain parallel when examining the infinite case. Advanced college mathematics majors and mathematicians are at this level.

In the 1990s, Clements and Battista (1992) hypothesized that a level exists that is below visualization, called prerecognition. Children operating at this level wouldn't be able to distinguish a three-sided figure from a four-sided figure. Observing a child performing the task of putting a puzzle together at this level, the observer will notice the child does not recognize the need for a certain shape or the correct orientation of the correct shape.

Most children at the elementary level are at the visualization or analysis level; some middle-school children are at the informal deduction level; and successful completion of a typical high school geometry course requires an understanding at the formal deduction stage. The NAEP noted that "most of the students at all three grade levels (fourth, eighth, and twelfth) appeared to be performing at the 'holistic' level [visualization] of the van Heile levels of geometric thought" (Struchens & Blume 1997, p. 166). It is desirable to have a child at the informal deduction level or above by the end of middle school.

For convenience, each of the activities in this chapter has been cross-referenced with the appropriate van Hiele level(s) of geometric thinking. When a range is given, it is because the level is dependent on which questions in the activity are being presented and the complexity of the figure being made.

Comments on the Levels of Thought

The following additional points must be considered:

- The levels are not age dependent but are related more to the experiences students have had.
- The levels are sequential, that is, children must pass through the levels in sequence as their understanding increases. (The only exception is highly gifted children who appear to skip levels because of their highly developed logical reasoning ability.)

- To move from one level to the next, children need to have many experiences in which they are actively involved in exploring and communicating about their observations of shapes, properties, and relationships.

- For learning to take place, language must match the child's level of understanding. If the language used in instruction is above the child's level of thinking, the child may only be able to learn procedures and memorize relationships without truly understanding geometry.

- It is difficult for two people who are at different levels to communicate effectively. For example, a person at the informal deduction level who says "square" thinks about the fact that a square has four congruent sides and four congruent angles and will know the properties of a square, such as having the opposite sides parallel and the diagonals perpendicular bisectors. A person at the visualization level may think of a compact disc case, because that is what a square looks like to that person. A teacher must realize that the meaning of many terms is different to the child than it is to the teacher and thus adjust communication accordingly yet precisely.

Thus, it is important for teachers to assess the van Hiele levels of thinking of the children in their classes and use this information to plan instruction on geometry and spatial sense that is appropriate and relevant to the children's level of thinking.

OTHER INSTRUCTIONAL NOTES

Developing the Language

The formal language of geometry develops over time. Therefore, the use of informal terms and expressions should be accepted in the elementary grades. For example, both teacher and children can use such terms as *corners, square corners, flips,* and *slides;* these terms eventually will be replaced with *vertices, right angles, reflections,* and *translations,* respectively. When children talk about what they are doing, their descriptions will become more precise and correct.

Method of Instruction

There is strong agreement among educators that geometry learning for elementary-school children should be informal, involving explorations, discovery, guessing, and problem solving. The capabilities of formulating precise descriptive statements using formal terminology and symbols are developed from many geometric experiences. Indeed, a child may progress through more than one grade level before being able to intelligently use both

The Annenberg/CPB Math and Science Collection

VIDEO LINK 14-1
Geometry and Spatial Sense

Brief Summary: In "Thanksgiving Quilt," teacher Elaine McAlear's first graders are making quilts from geometric shapes.

1. How was communication used in this lesson? How did it support the development of children's understanding?
2. What did the teacher do to support the children's working in pairs?
3. What is the teacher's role in this lesson? What do you think her objectives were for this lesson?
4. What were you able to learn about children's understanding from this lesson? What lessons might the teacher do next with this class?

Video Source: Teaching Math: A Video Library, K–4; Tape 8 from The Annenberg/CPB Math and Science Collection.

symbols and precise terminology to communicate an idea or relationship.

Although the study of geometry is to be informal in elementary school, experiences should not be haphazard and totally unstructured. There should be a sequence of activities that is developed systematically so that some direction and progress become evident to the children and children's thinking progresses through the van Hiele levels.

To make good decisions about the type of activity suitable for children, a teacher must try to discern their geometric thinking level. Engaging children in open-ended geometry explorations is one way to accomplish this. The following are examples of open-ended tasks:

- Look at a wooden block. Use sticks and marshmallows to make a skeleton model of the shape. (van Hiele level 0)

- Draw as many different four-sided figures as you can. Write about how they are different and how they are the same. (van Hiele level 1)

- How many different ways can you connect six square tiles with at least one side attached? (van Hiele level 2)

Open-ended tasks such as these allow all children to engage in a common activity. Although their output from these tasks will differ, children will have had a common experience that could successfully be followed by a class discussion. Such sharing enables some children to see relationships that, left to themselves, they might not have seen.

As children engage in discovery-oriented activities, a teacher can, as she or he mingles with the children, ask questions such as, "What do you notice?" "How would you describe this?" and "Can you make a different shape?" Responses can provide insight into the children's level of geometric thinking.

Connecting With the World

Geometry provides children an opportunity to connect mathematics to their world. Teachers should choose activities that involve the recognition and classification of shapes and figures and operations on objects that are familiar to children. A collection of boxes and other containers that the children bring to school can be the focus of discussions about different shapes and figures. Likewise, a "geometry walk" on a city street or on a nature trail can serve to connect geometry work to the environment.

Geometric ideas such as patterns, symmetry, and similarity can be explored in the school environment or neighborhood by examining both living and nonliving things. Upper-elementary- and middle-school children can, for example, explore packaging possibilities for different commodities in response to environmental concerns or the architectural design of the local school.

LEARNING ABOUT TOPOLOGY

A child's world view is first topological, that is, the child sees objects as changeable, depending on perspective or position (Piaget, Inhelder, & Szeminska, 1960). Gradually, the view changes to recognition of the rigidity of objects despite transformations in space.

Topology is the study of the properties of figures that remain unchanged even under distortions, excluding tearing or cutting. By stretching and reforming, something like a doughnut can be transformed into a coffee cup. Aspects of topology should be included in elementary-school geometry programs.

Things that Change and Things that Do Not Change

Using a balloon with markings on it, Robinson (1975) asked children to indicate which features changed and which did not as the balloon was being inflated. For example, a round balloon with facial features drawn on it can serve to exemplify the following properties that do not change when the balloon is inflated:

- Something *inside* something (the eyes in the face);
- Something *not closed* (nose drawn this way);
- Something involving *order* (the nose above the mouth);
- Something *intersecting* (eyelashes with the eyes); and
- Something *connected* and something *not connected* (any of the features on the face). (p. 213)

Things that could change when the balloon is being inflated would be that one eye might be larger than the other or the mouth could become nonsymmetrical.

After real balloons have been examined, Robinson suggests that children be shown pictures of balloons with faces drawn on them properly and improperly and be asked to tell which picture the balloon could look like (Figure 14-1). This activity can be repeated with other characters drawn on a balloon or piece of sheet rubber. Children can experiment with pieces of sheet rubber that have figures drawn on them to find out how they can transform the figures by stretching the rubber (Robinson, 1975).

Place and Order

The concepts of *place, order, betweenness, inside,* and *outside* can also be studied using real objects or pictures. For example, a teacher could set up classroom furniture or equipment, or group children in such a way that the children could respond to questions in the following manner: "Tom is sitting *on* the rug," "Annette is *behind* the chair," "The geoboards are *inside* the cupboard," or "The box of centi-cubes is *under* the table." Suitable large pictures can replace real objects for similar activities. Children can be taken outside and asked to describe what they notice. Statements showing order like the following should be encouraged: "The fir tree is *after* the maple tree," "The white house is *between* the brick house and the store," and "We walk through the door before we enter the building."

Mazes and Networks

Mazes of suitable complexity can be presented to young children to solve, whereas upper-elementary school children can work with networks. A study of networks will reveal which can be traversed and which cannot. A "tra-

FIGURE 14-1

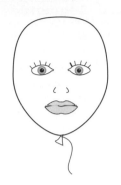
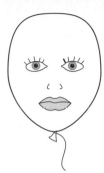
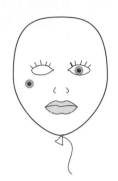
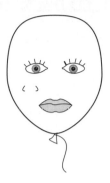

Could the balloon face look like this? If not, what's wrong?

Source: "Geometry" (p. [rule]), by G.E. Robinson, 1975, in Joseph N. Payne (Ed.), *Mathematics Learning in Early Childhood. Yearbook.* Reston, VA: Author.

versable" network is one that can be traced in one continuous motion without retracing over a line. This activity leads to an explorations of Euler circuits and Hamiltonian circuits. Try to discover which types of networks can be traversed by experimenting with figures that have

- All even vertices (two or four lines meeting at a point).
- All odd vertices (three or five lines meeting at a point).
- Only two odd vertices, others are even.
- More than two odd vertices.

Some networks are portrayed in Figure 14-2.

Distortion of Figures

Earlier, activities about distortion of figures were presented using the example of inflating a balloon. Besides stretching, distortions can be achieved by twisting, bending, and shrinking. Experimenting with Möbius strips is one type of activity that involves figure distortion by twisting (see Activity 14-1).

FIGURE 14-2

EXAMPLES OF NETWORKS

(a)   (b)

(c) 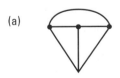   (d)

ACTIVITY 14-1

EXPLORATIONS WITH MÖBIUS STRIPS (VAN HIELE LEVELS 1-2)

MATERIALS

Use strips of narrow adding machine tape approximately 1 m in length. Mark each end of the strip with a large dot on the same side.

PROCEDURE

1. Take one strip, twist it once, then glue the ends together (the dots should touch each other).
   - Cut the strip in half following the lengthwise direction. Describe the results.

   - Use another strip and locate a line that is about one-third of the way across the strip. Cut along this line until you reach the "end." Describe what happened.

   - What would happen if you wanted to make one side of a strip one color and the other side another color? Try this and describe what you found.

2. Make Möbius strips with two twists and conduct cutting and coloring experiments.

LEARNING ABOUT EUCLIDEAN GEOMETRY

Three-Dimensional Shapes

Concurrent with activities of a topological nature, children can begin the study of rigid shapes or ideas related to Euclidean geometry. Children in kindergarten and grade 1 should be involved in manipulating different three-dimensional shapes to find out similarities and differences. When children explore such shapes, they should be asked to describe them: some shapes can roll, some have flat faces, some have pointed corners. The sophistication of the responses will depend on the children's geometric knowledge. Possible descriptions of faces are:

- Some faces are round, some have pointed corners.
- Some faces are squares, some are triangles.
- Some faces have four sides, some have three sides.

Children learn to recognize two-dimensional figures and name them (van Hiele Level 0) well before they are able to articulate their properties (van Hiele Level 1). Middle-school children should be able to classify three-dimensional shapes and two-dimensional figures by explaining some relationships between properties within a shape or figure and among shapes or figures (van Hiele Level 2).

Polyhedra   Polyhedra are three-dimensional shapes with *faces* consisting of polygons, that is, plane figures (two-dimensional) with three, four, five, or more straight sides. In a polyhedron, the lines where the sides of two polygons meet are the *edges* of the shape, and the point where edges meet are the *vertices* of the polyhedron.

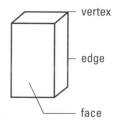

Regular polyhedra.   *Regular polygons* are plane figures with sides that are all the same length and angles of equal measure, as, for example, an equilateral triangle or a square. A *regular polyhedron* is one whose faces consist of the same kind of regular congruent polygons (e.g., all squares or all equilateral triangles) with the same number of edges meeting at each vertex of the figure (Billstein, Libeskind, & Lott, 1990). It is possible to construct five regular polyhedra:

PRINCIPLES AND STANDARDS LINK 14-3
Content Strand: Geometry

Geometry offers students an aspect of mathematical thinking that is different from, but connected to, the world of numbers. . . Some students' capabilities with geometric and spatial concepts exceed their numerical skills. Building on these strengths fosters enthusiasm for mathematics and provides a context in which to develop number and other mathematical concepts. (NCTM, 2000, p. 97)

Shape	Type and Number of Faces
Tetrahedron	4 equilateral triangles
Octahedron	8 equilateral triangles
Icosahedron	20 equilateral triangles
Hexahedron	6 squares
Dodecahedron	12 regular pentagons

The study of polyhedra is thought to have begun with Pythagoras (582–500 B C). Historians relate that Pythagoras probably brought his knowledge of the cube, the tetrahedron, and the octahedron from Egypt, but the icosahedron and the dodecahedron seem to have been developed in his own society. The study of the five regular polyhedra was passed on to the school of Plato, a Greek philosopher (427–347 BC), and subsequently these polyhedra became known as the *Platonic Solids* (Figure 14-3).

Semi-regular polyhedra.   Another set of polyhedra, known as the *Archimedean solids,* are semiregular shapes composed of more than one kind of regular polygon. There are 13 semiregular solids, all of which are ascribed to Archimedes (287–212 BC), who wrote about the entire set. Semiregular solids are shown in Figure 14-4.

Truncated and stellated polyhedra.   The study of polyhedra did not end with the discovery of the solids. In the middle ages, the systematic study of solids by the astronomer Johannes Kepler (1571–1630) led him to create other solids through a process called *stellating.* This process consists in building onto solids to form different solids. For example, attaching a tetrahedron to each face of an octahedron produces a solid known as the stella octangula or the eight-pointed star (see Figure 14-5). It also is possible to modify solids by cutting off sections in a systematic way. This process is known as *truncating* and also can lead to the formation of new solids. Figure 14-5 also shows examples of a stellated icosahedron and a truncated cube. Stellating and truncating solids are interesting enrichment activities for upper-elementary- and middle-school children that can be modeled with clay, Play-Doh, or commercially available polydron forms.

FIGURE 14-3

PLATONIC SOLIDS

tetrahedron

hexahedron

octahedron

dodecahedron

icosahedron

FIGURE 14-4

SEMI-REGULAR SOLIDS

FIGURE 14-5

Stella Octangula

Truncated Cube

Stellated Icosahedron

Other three-dimensional shapes.   Other three-dimensional shapes also are included in the elementary- and middle-school mathematics curriculum. These shapes include prisms, pyramids, cylinders, and cones, which are described below and shown in Figure 14-6.

A *prism* is a polyhedron with two congruent, parallel bases that are polygons, and with all remaining faces parallelograms. A cube is a special type of prism, with squares for all its faces.

A *pyramid* is a polyhedron whose base is a polygon and all the rest of the faces are triangles, which meet at a common point called the vertex A pyramid is regular if the base is a regular polygon and the other faces are congruent isosceles triangles. Special types of pyramids include *square pyramids,* with a square base, and *triangular pyramids,* with a triangular base.

A *cylinder* is a surface generated by a family of all lines parallel to a given line and passing through a curve

FIGURE 14-6

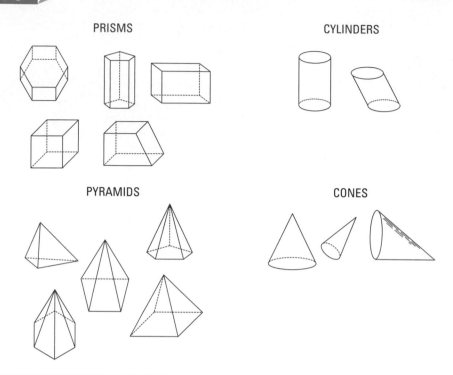

FIGURE 14-7

POLYHEDRON	FACES	VERTICES	EDGES
Tetrahedron			
Cube			
Octahedron			
Triangular Prism			
Square Pyramid			
What relationship do you notice among the shapes?			

in a plane. Special types of cylinders include *circular cylinders,* whose bases are circles, and *right circular cylinders,* whose axes are perpendicular to the bases. Other cylinders can have bases that are ellipses.

A *cone* is a surface generated by a family of all lines through a given point and passing through a curve in a plane. The base of a cone can be a circle or an ellipse.

Discovering Euler's rule. A special relationship, known as Euler's rule, exists among the number of faces (F), vertices (V), and edges (E) of polyhedra. The relationship is such that given the value of two of the three variables (F, V, and E), one can calculate the value of the third variable. Examine some models and complete a table similar to the one in Figure 14-7, then look for a pattern in the data.

LEARNING ABOUT THREE-DIMENSIONAL SHAPES

Comparing Polyhedra

Children can be given a collection of various three-dimensional shapes and asked to classify and describe them. Some classification activities are described below. Each activity has children verbalize what they notice about shapes. The teacher should attempt to provide frequent opportunities for children to express geometric ideas orally, as in Activities 14-2 through 14-5. Activity 14-2 is appropriate for primary-grade children, whereas Activity 14-5 can be challenging for upper-elementary school children. This kind of task can provide information about children's geometric thinking level.

PRINCIPLES AND STANDARDS LINK 14-4
Content Strand: Geometry

Beginning in the early years of schooling, students should develop visualization skills through hands-on experiences with a variety of geometric objects and through the use of technology that allows them to turn, shrink, and deform two- and three-dimensional objects. Later, they should become comfortable analyzing and drawing perspective views, counting component parts, and describing attributes that cannot be seen but can be inferred. Students need to learn to physically and mentally change the position, orientation, and size of objects in systematic ways as they develop their understandings about congruence, similarity, and transformations. (NCTM, 2000, p. 42)

ACTIVITY 14-2

DESCRIBING SHAPES
(VAN HIELE LEVELS 0-1)

MATERIALS
An assortment of three-dimensional shapes

PROCEDURE
1. Find shapes that can roll.
2. Find shapes that cannot roll.
3. How are the shapes different? How are they the same?

ACTIVITY 14-3

CLASSIFYING SHAPES
(VAN HIELE LEVELS 1-2)

MATERIALS
A set of three-dimensional shapes

PROCEDURE
1. Put the shapes in two different groups.
2. Tell why the shapes in each group belong together.

Constructing Three-Dimensional Shapes

A study of three-dimensional shapes should involve children in construction activities. Polyhedra can be constructed using various mediums such as Play-doh and stiff paper (see Activity 14-6). Children can construct *skeleton* or *edge models* of polygons and polyhedra using different materials. These can include:

ACTIVITY 14-4

COMPARING TWO SHAPES
(VAN HIELE LEVELS 1-2)

MATERIALS
A set of three-dimensional shapes

PROCEDURE
1. Choose two shapes and
   • tell how they are alike.
   • tell how they are different.

ACTIVITY 14-5

WRITING ABOUT SHAPES
(VAN HIELE LEVELS 1-2)

MATERIALS
A set of three-dimensional shapes

PROCEDURE
1. Examine a shape and write several statements about its characteristics.

ACTIVITY 14-6

CONSTRUCTING THREE-DIMENSIONAL SHAPES WITH PLAY-DOH
(VAN HIELE LEVELS 0-1)

MATERIALS
A set of three-dimensional shapes Play-doh

PROCEDURE
1. Select a three-dimensional shape.
2. Construct a similar shape using Play-doh.

• Toothpicks and miniature marshmallows or small gumdrops
• Struts made of rolled paper and taped together
• Straws and pipecleaners or some thin cord (crochet cotton, twine, or elastic thread) (see Figure 14-8).

A net is a flat version of a three-dimensional shape that, when folded along the connecting edges of the faces of the solid, forms a shape where all faces are connected edge to edge with no faces overlapping or leaving open gaps. As children construct polyhedra from nets they have drawn (Activity 14-7), they will learn that the beauty of the finished product is proportional to the care taken in accurately measuring, drawing, and cutting the nets.

FIGURE 14-8

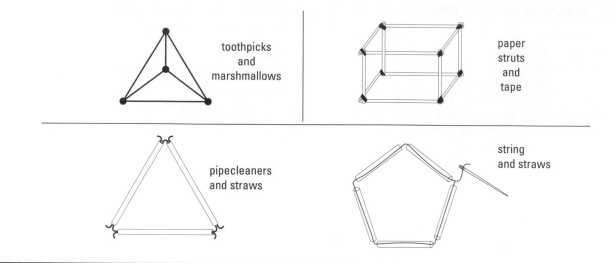

toothpicks
and
marshmallows

paper
struts
and
tape

pipecleaners
and straws

string
and straws

A set of polygons with tabs made from stiff paper (Figure 14-9) enables children to engage in investigative work regarding the composition of polyhedra. If available, the commercial set of Polydrons provides excellent pieces for explorations in polyhedra. Children can experiment with regular and nonregular polygons and try to construct shapes.

Constructions should be followed by descriptions and comparisons and by discussions about successful and unsuccessful construction attempts. Activities 14-8 through 14-12 are sample investigations students can be asked to do using the materials described in Figure 14-10.

Polyhedra can also be constructed with modeling clay. The stroke of a knife through a clay model serves to exemplify a plane passing through at given angles. In this manner, truncated figures can be formed to display different sections of solids. Predicting and testing the face of the slice made in the solid will encourage an improve-

ACTIVITY 14-7

CONSTRUCTING POLYHEDRA FROM NETS (VAN HIELE LEVELS 1-2)

MATERIALS
Nets of shapes drawn on paper

PROCEDURE
1. Cut out nets of shapes (see Figure 14-9).
2. By folding and taping, construct models of polyhedra.
3. As an alternative, draw 1-cm tabs around some edges of the nets and then construct models of polyhedra by cutting and pasting.

ACTIVITY 14-8

CONSTRUCTING POLYHEDRA (VAN HIELE LEVELS 1-2)

MATERIALS
Equilateral triangles with tabs, elastics

PROCEDURE
1. Using a set of equilateral triangles and elastics, try to construct some polyhedra.
2. Can you construct a shape with four triangles? with eight triangles? Can you name the shapes?
3. An icosahedron is made up of 20 equilateral triangles. Try to construct one.

ACTIVITY 14-9

CONSTRUCTING POLYHEDRA: EXPERIMENTING WITH IRREGULAR POLYGONS (VAN HIELE LEVELS 1-3)

MATERIALS
A set of isosceles triangles with tabs, elastics

PROCEDURE
1. Try to construct a three-dimensional shape using a set of isosceles triangles and elastics.
2. Can you construct a shape with four triangles? with eight triangles?
3. Can you construct another shape?
4. Comment on the regularity and nonregularity of the shape(s).

FIGURE 14-9

NETS

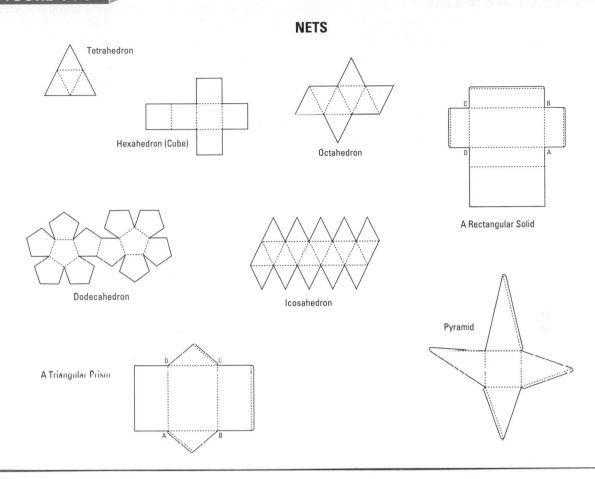

Tetrahedron

Hexahedron (Cube)

Octahedron

A Rectangular Solid

Dodecahedron

Icosahedron

Pyramid

A Triangular Prism

ment in mental imagery, which leads to an improvement in spatial sense. Children can experiment with different cuts on a solid as shown in Figure 14-11. A dissection activity is presented in Activity 14-13. Exploring the faces of a polydron can be accomplished in several ways: cast-ing the shadow of the shape on the wall with a flashlight or overhead projector, pressing the solid into moldable material, making jackets out of centimeter paper to fit the solid, or using finger paint and pressing the solid into the paint. Commercially available clear geometric solids that

ACTIVITY 14-10

CONSTRUCTING SEMIREGULAR POLYHEDRA (VAN HIELE LEVELS 1-2)

MATERIALS
Squares and equilateral triangles with tabs, elastics

PROCEDURE
1. Can you construct a three-dimensional shape using equilateral triangles and squares with the same side length? Describe your shape.*

2. Compare your shape with an icosahedron. What are the similarities? What are the differences?

*Children could be provided with a picture of the semiregular shape that they are to construct.

ACTIVITY 14-11

CONSTRUCTING PYRAMIDS AND PRISMS (VAN HIELE LEVELS 1-2)

MATERIALS
Various polygons with tabs, elastics

PROCEDURE
1. Using different polygons and elastics, construct three different pyramids.

2. Construct three different prisms.

3. Tell how the pyramids are different; how they are similar.

4. Tell how the prisms are different; how they are similar.

ACTIVITY 14-12

CONSTRUCTING POLYHEDRA: EXPLORATIONS (VAN HIELE LEVELS 2-3)

MATERIALS
Parallelograms

PROCEDURE
1. Can you construct a three-dimensional shape with parallelograms?
2. Describe the shape.
3. Compare it with a rectangular prism.

FIGURE 14-10

1. Cut out regular triangles.
2. Draw an 8-mm tab on each side.
3. Punch a hole near each vertex and clip off the point. Fold each tab outward.
4. Use elastic bands to construct 3-D shapes.
5. Cut out squares and other kinds of polygons. Follow steps 2 through 4.

allow the entry of water into the center of the solid enable students to examine the slice of a plane without actually slicing the solid.

LEARNING ABOUT TWO-DIMENSIONAL FIGURES

Polygons

Polygons can be described as two-dimensional figures with straight-line segments. Polygons are examples of *simple closed geometric curves* composed of straight-line segments. A geometric curve in a plane may be straight or curved. Therefore, parallelograms and circles are both simple closed curves. They are simple curves because no lines in the figure cross each other; only one region is formed. Examples of open and closed curves and simple and complex curves are shown in Figure 14-12. The line segments of a polygon are sides, and each point where two line segments meet is a *vertex*. A *diagonal* of a polygon is formed by drawing a line segment that connects two nonadjacent vertices (see Figure 14-13).

Polygons can be *convex* or *concave*. A convex polygon is one whose interior angles are all less than 180°, that is, any two points in a figure can be connected by a line segment that will be completely within the figure and all diagonals will remain inside the figure. A nonconvex polygonal region is called a concave polygon (see Figure 14-13).

FIGURE 14-11

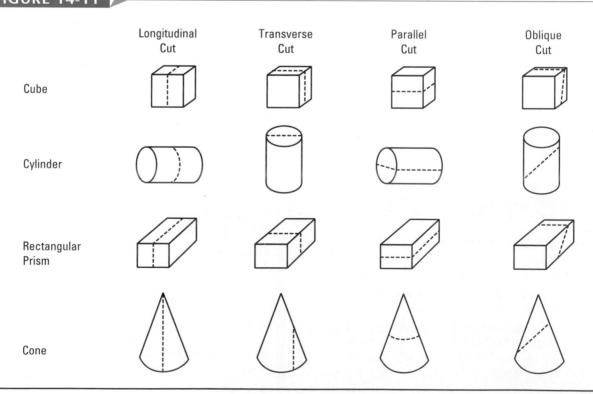

ACTIVITY 14-13

DISSECTION OF A CUBE
(VAN HIELE LEVELS 1-3)

MATERIALS
Modeling clay
Knife

PROCEDURE
1. What various polygons do you get when a plane cuts through a cube? Experiment to find out.

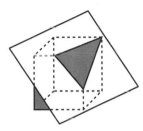

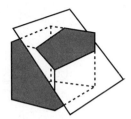

- Are all cross-sections of a cube bounded by quadrilaterals?
- What kinds of polygonal regions could be cross-sections of a cube?
- Find as many types of cross-sections as you can.
- What is the least number of edges that a cross-section can have?
- What is the greatest number of edges that a cross-section can have?

2. Make predictions for the answers to the following questions. Then, using a clay model of a cube and a knife, verify your predictions. Record both your predictions and your final answers.

3. Make predictions about the cross-sections of a rectangular solid, a cone, and a right cylinder. Verify your predictions in the same manner as for the cube.

Convex polygons are named according to the number of sides:

Number of Sides	Name of Polygon
3	triangle
4	quadrilateral
5	pentagon
6	hexagon
7	heptagon
8	octagon
9	nonagon
10	decagon

Triangles Triangles are classified according to their sides, angle measures, or both. Figure 14-14 shows a classification of triangles according to angles and sides.

Children's experiences with triangles should be with different sizes in different orientations. A geoboard is a good tool for explorations with such plane figures. Constructions on a geoboard can be recorded on dot paper. Activities 14-14 through 14-16 have children explore different triangles.

As a related activity to Activity 14-14, provide children with a set of plane figures, as in Figure 14-15, and ask them to find the triangles. Follow this with a class discussion by asking, "In what ways are some alike? Different?"

Quadrilaterals Like triangles, quadrilaterals are classified according to their sides, angle measures, or both. A quadrilateral refers to any simple closed figure consisting of four straight lines.

A *trapezoid* is usually defined as a quadrilateral with at least one pair of parallel sides. Sometimes this definition is modified slightly to "exactly one pair of parallel

FIGURE 14-12

GEOMETRIC CURVES

(a)

Open Curves

(b)

Simple Closed Curves

(c)

Complex Closed Curves

FIGURE 14-13

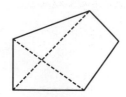
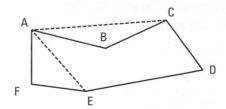

(a) Convex Polygons.
All angles are less than 180°

(b) Concave Polygons
Segment AC is outside the figure.
Interior angle ABC is greater than 180°

FIGURE 14-14

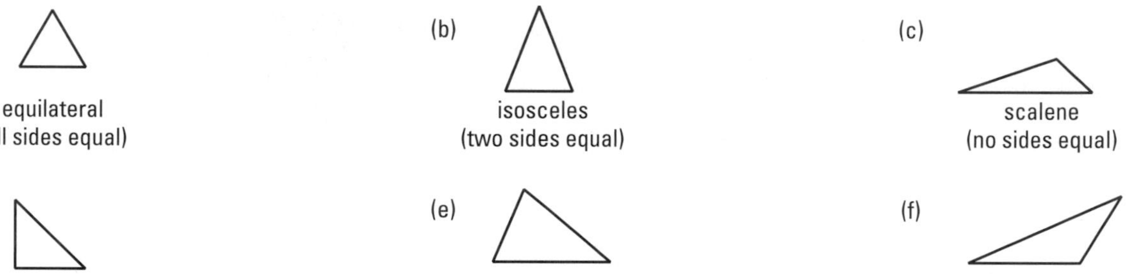

DIFFERENT TRIANGLES

(a)

equilateral
(all sides equal)

(b)
isosceles
(two sides equal)

(c)
scalene
(no sides equal)

(d)

right triangle
(1 angle = 90 degrees)

(e)

acute triangle
(angles < 90 degrees)

(f)
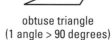
obtuse triangle
(1 angle > 90 degrees)

sides." Teachers should be aware which definition is used in their textbook and in any state content standards and use that definition consistently.

A *parallelogram* is a polygon with two pairs of parallel sides. A *rectangle* fulfills that requirement, and there-

ACTIVITY 14-14

DRAWING DIFFERENT TRIANGLES (VAN HIELE LEVELS 1-2)

MATERIALS
Paper
Pencil
Ruler

PROCEDURE
1. Draw three different triangles.
2. How are they different?
3. How are they alike?
4. Draw others that are different.

fore is a parallelogram, but it is a special parallelogram that has right angles. A *rhombus* also has parallel opposite sides and is also a special parallelogram because it has equal sides. A *square* also is a parallelogram. Because a square has four right angles, it is a rectangle; and it has equal sides, so it is also a rhombus. A *kite* is a quadrilateral with two pairs of adjacent sides that have equal lengths.

Children will recognize properties of shapes according to their geometric thinking level. For example, primary-grade children may articulate only the number of sides and corners; upper-elementary grade children may note that sides are equal or parallel and that angles are right or equal; middle-school children will be able to provide formal descriptions and classify figures in "families," such as the family of parallelograms (see Figure 14-16). Concise definitions of quadrilaterals are included in Figure 14-17.

In preparation for an oral activity, display a set of different polygons. Ask the children to choose a figure and examine it, then ask, "What can you say about the figure?" Activities 14-17 through 14-20 suggest some explorations with polygons, including quadrilaterals.

CONSTRUCTING TRIANGLES (VAN HIELE LEVELS 1-2)

MATERIALS
Geoboards
Rubber bands
Dot paper

PROCEDURE
1. Make different triangles on a geoboard.

2. Draw a picture of the triangles you made on dot paper.

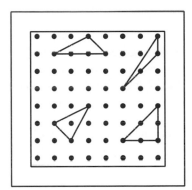

3. Is there one type of triangle that you cannot make on the geoboard? Why?

DESCRIBING TRIANGLES (VAN HIELE LEVELS 1-2)

MATERIALS
Geoboard

PROCEDURE
1. Make different triangles like these on a geoboard, then draw them on dot paper.

2. Describe each triangle.

FIGURE 14-15

FIND THE TRIANGLES

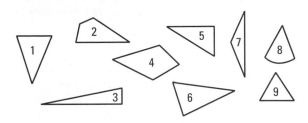

FIGURE 14-16

QUADRILATERALS

Trapezoid   Kite

Parallelogram

Rectangle   Rhombus

Square

FIGURE 14-17

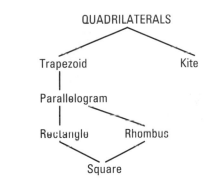

Parallelogram	A quadrilateral with 2 pairs of parallel sides.
Rectangle	A parallelogram with 90-degree angles.
Square	A rectangle with equal sides.
Rhombus	A parallelogram with all sides equal.
Trapezoid	A quadrilateral with at least one pair of parallel sides.
Isosceles Trapezoid	A trapezoid with 2 nonparallel sides equal.
Kite	A quadrilateral with 2 pairs of adjacent sides equal.

LITERATURE LINK 14-1
Geometry

Dodds, Dayle Ann. (1994). *The Shape of Things.* Cambridge, MA: Candlewick Press.

Children's spatial abilities often exceed their numeric skills. Therefore, it is important to give children many opportunities to explore both two- and three-dimensional shapes using concrete materials. *The Shape of Things* introduces young children to common shapes and shows where such shapes can be seen in the world around them.

- Draw or create a picture using only the shapes in the story. Using each of the shapes cut from colored construction paper, draw each shape into a picture using the correct name of the shape on the page. Combine the pages to create a shapes book for each child.
- Find pictures in magazines that show shapes in nature, in architecture, and other places. Design a shapes book with the pictures.
- Identify both two- and three-dimensional shapes hidden in a shoebox by using Attribute blocks or wooden solids. Record the features of each shape that are identified by touch.
- Explore three-dimensional geometry by using cutouts of various two-dimensional shapes and taping them together to see what three-dimensional shapes can be constructed from them. This helps children to connect the two-dimensional attributes with a three-dimensional shape and to visualize three-dimensional solids.

- Using large chart paper, write the name of a two- or three-dimensional shape, such as "parallelogram" or "cylinder," at the top of each piece of paper. Under the name of the shape use precise mathematical language to write as many descriptive words as possible to distinguish the attributes of this shape from other shapes. As shapes are added to the display, check to be sure that each shape has its own characteristics that make it distinct from other shapes.
- In *The Greedy Triangle* (Burns, 1998), children learn correct mathematical terminology for identifying polygons by the number of sides. Children can use toothpicks and minimarshmallows to create a triangle, then a quadrilateral, then a pentagon, and so on, modeling the shape changes the triangle makes in the story.
- Other books that introduce children to basic concepts about two-dimensional shapes include *Shapes, Shapes, Shapes* (Hoban, 1996), *Bear in a Square* (Blackstone, 1998), and *Brown Rabbit's Shape Book* (Baker, 1994).

Source: Dr. Patricia Moyer, George Mason University.

ACTIVITY 14-17

RECTANGLES (VAN HIELE LEVELS 1-2)

MATERIALS
Polygons as shown below

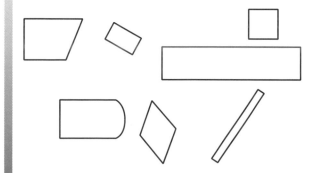

PROCEDURE
1. Which of the figures are rectangles?
2. Tell why you think the nonrectangles are not rectangles.

ACTIVITY 14-18

DESCRIBING AND COMPARING POLYGONS (VAN HIELE LEVEL 2)

MATERIALS
A set of polygons

PROCEDURE
1. Select a polygon. Write about the figure, mentioning as many characteristics as you can.
2. Choose another polygon and write about how it is different from and how it is similar to the first one.
3. Now examine the whole set of polygons. Make a list of all the different characteristics you notice as you examine the polygons. Which polygons have one or more characteristics in common?

ACTIVITY 14-19

HOW MANY SQUARES CAN YOU FIND? (VAN HIELE LEVELS 0-2)

MATERIALS
Geoboards
Rubber bands
Dot paper
Pencils

PROCEDURE

1. Make different squares on a geoboard.

2. Sketch each of the squares you make on the dot paper. Some possible squares are shown below:

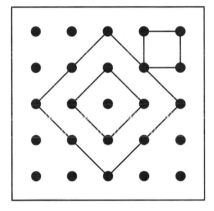

3. How many squares did you find? How do you know you have found all the squares possible? Extension: How many different rectangles can you make on a geoboard?

Diagonals. Creating a table of shapes where the sides increase by one each time and finding the number of diagonals in each figure is another aspect of the study of polygons that leads to a numerical pattern and a possible algebraic generalization. A *diagonal* is a line segment joining any two nonadjacent vertices of a figure, with the line segment completely in the interior of the figure (Henderson & Collier, 1973). For example, in the diagram the line segment FD is a diagonal, whereas the line segment AC is not. Activity 14-21 is about diagonals.

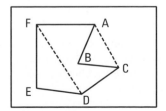

ACTIVITY 14-20

NAMING FIGURES (VAN HIELE LEVELS 0-1)

MATERIALS
The 12 figures shown below

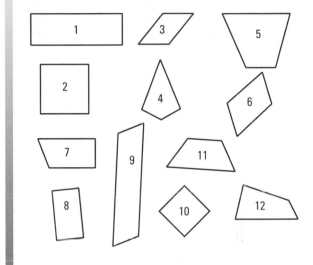

PROCEDURE

1. Examine the 12 figures.

2. How many figures can you name? Can you give more than one name for some figures?

ACTIVITY 14-21

FINDING DIAGONALS (VAN HIELE LEVELS 1-2)

MATERIALS
A set of convex polygons with 4, 5, 6, 7, 8, 9, and 10 sides drawn on paper

PROCEDURE

1. Find the number of diagonals in a four-sided polygon; in a 5-sided polygon; in a 10-sided polygon.

2. Look for a pattern that tells the number of diagonals in an *n*-sided polygon.

Circles A *circle* is a plane figure that has all its points the same distance from a fixed point, called the *center* of the circle. The distance from the center to the edge of the circle is called a *radius,* and a segment connecting two points on the edge of the circle is a *chord.* A chord passing through the center of the circle is a *diameter.* The length of the circle (distance around) is the *circumference.* A segment of the circle is called an *arc.*

LITERATURE LINK 14-2
Perimeter and Area of Polygons

Burns, Marilyn. (1997). *Spaghetti and Meatballs for All!* New York: Scholastic.

Being able to connect conceptual understanding to the processes for determining perimeter and area is crucial for children, who often have great difficulty explaining or illustrating these two ideas. When formulas for determining perimeter and area of common polygons are presented, children become easily confused because the procedures for finding the area and perimeter of squares and rectangles are quite similar. In *Spaghetti and Meatballs for All!*, Mrs. Comfort is planning a family reunion and designs a seating chart with square tables based on these ideas of perimeter and area. As the tables in the story are arranged and rearranged, children make some discoveries about these concepts.

- Model the arrangement and rearrangement of the tables in the story using blocks or color tiles. Note that shapes with the same area can have different perimeters (or combined perimeters).

- Design different table arrangements using 1-in. square tiles. As children create their own table arrangements, they can measure these perimeters and areas using various tools and methods.

- Create a class chart of the perimeters and areas of the different table arrangements created by the class. Compare arrangements with the same areas and different perimeters and recognize patterns in the measurements.

- Create and record the perimeters and areas of various table arrangements using geoboards and dot paper.

- Explore different kinds of quadrilaterals such as a square, rhombus, rectangle, parallelogram, and trapezoid. Write descriptions that show the distinct characteristics of each shape.

Source: Dr. Patricia Moyer, George Mason University.

LEARNING ABOUT SYMMETRY, CONGRUENCE, AND SIMILARITY

Symmetry

The idea of *symmetry* can first be introduced to children with examples from nature, art, and pictures of familiar objects. Symmetrical figures possess the quality that when the figure is bisected into two congruent parts, every point on one side of the bisection line (referred to as the line of symmetry) will have a reflective point on the other side of the bisection line. Folding is a means of testing for line symmetry. For example, by folding, one will find out that a square has four lines of symmetry, a rectangle has two lines of symmetry, whereas some other parallelograms have none. Exploring all parallelograms provides excellent examples and nonexamples of lines of symmetry. Figures can be classified according to the number of lines of symmetry in each. For polygons, lines of symmetry can be of three types: a line connecting two vertices, a line connecting a vertex to a midpoint of a side, and a line connecting the midpoints of two sides.

A mira is a good instrument to test for lines of symmetry in a figure. A mira is a piece of colored Plexiglas that allows one to view the reflection of a figure through the glass rather than on it, as with a mirror. The process of paper folding, known as origami, offers ample opportunities to improve spatial sense as students bend and fold square sheets of paper to make many three-dimensional shapes and objects.

Children can be asked to create symmetrical designs using pattern blocks, construct some symmetrical figures on a geoboard, or draw some on graph paper. Activities 14-22 and 14-23 are about creating symmetrical figures using pattern blocks and graph paper.

ACTIVITY 14-22

MAKING SYMMETRICAL DESIGNS WITH PATTERN BLOCKS (VAN HIELE LEVELS 1-2)

MATERIALS
Pattern blocks

PROCEDURE
1. Select a triangle and surround it with triangles and squares. How many lines of symmetry does the figure have?

2. Select a square and surround it with triangles. How many lines of symmetry does the figure have?

3. Select one of the blocks and surround it with other blocks to make regular figures. Count the lines of symmetry each figure has.*

*Idea from Eperson, 1982a.

ACTIVITY 14-23

SYMMETRICAL PATTERNS ON GRAPH PAPER (VAN HIELE LEVEL 2-3)

MATERIALS
Graph paper

PROCEDURE
1. Draw 3-by-3 squares on graph paper. Shade three of the small squares so that the figure created has one line of symmetry. Two examples are shown here.

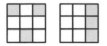

2. How many different patterns with one line of symmetry can you make by shading in three small squares?

3. Can you make patterns with two lines of symmetry?

4. Shade in four small squares and make figures with one line of symmetry; with two lines of symmetry.

5. Can you make figures with more than two lines of symmetry?

6. Compare your work with your classmates.*

*Adapted from Eperson, 1982b.

The following nine numbered activities have children examine familiar objects (leaves, windows), pictures of familiar objects (magazine pictures), and geometric figures for symmetry. Children are asked to construct symmetrical pictures and figures. In all of these activities, it is important to listen to children as they tell what they observe and what they are doing.

1. Symmetry
   • Provide children with a set of leaves to examine.
   • Have them discuss what they observe. Listen for observations about "sameness" within a shape ("I think this side is the same as this side because. . . .").

2. Symmetry
   • Provide children with a set of pictures from magazines, some symmetrical, others not.
   • Have children examine the pictures, looking for some that are the same on two sides of a central line, and describe what they notice.

3. Symmetry
   • Provide a set of pictures of homes or windows.
   • Have children examine the pictures to find windows that are symmetrical.
   • Have them tell why they think some windows are not symmetrical.
   • Have them verify the shapes are symmetrical with a mira.

4. Line symmetry
   • Have children construct symmetrical figures on a geoboard.
   • Have them tell how they know the figures are symmetrical by identifying the line of symmetry.

5. Line symmetry
   • Have children draw on paper different figures that have line symmetry.
   • Have them cut out the figures and test for symmetry by folding.

• Be sure to examine the diagonal cuts of parallelograms and rectangles to serve as nonexamples of line symmetry.

6. Line symmetry
   • Draw symmetrical shapes on patty paper or some type of transparent paper.
   • Have student fold the paper along the line of symmetry to see that one side of the shape can be placed directly on top of the other shape.

7. Line symmetry
   • Provide children with a set of different polygons drawn on paper.
   • Have them examine the figures for lines of symmetry and tell where each line of symmetry is.
   • Listen to find out how children describe each line of symmetry in a figure.

8. Line symmetry
   • Have children draw on paper figures with only one line of symmetry.
   • Ask, "Can you draw figures with two lines of symmetry? Can you draw one with three lines of symmetry? With more than three lines of symmetry?"

9. Drawing triangles and quadrilaterals
   • Have children draw or construct triangles on a geoboard with exactly one line of symmetry, with more than one line of symmetry, and one with no lines of symmetry.
   • Repeat the above steps with quadrilaterals.

Upper-elementary grade and middle-school children can study three-dimensional shapes for planes of symmetry. A three-dimensional shape has *plane symmetry* if a plane passing through the figure bisects it such that every point of the figure on one side of the plane has a reflection image on the other side of the plane. Activity 14-24 explores planes of symmetry.

> **ACTIVITY 14-24**

PLANES OF SYMMETRY (VAN HIELE LEVEL 2-3)

MATERIALS
A cube

PROCEDURE
Consider a cube.

1. How many horizontal planes of symmetry does a cube have?

2. How many vertical planes of symmetry does a cube have?

3. How many planes of symmetry pass through each pair of opposite edges?

4. How many planes of symmetry can you find for a cube? Consider other solids.

5. Does the tetrahedron have the same number of planes of symmetry as the cube?

6. Does an octahedron, an icosahedron, or a dodecahedron have planes of symmetry?

7. Record your findings on a chart. Compare your findings with those of some classmates.

Some three- and two-dimensional shapes and figures have *rotational symmetry*. A shape is said to have rotational symmetry if, when rotated about a point for an amount less than 360°, the rotated shape matches the original shape. For example, a square has 90°, 180°, and 270° rotational symmetry (Figure 14-18). Children can be asked to examine shapes and figures for rotational symmetry. For example, in explorations with figures, they will find that some figures have rotational symmetry but not line symmetry (e.g., a parallelogram), some have line symmetry but not rotational symmetry (e.g., an isosceles triangle), and regular polygons have both line and rotational symmetry, whereas some figures have neither. Letters of the alphabet, numbers, or commercially made pentomino shapes are excellent tools for exploring rotational symmetry (see Figure 14-23).

Congruence and Similarity

Congruent figures are those that have the same size and shape, that is, all corresponding angles and the length of corresponding sides are equal. Superimposing figures is one way to test for congruency. Another is by measuring sides and angles to identify that each shape has corresponding parts.

Similar figures have the same shape but not necessarily the same size. If two figures are congruent, they are also similar. Similar polygons have equal angles and proportional sides. Examples of similar figures can be obtained by enlarging or reducing a picture on a photocopying machine. Similar shapes possess the quality that when creating a ratio of two sides of one shape, the same ratio will exist in the similar figure. Or when selecting a side of one shape to its corresponding side of another shape, the same ratio will exist when comparing a different side of the first shape to the corresponding side of the other shape. This ratio can represent the scale value of the second object to the first object. For example a ratio of 1:2 indicates the second figure has each dimension of the shape twice as big as the first shape's dimensions. Each dimension has been increased, but students should explore what effect this will have on the area of the shape. Congruent and similar figures can be constructed on a geoboard, patty paper, and graph paper.

> **FIGURE 14-18**

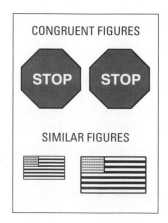

**The Annenberg/CPB
Math and Science Collection**

Classroom Clips:
Shapes from Squares

Previewing the Video

Teacher Marco Ramirez is helping his bilingual second and third graders learn about geometry by folding a paper square into different shapes. Mr. Ramirez begins the lesson with the children sitting together on the rug in front of the classroom. Each child has a square of construction paper, which they fold by following Mr. Ramirez's instructions. Mr. Ramirez has plenty of extra squares for children to use if they need to start again. He carefully models each of his verbal instructions by folding his square as he gives an instruction. Mr. Ramirez repeats the instructions in Spanish to assure that all the children understand the instructions.

The Task: **Folding the Square**

- Begin with a 5-inch by 5-inch square of paper. Fold it in half. Mr. Ramirez asks, "What shape do I have?" (a rectangle)

- Open the paper; place it with the fold line going up and down. Then make an airplane fold: "Fold one corner down to where the middle line (fold) is. Then fold the other side, too."

- "Turn the paper upside down and do the exact same thing: do another airplane fold. You're going to end up with a shape that looks something like this."

- "Then you're going to open it up. Now if you look you're going to have these lines right here, and this is called a *crease*. This is where you can fold your shapes, your square. What we're going to do is try to make as many different shapes as you possibly can, but we have one rule: **you can fold only where there's a crease.**"

The Final Product:
The Shape for Folding

Classroom Clips: **Shapes from Squares**   **D–1**

Focus on Standards

How does Mr. Ramirez address aspects of reasoning and proof in this lesson to encourage children to:

- extend their reasoning?
- develop and evaluate arguments and proofs?

Process Standard: **Connections**

At the end of class time, Mr. Ramirez reconvenes the class as a whole group on the rug to help the children summarize the relationships they are able to visualize among geometric shapes. **How does Mr. Ramirez help children understand spatial relationships and how they interconnect?**

Focus on Standards

How does Mr. Ramirez address connections in this lesson to encourage students to:

- understand how mathematical ideas interconnect and build on one another to produce a coherent whole?

How could this lesson be extended to help children understand links between geometry, measurement, and numbers?

For other connection ideas, including lesson plans and games for helping children understand geometry and learn more about tessellations, polyhedra, tangrams, and geoboards, please visit Chapter 14 of our website at **www.prenhall.com/cathcart**

Try This!

Shape Bingo

For two players

Materials: 5 disks each of two different colors
2 cubes (labeled as below)
1 gameboard

Label one cube with the following faces:

Rectangle	Triangle	Four sides	Three sides	Polygon	Quadri-lateral

Label one cube with the following faces:

No 45-degree angles	A 45-degree angle	A right angle	No right angles	Parallel lines	No parallel lines

Rules:

1. The first player rolls both cubes and puts a disk on any shape on the gameboard that matches the information on the two top faces of the cubes. If a player cannot find a shape that matches, he or she loses a turn.

2. Players take turns rolling cubes and covering a shape.

3. The first player to get three disks in a row, either horizontally, vertically, or diagonally, wins.

Adaptations: The teacher can modify this game to match the concepts children are learning by changing the labels on the faces of the cubes and changing the shapes on the gameboard.

Try This! activity from: *Mathematics Games for Fun and Practice* by Barson. ©1992 by Dale Seymour Publications. Used by permission.

LEARNING ABOUT TRANSFORMATIONAL GEOMETRY

Rigid Transformations

The idea that objects can be moved from one position to another without changing shape and size is a fundamental part of the study of transformation geometry. Movements of an object where the object itself is not distorted or changed in any way are called *rigid transformations*. Rigid transformations can be contrasted with topological transformations (e.g., stretching), in which the shape and size of objects change.

Transformation geometry (also called motion geometry) can be introduced by discussing different movements observed in nature and in the environment, such as a falling leaf, an airplane taking off, a boat moving on a river, or a door being opened.

Elementary school children study three fundamental types of rigid transformations: translations, reflections, and rotations. Children usually name these motions "slides," "flips," and "turns," respectively. A *translation* is a movement along a straight line. It has direction and distance. The direction can be horizontal, vertical, or oblique. A *reflection* is the movement of a figure about a line outside the figure, on a side of the figure, or intersecting with

a vertex. A *rotation* is the movement of a figure around a point. The turning point may be inside the figure, on the figure, or outside the figure (see Figure 14-19).

Materials used in the following 12 transformation geometry activities include a mira, paper cutouts, patty paper, figure templates, tracing paper, Attribute blocks, pattern blocks, and a geoboard.

1. Constructing Reflections
   - Provide children with a set of Attribute blocks.
   - Have them construct a figure such as a house or animal.
   - Have them construct a horizontal and vertical reflection of the figure.
2. Transformations on a geoboard
   - Ask children to make a figure on a geoboard.
   - Show a slide of the figure; a flip; a turn.
3. Drawing reflection images
   - Provide children with a mira and some figures printed on a page.
   - Have them draw reflection images about given lines.
4. Modeling transformations
   - Using several paper cutouts of nonsymmetrical figures (e.g., boats, birds), have children explore different motions on their desks. For example,

---

FIGURE 14-19

TRANSLATIONS (Slides)

horizontal slide

vertical slide

oblique slide

REFLECTIONS (Flips)

reflection about a line on the figure

reflection about a line not on the figure

reflection line intersects with a vertex

ROTATIONS (Turns)

turning point inside figure

turning point on the figure

turning point outside figure

have them demonstrate different slides (horizontal, vertical, oblique).
- Have children record their work.

5. Constructing reflections
- Provide children with an irregular figure or a shape made from pattern blocks
- Have them draw the figure.
- Then have them draw the figure showing a horizontal reflection; a vertical reflection; an oblique reflection across a diagonal.
- Utilize miras to verify their answers or use a hinged mirror where part of the shape is placed at the vertex of the hinged mirror. The image they drew should match the shape they see in the mirror.

6. Making a transformation
- Have children make a shape on paper.
- Have them trace the shape on patty paper or some type of transparent paper.
- Have them flip over the transparent version from left to right.
- Children should compare the two shapes to see that when they are placed adjacent to each other, a line of symmetry exists between the two shapes.
- Orient the two on top of each other again and explore a slide, a rotation, and an oblique flip.

7. Making reflective inkblots
- Take a piece of paper and place paint on one half of the paper.
- Have students fold the paper onto the wet paint.
- Open the paper and examine the reflective image that appears.

8. Constructing rotations
- Provide children with a paper cutout of a nonsymmetrical figure such as an animal.
- Have children explore with different rotations on their desks. In time, children should be able to demonstrate a rotation about a point on a figure, a rotation about a point outside a figure, and a rotation about a point inside a figure.

9. Constructing rotations
- Provide children with a template of a small nonsymmetrical figure.
- Have them trace the figure and then draw a half turn; a quarter turn clockwise; a quarter turn counterclockwise; combinations of rotations.

10. Constructing rotations
- Direct children to make a figure using pattern blocks.
- Have them make one that is a quarter turn of the first figure; a half turn; a three-quarter turn.

11. Constructing a pattern showing transformations
- Provide each child with a 4-by-4 square grid, with each small square measuring approximately 5 cm, and a cutout of a small figure.
- Ask children to trace the figure in each square following a pattern of rigid motions (for example, horizontal reflections and vertical half turns).

12. Constructing a pattern showing transformations
- Provide each child with a figure to use as a template (or use tracing paper or patty paper).
- Invite children to create borders for a bulletin board by using translations, reflections, and rotations of a figure.

At the middle-school level, children can conduct explorations with combinations of motions. Explorations to pursue include the following:

1. Draw any Figure A and then make two successive translations to produce Figures B and C. Compare Figures A and C. Is the result of a single translation different from the result of two successive translations? Why?

2. Draw any Figure A and then make two successive flips to produce Figures B and C. Compare Figures A and C. Are the results the same as for translations? Why not?

3. Compare the results of other successive motions:
- A slide followed by a flip and a flip followed by a slide.
- A turn followed by a flip and a flip followed by a turn.
- Other combinations including oblique flips and their reverse.

Write about your findings.

LEARNING ABOUT TESSELLATIONS

When considering *tessellations,* one generally thinks of a flat region being covered with repetitions of the same figure without any overlapping. A floor covered with square tiles is an example of a tessellation. Young children can be provided with a sufficient number of different types of regular figures and invited to explore which figures can cover a region (Activity 14-25). This is best explained by placing a large dot on the paper and having children take a vertex of the shape and placing it on the dot. Follow with more vertices of the additional shapes being places on the dot until no gaps or overlaps occur, if possible. Eventually, they will not need to place just the vertices on the dot. They will discover that triangles, convex quadrilaterals, and regular hexagons will tessellate by themselves, as will varied kinds of irregular shapes (Figure 14-20). Children can be challenged to explore why some figures tessellate and why others do not as they explore the concept of angles. This exploration could begin with triangles by asking the question: "Will all types of trian-

TECHNOLOGY LINK 14-1
Tessellation Tutorials

Learn more about creating tessellations with this site! Tessellations integrate mathematics and art and are motivating for children. This site defines tessellations, discusses the mathematics involved in creating tessellations, discusses tessellations from different cultures, and includes lesson plans and connections to technology. Visit this site and you'll be creating a tessellation within minutes!

Visit http://mathforum.org/sum95/suzanne/tess. intro.html or link from our Companion Website at **www.prenhall.com/cathcart.**

ACTIVITY 14-25

TILING A FLOOR (VAN HIELE LEVELS 1-2)

MATERIALS
Several equilateral triangles, squares, and regular pentagons, hexagons, and octagons with sides of equal length

PROCEDURE
1. Pretend that the shapes are ceramic tiles. What kind of shape could you use to tile a bathroom floor using only one kind of shape?
2. Could you tile a floor using two different shapes?
3. Draw pictures of different tiled floors.

gles tessellate?" Next, the questions "Why do all rectangles tessellate?" and "Will all convex quadrilaterals tessellate?" can be explored. Further investigations can be done with other polygons and with combinations of figures, including the use of hinged mirrors to see the tessellation about a point. By modifying tessellating polygons a certain way, Escher-type designs that will also tessellate can

be made. Explorations in Escher-type tessellations offer children opportunities to extend their understanding of symmetries, such as translation, reflection, rotation, and glide-reflection symmetry (Haak, 1976). Figure 14-21 shows the process of creating a simple Escher-type tessellation. Tessellation activities are described in Activities 14-25 through 14-28.

FIGURE 14-20

TESSELLATIONS

Regular tilings

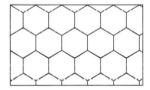
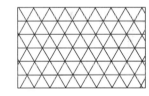

Tilings with different polygons

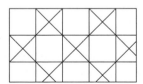
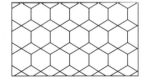
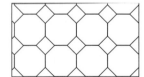

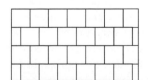

Tilings that are not edge-to-edge

FIGURE 14-21

CONSTRUCTING ESCHER-TYPE TESSELLATIONS

Step 1. Select a polygon; for example, a square.

Step 2. Select a transformation, for example, a rotation. Label the vertices and sides of the square. Rotating the square four times around vertex C produces the diagram at the right. One can see that sides 2 and 3 fit together. If the four-square pattern was translated horizontally and vertically, it would show that sides 1 and 4 fit together.

Step 3. Modify the square. The example shows that the piece removed from side 1 has been attached to side 4. Sides 2 and 3 could similarly be modified. The modified square has the same area as the original square, and it will tessellate in the same manner as did the original square.

Step 4. Invite children to use their ingenuity to make cuts on a square to produce a tessellation. An example follows.

Source: "Transformational geometry and the artwork of M.C. Escher," by S. Haak, 1976, *Mathematics Teacher, 69*(B), p. 650.

LITERATURE LINK 14-3
Geometric Designs: Patterns, Symmetry, and Tessellations

Friedman, Aileen. (1994). *A Cloak for the Dreamer.* New York: Scholastic.

Although children may lack the vocabulary and conceptual understanding necessary to express geometric relationships in formal terms, teachers can develop their repertoire by providing meaningful investigations that begin at the very basic level and move to more complex analytical activity. *A Cloak for the Dreamer* describes a tailor and his sons who sew together pieces of cloth to create beautiful cloaks. The geometric designs throughout the text can be used to begin a variety of mathematical investigations.

• The pictures in the text show children a variety of geometric designs that tessellate. Model these geometric patterns using commercially made blocks (such as pattern blocks, tangrams, Attribute blocks) or construction paper cutouts of different shapes.

• Recognize examples of tessellating patterns that have elements that repeat, highlighting that there are no gaps or spaces between the shapes. Pattern blocks can be used to create *tessellations* and patterns that have *symmetry*. These mathematical terms and their

properties should be discussed as they emerge naturally from children's investigations.

• Analyze and represent geometric designs found in different cultures. Tessellating and repeating patterns are found in Islamic culture, where designs decorate mosques and palaces; in Navajo culture, where they appear on blankets; and in the pueblo homes of the Hopi people. Use pattern blocks to re-create these tiling patterns.

• Investigate the rotational symmetry found in Native American intricate basket designs. Create a design that demonstrates rotational symmetry using a computer drawing program.

• Other books that explore geometric shapes and patterns and are representative of designs found in various cultures include *The Sultan's Snakes* (Turpin, 1990) and *Grandfather Tang's Story* (Tompert, 1990). Geometric designs can be explored using concrete materials such as tangrams, children's drawings, or computer programs such as Geometer's Sketchpad and Tessellmania.

Source: Dr. Patricia Moyer, George Mason University.

ACTIVITY 14-26

CONSTRUCTING TILING PATTERNS (VAN HIELE LEVELS 0-2)

MATERIALS
A set of rectangular-shaped tiles in two colors

PROCEDURE
1. Use the tiles to create an interesting pattern for a bathroom floor. Extension: Repeat using tiles in three colors; four colors; etc.

ACTIVITY 14-27

CONSTRUCTING A QUILT BLOCK (VAN HIELE LEVELS 1-2)

MATERIALS
Sixteen 8-cm squares (8 white and 8 of a solid color): A piece of paper 24 cm^2

PROCEDURE
1. Cut each square along one diagonal to form two congruent triangles.
2. Arrange the triangles in an interesting pattern to create a "block" pattern for a quilt.
3. When you have decided on a pattern, glue the triangles on a piece of paper.
4. Display your finished product on a bulletin board or on a large wall as a "quilt."

LEARNING ABOUT FRACTALS

Fractals are complex yet simplistic in design. A fractal is generated by a repetitive process where an alteration is made to each stage of the fractal design. Many rota-

ACTIVITY 14-28

TESSELLATIONS (VAN HIELE LEVELS 1-2)

MATERIALS
Graph paper

PROCEDURE
1. Draw an outline of a figure that will tessellate on the graph paper.
2. Color or shade in the figure.
3. By alternating white and color, create an interesting tiling pattern with the figure.

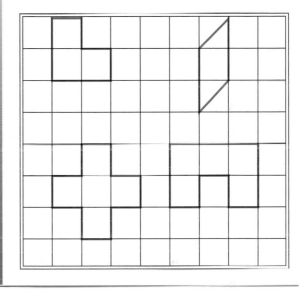

tions, reflections, and slides are made, as well as a change in reduction of the stage before and a replication of the previous stage to make the next stage. An interesting observation about fractals is that a certain portion of a fractal takes on the shape and image of the original fractal, only in a miniaturized form. Making a fractal can start with a simple geometric shape. For instance, the Sierpinski triangle begins with a simple equilateral triangle (Stage 0) and then, by connecting the midpoints of each side, a smaller equilateral triangle one-fourth the size of the original will be formed in the center. This triangle is removed, and three congruent triangles (at the top, left, and right) remain. The area of this new shape is three-fourths that of the original shape. This process is repeated for each of the smaller triangles to make the next stage, and so on. Other fractal drawings, such as the Koch curve, are generated by reducing, replicating, translating, and rebuilding the previous stage to form the next stage.

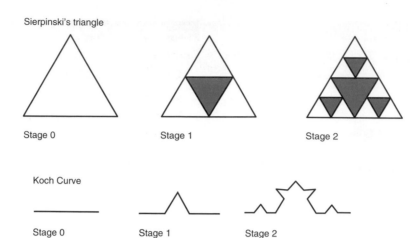

Sierpinski's triangle

Stage 0   Stage 1   Stage 2

Koch Curve

Stage 0   Stage 1   Stage 2

DEVELOPING SPATIAL SENSE

Spatial sense involves a visualization and an orientation factor (Owens, 1990). *Visualization* is the ability to mentally picture how objects appear under some rigid motion or other transformation. *Orientation* includes the ability to note positions of objects and to maintain an accurate perception of the objects under different orientation. Research shows that the two types of ability do not always reside within the same individual and that generally, boys score higher than girls on tests of spatial abilities (Owens, 1990).

Beginning at the primary level, geometry activities should aim to develop children's spatial abilities. Many of the activities described in this chapter can contribute to the development of visual perception. Activities involving tangrams and polyominoes, as well as the process of describing figures and dissecting figures, help to develop spatial sense.

Tangram Puzzles

A *tangram* is a seven-piece puzzle consisting of five triangles (2 large, 1 medium, and 2 small), one square, and one parallelogram cut from a square and that can be arranged to create different shapes, such as a rectangle, a large triangle, or an animal (see Figure 14-22). In *Grandfather Tang's Story* (Tompert, 1990), the tangram pieces are used to create many animals. Children can be asked to compare the tangram pieces:

- Compare the small triangle to the two larger triangles.
- Compare the small triangle to the parallelogram and then to the square.
- Compare the square to the largest triangle.

Such comparisons can elicit fraction language, as "The square is one-half the size of a large triangle" or "A small triangle is one-fourth the size of a large triangle." Making the square worth 1 whole and deciding on the fractional value of each piece can encourage discussions of one-fourth, one-eighth, and one-sixteenth.

A common activity uses the pieces to construct or "cover" different figures, as shown in Figure 14-22. Other activities can involve children in constructing geometric figures with some or all of the pieces, as in the following examples:

- Use two tangram pieces to make a square. Can you make a square with two other pieces? With four pieces? With all seven pieces?

 PRINCIPLES AND STANDARDS LINK 14-5
Content Strand: Geometry

Spatial visualization can be developed by building and manipulating first concrete and then mental representations of shapes, relationships, and transformations. Teachers should plan instruction so that students can explore the relationships of different attributes or change one characteristic of a shape while preserving others. (NCTM, 2000, p. 100)

 PRINCIPLES AND STANDARDS LINK 14-6
Content Strand: Geometry

Teachers should choose geometric tasks that are accessible to all students and sufficiently open-ended to engage students with a range of interests. For example, a second-grade teacher might instruct the class to find all the different ways to put five squares together so that one edge of each square coincides with an edge of at least one other square. (NCTM, 2000, p. 99)

FIGURE 14-22

Tangram Puzzle Pieces

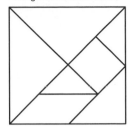

Use the tangram pieces to make the following figures.

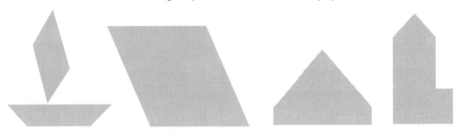

- Can you make a parallelogram with two pieces? With three pieces?
- How many different trapezoids can you make?
- Can you make a rectangle? A pentagon? A hexagon? A large triangle?

Children can be asked to keep a record of the different geometric figures they constructed and the number of tangram pieces they used.

Polyominoes

Polyominoes are arrangements of different numbers of squares: a triomino is constructed with three squares, a tetromino has four squares, a pentomino has five squares, a hexomino had six squares, etc. Combining color tiles or squares edge to edge and recognizing that a reflection or rotation of the shape does not create a new shape, students can discover the shapes for themselves. In Activity 14-29, children create figures using triominoes. The

ACTIVITY 14-29

TRIOMINOES (VAN HIELE LEVELS 1-3)

MATERIALS
A set of small ceramic or paper square tiles

PROCEDURE
1. Try to visualize which of the figures below can be made from two triominoes. Test your responses.

2. Use your triominoes to make figures that can be covered with three triominoes. Draw the outline of the figures on graph paper.

3. Draw the outline of some 9 square-unit figures on graph paper that cannot be covered with three triominoes. Ask a classmate to "solve your puzzles."*

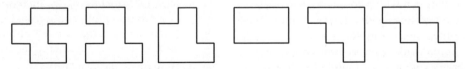

*Adapted from Eperson, 1983.

study can be extended to tetrominoes through, for example, the four-stamp problem.

Four-Stamp Problem

Stamps are sometimes printed in sheets of 100 stamps (10 rows of 10 stamps). How many different four-stamp arrangements could you buy?

 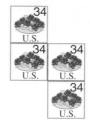

Pentominoes and hexominoes can be explored in the context of a packing box problem, as described in Activity 14-30. Activities 14-31 and 14-32 also help to develop spatial sense. The 12 pentominoes that can be constructed (Activity 14-32) are depicted in Figure 14-23. Although some are a bit difficult to see, the 12 shapes form the letters in the phrase "FLIP N TUVWXYZ". This same process of combining geometric shapes also can be formed with equilateral triangles.

Describing Figures

An activity that encourages children to verbalize what they visualize is to have them describe a figure through feeling. Using a feely bag and placing a pentomino shape inside the bag, have children reach in and describe the shape to the class. Or group the children into pairs and provided each pair with an irregular figure cut from poster board. One child holds the figure under the desk cover (neither child has seen the figure) and, through feeling it, describes the figure to a partner, who attempts to draw the figure. The roles of describing and drawing can be interchanged. The exercise can be simple or complex depending on the figure. This activity often does not produce a correctly drawn-to-scale or size-oriented replica and emphasizes the need for communication in mathematical drawings.

Another activity is to have a figure drawn on a card and to ask one child to describe the figure to a partner, who draws the figure as she or he visualizes what has been described (Sgroi, 1990). Another type of visualization is to provide children with a complex figure and ask them to find different figures within it (see Figures 14-24 and 14-25). Another more complex visualization is to provide the children with a three-dimensional object made up of interlocking cubes or multilink cubes and to have them draw on graph paper, the side view, the front

---

ACTIVITY 14-30

PACKING BOX PROBLEM (VAN HIELE LEVELS 1-2)

MATERIALS
Graph paper

PROCEDURE
1. Imagine you are a box manufacturer and you want to ship boxes flattened out. How many possible ways can you do this?
- Case I. The boxes you are presently making have no tops. If each side is a square, a box flattened out could resemble the pattern shown below.

Can you think of other patterns? Use graph paper and draw all possible patterns that can be made with five squares. (Two patterns are the same if they can be covered by the same paper cutout.) How many of your patterns fold into boxes? These are called "box-makers." Draw a set of "box-makers" for display.
- Case II. Now think about patterns for boxes that have tops. Draw as many patterns as you can for six-sided squares. How many of the patterns are "nets of cubes"? Draw a set of "nets of cubes" for display.

ACTIVITY 14-31

QUADROMINOES (VAN HIELE LEVELS 1-2)

MATERIALS
Interlocking cubes

PROCEDURE
1. Construct different arrangements using only three cubes.
2. How many arrangements did you find?
3. Now construct as many different arrangements as you can using four cubes (quadrominoes). (Arrangements that are reflections or rotations of another are not considered different.)
4. How many did you find?

view and the top view. Then, reverse the task by giving them a drawing of a shape's side, front, and top view and have them construct the object.

Figures 14-26 and 14-27 show two kinds of activities that help develop visualization skills and orientation abilities. Figure 14-26 can lead to interesting numeric patterns as the cube begins to increase in size. A generalization of the *n*th size cube can challenge many middle-school students.

Dissection Motion Operations

Spatial sense can be developed through dissection motion operations on figures. A *dissection motion operation* (DMO) is the operation of partitioning and then dissecting a figure for the purpose of rearranging the pieces (Rahim & Sawada, 1986). DMO has not commonly been a part of geometry programs, although children use such motions spontaneously when partitioning figures to attain equal-sized parts (Pothier & Sawada, 1990). Activity 14-33 is an example of a dissection activity.

ACTIVITY 14-32

CONSTRUCTING PENTOMINOES (VAN HIELE LEVELS 1-2)

MATERIALS
Five square tiles
Graph paper

PROCEDURE
1. Use the tiles to construct different arrangements of five squares. Each tile has to connect with other tiles along a full side.
2. Draw the different arrangements on graph paper.

FIGURE 14-25

How many different-sized squares can you make on a 5-by-5 geoboard?

FIGURE 14-23

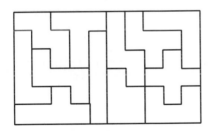

FIGURE 14-24

How many triangles do you see in the figure?

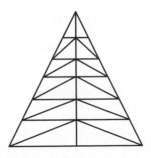

FIGURE 14-26

VISUALIZING CUBES

1. Let us say that a 1-by-1-by-1 cube has "order 1." Suppose that you were to dip such a cube into a can of paint. How many sides of the cube would be covered with paint?

2. Now imagine a 2-by-2-by-2 cube or a cube of order 2. Again, suppose you dip the cube into a can of paint and after the paint has dried, you sawed along each of the lines of its faces to obtain eight smaller cubes. How many of the small cubes have six sides painted? How many of the small cubes have five sides painted? Four sides painted? Three sides? Two sides? One side? No side?

3. BIG DIP! Now consider a cube of order three. Once again, you follow the procedure of dipping and sawing. Can you answer the questions in part 2 for a cube of order three?

FIGURE 14-27

VISUALIZING PAPER UNFOLDED

Take large rectangular pieces of paper, fold each one, and cut holes as indicated in the diagrams. ------ indicates a fold.

Draw the picture of the paper as it would look when unfolded.

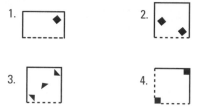

1.   2.

3.   4.

ACTIVITY 14-33

DISSECTING FIGURES (VAN HIELE LEVELS 1-2)

MATERIALS
Several paper rectangles (the same size) for each child

PROCEDURE
1. Select one rectangle.

2. Cut it into two pieces so that the pieces can be put together again to make a large triangle.

3. Cut other rectangles into two pieces to make the following:
   • A parallelogram
   • A rhombus
   • A right-angled triangle
   • A trapezoid
   • Other figures

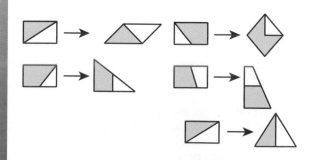

Subsequent to Activity 14-34, children could be challenged to "prove" that the area of noncongruent parts of figures, as in the figures shown here, are equal by DMO.

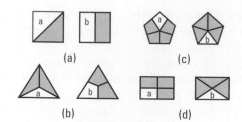

(a)   (c)

(b)   (d)

ACTIVITY 14-34

DISSECTING SQUARES (VAN HIELE LEVELS 1-2)

MATERIALS
Scissors
Paper

PROCEDURE
1. Cut a square into four parts to make the following:
   • A rhombus
   • A parallelogram
   • Other figures

LEARNING ABOUT COORDINATE GEOMETRY

Upper-elementary school children are introduced to notions of coordinate geometry. A first introduction could be with real-life situations such as finding a seat in a theater or sports arena or a car in a parking lot. Rows and columns could be labeled with letters and numbers

---

ACTIVITY 14-35

NAMING POINTS ON A GRID (VAN HIELE LEVELS 1-2)

MATERIALS
A grid with points labeled as in the figure

PROCEDURE
1. Name the points labeled A, B, C, D, and E.

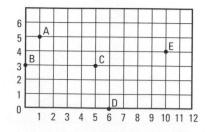

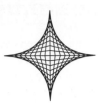
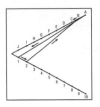
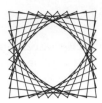

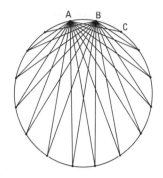

ACTIVITY 14-36

LOCATING POINTS ON A GRID (VAN HIELE LEVELS 1-2)

MATERIALS
Graph paper

PROCEDURE
1. Mark off a grid in at least 6-by-6 squares on the graph paper.

2. Label the axes.

3. Locate and label the following points on your grid:
   A (2,4); B (3,3); C (0,5); D (5,3); E (4,0)

(e.g., Row F, Seat 8) and later changed to numbers only (e.g., Row 6, Column 8). The ordered pair notation (6,8) can be presented by drawing graphs. Children may connect locating points on a coordinate grid with the popular game *Battleship*. Activities for children can consist of drawing figures on a coordinate grid by plotting points from sets of given ordered pairs or by identifying points on a grid figure (Activities 14-35 and 14-36). Geoboards and pegboards are good materials for coordinate geometry activities.

LEARNING ABOUT CURVE STITCHING

String sculpture or curve stitching is the process of connecting sequences of points with straight lines in such a manner that curves are formed. The materials required are poster board or stiff paper, a needle, and colored embroidery thread. Steps for creating designs with angles and circles follow.

Angles

- Draw an acute angle on a square piece of poster board. On each arm of the angle, mark off 1-cm intervals. Label the points with a pencil as in the diagram.

- With a needle, punch holes along the arms at each interval.

- Thread a needle and tape the end of the thread on the underside of the card. Pull the needle up at Point A and then down at 1. Cross over to 2 underneath and pull up at 2, then go down at Point B. Then up at Point C, down at 3, up at 4, down at Point D, and so on.

Circles

- Divide the circumference of a circle into 24 (or more) equal parts.

- Using needle and thread, begin at Point A, cross over and push down at Point B, then up at Point C, over to and down at Point A, up at Point D, over to and down at Point A, up at Point E, and so on.

- Upon completion, each point will be joined with every other point.

Varied designs can be constructed by changing the angle size and the distance between points. It is also possible to create three-dimensional curve stitching sculptures as shown in Figure 14-28.

The art of string sculpture can provide insights into relationships between lines and curves. It also exemplifies the aesthetics of geometry. String sculpture activities can be integrated with art classes.

FIGURE 14-28

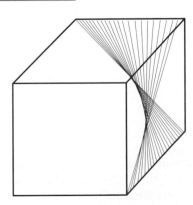

CONCLUSION

In this chapter, introductory aspects of different geometries have been presented. Elementary-school children should be introduced to ideas of each type in an informal manner. As children's geometric thinking progresses, the topics should be discussed in a progressively more formal manner. The development of spatial abilities should be a focus of geometry activities at all grade levels. Teachers should pay particular attention toward helping children progress on the van Hiele levels of geometric thought.

For Your Journal

When you have finished studying this chapter, reflect on the following questions in your math journal:

1. Give an example of an activity at each of the five van Hiele levels of geometric thought.

2. Visit an elementary-school classroom and a middle-school classroom and informally interview several children to assess their understanding of geometry. Describe their understandings and misconceptions. Where would you place their thinking related to the van Hiele levels of geometric thought?

3. Explain how to develop spatial sense in children.

For Your Portfolio

When you have finished studying this chapter, complete the following activities to include in your professional portfolio:

1. Examine a textbook's section on geometry and describe it in relation to the van Hiele levels.

2. Write a lesson plan to introduce a geometry concept of your choice to children at van Hiele Level 0. Then write a lesson to introduce a related topic to children at van Hiele Level 1.

3. Write a lesson plan to help children develop spatial sense.

Resources for Teachers

Children's books

Burns, M. (1994). *The greedy triangle.* New York: Scholastic.

Ehlert, L. (1989). *Color zoo.* New York: J. B. Lippincott.

Hewitt, S. (1996). *Taking off with shapes.* Texas: Raintree Steck-Vaughn.

Pinkney, J. (1985). *The patchwork quilt.* New York: Dial Books for Young Readers.

Pluckrose, H. (1995). *Math counts: Shapes.* Chicago: Children's Press.

Ringgold, F. (1991). *Tar beach.* New York: Scholastic.

Tompert, A. (1990). *Grandfather Tang's story: A tale told with tangrams.* New York: Crown.

Books on geometry

Creative Publications. (1994). *Beyond activities project: Mathematics replacement curriculum: Polyhedraville.* Mountain View, CA: Creative Publications.

Del Grande, J. (1993). *Geometry and spatial sense: Curriculum Evaluation Standards for School Mathematics Addenda Series, Grades K-6.* Reston, VA: National Council of Teachers of Mathematics.

Geddes, D. (1992). *Geometry in the middle grades: Curriculum Evaluation Standards for School Mathematics Addenda Series, Grades 5-8.* Reston, VA: National Council of Teachers of Mathematics.

Picciotto, H. (1984). *Pentomino activities, lessons, and puzzles.* Sunnyvale, CA: Creative Publications.

Rectanus, C. (1994a). *Math by all means: Geometry grade 2.* Sausalito, CA: Math Solutions Publications.

Rectanus, C. (1994b). *Math by all means: Geometry grade 3.* Sausalito, CA: Math Solutions Publications.

Sakata, H. (1984). *Origami.* Tokyo: Graph-Sha.

Seymour, D., & Britton, J. (1989). *Introduction to tessellations.* Palo Alto, CA: Dale Seymour Publications.

Tremaine, J. (1997). *Step by Step Origami.* Surrey, UK: Combe Books.

Walker, K., Reak, C., & Stewart, K. (1995a). *20 thinking questions for geoboards, grades 3-6.* Mountain View, CA: Creative Publications.

Walker, K., Reak, C., & Stewart, K. (1995b). *20 thinking questions for geoboards, grades 6-8.* Mountain View, CA: Creative Publications.

Winter, M., Lappan, G., Phillips, E., & Fitzgerald, W. (1986). *Middle grades mathematics project: Spatial visualization.* Menlo Park, CA: Addison-Wesley.

Links to the Internet

Math Forum: Tessellation Tutorials

http://www.mathforum.org/sum95/suzanne/tess.intro.html

Contains information about tessellations, including what they are and how to create them.

Geoboards in the Classroom

http://www.mathforum.org/trscavo/geoboards/

Contains a unit on exploring the length and area of two-dimensional geometric figures using geoboards.

Tangrams

http://www.mathforum.org/trscavo/tangrams.html

Contains a unit on using tangrams to find the area of polygons without employing formulas.

Explorer: Geometry

http://explorer.scrtec.org/explorer/explorer-db/browse/static/Mathematics/browse/f66.html

Contains many lessons on geometry and lists of other resources.

CHAPTER 15

Developing Measurement Concepts and Skills

KEY CONCEPTS ▶

✔ **Standard units of measure**

✔ **Nonstandard units of measure**

✔ **Meaning of** *length, area, volume, capacity, mass, time, temperature,* **and** *angle*

FOCUS QUESTIONS ▶

When you have finished studying this chapter, you should be able to answer the following questions:

1. What is the difference between standard and nonstandard units of measure?

2. What are some examples of situations in which measurement is needed? Choose at least one example for each attribute: length, area, volume, capacity, mass, time, temperature, and angle.

NCTM CONTENT STANDARDS AND EXPECTATIONS ADDRESSED IN THIS CHAPTER

STANDARD	EXPECTATIONS FOR GRADES PRE-K–2	EXPECTATIONS FOR GRADES 3–5	EXPECTATIONS FOR GRADES 6–8
Measurement Standard Instructional programs from pre-K–12 should enable all students to—	In prekindergarten through Grade 2 all students should— (NCTM, 2000, p. 102)	In Grades 3–5 all students should— (NCTM, 2000, p. 170)	In Grades 6–8 all students should—(NCTM, 2000, p. 240)
Understand measurable attributes of objects and the units, systems, and processes of measurement	• recognize the attributes of length, volume, weight, area, and time. • compare and order objects according to these attributes. • understand how to measure using nonstandard and standard units. • select an appropriate unit and tool for the attribute being measured.	• understand such attributes as length, area, weight, volume, and size of angle and select the appropriate type of unit for measuring each attribute. • understand the need for measuring with standard units and become familiar with standard units in the customary and metric systems. • carry out simple unit conversions, such as from centimeters to meters, within a system of measurement. • understand that measurements are approximations and how differences in units affect precision. • explore what happens to measurements of a two-dimensional shape such as its perimeter and area when the shape is changed in some way.	• develop an understanding of large numbers and recognize and appropriately use exponential, scientific, and calculator notation. • understand both metric and customary systems of measurement. • understand relationships among units and convert from one unit to another within the same system. • understand, select, and use units of appropriate size and type to measure angles, perimeter, area, surface area, and volume.

STANDARD	EXPECTATIONS FOR GRADES PRE-K–2	EXPECTATIONS FOR GRADES 3–5	EXPECTATIONS FOR GRADES 6–8
Measurement Standard (*continued*) Instructional programs from pre-K–12 should enable all students to—	In prekindergarten through Grade 2 all students should— (NCTM, 2000, p. 102)	In Grades 3–5 all students should— (NCTM, 2000, p. 170)	In Grades 6–8 all students should—(NCTM, 2000, p. 240)
Apply appropriate techniques, tools, and formulas to determine measurements	• measure with multiple copies of units of the same size, such as paper clips laid end to end. • use repetition of a single unit to measure something larger than the unit, for instance, measuring the length of a room with a single meterstick. • use tools to measure. • develop common referents for measures to make comparisons and estimates.	• develop strategies for estimating the perimeters, areas, and volumes of irregular shapes. • select and apply appropriate standard units and tools to measure length, area, volume, weight, time, temperature, and the size of angles. • select and use benchmarks to estimate measurements. • develop, understand, and use formulas to find the area of rectangles and related triangles and parallelograms. • develop strategies to determine the surface areas and volumes of rectangular solids.	• use common benchmarks to select appropriate methods for estimating measurements. • select and apply techniques and tools to accurately find length, area, volume, and angle measures to appropriate levels of precision. • develop and use formulas to determine the circumference of circles and the area of triangles, parallelograms, trapezoids, and circles and develop strategies to find the area of more-complex shapes. • develop strategies to determine the surface area and volume of selected prisms, pyramids, and cylinders. • solve problems involving scale factors, using ratio and proportion. • solve simple problems involving rates and derived measurements for such attributes as velocity and density.

easurement can be one of the most interesting and useful topics in the elementary curriculum. Children and adults use measurement ideas in their everyday lives, and questions involving measurement can be identified in virtually every subject taught during the school day. Learning the concepts and processes associated with measurement requires active participation in a wide variety of physical and mental situations; instruction naturally lends itself to a problem-solving approach. As children study measurement, they apply concepts from number and geometry and thus have opportunities to gain new insights and discover new connections within and between these mathematical topics (Lindquist, 1989).

What do we know of U.S. children's understanding of measurement? The sixth National Assessment of Educational Progress (NAEP) noted that most fourth and eighth graders show an "incomplete conceptual understanding of area, sometimes confuse area and perimeter, and have difficulty applying area concepts to complex situations" (Kenney & Kouba, 1997, p. 142). Likewise, twelfth graders had limited understanding of the concepts of volume and surface area. As with other math topics, teachers must make sure that children understand concepts before proceeding to practice skills. In measurement, children must understand what it means to measure and what different types of measurement, such as length, perimeter, area, and volume, *mean* before focusing on formulas to calculate those measures.

This chapter consists of two major sections. The first discusses measurement concepts and processes along with a recommended instructional sequence. The second section presents teaching strategies and learning activities for each of the following elementary- and middle-school measurement topics: length, area, volume, capacity, mass, time, temperature, and angle. ✔

CONCEPTS AND INSTRUCTIONAL SEQUENCE

What Is Measurement?

Although counting involves discrete objects, measuring involves continuous properties. A *measurable attribute* of an object or event, such as mass or time, is a characteristic that can be quantified by comparing it to a *unit*. The *process* of measuring is the same for each attribute: An appropriate unit is chosen and the object or event being measured is compared to the unit. The result of measuring is a number and a unit, such as 27 kg or 9.8 seconds.

To illustrate, if you had a large box to measure, you would first have to decide which attribute of the box you were interested in and then select a unit that possesses that same attribute. If you wanted to know how long the box was, possible choices for the unit would include your hand span, a paper clip, or the centimeter. Depending on the unit chosen, the length of a given box might be 3 spans, 20 paper clips, or 62 cm. If you wanted to know how heavy the box was, you could use a balance scale to compare it with a unit of mass such as a book or the pound. To measure how much the box holds, you could find how many smaller boxes of a particular size would fit into it or measure its length, width, and height in *centimeters* and compute the volume in *cubic centimeters* using the formula $V = lwh$.

Instructional Sequence

Although the meanings, units, instruments, and formulas associated with the various attributes are different, the process, concepts, and instructional sequence for each measurement topic is basically the same (Inskeep, 1976). First, the meaning of the attribute is developed through activities involving perception and direct comparison. Second, children begin to measure using arbitrary or nonstandard units. Third, they measure and estimate using standard units. Related experiences involve learning to use instruments and read scales and developing formulas to determine measurements. The following paragraphs

present key concepts and principles for teaching measurement in each of these phases.

Perception and direct comparison This first stage is sometimes referred to as "premeasurement," because it does not require a unit and it does not involve assigning a number to the object being measured. Activities such as those that follow in this chapter allow children to experience the properties of the attribute and to use sight and touch to compare and order objects with respect to those properties. The focus is on the development of conceptual understanding.

The use of appropriate *language* in direct comparison tasks is critical to allow the children to relate the concept to their experience and to distinguish among the various attributes. Deciding which of two objects is "bigger" depends on the meaning of the term *big*. Children also appreciate the need for different words to describe different attributes. For determining length, the child can be asked which of two sticks is *longer*. The problem can be solved by placing the sticks side-by-side. For determining capacity, the child can be asked to determine which of two cups *holds more*. Pouring from one cup into the other allows the child to answer without knowing how much either cup holds. Similarly, questions such as the following can be used to introduce mass, area, and temperature: Which book is *heavier?* Which paper *covers more surface?* Which liquid is *hotter?*

Classical Piagetian *conservation* tasks can be used at this stage to provide insight into the child's thinking (Steffe & Hirstein, 1976). To test for conservation of length, the child is asked to find a stick as long as a given stick and to show this by placing the sticks side-by-side. One stick is then moved forward and the child is asked whether that stick is now longer than, shorter than, or as long as the other stick. Children who do not conserve length believe that the length of an object changes when it is moved.

The teacher should not attempt to "correct" nonconservers and should not conclude that such children are not "ready" to learn basic measurement ideas and skills (Hiebert, 1984). Maturation and experience, particularly in settings in which children discuss their work with each other and the teacher, are factors that contribute to cognitive development, and over time children become conservers. Both nonconservers and conservers can benefit from comparison and other early measurement activities. Conservation tasks can also be presented as problems to be solved by the class or by small groups of children. It is through experiences such as these that children construct and modify their view of reality. Children can discuss conflicting answers and different reasons for them. Children who conserve generally give one of three arguments to explain why the quantity still is the same after a transformation: (1) reversibility—"you can move it back the way it was"; (2) identity—"you didn't add any or take any away"; and (3) compensation—"this one sticks out more here but this one sticks out more here" (Cathcart, 1971).

Seriation tasks involve ordering three or more objects according to a particular attribute. For example, the child might be given six containers and asked to order them by capacity. Although this requires a series of direct comparisons, other properties are also involved. The child uses *transitivity* when he or she reasons as follows: "I found that the bottle holds more than the jar and the jar holds more than the can, so I know that the bottle holds more than the can without actually pouring."

Nonstandard units At this stage the question is "How big?" rather than "Which is bigger?" and invites the further question "Compared to what?" When children see a need for a referent, they are encouraged to choose a variety of units with which to measure the object. The first criterion for selecting an *appropriate* unit is that it has the same attribute as that to be measured. Thus, a long thin object such as a pencil would be a good unit for measuring length but it would not be a very good unit for measuring area or angles. Another consideration is the size of the unit relative to the object to be measured. The unit should usually be smaller than the object but large enough so that the counting can be completed in a reasonable time and the resulting number has a reasonable magnitude; one would not want to measure the thickness of a page with an eraser or the length of a classroom with a paper clip.

An important concept is that physical measurement of continuous quantities is always *approximate* (Kastner, 1989). Children are exposed to this reality when they measure the length of a pen in paper clips and find that a whole-number multiple of this unit does not exactly match the object's length. In the drawing shown, the length of the pen is closer to 5 paper clips than to 6; we can say that the pen is about 5 paper clips long, the pen is a bit more than 5 paper clips long, or to the nearest paper clip the length of the pen is 5. Similarly, children might find that the capacity of a large juice can is about 10 paper cups and that the mass of an eraser is a bit more than 5 pieces of chalk.

As children gain experience working with nonstandard units, they should be encouraged to *estimate* their answers before they measure. In particular, they should be challenged to predict the effect of using a larger or smaller unit: Will the number obtained be larger or smaller? Examining the results of measuring an object using several different units leads children to discover the inverse relationship between the size of the unit and the number of units required to match the object. Learners should be encouraged to verbalize this concept in their own words. A child might say, "If the unit is shorter, it will take more of them to be as long."

The idea of *subdividing* a unit so that the number of units more closely matches the object introduces the concept of *precision* in relation to the approximate nature of measurement. Dividing the unit into smaller parts results in a more precise answer. The length of the pen below is about 5 of the larger units and 10 of the smaller units.

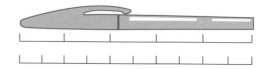

When two children accurately use the same unit to measure a particular object, both should get the same number. However, if they use different units, two different answers can be correct. It is helpful to discuss this idea when using body parts as arbitrary units. An example is measuring the width of the room in shoe lengths. Thus, another characteristic of a good unit is that others can easily replicate and understand it. It is interesting to discuss historical measures such as the cubit (the distance from the elbow to the tip of the middle finger) in this connection.

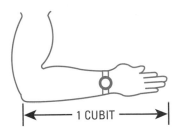

1 CUBIT

Standard units Even though the children all get the same answers using arbitrary classroom units and know what these units mean, they can appreciate the problems associated with trying to communicate such measures outside their class or school. They might discuss telling their parents about a rock with a mass of 23 blocks or trying to buy a board 13 textbooks long. But children will come to see that it is difficult to communicate measurements done with nonstandard units to other people. So something else is needed.

That something is *standard units.* Standard units are units agreed upon and accepted by a group of people. In the United States, two systems of standard units are used: the customary system and the metric system. Table 15-1 lists common units of measure in each system to measure different attributes.

The customary system may seem to be easier to most adults, because it is widely used in the United States. But this system has difficult equivalences: for example, there are 5280 feet in a mile and there are 16 ounces in a pound. The equivalences in the metric system are much easier to learn, because the metric system is based on powers of 10. For example, there are 1000 millimeters in a meter and 1000 milliliters in a liter. In the metric system there are three prefixes for smaller units: *milli-* (one thousandth), *centi-* (one hundredth), and *deci-* (one tenth). Likewise, there are three prefixes for larger units: *kilo-* (one thousand), *hecto-* (one hundred), and *deka-* (ten). So a child can use these prefixes to help understand the following:

There are	1000 millimeters in 1 meter
	100 centimeters in 1 meter
	10 decimeters in 1 meter
And that	1 dekameter is equal to 10 meters
	1 hectometer is equal to 100 meters
	1 kilometer is equal to 1000 meters

These same equivalences are true for all different units of measure, including meters, grams, and liters, and make the metric system easy to use.

TABLE 15-1

COMMON STANDARD UNITS OF MEASURE

ATTRIBUTE BEING MEASURED	CUSTOMARY SYSTEM	METRIC SYSTEM
Length	inch foot yard mile	millimeter centimeter meter kilometer
Area	square inch square foot square yard acre	square centimeter square meter hectare
Volume	cubic inch cubic foot cubic yard	cubic centimeter cubic meter
Capacity	fluid ounce cup quart gallon	milliliter liter
Weight	ounce pound ton	gram kilogram metric ton
Temperature	degrees Fahrenheit	degrees Celsius
Time	second minute hour day week month year	
Angles	degrees radians	degrees radians

It is important that children learn to use both systems of measurement. Note, however, that the teacher should *not* spend important instructional time converting measurements from one system to the other. Instead, instruction should focus on developing understanding of and skill in measuring using both systems of units. Table 15-2 lists a common scope and sequence for teaching measurement.

Knowledge of the units appropriate for a given task and the ability to decide when and how to *estimate* are components of "measurement sense" (Shaw & Cliatt, 1989). Thus, a child would identify the kilometer or mile, as opposed to the meter or centimeter or yard or foot, as the most appropriate unit for describing distances between two cities and would want to know only the approximate distance in order to estimate how long it would take to drive that far. Strategies used by good estimators include *referents* (using a known quantity such as your own height to estimate another person's height), *chunking* (estimating the area of a room by first breaking it into

TABLE 15-2 ▶

SCOPE AND SEQUENCE CHART FOR TEACHING MEASUREMENT

GRADE LEVEL	K	1	2	3	4	5	6
Length	direct comparison, nonstandard units, cm, in. ruler	m, ft	dm, yd	mm, km, mi perimeter rectangle			prefixes circle
Area		direct comparison, nonstandard units	cm², in.²	m², ft², yd² rectangle	km², parallelogram, circle	mm²	ha surface area
Volume			direct comparison, nonstandard units	cm³, in.³	m³, ft³, yd³	rectangular prism	dm³ = L cm³ = mL m³ = kL
Capacity	direct comparison, nonstandard units	L, C	mL	graduated beaker	pt, qt, gal	kL	
Mass	direct comparison, balance	nonstandard units	kg	g	t	mg	g − mL kg − L t − kL
Time	sequencing events, direct comparison, nonstandard units, calendar	minute, hour, second, digital clock	dial clock	date notation	A.M., P.M. 24-hr clock	time zones	
Temperature	weather	temperature, direct comparison	°C, °F thermometer		Celsius referents		
Angles					right, obtuse, acute, straight	degree protractor	interior angles in triangle

several workable parts), and *unitizing* (estimating the volume of a pitcher by mentally dividing it into smaller, equal parts such as glassfuls of 250 mL) (Lindquist, 1987). Children should have referents for common metric units (an average adult male's mass is about 80 kg, a quart of milk is about a liter, a dime is about 1 mm thick, room temperature is about 70°F).

Relationships among metric units can often be discovered directly. For example, it takes 10 cm to make a train one dc long. To successfully convert from one unit to another, the child needs to know the meaning of the prefixes, be able to multiply and divide by powers of 10, and understand that the larger unit will be associated with the smaller number. Generally, conversion questions should

occur in the context of realistic problem-solving situations rather than as sets of contrived exercises.

Instruments In the elementary grades, children learn to use the following measuring instruments: ruler (length), pan balance (mass), graduated beaker (capacity), protractor (angles), thermometer (temperature), and clock (time). Although these instruments are based on standard units, children should invent and construct their own instruments to simplify various tasks at earlier stages. For example, a balance is used to find which of two objects is heavier, a paper clip chain ruler is used to measure length in these arbitrary units, and a clear bottle is calibrated to show the water heights for whole numbers of paper cup

LITERATURE LINK 15-1
Developing Measurement Concepts

Adler, David. (1999). *How Tall, How Short, How Faraway.* New York: Holiday House.

Hightower, Susan. (1997). *Twelve Snails to One Lizard.* New York: Simon & Schuster.

Lasky, Kathryn. (1994). *The Librarian who Measured the Earth.* New York: Little, Brown and Company.

Lionni, Leo. (1960). *Inch by Inch.* New York: Astor Book.

Maestro, Betsy. (1999). *The Story of Clocks and Calendars: Marking a Millennium.* New York: Lothrop, Lee & Shepard Books.

Neuschwander, Cindy. (1997). *Sir Cumference and the First Round Table.* Watertown, MA: Charlesbridge Publishing.

Neuschwander, Cindy. (1999). *Sir Cumference and the Dragon of Pi.* Watertown, MA: Charlesbridge Publishing.

Older, Jules. (2000). *Telling Time.* Watertown, MA: Charlesbridge Publishing.

Measurement is a common and practical mathematics skill used in science and in everyday life. Children need experiences in measuring attributes of objects using both standard and nonstandard units. *Twelve Snails to One Lizard* is the story of mischievous Bubba the Bullfrog, who uses nonstandard units (like snails, lizards, and a boa constrictor) to help Milo Beaver build a dam. The humorous illustrations demonstrate for children the importance of using standard units of measure.

- Challenge children to develop their own nonstandard units of length measure. For example, what unit would children use to measure the length of their thumb, a desk, their classroom, the hallway, or a football field?

- Collect groups of objects that measure 1 inch, 1 centimeter, 1 foot, 1 yard, or 1 meter in length so that students begin to recognize when an object is approximately 1 centimeter or 1 foot. Use these objects as length referents for estimating the lengths of other objects in the classroom.

- Children can read the book *Inch by Inch* and use commercially-made inch worms or inch tiles to measure various objects in the classroom. After exploring nonstandard measuring units, they will gradually discover the need for more standard units of length.

How Tall, How Short, How Faraway also explores length measurement.

- *The Story of Clocks and Calendars: Marking a Millennium* show the evolution of time measurement exploring a variety of clocks and calendars. Children can investigate different time zones using maps and globes. They can create an eight-panel storyboard to show the time and what students in different time zones might be doing when it is noon in New York. *Telling Time* teaches children about minutes, hours, days, weeks, years, decades, and how to tell time.

- There are several books for older children that investigate the measurement of circles. *The Librarian Who Measured the Earth* is the story of Eratosthenes and his quest to find a way to measure the circumference of the earth. Children can use the library or the Internet to explore other contributions Eratosthenes made to mathematics, history, and geography. *Sir Cumference and the First Round Table* introduces students to the vocabulary of circle measurement (circumference, diameter, and radius) and *Sir Cumference and the Dragon of Pi* reveals how the diameter and circumference measures of circles arrive at pi (π).

---

units. Such devices help children see the connection between the attribute and the standard instrument. Careful teaching, demonstration, and appropriate classroom activities are required to ensure that children use measuring instruments correctly and with understanding.

Formulas   According to Bright and Hoeffner (1993), "formulas should be a product of exploration and discovery" (p. 81). The authors recommend that children must have hands-on experiences with measuring, "with emphasis more on understanding the underlying concepts than on applying formulas" (p. 82).

In the intermediate grades, children learn and apply *formulas* for finding the perimeter, area, and volume of simple two- and three-dimensional figures. Children can often discover these relationships on their own. For example, children who have been finding the distance around a number of different polygons by measuring the individual sides notice that when a rectangle is involved, only two sides need to be measured; the perimeter can be found by doubling the sum of the length and the width or by adding twice the length and twice the width. Developing formulas in this way is meaningful and makes it possible for children to solve problems when rules are forgotten. Formulas for the area of a rectangle, parallelogram, and triangle and for the surface area and volume of a rectangular prism can similarly be discovered by children. The relationship between the circumference and the diameter of a circle (pi) can be explored by children at various grade levels. Primary-grade children can use string to compare the distances around and across discs of varying sizes; intermediate-grade children can measure these distances in millimeters and find their ratio using a calculator.

Problem solving and applications   There are a number of interesting problems in which relationships between two attributes are investigated. For example, children can make as many different rectangles as they can having a fixed perimeter and find the area of each. Activities of this nature are appropriate at various grade levels, since formulas and relationships do not depend on particular units. Practical real-life problems might include finding the cost of painting or carpeting a room. Cooking, carpentry, and outdoor education are other settings in which measurement skills can be learned and applied.

Summary of Teaching Sequence

The first part of this chapter described the measurement process and an instructional sequence for the important concepts and skills. The early emphasis is on developing understanding and vocabulary through activities involving visual perception, direct comparison, and measuring with arbitrary units. Later, children learn to estimate and measure with appropriate metric units, use measurement instruments, and discover formulas and relationships. Finally, teachers should use an active learning, problem-solving approach at all levels.

The remainder of the chapter describes sample teaching strategies and learning activities for the three stages of the instructional sequence for each of the attributes. Teachers can adapt questions and activities for use in whole class, small group, and individual learning settings.

TEACHING STRATEGIES AND LEARNING ACTIVITIES

Length

In studying linear measure we refer to the *length* of an object and to the *distance* between two objects. We also talk about the *height* of a building, the *width* of a hall, and the *thickness* of a piece of paper. Related vocabulary includes the terms *long* and *short, near* and *far, tall* and *short, narrow* and *wide,* and *thick* and *thin. Perimeter* is the total distance around a closed figure.

Research on children's knowledge of measuring has identified several difficulties (Wilson & Rowland, 1993). To assess children's understanding of the inverse relationship between the size of the unit and the number of units used, first and second graders were shown two identical strips. When one strip was covered with small units and the other with larger units, children said that the strip covered by the smaller units was longer because there were more units. In another study, third-grade students were told the number of sheets of paper used by two different people to measure the height of a door. Over half of the children claimed that the person who had used the most sheets had the longest sheets. On a task involving measuring with a ruler in an unfamiliar situation, most third-grade children and half of the seventh-grade children could not give the length of a line segment placed on a pictured ruler such that the end of the ruler was not aligned with the end of the segment.

Length: Perception and direct comparison
Beginning activities focus on language and concept development (Jensen & O'Neil, 1981). The following are sample questions and directions a teacher might use with a group of children provided with a set of rods or cardboard strips cut into different lengths.

- Find a strip that is long (short). Find another strip that is longer (shorter) than this strip. Can you tell by looking? How do you place the strips to know? Find another strip as long as your strip. Show how you know these two strips have the same length.

- Now choose any strip and sort the other strips into three groups: longer, shorter, and the same length. Choose any five strips and put them in order from longest to shortest.

Many young children do not understand that the length of an object is the distance between the two endpoints. They focus on only one aspect of the situation and consider only the position of the endpoint. The test for conservation of length was described earlier in this chapter. After the child has stated whether the moved stick is longer, shorter, or the same length as the other stick, the child is asked to "explain how you know."

The idea of the length of a curved path can be investigated with string. The child is asked to cut two pieces the same length. The teacher then bends one of them and asks if it is still the same length.

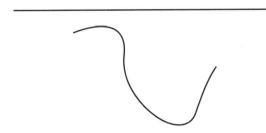

As a further activity, children can sort and order pieces of string of different lengths.

Activities and questions such as the following are useful for introducing related vocabulary and further exploring basic concepts.

- Name something in the room that is *near* to you (*far* from you). Find something that is *nearer* (*farther*). Is it farther from you to the door or from the door to you?
- Name someone who is *tall* (*short*). Who is taller, Marie or Peter? How do you know? Find a child who is *taller than*, *shorter than*, and *as tall as* Pam.
- We can see that Paul and Kim have the same *height*. (Have Paul stand on a chair.) Are Paul and Kim still the same height? Can you tell by looking? How do you know?
- Form a group of three or four children. Who is the tallest and who is the shortest? Show how you know. With their backs against the chalkboard, have the children in the group stand side-by-side in a line from tallest to shortest. Have another classmate mark the height of each member of the group on the chalkboard.
- Tell or write a story about the members of your family using the words *tall, taller, tallest, short, shorter, shortest*.
- If Jim is taller than Kate and Kate is taller than Don, is Jim shorter or taller than Don? Can you tell without seeing them together?

To introduce the idea that objects have more than one linear dimension and that the children need additional vocabulary to describe them, the teacher shows a pencil and a shorter, thicker crayon and asks the children which they think is *bigger*. The children might say that the pencil is longer but that the crayon is *thicker* or *fatter* or *wider*. The teacher then assembles a collection of pencils, felt pens, markers, and crayons and asks the children to sort them and to order them according to size. Next, the teacher can challenge the children to sort the objects in another way.

Length: Nonstandard units   As a transition to the idea of using a unit, the children can compare two lengths or distances where direct comparison is not possible. *Indirect comparison* involves comparing representations of the objects (Hiebert, 1984). Sample problems and possible solution strategies are as follows:

- Which is longer—the distance around your wrist or the length of an eraser? (String might be used.)
- Which is higher—the doorknob or the top of the filing cabinet? Because we cannot move the door or the filing cabinet, how can we find out? (The children might stand by the doorknob and use masking tape to mark a point on their bodies, then walk to the filing cabinet and compare its height with the tape mark.)
- Could we move the teacher's desk through the door without first tipping the desk on its side? (Provide an unmarked stick about a meter in length.)

To introduce the idea of measuring with a unit, students can find how many paper clips it would take to make a train *as long* as their pencils. The teacher tells the class that they are *measuring the length* of their pencils in paper clips. The teacher points out that a whole number of paper clips will not exactly match a pencil length but that the number that most closely fits is to be reported. The teacher demonstrates the correct procedure for measuring with this unit and also shows common errors and invites the children to tell what is wrong in each case.

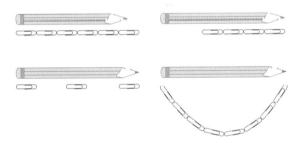

At first, teachers should provide the children with enough paper clips to measure the selected objects. Later, children may move a single paper clip along the object. This procedure is called "iteration of the unit." After children have had some practice, they are encouraged to estimate before they measure. Children can record their work on a chart such as the following.

Object	Estimate	Measure
pencil	9 paper clips	6 paper clips
eraser	_____	_____
book	_____	_____
_____	_____	_____

Another beneficial exercise is to invite children to use paper clips to make straight paths the same length as broken or curved paths. In one setting for this task, children are shown a "road" that has curves or bends and are instructed to use short rods to make a straight road that would be just as far to walk on.

The teacher then explains that the paper clip is a *unit* for measuring length and asks the children to suggest other objects that could be used as units. The children then use several different units to measure the length of a page of their notebook and record their findings on a chart as follows.

Unit	Estimate	Measure
chalk	5	4
eraser	9	7
pencil	————	————
————	————	————

During and following this activity, teachers should ask questions such as the following to focus attention on the role of the unit: Why did you get different answers for the length of the page? If you were told that the length of a page was 4, would you know how long the page was? What else would you need to know? Did you need more units for measuring the page when you used a long unit or a short unit? Why?

Other questions relate to the choice of an appropriate unit. Do you think an eraser would be a good unit for measuring the length of our classroom? Why or why not? Is a new pencil a good unit for measuring the length of a piece of chalk? Why or why not?

Body parts can also be used as nonstandard units of length. For example, children can use their *span* (the distance between the thumb and little finger on an outstretched hand) to measure the length of their desk. To increase their understanding the children should discuss the reason different children get different answers when they use this unit.

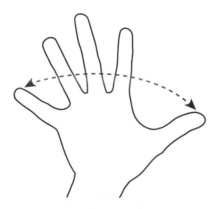

To introduce the idea of a *ruler*, have children make a paper clip chain. Then ask, "How do you think you can use your chain to measure the length of your pencil?" The children could also connect about 10 interlocking cubes together and use this device to measure the lengths of various objects in cubes. They could discuss whether it is easier or harder to measure using individual cubes or the cube stick.

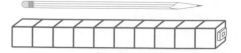

Children can use squared paper (Activity 15-1) and geoboards (Activity 15-2) to explore interesting and worthwhile problems involving the lengths of broken line segments and distances around polygons. Using string, children can find relationships among distances around a person's wrist, neck, and waist (Activity 15-3) and discover the relationship (pi) between the distance around and across circular objects (Activity 15-4).

ACTIVITY 15-1

EXPLORING DISTANCES ON SQUARED PAPER

MATERIALS
Squared paper

PROCEDURE
1. Copy Figures A and B on a piece of squared paper.

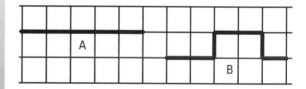

2. If the unit is the distance between two lines, the total length of Figure A is 5 units. Figure B has a length of 7 units.
   • By tracing over grid lines, draw some other figures and find their length.
   • How many different figures can you draw that have a total length of 10 units?

3. Figure C is closed. The distance around it is 16 units.
   • Draw some other closed figures by following grid lines and find the distance around each of them.
   • How many different closed figures can you draw that have a distance around of 12 units?

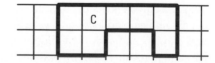

PERIMETERS ON A GEOBOARD

MATERIALS
Geoboard or dot paper

PROCEDURE
1. The distance around a closed figure is called its perimeter. How many different figures that have a perimeter of 10 units can you make on a 5 × 5 geoboard?

WRIST, NECK, AND WAIST

MATERIALS
String

PROCEDURE
1. Use string to measure the distance around your wrist, neck, and waist.
2. Cut pieces of string matching these lengths and compare them.
   • How many wrist lengths are as long as a neck length?
   • How many wrists make a waist?
3. Compare your findings with those of your classmates.

MEASURING A CIRCLE

MATERIALS
Different-sized circular shapes (bottle lids, cans, etc.), string

PROCEDURE
1. For each shape, cut pieces of string as long as the distance across and the distance around the outside edge.
2. Use the shorter piece to measure the longer one. What do you notice for each shape?

that five centimeters is written 5 cm. They then practice measuring and estimating length using this unit, recording their findings on a chart such as the following:

Object	Estimate	Measure
pencil	12 cm	14 cm
eraser	___ cm	___ cm
your span	___ cm	___ cm

Before demonstrating the standard ruler, invite children to use the ten rod from the base-ten materials or a connected centicube stick to find lengths in centimeters (Thompson & Van de Walle, 1985). The first ruler they use should have centimeter markings without numbers along one edge so they see that the unit on the ruler is represented by the space, not the mark. Children then learn to measure using the other edge that has numbers under the markings. The teacher needs to demonstrate the correct procedure for using this tool, emphasizing the importance of placing the zero mark at the beginning of the object. Children should also realize that a ruler with the front end broken off still can be used to find the length of an object (by subtraction or counting units between the endpoints).

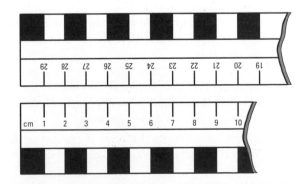

As a practice activity, children can work in pairs. One person draws a line segment on a piece of paper. The partner estimates its length in centimeters and then measures it using a ruler. The children then switch jobs.

Length: Standard units Children who have measured lengths using a variety of units can appreciate the need for a unit that can be understood and communicated beyond the classroom. The book *How Big Is a Foot?* by Rolf Myller (1990) makes this point in a delightful way. The king in the story orders an apprentice to make him a bed 6 feet long and 3 feet wide. The apprentice uses his own foot to measure the bed, with predictable results.

The centimeter is usually the first standard unit taught to children. It is presented as a unit of length known throughout the world. Children become familiar with the size of the centimeter by using the small cubes from the base-ten blocks or interlocking centimeter cubes (called "centicubes") to measure objects. They should note that one of their fingernails is about a centimeter in length. They are told that the *symbol* for centimeter is cm and

10 dm = 1 m   10 cm = 1 dm   100 cm = 1 m

They might also try this with broken-line or curved paths. Similar activities can be done using inches.

The *meter* is introduced as a standard unit for measuring longer distances, such as the length of the classroom. Activities such as the following help children gain an appreciation for the size of this unit and relate it to the centimeter:

• Use an unmarked meter stick to find a point on your body that is one meter from the floor. Put the meter stick on the floor. How many of your steps make a meter. Find objects in the classroom that are about one meter in length or have a height of about one meter. How many meters long (wide) do you think the classroom is? Measure and compare the actual length with your estimate.

• Use a trundle wheel to measure the length of the hall, the distance around the gym, and so on. Estimate before you measure.

• How many centimeters does it take to make a meter? Estimate first, then look at the side of the meter stick marked in centimeters to find out. If an object is 2 m long, how many centimeters is that?

Similar activities can be done for feet, inches, and yards.

To measure in *decimeters* children can use the 10-cm Cuisenaire rod, the "long" from the base-ten materials, or a 10 centicube stick. The meter stick pictured is marked to show the relationships among the meter, decimeter, and centimeter. The meaning of the prefixes *centi* and *deci* can be discussed in this connection.

In relation to the concept of precision, children can measure the length of the chalkboard to the nearest meter, decimeter, and centimeter. They can discuss which unit is most appropriate in this case and which of the three results is the most precise.

The *millimeter* is introduced as a unit to measure very small things, such as insects. Two sample activities involving this unit are:

• Use a ruler marked in centimeters and millimeters to measure to the nearest millimeter the length of several objects or line segments drawn on paper.

• Make a stack of 10 dimes. Measure the height of the stack. What is the approximate thickness of one dime?

Sample questions and activities relating to the *kilometer* are as follows:

• What place would be about 1 kilometer (km) from your home (the school?) How long does it take you to walk (jog, run) a kilometer? Identify places that are about 2 km (10 km) apart.

• Use a road map or atlas to find the distances between your town or city and other cities you have visited or would like to visit. How far is it from Los Angeles to New York? From Chicago to Seattle? What is the distance around the earth? How far is it to the moon?

In Activities 15-5 through 15-8, children measure in metric units to collect data to develop formulas or discover relationships.

ACTIVITY 15-5

PERIMETER OF A RECTANGLE

MATERIALS
Ruler, meter stick

PROCEDURE
1. Find and record the *perimeter* of (distance around) your textbook, the door, a window, the top of the filing cabinet. Use appropriate units.

2. How many different sides did you need to measure to find the perimeter of these things? Write a sentence telling how to find the perimeter of a rectangle.

ACTIVITY 15-6

CIRCUMFERENCE OF A CIRCLE

MATERIALS
Circular objects
Tape measure
Calculator

PROCEDURE
1. Using a tape measure marked in millimeters, measure the *diameter* (distance across) and the *circumference* (distance around) of several circular objects. Enter these numbers in the chart and use a calculator to compute the ratios.

Circumference (C)	Diameter (d)	C ÷ d
273 mm	85 mm	3.21

2. Can you state a relationship between the diameter and the circumference of a circle?

ACTIVITY 15-7

ARE YOU SQUARE?

MATERIALS
Meter stick or tape measure

PROCEDURE
1. Measure your height and armspan (the distance between your outstretched fingertips) in centimeters. Are you square?
2. Compare with your classmates.

ACTIVITY 15-8

BODY PARTS

MATERIALS
Tape measure

PROCEDURE
1. Use a tape measure marked in centimeters to find the distance around your wrist, neck, and waist.
2. Do this for several people.
3. Can you state a relationship among these measurements for people?

Name	Wrist	Neck	Waist

Area

Area is the amount of surface enclosed by a curve in the plane. We consider area when we hang wallpaper, carpet a floor, or wrap a present. Although any plane region that tessellates can be used as a unit for measuring area, the standard unit is the measure of a square having an edge with a length of one unit. Children should learn about measuring area by covering figures with square tiles and by drawing figures on squared paper before being taught to use formulas. Units of area are derived from corresponding linear units.

TECHNOLOGY LINK 15-1
The Learning Network's Shape Surveyor

Integrate measurement and geology with this site! First, set your own difficulty level (easy, medium, hard, or super brain). Then choose to work on area, perimeter, or a combination of the two, and start digging! Each correct answer provides you with a piece of an archeological puzzle. The game is over when you get all the puzzle pieces. It's a fun way to work on measurement skills!
Visit http://www.funbrain.com/poly/index.html or link from our Companion Website at **www.prenhall.com/cathcart.**

Area: Perception and direct comparison

To introduce the notion of area the teacher might show the class two rectangular pieces of cardboard, one measuring about 30 cm by 3 cm and the other 20 cm by 10 cm, and ask the question, "Which is bigger?" Even though the first piece is longer, children will generally say that the other looks bigger in the sense that it *covers more surface.* They might also argue that the two areas could be compared directly if the long strip was cut into two pieces.

As a follow-up activity, children working in small groups can compare the areas of pairs of rectangles having the following dimensions: 10 cm by 6 cm and 8 cm by 8 cm; 6 cm by 8 cm and 12 cm by 4 cm.

To test for conservation of area, two squares of the same size are shown. The teacher cuts one square along a diagonal and rearranges the two pieces to form a triangle or parallelogram. Then the teacher asks the students whether the two shapes have the same area and to explain their answer.

Area: Nonstandard units To introduce the idea of a unit of area, the teacher can ask the class how many pieces of construction paper would be required to cover the bulletin board. At their seats they could use small file cards to cover a page or the surface of their desks. Children could also find out how many of their hands it takes to cover their desks and then compare and discuss their results.

In another activity, children can be given small squares and asked if they can use them to find which two of three specially constructed figures cover the same amount of surface. The number of squares covering each figure is the area measure of the figure with respect to that unit.

Given pattern blocks such as the six shapes shown, children can be asked to find how many copies of each shape are required to cover a card measuring about 10 cm by 13 cm.

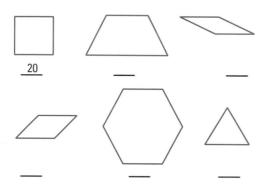

Asking children to use objects such as toothpicks and circular counters to cover a surface can lead to a discussion about the desirable characteristics of a unit of area. Key ideas are that the unit should possess the attribute of covering and that it should cover without overlapping; the figure tessellates the plane. Children should also use three different sizes of squares to measure a particular surface and note the relationship between the number of units needed and the size of the unit.

Several geoboard tasks involving area are shown in Activity 15-9. Activity 15-10 leads children to discover the formula for the area of a rectangle; other excellent activities with squared paper are described by Shaw (1983). In Activity 15-11, children use tiles to find the perimeters of rectangles having a fixed area. See Blackline Masters

ACTIVITY 15-9

GEOBOARD AREAS

MATERIALS
Geoboard

PROCEDURE
1. Copy the figure below on your geoboard. The unit is the square region formed as shown. The area of the figure is 7 units.

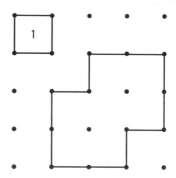

2. On your geoboard, enclose figures with areas of 3, 6, and 11 units.
3. On your geoboard, how many different figures can you make having an area of 5 units?
4. Find the perimeter of each figure in 3.

11 and 12 in the Appendix for a geoboard template and geoboard recording paper.

Area: Standard units The basic units of area are the *square meter,* the *square inch,* and the *square foot.* To give children a feel for the square meter, outline a square 1 m by 1 m on the chalkboard or on the floor (with masking tape). Children need to know that the symbol m² is read "square meter" and not "meter squared." The class could determine the number of square meters of carpet needed to cover the classroom floor and the area of the gym floor in square meters. Similar activities can be done for square inches and square feet.

Children can become familiar with the *square centimeter* (cm²) by using centimeter graph paper (Horak &

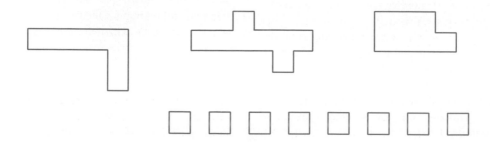

ACTIVITY 15-10

AREAS OF RECTANGLES

MATERIALS
Squared paper

PROCEDURE
1. Draw several different rectangles on squared paper.

2. For each rectangle find the length and width in linear units and the area in square units.

Length	Width	Area
3	2	6
___	___	___
___	___	___

3. State a rule for finding the area of a rectangle given its length and width.

ACTIVITY 15-11

PERIMETER AND AREA

MATERIALS
36 square tiles

PROCEDURE
1. Arrange 36 small square tiles to form a rectangular region with a base of 9 units and a height of 4 units, as shown.

2. Find the perimeter and area of this figure.

3. Using all 36 squares each time, make as many other different rectangular regions as you can.

4. Record your findings.

Base	Height	Perimeter	Area
9	4	26	36
___	___	___	___

5. What did you notice about the perimeters and areas of the various figures?

6. Which shape gives the greatest perimeter?

Horak, 1982). One task is to find the approximate area of their hand by tracing around it on graph paper and counting squares. Children also can be asked to outline polygons enclosing specified numbers of square centimeters. For example, enclose a region with an area of 43 cm². Do this in several different ways. (See Blackline Master 15 in the Appendix for centimeter grid paper.)

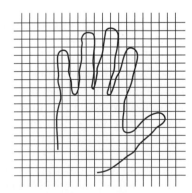

The faces of the small cube of the base-ten materials have sides 1 cm in length, and thus each face has an area of 1 cm². The 10-by-10 flat is a *square decimeter*. By

comparing these two blocks, children can find that 1 dm² = 100 cm². They should also be able to determine that 1 m² = 10 000 cm² by considering 100 rows of 100 square centimeters in a square meter.

From Activity 15-10, children found that the area of a rectangle is the product of its *length* and *width*. In Activity 15-11, the terms *base* and *height* were used for the two dimensions of a rectangle. These latter concepts are needed in developing formulas for the area of a parallelogram and a triangle. First, children can discover that a parallelogram can be transformed into a rectangle by cutting and sliding a triangular section as indicated in the diagram below.

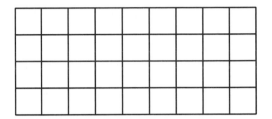

Thus, the area of a parallelogram is the product of its base and height. It needs to be stressed that the height is the perpendicular distance from the base to the opposite side, not the length of an adjacent side. Furthermore, any of the sides can be considered as the base.

Children can use geoboards to investigate triangular areas. Children see that a right triangle can be enclosed in a rectangle and because the two resulting triangles are congruent, the area of the original triangle is half that of the rectangle. A triangle without a right angle can also be enclosed in a rectangle, as illustrated, and its area found by subtracting the areas of the right triangles formed from the area of the rectangle.

 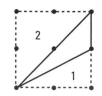

Area = $\frac{1 \times 2}{2}$ = 1   Area = 4 − 1 − 2 = 1

In general, two copies of any triangle form a parallelogram, as shown in the following diagram. Children can reason that since the triangle and the parallelogram have the same base and height, the area of a triangle can be computed by finding half the product of its base and height.

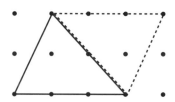

Activities 15-12 through 15-15 are problems and investigations relating to the areas of rectangles, parallelograms, and triangles. The surface area of a rectangular solid is introduced in Activity 15-16.

To help children see that the formula for the area of a circle, $A = \pi r^2$, is sensible, show a diagram in which a circle of radius r is inscribed in a square of side $2r$ (see illustration). The area of the square is $4r^2$. It appears that the area of the circle is about three-fourths of the area of the square, or about $3r^2$. Children can also draw circles

ACTIVITY 15-12

MAKING A FENCE

Julie has 100 m of fencing to make a pen for her horse. She wants the pen to be rectangular in shape. Find the dimensions of the pen that encloses the greatest area.

ACTIVITY 15-13

PARALLELOGRAM AREAS

* How are the parallelograms the same?
* How are they different?
* Find the area of each.

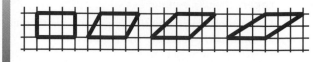

on squared paper and find their approximate areas by counting squares. They will find that the ratio of the area to the square of the radius is a bit more than three. This ratio is known as pi (π), which is approximately 3.1416.

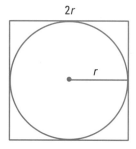

Volume

Volume measure associates a number with a closed space region. *Volume* is the amount of space occupied by a three-dimensional object. *Interior volume* refers to the amount of space confined within the boundaries of a container such as a box. The unit is the measure of a cube having an edge with a length of one unit. Concept development activities include building solids with cubes and filling boxes with cubes (Hart, 1984). Units for volume are derived from linear units.

Volume: Perception and direct comparison
To introduce the concept of cubic volume the teacher might hold up two solid rectangular prisms and ask which is "bigger." Although linear dimensions and surface areas of these three-dimensional objects could be compared, the discussion should lead to the question of which one *occupies more space.* Two empty boxes, one of which fits within the other, are then shown and compared directly for *volume.* The teacher and children can generate a list of everyday examples of objects that have a large volume or a small volume, but in most cases direct comparison cannot be carried out and beginning instructional activities involve the use of nonstandard units.

To determine whether a child conserves volume, the teacher can use wooden cubes to build a solid shape, such

ACTIVITY 15-14

GEOBOARD TRIANGLES

MATERIALS
Geoboard

PROCEDURE
1. Find the areas of these geoboard triangles by enclosing them in rectangles and subtracting the areas of the right triangles formed.

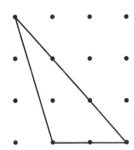

2. On a 25-nail geoboard it is possible to make 8 different triangles that have an area of 1. How many can you find?

ACTIVITY 15-15

AREAS OF TRIANGLES

MATERIALS
A compass and a ruler

PROCEDURE
1. Construct a triangle with sides measuring 9 cm, 10 cm, and 12 cm.

2. From each of the vertices construct the perpendicular to the opposite side.

3. Using the standard formula compute the area of the triangle three times, each time using a different side as base. Are the three answers the same?

4. Construct other triangles with sides of different lengths and repeat the activity.

ACTIVITY 15 16

COVERING A BOX

MATERIALS
Shoebox (or similar box)
Paper
Scissors

PROCEDURE
1. Cut pieces of paper to match each of the faces of the box. Use them to completely cover the box.

2. How many pieces of paper did you cut? How many different sizes were there?

3. Find the dimensions of each rectangular piece of paper in centimeters and compute the areas.

4. The *surface area* of a box is the sum of the areas of its faces. Find the surface area of the box in square centimeters.

5. State a rule for finding the surface area of a box given its length, width, and height.

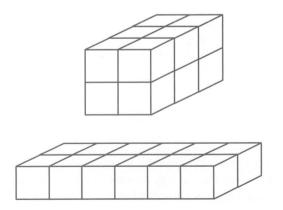

as a $2 \times 3 \times 2$ prism. The teacher explains that she or he is making a house with blocks and that each block is a room. The teacher instructs the child to copy the house and to confirm that the two structures have the same number of rooms. The teacher then rearranges the 12 blocks to form a prism with different dimensions, such as $6 \times 2 \times 1$, and asks the child if this house has more, fewer, or the same number of rooms as the child's house. The child is asked to justify her or his explanation.

Volume: Nonstandard units Common (2.5-cm cube) wooden or plastic blocks can be used as a unit of volume in many concept development activities. For one task, the teacher constructs open boxes that can be filled by the cubes arranged in the following ways: $3 \times 3 \times 3$, $4 \times 3 \times 2$, and $5 \times 5 \times 1$. The children first predict which of the boxes will hold the most cubes and then carry out the measurement.

Children can also use the blocks to make solid shapes with a given volume (such as 7 or 13) and to make as many different rectangular solids as possible using a fixed number of blocks (12, for example). Activity 15-17 is designed to lead children to discover the formula for the volume of a rectangular prism. In Activity 15-18 children investigate the surface areas of rectangular solids with a constant volume.

Teachers should discuss with children the problem associated with using spherical-shaped objects such as marbles or Ping-Pong balls as units of volume. Using different-sized cubes (such as sugar cubes and interlocking cubes) to measure the volume of a box provides a setting for reviewing the relationship between the unit size and the number of units needed.

ACTIVITY 15-17

VOLUME OF A RECTANGULAR SOLID

MATERIALS
25 wooden or plastic cubes

PROCEDURE
1. Use cubes to build the rectangular solid pictured here. Its length is 4, its width is 2, and its height is 2.

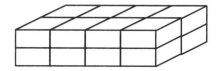

2. Find its volume by counting the number of blocks used to build the solid.

3. Build other rectangular solids with different dimensions.

4. Record their length, width, height, and volume.

Length	Width	Height	Volume
4	2	2	16
5	1	3	——
——	——	——	——

5. Can you state a rule for finding the volume of a box given its length, width, and height?

Volume: Standard units A model for a *cubic meter* can be constructed using 12 meter-length sticks. After the teacher introduces the symbol m^3, the class might calculate the approximate volume of the classroom using its length, width, and height in meters. A similar activity can be done for yd^3 and ft^3.

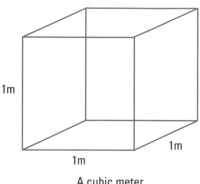

1m
1m
1m

A cubic meter

The cubic centimeter (cm^3) is modeled by the small cube of the base-ten materials and by the centicube block. Children should use these blocks to build solids having volumes of given numbers of cubic centimeters. They should also use a ruler to measure the length, width, and height of a box to the nearest centimeter and compute the approximate volume in cubic centimeters.

The large cube of the base-ten materials provides a model for a *cubic decimeter* (dm^3). Comparing the small cube to the large cube, children find that $1 \text{ dm}^3 = 1000 \text{ cm}^3$.

Children can also determine that there are a million cubic centimeters in a meter. A centimeter cube can be placed inside the model of the cubic meter to help students visualize this large number.

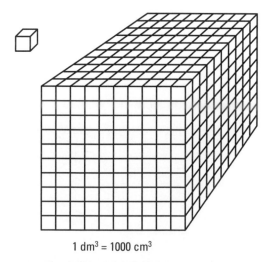

$1 \text{ dm}^3 = 1000 \text{ cm}^3$

Activity 15-19 describes an interesting small-group problem-solving activity relating to the construction of an open box of maximum volume.

ACTIVITY 15-18 ▶

SURFACE AREA OF A RECTANGULAR SOLID

MATERIALS
24 wooden or plastic cubes

PROCEDURE
1. Arrange 24 cubes to form a rectangular solid 4 blocks long, 2 blocks wide, and 3 blocks high.

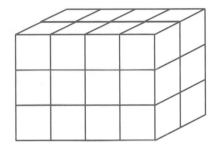

2. Find the prism's surface area—the total number of squares (the size of a face of a unit cube) needed to cover all faces of the prism.

3. Using all 24 cubes each time, make as many other different solid rectangular prisms as you can.

4. Record your findings.

Length	Width	Height	Surface Area
4	3	2	52
12	2	1	_____
_____	_____	_____	_____

5. These prisms all have the same volume. Which has the greatest/least surface area?

6. Suppose you wanted to build an apartment building containing 24 rooms of equal size. How would you arrange the 24 rooms? Consider factors such as cost, view, heating, availability of land, need for elevators.

ACTIVITY 15-19 ▶

MAKE THE BIGGEST BOX

MATERIALS
Centimeter grid paper 12 cm by 9 cm
Scissors

PROCEDURE
1. Cut a square of size 1 cm from each corner of the grid paper.

2. Fold the resulting edges to make an open box.

3. Find its volume.

4. What size square should you cut out of the corners of the original square to make the box with the greatest volume?

Length of Cut	Height	Length	Width	Volume
1 cm	1 cm	10 cm	7 cm	70 cm³
2 cm	____	____	____	____
____				

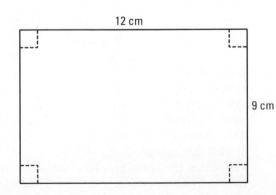

12 cm

9 cm

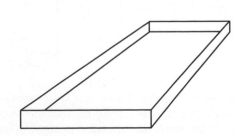

Capacity

While volume is the amount of space occupied by an object, the term *capacity* is often used to refer to the amount of space that can be filled. Capacity is usually used in connection with liquid measure. In the elementary curriculum, children learn about capacity in kindergarten and Grade 1, whereas cubic volume is first encountered in Grade 3 or 4.

Capacity: Perception and direct comparison To introduce the attribute of capacity, children can be shown two containers and asked which one *holds more*. If one container fits into the other, the children can see that the large container will hold more. If not, the question is answered by filling one container and pouring it into the other. Substances used to explore capacity in the classroom include dried peas, sand, and water. Children require a great deal of hands-on experience with a variety of cans, bottles, paper cups, and other containers of different sizes and shapes. The following instructions might be given:

• Find which container holds the most/least. Estimate first, then check by pouring.

• Can you find two different containers that hold about the same amount?

• Order the containers according to how much they hold.

To check for conservation, the teacher shows two identical glasses sitting side-by-side, pours water into one of the glasses, and asks a child to fill the other glass so that it contains the same amount. The child pours water into the glass until the water level is the same in the two glasses. The teacher then pours the water from the first glass into a tall narrow container and asks if it contains more water, less water, or the same amount of water as the child's glass. The teacher then asks the child to explain or justify her or his answer.

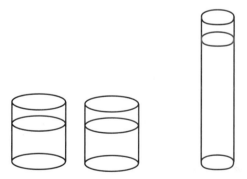

Capacity: Nonstandard units To describe *how much* a container holds, the children find how many times a smaller container must be filled to hold the same amount as the larger container. Again, children should be

encouraged to estimate before they measure and to record their results as they find the capacities of a variety of containers using a nonstandard unit. Children will find that the container will not be filled exactly by a whole number of units. They are instructed to measure to the nearest unit, but answers such as $4\frac{1}{2}$ cups are not uncommon.

Container	Estimate	Measure
mug	8 ounces	10 ounces
yogurt carton	_____	_____
_____	_____	_____

Next, children can use units of different sizes to measure an object such as a cottage cheese container. They should predict what will happen when a smaller unit is used and explain why more of these units will be needed to fill the container.

Unit	Estimate	Measure
paper cup	4	5
ladle	_____	_____
_____	_____	_____

A body unit for capacity is the "handful." Several different children can be asked to find how many handfuls of corn it takes to fill a margarine tub. Children can compare results and discuss the problems associated with using handfuls as a unit of measurement.

Children can make their own *calibrated beaker* by adhering a strip of masking tape to the length of a tall, clear glass and marking with a felt pen the water level for 1, 2, 3, and 4 smaller containers. They can then use this device to find the approximate capacities of various containers with respect to the given unit.

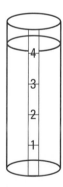

Capacity: Standard units A teacher can instruct children about measuring capacity in standard units by first telling them that a standard unit for measuring how much a container holds is a *liter* and that its symbol is L. Then the teacher can show the children several different-shaped liter containers and give them the opportunity to verify that the containers have the same capacity. An early activity with this unit is to sort a variety of containers using the categories "more than a liter," "about a liter," and "less than a liter." Familiar containers such as a 1-L water bottle should be displayed and referred to in connection with this unit. Similar activities can be done using quarts and gallons.

The *milliliter* (mL) is a very small unit, and children usually first experience it by measuring with a set of un-calibrated beakers of sizes 500 mL, 250 mL, 100 mL, and 50 mL. Spoon sets including sizes 1 mL, 2 mL, 5 mL, 15 mL, and 25 mL can also be used to measure smaller amounts. Children can then learn to use graduated 1000-mL beakers marked in 100-mL or 50-mL intervals to measure capacity. They note that reading the scale is similar to using a ruler to measure length.

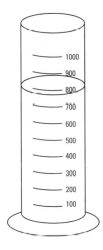

The problem in Activity 15-20 explores the relationship between volume and lateral surface area. Predict which one has the greater volume before performing the experiment. Computing the volumes of the two cylinders confirms that their ratio is 2:1.

ACTIVITY 15-20

COMPARING CYLINDERS

MATERIALS
Paper
Scissors
Popcorn

PROCEDURE
1. Cut two pieces of paper to measure 8 cm by 16 cm.

2. Roll each sheet to form a cylinder, one 8 cm high and the other 16 cm high.

3. Tape the edges together and stand them on a flat surface.

4. The two cylinders have the same lateral surface area. Do you think they have the same volume?

5. Fill each with popcorn to compare volumes.

6. Repeat with two papers measuring 8 cm × 24 cm.

Mass

Mass is a measure of the amount of matter in an object, whereas *weight* is the force of gravity acting on that mass. When astronauts orbit the earth in the space shuttle, their weight is less than it is on earth but their mass does not change. To compare two masses or to quantify mass, children first use a *two-pan balance*. Because this apparatus does not directly show what mass means, the concept is a difficult one for children to grasp. Whereas the pound is a unit of weight in the customary system of measurement, the *kilogram* is a metric unit for mass. Compression scales and spring balances are calibrated to measure mass in standard units.

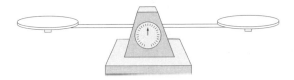

Mass: Perception and direct comparison

To test for conservation of matter, the teacher can use clay to make two balls that the children judge to have the same amount of clay. The teacher then rolls one ball into a sausage shape and asks the children whether it has more clay, less clay, or the same amount of clay as the other ball. The teacher then asks the children to elaborate on their answers.

To introduce the concept of mass, the teacher might hold a brick in one hand and a basketball in the other and ask, "Which is bigger?" From their experience, children will likely know that although the ball has a larger volume, the brick is *heavier*. The teacher asks the class to name some things that are *heavy* and *light*. These ideas are further developed as the children hold objects and feel the pull of gravity. In most cases, the masses of two objects cannot be compared by sight; they must be held to determine which is heavier. Activity 15-21 describes a task for partners.

The pan balance is helpful for making more accurate comparisons. Children should discuss why the side with the heavier object is lower. In Activity 15-22 children first estimate which of two objects is heavier, then check using a pan balance.

Mass: Nonstandard units
Objects that can be used as nonstandard units of mass include common wooden or plastic blocks, interlocking cubes, paper clips, and bolts or nuts. The children might be asked to estimate how many wooden blocks are *as heavy as* a glue stick and to use the pan balance to measure. If five blocks are required, the teacher explains that the *mass* of the glue stick is about five blocks. The teacher should then repeat the procedure with several other objects.

ACTIVITY 15-21 ▶

WHICH IS HEAVIER?

MATERIALS
Various objects

PROCEDURE

1. Choose two objects.

2. Decide which is heavier first by looking, then by holding one object in each hand.

3. See if your partner makes the same decision.

4. Do this for other pairs of objects.

5. Record what you do and find.

Heavier	Lighter	Partner Agrees
book	ball	yes
scissors	stapler	no
————	————	————

ACTIVITY 15-22 ▶

USING A PAN BALANCE TO COMPARE

MATERIALS
Pan balance
Various objects

PROCEDURE

1. Use the pan balance to compare pairs of objects. Estimate first. Then record which is heavier.

Objects	Estimate	Balance
book and ball	book heavier	book heavier
scissors and tape	same	scissors heavier
————	————	————

2. Arrange the objects in order from lightest to heaviest.

3. Are big things always heavier than small things? Why or why not?

Object	Estimate	Measure
glue stick	7 cubes	5 cubes
eraser		
————	————	————

To explore the relationship between the size of the unit and the number of units required to measure an object, the mass of a particular object, such as a glue stick, is then found using several different units.

Unit	Estimate	Measure
wooden cube	7	5
interlocking cube	12	15
bottle cap	————	————

Mass: Standard units The *kilogram* (kg) is introduced as a standard unit for measuring mass. Sample activities include the following:

- Hold a kilogram mass. Use clay to make a ball with a mass of 1 kg. Check using a pan balance. Make another shape using this same clay. Is its mass still 1 kg? How do you know?

- Find things in the room that have a mass of about 1 kg, greater than 1 kg, and less than 1 kg. How many notebooks does it take to make a mass of 1 kg?

- At home use your bathroom scale to find your mass in kilograms. Ask your family members to do the same.

Similar activities can be done using pounds.

The *gram* (g) is one-thousandth of a kilogram. The centicube is designed to have a mass of one gram. Children can use individual gram units to compare masses of objects, such as the small cube from the base-ten materials and a paper clip, and find the mass of various objects in grams.

Object	Estimate	Measure
nickel	10 g	5 g
eraser	————	————
pen	————	————
————	————	————

Children can also use a set of standard masses (1 kg, 500 g, 200 g, 100 g, 50 g, 20 g, 10 g) to find the masses of various objects to the nearest 10 g.

Object	Estimate	Measure
glue bottle	200 g	250 g
stapler	————	————
————	————	————

At home, children should look for products that are packaged or sold by mass and report these to the class (e.g., a sack of sugar, a cake mix, a box of cereal, a candy bar, a bag of apples).

Children learn relationships between metric units of volume and mass when they find that the mass of a liter (cubic decimeter) of water is close to a kilogram. It follows that a milliliter (cubic centimeter) of water has a mass of one gram. Furthermore, because a cubic meter is 1000 cubic decimeters, the mass of water required to fill a tub of length, width, and height 1 m is 1000 kg, which is a *tonne* (t). Because an average football player has a mass of about 100 kg, it would take about 10 football players to make a tonne.

Time

We use *time* to specify *when* an event occurred or will occur and also to describe *how long* an event lasted. Can you identify both aspects of time in the following sentence?

In 2000, Maurice Green set a new Olympic record of 9.87 sec. in the 100-m dash.

Judging the passage of time is not an easy task for children, and adults remark that "time flies when you're having fun." Learners should have many concept development experiences related to the *sequencing* of events and the *duration* of time periods before they are taught the complex process of *telling time* by reading a clock (Horak & Horak, 1983).

Time: Perception and direct comparison

Questions such as the following help children develop concepts and vocabulary related to the sequencing of events:

- When you get dressed, which do you put on *first*—your shoes or your socks? When you get ready for bed do you brush your teeth *after* you put on your pajamas or *before* you put on your pajamas? What is the *last* thing you do before you go to bed?
- Name some things we do in class *before* lunch and some things we do *after* lunch.
- List in order five things you do *after* you wake up on Saturday mornings.

Early comparison tasks rely on memory. The teacher may describe two events and ask the child which takes longer or more time to complete. Examples are eating breakfast or walking to school, watching a cartoon or playing a soccer game. The class might also make a list of activities done during a school day (such as music, sharing time, and recess) and vote on which takes the least amount of time and which takes the most amount of time. A related task is to list several events in order according to how much time each takes.

To check for conservation of time, a teacher can place two toy animals side-by-side on a table. The teacher then tells the children that the animals are going for a walk and to say when to start and when to stop. When the children say "go," the teacher hops the animals along the table so that they remain side-by-side. At "stop," the teacher asks the children if the animals started and stopped at the same time. The procedure is then repeated but with one animal taking longer hops so that when they stop, it will be farther ahead. The teacher then asks the children if the animals started and stopped at the same time.

Although we cannot see time, it is sometimes possible to observe which of two events takes longer. To carry out direct comparisons of time, the two events must start simultaneously. Children are familiar with the idea that in a race the two runners must start at the same time. Comparing two different activities can help children focus on the concept of time duration rather than on "who won." For example, one children jumps up and down 10 times while another stacks seven blocks. The class observes which event took more time to complete.

Time: Nonstandard units To establish the need for a unit for measuring time, the children should compare the times of two events that cannot be carried out concurrently; for example, the children may be asked how they might find out whether it takes Samantha longer to print her name neatly or tie the laces on her shoes. The problem then becomes one of determining how to measure *how long* an event takes.

Any repeated, regular action can serve as a nonstandard unit. One procedure is to have one child tap a pencil on a table according to a steady beat while another counts the taps. The number of taps required by other children to perform various tasks is then recorded. Later, children experiment with increasing and decreasing the rate of tapping and discuss the relationship between this variable and the number of taps associated with a given event.

Children could make a *pendulum* as an instrument for measuring time by attaching a metal nut to a piece of string. Working in pairs, one partner counts the number of times the string swings back and forth while the other performs a task.

Task	Estimate	Measure
saying the alphabet	6 swings	5 swings
joining 10 interlocking cubes	————	————
	————	————

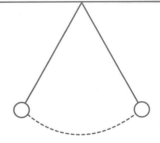

A *metronome* also is useful for measuring time. One person performs a task while others count the "ticks." The class can observe and discuss the effect of adjusting the device to tick at different speeds. The children might also use a *sand timer* to find how many times they can perform various actions, such as jumping up and down, before the sand runs out.

Time: Standard units To introduce the *second* (s), the teacher should set the metronome so that its ticks are 1 second apart. If a metronome is not available, a pendulum of length 25 cm may be used. Children count in time with the metronome or the swing of the pendulum so that they are saying one number per second. They then measure the time required to do various tasks in seconds.

The following activities acquaint the children with the *minute:*

- Put your heads on your desks and close your eyes. I will tell you when a minute has passed. Now I will read to you for 1 minute. Next we will jump up and down for 1 minute. Did the length of these minutes seem the same to you? What are some things you can do that take about a minute? Less than a minute? More than a minute? Now close your eyes again and raise your hand when you think 1 minute has passed.

- Make a minute book. On each page describe something you can do in a minute or how many times you can do some activity in a minute. For example, how many sit-ups can you do in a minute? How many times can you bounce a ball?

If there is a dial clock in the classroom with a second hand, the minute can be related to the time it takes this hand to make a complete revolution. The class might also discuss the fact that this is equivalent to 60 seconds. Longer periods of time can then be referred to: recess is 15 minutes long; a music class lasts for 40 minutes.

The *hour* can be related to the child's experience as follows: lunch break is 1 hour; we go to school for 3 hours in the morning; movies last about 2 hours; you should get about 10 hours of sleep each night. Children are familiar with the concept of a *day* and the ideas of *yesterday* and *tomorrow.* They might be asked to make a list showing how many of the 24 hours in a day they spend on the following activities: sleeping, eating, going to school, playing, doing chores, and watching television.

The *week, month,* and *year* are studied in connection with the *calendar.* In problems such as the following children use equivalencies among these units.

- How many years have you lived? How many months?
- Can you give your age in weeks? Days? Hours? Minutes? Seconds? You may want to use a calculator.

We now turn our attention from questions related to measuring *how long* an event took to questions about describing when an event occurred or is scheduled to occur. Children should be familiar with the dates of special events such as their birthday. The idea of *telling time* is motivated by the need to specify when events occur during the day. The related question is, "What time is it?" To introduce this concept the teacher might draw an hour timeline on the board starting and ending at midnight. A dialogue such as the following might be used:

At 1 o'clock in the *morning,* most people are asleep. You probably wake up at about 7 o'clock. School starts at 9 o'clock and ends in the morning at 12 o'clock which is also called *noon.* An hour later it is 1 o'clock in the *afternoon.* School lets out at 3 o'clock. You might have dinner at 6 o'clock and go to bed at 8 o'clock. 12 o'clock at night is also called *midnight.*

We write 4 o'clock like this—4:00. Between 1 o'clock and 2 o'clock we indicate the number of minutes past the hour. If it is 23 minutes past 1 o'clock, we write the time like this—1:23. Four minutes past 1 o'clock is written 1:04 and one minute before 2 o'clock is 1:59. Times such as 1:23 are also read "one twenty-three."

Digital clocks show the time of day in this way. If a digital clock shows 5:40, what would it show 1 hr later? 7 hr later? 8 hr later? 10 min later? 20 min later?

To introduce the *dial clock* the teacher might draw a horizontal 12-hour timeline and then discuss and draw how this looks when it is rearranged to form a circle with the number 12 at the top. The teacher then shows a demonstration clock and asks questions such as the following: Which number is at the top (bottom)? Which number comes before 8? After 3? Before 12? After 12? The hour hand and the minute hand are identified and the positions of these hands for 5 o'clock, 8 o'clock, and 12 o'clock are shown. Children note how these clock times are the same and how they are different and then use individual demonstration clocks to practice showing times on the hour.

To teach children to tell time between hours, teachers should use a clock with a minute scale as well as an hour scale (Thompson & Van de Walle, 1981). Prerequisite skills include counting by fives and reading a number line scale with numbers provided only for the multiples of five. Children first learn to place the minute hand for times such as 20 or 50 minutes past the hour and later for 23 or 57 minutes past the hour. They should realize that at 5:40 the hour hand will be between 5 and 6, but precise placement is not important at this stage. Later they will relate the fraction of the circle traversed by the minute

12	1	2	3	4	5	6	7	8	9	10	11	12	1	2	3	4	5	6	7	8	9	10	11	12
Midnight							Wake	School				Noon					Dinner		Bed				Midnight

hand to the fractional part of the distance between two numbers moved by the hour hand. The ideas of "half past" and "quarter past" the hour and "before the hour" are taught after children can express all clock times "after the hour."

Other time topics usually found in the later elementary curriculum include A.M. and P.M. and the 24-hour clock.

Temperature

Temperature is a measure of how hot or cold an object is. A reading of a *thermometer*, the instrument used to measure temperature, does not reflect the quality of heat or temperature, and this can cause difficulties for some children. The *Celsius scale* is commonly used for recording temperature in the metric system.

Temperature: Perception and direct comparison   Although temperature is not visible, large differences can be sensed by feel, and we notice even relatively small changes in room temperatures. Questions using the expressions "hot and cold" and "warm and cool" are used in concept development activities.

• Is it *hotter* in summer or in winter? Is it *cooler* on a sunny day or on a cloudy day? Is it *warmer* inside our classroom or outside today?

• How do you dress when you go outside on a *cold* day? Name something you drink when it is *cold/hot* outside. We use the word *temperature* when we talk about how hot or cold something is.

The teacher can collect and display pictures clearly indicating heat. The class could discuss how these pictures might be ordered using the idea of hot and cold. For a hands-on activity, the teacher prepares several containers with water of varying temperatures: hot and cold tap water, water at room temperature, and water from a refrigerator. The children feel the water in each container and order them from warmest to coldest.

The class can discuss what happens to water when it gets very hot and very cold and how you can tell when some objects are very hot (for example, coals in a barbecue grill or an element of an electric stove).

Temperature: Standard units   No activities for measuring temperature using nonstandard units are suggested. Children will be familiar with hearing temperatures reported in *degrees Fahrenheit*. The teacher can state that the temperature in the room is about 70°F. The class should also discuss temperature readings on hot and cold days, the meaning of 32°F, and temperatures below zero.

Introduce the *thermometer* as an instrument for measuring temperature. To make a demonstration thermometer, join a piece of white ribbon and a piece of red ribbon and fit the ends through horizontal slits in a piece of cardboard. Mark a scale on the cardboard and slide the ribbon up and down to indicate the temperature rising and falling. The height of the red section indicates the temperature. The teacher should demonstrate how to read the scale, first at 10- or 5-degree intervals and then to the nearest degree.

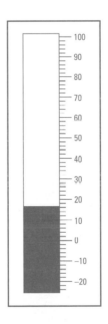

The teacher can explain that in a real thermometer the liquid in the tube expands as the temperature increases and the level rises. Children can then use a thermometer to find the temperature of water under several conditions to the nearest degree Fahrenheit.

	Estimate	**Measure**
water left sitting	20°C	18°C
hot tap water	_____	_____
cold tap water	_____	_____
ice water	_____	_____

Two useful benchmarks are the temperature at which water boils (212°F) and normal body temperature (about

98.6°F). As an ongoing activity, children can record and graph the outside temperature (or the high and low temperatures) for a month. As a telecommunications project students could share these data with schools in different parts of the world.

Angle

As a geometric figure, an *angle* is the union of two rays that have the same endpoint. When we measure an angle, we assign a number to the *spread* between the two arms, or rays. Angular measure can also be thought of in terms of the *amount of turning* about a point, which is used in defining the degree. For children to use a *protractor* correctly and understand what is being measured, they first require experiences in comparing angles directly and in using arbitrary units of angular measure.

Angle: Perception and direct comparison
Developing the concept of angle as a turn is particularly appropriate in the early elementary years (Wilson & Adams, 1992). Children can explore turning their bodies to make half, full, and quarter turns and use their arms to represent clock hands. They can also examine and discuss angles made by a swinging door.

To introduce the notion of the size of an angle, the teacher might open a pair of scissors and direct attention to the *angle* formed by the two blades. The teacher asks the students whether they think this angle is "big" or "small" and how a bigger or smaller angle might be formed. The key idea is that the size of an angle has to do with the *spread* between the two blades, not their length. To make this point, compare angles formed by two pairs of scissors of different sizes, paying special attention to examples in which the angle formed by the larger scissors is smaller than the angle formed by the scissors with shorter blades.

Drawing representations of angles on a chalkboard or paper introduces the static view of angle. To develop basic concepts, the teacher might use an overhead projector to display two angles, as indicated below, and ask the class members which angle they think is bigger and how they might check their estimate.

Again, children find that they must focus on the relationship between the arms and not their length. Mention

that geometrically, the arms of an angle are rays and thus extend indefinitely. To compare the two angles, one first makes a tracing of one of them and directly compares the tracing with the other angle. When the vertices and one of the arms are matched, the other arm of the smaller angle lies in the interior of the larger angle.

Next, teachers can give the children tracing paper and a sheet containing angles of various measures in a number of different positions, with instructions to order the angles according to size. Two of these angles should have the same measure.

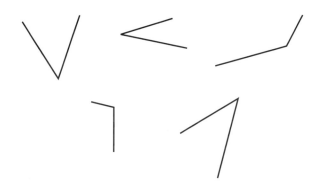

Angle: Nonstandard units
The teacher can draw an angle on the chalkboard and ask the children how they might determine "how big" the angle is. One strategy that is often suggested is to use a ruler to measure the distance between the arms. It should be recognized that children can use this procedure to compare and quantify angular measure, provided that they take the measurement at a fixed distance from the vertex along the arm(s).

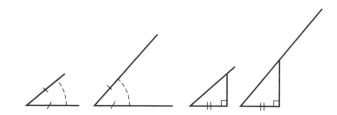

When children are reminded that an important characteristic of a unit is that it has the same attribute as that to be measured, they should realize that a small angle can be used as a unit. The question then is how many copies of this small angle fit inside the angle to be measured. A wedge cut from cardboard is useful as a unit to measure the angle on the chalkboard.

Children should predict and verify the result of using a smaller unit angle to measure the angle in question. As an activity, children could prepare several copies of cardboard wedges representing angles of three different sizes. They would then draw an angle on paper and measure it using the three different units. Teachers should remind children to estimate before measuring and to measure to the nearest unit.

Children can create an instrument for measuring angles by partitioning a paper half circle into equal sectors by folding. The teacher can then challenge them to use this "protractor" to find the measures of angles of various cardboard wedges.

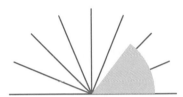

Angle: Standard units Before children learn about the degree as a standard unit of angular measure, they can use the familiar *right angle* as a referent. This special angle can first be introduced in relation to body turns. Some children reason that because a quarter turn right is called a right angle, a quarter turn left is called a "left" angle. Later, children should be shown how to fold a piece of paper twice to produce a right angle. They then use this "right angle tester" to identify right angles on familiar objects at their desk and in the room and to classify other angles as greater than or less than a right angle. To illustrate a *straight angle,* two right angles can be placed together. Tell the children that an *acute* angle has a measure that is less than a right angle and an *obtuse* angle has a measure greater than a right angle but less than a straight angle (see illustration).

Children explore the measures of angles of triangles and quadrilaterals in Activities 15-23 and 15-24.

The *degree* can be defined as the amount of turning (or the size of unit angle) such that the measure of a quarter turn (or right angle) is 90°. It follows that the measure of a half turn (or straight angle) is 180° and the measure of a full turn is 360°.

Because the number 360 is not a power of 10, children may be interested in knowing the origin of the degree. This unit originated with the Babylonians, who observed

ACTIVITY 15-23

ANGLES OF TRIANGLES

MATERIALS
Straight edge

PROCEDURE
1. Draw a triangle with a right angle.

2. Can you draw a triangle with two right angles? Why or why not?

3. Try to draw triangles with angles as follows:
   • one obtuse angle
   • two obtuse angles
   • three acute angles

4. If possible, draw a quadrilateral with:
   • exactly one right angle
   • exactly two right angles
   • exactly three right angles
   • four right angles

ACTIVITY 15-24

TRIANGLE ANGLES

MATERIALS
Light cardboard
Scissors

PROCEDURE
1. Cut a triangle out of cardboard.

2. Cut off each of the corners as shown and place the three angles together. What kind of angle is formed?

3. Repeat with a different-shaped triangle. Did you get the same result?

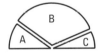

4. Cut a cardboard quadrilateral.

5. Cut off the four corners and place the four angles together. What did you find?

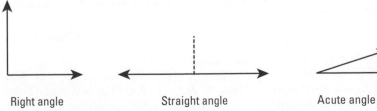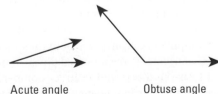

Right angle   Straight angle   Acute angle   Obtuse angle

ACTIVITY 15-25

SUM OF ANGLES IN A POLYGON

MATERIALS
Straight edge, protractor

PROCEDURE

1. Draw several different-shaped triangles.

2. Measure each of the interior angles and find the sum of the three angles of each triangle.

3. What do you notice?

4. Repeat for quadrilaterals, pentagons, and hexagons.

5. Can you find a pattern?

that the position of the sun changes by the same amount each day. They called the amount of turn the earth makes each day from the viewpoint of the sun 1°. Because 365 has few divisors, they decided to divide the circle into 360 parts instead (Newton, 1988).

At this point, teachers can ask the class to estimate the measures of various acute and obtuse angles drawn on the board by the teacher, and draw angles of approximately 45°, 60°, 135°, and 170°. The teacher then demonstrates how to use a *protractor* to measure angles in degrees, emphasizing the correct placement of the baseline and the vertex. Children practice using a protractor to measure angles and construct angles with given measures. Working in pairs, one child draws an angle and the other estimates and then measures it. Next, the children reverse roles. Later, children learn to measure and construct angles greater than 180°.

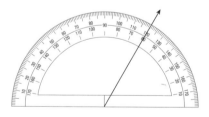

In Activity 15-25 children use protractors to investigate the sum of the interior angles of various polygons.

CONCLUSION

When we measure, we assign a number to a physical property of an object or to an event by comparing it with a unit. Beginning instruction in measurement stresses language development and involves activities that give meaning to the attribute. Perception and physical materials are used to make direct and indirect comparisons. Measuring should be carried out first with nonstandard

units, then with standard SI units. Children need to be able to identify appropriate units for given situations and estimate and use instruments or formulas to measure with those units. As they learn measurement concepts and skills, learners are actively involved in solving problems.

Measurement is a practical, useful skill. Children should appreciate the role it plays in their everyday lives and in modern society. Measurement ideas should be identified, applied, and reinforced in other school subjects, including science, social studies, physical education, art, and music. Children should enjoy measuring and have confidence in their ability to use their knowledge and skills to solve problems in the real world.

For Your Journal

When you have finished studying this chapter, reflect on the following questions in your math journal:

1. What are some examples of real-world situations in which nonstandard and standard units of measure are used? Discuss the reasons for each.

2. How does measuring with nonstandard units help children use standard units?

3. How were you taught to find perimeter, area, and volume when you were in elementary school? Compare and contrast your experiences with the recommendations of this chapter.

4. Visit a middle-school classroom and informally interview several children to assess their understanding of area and perimeter. What were their understandings and misconceptions about these concepts?

For Your Portfolio

When you have finished studying this chapter, complete the following activities to include in your professional portfolio:

1. Examine a textbook's section on measurement. Discuss it in relation to the content of this chapter. How is actual measurement provided for in the textbook activities?

2. Write a lesson plan to introduce nonstandard measurement of an attribute of your choice (either length, area, volume, capacity, mass, time, temperature, or angle).

3. Write a lesson plan to introduce standard measurement of an attribute of your choice (either length, area, volume, capacity, mass, time, temperature, or angle).

Resources for Teachers

Children's books

McMillan, B. (1989). *Time to . . . .* New York: Scholastic.

Olney, R., & Olney, P. (1984). *How long? To go, to grow, to know.* New York: William Morrow.

Pluckrose, H. (1995). *Math counts: Length.* USA: Children's Press.

Books on measurement

Geddes, D. (1994). *Measurement in the middle grades: Curriculum Evaluation Standards for School Mathematics Addenda Series Grade 5–8.* Reston, VA: National Council of Teachers of Mathematics.

Rectanus, C. (1997). *Math by all means: Area and perimeter Grades 5–6.* Sausalito, CA: Math Solutions.

Shroyer, J., & Fitzgerald, W. (1986). *Middle grades mathematics project: Mouse and elephant: Measuring growth.* Menlo Park, CA: Addison-Wesley.

Links to the Internet

Explorer: Measurement

http://explorer.scrtec.org/explorer/explorer-db/browse/static/Mathematics/browse/f55.html

Contains many lessons on measurement and lists of resources.

Shape Surveyor

http://www.funbrain.com/poly/index.html

Contains a game on finding area and perimeter.

CHAPTER 16

Collecting, Organizing, and Interpreting Data

FOCUS QUESTIONS ▶

When you have finished studying this chapter, you should be able to answer the following questions:

1. What are the stages of graphing experiences that children should encounter? Give an example of each stage.

2. What different types of graphs are used in organizing and interpreting data? Give an example of each type.

3. What are the three measures of central tendency? How can teachers help children to better understand each of these measures?

4. What are some ways to use technology to help in collecting, organizing, and interpreting data?

NCTM CONTENT STANDARDS AND EXPECTATIONS ADDRESSED IN THIS CHAPTER

STANDARD	EXPECTATIONS FOR GRADES PRE-K–2	EXPECTATIONS FOR GRADES 3–5	EXPECTATIONS FOR GRADES 6–8
Data Analysis and Probability Standard Instructional programs from pre-K–12 should enable all students to—	In prekindergarten through Grade 2 all students should— (NCTM, 2000, p. 108)	In Grades 3–5 all students should— (NCTM, 2000, p. 176)	In Grades 6–8 all students should—(NCTM, 2000, p. 248)
Formulate questions that can be addressed with data and collect, organize, and display relevant data to answer them	• pose questions and gather data about themselves and their surroundings. • sort and classify objects according to their attributes and organize data about the objects. • represent data using concrete objects, pictures, and graphs.	• design investigations to address a question and consider how data-collection methods affect the nature of the data set. • collect data using observations, surveys, and experiments. • represent data using tables and graphs such as line plots, bar graphs, and line graphs. • recognize the differences in representing categorical and numerical data.	• formulate questions, design studies, and collect data about a characteristic shared by two populations or different characteristics within one population. • select, create, and use appropriate graphical representations of data, including histograms, box plots, and scatterplots.

STANDARD	EXPECTATIONS FOR GRADES PRE-K–2	EXPECTATIONS FOR GRADES 3–5	EXPECTATIONS FOR GRADES 6–8
Data Analysis and Probability Standard *(continued)* Instructional programs from pre-K–12 should enable all students to—	In prekindergarten through Grade 2 all students should— (NCTM, 2000, p. 108)	In Grades 3–5 all students should— (NCTM, 2000, p. 176)	In Grades 6–8 all students should—(NCTM, 2000, p. 248)
Select and use appropriate statistical methods to analyze data	• describe parts of the data and the set of data as a whole to determine what the data show.	• describe the shape and important features of a set of data and compare related data sets, with an emphasis on how the data are distributed. • use measures of center, focusing on the median, and understand what each does and does not indicate about the data set. • compare different representations of the same data and evaluate how well each representation shows important aspects of the data.	• find, use, and interpret measures of center and spread, including mean and interquartile range. • discuss and understand the correspondence between data sets and their graphical representations, especially histograms, stem-and-leaf plots, box plots, and scatterplots.
Develop and evaluate inferences and predictions that are based on data	• discuss events related to students' experiences as likely or unlikely.	• propose and justify conclusions and predictions that are based on data and design studies to further investigate the conclusions or predictions.	• use observations about differences between two or more samples to make conjectures about the populations from which the samples were taken. • make conjectures about possible relationships between two characteristics of a sample on the basis of scatterplots of the data and approximate lines of fit. • use conjectures to formulate new questions and plan new studies to answer them.
Understand and apply basic concepts of probability		• describe events as likely or unlikely and discuss the degree of likelihood using such words as *certain, equally likely,* and *impossible.* • predict the probability of outcomes of simple experiments and test the predictions. • understand that the measure of the likelihood of an event can be represented by a number from 0 to 1.	• understand and use appropriate terminology to describe complementary and mutually exclusive events. • use proportionality and a basic understanding of probability to make and test conjectures about the results of experiments and simulations. • compute probabilities for simple compound events, using such methods as organized lists, tree diagrams, and area models.

Data are all around us. Indeed, sometimes data overwhelm us. Children, too, are bombarded with all kinds of data that they would like to understand. How? What? When? Where? Who? Why? are real-life questions that often require the collection, organization, and interpretation of data to be answered.

What do we know of U.S. children's understanding of data analysis, statistics, and probability? The sixth National Assessment of Educational Progress (NAEP) assessment noted that most 4th, 8th, and 12th graders tested were able to read and use data presented in tables. But children in all three grade levels tested had "difficulty communicating their reasoning about data representation" (Zawojewski & Heckman, 1997, p. 196). Teaching about data analysis must be more than just creating and reading graphs. Instruction must help children to understand, interpret, and apply reasoning in studying data.

In this chapter, we will describe data collection techniques, examine methods for organizing and displaying data, and discuss ways of interpreting data to make predictions—all with the intent of designing mathematics instruction to help children use and interpret data in decision making. ✔

COLLECTING AND ORGANIZING DATA

There must be a reason for collecting data. Children need to have some question they want to answer—a question they agreed upon after a brainstorming session, perhaps, or a question that arises from a class discussion in some other subject area or from someone's recent experience. A provocative question by the teacher may also give rise to the need to collect data. For example, "Do more children have dogs than cats for pets?" or "I think vanilla is the favorite flavor of ice cream by children in this class." These questions arouse interest. Children want to find out—even to prove that the teacher's supposition is wrong.

Scenarios such as those just described suggest that we are involved with an investigation or research project rather than a short in-class activity. The first two steps in a research model appropriate for elementary school mathematics proposed by Bohan, Irby, and Vogel (1995) involve choosing a question to answer or problem to solve. The complete model consists of seven steps:

Step 1: Brainstorm for questions that children would like answered.
Step 2: Choose one of the questions or problems.
Step 3: Predict what the outcome will be.
Step 4: Develop a plan to test the predicted outcome.
Step 5: Carry out the plan.
Step 6: Analyze the data. Is the hypothesis supported?
Step 7: Look back. Answer the question. Should the information be shared? With whom? How could it be shared?

It is very important that children collect their own data (Russell & Friel, 1989). This contributes ownership, interest, and reality to their experience. A class survey is one of the most obvious and easy ways of getting information with which all children can identify. The following section presents a number of ideas for surveys, including children's favorites—one of the most fruitful sources of data (Young, 1991). Children can make surveys on favorite pets, fruits, ice cream flavors, colors, and so on and graph the data. For some topics, children can extend the survey to include other classes or the whole school. For example, older children can take surveys of traffic outside the school, type of clothing worn by people who enter a nearby mall, or the amount of sugar or fiber in several brands of cereal.

Hofstetter and Sgroi (1996) used cereal boxes as the basis for a data management project. After collecting a variety of empty boxes of different brands of cereal, the

---

PRINCIPLES AND STANDARDS LINK 16-1
Content Strand: Data Analysis and Probability

Instructional programs from prekindergarten through grade 12 should enable all students to—

- formulate questions that can be addressed with data and collect, organize, and display relevant data to answer them;
- select and use appropriate statistical methods to analyze data;
- develop and evaluate inferences and predictions that are based on data;
- understand and apply basic concepts of probability. (NCTM, 2000, p. 48)

PRINCIPLES AND STANDARDS LINK 16-2
Content Strand: Data Analysis and Probability

The Data Analysis and Probability Standard recommends that students formulate questions that can be answered using data and addresses what is involved in gathering and using the data wisely. Students should learn how to collect data, organize their own or others' data, and display the data in graphs and charts that will be useful in answering their questions. (NCTM, 2000, p. 48)

Food seems to be a popular basis for data management activities. Hitch and Armstrong (1994) and Shannon (1995) also use it. In addition, children's literature can provide a rich source of ideas for data management projects (Litton, 1995). Bankard and Fennell (1991) and Brahier and Speer (1995) also provide some projects that would involve gathering data firsthand, then organizing and displaying them in graphical form.

The Internet and electronic mail can be interesting media for collecting data. Comparing data collected and shared by children from different countries can lead to some valuable learning in mathematics and beyond.

A useful technique for recording data is a tally. The teacher can demonstrate this technique to the whole class by taking a survey of children's favorite fast food, weekend activity, or some other topic. Demonstrate making a tally for each child's preference as in Figure 16-1.

Young children should also have opportunities to discover that the way data are organized varies with the kinds of questions one wants to ask. Figure 16-2 shows three ways in which data from a survey of class members' favorite fruit could be organized. Figure 16-2(a) would be the best display if you wanted to know Nathan's favorite fruit. On the other hand, if you were interested in the number of people who prefer oranges or were determining the most popular fruit in the class, you would consult the display in either (b) or (c) of Figure 16-2.

FIGURE 16-1

Favorite Fast Food

Hamburger	$\cancel{||||}\,|$
Fried Chicken	$|||$
Taco	$||$
Hot Dog	$\cancel{||||}\;\cancel{||||}\;||$
Other	$||$

GRAPHING DATA

Graphs summarize data in a concise and pictorial form. Graphing, while a legitimate mathematics education topic in its own right, is best thought of as an integrative component of the program. It is integrative within mathematics in that graphs can be used when developing other mathematical topics. Graphs, for instance, can be used as a means of generating computational exercises, for showing the number of prismatic as opposed to pyramidal

children described the boxes (geometry) and then classified and ordered them using different criteria. Later, they analyzed and graphed the food content.

M&Ms or other candy can also be used by children as firsthand data (Brosnan, 1996; Browning, Channell, & Meyer, 1994). The children can predict the number of each color of candy to be found in one box, then count and graph for themselves.

FIGURE 16-2

Fruit Survey	
Name	Fruit
Wendy	Apples
Seyi	Oranges
Nathan	Bananas
Mavis	Oranges
John	Apples
	Grapes

(a)

Fruit Survey	
Fruit	Choices
Oranges	✓ ✓ ✓ ✓ ✓ ✓ ✓
Apples	✓ ✓ ✓ ✓ ✓ ✓
Bananas	✓ ✓ ✓
Grapes	✓

(b)

Fruit Survey	
Fruit	Frequency
Oranges	12
Apples	6
Bananas	3
Grapes	1

(c)

shapes children can find in the classroom, the variability in the noon-hour temperature outside the classroom over a period of a week, and many other relationships. An understanding of ratios, proportions, percents, fractions, and other topics is often required in constructing or interpreting more advanced graphs.

Graphing is also integrative in the sense that it brings together mathematics and other curriculum subjects such as science, physical education, and social studies. Thus, from a teaching standpoint graphing should be thought of not as a strand to be covered in a 4-week unit but as something to be done throughout the school year.

Children may be introduced to graphing as early as the first grade. Skills associated with graphing include constructing graphs, reading information from graphs, and interpreting the information by discussing or writing about it.

Early Experiences

Most graphic representations at the primary level will be some form of bar graph. Some introduction to coordinate graphing is often included before the end of the primary grades. At this level, children's graphing experiences generally progress through four overlapping stages: concrete, concrete-pictorial, pictorial-abstract, and abstract.

Concrete stage Children's early graphing experiences should involve constructing graphs with concrete materials. Each object, such as a block, should represent only one thing, and children should compare only two events or things.

There are numerous dichotomous events that young children enjoy graphing. Some of them include:

- eyeglasses—no eyeglasses
- walked to school—rode to school
- left-handed—right-handed

When modeling graphs concretely, children like to be the objects. An initial query might be, "I wonder if more children walked to school than rode to school this morning." Children could form two straight lines, those who walked standing in one line and those who rode in the other. Depending on the ratio in the class, children may or may not be able to perceive a difference in the length of the lines. If children formed two lines on the basis of whether they printed with their right hand or left hand, the lines would most likely be very different in length. In these examples, the line is analogous to a bar in a bar graph, so you may want to discuss the following aspects of graphing with the children:

- the beginning of the lines should be along the same line (axis).
- distance between children in line should be uniform.

Although children like to "act out" the graph, there are a number of disadvantages to this approach. The most significant is that children have difficulty perceiving which line is longer because they are part of a line. They often need to "get out of line" to check, which can create problems with the line as it was initially constituted. Other disadvantages include the possible lack of uniformity in spacing and the possibility of the lines not starting at the same imaginary axis.

Experiences such as the one described in Activity 16-1 avoid such difficulties. This activity is probably best done in a group of about one-half the class; otherwise, the stacks of blocks used in the activity may become too high and topple before all the blocks are placed. The two groups can compare their graphs afterward.

An activity that might serve as a transition to the next level would be to have children draw a picture of themselves on an index card. A query to the children might be, "Would you like to be younger or older than you are?" Each child would then tack his or her picture in the appropriate section of a bulletin board chart the teacher prepares beforehand (see Figure 16-3).

Because the pictures will be somewhat randomly placed in the boxes, it may not be easy to see whether there is a difference. Children could count to decide, or they might be asked to organize the cards in each box into an array.

A by-product of this activity may be some further insight into the thoughts of the children. These thoughts could be elicited as an extension of the reading/interpretation questions, that is, you could follow a question such as "Do more children prefer to be younger or do more prefer to be older?" with "Why would you like to be older (younger)?"

PRINCIPLES AND STANDARDS LINK 16-3
Content Strand: Data Analysis and Probability

A fundamental idea in prekindergarten through grade 2 is that data can be organized or ordered and that this "picture" of the data provides information about the phenomenon or question. In grades 3–5, students should develop skill in representing their data, often using bar graphs, tables, or line plots. They should learn what different numbers, symbols, and points mean. Recognizing that some numbers represent the values of the data and others represent the frequency with which those values occur is a big step. . . . Students in grades 6–8 should begin to compare the effectiveness of various types of displays in organizing the data for further analysis or in presenting the data clearly to an audience. (NCTM, 2000, p. 48)

ACTIVITY 16-1

CONCRETE GRAPH (LIGHT VERSUS DARK HAIR)

MATERIALS

- Two sheets of paper on which the words *light* and *dark* have been printed (or a light and dark sheet of colored construction paper.)
- Selection of light- and dark-colored blocks that can easily be stacked.

PROCEDURE

1. Each child should
- select a block that he or she thinks most resembles his or her hair color.
- place the block on the stack on the appropriate sheet, as shown in the figure.

2. Talk about what the graph tells you.

3. Talk about things the graph does not tell you. (The teacher may need to ask a leading question, such as "Does this graph tell us how many children are absent today?")

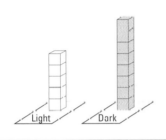

FIGURE 16-3

I Would Like to Be:

Younger	Older

FIGURE 16-4

I Would Like to Be:

Younger	Same Age	Older

Concrete pictorial stage In this stage, children will use pictorial representation of objects in addition to concrete materials. They may compare more than two events but will still maintain the one-to-one correspondence between object or picture and what is being graphed.

The last example in the previous section was a transition to this level. To make it a true Stage 2 activity, change the bulletin board chart to include three boxes, as in Figure 16-4.

Children like to talk about their birthday. They could make a block graph of birthday months. Normally, a comparison of 12 things is too much for primary-grade children, but birthdays may be an exception because of familiarity and interest. Furthermore, such an activity will reinforce the children's learning of the months of the year. Figure 16-5 shows one form that this graph might take. If you had photocopies of the children's photos, each child could tack his or her picture above the appropriate month to make a bulletin board graph.

Children's favorites is an excellent setting for a variety of Stage 2 graphing activities; favorite flavor of ice cream is one possibility. An introductory motivational query might be, "I think most children in the class like

chocolate ice cream the best." A bulletin board display like the one in Figure 16-6 could be prepared as well as several cutouts of each of the anticipated flavors. Ask the children to take one of the paper cones representing their favorite flavor and pin it above the appropriate model.

A primary grade teacher could capitalize on the variety of characteristics of buttons to develop Stage 2 graphing experiences. For example, children in cooperative learning groups could each take a handful of buttons, put their selections together, and create a graph as shown in Figure 16-7. Some possible comparisons include

- number of holes: 0, 2, 4
- flat versus raised
- material: plastic, metal, wood
- shapes: round, square, other
- texture: smooth, rough, fabric-covered, other

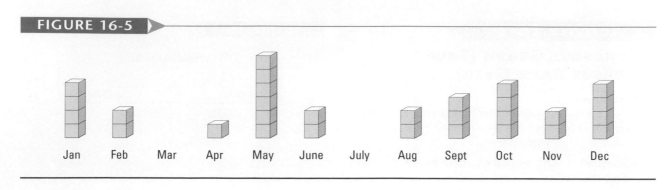

FIGURE 16-5

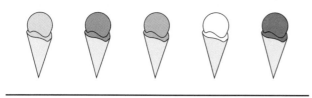

FIGURE 16-6

My Favorite Ice Cream

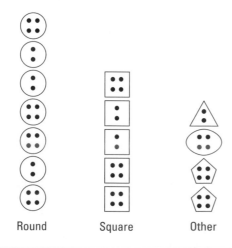

FIGURE 16-7

Round   Square   Other

Encourage the children to "interpret" the graph by asking one or two leading questions, such as "What does the graph tell you?" or "What can you learn from the graph?" Children might also discuss how this graph could help them if they were a button maker. Once chil-

dren's writing skills have developed sufficiently, they could write a report about what they learned.

Pictorial-abstract stage   At the third level, pictorial-abstract, primary children continue to make bar graphs with pictures, but they also make a transition to the abstract by using gummed stickers, colored cards, etc., to form the graph.

Any of the topics used in the previous two levels could be used at Stage 3. Children could pin objects or pictures of objects on the bulletin board or on paper as before. Then they could construct the same graph by putting gummed stickers on a chart. In Figure 16-8(a), the children pinned pictures of their favorite fruit on a bulletin board chart. Figure 16-8(b) shows the same information using gummed stickers.

A transition to the next level could be developed by having children fill in squares, one square for each tally on their survey. This could easily be done with the favorite fruit activity. Provide children with a template as in Figure 16-9 (without the shading) and challenge them to figure out how they could represent the same information on this graph.

Pictographs.   Although most pictographs are a Stage 4 (abstract) activity, they can be introduced at Stage 3 in a setting in which the one-to-one correspondence is convenient. For example, children could be given the graph in Figure 16-10 and asked to read, interpret, and discuss it through questions such as the following:

• How many brothers and sisters does Heather have?
• Who has the most brothers and sisters?
• Does Kerri have more brothers and sisters than Heather?
• What else does the graph tell you?

To construct a simple one-to-one pictograph, children could be given a template as shown in Figure 16-11. They would tally the number of library books in their desk, print their name in one of the rows, then draw one square for each book they found. Some may have no books, in which case they would only print their name. Children could follow this by writing a short paragraph about the graph.

FIGURE 16-8

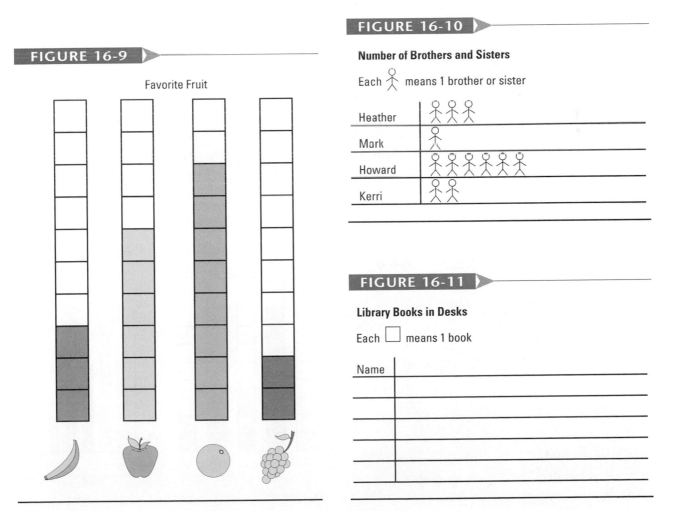

(a)

(b)

FIGURE 16-9

Favorite Fruit

FIGURE 16-10

Number of Brothers and Sisters

Each 👤 means 1 brother or sister

Heather	👤👤👤
Mark	👤
Howard	👤👤👤👤👤👤
Kerri	👤👤

FIGURE 16-11

Library Books in Desks

Each ☐ means 1 book

Name	

Glyphs. *Glyphs,* another form of picture graph, are a great way to represent or communicate data. They have their origin in ancient *hieroglyphics* or picture writing and have been used more recently in medical and scientific applications. Children and teachers in the primary grades are now using glyphs to represent information (Cartland, 1996; Harbaugh, 1995). Because glyphs are a form of picture graph, they are easily incorporated into data management experiences.

Children find glyphs both easy and fun to construct. Harbaugh (1995) describes the process as follows:

Simply (1) decide to create either a facial glyph or a shape glyph, (2) determine the various characteristics to be explained, (3) assign glyph features to the characteristics, (4) print the corresponding key, and (5) draw the glyph. (p. 511)

The following example has been adapted from Cartland (1996). After seeing some hot air balloons float over the school, children might decide to use a hot air balloon shape for a glyph. Children might decide to use:

1. A different basket shape to represent their position in the family.

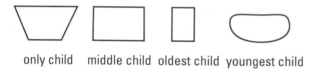

only child   middle child   oldest child   youngest child

2. The number of strings attaching the basket to the balloon to represent the number of people in their home.

3. The design on the basket to represent the main language spoken at home.

English: **+++**   Japanese: ✓✓✓

French: ▲▲▲   Spanish: ✳✳✳

Vietnamese: Ŏ Ŏ Ŏ   Other: ❖❖❖

Two children's hot air balloon glyphs might look like this:

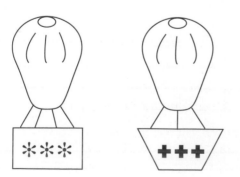

Harbaugh (1995) and Sacco, Copes, Sloyer, and Stark (1987) present other samples of glyphs that young children have constructed.

Abstract stage   If adequate experiences have been provided in Stages 1 to 3, the move to abstract representation should be relatively easy. At this stage, one-to-one correspondence of objects to events is replaced with a one-to-many correspondence. This normally requires a scale for one of the axes. Rectangular bars replace the colored squares and line graphs can be introduced.

Again, many of the topics graphed earlier could be used at this level. It is not the topic but rather the way the data are presented that determines the level. Consider the query, "I wonder which vowel occurs most often in writing." At Stage 3, children might select a sentence from their reader or library book, tally the occurrence of each vowel, and then color squares, one square for each occurrence, as in Figure 16-12(a).

At Stage 4 (abstract level), children could choose a paragraph and tally the occurrence of vowels as before. A paragraph may provide more vowels than they wish to handle on their graph using one square for each occurrence. A scale of 1 square representing 2 occurrences may be convenient. Later the squares can be replaced with rectangular bars. The graph shown in Figure 16-12(b) may result.

The one-for-many relationship leads naturally into pictographs in which the object may represent 2, 5, 10, or some other convenient number of things. Figure 16-13 shows a pictograph of the number of soda can tabs a few children brought to school as part of a class project investigating how much room 1000 soda can tabs would take up.

Another activity that would involve Stage 4 graphing could be instigated with the query, "What kind of vehicle

FIGURE 16-12

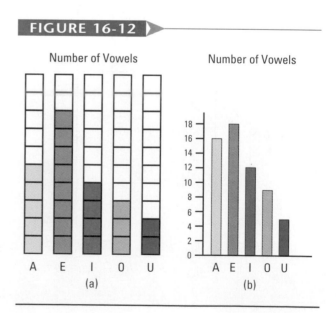

FIGURE 16-13 ▶

Soda Can Tabs Collected

Each ◎ = 10 tabs

Wendy | ◎ ◎ ◎ ◎ ◎ ◎ ◎ ◎

Bill | ◎ ◎ ◎ ◎ ◎ ◎

Carlo | ◎ ◎ ◎ ◎ ◎ ◎ ◎ ◎ ◎ ◎ ◎ ◎

Heather | ◎ ◎ ◎ ◎

Joy | ◎ ◎ ◎ ◎ ◎ ◎ ◎

FIGURE 16-13 ▶

FIGURE 16-15 ▶

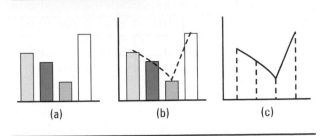

(a)   (b)   (c)

passes by our school most often?" This should be done on a day when a parent volunteer or teacher assistant is available to help. One or two small groups could go out with the parent or aide for a 20- or 30-minute period to collect the data by keeping a tally of the different kinds of vehicles that pass by.

Afterward, children could color a rectangular bar, as shown in Figure 16-14, rather than preexisting squares. An excellent interpretation activity could involve writing a letter to the principal describing the vehicular activity and perhaps making some safety recommendations.

Line graphs are another way to represent information at Stage 4. For example, children could record the outside temperature at a given time each day for a week. The data could be graphed using a bar graph as shown in Figure 16-15(a). Discuss how each data point can be joined with a line, as shown in Figure 16-15(b). Line graphs are not so mysterious for young children if they understand this difference, namely that in a bar graph, data points deter-

mine the height of a rectangle (the bar) from the axis, whereas in a line graph the same data points are simply joined with a line. Figure 16-15(b) and Figure 16-15(c) show this distinction.

One important distinction, however, between line and bar graphs that children need to understand is that bars represent a category or event, whereas line graphs represent continuous data, such as temperature. Both axes on a smooth line graph involve a continuous scale. In the case of a broken line graph, one scale may not be numeric but is at least ordered, as in the case of the months of the year (see Figure 16-16).

A good reading/interpretation activity is to give children a line graph with a title and the nature of the units for each axis and ask them to describe orally or in writing what is happening. This will also reinforce the continuous nature of the data. Activity 16-2 is an example of this type of exercise.

ACTIVITY 16-2 ▶

GAS STOP

MATERIALS
Graph (below)

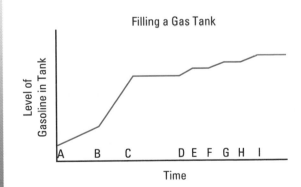

Filling a Gas Tank

Level of Gasoline in Tank

A   B   C   D E F   G H   I

Time

PROCEDURE
This graph shows the level of gasoline in the tank of a car as it is being filled. Write as interesting a story as you can about this. Include what happened at points (Time) A, B, C, D, E, F, G, H, and I.

FIGURE 16-14 ▶

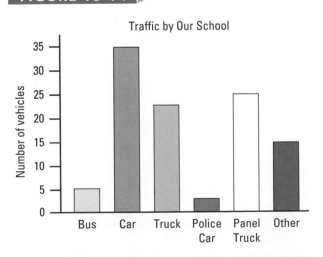

Traffic by Our School

Number of vehicles

35
30
25
20
15
10
5
0

Bus   Car   Truck   Police Car   Panel Truck   Other

FIGURE 16-16

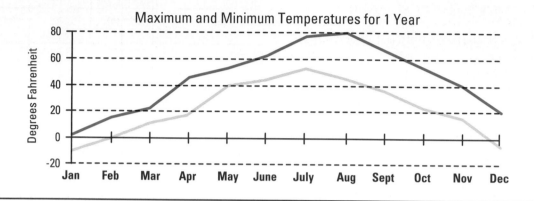

	Jan	Feb	Mar	Apr	May	June	July	Aug	Sept	Oct	Nov	Dec
Maximum	2	16	22	48	56	62	78	80	62	56	40	20
Minimum	−18	0	10	18	40	44	56	46	38	24	16	−6

Once this basic understanding is developed, upper-elementary and middle-school children are ready for more advanced line graphs. But first, a transitional activity such as Activity 16-3 would help children think about the kind of continuous activity or relationship represented by both straight-line and curved-line graphs.

Upper-elementary and junior high school children can use a multiple-line graph to compare two or more things. For example, a group of children could obtain the maximum and minimum temperatures for each month of the year from the local weather office. They would plot two line graphs on the same chart, one showing the maximum, the other the minimum temperature each month, and orally report their observations and conclusions to

the class or prepare a written report. Upper-elementary or junior high children who have had a little experience with a computer spreadsheet may volunteer to enter the data and have the computer produce the graph. Figure 16-16 shows a line graph and the spreadsheet from which it was generated.

Coordinate Graphing

Coordinate graphing is normally introduced at about the Grade 3 level. Smith (1986) found that "third graders are able to understand the concepts and master the skills required" (p. 11). He recommends that pedagogically, coordinate graphing should be presented "as an integrated

ACTIVITY 16-3

COLLECTING WATER

MATERIALS
Graphs (below)

PROCEDURE
Write a story about each graph.

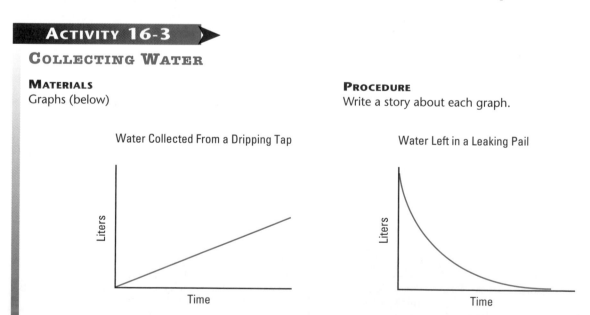

unit rather than in a piecemeal fashion" (p. 11). Superimposing a grid on a "community" and using coordinates to locate buildings on a map might be an example of an integration of a social studies unit with mathematical skills.

To introduce coordinate graphs, Smith (1986) suggests beginning with the geoboard. Children can decide on how to label each nail or peg on a 5-by-5 square geoboard. They might begin by simply labeling them from A through Y, as shown in Figure 16-17(a). With some guidance, they can be led to name just the rows and columns, as in Figure 16-17(b). The need for the 0 coordinates can be elicited by presenting a grid similar to Figure 16-17(c) on the overhead projector. Place a small object such as a small plastic animal (it is all right that children will see only the outline) at a particular location and ask the children to tell you where the animal is hiding. After a few repetitions, place the animal on one of the points on one of the axes, say (0,3) and ask where the animal is hiding. Children could now suggest labels for the points on each of the axes.

Using the geoboard or dot paper, children can engage in activities such as copying shapes from coordinate descriptions and playing simple versions of tic-tac-toe and *Battleship* (Smith, 1986).

Initially the language needs to be the language of the child. A teacher might project a simple grid, as in Figure 16-18, and ask the children to describe how to find the lost puppy if they are standing at the origin (0,0). They will likely use statements such as "go over 3 and up 2." Initial activities use terms such as *over, across,* and *up.* Once children understand the concept, it is relatively easy to introduce notation such as ($\rightarrow$ 3, $\uparrow$ 2) and then the standard notation (3,2). Once children reach this stage of understanding they can apply their understanding to some more practical or integrative activities, as in Figure 16-19 (Smith, 1986).

Next, the grid can be expanded to include 10 or more coordinate points on each axis. Children could be given

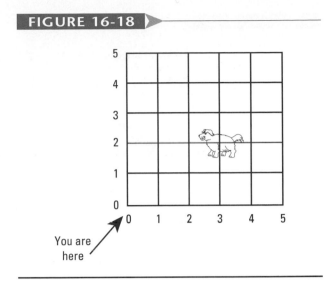

FIGURE 16-18

You are here

coordinates, be asked to plot them, and join them to discover a design, as in Figure 16-20. They could extend this by creating a design, recording and giving only the ordered coordinates to a friend, and asking the friend to draw the design.

Vissa (1987) suggests an activity in which the teacher gives the children half of a design on a coordinate grid. The children are to complete it and list the coordinates of each corner. Figure 16-21 is a similar activity. Vissa also extends coordinate graphing to three dimensions using an airplane in space and fish in an aquarium (negative coordinates).

Circle or Pie Graphs

Circle or pie graphs appear frequently in newspapers, brochures, and many business documents. A circle graph clearly shows how a whole is broken into parts. Sources of revenue or a breakdown of expenditures are usually

FIGURE 16-17

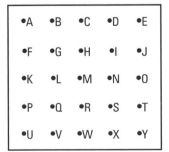

(a) Coordinates named A - Y

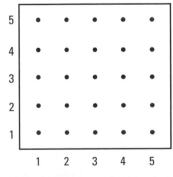

(b) Coordinates named by rows and columns

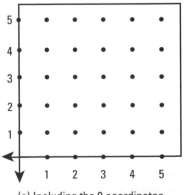

(c) Including the 0 coordinates

FIGURE 16-19

(a) What are the coordinates of the different sites?

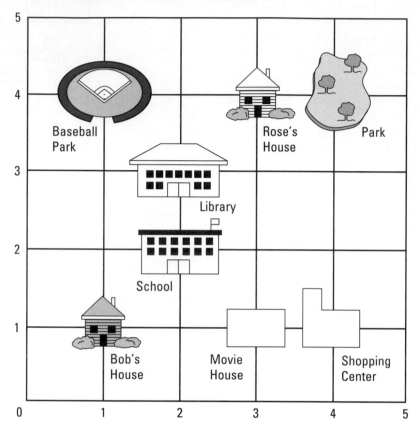

(b) What are the coordinates of the different sites?

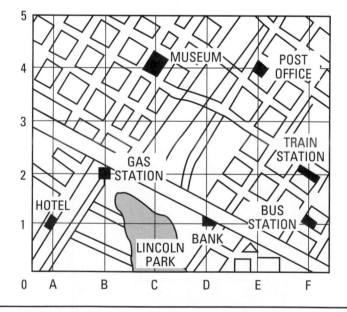

Source: "Let's do it: Coordinate geometry for third graders," by R.F. Smith, 1986, *Arithmetic Teacher,* 33(8), 6–11.

FIGURE 16-20

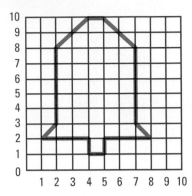

FIGURE 16-22

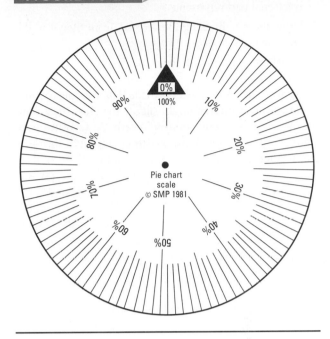

shown with a circle or pie graph. Temperatures are appropriate for a line graph but not normally for circle graphs. Likewise, a circle graph clearly portrays the amount of time that a child devotes to various activities during the day. A line graph of such data would not be as easy to understand. Although bar graphs could show this information, the relationship among the activities and of each activity to the whole is more clearly seen in a circle graph.

Reading and constructing circle graphs is generally delayed until Grade 6 or later because children need to have an understanding of fractions, percents, and angular measure before they can work with circle graphs in a meaningful way.

A device designed by the School Mathematics Project in England (cited by Ewbank, 1987), shown in Figure 16-22, may allow children to draw circle graphs in earlier grades before they have done much with angular measure.

Most school texts include a family budget as an example of a circle graph. In this case, the circle represents the total budget, and each sector represents a budget category as a percent of the total budget. The family whose budget is represented in Figure 16-23 spent 25% of its budget for food, 18% for clothing, and so on.

To construct a circle graph, children should be guided through six steps.

1. Collect the data and calculate the total.

2. Calculate the fractional part each data piece is of the total.

3. Express each fraction as a percent. This is not mandatory, although many circle graphs include the percent as part of the labeling process.

FIGURE 16-21

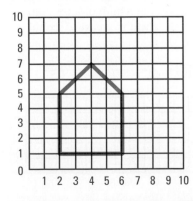

Name the shape. _____

List the coordinates of each corner.

(___,___) (___,___)

(___,___) (___,___)

(___,___)

FIGURE 16-23

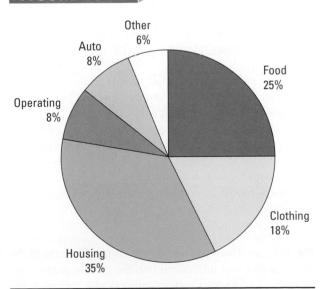

4. Calculate the number of degrees out of 360° that each fractional part represents.

5. Draw the graph, using the degrees from Step 4 to determine the size of each sector.

6. Label the graph and each sector.

Again, class surveys can provide data for constructing circle graphs. Children might survey the class (or a sample of the school population) to determine favorite sport, ice cream flavor, TV show, month or season of the year, etc. Rather than draw bars as they did earlier, children would determine the fraction of children who responded in each category, calculate the corresponding angle, and construct the circle graph. Statistics from government documents and newspaper articles also provide suitable graphing data that are of interest to children. Again, children need to talk or write about what the graph tells them and, perhaps, what it does not tell.

Histograms, Line Plots, and Stem-and-Leaf Plots

Histograms, line plots, and *stem-and-leaf plots* are different forms of graphs often used to represent characteristics of a set of scores. They are often discussed and used in the context of statistical topics. We include them here because of their graphical nature. Another display, *box-and-whisker plots,* is discussed later in this chapter. These forms of representation are often introduced in the later middle grades.

Histograms and line plots   The histogram is a graphical representation of the frequency with which scores occur. To construct a histogram, separate the data into categories (usually equal intervals), tally the occurrence of each value in the appropriate category, and then plot the total count in each category.

Suppose a group of children found last year's monthly precipitation in inches in their city to be 25, 19, 23, 35, 22, 19, 15, 24, 42, 29, 13, 9. Figure 16-24 is a histogram of these data using intervals: 0–9, 10–19, 20–29, 30–39, 40–49.

Line plots have replaced histograms in many cases. To construct a line plot, draw a number line and label it with appropriate values. For each data value, place a symbol, such as an X, above the corresponding point on the scale. If appropriate, the data may be rounded to make plotting easier. Figure 16-25 shows the precipitation data on a line plot. The grid format used in Figure 16-25 is not required but makes plotting easier, especially when some values have higher frequencies than those occurring in the precipitation data.

Stem-and-leaf plots   In the early 1990s, the *stem-and-leaf* plot was introduced into the middle grades curriculum. To construct a stem-and-leaf plot, select a cer-

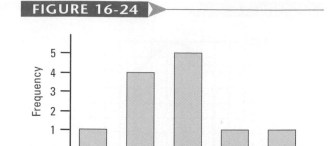

FIGURE 16-24

tain number of "front-end" digits at the beginning of each value to form the *stem.* The next digit to the right of the stem forms the *leaf.* For example, in the precipitation data above, the tens digits would be selected for the stems and the ones digits would form the leaves.

To form a stem-and-leaf display, first place the stems in either ascending or descending order, as shown in Figure 16-26(a). Next, draw a vertical line to the right of the stems. Now place the leaves (units digits) to the right of the vertical line but on the same horizontal line as their corresponding stems. The precipitation data would look like Figure 16-26(b). The use of grid paper is not necessary but will ensure that the leaves are evenly spaced, making it easier to interpret the graph. Note the addition of a key to inform the reader of what the data values represent. For clarity and ease of reading, it is also wise to sort the leaves. The final stem-and-leaf display in this case is shown in Figure 16-26(c).

Note that these stem-and-leaf plots bear some resemblance to a histogram. However, in a stem-and-leaf display, all the data values are retained and can be identified, the categories are not arbitrary, construction is easier, the data can be easily ordered, and other descriptive statistics can be calculated from the display.

Applications.   Measurement activities provide an excellent setting for collecting data that could be displayed in a stem-and-leaf plot. An example from the Curriculum Standards (NCTM, 1989, p. 117) suggests that children use a meter tape to measure the length of a room to the nearest centimeter. Each child's measure could be

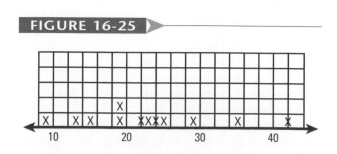

FIGURE 16-25

FIGURE 16-26

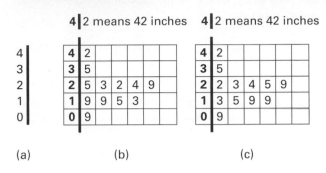

4│2 means 42 inches   **4│2 means 42 inches**

4		**4**	2							**4**	2				
3		**3**	5							**3**	5				
2		**2**	5	3	2	4	9			**2**	2	3	4	5	9
1		**1**	9	9	5	3				**1**	3	5	9	9	
0		**0**	9							**0**	9				

(a)   (b)   (c)

FIGURE 16-28

                    GIRLS   BOYS

			GIRLS		stem	BOYS			
			4	7	15	4			
	2	5	6	7	14	6	8		
1	2	5	6	6	8	13	1	4	4	6
			2	4	12	0	4	4	7	9
				3	11	7			

15│4 means 154 centimeters

recorded on the chalkboard and then pairs of children could construct a stem-and-leaf plot for the data. Figure 16-27 illustrates a possible stem-and-leaf display resulting from this activity. Notice how the one extreme value is handled. Note also how the remainder of the data clusters between 85 and 86. These values still serve as stems, but the leaves between them are partitioned into pairs (0 and 1, 2 and 3, etc.) marked in this example, with a bullet (•).

Children could also measure their heights or masses and prepare a stem-and-leaf display of the class data (Bankard & Fennell, 1991). This may be an ideal setting in which to develop a stem-and-leaf plot comparing two groups. Suppose the height measurements (cm) turned out to be:

Girls: 154, 136, 138, 113, 122, 145, 131, 136, 124, 132, 146, 135, 147, 157, 142

Boys: 117, 136, 148, 154, 146, 129, 124, 131, 124, 120, 134, 134, 127

Figure 16-28 is a stem-and-leaf display comparing these two sets of data.

Children enjoy collecting data over a reasonable period of time. (If the time frame is too long, they lose interest.) For example, they might determine the temperature at a particular time each day for 2 weeks. Daily precipitation, maximum temperatures, value of a particular stock, and other things could provide data that could be displayed by a stem-and-leaf plot.

For each stem-and-leaf plot, children should make observations about and discuss, orally or in the form of a written paragraph, features such as:

- how wide a range there is in the data values.
- the smallest value—the largest value.
- how concentrated the values are.
- the symmetry of the distribution.
- gaps in the data.
- extreme values.
- what was learned from the plot.

Computer-Generated Graphs

There are a number of commercial graphing programs that elementary- and middle-school children can use easily.

Graphers (Sunburst) and GraphPower (Ventura Educational Systems) are two software packages that younger children can use to produce a variety of types of graphs. Data Insights and Statistics Workshop, both available from Sunburst, are more suitable for middle-school children. See Kader and Perry (1994) for some examples of graphs produced by the last two programs.

The Cruncher from Davidson and Associates is an example of a fairly simple spreadsheet/charting program suitable for the middle grades. It is appealing for classroom use because it is easy to learn, includes a variety of chart types, and allows a child to instantly see the effect that changing one cell in the spreadsheet has on a graph.

Most integrated productivity packages such as MicrosoftWorks (Microsoft) and ClarisWorks (Claris Corporation) also have graphing capabilities. Figure 16-29 shows two graphs of the same data produced by ClarisWorks.

FIGURE 16-27

95	4
86	
•	8 9 9
•	6 6 6 6 7 7 7
•	4 4 5 5 5 5
•	2 3
85	
85	3 means 853 cm

Source: Adapted from *Curriculum and evaluation standards for school mathematics* (p. 117), by NCTM, 1989, Reston, VA: Author.

FIGURE 16-29

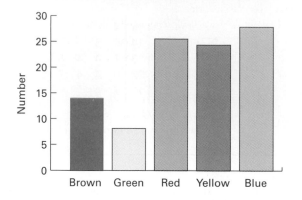

Color of Peanut Butter M&Ms (One 153 g bag)

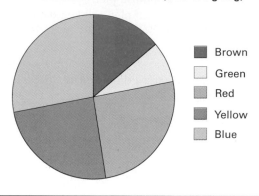

Color of Peanut Butter M&Ms (One 153 g bag)

The reader should consult suppliers' catalogs for information on the newest versions of these and other software packages.

INTERPRETING DATA: STATISTICS

Statistics is a topic that is found with increasing frequency in elementary- and middle-school mathematics textbooks. Some years ago the *average* was about the only statistical topic introduced prior to junior high school. Now other topics such as *median, mode,* and even some rudimentary notions of *dispersion* can be found in elementary texts. Middle-school children will study these topics in more depth, particularly the notion of dispersion or variation in data.

Descriptive statistics is a general term used to refer to the collection, organization, presentation, and interpretation of data. Even young children are exposed to statements that *describe* data. For example:

• "The average high temperature last week was only 13°F."

• "Most children in this room are 11 years old."

Shulte and Smart (1981) identify five reasons statistics and probability should be included in the school mathematics program:

• They provide meaningful applications of mathematics at all levels.

• They provide methods for dealing with uncertainty.

• They give us some understanding of the statistical arguments, good and bad, with which we are continually bombarded.

• They help consumers distinguish sound use of statistical procedures from unsound or deceptive uses.

• They are inherently interesting, exciting, and motivating topics for most children. (p. ix)

Frequency

The notion of how often something occurs is inherent in many of the graphing activities that involve collecting data and discussing the relative frequency of different events, as discussed earlier in this chapter. For example, oranges were more frequently mentioned as a favorite fruit than grapes; *e* occurred more frequently than any of the other vowels in a piece of writing; 5 buses, 35 cars, 22 trucks, 3 police cars, 25 panel trucks, and 15 other vehicles passed the school in one-half hour.

Older children could make more elaborate frequency distributions. If each member of a team tossed counters at a target with possible scores ranging from 0 to 20, the team might prepare a distribution table like the one shown in Figure 16-30. A histogram could then be drawn for their data. Some children may prefer to tally each score and show the frequency through a stem-and-leaf display.

Central Tendency

Measures of *central tendency* attempt to describe what is "typical" or "average" in a set of data. At the elementary- and middle-school levels, three types or measures of central tendency are normally considered: mode, median, and arithmetical average (mean).

FIGURE 16-30

Distribution of Team Scores		
Score	Tally	Frequency
0–4		
5–9		
10–14		
15–19		
20		

FIGURE 16-31 ▶

Size	Tally	Count
7	/	1
6	////	4
5	//	2
4	//	2
3	/	1

Mode The concept of the *mode,* but not the term, is introduced informally early in a child's school experience when a child examines a graph and reports:

- "September has the most birthdays."
- "Most members of the class like chocolate ice cream the best."
- "The vowel that occurs most often is *e.*"

The mode is the most frequently occurring value in a set of data. Sometimes one or two values in a data set can distort the "typical" value described by the mean. In these cases, the mode is sometimes the preferred measure of central tendency. For example, a shoe manufacturer is more interested in the most frequently sold shoe size than the mean size of shoes.

The mode is usually easily determined from a frequency distribution. For example, 10 children in a classroom reported the following shoe sizes: 6, 5, 4, 6, 7, 4, 6, 3, 5, 6. The mode is not easy to see in this list, but once a frequency table (Figure 16-31) is prepared, the mode, 6, is apparent. Line plots as shown in Figure 16-25 and stem-and-leaf plots also provide good visual representation of the mode.

Median A second measure of central tendency, the *median,* often is not introduced until the middle grades. Computational procedures should be left until the middle grades, but the concept of the median should be introduced to elementary-school children because they "need many experiences with data sets and the median before they can understand how the mean represents the data" (Russell & Mokros, 1996, p. 362).

The median is the middle number in a set of numbers. Some children may have seen the highway sign, DO NOT CROSS MEDIAN. Here the term is used to refer to the section between two parts of the highway, that is, the middle position. Reference to the use of the term outside of mathematics may help children understand the concept.

The concept of the median can also be easily modeled. Suppose that in one learning group, five children record their ages on index cards: 11 10 13 12 10 . To find the median age, the children order the cards from youngest to oldest, 10 10 11 12 13 ,or vice

versa. The children might discover the need for sorted data by first working with unsorted data. They will soon recognize that with unsorted data the middle card could have any number on it.

Children now simultaneously remove a card from each end and continue this process until there is only one card left. This card is the midpoint or middle value, because the cards were ordered.

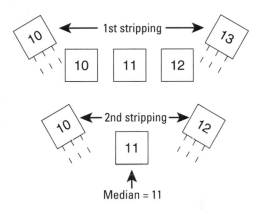

What happens if there is an even number of children in the group? Again the children order the cards and remove the first and last as before. This time, however, there will be two cards left in the middle, and children should be challenged to talk about what the median should be.

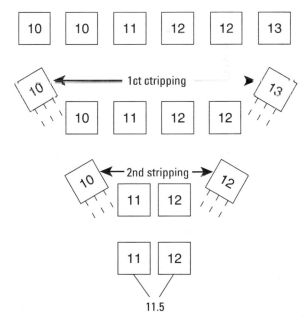

Median = mean of 11 and 12
or 11.5

From these manipulative experiences children should understand that the median is the midpoint of a set of values. If the number of values is odd, the median is the middle number; if the number of values is even, the median is the mean of the *two* middle values.

FIGURE 16-32

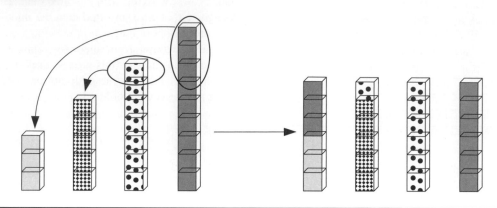

Mean The mean is the most commonly used measure of central tendency. It is what most people speak of simply as the *average*. It is found by dividing the sum of a set of numbers by the number of numbers in the set. This is a rule that is easily forgotten by children unless they have some understanding of the concept. A good introduction might be to have children engage in a discussion about "being average" (Paull, 1990). What does it mean? Is being average desirable? Is anyone average?

An understanding of the mean can be developed through concrete and visual manipulation (Rubenstein, 1989). Begin with two numbers. Using interlocking cubes, ask the children to build a tower with four blocks and another with eight blocks. They should now talk about what they would have to do to make both towers the same height, using only the blocks they have used to construct the towers. After several examples with two numbers, children should apply their strategy to three or four numbers, say, 3, 5, 7, and 9. Figure 16-32 illustrates the process of concretely determining the mean of these numbers. Later, children can attempt to apply the process and discuss a situation in which the cubes cannot be evenly shared. Allow the children to use their own language, but the end result should be an understanding that the mean is simply one number that describes or characterizes all the numbers in the data set.

Once the children understand the concept, the teacher should provide an activity that more closely matches the computational algorithm. A problem such as the following would serve that purpose:

While trick-or-treating on Halloween, Trevor collected 4 chocolate bars, Heather collected 8, Betty got 3, and Harold found 5 in his sack. What is the average number of bars collected by the 4 children?

HINT: To find the average, put all 4 collections together and share them equally.

The process could be simulated with pictures or counters (Figure 16-33). First find the sum (put everybody's bars into one pile), then separate the total pile into four equal piles (the number of people to share). Finally, count to see how many bars each person received. This process parallels the computational algorithm. To help children discover the "add-'em-up and then divide" rule, Zawojewski (1988) suggests giving children

. . . a bundle of eight pencils of varying lengths and ask them to cut a straw to the length that they would estimate as the average length of all the pencils. After the estimates are in, lay the pencils end-to-end and cut a strip of adding machine tape the same length. This action illustrates the "add-em-up" step. Then fold the strip into eight equal parts to illustrate the division step. (p. 26)

FIGURE 16-33

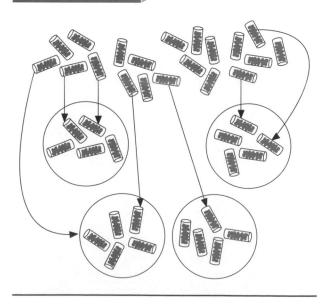

Russell and Mokros (1996) use "construction" problems (given a statistic, children construct the data) to help children understand the concepts of central tendency. One type of problem involves an "unpacking" task to construct the data given the mean. The authors use an example in which the mean family size is 4. Assuming there were 8 families, a line plot could be constructed by placing eight stick-on notes above the 4 on the line. At an early level, children could "unpack" the data by taking one stick-on note from the set and placing it above the 3. To balance this, the next one would go above the 5, and so on as in Figure 16-34(a).

After a series of symmetrical balancing as above, children might be asked what would happen if one family had 8 members. Clearly, one stick-on note could be moved above the 8 on the line, but it does not make sense to balance this with a note above 0. Russell and Mokros maintain that in their work "students have always come up with the idea of moving two different stick-on notes down a total of 4 units so as to balance the upward move of 4" (p. 363). This is illustrated in Figure 16-34(b).

Integrating activities. Problems such as the following will stimulate small group discussion resulting in increased understanding of the mean, median, and mode. They will also stimulate discussion about the relationships among the measures.

> *Seven girls are at a slumber party. Their shoe sizes range from $5\frac{1}{2}$ to 9 (with half-sizes included). If the median shoe size for the girls is 7, what are some possible combinations of shoe sizes for the girls?*
>
> *The mean of five brothers' ages is 4, and the mode is 3. What are some possible ages for the five brothers? (Zawojewski, 1988, p. 26)*

See Loewen (1991) for some other integrating activities based on a card game.

Variation

Children are often interested in learning about the longest and shortest jump distances achieved at the school field day, the tallest and shortest heights in class, or the highest and lowest grades given on an examination. These children are inquiring about the *range* or the difference between the greatest and least number in a set of numbers. The range is a simple measure of the spread or dispersion of scores. The range of shoe sizes (Figure 16-31) is 7 − 3, or 4. In addition to central tendency, spread or variation is another way to describe or characterize data.

The range, like the mean, is often not a good characterization of the data, however, because it is directly affected by extreme scores. For example, consider these two sets of data:

SET 1: 3, 3, 13, 13   Mean = 8; Range = 10

SET 2: 3, 8, 8, 13   Mean = 8; Range = 10

Although the mean and range are the same for each set, the dispersion or scatter of scores is quite different. The first set has scores clustering around the extremes, while the second set has scores more uniformly distributed about the mean. Histograms, line plots, and stem-and-leaf plots discussed earlier in this chapter provide more useful representations of the variation in scores. Another representation, the box-and-whiskers plot, is discussed here.

Box-and-whisker plots In the NCTM Curriculum Standards for grades 5–8, box-and-whisker plots are mentioned as appropriate activities for these grades in both Standard 10 (Statistics) and Standard 13 (Measurement). A box-and-whiskers plot includes the median and charts the dispersion of data in a way that adds information about the spread of scores not directly available from a stem-and-leaf display. To construct a simple (sometimes referred to as a *skeletal*) box-and-whiskers plot, five values are required; median, *upper quartile, lower quartile, upper extreme,* and *lower extreme.* These terms will be explained in the following paragraphs as they are used. Note that the median is the middle quartile.

The median, quartiles, and extremes can be readily obtained by sorting the data into ascending order and adding a *depth* column beside the sorted data. The depth simply indicates how far a particular value is from the high or low end of the set of values. The lowest and highest value each have a depth of 1, the next highest and next lowest a 2, and so on. The life expectancy at birth for males in 15 selected countries (excluding Canada) is shown in Table 16-1, with the depth of each value listed to the left of the data.

When the number of data values is odd, the median is the "deepest" value. The eighth value from both the top and the bottom is 71.45. If the equivalent statistic for Canada, 72.92, were incorporated into the list, both 71.50 and 71.45 would have a depth of 8. The median then would be the mean of 71.50 and 71.45 or 71.48.

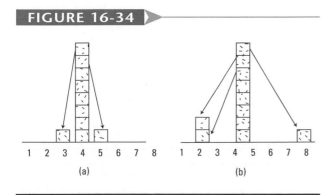

FIGURE 16-34

1 2 3 4 5 6 7 8   1 2 3 4 5 6 7 8
        (a)   (b)

TABLE 16-1

LIFE EXPECTANCY AT BIRTH FOR MALES

DEPTH	LIFE EXPECTANCY
1	74.54
2	73.62
3	72.75
4	72.70
5	72.52
6	72.09
7	71.50
8	71.45
7	71.34
6	71.00
5	70.41
4	70.41
3	69.69
2	67.04
1	65.09

Source: Canada Yearbook 1990, (p. 3–18), Statistics Canada, 1989. Ottawa, ON: Author, Publications Division.

The *upper* and *lower quartiles* are roughly the medians of the two halves of the data determined by the median. The quartiles can therefore be found by repeating the depth-finding process using the median as the starting point and going both directions. The following simplified examples should clarify the process.

Example 1

DATA	MEDIAN	DEPTH FOR UPPER QUARTILE	LOWER QUARTILE
63	1	1	
60	2	2	
59	3	59.5 2	
55	← 4	1	1
48	3		2
46	2		47 2
45	1		1

Example 2

DATA	MEDIAN	DEPTH FOR UPPER QUARTILE	LOWER QUARTILE
63	1	1	
60	2	60 2	
59	3	1	
55	← 3		1
48	2		48 2
46	1		1

Example 3

DATA	MEDIAN	DEPTH FOR UPPER QUARTILE	LOWER QUARTILE
63	1	1	
60	2	60 2	
59	← 3	1	
55	2		55 1 2
48	1		2

Using the life-expectancy data for 15 countries, the median has a depth of 8. The greatest depth for the upper quartile would be 4, corresponding to both 72.70 and 72.52. The upper quartile would then be the average of these, or 72.61 years. What is the value of the lower quartile? What are the upper and lower quartiles when the value for Canada, 72.92, is included?

The *extremes* (highest and lowest scores) are 74.54 and 65.09. The five values needed to construct a box-and-whiskers plot (Figure 16-35) are now available. Begin by drawing a number line horizontally or vertically that encompasses both extremes and as many other reference points as desired. On the side of the line opposite the reference points construct a *box* (rectangle) with one pair of opposite sides perpendicular to the number line at the points corresponding to the quartiles, as illustrated in Figure 16-35. Draw another line through the box parallel to the quartiles at the point on the number line corresponding to the median. Now draw a *whisker* (line) parallel to the number line from the midpoint of the side corresponding to the lower quartile to a point corresponding to the lowest value in the data set. Similarly, draw a whisker from the upper quartile to the point corresponding to the greatest data value.

Two or more box-and-whisker plots could be superimposed on the same reference line. Box charts for the heights of boys and girls (data from Figure 16-28) could be placed side-by-side, as shown in Figure 16-36.

Children and box-and-whisker plots. Box-and-whisker plots are relatively new in school curricula. For this reason, the preceding explanation was more extensive and formal than is necessary for children in the middle grades. To find the median, children already know that they need to work with sorted data. Rather than use a depth column, they could simply count up from the bot-

FIGURE 16-35

Age in years

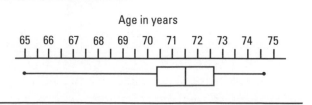

FIGURE 16-36 ▶

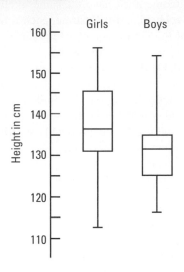

tom or down from the top to the middle value or middle pair of values. For the upper quartile, they could count down from the top to the score that represented one-quarter of the scores. Similarly, they could count one-quarter of the scores from the bottom to find the lower quartile. They could then draw the box-and-whisker plot.

Of greater importance than the precision of the construction is the interpretation or discussion that takes place as a result of the data. Children should write a paragraph or two stating their observations. If necessary, the teacher can draw attention to such features as the extremes, the range, and the range within which most of the scores fall (the box contains the middle 50%). Children should also discuss such questions as "What does a long box tell you?" and "What does a short box with long whiskers mean?"

We have provided some data for illustrative purposes. It is important, however, that children draw box-and-whisker plots for data they collect themselves. Activity 16-4, adapted from Brosnan (1996), provides one idea for doing this.

INTERPRETING DATA: PROBABILITY

I think it will snow today.
If I drop this rock in the pool it will sink.
I want to roll a 4.

These sorts of statements could easily have been uttered by young children who are exposed to probability in their life outside school. In school we need to provide children with activities that will ensure that misconceptions do not develop. Activities involving probability

ACTIVITY 16-4 ▶

COUNT THE RAISINS

MATERIALS
14g box of raisins for each child
1-cm grid paper

PROCEDURE
- Don't open the box. Each person write down an estimate of how many raisins he or she thinks is in the box. (The teacher records all the estimates from each group on the board.)
- Count the number of raisins in each box. (Again, the teacher records the actual count for each box on the board.)
- Construct a back-to-back stem-and-leaf plot. One side will show the estimates, the other side the actual counts.
- Construct a box-and-whiskers plot for both the estimates and the counts. Use one number line to show both box plots.
- Answer these questions:
  1. Which actual count occurred most often? Which plot tells you this?
  2. What is the lowest count? The highest count? What is the range?
  3. What is the lowest estimate? The highest estimate? What is the range?
  4. How can you find the medians from your plots?
  5. What can you say about the estimates compared to the actual counts?

 PRINCIPLES AND STANDARDS LINK 16-4
Content Strand: Data Analysis and Probability

In prekindergarten through grade 2, the treatment of probability ideas should be informal. Teachers should build on children's developing vocabulary to introduce and highlight probability notions, for example, We'll *probably* have recess this afternoon, or It's *unlikely* to rain today. Young children can begin building an understanding of chance and randomness by doing experiments with concrete objects, such as choosing colored chips from a bag. (NCTM, 2000, p. 51)

contribute to the development of problem-solving skills because children do experiments and collect and organize data to determine the probability of an event. Probability activities can also be used to reinforce other concepts and skills. Furthermore, activities in probability can be fun, adding motivation, excitement, and variety to the mathematics program. "Classroom activities involving probability should be active, involve physical materials, and furnish opportunities for questioning, problem solving, and discussion" (Fennell, 1990, p. 18). And according to Bright and Hoeffner (1993), "students need to be exposed to problems for which intuitions alone are insufficient for finding solutions" (p. 87).

Overview

Probability is the area of mathematics that analyzes the chance of something occurring. The probability that a given *event* will occur is the ratio of the number of *favorable* or *desirable outcomes* to the total number of *possible outcomes*. This is often written in the form:

$$P(\text{event}) = \frac{\text{Number of Desired or Favorable Outcomes}}{\text{Number of Total Possible Outcomes}}$$

For example, if you flip a coin, the probability of its landing with the head up is $\frac{1}{2}$, because there is one desired outcome (landing heads) and two possible outcomes (head, tail). This provides another setting in which children can use some of the ratio and percent ideas (Chapter 13) they have learned.

PRINCIPLES AND STANDARDS LINK 16-5
Content Strand: Data Analysis and Probability

In grades 3–5 students can consider ideas of chance through experiments—using coins, dice, or spinners—with known theoretical outcomes or through designating familiar events as impossible, unlikely, likely, or certain. Middle-grades students should learn and use appropriate terminology and should be able to compute probabilities for simple compound events, such as the number of expected occurrences of two heads when two coins are tossed 100 times. (NCTM, 2000, p. 50)

PRINCIPLES AND STANDARDS LINK 16-6
Content Strand: Data Analysis and Probability

Through the grades, students should be able to move from situations for which the probability of an event can readily be determined to situations in which sampling and simulations help them quantify the likelihood of an uncertain outcome. (NCTM, 2000, p. 50)

In an experiment, events must be *random,* and each event or outcome must have the same likelihood of occurring on each trial. To illustrate, each time you roll a die, each of the six outcomes is equally likely and the probability of the die landing with a 2 on top is the same for each trial. On the other hand, if you drew a card from a deck of ordinary playing cards, replaced it at the bottom of the deck and drew again, the probability of drawing the same card would not be the same the second time. The deck would need to be thoroughly shuffled after each draw to ensure randomness. This does not mean that all possible outcomes have the same probability. For example, if a styrofoam cup is tossed into the air and allowed to land on the table, the probability of its landing on its side is greater than landing on either its top or bottom, but the likelihood of its landing on its side does not change from toss to toss. Based on studies in the United States and England, it is evident that many children do not have a good understanding of randomness (Dessart, 1995).

Rolling a die is an example of a *sample space* with *equally likely* outcomes because each of the six faces has the same chance of turning up. Tossing a styrofoam cup involves a sample space with outcomes that are *not equally likely.* Experiments such as these involve events that are *independent.* The fact that a 2 turned up last time has no bearing on what will come up on the next shake of a die. The probability of getting a 2 is always $\frac{1}{6}$ regardless of how many times 2 came up previously. This is sometimes a difficult concept for adults to understand, let alone children.

Dependent events are events in which the probability of a second outcome is different, given the nature of an earlier outcome. If a bag contains eight yellow and four red marbles, the initial probability of drawing a red marble at random is $\frac{4}{12}$, or $\frac{1}{3}$. If, after each draw, the marble is replaced and the bag is shaken, the probability of drawing a red marble on subsequent draws remains at $\frac{1}{3}$, since these events are independent. If, however, the marble is not replaced, the probability on subsequent draws changes. If a red marble was drawn on the first trial, the probability of a red on the second draw would now be $\frac{3}{11}$ since there are now 11 marbles in the bag, three of which are red. If a yellow marble was drawn on the first trial, the probability of a red on the second draw would now be $\frac{4}{11}$.

In some situations the number of favorable outcomes is equal to the number of possible outcomes. In this case, the event is said to be *certain* and has a probability of 1. If there are no favorable outcomes, the event has a probability of 0 and is said to be *impossible.*

General Teaching Considerations

Early experiences Teachers can introduce some informal, nonnumeric (no values) probability activities to young children to help them think about concepts such as

The Annenberg/CPB Math and Science Collection

Classroom Clips:
The Missing Link—
Essential Concepts for Middle School Math Teachers

Previewing the Video

In this video, middle school teachers learn constructivist strategies for presenting important math topics identified by the Third International Mathematics and Science Study (TIMSS). Master teacher Jan Robinson works with a group of learner–teachers, helping them see ways to engage themselves and their students in collaborative problem solving. Teachers tackle hands-on activities to investigate angle measurements and their geometric relationships in triangles, quadrilaterals, pentagons, and other polygons.

CORE CONCEPTS

- ☑ Angles occur as rotations, wedges, and sides with a common vertex.

- ☑ Angles are measured in degrees.

- ☑ Angle measures range from 0° to 360°.

Ms. Robinson begins with a paper-folding activity, where learner–teachers work together to fold and refold a piece of paper, always using the same corner as a vertex, looking for as many angle measurements as possible. Robinson moves on to the next activity, where learner–teachers use hinged mirrors to explore geometric concepts, *building on the core concepts* from the paper-folding activity.

As the learner–teachers explore the activities on their own, they begin to more fully understand the concepts, procedures, and engaging qualities of constructivist activities. These teachers will take this activity back to their own middle school classrooms to help their students help one another to recognize patterns and relationships between sides and angles of different polygons and to use those concepts to build patterns and structures.

> "I think this prepares the students for what they're going to encounter in life. No matter what their profession—doctors, lawyers, teachers—they're going to work with somebody together, and they're not going to be given a formula to solve something. They're going to have to figure things out for themselves."
>
> — Saundra, learner–teacher

Process Standard: **Problem Solving**

The hinged-mirror lesson focuses on understanding what a degree is and how it is used to describe the size of an angle. Students also relate a full-circle rotation to an angle of 360°.

The problem to be solved: **How do I use these mirrors and dots to figure out angle measure?**

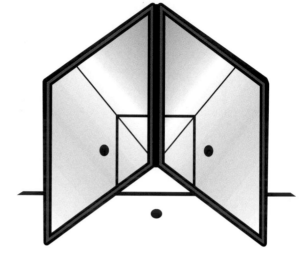

Ms. Robinson gives her learner–teachers and her 7th grade students the hinged mirrors and papers with a 3-inch line and a dot approximately one-half inch below the line. Learners place the vertex of the hinged mirror above the line, so that the dot is reflected in the mirror.

She asks the learners to:

- create as many shapes and angles as possible with the mirrors
- go inside the mirrors to trace the angle
- probe the angle measure with math
- count dots to get hints to angle size
- label angles and show math

Try this exercise yourself. **What is the relationship between the number of sides of a polygon and the sum of the interior angles? How many different ways can this relationship be stated?**

Samuel, one of the learner–teachers, comments that using the hinged mirrors will reinforce for students that a complete rotation is 360°. **Is that true? If so, how? What additional math concepts should students understand with this lesson?**

Focus on Standards

How have Ms. Robinson's open-ended activities set up her learners to:

- apply and adapt a variety of appropriate strategies to solve problems?
- monitor and reflect on the process of mathematical problem solving?

"They'd love it because it's discovery."
— Romeo, learner–teacher

Ms. Robinson begins the hinged-mirror lesson with a series of questions that prompt prior knowledge, asking her learner–teachers to (a) explain what a degree is and how it is used to describe the size of an angle, (b) discuss benchmarks and what angles they would consider to be benchmark angles, and (c) describe why angle measures need to be precise. In this way she gets her learner–teachers thinking about core teaching concepts as they prepare to undertake the activity. **What other reason might she ask these questions? How do her questions model constructivist teaching?**

Process Standard: **Representation**

While the math concepts in these lessons could easily be covered with worksheets, Ms. Robinson helps middle school teachers see ways to actively engage their students in learning by using manipulatives and exploration, connecting the discoveries with the core concepts through questions. She incorporates multiple representations by asking her learners to include written math to prove the angle estimations. How else can basic computational skills be incorporated into these lessons?

Focus on Standards

Notice the way Ms. Robinson includes basic computational skills in the written proof and leads a discussion about wedges, turns, and angles in everyday life to help her learners realize that they can:

- create and use representations to organize, record, and communicate mathematical ideas
- use representations to model and interpret physical, social, and mathematical phenomena

> "You really start thinking. It's actually incorporating a lot of methods usually done in isolation."
>
> — *Romeo, learner–teacher*

Process Standard: **Communication**

Jan Robinson tells her learner–teachers that students should be encouraged to discuss and share their findings with a partner as they work. She believes teachers should have questions and extension activities ready for students who need an additional challenge.

- How does Jan Robinson engage the teachers in communication prior to the lesson?
- How might this help clarify ideas for the teachers?
- Will this make their teaching more effective?

Notice how the summary phase of the lesson gets students communicating about the lesson as they clarify concepts and share strategies. What questions could be asked to help students who are having difficulty? What extension questions or activities are appropriate for students who are ready to move on?

> "When you're planning your lessons, you seed yourself with questions. You have to have questions for the group that gets stuck, and you have to have questions for the group who've gone beyond."
>
> — *J. Robinson*

> "All it takes to get a group started again is a good question."
>
> — *J. Robinson*

Focus on Standards

Ms. Robinson writes important terms, such as benchmark angles, on the board as they come up in class discussion. How else might she:

- use the language of mathematics to express mathematical ideas precisely?

Process Standard: **Reasoning and Proof**

You'll see that Ms. Robinson expects to see reasoning and proof even from her learner–teachers, pointing out the mathematical processes written next to the traced angles.

$$\begin{array}{r} 22.5 + 45 \\ \hline 2\,)\overline{45} \end{array}$$

INTEGRATING STANDARDS, TECHNOLOGY, AND TEACHING

Reasoning and Proof continued...

After this investigation, students should have a better understanding of angles as turns and rotations. To make sure students understand the core concepts, Ms. Robinson asks students to draw several angles, estimate the angle measures, and then measure with a protractor or angle ruler to check the accuracy of the estimates. **How do the teacher–learners prove their understanding of the core concepts? How does Ms. Robinson use questions to keep students reasoning through their lesson?**

Focus on Standards

Ms. Robinson tells her learner–teachers that dialoguing is an acceptable way for them to work through their own mathematical reasoning, but that she prefers to have students put their proof in writing. How else might she ensure that her students are

- selecting and using various types of reasoning and methods of proof?
- recognizing reasoning and proof as fundamental aspects of mathematics?

Process Standard: Connections

Jan Robinson launches her lesson by asking her learner–teachers, as well as her 7th graders, to think about where they find wedges, turns, and sides with a common vertex in the world. **What effect might this opening have on the learners' experience with the hinged-mirror activity? Why is it important for students to connect geometric concepts with everyday life?**

Focus on Standards

Ms. Robinson begins with the paper-folding activity in the Try This! box. How else could Ms. Robinson help her students:

- recognize and use connections among mathematical ideas?
- understand how mathematical ideas interconnect and build on one another to produce a coherent whole?

How else could this lesson be expanded to help children understand how mathematical ideas interconnect and build on one another to produce a coherent whole?

 For other connection ideas, as well as a full lesson plan for the hinged-mirror and paper-folding activities, please visit Chapter 16 of our website at **www.prenhall.com/cathcart**

Hinged-Mirror Lesson CORE CONCEPTS

☑ A complete rotation around a given point is 360°.

☑ Benchmark angles such as 90° and 180° help to make accurate estimates.

Try This!
Folding Paper Angles

In this lesson, students construct variously sized angles without a protractor, while making connections between angles and their measures to strengthen their ability to estimate angle size. Your goal is to help students understand that the measure of an angle is the size of the opening (or turn) between its sides, and that a full turn is 360°, a half turn is 180°, and a quarter turn is 90°. This activity makes a great precursor to the hinged-mirror activity.

Have your students:

- take a sheet of paper and identify the measure of the angle formed by the corner (90°);
- trace and label this angle on another sheet of paper;
- fold this angle in half, measure the new angle, and trace and record this new angle;
- find as many different angles as possible simply by folding the paper at its chosen vertex; and
- show and explain their work, documenting their findings mathematically.

Ms. Robinson warns that students often get stuck, choosing simply to continue to fold each angle in half again and again until the paper can no longer be folded. **How can you help your students avoid this trap? What questions might you ask them to keep them experimenting with the angles?**

FIGURE 16-37

Draw number	1	2	3	4	5	6	7	8	9	10
Color										

certain, impossible, equally likely, more likely, and less likely. Terms such as these may or may not be used explicitly. *Prediction* and *experimentation* are major components of many of the activities in the early years.

Capitalize occasionally on the natural language of the children to help them think in probability terms. For example, a child may come bounding in one morning and say, "It's going to rain today." Many times you will accept this statement, but on occasion you might respond, "Are you *certain* it is going to rain today, or do you think it *might* rain today?"

The following four activities are samples of experiences children in the late primary grades might find interesting and which would help develop intuitive understanding as a foundation for later work.

1. What's in the bag?
   - Without the children's knowledge, place 3 blue blocks in a bag.
   - Tell the children that you have some blocks in the bag and that you are going to draw one out, note the color, and then replace it in the bag.
   - Ask the children to keep a record of the color drawn.
   - Draw and replace two or three times, then ask the children to make a prediction about the color of the block you will draw next time. Record their guesses.
   - Draw two or three more times. Ask again for a prediction for the color of the next block.
   - Ask, "Can anyone guess what is in the bag?" "What are the chances that I will draw a red block?"

2. One of Each
   - Place 1 red and 1 blue block in a bag, shake, and draw one block out.
   - Give the children a recording sheet like the one in Figure 16-37. Ask them to color the square under "1" the color of the first block drawn.
   - Return the block to the bag, shake the bag and draw another block without looking, and have the children color each square as you go along.
   - Do this a total of 10 times.
   - Ask, "How many red blocks were drawn?" and "How many blue blocks were drawn?"

3. Guess the Color
   - Use the setting from the previous activity, but this time have the children record their guess of the outcome before a block is drawn (see Figure 16-38).

- Have the children shade in the first square opposite "Guess" with either blue or red before the draw. After the draw they should color the square opposite "Color drawn" with the color of the block drawn.
- After 10 draws, have the children complete the totals below the chart.

   Total guessed: _____ red and _____ blue.

   Total drawn: _____ red and _____ blue.

4. Sort the Statements
   - Give the children a set of cards with probability statements on them or have the children make up their own statements. For example:

It will snow today.	The sun will set in the east today.
There are more left-handed people in the class than right-handed.	I will drink milk at lunch.

Tomorrow will be here in less than 24 hours.

   - Prepare containers so that the children can sort the statements into groups

CERTAIN   LIKELY   UNLIKELY   IMPOSSIBLE

   - Have the children compare their groupings and discuss any differences.

FIGURE 16-38

Draw number	1	2	3	4	5	6	7	8	9	10
Guess										
Color drawn										

Burbank (1987) outlines several useful activities. One that will help with the notion of the range of probability going from impossible (0) to certain (1) involves initially placing five cubes under five glasses. The children discuss the number of choices, the number of cubes, and the chance of selecting a glass with a cube. Then they replace one cube with one ball and repeat the discussion and then replace a second cube with a ball and again discuss the chances of selecting a cube. They continue until all five glasses have balls under them (no cubes) and again discuss the chances of picking a glass with a cube under it.

Upper elementary   In the upper elementary grades children will begin to use some of the conventional probability terms and can start to assign probability values to some events. The emphasis still is on experimental probability as opposed to *theoretical* probability, although theoretical values can be assigned to some simple events such as flipping a coin or shaking a die. Some simple *simulations* can be done at this level. Children could also be exposed to examples of *fair* and *unfair* experiments or games. Here, and at higher grade levels, considerable integration of graphing and statistics with probability can take place.

Wilkinson and Nelson (1966) observed that children often demonstrate biases when dealing with familiar material such as coins or dice. Biases did not seem apparent when using thumb tacks, styrofoam cups, or other unfamiliar material. It might be wise, then, to start a more formal development of basic probability concepts in the upper elementary grades with relatively unfamiliar objects. Activity 16-5 is one example. Before starting this activity, a number of washers (or equivalent) will need to have a small piece of masking tape placed on one side.

Children who are ready to begin quantifying the probability of an outcome could complete a recording sheet, as shown in Figure 16-39. Tossing a single die is essentially the same experiment except that the sample space now contains six possible outcomes rather than two. However, each outcome still is equally likely.

Experiments in which different outcomes have different chances of occurring add another element of interest for children. Figure 16-40 illustrates the three possible outcomes, each with a different probability, when a styro-

ACTIVITY 16-5

FLIP A WASHER

MATERIALS
Washers with masking tape on one side

PROCEDURE
- Predict how many times the washer will land tape side up in 10 tosses.
- Toss a washer 10 times and keep a record of how it lands.
- Compare your results with your prediction.
- Repeat the experiment several times and calculate a total for each outcome.
- Compare your results with those of another group and discuss similarities and differences.

FIGURE 16-40

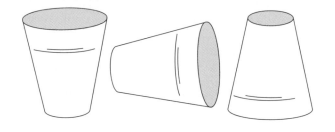

foam cup is tossed. Children should toss the cup a large number of times to feel confident that they have a reasonable estimation of the actual probability.

Children should be challenged to think about factors that could affect the probability of a particular event. Would the probabilities be different if the cup landed on a piece of plush carpet? Would the size of the cup change the probabilities? These challenges could serve as the basis for a long-term project for one or two groups of children.

Tossing a thumb tack is another popular activity using unfamiliar probability materials with outcomes not equally likely. There are only two possible outcomes if

FIGURE 16-39

	After 10 Tosses		After 40 Tosses	
Outcome	Number	Fraction	Number	Fraction
Tape up		$\overline{10}$		$\overline{40}$
Tape down		$\overline{10}$		$\overline{40}$

ACTIVITY 16-6

HIT THE TARGET

MATERIALS
Game board
Bingo chips or similar counters

PROCEDURE
1. Take turns tossing a chip at the board 10 times from a distance of about 1 m, recording each time where the chip lands.

2. Guess how many times you would hit both A and B (overlap) if you tossed your counter 100 times.

3. Combine the results from 10 children and compare the total with your guess.

PART HIT	TALLY	FRACTION OF TOTAL HITS
Circle A but NOT B		$\overline{10}$
Circle B but NOT A		$\overline{10}$
Both A AND B (overlap)		$\overline{10}$
Outside circles (on board)		$\overline{10}$
Off the board		$\overline{10}$

children toss the tack on the floor or their desk. Here is a case in which tossing the tack on a plush carpet might not only change the probabilities associated with each outcome but also add a third possible outcome to the sample space, namely, the point going down into the carpet.

Activity 16-6 and the following teacher-directed activity also involve events that are not equally likely.

Drawing Numbered Balls

- Write the numeral 5 on one Ping-Pong ball (or card), 6 on two balls, 7 on four balls, 8 on two balls, and 9 on one ball.

- Place all 10 balls in a bag. Tell the children that you have 10 balls in the bag but give no other information.

- Have one child record the outcomes on the chalkboard or overhead projector as another child draws the balls from the bag.

- After 3 or 4 draws, solicit predictions as to what the 10 balls are.

- After approximately 20 draws, ask the recorder to organize the data on the chalkboard.

- Then tell the children that each ball had either a 5, 6, 7, 8, or 9 on it.

- Divide the children into groups to discuss and write a new prediction.

- Have one child count the number of times each number was drawn and announce this to the class so that children can compare the count with their prediction.

For Activity 16-6, children will need a game board similar to the one shown here. This activity should be done in groups of three or four.

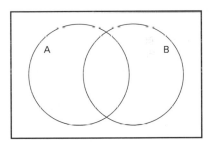

Teachers can incorporate probability discussions into some of the graphing and statistics activities suggested previously. For example, one activity suggested earlier in this chapter involved selecting a paragraph, recording the number of vowels, and then graphing these data. Children could also use the data to calculate statistics such as the mean, median, and mode; to draw a stem-and-leaf display; and to make a box-and-whiskers plot. Some probability questions could then be explored. For example, suppose you were blindfolded and randomly placed the tip of your pencil anywhere on a page from a book. Suppose also that your pencil pointed to a word. Based on your data,

- What would be a "good" guess for the length of the word?

- What would be some "poor" guesses?
- What is the probability that the word has one letter? three letters? eight letters?

Survey activities could also be expanded to include some probability questions. For example, children might take a survey of the class to determine how many children are left-handed. What is the probability that the next child to walk through the door is left-handed? Use the data from your room to guess how many children in the room next door are left-handed. Survey that class to find out. Use these data to predict how many children in the school are left-handed. Bankard and Fennell (1991) suggest a similar activity based on hair color.

Simulations are another popular probability activity. Simulating an experiment is known as the *Monte Carlo* method. Consider the following scenario:

> *A certain cookie manufacturer designs a set of six different hockey cards. One card is randomly inserted into each bag of cookies. On the average, how many bags of cookies would you have to buy to get at least one of each card?*
>
> *(Assume that equal numbers of each card are printed and distributed.)*

Teachers should challenge children to think of ways to simulate this problem. One suggestion is to place the numerals 1 through 6 on six different cards. Then have the children shuffle the cards, place them in a bag, draw one out, record the number, and replace the card, continuing the process until one of each of the six numbers is drawn. Have the children note how many draws were made to get one of each card, repeat this complete process a number of times, and then calculate the mean to get a better estimate of the answer to the problem. Most problems can be simulated in a variety of ways. A regular die could also be used for this problem, because there are six different and equally likely outcomes.

Children in the upper elementary grades could also explore the concept of a *fair game*. For example, you might take a few minutes one day to suggest to your children that you will play a game with them. Shake a die; if it shows a number greater than 4 they win, otherwise you win. Each game consists of 10 shakes. Keep a tally on the chalkboard for each game and note the winner beside each set. It likely won't take long for someone to object to this game because "It's not fair!"

Middle grades In the middle school and junior high school grades, more emphasis is placed on determining theoretical values, although the experimental aspect should not be neglected. More advanced work can be done with simulating events and with some of the other ideas developed earlier.

An activity commonly done at this level is to have children shake and roll a pair of dice and record the sum. Activity 16-7 is a good opportunity for children to compare experimental with theoretical probability.

A related but more complicated activity involves tossing two styrofoam cups. The three possible outcomes for one cup (top, bottom, side) are not equally likely and their theoretical probability cannot readily be determined. Furthermore, the probability will vary with the size of cup, type of landing surface, etc. Encourage the children to toss the two cups many times to gain some assurance that their experimental probability is reasonable. If the children worked in pairs and each pair tossed the cups 50 times and then pooled their results, they would have at least 500 tosses. Each group could complete a chart like the one shown below.

Cup 1	Side	Top	Bottom
Side	50	50	50
Top	50	50	50
Bottom	50	50	50

Cup 2

Activity 16-8 is another type of experiment.

In some cases the probability of a second event is *dependent* on the result of an earlier event. Such cases are more difficult for children to conceptualize. A tree diagram is helpful for analyzing this type of situation.

An approach that should help children understand dependent events involves giving children a problem that they can simulate and then having them develop and discuss a tree diagram of the problem. For example, prepare two identical boxes, one containing one hockey card and two baseball cards, the other containing one of each. Label the bottom of the first box A and the bottom of the second B; place a label on the bottom of each box so that the label is not visible when a box is selected. In groups of three, one child shuffles the boxes, one keeps a record, and the other randomly chooses a box, then randomly chooses a card from that box, and then checks the label so the recorder can keep a proper record. Each group

Trial	Box A		Box B	
	H	B	H	B
1		✓		
2			✓	
3		✓		
4				✓

ACTIVITY 16-7

DICE SUM

MATERIALS
Dice (different colors)

PROCEDURE

1. Shake and roll a pair of dice 36 times. Tally and record each result in the first chart below. Write the probability for each outcome based on your experiment.

2. Now compare your results with the *theoretical probability.* Analyze how many possible ways there are for each sum to occur by completing the chart at right.

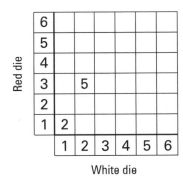

Outcome	2	3	4	5	6	7	8	9	10	11	12
Frequency											
Experimental Probability	$\frac{}{36}$	$\frac{}{36}$	$\frac{}{36}$	$\frac{}{36}$	$\frac{}{36}$	$\frac{}{36}$	$\frac{}{36}$	$\frac{}{36}$	$\frac{}{36}$	$\frac{}{36}$	$\frac{}{36}$

Outcome	2	3	4	5	6	7	8	9	10	11	12
Frequency											
Theoretical Probability	$\frac{}{36}$	$\frac{}{36}$	$\frac{}{36}$	$\frac{}{36}$	$\frac{}{36}$	$\frac{}{36}$	$\frac{}{36}$	$\frac{}{36}$	$\frac{}{36}$	$\frac{}{36}$	$\frac{}{36}$

3. Count the frequency of each sum and record it in the first line of the chart immediately above. Write the theoretical probability in the last line.

4. Compare the *experimental* with the *theoretical* results

by drawing a bar graph with the bars for each type of result adjacent and in a different color.

5. Write a paragraph describing similarities and differences.

---

member should perform each role 10 times, then the group should discuss their results. One expected observation is that, if Box B is chosen, the chance of getting a hockey card is better than if Box A is chosen. After children have discussed this problem, develop a tree diagram for the problem (Figure 16-41).

More advanced *simulation* activities are appropriate for the middle grades. Consider the following problem:

Ten hunters are in a blind together. All 10 are perfect shots, that is, they never miss. Ten Canada geese fly up at the same time. The 10 hunters rise together, randomly choose a goose, and simultaneously shoot. On the average, how many geese would survive?

In the earlier simulation, shaking a die or drawing a card from a set of six worked well. Although the cards would work here as well, teachers should challenge children to think of other ways to simulate this problem. Children may suggest that 10 children each should write the number of the goose he or she chooses (0 to 9 or 1 to

10) on a piece of paper. Then they could record all numbers chosen and determine which numbers were not chosen by any of the group.

This may also be an opportune time for children to explore a table of random numbers. Give children a table of random numbers and challenge them to use it to solve the hunters and geese problem. The partial table in Figure 16-42 suggests that you begin at any random position and list off the next 10 digits either horizontally or vertically. Digits from 0 to 9 not included in the list would represent the geese that survived. Repeat the experiment several times to answer the question, "On the *average,* how many geese would survive?"

The concept of a fair game was introduced earlier in this chapter. In the middle or junior high grades, this concept can be expanded with some more involved examples. Bright, Harvey, and Wheeler, (1981) describe eight pairs of games to introduce the notion of "fairness." Each game requires two players. Activity 16-9 is an adaptation of one of the pairs of games. Note the reinforcement of fraction concepts.

◀ ACTIVITY 16-8 ▶

FLIPPING A COIN

MATERIALS
Marker

PROCEDURE

1. Flip a coin five times to move from START to one of the letter boxes at the bottom.

2. When you reach the bottom record the letter box you ended in.

3. Do the experiment 50 times.

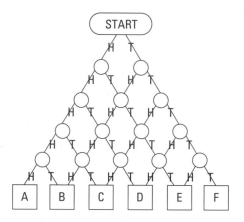

4. Graph the results of your 50 trials.

5. Which letter or letters did you finish on most often? Least often?

6. Write a paragraph about your experiment.

FIGURE 16-42 ▶

Partial Table of Random Numbers

10480	15031	01536	02011	81647
22368	46573	25595	85393	30995
24130	48360	22527	97265	76393
42167	93093	06243	61680	07856
37570	39975	81837	16656	06121

Beginning from the point of the pencil, 10 random numbers reading horizontally are: 5, 7, 3, 2, 5, 5, 9, 5, 8, 5. Digits not included are: 0, 1, 4, 6. For this trial, 4 geese survived.

TECHNOLOGY AND DATA

Analyzing data can lead to a significant amount of computational work. This may, at times, be used to reinforce paper-and-pencil computation. However, because the emphasis should not be on computation but on obtaining, understanding, and using the calculated results, teachers should permit children to do most of the computation on a calculator or computer.

The graphing software mentioned earlier in this chapter can be used to graph collected data. The visual display facilitates and clarifies interpretation of the data. In most cases, computers construct graphs from data entered into a spreadsheet. A spreadsheet is also a useful medium for conceptualizing measures of central tendency and other statistics. Most spreadsheets have built-in functions for mean, median, mode, maximum, and minimum, as well as procedures for sorting data. Given a set of data, children could be encouraged to change one or more values, predict what effect the change will have on one or more

FIGURE 16-41 ▶

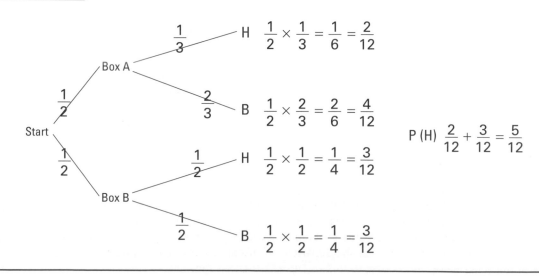

ACTIVITY 16-9

FAIR GAMES

Game 1: Fractions Less Than or Equal to 1

MATERIALS

2 standard dice and a recording sheet.
   One player will be 'A,' the other 'B.'

PROCEDURE

1. Roll the dice and make a fraction less than or equal to 1, with the numbers showing. If the fraction is in lowest terms, player A scores a point; otherwise, B scores a point.

2. Do this 20 times for 1 game. The player with the most points after 20 rounds is the winner.

3. Play several games, then answer these questions:
   - Did the same player win each time?
   - Do both players have the same chance of winning?
   - Is this a fair game?

Game 2: Proper and Improper Fractions

MATERIALS

2 standard dice (one red and one green) and a recording sheet. (The number on the red die will be the numerator and the number on the green die will be the denominator.)
   One player will be 'A,' the other 'B.'

PROCEDURE

1. Roll the dice. If the fraction formed is greater than 1, player A scores a point. If the fraction is less than 1, player B scores. If the fraction is equal to 1, both players score one point.

2. Repeat this 15 times for one game. The player with the most points after 16 rolls wins that game.

3. Play several games, then answer these questions:
   - Did the same player win each time?
   - Do both players have the same chance of winning?
   - Is this a fair game?

of the measures of central tendency, and then observe the change or changes. This kind of exploration could help children understand the key ideas before they learn computational procedures (Wilson & Krapfl, 1995).

CONCLUSION

In today's technological age, the collection, organization, and interpretation of data are important to almost everyone of almost every age. Children need to have experiences with data analysis to help them deal with the large amount of information that is available to them.

   Initially, children should collect data themselves through surveys or other means to answer questions they have identified. Later, they can gather information from secondary sources such as encyclopedias, newspapers, and the Internet.

   Similarly, the first approach to probability needs to be experimental. Children should do experiments to determine the probability of particular events occurring. This active approach will make these topics interesting and enjoyable but, more important, it will enable children to develop conceptual understanding that will serve them well in their everyday lives and careers.

For Your Journal

When you have finished studying this chapter, reflect on the following questions in your math journal:

1. What are some uses for each of the different types of graphs discussed? Describe situations in which some types of graphs are more appropriate or useful than others, and why.

2. What are the three measures of central tendency? How can teachers help children to understand each measure?

3. Visit a middle-school classroom and informally interview several children to assess their understanding of data analysis, statistics, and probability. What are their understandings and misconceptions?

4. Examine a textbook's section on data analysis, statistics, and probability. Discuss the textbook in terms of the concepts included in this chapter.

5. Imagine that you are a classroom teacher and a parent of one of the children in your class is concerned that you are devoting too much instructional time to data analysis, statistics, and probability. How would you respond?

For Your Portfolio

When you have finished studying this chapter, complete the following activities to include in your professional portfolio:

1. Write a series of lesson plans focusing on the stages of graphing experiences children should encounter.

2. Write a series of lesson plans to introduce the three measures of central tendency.

3. Use software to assist with the organization and interpretation of data.

Resources for Teachers

Books on data and statistics

Corwin, R., & Friel, S. (1990). *Used numbers: Statistics: Prediction and sampling.* Palo Alto, CA: Dale Seymour Publications.

Friel, S., Mokros, J., & Russell, S. (1992). *Used numbers: Statistics: Middles, means, and in-betweens.* Palo Alto, CA: Dale Seymour Publications.

Lindquist, M. M. (1992). *Making sense of data: Curriculum Evaluation Standards for School Mathematics Addenda Series, Grade K-6.* Reston, VA: National Council of Teachers of Mathematics.

Russell, S., & Corwin, R. (1989). *Used numbers: The shape of the data.* Palo Alto, CA: Dale Seymour Publications.

Russel, S., & Corwin, R. (1990). *Used numbers: Sorting: Groups and graphs.* Palo Alto, CA: Dale Seymour Publications.

Zawojewski, J. S. (1991). *Dealing with data and chance: Curriculum Evaluation Standards for School Mathematics Addenda Series, Grade 5–8.* Reston, VA: National Council of Teachers of Mathematics.

Books on probability

Burns, M. (1995). *Math by all means: Probability, Grades 3–4.* Sausalito, CA: Math Solutions Publications.

Phillips, E., Lappan, G., Winter, M., & Fitzgerald, W. (1986). *Middle Grades Mathematics Project: Probability.* Menlo Park, CA: Addison-Wesley.

Shulte, A., & Choate, S. (1977). *What are my chances? Book* A. Sunnyvale, CA: Creative Publications.

Links to the Internet

Government Information Sharing Project

http://govinfo.kerr.orst.edu/

Contains information about the current U.S. census data, including profiles of geographical areas. This is a great source of data.

Exploring Data

http://www.mathforum.edu/workshops/usi/dataproject/

Contains lesson plans for collecting, analyzing, and displaying data, links to statistics software on the Internet, and suggested discussion questions.

Explorer: Statistics and Probability

http://explorer.scrtec.org/explorer-db/browse/static/Mathematics/browse/f75.html

Contains many lessons on statistics and probability and lists of additional resources.

CHAPTER 17

Developing Algebraic Thinking

Revised by Dr. Sally Robison and Judy Bippert, M.A.

KEY CONCEPTS ▶

✔ Models for understanding integers and operations on integers

✔ The role of geometric and numeric patterns in algebraic thinking

✔ The meaning of variables

✔ Relationships and functions

✔ Expressions, equations, and inequalities

FOCUS QUESTIONS ▶

When you have finished studying this chapter, you should be able to answer the following questions:

1. What models are useful for helping children understand operations on integers? Give an example of a model for each operation.

2. What is a pattern and how does work with patterns help children think algebraically?

3. What should children understand about variables?

4. What models are useful for helping children understand equations, inequalities, functions, and formulas and how do children learn to use such models to solve them?

5. What models are useful for developing an understanding of the difference between relations and functions?

NCTM CONTENT STANDARDS AND EXPECTATIONS ADDRESSED IN THIS CHAPTER

STANDARD	EXPECTATIONS FOR GRADES PRE-K–2	EXPECTATIONS FOR GRADES 3–5	EXPECTATIONS FOR GRADES 6–8
Algebra Standard Instructional programs from pre-K–12 should enable all students to—	In prekindergarten through Grade 2 all students should— (NCTM, 2000, p. 90)	In Grades 3–5 all students should—(NCTM, 2000, p. 158)	In Grades 6–8 all students should—(NCTM, 2000, p. 222)
Understand patterns, relations, and functions	• sort, classify, and order objects by size, number, and other properties. • recognize, describe, and extend patterns such as sequences of sounds and shapes or simple numeric patterns and translate from one representation to another. • analyze how both repeating and growing patterns are generated.	• describe, extend, and make generalizations about geometric and numeric patterns. • represent and analyze patterns and functions, using words, tables, and graphs.	• represent, analyze, and generalize a variety of patterns with tables, graphs, words, and when possible, symbolic rules. • relate and compare different forms of representation for a relationship. • identify functions as linear or nonlinear and contrast their properties from tables, graphs, or equations.

STANDARD	EXPECTATIONS FOR GRADES PRE-K–2	EXPECTATIONS FOR GRADES 3–5	EXPECTATIONS FOR GRADES 6–8
Algebra Standard (continued) Instructional programs from pre-K–12 should enable all students to—	In prekindergarten through Grade 2 all students should— (NCTM, 2000, p. 90)	In Grades 3–5 all students should—(NCTM, 2000, p. 158)	In Grades 6–8 all students should—(NCTM, 2000, p. 222)
Represent and analyze mathematical situations and structures using algebraic symbols	• illustrate general principles and properties of operations, such as commutativity, using specific numbers. • use concrete, pictorial, and verbal representations to develop an understanding of invented and conventional symbolic notations.	• identify such properties as commutativity, associativity, and distributivity and use them to compute with whole numbers. • represent the idea of a variable as an unknown quantity using a letter or a symbol. • express mathematical relationships using equations.	• develop an initial conceptual understanding of different uses of variables. • explore relationships between symbolic expressions and graphs of lines, paying particular attention to the meaning of intercept and slope.
Represent and analyze mathematical situations and structures using algebraic symbols			• use symbolic algebra to represent situations and to solve problems, especially those that involve linear relationships. • recognize and generate equivalent forms for simple algebraic expressions and solve linear equations.
Use mathematical models to represent and understand quantitative relationships	• model situations that involve the addition and subtraction of whole numbers, using objects, pictures, and symbols.	• model problem situations with objects and use representations such as graphs, tables, and equations to draw conclusions.	• model and solve contextualized problems using various representations, such as graphs, tables, and equations.
Analyze change in various concepts.	• describe qualitative change, such as a student's growing taller. • describe quantitative change, such as a student's growing two inches in one year.	• investigate how a change in one variable relates to a change in a second variable. • identify and describe situations with constant or varying rates of change and compare them.	• use graphs to analyze the nature of changes in quantities in linear relationships.

Algebra is a language of relationships and patterns of symbols and is an abstract system with its own rules, operations, and definitions (Usiskin, 1992, p. 27). Algebra is best learned in context and is more easily understood if pre-algebraic topics are a part of the mathematics curriculum throughout children's early and intermediate school years. Thus, mathematics in the middle grades can bridge the transition between the concretely based elementary mathematics curriculum and the more abstract, symbolic secondary curriculum.

What do we know of U.S. children's understanding of algebra? In the Third International Mathematics and Science Study (Peak, 1996) eighth-grade students scored close to the international average in algebraic patterns, relations, expressions, and equations. Compared with the top-scoring countries such as Singapore, Japan, Hong Kong, and Korea, the U.S. eighth graders performed at the seventh grade levels. Nonalgebra class textbooks focused more on arithmetic skills rather than algebra, geometry, and measurement, and what little algebra was included was found to be at a low level of knowledge and skills (Silver, 1998). The Sixth National Assessment of Educational Progress (NAEP) noted that more than half of the eighth graders tested correctly answered items dealing with algebra concepts treated informally. However, most 8th and 12th graders "had difficulty solving equations and inequalities other than fairly simple ones" (Blume & Heckman, 1997, p. 226). It is clear that we must do a better job helping children understand the many algebraic concepts and connecting that understanding with the processes and skills that help make algebra accessible to more children by laying a foundation for algebraic thinking in earlier years.

Algebra is often defined as generalized arithmetic and is identified as a gateway to higher mathematical development. Kaput (1998) comments that it is difficult to identify an area of mathematics that does not require some degree of algebraic reasoning. Nasser and Caritio (1995) believe that algebraic reasoning is the entry level skill in most sciences as well as for business, industry, and technical jobs. Yet, 8% of 17-year-olds reported that their highest mathematics course taken in high school was below the level of algebra. However, the inclusion of algebra as one of the five content standards in Principles and Standards for School Mathematics (NCTM, 2000) indicates the seriousness of the effort to engage teachers in seeing the need for providing children the opportunity to learn to reason algebraically.

According to House (2001), in order to think algebraically, children must able to do the following:

✔ Understand patterns, relations, and functions;

✔ Represent and analyze mathematical situations and structures using algebraic symbols;

✔ Use mathematical models to represent and understand quantitative relationships; and

✔ Analyze change in various contexts. (p. 2)

This chapter describes how teachers can focus on these concepts to help children develop algebraic thinking. ✔

WHAT IS ALGEBRA?

Algebra, as defined by *Random House Word Menu* (1992), is a "theory and practice of arithmetic operations that uses symbols, especially letters, to represent unknown variables in equations" (p. 143). Algebraic reasoning requires representing, generalizing, and formalizing patterns and regularities found in all aspects of mathematics. In algebra, these patterns are generalized through the use of symbolic notation with variables. Equations and formulas are developed to represent the relationships that occur from the patterns. The study of relationships that develop from these meaningful contexts leads to the study of functions.

The goal of this chapter is to show how the whole-number system can be extended and how concepts related to integers, patterns and relationships, variables, expressions, functions, and graphing can be developed so that children learn how to use the powerful language of algebra. When algebraic thinking is taught in a meaningful way, children can learn to utilize that thinking as a useful tool for solving many real-world problems.

INTEGERS

The study of integers provides children with an opportunity to extend the whole-number system. Fremont (1969) stated that "Everything that is done in any future work in algebra will involve using these new numbers and using them with ease. Our start in this area should be unhurried and as meaningful as we can make it" (p. 203).

Integers provide a way for us to express numbers as positive and negative. Even though models for negative numbers may be less intuitive to children than models for fractions and decimals that they may have previously learned, children generally find learning about the system of integers to be easier than working with the positive rational numbers. The notation for negative numbers is less complex than that for rational numbers, and typically only one- or two-digit numbers are used in examples and problems. Furthermore, the rules for operating on integers are easier to learn and apply than the corresponding algorithms with fractions. The challenge for teachers is to assist children in understanding *why* as well as *how* these rules work. The following sections describe an instructional approach that connects computational procedures to number properties and patterns and to the meaning of operations using integers in the context of real-world applications.

Introducing Integers

There are many situations in everyday life that require numbers that deal with direction as well as magnitude. Children know, for example, that a temperature of 5° Fahrenheit below zero is referred to as "five below" and written -5°F. Young children encounter negative numbers when they use calculators to find answers for expressions such as 2–5 or continue to "count down" past zero and see -1, -2, -3, and so on, appear in the display.

The concept of a negative number is used when a person spends more money than he or she earns and when a football team loses more yards than it gains. Hockey players' "plus-minus" statistics are the difference between the number of goals scored by and against that player's team when they are on the ice. Other real-world examples include profit and loss, credits and debits, above and below sea level, winning and losing points, golf scores above and below par, and positive and negative electrical charges.

Teachers can introduce negative numbers as *opposites* of counting numbers. To make the distinction between the sign of the number and the operation of subtraction, the *opposite* of 3 is written -3 and is read *negative* 3 rather than *minus* 3. The counting numbers, their opposites, and zero form the set of integers: . . . -3, -2, -1, 0, 1, 2, 3, ... Teachers can now refer to the counting numbers as the positive integers; the number 3 is sometimes called *positive* 3 and written +3. The integer 0 is neither positive nor negative. Integers are sometimes referred to as "signed" or "directed" numbers.

A number line can help children visualize integers. Even in the early grades it is important to have an integer number line so children begin to have a sense of the relationships among numbers. To construct the integer number line, first mark a point to represent 0 and measure equal segments to the right to identify the positive points 1, 2, 3, . . . and equal segments measured to the left to determine the negative points -1, -2, -3, ...

Teachers can provide children with a real-world context for integers by using the idea of the negative direction as heading west and the positive direction as heading east, with the student's home at position zero (see Figure 17-1).

If children walk 5 blocks east to the local school and 7 blocks west to the library, they will be at the position -2 or rather 2 blocks west of home. Figure 17-1 shows several similar scenarios that will help children see that negative number operations are easy to visualize. Another possibility is to place a number line on the classroom floor. Designate a middle location that can be labeled 0 and designate one side with positive values and the other with negative values; include + or - signs at the end of the respective sides. Have one student stand on the 0 and move 5 spaces in the positive direction, and have another student begin at 0 and move 5 spaces in the negative direction. Ask children to identify who is farther from 0. Children can then model 5–7 and -3 + 4 on the number line.

Opposites, such as 3 and -3, are equal distances from zero on the number line. Integers may also be thought of as directed distances on the number line rather than points. As such, integers may be represented by arrows that indicate both length and direction. Thus, -3 can be represented as an arrow 3 units in length and pointing left. Note that the arrow can be moved along the line to positions other than the 0 to -3 segment. Using this type of explanation and the previous example involving the number line on the floor, children can come to understand the idea that the absolute value of a number is the distance to the point from 0. For instance, $|3| = |-3| = 3$, and $|2 - 5| = |-3| = 3$. In addition, the use of arrow notation will be useful when working with the operations on integers in the following sections.

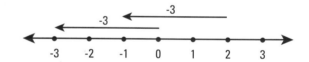

FIGURE 17-1

REAL-WORLD INTEGER MODELS

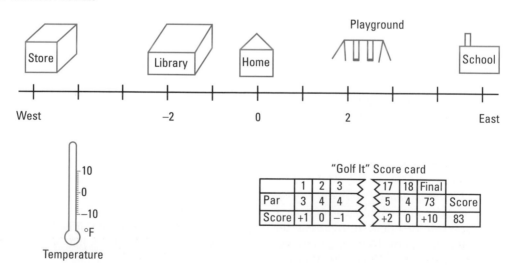

Ordering Integers

The number line is a particularly useful model for ordering integers. For the whole numbers the greater of two numbers is situated to the right of the preceding number on the number line; this is also true for the negative integers. Children need to use words and symbols to indicate order relations between particular pairs of integers, such as -3 < 2 and 4 > -5. Teachers should encourage children to look for these patterns in words or in writing. Children might note, for example, that any negative number is less than zero and is also less than any positive number. The fact that -7 < -4 may at first seem confusing, however, a basic explanation that -7 is further to the left on the number line makes it smaller than -4 should rapidly clear up any confusion. Thinking in terms of temperature, teachers may ask questions such as "Is it colder at -7°C than it is at -4°C"; or, considering depth, "Is 700 m below sea level deeper than 400 m below sea level?" Extensive practice in ordering negative and positive integers, identifying the direction from zero, and labeling points on the number line will familiarize children with a basic knowledge of integers.

Before engaging children in operations on integers, teachers should have them consider real-life situations that require the process of ordering negative and positive integers. Ask children to draw models to represent their ideas. The following are some examples:

1. What happens if the temperature fell 16° at night, but rose 20 degrees during the day? If the temperature started off at 60 degrees, what is the ending temperature?

2. You are in an elevator that moved up 6 flights and then down 9 flights. If you are now on the seventh floor, on which floor did you start?

Providing real-world settings will motivate children to explore and understand the concept of integers.

Addition of Integers

Of all the operations on integers, addition is the easiest for children to understand. Two approaches suggested for developing integer addition include the electric charges model (Grady, 1978) and the number line. Before receiving any direct instruction, however, children should have opportunities to draw on their previous knowledge to construct solutions to addition problems. The teacher might begin with real-world situations involving earning and spending money. For example, the situation of borrowing $7 and then repaying $10 prompts children to find the sum of -7 + 10. Teachers should ask children to solve the problems and write corresponding number sentences (Chang, 1985). An alternative approach would be to give integer addition questions, such as 5 + -7, and ask children to write corresponding real-life problems and find solutions for them.

Electric charges model for addition of integers To model positive and negative charges concretely, the teacher can use chips of two different colors, for example, white (positive) and black (negative). Children may find it easier if the teacher represents the charges pictorially using the symbols + and - on regular chips. The key idea in the model is that a positive and a negative charge "cancel" each other; symbolically, 1 + -1 = 0. This has been depicted as "Zero, my Hero" in some classrooms and in the short film *Multiplication Rock*. By combining required numbers of white (+) and black (-) chips, children easily find answers for different types of addition questions (see Figure 17-2). Note that in Figure 17-2, 5 + -2 can also be viewed as the solution to a comparison subtraction problem for whole numbers—how many more white chips than black chips? Special attention should be made to finding solutions that equal zero, such as -1 + 1, 2 + -2, etc. This fact will prove essential in the conceptual development of integer subtraction problems where the minuend (first number) is smaller than the subtrahend (second number), such as 3 – 6. One child wrote the following in her journal after a lesson on addition of integers:

The interesting thing was how you would add a negative and a posetive [sic] you ended up with a lower number than you started with so it would be like subtracting. (Vance, 1995, p. 14)

Number line model for addition of integers To use the number line to add two numbers, begin at the point represented by the first addend and move the distance and direction (positive—right, negative—left) indicated by the second addend. Thus, for 2 + -5, start at 2 and move five spaces to the left (negative direction). Children will find that although the number line solution for -5 + 2, where they begin at -5 and move right (positive direction) two spaces, looks different from the previous explanation for 2 + -5, the final result is the same as shown in Figure 17-3.

FIGURE 17-2

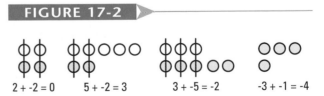

2 + -2 = 0   5 + -2 = 3   3 + -5 = -2   -3 + -1 = -4

FIGURE 17-3

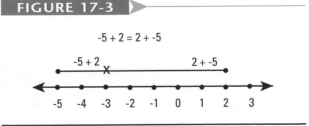

-5 + 2 = 2 + -5

Children who have many experiences solving integer addition problems using the two models begin to develop mental procedures for getting answers quickly (see examples in Figure 17-4). As children use these models, teachers should help children discover that the commutative property for addition also holds true for integers. Teachers should help children demonstrate this property as they practice using the models.

Teachers should ask students who are at this stage to verbalize how they determine the value and sign of the sum when the two integers have the same sign and when one is positive and one is negative. Some children will begin to generalize the procedure that includes the following:

1. When the signs are the same, add the numbers and maintain the sign.

2. When the signs are different, subtract the smaller number from the larger number and use the sign of the larger number.

Subtraction of Integers

The general rule that states "to subtract an integer, add its opposite" is fairly easy to remember and apply. In fact, because subtraction can always be changed to an addition problem, the previous discussion applies. However, rather than simply giving this procedural rule that offers very little conceptual development about subtraction, the teacher needs to provide opportunities for children to engage in problem-solving and sense-making experiences involving subtraction of integers, so that they understand this important concept. For example, ask children to think about the temperature being -3° and dropping another 6°, resulting in an expression of -3 − 6, and a final temperature of -9°. Children can work in small groups to make up problems and decide on answers for number sentences and explanations for integer subtraction problems, such as 3 − 5 = ☐ and 3 − -2 = ☐. Procedures for developing subtraction using patterns, the number line, and electric charges are discussed in the following paragraphs.

Number pattern approach for subtraction of integers   Teachers can ask children to continue patterns such as the following, and discuss possible rules suggested by the results.

3 − 1 = 2	3 − 2 = 1
3 − 2 = 1	3 − 1 = 2
3 − 3 = 0	3 − 0 = 3
3 − 4 = ☐	3 − -1 = ☐
3 − ☐ = ☐	3 − ☐ = ☐

In some cases, the use of a calculator and the repeated pressing of the ☐= sign may assist in conceptual understanding. For instance, begin-

ning with 3 and subtracting 1, then pressing ☐=, ☐=, ☐=, ☐=, ☐=, produces results of 2, 1, 0, -1, -2 and develops the pattern shown above. Next try -3 and subtract 1, then ☐=, ☐=, ☐=, ☐= will result in -4, -5, -6, -7. The final outcome should be that children notice subtracting a negative integer is like adding a positive integer, and that subtracting a positive integer is like adding a negative integer.

Number line model for subtraction of integers   Subtraction on the number line is similar to missing addend addition. If we think of fact families, we know 5 − 2 = _____ can also be thought of as 2 + _____ = 5. The solution, 3, is found on the number line by starting at 2 and moving right to 5. Beginning on the 2 and moving 3 spaces to the right (or the positive direction three spaces) results in the final value, 5. Similarly, 3 − 5 = _____ is equivalent to 5 + _____ = 3. To solve, we begin at 5 and move two spaces to the left (or the negative direction 2) to land on 3. The final answer reflects the *number* of spaces moved and the *direction* of the move. This example and those for 3 − -2 = _____ and -1 − 3 = _____ are shown in Figure 17-5. Although it requires a bit of practice, this "think addition" strategy will help students develop an understanding of integer subtraction.

Electric charges model for subtraction of integers   The electric charges model of integers lends itself nicely to the "take away" interpretation of subtraction. To solve 5 − 2, we start with 5 white chips and remove 2 white chips; obviously, the answer is 3. To solve -5 − -2, we start with 5 black chips and remove 2 black chips; the 3 remaining black chips represent the answer -3. As with whole numbers, addition from the fact family can be used to check the result: -5 − -2 = -3 because -2 + -3 = -5.

Using chips to solve problems such as 3 − 5 requires another step. Because adding zero (1 + -1, 2 + -2, etc.) to a number does not change its value, an integer can be named as the sum of two integers in many ways. For example, 3 = 3 + (1 + -1) = 3 + (2 + -2), and so on. In the electric charges model, the value of a set of chips remains the same if equal numbers of white and black chips are added to (or taken from) the pile so the indicated number of chips can be removed from the pile. It follows that an integer, such as 3, can be represented by many different combinations of white and black chips, including 4 white and 1 black chips, 5 white and 2 black chips, and so on.

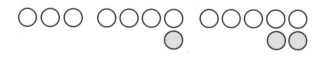

| 3 | = | 4 + -1 | = | 5 + -2 |

FIGURE 17-4

USING NUMBER LINE MODEL AND ELECTRIC CHARGES MODEL FOR ADDITION OF INTEGERS.

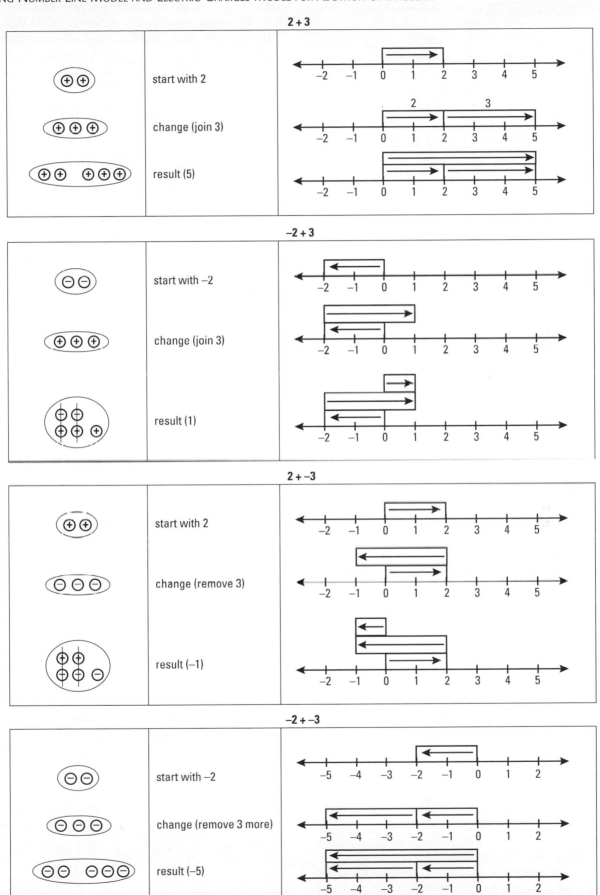

FIGURE 17-5

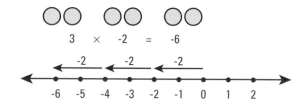

$$3 - 5 = \square \leftrightarrow 5 + \square = 3$$

$$3 - -2 = \square \leftrightarrow -2 + \square = 3$$

$$-1 - 3 = \square \leftrightarrow 3 + \square = -1$$

To represent $3 - 5$, we cannot perform the subtraction when starting with only 3 white chips, because we need to remove 5 white chips from pile. Therefore, we add equal numbers of white and black chips until we have enough white chips to remove 5. In this case, we can add 2 chips of each color (representing +2 and -2 for a total of 0) and then remove the 5 white chips, leaving 2 black chips; the answer is -2. Thus, $3 - 5 = 3 + (2 + -2) - 5 = 3 + 2 + -2 - 5 = -2$.

The same process applies when subtracting a negative number. For example, to find the solution to $3 - -2$, start with 3 white chips, then add 2 white and 2 black chips, and then remove 2 black chips, which leaves 5 white chips. Therefore, $3 - -2 = 5$.

Note that after the 3 negative chips are removed, the diagram for $2 - -3$ is the same as for $2 + 3$. If we examine the example solving for $3 - 5$, 5 positive chips and 5 negative chips would be added to the pile and the diagram would eventually look like $3 + -5$. The rule "to subtract an integer, add its opposite" follows from an examination of several examples of this type. Another approach is to have children find the answers to two related sets of questions using any of the methods previously developed.

Compare	$5 - 2 =$	to	$5 + -2 =$
Compare	$3 - -4 =$	to	$3 + 4 =$
Compare	$-2 - 5 =$	to	$-2 + -5 =$
Compare	$-6 - -2 =$	to	$-6 + 2 =$

The class then can examine the two groups of problems and discuss how the problems are the *same* (first number and answer) and how they are *different* (the first set of problems are subtraction sentences, whereas the other set are addition sentences; the second numbers in corresponding sentences are opposites). Once again, the

repeat feature of the calculator will help generalize the rule for subtracting integers. Teachers might then ask children to verbalize a "short-cut" procedure for subtracting an integer. The result "to subtract an integer, add its opposite" could then be compared with the rule "to add a negative, subtract its positive value" (Figure 17-6).

Additional number line and electric charges models for subtraction are provided in Figure 17-7.

Multiplication of Integers

The rules for multiplying integers are straightforward; the product of two positive or two negative integers is positive and the product of a positive and a negative integer is negative. But it is important that children also understand the meaning of multiplication of integers. When the first factor is positive, children can apply the interpretation of multiplication as repeated addition to find the product. For example, 3 times -2 is the same as three groups of negative 2:

$$3 \times -2 = 3 \text{ groups of } -2 = -2 + -2 + -2$$

Teachers can use either the electric charges model or the number line model in this case (Figure 17-8). Sometimes the electric charges model will seem clearer to children.

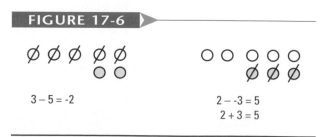

Electric charges model for multiplication of integers   Another way to model integer multiplication is the electric charges model, which begins with an empty circle from which chips will be removed or added. In multiplication with integers, the first factor will be either positive or negative. When the first factor is negative, children will think about removing chips and when the first factor is positive, children will think about adding chips. The value of the first factor indicates the number of groups of chips that are to be added or removed. For example, a first factor of -2 means to remove two groups of chips, and a first

FIGURE 17-6

$$3 - 5 = -2$$

$$2 - -3 = 5$$
$$2 + 3 = 5$$

FIGURE 17-7

Using Number Line Model and Electric Charges Model for Subtracting Integers

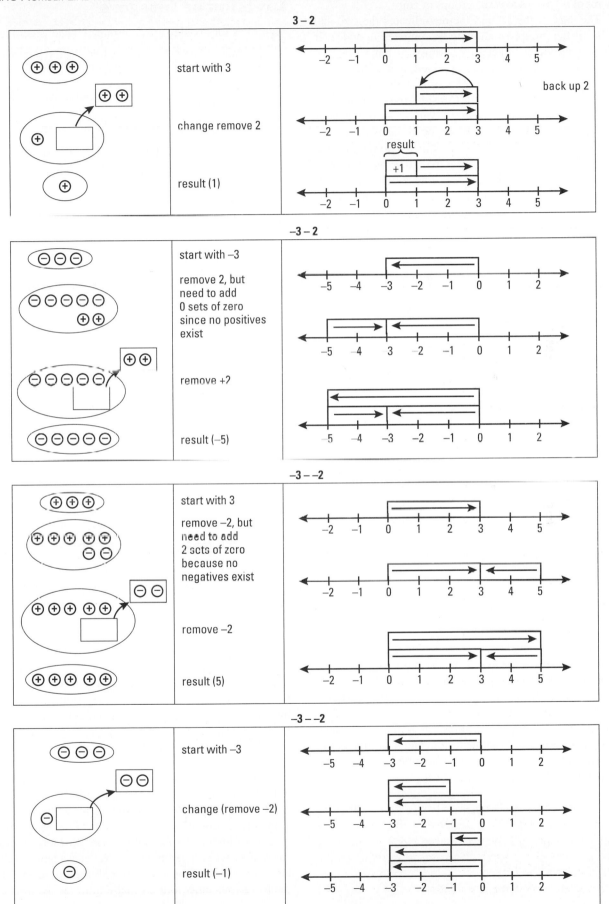

factor of +3 means to add 3 groups of chips.

The sign of the second factor indicates the size and color of the groups of chips to be removed or added. If the second factor is negative, groups of black chips of that size should be removed or added, and if the second factor is positive, groups of white chips of that size should be removed or added. Consider the problem -2 × 3. The first factor of -2 means to remove two groups of chips, whereas the second factor of 3 means to remove groups of 3 white chips, so -2 × 3 means to remove two groups of 3 white chips. In order to do this, we must once again consider the concept of inserting zero; in this case 6 zero pairs of white chips and black chips must be inserted. Now it is possible to remove 2 groups of 3 white chips, which results in 6 black chips, or -6 (see Figure 17-8). Subsequent explanations will explain the other situations, such as -2 × -3 as meaning to remove two groups of 3 black chips, and 2 × -4 meaning to add two groups of 4 black chips.

Number line model for multiplication of integers. Another way to model multiplication of integers is the number line model, which starts at zero on a number line and moves the number of "jumps" in the indicated direction.

The first factor indicates the number of jumps and the direction of the jumps, with a negative factor meaning to jump to the left and a positive factor meaning to jump to the right. The second factor indicates the length of each jump. For example, consider the problem -2 × 3. The first factor of -2 means to make two jumps to the left. The second factor of 3 means that each jump will be three units long. The jumps will end at -6, which is the answer.

The problems get a little more complicated when the second factor is negative. For example, consider the problem -2 × -3. The first factor of -2 means to make two jumps to the left. The second factor -3 means that each jump will be three units long *in the opposite direction,* or in other words, two jumps each three units long *to the right.* The jumps will end at 6, which is the answer, and is the same result as 2 × 3 (see Figure 17-8).

Products such as a negative number times a positive number (e.g., -3 × 2) or a negative number times a negative number (e.g., -3 × -2) do not lend themselves easily to physical models of repeated addition. One approach to understanding these situations involves extending whole-number properties and patterns. If 3 × -2 = -6, then -2 × 3 should also be -6 because of the commutative property. A pattern leading to this conclusion, and also for a negative number times a negative number (e.g., -3 × -2 = 6) follows:

2 × 3 = 6	-3 × 2 = -6
1 × 3 = 3	-3 × 1 = -3
0 × 3 = 0	-3 × 0 = 0
-1 × 3 = ☐	-3 × -1 = ☐
-2 × 3 = ☐	-3 × -2 = ☐

Division of Integers

Sign rules for division are determined by considering the fact families and the relationship between division and multiplication. Children recall that the sentence 6 ÷ 2 = ☐ can be expressed as 2 × ☐ = 6. The three cases in which at least one of the terms is negative are as follows:

$$-6 \div 2 = -3, \text{ because } 2 \times -3 = -6$$

$$6 \div -2 = -3, \text{ because } -2 \times -3 = 6$$

$$-6 \div -2 = 3, \text{ because } -2 \times 3 = -6$$

Therefore, the rules for determining the sign of the quotient of two integers are the same as those for multiplication.

Electric charge model for division This model extends the meaning of division of whole numbers. Once again, division is simply viewed as repeated subtraction. Recall that 12 divided by 3 can have two possible meanings: partitive and measurement. In partitive division, we think "Three sets of what size make 12?" In measurement division, we ask "How many sets of 3 are in 12?" Generally, the second approach is used with integer division.

Figure 17-9 shows concrete examples for division of integers using the electric charges model and the number line model. The examples 8 ÷ 4, -8 ÷ 4, 8 ÷ -4, and -8 ÷ -4 are illustrated using both models. These models match the procedures for multiplying integers and make more sense when we consider fact families.

Number line model for division of integers As with the discussion of multiplication of integers, the number line model can be used best with the measurement approach to division. Although it can be a bit confusing at first, the model will come to make more sense with practice. Always begin with a whole-number example, for instance 8 ÷ 4, to reacquaint students with the meaning of division and the use of the number line as a model. For example, with 8 ÷ 4, a child can look at a segment on the number line from 0 to 8 and determine the number of four-unit-long segments into which this eight-unit-long segment can be split, or in other words: How many fours are in 8? Another way to think about it is that we can begin at 0 and move forward from 0 in four-unit-long jumps two times to reach 8. And because we moved to the right to get to 8, the answer will be positive. Similarly, for -8 ÷ -4, children again start at 0 once and move toward -8 in two segments or "jumps" each -4 units long; thus, -8 ÷ -4 = 2.

The following two examples are bit more complicated. First we will examine -8 ÷ 4. Once again, children begin on the number line at 0 and attempt to move in jumps of four units long as many times as necessary to

FIGURE 17-8

Using Electric Charges Model and Number Line Model for Multiplication

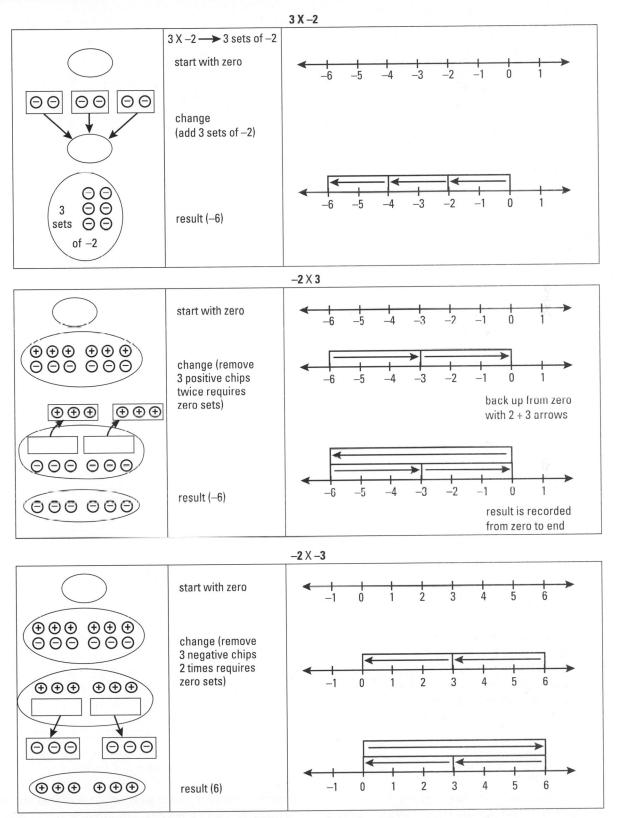

FIGURE 17-9

USING ELECTRIC CHARGES MODEL AND NUMBER LINE MODEL FOR DIVISION OF INTEGERS.

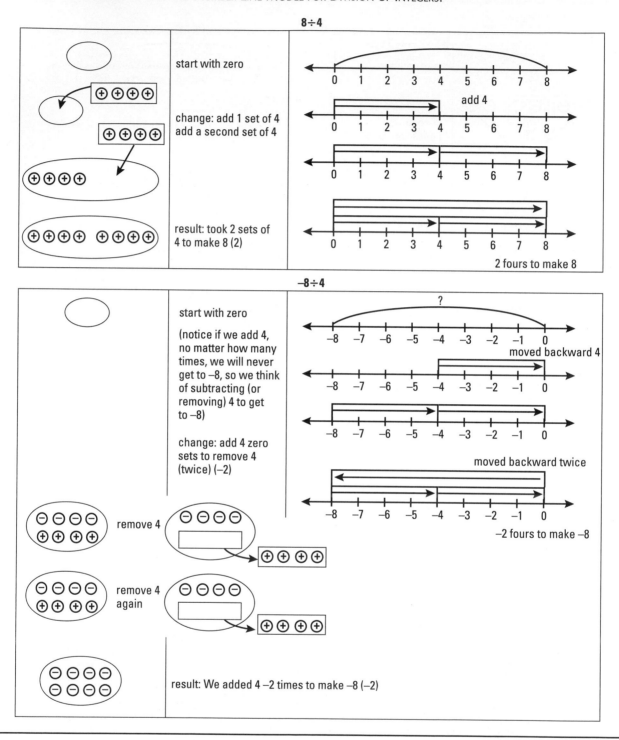

reach -8. However, they are unable to jump from 0 to the right to reach -8. It will actually require 2 jumps moving backward (or left) to reach the -8, resulting in an answer of -2. The negative comes from the fact that children

must back up (in this case move left), rather than moving forward (in this case moving right) from 0.

For 8 ÷ -4, children begin at 0 and try to move in jumps of -4 units (in other words, to the left) to reach 8.

FIGURE 17-9

CONTINUED

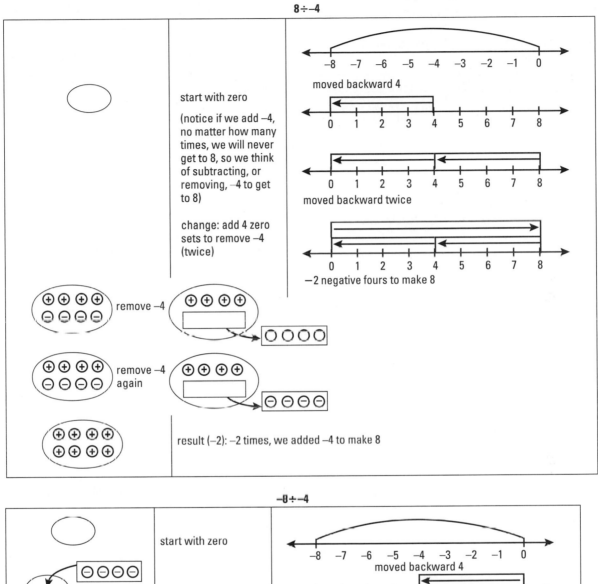

$8 \div -4$

start with zero

(notice if we add −4, no matter how many times, we will never get to 8, so we think of subtracting, or removing, −4 to get to 8)

change: add 4 zero sets to remove −4 (twice)

remove −4

remove −4 again

result (−2): −2 times, we added −4 to make 8

moved backward 4

moved backward twice

−2 negative fours to make 8

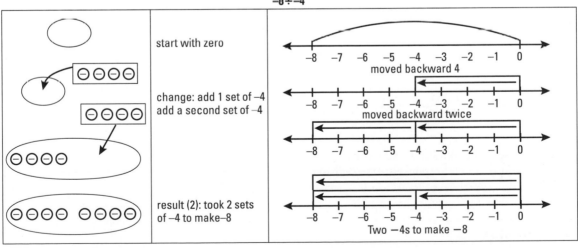

$-8 \div -4$

start with zero

change: add 1 set of −4
add a second set of −4

result (2): took 2 sets of −4 to make −8

moved backward 4

moved backward twice

Two −4s to make −8

Once again, children will find that jumps to the left from 0 will not get them to 8. Instead, they will need to change directions (or move to the right) in two jumps that are 4 units long to reach the 8. The process of changing direction (moving right instead of left, as indicated by the negative sign of -4) will result in a negative answer, in this case, -2. Additional examples are shown in Figure 17-9.

Integer Assessment

As discussed in previous chapters, assessment should be consistent with the goals of instruction. A test should include questions that require the children to relate integers to everyday life and to justify rules for the operations. Some test questions (Q) and sample responses (R) by sixth and seventh graders follow:

Q: *Write and solve a story problem for -5 + 13.*

R: *Pavel Bure was on the ice for 5 goals scored against his team during one game. The next game he was on for 13 goals that his team scored. What was his positive-negative rating? -5 + 13 = 8. His rating was +8.*

Q: *Write a question to make a problem using the following information. "At noon the temperature was 8°F. At midnight the temperature was -5°F." Solve the problem.*

R: *How many degrees did the temperature fall? (A diagram of a thermometer was drawn.) 8 − -5 = 13. The temperature fell 13°.*

Q: *Write a story problem for 3 × -4. Solve using a number line.*

R: *Stephen had 3 library cards. If he owed $4.00 on each, how much does he owe? (A number line showing 3 jumps of 4 starting at 0 and moving to the left to -12 was drawn.) 3 × -4 = -12. He owed $12.00.*

Q: *Write and solve a story problem for -8 ÷ 2. Show how you would check that your answer is correct.*

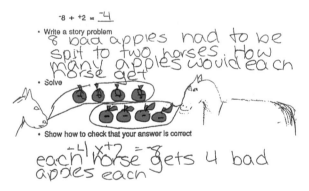

How would you assess the skill and understanding of the child who gave the above response to the division question?

Practice Settings

As discussed in the previous sections, children should be able to use models and mathematical reasoning to justify the rules for adding, subtracting, multiplying, and dividing integers. Children also need to be able to execute these procedures automatically when solving problems and learning algebraic concepts. Activities 17-1 and 17-2

ACTIVITY **17-1**

INTEGER TARGET

Use the first three listed integers together with two operations to make a number sentence having the fourth integer as the answer (target). The three numbers can appear in any order in the sentence.

EXAMPLE:	7	-2	-5	-6
SOLUTION:	(7 − -5) ÷ -2 = -6			

1.	-9	4	3	-23
2.	-8	2	-7	3
3.	6	-9	6	0
4.	-7	1	12	-2

ACTIVITY **17-2**

TWO-COLOR GAME

MATERIALS

10 two-color counters (chips with a different color on each side)

PROCEDURES

Use 10 chips that are two sided, one color on one side, another color on the other side. Designate that one color will represent a negative number and the other a positive number. Put the chips in a cup. Students will shake up the chips and pour them out on the table. They will count the number for each color to determine the two numbers. For example, two reds and 5 whites will mean -2 + 5. Students will add the two numbers for their score for that turn. The student with the highest score at the end of 10 turns is the winner.

ALTERNATIVES:

a) Select another operation (−, ×, ÷) for the game.

b) Use two spinners or two dice instead of the chips.

c) Scoop out two colors of beans for them to add.

d) Use more than 10 chips.

e) Make a game board like that given below.

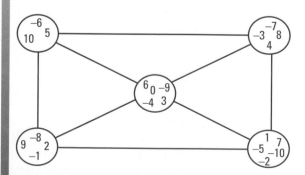

Move from one corner across to the opposite corner.

PRINCIPLES AND STANDARDS LINK 17-2
Content Strand: Algebra

By viewing algebra as a strand in the curriculum from prekindergarten on, teachers can help students build a solid foundation of understanding and experience as a preparation for more-sophisticated work in algebra in the middle grades and high school. For example, systematic experience with patterns can build up to an understanding of the idea of function (Smith, forthcoming), and experience with numbers and their properties lays a foundation for later work with symbols and algebraic expressions. (NCTM, 2000, p. 37)

are examples of problem-solving activities that provide practice with integer operations.

The remaining sections of this chapter describe a variety of activities that allow children to examine patterns and relationships, evaluate expressions, apply order of operations, illustrate properties of operations, solve equations and inequalities, and explore functions using contextual situations, tables, graphs, and symbols that are aimed at helping children think algebraically.

PATTERNS

Algebra can be defined as the study of patterns, which form the basis for the logical connections in all of mathematics. Through the study of patterns, children can learn to see relationships and make connections, generalizations, and predictions about the world around them. According to NCTM's Principles and Standards for School Mathematics, studying patterns leads to generalizations about relationships and the development of supporting logical arguments, which is an important aspect of algebraic thinking. To help children think algebraically, teachers should encourage them to analyze existing patterns, extend the patterns they see, recognize when a similar pattern has occurred, and generate patterns of their own.

Through experiences with their world, young children explore patterns. Teachers can build on children's interest in patterns by providing experiences in the classroom in which children sort, describe, compare, predict, and create patterns. In higher levels, children look for relationships in concrete materials, tables, charts, and graphs; describe these patterns in numbers, symbols, words, and graphs; and make predictions.

Children's first experiences with patterns should focus on repeating patterns, with children participating in hand-clap exercises, listening to the rhythmic beat of music, looking at pattern shape cards, and examining natural patterns found in nature. No matter what the medium,

exposure to a wide variety of patterns is invaluable in the understanding of patterns and the relationship of the component parts that form them.

Another way to help children make sense of the patterns in their mathematics world is through the hundreds chart. For example, have groups of children color in all the numbers that have a 4, or 8, or 6. Display the patterns for the entire class and discuss what children observe. Give children a number, for example, 37, and ask what number would be above (27), below (47), to the right (38) or to the left (36) in the hundreds chart. Ask children to describe the patterns they notice.

Repeating Patterns

As children are involved in experiences with patterns, they should be encouraged to describe the patterns they see or hear in a variety of ways. One way to describe patterns is by classifying the *core,* which includes two complete repetitions of the repeating pattern segment, or in other words, the shortest string of elements that repeats in a pattern. A core pattern might be a boy-girl-boy-girl arrangement, or square-circle-square-circle arrangement. We refer to this type of pattern as an AB pattern.

Experiences with patterns using manipulatives such as pattern blocks, attribute blocks, Unifix cubes, and other assorted shapes such as those found in Figure 17-10 support children's ideas of order in their world. Many experiences with patterns are crucial to the development of algebraic concepts in young learners. It is helpful for children to name patterns in a variety of ways, such as ABAB; 1, 2, 1, 2; or red, green, red, green. When these patterns are described orally and written in words or symbols, children start making sense of the concept of the pattern. As children become more confident with simple patterns, they should be encouraged to make more complicated patterns such as ABBCC or ABBAABBA, using a variety of symbols, numbers, or manipulatives. Teachers should challenge children to generate their own

FIGURE 17-10 ▶

EXAMPLES OF REPEATING PATTERNS

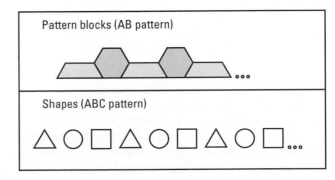

ACTIVITY 17-3

MATCH THE PATTERNS

PROCEDURE:

1. The teacher demonstrates creating ABC patterns, first using learning links then using color tiles.

2. Provide groups of children with various materials, such as colored beads and string, interlocking links or cubes, attribute shapes, bags of buttons, etc.

3. Ask children to generate various patterns using the above materials and have them discuss what materials their groups used to represent the pattern.

patterns using a variety of materials and to look for patterns that are similar or explain patterns using letters in the alphabet.

Growing Patterns

Repeating patterns lead into *growing patterns,* which are patterns that grow or change. At first, children need lots of exposure to different growing patterns until they begin to see how patterns continue. Next comes identifying the "rule" for the pattern. Once children are able to verbalize the rule, they can use symbolic notation to represent the changes. Graphs are another component. They help visual learners see the relationships. The pattern (usually described in a T-Table), the rule, the symbolic notation, and the graph form a link of understanding for algebraic relationships that become more complex in the middle grades.

Once children have fully explored an assortment of progressively more complicated experiences and exposure to natural and musical patterns, manipulatives (e.g., pattern blocks, color tiles, Cuisenaire rods) and abstract representations (e.g., using letters or numbers), they will be ready to begin understanding growing patterns. Introducing children to growing patterns should begin early and extend into the study of sequences, which are basically growing patterns, and their related functions at upper-level mathematics. Using real-world objects or

pictures helps children make connections with what they already understand. Typically, children begin displaying growing patterns by recording a pattern in a T-Table. The first experience with this could be a class lesson comparing the number of people with their number of eyes, as in Figure 17-11. Another example is Activity 17-4, "The Growing Worm."

Once children have about three entries in the T-table, ask them to predict what the next result will be. Questioning such as this helps children to begin to examine the way the T-table works. When children are able to make some accurate predictions, ask them to explain their thinking. See if they can predict what would happen for the 10th case. The aim is to have children see a pattern that they can generalize into a rule. As students become more experienced with verbalizing a rule, teachers can show how the rule can be written using symbolic notation with letters from the T-table and numbers. Figure 17-12 shows a sample of a child's work on this problem.

Sometimes children in lower grades have difficulties writing letters—capital letters are acceptable in these problems. As children advance through the grades, it is preferable for children to use lower-case letters to represent patterns in order to better prepare them for more formal algebraic learning.

Relationships

Children need to be encouraged to describe and analyze the relationship that exists among objects or numbers. As they become proficient in recording patterns in T-tables and discovering the rules for growth, children are ready for more complicated patterns and are ready to display the rule in graph form to "see" the relationship. For example, consider using toothpicks to make triangles. If the triangles are separate from one another, three toothpicks are needed for each triangle and the pattern rule is *toothpicks* $= 3 \times \square$. Suppose, however, that triangles can share a common side. Looking at the table, children predict that 21 toothpicks are needed to make 10 triangles. The rule can be expressed as *toothpicks* $= 2 \times \square + 1$.

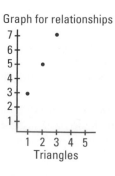

triangles	1	2	3	4 . . .	10
toothpicks	3	5	7	9 . . .	—

Graph for relationships

FIGURE 17-11

T-TABLE: GROWING PATTERNS

N Number of People	E Number of Eyes
1	2
2	4
3	6
4	

ACTIVITY 17-4

THE GROWING WORM

MATERIALS:
Pattern blocks

PROCEDURES:

1. Using an overhead projector, display three pattern blocks (as in the diagram below) to represent the worm. Tell the class that this is a worm, and this worm eats a lot and grows a lot every day.

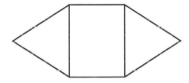

2. Ask students how many blocks were used for the first day. Make a T-table to record the days and number of blocks used.

3. On Day 2 the worm gets larger, and now is made up of four pattern blocks, as in the diagram below. Record this data in the T-table.

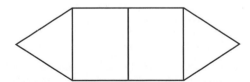

4. The worm's body gets one square longer every day. Model how the worm grows by adding one square in the body and record the data in the T-table.

5. Have the children use pattern blocks to continue to build the figures and draw them on a recording sheet, recording the numbers in the T-table each time.

6. As a class, discuss the pattern and move toward discovering the "rule" and recording the rule in symbolic equation.

FIGURE 17-12

EXAMPLE OF STUDENT WORK ON "THE GROWING WORM" PROBLEM

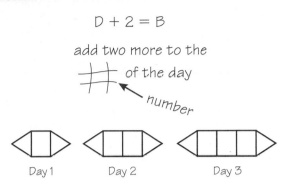

$$D + 2 = B$$

add two more to the ⊞ of the day number

| Day | Day 1 | Day 2 | Day 3 |

Day	# of Blocks
1	3
2	4
3	5
4	6
5	7
6	8
7	9
8	10
9	11
10	12
25	27

By representing this pattern as a graph, children have another way to understand the relationship between toothpicks and triangles in this problem. The idea that the pattern continues is more evident in the visual form and helps to confirm the relationship. Enabling children to see the connections among the data, the rule, and the graph also lays the groundwork for understanding functions.

VARIABLES

According to Peck and Jencks (1988), "algebra can and should arise as a by-product of making arithmetic sensible" (p. 85). Children can represent mathematical situations and properties first with objects and numbers and later with symbols, including variables, which are letters that represent quantities that may or may not vary or change.

Mathematicians often think of a *variable* as a symbol for an element from a specified replacement set (Usiskin, 1988). A variable provides students with a new language they can use to generalize patterns and complex situations.

According to Kieran and Chalouh (1993), instruction should focus on the exploration of key algebraic ideas in which children "(a) think about the numerical relations of a situation, (b) discuss them explicitly in simple everyday language, and (c) eventually learn to represent them with letters or other nonmisleading notation" (pp. 181–182).

Meanings of a Variable

Variables are letters that represent quantities that may or may not vary, or change. Quantities that do not vary are often referred to as "unknowns" or "missing elements" when they are used in number sentences. In primary grades, children encounter the notion of a variable, or unknown quantity, when they solve missing addend problems and when they use words to generalize patterns. Consider the following examples:

$$4 + \square = 9 \quad \square + 7 = 15 \quad 12 + 7 = \square$$
$$14 - \square = 5 \quad 3 \times \square = 12 \quad 25 \div \square = 5$$

In the example $4 + \square = 9$, the square represents the unknown, or missing addend, 5. In the example $3 \times \square = 12$, the square represents the unknown, or missing factor, 4.

In later experiences, children can begin to work with variables that change. Earlier experiences with repeating and growing patterns and generalizing to a stated rule and symbolic notation form the foundation for more complex ideas. It continues to be important to link concepts with real-world situations. Experiencing and recording the pattern helps consolidate understanding of the pattern. After practicing and generalizing many patterns, recording the rule can easily be shifted to the more standard (x, y) notation. Consider Activity 17-5, which asks children to use symbols to generalize a pattern they observe after making sets that add to 10.

Letters may be used to represent numbers in different mathematical contexts and, consequently, variables take on several different meanings. A symbol or variable may represent one or more numbers, called values of the variable. The term *variable* also may imply a symbol that may have two or more values in a particular situation. Variables can be used as follows:

1. In equations as a specific unknown number.

   Example: $3 + x = 7$

PRINCIPLES AND STANDARDS LINK 17-4
Content Strand: Algebra

Instructional programs from pre-kindergarten through grade 12 should enable all students to—

- understand patterns, relations, and functions;
- represent and analyze mathematical situations and structures using algebraic symbols;
- use mathematical models to represent and understand quantitative relationships;
- analyze change in various concepts (NCTM, 2000, p. 37)

PRINCIPLES AND STANDARDS LINK 17-5
Content Strand: Algebra

Instructional programs for grades 3–5, all students should enable all students to—

- represent the idea of a variable as an unknown quantity using a letter or a symbol . . . (NCTM, 2000, p. 158)

PRINCIPLES AND STANDARDS LINK 17-6
Content Strand: Algebra

An understanding of the meanings and uses of variables develops gradually as students create and use symbolic expressions and relate them to verbal, tabular, and graphical representations (NCTM, 2000, p. 225).

ACTIVITY 17-5

WAYS TO MAKE 10

MATERIALS:
2 small cups for each child and 10 chips for each child

PROCEDURE:
- Ask children to find all the different ways they could distribute the chips, always using all 10 chips.
- Record a number sentence for each way to distribute the chips (for example, $1 + 9 = 10$).
- Compare the list of number sentences developed.
- Ask: What is the same in each number sentence? (the sum is 10)
- Ask: What changes (or varies) in each number sentence? (the two addends)
- Ask: How could we write a general equation to represent this situation? Possible answers include the following:

  $\square + \triangle = 10$ and $x + y = 10$

2. To state properties or to generalize a pattern.

Example: $a + 0 = a$, or $ab = ba$

3. To describe functions or sequences of quantities that are joint variations.

Example:

in: n 7   4   12
out: $3n - 1$ 20 11 35

Example: 2, 5, 8, . . ., $3n - 1$

4. In formulas to express relationships.

Example: $C = \pi d$

In the first case, the variable x is used as a placeholder for a specific unknown. The task is to solve for x, that is, find a single number to substitute for x that will make the sentence true. In the other cases, the variable represents a range of values. In the second case, the statements are true for all numbers. In the third case, the expression $3n - 1$ defines a function; for any number n that is input, the output number is found by the applying the relationship "multiply n by 3 and subtract 1." A variable can also be used to describe a sequence; successive terms are found by replacing the variable with the numbers 1, 2, 3, and so on. In the fourth case, the formula expresses the relationship between the diameter and the circumference of a circle; the circumference varies as the diameter changes and, given one of the quantities, the other can be determined. This also describes a function relationship of independent and dependent values. Teachers should provide middle-school children many experiences with different variable situations so children can build their own understanding of the different uses of a variable. Interestingly, Willoughby (1997) and Sulzer (1988) found that fourth graders who were exposed to variable notation could use the notation "$x + 5$" versus simply saying "add 5."

After working with many examples involving one variable or one unknown, children may begin to work with two variables or two unknowns. For example, in the previous comparison examples of Cuisenaire rods, children learn that 2 red = 1 purple (2R = P) and that 1 nickel = 5 cents ($n = 5c$). Later, children can note that 5 nickels + 3 pennies = 18 cents. This slow progression lends itself nicely to an introduction to equations and the procedures of solving equations.

Misconceptions About Variables

Several types of misunderstandings are associated with the use of letters to represent numbers (Booth, 1988). Some children believe that variables represent objects rather than numbers. Children sometimes think that the particular letter used as the variable in an expression corresponds to the first letter in the quantity being represented. For example, in one study a subject said that $8y$ would have to mean eight yachts or yams or some other word starting with y, and could not represent apples or dogs or any quantity *not* beginning with the letter y. Writing "5 times n" as $5n$ also leads some children to write 56 when $n = 6$.

Wagner (1981) found that many children believe that changing the letter in an equation changes the problem. Subjects were shown the equations $7 \times W + 22 = 109$ and $7 \times N + 22 = 109$ and asked whether W or N would have a larger value. Some children said that they couldn't tell without solving the equation, whereas others believed that the order of the letters alphabetically must correspond to the order of the size of the numbers, so W would be larger because it comes after N in the alphabet.

Many children have difficulty accepting algebraic expressions, particularly those containing addition or subtraction symbols, as answers to problems. Typical computational error finds children rewriting $3 + 4b$ as $7b$ and $2x + 3y = 5xy$. A basic misunderstanding of the meaning of a variable is quite noticeable. The conventions of writing the product of variables creates the fact that $4ab$ means $4 \times a \times b$ and 4×5 is not equal to 45. We often express the commutative property as $ab = ba$, but notice that 35 is not equal to 53.

Translation errors sometimes occur when children write comparison relationships with variables. For instance, when children are asked to translate the relationship "twice as many feet as noses," the typical response is to write "2 × Feet = Noses." However, a closer examination indicates that "Feet = 2 × Noses" would be more accurate.

Activity 17-6 encourages children to think and use reasoning skills and see consistency in the relationship

ACTIVITY 17-6

DETECTIVE WORK

PROCEDURE:
Explain the rules:

• The same shapes have the same value.

• Different shapes have different values.

• No shape has a value of zero.

Have children examine the following equations and answer these questions:

$\bigcirc + \bigcirc + \bigcirc = 24$ $(\bigcirc - \triangle) + 10 = 12$

$\bigcirc =$ $\triangle =$

Have children explain how they got their answer and why their answer makes sense.

UNDERSTANDING EQUALITY AND EXPRESSIONS

Many adults may have memories of solving equations in an algebra course. But before children can learn how to solve equations, a strong foundation based on understanding the notion of equality must be established.

Understanding Equality

In a recent study (Falkner, Levi, & Carpenter, 1999), a group of 145 sixth graders were asked to identify the number that should go in the box in the equation below:

$$8 + 4 = \Box + 5$$

All of the children thought that either 12 or 17 should go in the box. What do these responses indicate about these children's understanding of equality and the equals sign, and what can teachers do to help them develop richer understandings?

According to Falkner, Levi, and Carpenter (1999), elementary-school children often think that the equals sign means that "they should carry out the calculation that precedes it and that the number after the equals sign is the answer to the calculation. [They] generally do not see the equals sign as a symbol that expresses the relationship 'is the same as'" (p. 233).

It is important for children to understand that equality is a relationship which states that two mathematical expressions have the same value. This understanding not only helps children solve algebraic equations, such as $4x + 7 = 20$, but also helps younger children understand relationships expressed as number sentences, such as $8 + 9 = 8 + 8 + 1$, which is a useful thinking strategy in learning basic facts.

In the early grades, children can be introduced to the concept of equality through the idea of balance. Using a pan balance, children can explore how to maintain balance by adding or subtracting the same weight on each side of the balance, noting that replacing objects with other objects with the same weight will not make the pans go out of balance. Activity 17-7 challenges children to reason and examine patterns.

Understanding Expressions

An expression is different from an equation. An *expression* is a symbolic statement and can be either an arithmetic expression, such as $2 + 3$, or an algebraic expression, such as $2x + 3$. Expressions may be constants (e.g., 3, 4, -2), variables (e.g., *m, x, w*), operations (e.g., addition, subtraction), and grouping symbols (e.g., parentheses). An *equation* includes an equals sign and states the equality of two expressions. Equations that contain only numbers, such as $2 + 3 = 5$, are known as *number sentences*.

ACTIVITY 17-7

BALANCING ACT

MATERIALS:
Copy of Pan Balance Worksheet for each group (see below)

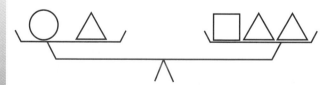

20 counters for each group

PROCEDURE:
1. Explain the rules:

   Find the value of each shape, given the following assumptions:

   • The pans must balance.
   • The same shapes have the same value.
   • No shape has a value of zero.

2. Ask how many counters will be on each side of the scale if there are 20 counters altogether.

3. Have children examine the pan balance and determine values for the shapes.

4. Have children explain how they got their answers.

5. Enter the values in a chart as below:

Pan Balance Chart

○	△	□
9	1	8
8	2	6
7	3	4
6	4	2

6. Discuss the patterns in the table. (This activity can be used with many other even numbers of counters.)

Children first encounter expressions and number sentences when they study addition. For instance, the number sentence expressing that two birds are joined by three other birds can be written in a number expression as $2 + 3$ or as a number sentence $2 + 3 = 5$. For example, if, the *expression* $2 + 3$ tells how many birds there are now, when we write the *number sentence* $2 + 3 = 5$, we are saying that 5 is another name for the total number of birds. The *equals* sign means that $2 + 3$ and 5 are different names for the same number. Children should be shown that this relation can also be written as $5 = 2 + 3$, and they should have experiences writing number sentences such as $2 + 3 = 3 + 2$ and $2 + 3 = 4 + 1$. Asking children to examine families of basic facts that have the same sum or product or to write expressions in order to name a particular number in many different ways allows these concepts to be discussed and reinforced. This process will also improve number-sense abilities for operations.

An important point here is that an arithmetic expression such as $2 + 3$ can be an answer as well as an instruction to add. Children with this understanding will later be better able to accept algebraic expressions such as $3 + a$ and $x + y$ as correct and meaningful final representations. The ideas that the addition symbol can show the result of an operation as well as the action of addition, and that the equals sign can indicate an equivalence relation as well as represent a signal to give the answer, are essential to algebraic understanding (Booth, 1988).

Throughout the elementary years, children have many opportunities to interpret, write, and evaluate arithmetic expressions by replacing the unknown values with a known quantity. As each of the four operations is introduced, children have experiences connecting physical actions and real-world situations with mathematical expressions. Learning the basic facts and computational algorithms involves finding single numbers to rename expressions. It is important to note that textbook and teacher-made exercises requiring children to "add," "find the product," or "complete" may or may not include the equals sign. Regardless of the format, the intent is that children learn the various ways to interpret expressions in order to find the "answer."

$$4 \quad \quad 5 \times 8 = \square \quad \quad 63 \div 7$$
$$\underline{+9}$$

Simplifying Algebraic Expressions

Other skills learned in beginning algebra involve simplifying and expanding expressions. Children learn that a *term* can be either a number, a variable, or a product or quotient including one or more variables. Terms are separated by addition or subtraction operation symbols to cre-

ate algebraic expressions. Thus, in the expression, $7x - 3xy + y - 8 + 2x$, there are five terms, with some common terms. In this example, $7x$, $3xy$, y, and 8 are *unlike terms*, whereas $7x$ and $2x$ are *like terms* because they contain the same variable, x. Like terms can be combined to simplify an expression. Thus, $7x + 2x$ can be written as $9x$, but the terms in $7x + y$ and $9x + 8$ cannot be combined.

Moving from numeric expressions to algebraic expressions is accompanied by the introduction of new notations for multiplication and division. The symbol $\times$ is no longer used to indicate multiplication; "3 times a" is written $3a$, "3 times the sum of a and b" is written $3(a + b)$, and "3 times 4" is written $3(4)$ or $3 \cdot 4$. As noted earlier, this notation can be a source of confusion for children. For division, the $\div$ symbol is most commonly used to denote "a divided by b." Children first make this connection when they study fractions and decimals. For example, they see that both $6 \div 3$ and $\frac{6}{3}$ are 2, and they find that the fraction $\frac{3}{5}$ can be expressed as a decimal by performing $3 \div 5$. Thus, the fraction bar can be either a number or an instruction to divide. The expression $(a + b) \div 3$ is written without parentheses as $\frac{a + b}{3}$.

The concept of an algebraic expression can be developed with materials such as straws, base-ten blocks, and Algebra Tiles. For instance, cutting straws of equal length to represent an unknown value, say x, and using straws of another length to represent units, children can model expressions such as $x + 2$, and $2x + 4$ using the materials. In using base ten blocks, the unit can remain units, whereas the rods become x values. These devices allow children to visualize the expression and leads them to understand why $3x$ is not the same as $3 + x$ and why $2(x + 3)$ is not the same as $2x + 3$. Various models for expressions are provided in Figure 17-13.

Children may use straws to represent the following relationship. Model the sides of a triangle with straws given the following conditions: the length of the second side of triangle is three times the first side, whereas the third side is twice the length of the first side. The same approach can be used to model a rectangle such that the length is three times the width. Many possible designs could be made and a table of the results can be kept. Teachers can also specify a perimeter, say 40 units, and ask children to use patterns and relationships to find the length and width.

Children can learn to write and interpret expressions involving variables. The phrase "4 more than a number" can be written $p + 4$; the letter p is a placeholder for a number. To evaluate the expression, a specific number is substituted for the variable p and the resulting number expression is evaluated. For $p = 2$ the value of the expression is 6, for $p = 5$ the value is 9, and so on. Carefully translating phrases to algebraic expressions as well as analyzing expression for contextual setting will prove

FIGURE 17-13

CONCRETE MODELS FOR EXPRESSIONS

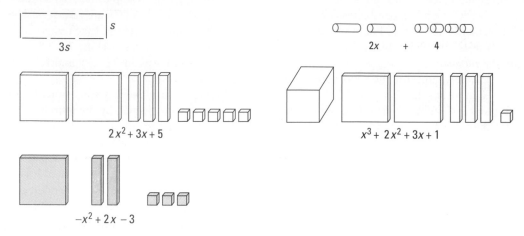

ACTIVITY 17-8

CANDY SALE

PROCEDURE:
Give children the following problem and have them generate a profit table to determine how much money they will have made in 10 days, 20 days, and *n* days.

You are working on the candy drive. You begin the campaign with $25 in your pocket. Each candy bar sells for 50 cents. You sell an average of 15 candy bars per day. Calculate the amount of money you will have on the 5th, 10th, 20th, and 50th days. Can you make a rule for finding your profit?

ACTIVITY 17-9

EXPRESS YOURSELF

Find the expression for each of the following:

a) 25 more than an integer

b) $4 less than the cost

c) Twice the width

d) Half the distance around

e) Three more than twice the value

Write a situation for each of the following:

a) $4x$

b) $3 + m$

c) $12 - w$

d) $4n + 2$

e) $\frac{d}{7}$

beneficial in the formation of algebraic thinking. Wraparound games, bingo-type games, and expression domino games like those described in Activities 17-8 through 17-10 can be used to help children connect the symbolic nature of an expression with the contextual expression.

Understanding Algebraic Properties

Children learned about arithmetic properties as they worked with number sentences, as discussed in Chapter 8. As children learn about algebra, they need to understand the similarity between arithmetic and algebraic properties.

In the early grades, children apply the *commutative* and *associative* properties of addition and multiplication but do not need to know these formal terms. In the intermediate years, the terms can be introduced and the properties described using variables, as in Table 17-1.

It is important for teachers to help children see the connections between the arithmetic properties they already understand and the algebraic statements of those

ACTIVITY 17-10

BINGO WITH EXPRESSIONS

PROCEDURE:
Use a standard bingo game, or generate your own bingo cards. Instead of reading coordinates like B5, provide children with an expression and a value to calculate. For instance, $3x + 1$ when $x = 4$ would mean students who have the number 13 on their card can cover it up.

TABLE 17-1

PROPERTY	ARITHMETIC EXAMPLE	ALGEBRAIC EXAMPLE
Commutative property of addition	$2 + 3 = 3 + 2$	$a + b = b + a$
Commutative property of multiplication	$2 \times 3 = 3 \times 2$	$ab = ba$
Associative property of addition	$(2 + 3) + 4 = 2 + (3 + 4)$	$(a + b) + c = a + (b + c)$
Associative property of multiplication	$(2 \times 3) \times 4 = 2 \times (3 \times 4)$	$(ab)c = a(bc)$
Distributive property of multiplication over addition	$2 (3 + 4) = 2 \times 3 + 2 \times 4$	$a(b + c) = ab + ac$
Addition property of 0	$2 + 0 = 2$	$a + 0 = a$
Multiplication property of 1	$2 \times 1 = 2$	$a * 1 = a$

same properties. One way to do this is to encourage children to express in their own words what each property means, and then give numerical examples to support each property. Teachers can then help children use their understanding of variables to represent these properties with variables, as in the third column of Table 17-1. The key idea is that the statements are true for all numbers. Although the properties are first examined for whole numbers, they are later found to also hold for integers, rational numbers, and real numbers. In this situation, variables are being used to generalize patterns. The goal is for children to come to appreciate the power and simplicity of this symbolic representation of the ideas. Activities 17-11 and 17-12 provide an opportunity for children to verify these properties.

Understanding the Order of Operations

Evaluate the expression $2 + 3 \times 4$. Is the correct answer 20 (found by adding 2 plus 3 and then multiplying by 4) or is it 14 (found by multiplying 3 times 4 and then adding 2)? Because two answers are possible in cases such as this, a hierarchy for performing operations, called the order of operations, was developed. The order of operations, listed below, should be used when evaluating an expression containing more than one operation.

1. Operations in parentheses. If multiple parentheses exist, perform the operations left to right and working from the inside to the outside.
2. Perform exponents calculations.
3. Perform multiplication and division from left to right.
4. Perform addition and subtraction from left to right.

A common abbreviation for these steps is the expression "Please Excuse My Dear Aunt Sally" (PEMDAS), which corresponds to "Parentheses, Exponents, Multiplication, Division, Addition, Subtraction." The following example shows the sequence of evaluating the expression $3 \times 5 - (12 + 8) \div 4 + 2^2$:

$$3 \times 5 - (12 + 8) \div 4 + 2^2$$
$$3 \times 5 - 20 \div 4 + 2^2$$
$$3 \times 5 - 20 \div 4 + 4$$
$$15 - 20 \div 4 + 4$$
$$15 - 5 + 4$$
$$10 + 4 = 4$$

ACTIVITY 17-12

COMBINING LIKE TERMS WITH MODELS

PROCEDURE:
Use base-ten blocks or Algebra Tiles to simplify the following problems:

1. $(x + 5) + (x - 3)$
2. $(x^2 - 3x + 3) + (x^2 + 5x - 4)$
3. $(x^2 + 2x + 7) - (x^2 - 2)$
4. $(2x + 3) (x - 3)$
5. $(x^2 + x + \text{-}7) / (x + 4)$

ACTIVITY 17-11

MODELING THE PROPERTIES

PROCEDURE:
Use color tiles, counters, graphing paper, or another manipulative to show the following true statements:

1. $3 + 5 = 5 + 3$
2. $4 \times 7 = 7 \times 4$
3. $4 \times (2 + 7) = 4 \times 9$

In evaluating expressions such as $3n + 6$ and $7 - ((\frac{n}{2}) - 3)$, the order of operation rules must be applied. When $n = 10$, the values for the above expressions are 36 and 5, respectively.

Writing the steps for solving the expression one stage at a time may seem cumbersome at first, but taking shortcuts at the beginning can result in inaccurate answers, especially when additional operations of multiplication and division are included later. Writing each stage of the solution process will allow for more accurate solutions and an easier process for checking answers.

Simple calculators perform operations in the order entered, for example, pressing $2 + 3 \times 4 =$ produces 20. This is referred to as *chain* computation. Also available for elementary-school children are low-cost calculators that are designed to follow order of operation rules. For example, on the Texas Instruments Math Explorer, pressing $2 \boxed{+} 3 \boxed{\times} 4$ and $\boxed{=}$ gives an answer of 14. Computers are programmed to utilize the order of operations rules.

Several computer programs that provide practice with order of operations are available. In the strategy game "How the West Was One + Two × Three" (Sunburst), players create equations using three randomly generated numbers with two different operations of their choice to produce answers in order to move a stagecoach or locomotive along a trail. For example, possible answers using the numbers 6, 2, and 5 include $6 \div 2 + 5 = 8$, $(6 - 5) \times 2 = 2$, and $6 - 5 \times 2 = -4$.

The commercial game "Krypto" (Creative Publications) for two to eight players is based on the same idea. The game includes a deck of 52 cards numbered as follows: three each 1 through 10, two each 11 through 17, and one each 18 through 25. Five cards are dealt to each player and a common objective card for all players is turned up. The first player to use his or her five numbers, together with any combination of the operations, to match the objective card number wins the hand.

The commercial game "24" (Creative Publications) has children compete to see who can find an arrangement of 4 given numbers to reach the designated value of 24 by incorporating the order of operations conventions. Given the numbers 5, 2, 2, and 1, a possible solution would include $5^2 - 2 + 1$. License plate mathematics is another way to practice the order of operation. A fictitious license plate is given with a combination of numbers. Children compete to find the largest value possible using the conventions of the order of operations and the numbers available. Another alternative is to use dice or number cubes to generate the numbers. A player shakes three to five dice and uses the numbers together with any combination of the operations to make an equation.

Several problem-solving activities requiring the use of grouping symbols to alter the order of operations are suggested by Sanfiorenzo (1991):

ACTIVITY 17-13

CALCULATOR EXPLORATIONS

PROCEDURE:
Perform the operations as they occur left to right on paper first and then explore the order of operations for the following problems using a calculator.

1. $12 - 3 + 5$
2. $24 + 3 \times 2$
3. $-3 - 8 - 1$
4. $3 + \frac{5}{2}$
5. $24 - 4^2$

1. Use grouping symbols to make a sentence true.

   Example: $11 - 5 \times 2 + 3 = 30$

   Solution: $(11 - 5) \times (2 + 3) = 30$

2. Use grouping symbols to produce multiple values for an expression.

   Example: $4 + 8 \div 4 - 2$

   Solution: $(4 + 8) \div (4 - 2) = 6$
   $\qquad\quad (4 + 8) \div 4 - 2 = 1$

3. Find operations and use grouping symbols to make a sentence true.

   Example: $5 \square 4 \square 2 = 2$

   Solution: $(5 - 4) \times 2 = 2$

Activities 17-13 and 17-14 will help students better understand order of operations.

UNDERSTANDING ALGEBRAIC EQUATIONS

An algebraic equation is formed when two or more algebraic expressions containing at least one variable are joined by an equal sign, such as $4x + 7 = 19$. The Sixth NAEP (Blume & Heckman, 1992) found that 48% of eighth graders were able to solve equations involving unknowns; however, only 25% could generate an equation when given a table of data containing missing values. These findings show that teachers should provide more real tables of data that require children to extend and generalize the pattern, and help children to use algebraic equations to do so.

ACTIVITY 17-14 ▶

ARITHMETIC RABBITS

PROCEDURE:

1. Draw a rabbit—4 squares, 2 ears, and 1 tail.

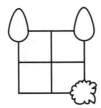

2. Write any four numbers in the four squares.

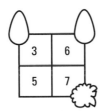

3. Add across and down and write the sums. Add diagonally and write the sums in the ears.

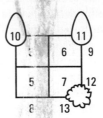

4. Add the two "across" sums. Write this number in the tail. Add the two "down" sums. Add the two "diagonal" sums. What do you notice?

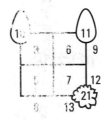

- Do this using your own four numbers. Is the final sum always the same? Why?
- Try this with multiplication instead of addition.
- Now try it using subtraction.

Early Equations Development

Nibbelink (1990) outlined an instructional sequence for teaching equations that provides a gradual transition from arithmetic to algebra. In the early stages (up to the middle of Grade 2), he recommends working with basic facts in vertical, rather than horizontal, format because young children can more easily discriminate up from down than right from left. Many children read $\square - 5 = 3$ as $3 = 5 - \square$ and write 2 or even 8 in the blank, yet this type of reversed reading rarely occurs when problems are written in vertical form. Nibbelink recommends the following gradual steps:

Step 1: *Hidden and missing numbers.* Story lines and special characters are used at this stage. For example, a cat wearing a large mitten covers a number with its paw and a gerbil eats a hole in the paper where a number was written (Figure 17-14).

Step 2: *Replaced numbers.* The character at this stage (which can begin about the middle of Grade 3) is a thief who steals numbers and leaves, as a mark, the letter of his or her first name at the scene of the crime. The idea is that the letter marks the spot and the task is to replace that letter with the number that will make the sentence true (Figure 17-15). In this context, it is reasonable that a given letter can replace different numbers in

FIGURE 17-14 ▶

Hidden Number	Missing Number

FIGURE 17-15 ▶

 Replaced numbers

$$\begin{array}{r} 23 \\ +B \\ \hline 29 \end{array}$$

$$4 \times H = 28$$
$$T - 3 = 18$$

PRINCIPLES AND STANDARDS LINK 17-7
Content Strand: Algebra

Most middle-grade students will need considerable experience with linear equations before they will be comfortable and fluent in transforming or solving them. (NCTM, 2000, p. 226) different problems, and that in a given problem any one letter will always represent the same number. This provides a beginning for the understanding of variables.

Step 3: *Number aliases (unknowns).* The idea in this stage (beginning in the middle of Grade 4) is that numbers use aliases that are letters of the alphabet. Note that different numbers can use the same alias in different problems and that a given number can choose different pseudonyms from problem to problem. The task in $P + 8 = 13$ is to find which number is using the name P in this instance. Thus, the letter is a name for a number. Solving equations is likened to detective work aimed at finding the true (number) identity of the letter. Children do not see a variable as only one number any longer, but rather as an unknown with many possibilities yet only one known value for the specific scenario.

Step 4: *Variables over specified domains.* The formal concept of a variable is studied in algebra courses.

In the early grades, children find missing or unknown numbers in open number sentences by using their knowledge of basic facts or by applying the guess-and-check strategy. For example, if $m - 6 = 8$, then $m = 14$ because $14 - 6 = 8$. If they had first selected, say 16 from a guess-and-check method, they would plug the value in to find that the expression $16 - 6$ is 10, which is high for the value of 8, and therefore in need of adjustment. In the intermediate years, children begin to learn procedures to solve equations that rely on inverse relationships, noting, for example, that because addition and subtraction are *inverse* operations (see Chapter 7), subtraction will undo addition and vice versa.

Kieran (1988) found two different perspectives on solving equations among children in beginning (Grade 7) algebra. One group used the guess-and-check approach by substituting different numbers for the letter until they found one that made the sentence true. Another group used inverses of the operations and transposed terms to the other side to solve for the variable. Kieran recommended that elementary-school experiences with placeholders should emphasize the substitution method, because this method lends greater meaning to the idea that the letter is really a number in its own right within the equation.

Modeling Algebraic Equations

As discussed in the previous section on equality, the notion of balance as a metaphor for an equation is powerful. Teachers should provide children with experiences using pan balance scales to help them recognize that any operation performed on one side of an equation must be balanced with the same operation on the other side. Balance scales help children understand that removing or adding something to one pan of the balance scale will offset the balance unless the same procedure is performed to the other pan.

Several models for balancing and solving equations, such as Hands-on Algebra, pan balances, base-ten blocks, and Algebra Tiles, are commercially available. Each model offers an interesting method of representing equations, balancing operational activities, and solving for unknown quantities. Figure 17-16 shows how an equation is represented with each model. Each model offers a method of "seeing" the equation and recognizing the significance of the equal sign, the need for balancing the equations as the solution is explored, and the concept of a unique solution to an equation, independent of the variable used.

Figure 17-17 shows a method of using colored chips (white for positive numbers, black for negative numbers) and some device to represent the unknown for the equation $x + 5 = 2x - 3$. This example moved slowly to remove an x and add a 3 to both sides to find the solution of 8. After finding the unknown value of the variable, this method also allows children to replace the unknowns to verify their answer.

The next step is to reconnect with the order of operations procedures discussed previously. Children may need to combine like terms in order to find solutions. Like terms refers to a single term (a *monomial* term) whose variables, as well as the powers of each variable, correspond. For example, $3x$ and $2x$, $5x^2$ and $7x^2$ can be combined with methods discussed previously, as shown in Figure 17-18.

Algebra Tiles, or base-ten blocks in two colors, can be used to model equations in one or two variables (see Figure 17-18). These devices allow the introduction of a *trinomial* (three-term) polynomial, in which the highest power of one variable is 2 or less.

Binomial linear expressions, which are two-term polynomials with a highest power of 1, such as $(2x + 1)$ or $(3x - 7)$, can be used to demonstrate multiplication in an array, much like that used with base-ten blocks earlier (Figure 17-19). The result is called a *quadratic expression,* which involves x to the second power, also known as "x squared." Although the process involves variables, teachers should take particular care when showing students how this process matches whole-number multiplication (see Figure 17-19). The reverse process is used with quadratics to demonstrate division, often referred to as finding factors of the quadratic. Most algebra classes teach the process of using FOIL (*F*irst, *O*utside, *I*nside, *L*ast) to find multiply two binomial expressions together, as in the following example:

$$(2x + 3)(x + 1) = 2x^2 + 5x + 3$$

First terms $(2x)(x)$, Outside terms $(2x)(1)$, Inside terms $(3)(x)$, Last terms $(3)(1)$

FIGURE 17-16

CONCRETE MODELS FOR $2x + 5 = 17 - 4$

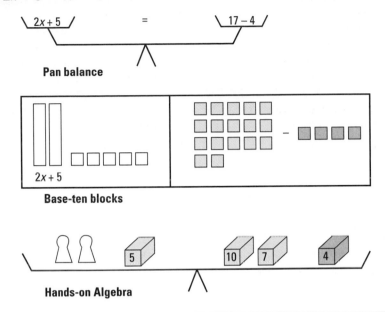

Pan balance

Base-ten blocks

Hands-on Algebra

FIGURE 17-17

MODEL FOR SOLVING $x + 5 = 2x - 3$

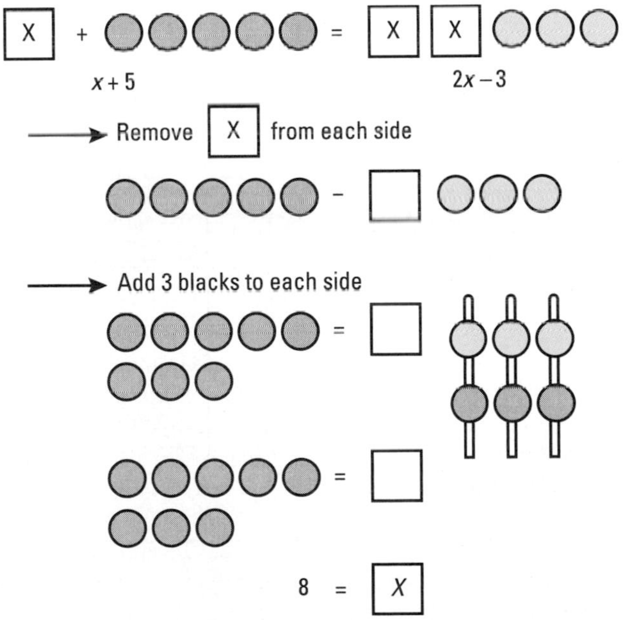

$x + 5$ $2x - 3$

Remove ☒ from each side

Add 3 blacks to each side

$8 = X$

Using the reverse thinking can help children find factors of a quadratic. For instance, when looking for factors of $2x^2 - 7x - 4$, students should first multiply 2 and 4 together. Next, they look for all the factors of 8, such as $(1, -8), (-1, 8), (2, -4), (-2, 4)$ that when added form -7. Now, decompose the -7x to be x and -8x. Rewrite the equation as four terms $(2x^2 - 8x + 1x - 4)$ and group the first two and the last two within parentheses $(2x^2 - 8) + (x - 4)$. Last, factor out any like terms in each set of parentheses $(2 \times (x - 4) + (x - 4))$. The final result will show that both terms possess a factor that is the same. Now, factor out the set of parentheses they share and the final result will be the factors $(x - 4)(2x + 1)$. Although the above technique is quite procedural, using Algebra

FIGURE 17-18

ALGEBRA TILES FOR ALGEBRA EXPRESSIONS AND EQUATIONS

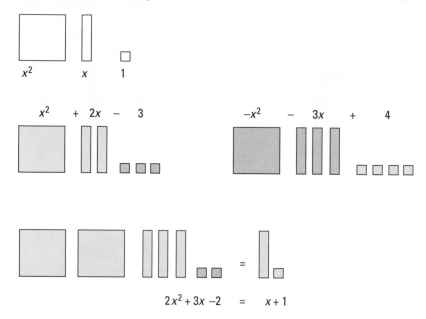

$$2x^2 + 3x - 2 = x + 1$$

FIGURE 17-19

MULTIPLICATION AND DIVISION MODELS USING ALGEBRA TILES

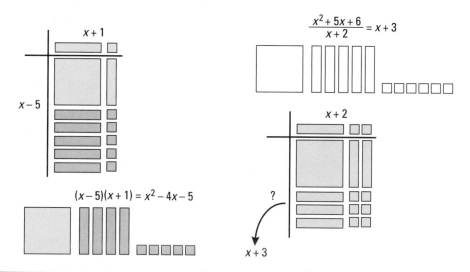

$$\frac{x^2 + 5x + 6}{x + 2} = x + 3$$

$$(x - 5)(x + 1) = x^2 - 4x - 5$$

Tiles to demonstrate the process and examining the graphs of quadratic expressions will make the process of finding factors a bit easier to understand (see Figure 17-20).

Spreadsheets or the table function on a graphing calculator should be used to examine the values and graphs of the linear equations: x, $2x$, $x + 1$. Examining many linear graphs and discussing the concept of the slope of a line and y intercepts will make graphing much more meaningful for

children. After exploring linear equations, try quadratics and cubic equations to help children generalize the typical graphing appearance of lines, parabolas, and cubic curves. Exploring graphing concepts is discussed later in this chapter.

Although these concepts usually occur in an algebra course, teachers should provide early informal lessons involving concrete models that illustrate the differences between a constant (or number), a binomial, or a trinomial

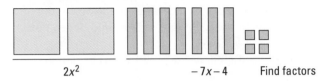

ALGEBRA TILES AND FACTORING

Reverse the multiplication process to find factors

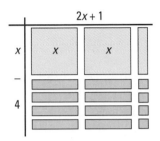

$2x^2$ $-7x - 4$ Find factors

$2x + 1$

x x x

$-$

4

Factors for $2x^2 - 7x - 4$

of power two (quadratic). Teaching lessons about the combining of like terms, performing simple operations, and solving equations will prove easier than expected and will lead to a better understanding of variables, expressions, equations, and functions.

Real-world Settings for Algebraic Equations

There are many real-world settings for problems using algebraic equations. Problems involving proportional reasoning, such as finding values of similar figure, identifying unit prices, and map/scale diagrams, can lead nicely into realistic algebraic equations in one variable. Although more than one approach can be used to solve a proportion, the traditional approach using a cross product will create an algebraic equation. The following are examples of real-world settings for which children can use algebraic equations to solve:

• A scale drawing of my backyard shows the length to be two more centimeters than twice the size of the width. The length was exactly 8 cm. If the scale factor of my diagram implies that every centimeter represents 3 yards, find the dimensions of my yard. Will I have enough fencing if I have 150 yards of material?

• Two out of 3 children drink 1 pint of milk at lunch each day. If the cafeteria sold 480 pints of milk today, how many people drank milk at lunch? How many people did not drink milk?

• Two ladders differ in length by 5 m. When the ladders are placed end to end, the total length is 70 m. What is the length of each ladder?

• A pet store always stocks 3 cats to every 2 dogs. All together there are 75 pets. How many of each pet do they have in stock?

• I have 43 cents in my pocket. What are the possible coins in my pocket?

• I have a recipe that serves 6 people. How many times should I make the recipe to serve 132 people?

Activity 17-15 will help children better understand algebraic equations.

Solving Inequalities

An *equation* is a statement that two expressions are equal. An *inequality* is a statement that one expression is greater than (or less than) the other. In the early grades, children learn to use the symbols $>$ and $<$ to write sentences expressing relationships between unequal numbers (for example, $2 < 5$ and $3 + 4 > 6$). Children need to practice using these symbols because they often confuse the signs or do not associate the terms "greater than" and "less than" with the proper symbols. When integers are introduced, additional practice is needed to see that $-4 > -8$. As with equations, the notion of balance applies to inequalities. However, with inequalities, the pan balance will show the two sides to be *out* of balance, with one pan higher than the other.

Solving an inequality containing a variable involves finding all possible values from the replacement set that will make the sentence true. For example, if the replacement set is the set of whole numbers, then the solution set for $x + 1 < 4$ consists of the numbers 0, 1, and 2. If the replacement set for this inequality is the integers, then the solution set consists of all integers less than 3—an infinite set. The solution in the set of rational numbers is expressed symbolically as $x < 3$, where x represents a rational number. Another method is to use the concept of infinity and parentheses, i.e. $(-\infty, 3)$. The solution sets

ACTIVITY 17-15

WHAT'S MY VALUE?

MATERIALS:
Algebra Tiles

PROCEDURE:
Use algebra tiles to simplify the following expressions

a) $4(x + 3) + 2(x - 1)$

b) $(3x^2 + 2x - 6) + (2x^2 - 4x + 5)$

c) $-3x - 7 - (-5x + 6)$

d) $(2x^2 - 4x - 5) - (x^2 - 4x + 7)$

Evaluate each expression when $x = 1$, when $x = 0$, and when $x = -1$.

should be found and can be expressed symbolically expressed on a number line such the following examples:

$4x + 2 < 14$ leads to $x < 3$ or $(-\infty, 3)$

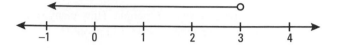

$4x - 8 > 2(x - 4)$ leads to $x \geq 0$ or $(0, +\infty)$

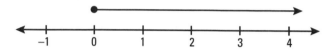

First, teachers should take special care to explain when the point is and is not included into the solution set and what it means to go to infinity. Next, show how to represent a combined solution set such as $x < -1$ and $x > 4$. All operational methods for solving equations and the order of operations apply to inequalities, with the exception of one specific situation. If the inequality requires the multiplication or division of a negative number, the result is that the sign flips the opposite way. This can be explained to children by comparing and contrasting the tables of data and the graphs for congruent inequalities such as $-x > 4$ and $x < -4$.

FUNCTIONS

The concept of function is one of the fundamental ideas in mathematics. In the school curriculum, a function is viewed both as a concept—the study of regularity—and as a process—analyzing relationships (Howden, 1989). "Joint variation is at the heart of understanding patterns and functions. As students grow in their ability to derive meaning for variables in contexts, they encounter variables that are changing in relation to each other" (Lappan, 1998, p. 57). This section discusses how teachers can help children understand functions.

What Is a Function?

When the value of one quantity (*dependent* variable) depends on or varies with the value of another (*independent* variable), we say that the first quantity is a function of the second quantity. For example, the height of a burning candle is a function of time: The longer the time it burns, the shorter the candle becomes.

In general, a *function* is a rule of correspondence connecting the elements of one set (the *domain* of the function) with the elements of another set (the *range* of the function) such that each member of the domain corresponds to a unique member of the range. For example, the perimeter of a square is determined by the length of

its sides. For each value of a side, there is one and only one corresponding value for the perimeter. The domain and the range of this function are the non-negative real numbers. In this case, the rule of correspondence can be expressed algebraically as an equation, $P = 4s$. It can also be represented as an arrow diagram, a table, and a graph (Figure 17-21). Using formal functional language and notation, we say that the perimeter of a square is a function of the length of its side and write $f(s) = 4s$.

Many equations written in two variables can be considered functions, if one variable depends on the input of the other variable. Another way of defining a rule of correspondence is to give all possible pairings of elements in a table or arrow diagram, as in Figure 17-22a. This

FIGURE 17-21

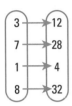

side s	perimeter 4 s
5	20
2	8
6	24
4	16

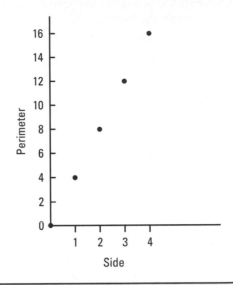

diagram is called a *mapping* of the relationship. The relation defined by the arrow diagram in Figure 17-22b is not a function because the element 3 in the domain corresponds to two different elements, 5 and 8, in the range. The relation represented in Figure 17-22c is a function even though two different elements in the domain are paired with the same element in the range. The key attribute of a function is that each first element corresponds to only one other element.

Developing Function Concepts

There are at least five different ways to represent a function. Each way communicates the same functional relationship. It is important that children be provided with as many different ways of viewing a function as possible so that they can meaningfully interpret situations. The representations include the following: contextual setting, table representations, language expressions, graphical representations, and symbolical representations

First and foremost, a function should begin with a contextual setting, preferably a real-world setting, to provide a meaningful experience with the function. Such settings help children understand the function.

Second, children should collect data and create a table. This is particularly important when the independent variable is ascending. With the help of a calculator and a few basic statistical options, data can be graphed to look for a pattern and an equation can be generalized. Starting with the data allows for a connection with the contextual problem. Using a calculator and the Computer-Based Lab (CBL™) probes to capture real data, such as the distance from a location or the temperature of an item, allows children to establish a pattern and make a generalization from the graph of the data. This technique will help students determine if each element is paired up to a unique functional value.

Language expression helps children describe the relationship in a meaningful and useful manner. The expression should be generated by describing, either in writing or in spoken words, the effects of one variable on the other and the relationship between the variables. This verbalization will provide a bridge to the other representations and provide an understanding of the function.

Graphical representation is the most commonly used mode of representing a function. A graph provides a visual representation of the function and can often help children understand the meaning of a situation. Children can interpret the relationship between the variables by analyzing the graphs as linear or nonlinear, increasing or decreasing, continuous or discontinuous. Analyzing graphs provides a close connection to the process of finding the equation. However, warning children that extrapolating the data to extend indefinitely may not make sense for the problem provided. Limitations may exist that are not being addressed through the extended graph or the data may not provide a clear functional relationship. For instance, if a teacher provides children with a list of student ID numbers and corresponding

FIGURE 17-22

(a) a function (b) not a function (c) a function

mathematics and science grades, they will see that a pattern does not necessarily emerge in all cases.

Converting the functional relationship into an equation results in a more abstract form than any of the previously mentioned representations. This method utilizes the symbolism often found in the mathematics curriculum. The general form assists in making calculations for any part of the function. The equation can be entered into a calculator to produce the table of data and the graph. This method allows us to explore the graph without the tedious job of plotting points.

The following problems can be used to practice using each representation of a function:

1. Suppose we need to convert the temperature reported to us in Fahrenheit into Celsius. The function $C(f) = \frac{5}{9}(f - 32)$ provides the converted value. Have children make a table of data for an assortment of temperatures. Encourage them to graph the ordered pairs (32, 0) and (212, 100). Connect the two points. Explore the connections between the table of data and the line they just created. Have children describe in their own words the reverse relationship for finding a temperature in Fahrenheit if the temperature is given in Celsius.

2. Imagine you are the vendor at a newspaper stand. *The New York Times* costs $1 per copy and the local paper costs 50 cents per copy. If you sell an average of 50 copies of each paper per day, find your weekly income based on this daily average. Make a chart showing the cumulative profits for the week and plot the data. Generalize the formula to find your cumulative income for any given day.

3. Explore all the possible rectangles that can be formed with a piece of string 24 inches long—the area and perimeter will vary in each. If you begin with the thinnest rectangle formed by integers, its dimensions will be 1 × 11 inches. List all possible integer dimensions in a table of data. Identify the shape that will produce the maximum area. Graph length and width and notice the functional relationship. Write a relationship that gives the area of the shape as the dimensions vary. In your own words, explain what occurs to the area as the length and width vary.

4. Ask children "Are you a square?" Have children measure the height and arm span of several classmates. Have them generate a table, plot the points, and generalize a pattern. Children should verbalize the relationship the look for other kinds of patterns that match this function. A student who is a short rectangle will have a height less than the arm span, a tall rectangle will have a height greater than the arm span, and a square's values will be equal.

5. Assign each group of children a different Cuisenaire rod. Have them calculate and tabulate the volume and surface area of their rod. Next, have them place another rod side-by-side, with the longest sides together. Have children calculate the volume and surface area again. Collect the data and graph the sequence number to the volume, the sequence number to the surface area, and the volume to the surface area. Ask children to explain in their own words what relationships they notice as they added a rod each time. Can they generalize this solution for each case? Examine the rods and the relationships in tabular, graphical, verbal form and as an equation of the other groups' findings.

Regardless of which representation is used, it is important to realize that each representation describes the relationship of the function. In fact, having children generate all five representations will provide a more diverse approach and provide different access routes for children with different learning styles.

Functional Patterns

In the primary grades, children's experiences with the concept of function focuses on number patterns and mathematical relationships. For example, children could explore the problem of finding the total number of eyes there are in a small group or in the class (Howden, 1989). They might do this by first counting, drawing pictures, or using chips or blocks to model the process and then making a table to record their findings (Figure 17-23). In the discussion, the teacher should encourage children to use words to describe the patterns and generalize the result. The children might relate the "eyes" pattern to skip counting, counting by twos, or adding two each time. The idea of a functional relationship is encountered in predicting (without continuing the pattern) the total number of eyes in a group of 10 children. When explaining their answer, children might say that the number of eyes is equal to the number of people added to itself or doubled (multiplied by 2). Writing the pattern rule in a generalized form as □ + □, or □ × 2, introduces the use of a variable as a placeholder for any (whole) number. In this example, the number of eyes is dependent on the number of children involved or f(children) $= 2 \times$ children. Similar problems involve finding the relationship between tricycles and the number of wheels or hands and the num-

FIGURE 17-23

children	1	2	3	4	10
eyes	2	4	6	8	—

ber of fingers. Children might also be asked to find real-world examples of relationships that match given rules, such as □ × 10.

Next, teachers should encourage the development of a functional relationship where one value is obviously dependent on another value by asking children to answer interesting questions that have a functional relationship. For instance, ask children "How many toothpicks are needed to make 10 triangles?" If the triangles are separate from one another, three toothpicks are needed for each triangle and the pattern rule is 3 × □. Suppose, however, that triangles can share a common side. Looking at the following table we predict that 21 toothpicks are needed to make 10 triangles. The rule can be expressed as 2 × □ + 1.

Try asking children the following questions:

- How many learning links or snap cubes can you connect together in relationship to the time given?

- How long will it take you to pass a ball around to 100 children?

- How far will a plastic car travel if the height of the ramp varies?

- How long will it take you to walk up a flight of stairs?

- What is the relationship between the time it takes you to get lunch and your position in line?

- How long do you spend on the bus given the distance the bus travels?

- How many Ping Pong balls would be needed to fill a room?

Function Machines and Tables

A popular way of introducing functions in the elementary grades is through "function machines." The idea is that something is fed into the machine (the "input") and operated on by a rule, and the resulting output comes out of the machine. Children's first exposure to a function machine should be with manipulatives at pre-K–2. For example, the rule may be that a shape drops in and the shape is shrunk down into one _ its size, or a given shape is dropped in and a shape with one more side out. Next, move into a number function machine. The rule "multiply by 3 and add 1" might first be described in words. Children can drop in several sequential numbers to see the effects of the function machine on their value. The task is to find for given "input" numbers the associated "output" numbers and record these numbers in a table, as in Figure 17-24a. Children can graph the values on a Cartesian graph to visualize the pattern. Later, this function would be represented using an algebraic expression: 3 × □ + 1 or 3n + 1.

A related activity is "guess my rule," in which the objective is to determine the rule used to produce a given set of values. The teacher should include special functions

FIGURE 17-24

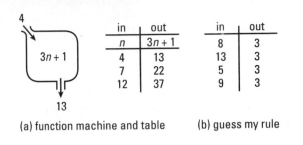

in	out
n	3n + 1
4	13
7	22
12	37

in	out
8	3
13	3
5	3
9	3

(a) function machine and table (b) guess my rule

such as the constant shown in Figure 17-24b. The rule might be verbalized as "the answer is always 3," or double the first number and add the second to get the third number. These explanations can then be expressed as a function and tested for the values provided to derive a set of values that fit the rule.

Sequences

A number *sequence* is an ordered set of numbers such that there is a *first term*, a *second term*, a *third term*, and so on. The arrangement proceeds from left to right, with each term separated by a comma. If the "in" values in a function table are 1, 2, 3, and so on, the corresponding "out" values constitute a sequence. Thus, a sequence is a function in which the "in" values are indicated by the position of the term (first—1, second—2, third—3, and so on).

Some sequences can be described algebraically by finding a pattern that relates the number of the term to the term itself. The pattern rule is called the general, or *n*th, term of the sequence. For example, the *n*th term of the sequence of positive even numbers 2, 4, 6, . . . is 2*n*, which means that every even number is the product of 2 and a counting number and that a given term of the sequence is found by replacing *n* in the general term by the term number. Thus, the 10th term is 2(10) = 20.

Other elementary sequences and their *n*th terms are:

NAME	SEQUENCE	NTH TERM
Counting numbers	$1, 2, 3, \ldots, n$	$f(n) = 2n$
Odd numbers	$1, 3, 5, \ldots, 2n - 1$	$f(n) = 2n - 1$
Multiples of 5	$5, 10, 15, \ldots, 5n$	$f(n) = 5n$
Skip counting	$4, 10, 16, \ldots, 6n - 2$	$f(n) = 6n - 2$
Square numbers	$1, 4, 9, \ldots, n^2$	$f(n) = n^2$
Triangular numbers	$1, 3, 6, \ldots, (n^2 + n)$	$f(n) = (n^2 + n)$

Given the first few terms of a sequence, children must find the rule for that pattern, write the next few terms, generalize the pattern to determine a term not found and, where possible, give the *n*th term.

The Fibonacci numbers are an interesting sequence, as follows:

$$0, 1, 1, 2, 3, \ldots\ldots f(n-1) + f(n)$$

Notice that each new value in the sequence is the sum of the previous two values. Explorations of the Fibonacci numbers can include generalizing the approximation for the golden ratio, 1618. . . . By looking at the ratio of $\frac{f(n)}{f(n-1)}$, the value will eventually approach the golden ratio.

Calculator Functions

Most inexpensive calculators have built-in constant features that permit the user to evaluate expressions such as $n + 3$, $n - 3$, $3n$, and $n \div 3$ for different values of the variable by entering a number and pressing $\boxed{=}$. For example, $3n$ is established by keying 3 $\boxed{\times}$. Successively pressing $5 \boxed{=}$, $8 \boxed{=}$, $12 \boxed{=}$ produces 15, 24, 36 in the display. To establish $n - 3$, press $\boxed{-} 3 \boxed{=}$. This calculator feature might be explored in conjunction with function machines to illustrate the idea of a machine operating on the input of sequential numbers according to a given rule to produce output numbers. Programmable calculators can, of course, handle more complex expressions.

Graphing calculators and CBL probes capture real data and generate a scatter plot of the data. Good exploratory questions can be asked to generate more interesting functional relationships. For instance, ask children to create a linear descending line, an increasing line, a parabola, a horizontal line, and a vertical line using a motion detector. They will find this challenging, perhaps even impossible. Asking them to speculate reasons why some functions work and some do not will lead to the generalization of the formula $d = rt$. Using probes and calculators allows one to look for patterns and to generalize many realistic formulas resulting from the graph of the data.

Collecting data that do not lend themselves well to analysis can often be entered into the calculator to identify the line of best fit. When collecting real data, the pattern is not always as obviously linear, or quadratic, as one might anticipate. The graphing calculator's statistical options allow for a formula or function relationship to emerge.

Graphing Functions

In geometry, children learn to plot ordered pairs of numbers on a coordinate system. A function can be represented graphically by thinking of the "in" and "out" elements in a table of values as the horizontal and the vertical coordinates, respectively, and plotting the points. The transition to naming the axes x and y is accomplished

by expressing the rule as an equation in x and y and using these variables as column headings in a table of values. Consider $y = 4x - 3$.

x	$y = 4x - 3$
1	1
2	5
3	7
4	?

Children's first experiences with graphing functions often involve familiar formulas such as $P = 4s$, which relates the length of a side of a square and its perimeter (Figure 17-25). Children can observe that the points lie on a line. Later, the points may be connected and extended. The teacher should encourage children to find how the relation "increasing the side by 1 increases the perimeter by 4" is manifested in the graph and how it directly relates to identifying the slope of a line of the given form $y = mx + b$. Children should be encouraged to examine two points and to calculate the rise versus the run. This value is called the *slope* and in the previous example will prove to be 4. The next interesting values result when the graph crosses the axes, in particular the y axis. Using the calculator to graph and adjust the m and b values will help children make generalizations about the role of the constants m and b. This is a particularly important development that many algebra students struggle with.

Graphs representing the formulas for the area of a square ($A = s^2$) and the volume of a cube ($V = s^3$) can also be constructed (Figure 17-26). Children will find that these are not straight-line graphs. A discussion of the family of graphs for lines, quadratics, and cubic equations will be more meaningful when the graphs are made available. The calculator can be used to explore many families of graphs and simple shifts in constants to see the effects of those shifts.

Children should be given a variety of graphs and asked to identify the type of graph, linear, quadratic, or cubic equation as well as a possible equation or scenario that matches the graph. This is an excellent exercise in making a connection between the symbolic, graphic, and contextual setting for function (see Figure 17-26).

Formulas

Children's first encounters with algebraic expressions usually involve *formulas* that contain more than one variable. For example, children discover that the perimeter of a rectangle can be found by adding twice the length and twice the width or by adding the length and width and doubling the result. After expressing this relationship in words, they write it using symbols: $P = 2l + 2w$, or $P = 2(l + w)$. The perimeters of different rectangles are then determined by substituting the values of their dimensions

FIGURE 17-25

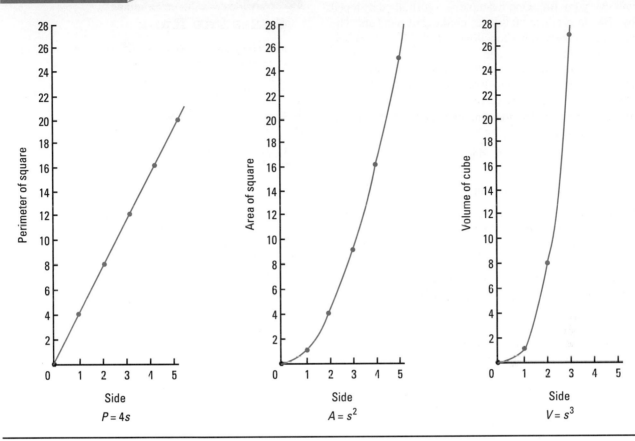

$P = 4s$

$A = s^2$

$V = s^3$

in the formula. Next, children quickly learn to cover up a shape with square color tiles; however, teachers do not always make it clear to children that this means finding the area of the rectangle. The dimensions become an integral part in the formula development of $A = lw$. Other well-known formulas include $V = lwh$ (volume of a rectangular prism), $A = \pi r^2$ (area of a circle), and $i = prt$ (simple interest).

FIGURE 17-26

GRAPHS MATCHED TO CONTAINERS

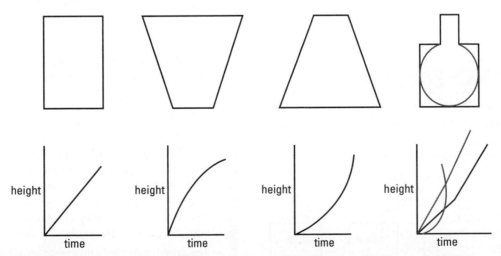

Have children verbalize the height of the water line of each container and match it to the appropriate graphs.

Mathematical formulas abound in science, business, and everyday life. One example is a formula developed by IBM to produce "fail-safe" credit card numbers. The last digit of the number functions as a check on the possibility that an error is made in transcribing the number into the computer. The last digit is determined using the following formula:

1. Add the digits in the odd-numbered positions and double this sum.
2. Count the number of odd-numbered digits greater than 4.
3. Add the even-numbered digits, except the last digit.
4. The last digit is the difference between the sum of (1), (2), and (3) and the next highest multiple of 10.

Example: Consider card number 3125-6001-9643-12

1. $(3 + 2 + 6 + 0 + 9 + 4 + 1) \times 2 = 50$
2. The number of these digits greater than $4 = 2$
3. $1 + 5 + 0 + 1 + 6 + 3 = 16$
4. $50 + 2 + 16 = 68$. The last digit is 2.

The computer receiving the credit card number is programmed to check the numbers entered against this formula. About 98% of the most common transcription errors are caught using this procedure.

Activities 17-16 through 17-20 will help children to better understand formulas.

Instruction and Assessment Activities

In addition to drawing graphs for formulas, children can take measurements or collect data for two related variables and plot the information on a graph. Problems of this nature include finding the relationship between height and armspan and between the distances around the

ACTIVITY 17-16

FUNCTION MACHINE

PROCEDURE:
Find the values returned from each of the function machines for the following input:

a) 3   b) -1   c) 5   d) $x + 1$

x2   −5   square   double −2

ACTIVITY 17-17

GUESS THE RULE

In each of the following sets of numbers, some kind of operation is performed on the first two numbers which are then combined with +, −, ×, or ÷ to obtain the third number. Try to determine the rule.

a) 1   3   5
    4   6   14

b) 2   3   13
    -1   5   26

c) 12   3   6
    45   12   21

d) 7   3   16
    5   2   9

ACTIVITY 17-18

CUISENAIRE ROD FUN

PROCEDURE:
Assign each group of children a different-sized Cuisenaire rod. Have children generate a table of data that records the stage, the volume, and the surface area of each stage. Stage one has just one rod, stage two has another rod right next to the first rod such that the long sides are connected. Stage three has three rods side-by-side (long sides together). Students should graph the following, look for generalized patterns, and discuss the concept of slope in the equation $y = mx + b$.

1. plot stage to volume
2. plot stage to surface area
3. plot volume to surface area

ACTIVITY 17-19

ANALYZE IT!

Calculate sample data values in the functional relationships below. Determine which is the dependent event and which is the independent event.

- The speed of a toy car compared with the height of ramp it runs down.
- The time it takes to pass a book along a line compared with the number of people in the line.
- The time it takes for the last person in line to go through the lunch line compared with the number of people in line.
- The time spent traveling in an airplane compared with the distance traveled.
- The time it takes an ice cube to melt compared with the temperature exerted on the ice cube.

ACTIVITY 17-20

WHICH IS MORE?

1. Determine which of two cylinders will hold more by taping a piece of paper with long sides together to form one cylinder and taping together a same-sized piece of paper with the short sides together. Have children experiment to see which container will hold more. To dramatize the difference, place the long, tall cylinder inside the short, fat cylinder. Fill the long cylinder to the top with popcorn. Ask children if they think the short, fat cylinder will hold the popcorn. Then, release the popcorn into the short, fat cylinder to see the result.

2. Give children a piece of ledger paper (11 in. × 14 in.) and have them make a box by cutting out squares from the corners. Have them find the dimensions of the box that has the maximum volume.

3. Present the following problem to students: A local pizza company offers a special on two 9-inch medium pizzas for the same price as a 15-inch large pizza. Which is a better deal: two medium pizzas or one large pizza? Why?

wrist and neck (Figure 17-27). If appropriate graphing software is available, some children may wish to construct these graphs on a computer.

Problems involving relationships between measurement concepts such as perimeter and area or volume and surface area provide further opportunities for children to generate data, organize them in a table, and construct a graph (Phillips, 1991). For example, if you had 100 m of fencing to enclose a rectangular garden plot, what dimensions would you choose? To investigate this problem, selected integer values for the base and height might be systematically listed and the areas of corresponding rectangles computed. A graph showing the relationship between the base and the area of these rectangles could then be drawn (Figure 17-28).

The table and graph reveal that the rectangle with the greatest area is actually a square with sides measuring 25 m. Long, narrow rectangles have small areas. In answering the original question of this example, other factors that might be considered in choosing the shape of the plot should also be identified.

Many of the activities to help children understand functions require them to describe patterns in words, extend patterns visually, represent relationships using tables and graphs, make predictions based on relationships, and generalize functional relationship. All of these components support the development of algebraic thinking.

FIGURE 17-27

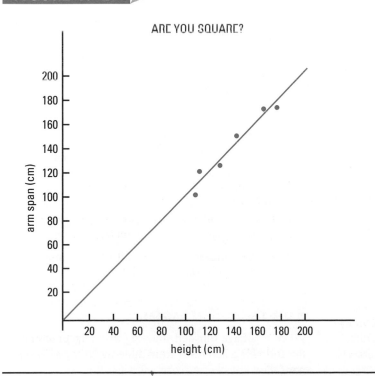

ARE YOU SQUARE?

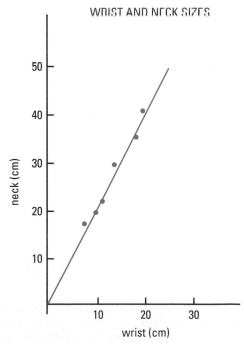

WRIST AND NECK SIZES

FIGURE 17-28

Perimeter = 100

Base	Height	Area
5	45	225
10	40	400
15	35	525
20	30	600
25	25	625
30	20	600
35	15	525
40	10	400
45	5	225

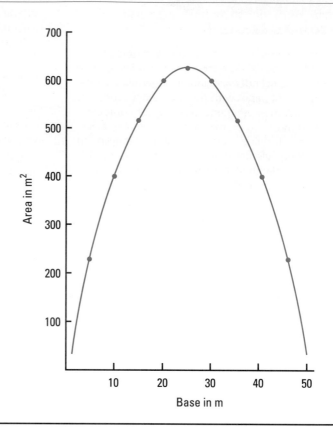

CONCLUSION

The development of algebraic thinking in the mathematics curriculum begins in the early grades and occurs as a gradual building from informal to formal concepts (Schultz, 1991). Key ideas that run through the grades include patterns, relationships, variables, exponents, expressions, properties, equations, inequalities, functions, and graphing. The transition from arithmetic to algebra provides many opportunities for children to engage in problem solving and to make connections. Experiences such as those described in this chapter will help children understand mathematics through sense-making activities as they study algebraic thinking during the primary years through to algebra in the middle-school and high-school years.

For Your Journal

When you have finished studying this chapter, reflect on the following questions in your math journal:

1. Give an example of a model to help children understand each operation on integers. Draw a picture to show how to solve each problem using the model you chose.

2. Discuss how to help children develop an understanding of variables and integers.

3. Describe how to teach children about integers in equations, including the order of operations, exponents, and problem-solving techniques. Be sure to utilize some of the models discussed.

4. Discuss several real-world situations that are functions. Illustrate each function using all five representations.

5. Visit a middle-school classroom and informally interview several children to assess their understanding of variables and integers. Ask the children questions such as the following:
- What does the expression $3b$ mean?
- What is n if $n - 4 = 9$? $2n = n$? $2n = 1$?
- Which is greater, $2n$ or $n + 2$? Explain.

6. Describe children's understandings and misconceptions about algebraic thinking.

For Your Portfolio

When you have finished studying this chapter, complete the following activities to include in your professional portfolio:

1. Write a lesson plan that would encourage children to develop a geometric pattern and connect it to a table of data that would generalize the nth term.

2. Examine a mathematics textbook's section on operations on integers. Describe the models used in the textbook to represent operations on integers.

3. Using a model and an operation of your choice, write a lesson plan to introduce an operation with integers to middle-school children.

4. Write a lesson plan using a real-world situation to introduce the concept of variables to middle-school children.

5. Using a model of your choice, write a lesson plan to introduce a method for solving an equation.

Resources for Teachers

Children's Literature
Anno, M. (1983). *Anno's multiplying jar*
Anno, M. (1994). *Anno's magic seed*
Pittman, H. (1986). *A grain of rice.* New York: Bantam Double-day Dell.
Schwartz, D. (1998). *How much is a million?* New York: Mulberry.
Scieszka, J. & Smith, L. (1995). *Math curse.* Viking.

Books on algebraic thinking
Charles, L. H. (1990). *Algebra thinking: First experiences.* Sunnyvale, CA: Creative Publications.
Dalton, L. (1983). *Algebra in the real world.* Parsippany, NJ: Dale Seymour Publications.
Picciotto, H. (1990). *The algebra lab: Middle school.* Sunnyvale, CA: Creative Publications.

Links to the Internet

Math Explorer: Algebra
http://explorer.scrtec.org/explorer/explorer-db/browse/static/Mathematics/browse/f83.html

Contains many lessons on and lists of other resources for algebraic ideas.

Eisenhower Regional Consortium
http://www.ael.org/eisen

A Web page from the Eisenhower Regional Consortium that uses building blocks to teach algebraic concepts as well as graphing calculator activities to download for free.

Project Interactivate
http://www.shodor.org/interactivate/activities/index.html

Activities on functions and algebra concepts such as linear functions, plotting, and graphs on the coordinate plane, function machines, and reading graphs.

K–12 Software
http://archives.math.utk.edu/K12.html software

An assortment of free and shareware software programs that will allow you to search for patterns and graph data as well as many other math programs and activities. Algebra Editor, Algebra +, and Algebra Grapher are a few of the programs available.

Learner
http://www.learner.org

Free or relatively inexpensive materials on algebraic thinking.

Appendix

Blackline Masters

1. BASE-TEN BLOCKS

2. TEN FRAMES

3. HUNDREDS CHART (0–99)

4. HUNDREDS CHART (1–100)

5. TEN-BY-TEN MULTIPLICATION ARRAY

6. FRACTION CIRCLES (*Whole, Halves, Thirds, Fourths*)

7. FRACTION CIRCLES (*Fifths, Sixths, Eighths, Ninths*)

8. FRACTION CIRCLES (*Tenths, Twelfths, Fifteenths, and Sixteenths*)

9. FRACTION BARS (*Whole, Halves, Thirds, Fourths, Fifths, Sixths, Eighths, Ninths, Tenths, and Twelfths*)

10. DECIMAL GRIDS

11. GEOBOARD TEMPLATE

12. GEOBOARD RECORDING PAPER

13. CENTIMETER DOT PAPER

14. TANGRAM

15. CENTIMETER GRID PAPER

16. INCH GRID PAPER

BLM-1 Base-Ten Blocks

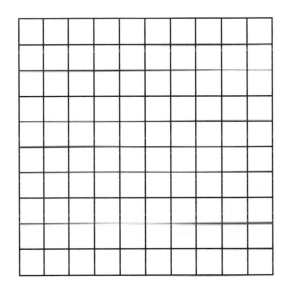

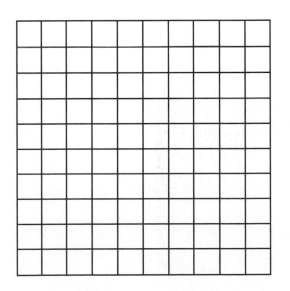

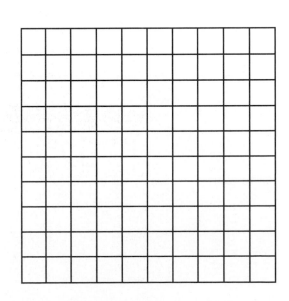

BLM-2 Ten Frames

BLM-3 Hundreds Chart (0–99)

0	1	2	3	4	5	6	7	8	9
10	11	12	13	14	15	16	17	18	19
20	21	22	23	24	25	26	27	28	29
30	31	32	33	34	35	36	37	38	39
40	41	42	43	44	45	46	47	48	49
50	51	52	53	54	55	56	57	58	59
60	61	62	63	64	65	66	67	68	69
70	71	72	73	74	75	76	77	78	79
80	81	82	83	84	85	86	87	88	89
90	91	92	93	94	95	96	97	98	99

BLM-4   Hundreds Chart (1–100)

1	2	3	4	5	6	7	8	9	10
11	12	13	14	15	16	17	18	19	20
21	22	23	24	25	26	27	28	29	30
31	32	33	34	35	36	37	38	39	40
41	42	43	44	45	46	47	48	49	50
51	52	53	54	55	56	57	58	59	60
61	62	63	64	65	66	67	68	69	70
71	72	73	74	75	76	77	78	79	80
81	82	83	84	85	86	87	88	89	90
91	92	93	94	95	96	97	98	99	100

BLM-5   Ten-by-Ten Multiplication Array

BLM-6 Fraction Circles

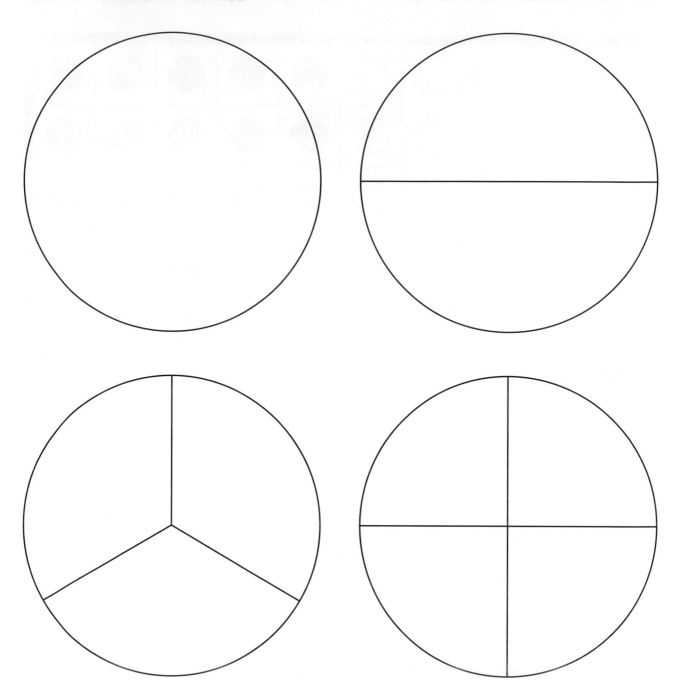

BLM-7   **Fraction Circles**

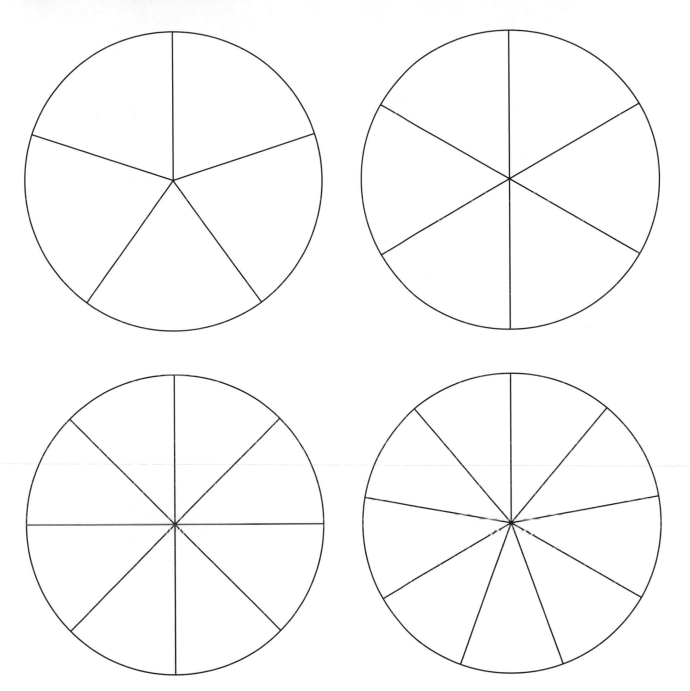

BLM-8 Fraction Circles

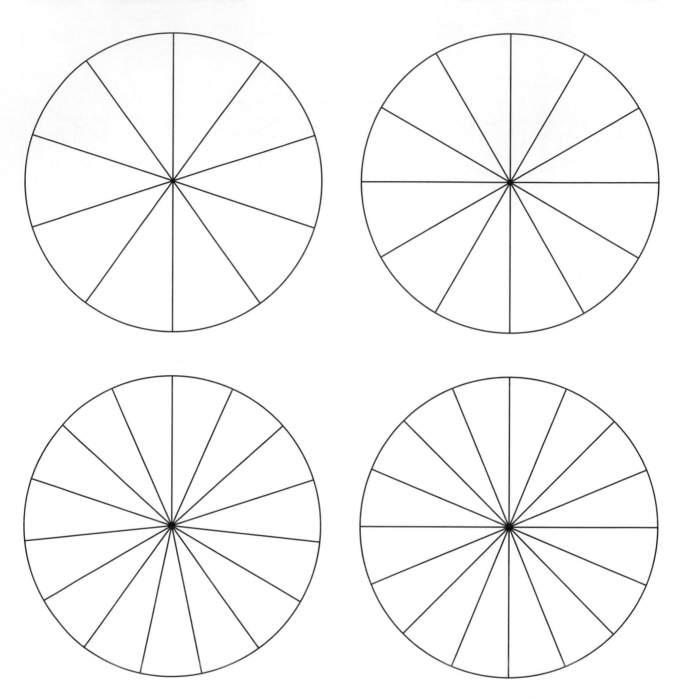

BLM-9 Fraction Bars

whole

| halves | $\frac{1}{2}$ | $\frac{2}{2}$ |

| thirds | $\frac{1}{3}$ | $\frac{2}{3}$ | $\frac{3}{3}$ |

| fourths | $\frac{1}{4}$ | $\frac{2}{4}$ | $\frac{3}{4}$ | $\frac{4}{4}$ |

| fifths | $\frac{1}{5}$ | $\frac{2}{5}$ | $\frac{3}{5}$ | $\frac{4}{5}$ | $\frac{5}{5}$ |

| sixths | $\frac{1}{6}$ | $\frac{2}{6}$ | $\frac{3}{6}$ | $\frac{4}{6}$ | $\frac{5}{6}$ | $\frac{6}{6}$ |

| eighths | $\frac{1}{8}$ | $\frac{2}{8}$ | $\frac{3}{8}$ | $\frac{4}{8}$ | $\frac{5}{8}$ | $\frac{6}{8}$ | $\frac{7}{8}$ | $\frac{8}{8}$ |

| ninths | $\frac{1}{9}$ | $\frac{2}{9}$ | $\frac{3}{9}$ | $\frac{4}{9}$ | $\frac{5}{9}$ | $\frac{6}{9}$ | $\frac{7}{9}$ | $\frac{8}{9}$ | $\frac{9}{9}$ |

| tenths | $\frac{1}{10}$ | $\frac{2}{10}$ | $\frac{3}{10}$ | $\frac{4}{10}$ | $\frac{5}{10}$ | $\frac{6}{10}$ | $\frac{7}{10}$ | $\frac{8}{10}$ | $\frac{9}{10}$ | $\frac{10}{10}$ |

| twelfths | $\frac{1}{12}$ | $\frac{2}{12}$ | $\frac{3}{12}$ | $\frac{4}{12}$ | $\frac{5}{12}$ | $\frac{6}{12}$ | $\frac{7}{12}$ | $\frac{8}{12}$ | $\frac{9}{12}$ | $\frac{10}{12}$ | $\frac{11}{12}$ | $\frac{12}{12}$ |

BLM-10   Decimal Grids

BLM-11   Geoboard Template

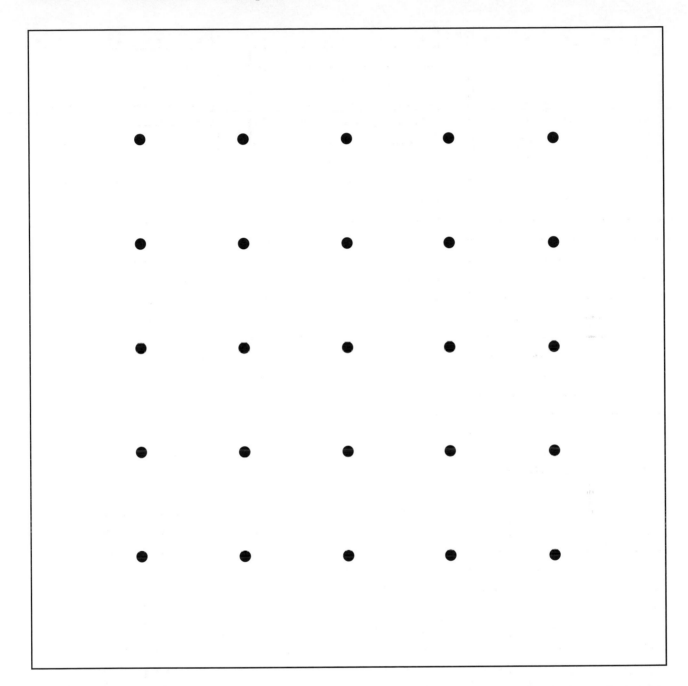

BLM-12 Geoboard Recording Paper

BLM-13 Centimeter Dot Paper

BLM-14   Tangram

BLM-15   Centimeter Grid Paper

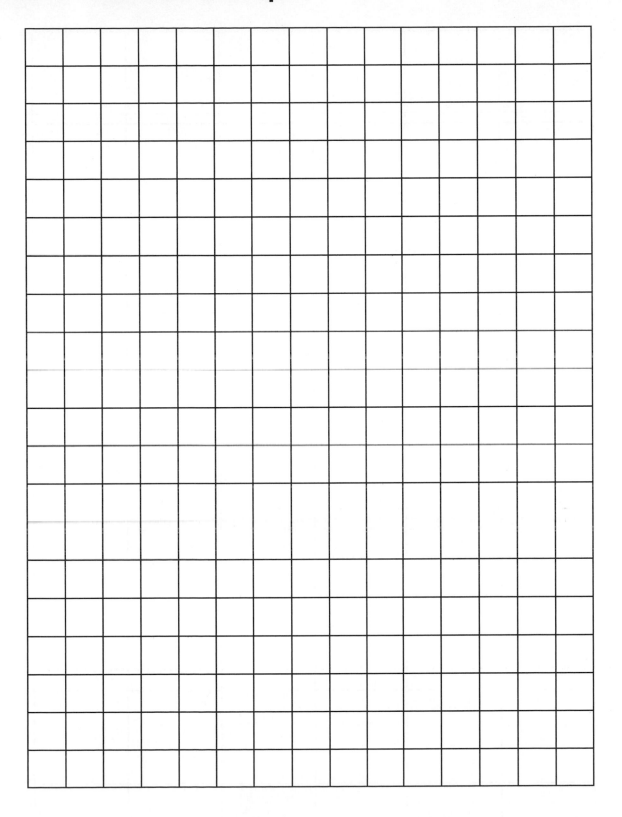

BLM-16 Inch Grid Paper

References

Chapter 1

Atherlay, S. (1995). *Math in the bath (and other fun places, too!)*. New York: Simon & Schuster Books for Young Readers.

Behr, M. J., Lesh, R., Post, T. R., & Silver, E. A. (1983). Rational number concepts. In R. Lesh & M. Landau (Eds.), *Acquisition of mathematics concepts and processes* (pp. 91–126). New York: Academic Press.

Bezuk, N. S., Whitehurst-Payne, S., & Aydelotte, J. (2000) Successful collaborations with parents to promote equity in mathematics. In W. G. Secada (Ed.), *Changing the faces of mathematics* Reston, VA: National Council of Teachers of Mathematics, 143–148.

Brownell, W. A. (1947). An experiment on "borrowing" in third grade arithmetic. *Journal of Educational Research, 41*(3), 161–171.

Brownell, W. A., & Moser, H. E. (1949). Meaningful vs. mechanical learning: A study in grade 3 subtraction. *Duke University Studies in Education 8,* 1–27.

Browning, C. A., & Channell, D. E. (1992). A "handy" database activity for the middle school classroom. *Arithmetic Teacher, 40*(4), 235–238.

Cappo, M., & Osterman, G. (1991). Teach students to communicate mathematically. *The Computing Teacher (How Learning & Leading with Technology), 18*(5), 34–39.

Clement, R. (1991). *Counting on Frank*. Milwaukee, WI: Gareth Stevens Publishing, (Grades 3–6)

Dossey, J. A., & Mullis, I. V. S. (1997). NAEP mathematics: 1990–1992: The national, trial state, and trend assessments. In P. A. Kenney and E. A. Silver (Eds.), *Results from the Sixth Mathematics Assessment of the National Assessment of Educational Progress* (pp. 17–32). Reston, VA: National Council of Teachers of Mathematics.

Edmark Corporation (1993). *Millie's math house* [Computer Software]. Redmond, WA: Author.

Friel, S. (1983). Lemonade's the name, simulation's the game. *Classroom Computer News, 3,* 34–39.

Glennon, V. J. (1963). Some perspectives in education. In *Enrichment mathematics for the grades* (27th Yearbook). Washington, DC: National Council of Teachers of Mathematics.

Hembree, R., & Dessart, D. J. (1986). Effects of hand-held calculators in precollege mathematics education: A meta-analysis. *Journal for Research in Mathematics Education, 17*(2), 83–99.

Hiebert, J. (1990). The role of routine procedures in the development of mathematical competence. In T. J. Cooney and C. R. Hirsch (Eds.), *Teaching and learning mathematics in the 1990s* (1990 Yearbook, pp. 31–40). Reston, VA: National Council of Teachers of Mathematics.

Hyde, J. S., Fennema, E., & Lamon, S. J. (1990). Gender differences in mathematics performance: A meta-analysis. *Psychological Bulletin, 109,* 139–155.

Jensen, R. J. (Ed.). (1993). *Research ideas for the classroom: Early childhood mathematics*. New York: Macmillan.

Kenney, P. A., & Silver, E. A. (Eds.). (1997). *Results from the Sixth Mathematics Assessment of the National Assessment of Educational Progress.* Reston, VA: National Council of Teachers of Mathematics.

Lapointe, A. E., Mead, N. A., & Phillips, G. W. (1989). *A world of differences: An international assessment of mathematics and science* (Report No. 19-CAEP-01). Princeton, NJ: Educational Testing Service.

Mathematical Sciences Education Board and National Research Council (1989). *Everybody counts: A report to the nation on the future of mathematics education*. Washington, DC: National Academy Press.

Mathematical Sciences Education Board and National Research Council. (1990). *Reshaping school mathematics: A philosophy and framework for curriculum*. Washington, DC: National Academy Press.

McKenzie, W. S. (1990). Meaning: The common element in both reading and mathematics. *Ontario Mathematics Gazette, 28*(3), 8–13.

Meyer, M. R. (1989). Gender differences in mathematics. In M. M. Lindquist (Ed.), *Results from the Fourth Mathematics Assessment*. Reston, VA: National Council of Teachers of Mathematics.

Meyer, M. R., & Fennema, E. (1992). Girls, boys, and mathematics. In T. R. Post (Ed.), *Teaching mathematics in grades K–8: Research-based methods* (pp. 443–464). Boston: Allyn & Bacon.

Morgan, M. T., & Robinson, N. (1976). The "Back to the Basics" movement in education. *Canadian Journal of Education, 1*(2), 1–11.

Mullis, I. V. S. (1997). *Benchmarking to international achievement: Attaining excellence: TIMSS as a starting point to examine student achievement*. Washington, DC: U.S. Department of Education, Office of Educational Research and Improvement.

National Council of Supervisors of Mathematics. (1977). Position statement on basic skills. *Arithmetic Teacher, 25*(1), 18–22.

National Council of Supervisors of Mathematics. (1988). Essential mathematics for the 21st century. Unpublished paper.

National Council of Teachers of Mathematics. (1977, October). Position statement on basic skills. *Arithmetic Teacher, 25*(1), 18.

National Council of Teachers of Mathematics. (1980). *An agenda for action.* Reston VA: Author.

National Council of Teachers of Mathematics. (1989). *Curriculum and evaluation standards for school mathematics.* Reston, VA: Author.

National Council of Teachers of Mathematics. (1991). *Professional standards for teaching mathematics.* Reston VA: Author.

National Council of Teachers of Mathematics. (1991, February). *Position statement on calculators and the education of youth.* Reston, VA: National Council of Teachers of Mathematics.

National Council of Teachers of Mathematics. (1995). *Assessment standards for school mathematics.* Reston VA: Author.

National Council of Teachers of Mathematics (2000). *Principles and Standards for School Mathematics.* Reston, VA: Author.

Owens, D. T. (Ed.). (1993). *Research ideas for the classroom: Middle grades mathematics.* New York: Macmillan.

Reys, B. J., & Reys, R. E. (1987). Calculators in the classroom: How can we make it happen? *Arithmetic Teacher, 34*(6), 12–14.

Scieszka, J., & Smith, L. (1995). *Math curse.* New York: Penguin. (Grades 2–6).

Suydam, M. N. (1984). Research report: Manipulative materials. *Arithmetic Teacher, 31*(5), 27.

Travers, K. J., & McKnight, C. C. (1984). *International Association for the Evaluation of Educational Achievement—Second Study of Mathematics—The International Mathematics Curriculum.* Urbana-Champaign, IL: International Coordinating Center.

U.S. Department of Education, National Center for Education Statistics. (1996). *Pursuing excellence: A study of U.S. eighth-grade mathematics and science teaching, learning, curriculum, and achievement in international context.* Washington, DC: U.S. Government Printing Office.

U.S. Department of Education, National Center for Education Statistics. (1997). *Pursuing excellence: A study of U.S. fourth-grade mathematics and science achievement in international context.* Washington, DC: U.S. Government Printing Office.

Chapter 2

Artzt, A. L., & Newman, C. M. (1990a). Implementing the standards: Cooperative learning. *Mathematics Teacher, 83*(6), 448–452.

Artzt, A. L., & Newman, C. M. (1990b). *How to use cooperative learning in the mathematics class.* Reston, VA: National Council of Teachers of Mathematics.

Ashlock, R. B., Johnson, M. L., Wilson, J. W., & Jones, W. L. (1983). *Guiding each child's learning of mathematics: A diagnostic approach to instruction.* Columbus, OH: Merrill.

Azzolino, A. (1990). Writing as a tool for teaching mathematics: The silent revolution. In T. J. Cooney and C. R. Hirsch (Eds.), *Teaching and learning mathematics in the 1990s* (1990 NCTM Yearbook, pp. 92–100). Reston, VA: National Council of Teachers of Mathematics.

Bartels, B. H. (1995). Promoting mathematics connections with concept mapping. *Mathematics Teaching in the Middle School, 1*(7), 542–549.

Behr, M. J., Lesh, R., Post, T. R., & Silver, E. A. (1983). Rational number concepts. In R. Lesh & M. Landau (Eds.), *Acquisition of mathematics concepts and processes* (pp. 91–126). New York: Academic Press.

Burns, M. (1998). *Math: Facing an American phobia.* Sausalito, CA: Math Solutions Publications.

Burton, G. M. (1985). Writing as a way of knowing in a mathematics education class. *Arithmetic Teacher, 33*(4), 40–45.

Butler, K. (1988). Learning styles. *Learning 17* (4), 30–34.

Clements, D. H., & McMillen, S. (1996). Rethinking "concrete" manipulatives. *Teaching Children Mathematics, 2*(5), 270–275.

Confrey, J. (1990). What constructivism implies for teaching. In R. B. Davis, C. A. Maher, and N. Noddings (Eds.). *Constructivist views on the teaching and learning of mathematics. (Journal for Research in Mathematics Education,* Monograph No. 4, pp. 107–122). Reston, VA: National Council of Teachers of Mathematics.

Davidson, N. (1990a). Small-group cooperative learning in mathematics. In T. J. Cooney and C. R. Hirsch (Eds.). *Teaching and learning mathematics in the 1990s* (1990 NCTM Yearbook, pp. 52–61). Reston, VA: National Council of Teachers of Mathematics.

Davidson, N. (1990b). *Cooperative learning in mathematics: A handbook for teachers.* Reading, MA: Addison-Wesley.

Davidson, D. M., & Pearce, D. L. (1988). Using writing activities to reinforce mathematics instruction. *Arithmetic Teacher, 35*(8), 42–45.

Evans, C. S. (1984, December). Writing to learn in math. *Language Arts, 61*(8), 828–835.

Fennell, F., & Ammon, R. (1985). Writing techniques for problem solvers. *Arithmetic Teacher, 33*(1), 24–25.

Gagné, R. M. (1985). *The conditions of learning and theory of instruction.* New York: Holt, Rinehart & Winston.

Ginsburg, H. P., & Baron, J. (1993). Cognition: Young children's construction of mathematics. In R. J. Jensen (Ed.), *Research ideas for the classroom: Early childhood mathematics* (pp. 3–21). New York: Macmillan.

Goldin, G. A. (1990). Epistemology, constructivism, and discovery learning in mathematics. In R. B. Davis, C. A. Maher, and N. Noddings (Eds.), *Constructivist views on the teaching and learning of mathematics. (Journal for Research in Mathematics Education,* Monograph No. 4, pp. 31–47). Reston, VA: National Council of Teachers of Mathematics.

Good, T. L., Reys, B. J., Grouws, D. A., & Mulryan, C. M. (1989/90). Using work-groups in mathematics instruction. *Educational Leadership, 47*(4), 56–62.

Hanselman, C. A. (1996). Using brainstorming webs in the mathematics classroom. *Mathematics Teaching in the Middle School, 1*(9), 766–777.

Hart, L. C., Schultz, K., Najee-Ullah, D., & Nash, L. (1992). The role of reflection in teaching. *Arithmetic Teacher, 40*(1), 40–42.

Hiebert, J. (1990). The role of routine procedures in the development of mathematical competence. In T. J. Cooney and

C. R. Hirsch (Eds.), *Teaching and learning mathematics in the 1990s* (1990 Yearbook, pp. 31–40). Reston, VA: National Council of Teachers of Mathematics.

Holmes, E. E. (1990). Motivation: An essential component of mathematics instruction. In T. J. Cooney and C. R. Hirsch (Eds.), *Teaching and learning mathematics in the 1990s* (1990 Yearbook, pp. 101–107). Reston, VA: National Council of Teachers of Mathematics.

Kamii, C. (1990). Constructivism and beginning arithmetic (K–2). In T. J. Cooney and C. R. Hirsch (Eds.). *Teaching and learning mathematics in the 1990s* (1990 Yearbook, pp. 22–30). Reston, VA: National Council of Teachers of Mathematics.

Kennedy, L. M., & Tipps S. (1991). *Guiding children's learning of mathematics* (6th ed.). Belmont, CA: Wadsworth.

Lerman, S. (1989). Constructivism, mathematics and mathematics education. *Educational Studies in Mathematics 20*(2), 211–233.

McIntosh, M. E. (1991). No time for writing in your class? *Mathematics Teacher, 84*(6), 423–433.

Morine-Dershimer, G. G. (1990). Instructional planning. In J. M. Cooper (Ed.), *Classroom teaching skills* (4th ed., pp. 17–49). Lexington, MA: D. C. Heath.

National Council of Teachers of Mathematics. (1989). *Curriculum and evaluation standards for school mathematics.* Reston, VA. Author.

National Council of Teachers of Mathematics. (1991). *Professional standards for teaching mathematics.* Reston, VA: Author.

National Council of Teachers of Mathematics (2000). *Principles and Standards for School Mathematics.* Reston, VA: Author.

Oberholtzer-Sutton, G. (1992). Cooperative learning works in mathematics. *Mathematics Teachers, 85*(1), 63–66.

Orlich, D. C., Harder, R. J., Callahan, R. C., Kauchak, D. P., Pendergrass, R. A., Keogh, A. J., & Gibson, H. (1990). *Teaching strategies: A guide to better instruction* (3rd ed.). Lexington, MA: D. C. Heath.

Pa, N. A. N. (1986). Meaning in arithmetic from four different perspectives. *For the Learning of Mathematics, 6*(1), 11–16.

Reuille-Irons, R., & Irons, C. J. (1989). Language experiences: A base for problem solving. In P. R. Trafton and A. P. Shulte (Eds.), *New directions for elementary school mathematics* (1989 NCTM Yearbook, pp. 85–98). Reston, VA: National Council of Teachers of Mathematics.

Riedesel, C. A. (1990). *Teaching elementary school mathematics* (5th ed.). Englewood Cliffs, NJ: Prentice Hall.

Ross, R., & Kurtz, R. (1993, January). Making manipulatives work: A strategy for success. *Arithmetic Teacher, 40* (5), 254–257.

Sawada, D. (1985). Mathematical symbols: Insight through invention. *Arithmetic Teacher, 32*(6), 20–22.

Schmandt-Besserat, D. (1999). *The history of counting.* New York: Morrow Junior Books. (Grades 2–6)

Schwartz, D. (1998). *G is for googol.* Berkeley: Tricycle. (Grades 4–6)

Skemp, R. (1989). *Structured activities for primary mathematics* (Vol. 1). London: Routledge.

Stigler, J. W. (1988). Research into practice: The use of verbal explanation in Japanese and American classrooms. *Arithmetic Teacher, 36*(2), 27–29.

Thompson, A. (1990). Letters to a math teacher. In N. Atwell (Ed.), *Coming to know: Writing to learn in the intermediate grades* (pp. 87–93). Concord, ON: Irwin.

Van de Walle, J. A. (1994). *Elementary school mathematics: Teaching developmentally* (2nd ed.). White Plains, NY: Longman.

Wentworth, N. M., & Monroe, E. E. (1995). What is the whole? *Mathematics Teaching in the Middle School, 1*(5), 356–360.

Chapter 3

Anno, M. (1995). *Anno's magic seeds.* New York: Philomel. (K–6)

Birch, D. (1988). *The king's chessboard.* New York: Puffin. (Grades 3–6)

Charles, R. I., & Lester, F. K., Jr. (1982). *Teaching problem solving: What, why, & how.* Palo Alto, CA: Seymour.

Charles, R. I., & Lester, F. K., Jr. (1984). An evaluation of a process-oriented program in mathematical problem solving in grades 5 and 7. *Journal for Research in Mathematics Education, 18*(2), 83–97.

Fennel, F., & Ammon, R. (1985). Writing techniques for problem solvers. *Arithmetic Teacher, 33*(1), 24–25.

Ford, M. I. (1990). The writing process: A strategy for problem solvers. *Arithmetic Teacher, 38*(3), 35–38

Hembree, R., & March, H. (1993). Problem solving in early childhood: Building foundations. In R. J. Jensen (Ed.), *Research ideas for the classroom: Early childhood mathematics.* Reston. VA: National Council of Teachers of Mathematics.

Kroll, D. L., & Miller, T. (1993). Insights from research on mathematical problem solving in the middle grades. In D. T. Owens (Ed.), *Research ideas for the classroom: Middle grades mathematics* (pp. 58–77). New York: Macmillan.

Moser, J. M. (1992). Arithmetic operations on whole numbers: Addition and subtraction. In T. R. Post (Ed.), *Teaching mathematics in grades K–8: Research-based methods* (pp. 123–155). Boston: Allyn & Bacon.

Moses, B., Bjork, E., & Goldenberg, E. P. (1990). Beyond problem solving: Problem posing. In T. J. Cooney (Ed.). *Teaching and learning mathematics in the 1990s* (1990 Yearbook, pp. 82–91). Reston, VA: National Council of Teachers of Mathematics.

National Council of Teachers of Mathematics (2000). *Principles and Standards for School Mathematics.* Reston, VA: Author.

National Research Council (1989). *Everybody counts.* Washington, DC: National Academy Press.

Polya, G. (1949). On solving mathematical problems in high school. Reprinted in S. Krulik and R. E. Reys (Eds.), *Problem solving in school mathematics* (1980 Yearbook, pp. 1–2). Reston, VA: National Council of Teachers of Mathematics.

Polya, G. (1957). *How to solve it* (2nd ed.). New York: Doubleday.

Pothier, Y. (1992). Writing to communicate mathematics. In D. Sawada (Ed.), *Communication in the mathematics classroom.* Edmonton, AB: Mathematics Council of the Alberta Teachers' Association.

Pothier, Y., & Sawada, D. (1990). Students value time and a patient teacher. *Mathematics in School, 19*(3), 38–39.

Suydam, M. (1984). Research reports: Problem solving. *Arithmetic Teacher, 31*(9), 36.

Chapter 4

California Mathematics Council. (1996). *Constructive assessment in mathematics.* San Diego: Author.

Collison, J. (1992). Using performance assessment to determine mathematical dispositions. *Arithmetic Teacher, 39,* 40–47.

Crowley, M. L. (1993). Student mathematics portfolio: More than a display case. *Mathematics Teacher, 86,* 544–547.

Lambdin, D. V., & Walker, V. L. (1994). Planning for classroom portfolio assessment. *Arithmetic Teacher, 41,* 318–324.

Lankford, M. D. (1998). *Dominoes around the world.* New York: Morrow Junior Books. (Grades 2–6)

Ledwon, P., & Mets, M. (2000). *Midnight math.* New York: Holiday House. (Grades K–4)

Maisner, H. (1996). *Planet monster.* Cambridge, MA: Candlewick. (Grades 2–6)

National Council of Teachers of Mathematics. (1995). *Assessment standards for school mathematics.* Reston, VA: Author.

National Council of Teachers of Mathematics (2000). *Principles and Standards for School Mathematics.* Reston, VA: Author.

Pandey, T. (1991). *A sampler of mathematics assessment.* Sacramento: California Department of Education.

Stenmark, J. K. (Ed.). (1991). *Mathematics assessment: Myths, models, good questions, and practical suggestions.* Reston, VA: National Council of Teachers of Mathematics.

Chapter 5

Anderson, L. (2000). *Tea for ten.* New York: R & S Books. (Grades K–2)

Anno, M. (1977). *Anno's counting book.* New York: HarperCollins. (Grades K–3)

Anno, M. (1982). *Anno's counting house.* New York: Philomel. (Grades K–3)

Baker, A. (1998). *Little rabbits' first number book.* New York: Scholastic. (Grades K–3)

Baker, A., & Baker, J. (1990). *Mathematics in process.* Portsmouth, NH: Heinemann Educational Books.

Baratta-Lorton, M. (1987). *Mathematics their way.* Palo Alto, CA: Addison-Wesley.

Barchas, S. E. (1975). *I was walking down the road.* New York: Scholastic.

Carle, E. (1968). *1, 2, 3 to the Zoo.* Trumpet Club. (Grades K–3)

Charles, F., & Arenson, R. (1996). *A Caribbean counting book.* New York: Houghton Mifflin. (Grades K–4)

Crews, D. (1968, 1986). *Ten black dots.* New York: Mulberry. (Grades K–2)

Ernst, L. C. (1986). *Up to ten and down again.* New York: Mulberry. (Grades K–3)

Falwell, C. (1993). *Feast for 10.* New York: Scholastic. (Grades K–2)

Feelings, M. (1971). *Moja means one: Swahili counting book.* New York; Dial. (Grades K–3)

Fleming, D. (1992). *Count!* New York: Scholastic. (Grades K–2)

Geisert, A. (1996). *Roman numerals I to MM.* New York: Houghton Mifflin. (Grades 2–6)

Gelman, R., & Gallistel, C. R. (1978). *The child's understanding of number.* Cambridge, MA: Harvard University Press.

Hoffman, M. (1990). *Nancy no-size.* London, UK: Little Mannoth.

Hughes, M. (1986). *Children and number: Difficulties in learning mathematics.* Oxford, UK: Basil Blackwell.

Hutchins, P. (1982). *1 hunter.* New York: Greenwillow. (Grades K–3)

Kamii, C., & Joseph, L. (1988). Teaching place value and double-column addition. *Arithmetic Teacher, 35*(6), 48–52.

Labinowicz, E. (1980). *The Piaget primer: Thinking, learning, teaching.* Palo Alto, CA: Addison-Wesley.

Labinowicz, E. (1985). *Learning from children: New beginnings for teaching numerical thinking.* Palo Alto, CA: Addison-Wesley.

Lottridge, C. B. (1986). *One watermelon seed.* Toronto: Oxford University Press. (Grades K–3)

McGrath, B. B. (1998). *The Cheerios counting book.* New York: Scholastic. (Grades K–3)

Marchand, L. C., Bye, M. P., Harrison, B., & Schroeder, T. L. (1985). *Assessing cognitive levels in the classroom.* Edmonton, AB: Alberta Education. (ERIC Document Reproduction Service No. ED 266 033.)

Mora, P. (1996). *Uno, dos, tres; one, two, three.* New York: Clarion Books. (Grades K–6)

National Council of Teachers of Mathematics. (1989). *Curriculum and evaluation standards for school mathematics.* Reston, VA: Author.

National Council of Teachers of Mathematics (2000). *Principles and Standards for School Mathematics.* Reston, VA: Author.

Oppenhiem, J., & Reid, B. (1986). *Have you seen birds?* Richmond Hill, ON: Scholastic-TAB.

Parker, J. (1988). *I love spiders.* New York: Scholastic.

Piaget, J. (1965). *The child's conception of number.* New York: Norton.

Serfoza, M. (1988). *Who said red?* New York: Scholastic.

Sierra, J. (1997). *Counting crocodiles.* San Diego: Gulliver. (Grades K–3)

Skemp, R. (1989). *Structured activities for primary mathematics (Vol. 1).* London: Routledge.

Sloat, T. (1991). *From one to one hundred.* New York: Dutton Children's Books. (Grades K–3)

Stinson, K. (1982). *Red is best.* Toronto, ON: Annick.

Tildes, P. L. (1995). *Counting on calico.* New York: Scholastic. (Grades K–3)

Trinca, R., & Argent, K. (1982). *One woolly wombat.* New York: Puffin. (Grades K–3)

Turner, P. (1999). *Among the odds & evens.* New York: Farrar Straus Giroux. (Grades K–6)

Van de Walle, J. A. (1994). *Elementary school mathematics: Teaching developmentally (2nd ed.).* White Plains, NY: Longman.

Walsh, E. S. (1991). *Mouse count.* Orlando: Voyager. (Grades K–2)

Walton, R. (1993). *How, many, how many, how many?* Cambridge, MA: Candlewick Press. (Grades K–3)

Wells, R. (2000). *Emily's first 100 days of school.* New York: Hyperion. (Grades K–3)

Wirtz, R. (1974). *Mathematics for everyone.* Washington, DC: Curriculum Development Associates.

Chapter 6

Anno, M., & Anno, M. (1983). *Anno's mysterious multiplying jar.* New York: Philomel. (Grades 3–6)

Bidwell, J. K. (1967). Mayan arithmetic. *Mathematics Teacher, 60*(7), 762–768.

Cowle, I. M. (1970). Ancient systems of numeration—stimulating, illuminating. *Arithmetic Teacher, 17*(5), 413–416.

Hampton-Burnett, P. (1981). A million! How much is that? *Arithmetic Teacher, 29*(1), 49–50.

Kamii, C., & Joseph, L. (1988). Teaching place value and double-column addition. *Arithmetic Teacher, 35*(6), 48–52.

Murphy, S. J. (1997). *Betcha.* New York: Harper Trophy. (Grades 2–6)

Murphy, S. J. (1996). *Too Many Kangaroo Things to Do!* New York: Harper Collins.

National Council of Teachers of Mathematics (2000). *Principles and Standards for School Mathematics.* Reston, VA: Author.

Payne, J. N. (1988). Research into practice: Place value for tens and ones. *Arithmetic Teacher, 35*(6), 64–66.

Reys, R. E., Suydam, M. N., & Lindquist, M. M. (1984). *Helping children learn mathematics.* Englewood Cliffs, NJ: Prentice Hall.

Ross, S. (1986). *The development of children's place value concepts in grades 2 through 5.* Paper presented at the American Education Research Association, San Francisco.

Ross, S. (1989). Parts, wholes, and place value: A developmental view. *Arithmetic Teacher, 36*(6), 47–51.

Schwartz, D. (1985). *How much is a million?* New York: Lothrop, Lee, and Shepard. (Grades 2–6)

Schwartz, D. M. (1989). *If you made a million.* New York: Mulberry.

Skemp, R. (1989). *Structured activities for primary mathematics (Vol. 1).* London: Routledge.

Smith, R. F. (1973). Diagnosis of pupil performance in place-value tasks. *Arithmetic Teacher, 20*(5), 403–408.

Tang, G. (2001). *The grapes of math.* New York: Scholastic.

Chapter 7

Anghileri, J., & Johnson, D. C. (1992). Arithmetic operations on whole numbers: Multiplication and division. In T. R. Post (Ed.), *Teaching mathematics in grades K–8: Research-based methods* (pp. 157–200). Boston: Allyn & Bacon.

Burns, M. (1991). Introducing division through problem-solving experiences. *Arithmetic Teacher, 38*(8), 14–18.

Carey, D. A. (1991). Number sentences: Linking addition and subtraction word problems and symbols. *Journal for Research in Mathematics Education, 22*(4), 266–280.

Carpenter, T. P., & Moser, J. M. (1982). The development of addition and subtraction problem-solving skills. In T. P. Carpenter, J. M. Moser, and T. A. Romberg (Eds.), *Addition and subtraction: A cognitive perspective* (pp. 9–24). Hillsdale, NJ: Erlbaum.

Fennema, E., Carpenter, T. P., Levi, L., Franke, M. L., & Empson, S. (1997). *Cognitively guided instruction: Professional development in primary mathematics.* Madison: Wisconsin Center for Education Research.

Friedman, A. (1994). *The king's commissioners.* New York: Scholastic. (Grades 2–5)

Greer, B. (1992). Multiplication and division as models of situations. In D. A. Grouws (Ed.), *Handbook of research on mathematics teaching and learning* (pp. 276–299). New York: Macmillan.

Hutchins, P. (1986). *The doorbell rang.* New York: Morrow. (Grades K–6)

Kouba, V. L., & Franklin, K. (1993). Multiplication and division: Sense making and meaning. In R. J. Jensen (Ed.), *Research ideas for the classroom: Early childhood mathematics* (pp. 103–126). New York: Macmillan.

McGrath, B. B. (1994). *The M & Ms counting book.* New York: Scholastic. (Grades K–3)

National Council of Teachers of Mathematics. (1989). *Curriculum and evaluation standards for school mathematics.* Reston, VA: Author.

National Council of Teachers of Mathematics (2000). *Principles and Standards for School Mathematics.* Reston, VA: Author.

Neuschwander, C. (1998). *Amanda Bean's amazing dream.* New York: Scholastic. (Grades 2–6)

Page, A. (1994). Helping children understand subtraction. *Teaching Children Mathematics, 1*(3), 140–143.

Pallotta, J. (2000). *Reese's Pieces count by fives.* New York: Scholastic. (Grades 2–4)

Pinczes, E. (1995). *One hundred hungry ants.* New York: Houghton Mifflin. (Grades 2–6)

Sowder, L. (1988). Children's solutions of story problems. *Journal of Mathematical Behavior, 7*(3), 227–238.

Stigler, J. W., Fuson, K. C., Ham, M., & Kim, M. S. (1986). An analysis of addition and subtraction word problems in American and Soviet elementary mathematics textbooks. *Cognition and Instruction, 3*, 153–171.

Trafton, P. R., & Zawojewski, J. S. (1990). Meaning of operations. *Arithmetic Teacher 38*(3), 18–22.

Chapter 8

Baroody, A. J. (1984). Children's difficulties in subtraction: Some causes and questions. *Journal for Research in Mathematics Education 15*, 203–213.

Feinberg, M. M. (1990, April 8). Using patterns to practice basic facts. *Arithmetic Teacher 37*, 38–41.

Isaacs & Carroll, 1999

Moser, J. M. (1992). Arithmetic operations on whole numbers: Addition and subtraction. In T. R. Post (Ed.), *Teaching mathematics in grades K–8: Research-based methods* (pp. 123–155). Boston: Allyn and Bacon.

NCTM, 2000

Rathmell, E. C. (1978). Using thinking strategies to teach the basic facts. In M. N. Suydam and R. E. Reys (Eds.), *Developing computational skills* (1978 Yearbook, pp. 13–38). Reston, VA: National Council of Teachers of Mathematics.

Thornton, C. A. (1978). Emphasizing thinking strategies in basic fact instruction. *Journal for Research in Mathematics Education, 9*, 214–227.

Watson, J. M. (1991). Models to show the impossibility of division by zero. *School Science and Mathematics, 9*(8), 373–376.

Weill, B. F. (1978). Mrs. Weill's hill: A successful subtraction method for use with the learning-disabled child. *Arithmetic Teacher, 26*(2), 34–35.

Chapter 9

Ashlock, R. B. (2002). *Error patterns in computation* (8th ed.). Upper Saddle River, NJ: Merrill.

Atweh, B. (1982). Developing mental arithmetic. In L. Silvey and J. R. Smart (Eds.), *Mathematics for the middle grades* (5–9) (1982 Yearbook, pp. 50–58). Reston, VA: National Council of Teachers of Mathematics.

Bidwell, J. K. (1991). Readers' dialogue: Susan's personal algorithm. *Arithmetic Teacher, 39*(3), 1.

Bohan, H. J., & Shawaker, P. B. (1994). Using manipulatives effectively: A drive down rounding road. *Arithmetic Teacher, 41*(5), 246–248.

Brownell, W. A. (1947). An experiment on "borrowing" in third grade arithmetic. *Journal of Educational Research, 41*(3), 161–171.

Brownell, W. A., & Moser, H. E. (1949). Meaningful vs. mechanical learning: A study in grade 3 subtraction. *Duke University Studies in Education, 8,* 1–207.

Cathcart, W. G. (1990). Implementation of an Apple Center for Innovation and year 1 results. In L. Pereira-Mendoza and M. Quigley (Eds.), *Canadian Mathematics Education Study Group: Proceedings 1989 Annual Meeting* (pp. 87–98). St. Johns, NF: Memorial University of Newfoundland.

Cathcart, W. G. (1991). Achievement in a computer-rich environment. In S. Gayle (Ed.), *Proceedings: NECC 91* (pp. 188–194). Eugene, OR: International Society for Technology in Education.

Hamic, E. J. (1986). Student's creative computations: My way or your way. *Arithmetic Teacher, 34*(1), 39–41.

Harel, G., & Behr, M. (1991). Ed's strategy for solving division problems. *Arithmetic Teacher, 39*(3), 38–40.

Kouba, V. L., Zawojewski, J. S., & Struchens, M. E. (1997). What do students know about numbers and operations? In P. A. Kenney and E. A. Silver (Eds.), *Results from the Sixth Mathematics Assessment of the National Assessment of Educational Progress* (pp. 87–140). Reston: VA: National Council of Teachers of Mathematics.

Lee, K. S. (1991). Left-to-right computations and estimation. *School Science and Mathematics, 91*(5), 199–201.

Madell, R. (1985). Children's natural processes. *Arithmetic Teacher, 32*(7), 20–22.

National Council of Teachers of Mathematics. (1989). *Curriculum and evaluation standards for school mathematics.* Reston VA: Author.

National Council of Teachers of Mathematics (2000). *Principles and Standards for School Mathematics.* Reston, VA: Author.

Neufeld, K. A. (1991). Computational pizazz: Teach your students to create puzzles for their peers—Magic cross-out. *Ontario Mathematics Gazette, 30*(2), 23–24.

Philipp, R. A. (1996). Multicultural mathematics and alternative algorithms: Using knowledge from many cultures. *Teaching Children Mathematics, 3*(3), 128–135.

Pinczes, E. (1995). *A remainder of one.* New York: Houghton Mifflin. (Grades 2–6)

Reys, B. J. (1985). Mental computation. *Arithmetic Teacher, 32*(3), 43–46.

Reys, B. J. (1986). Teaching computational estimation: Concepts and strategies. In H. L. Schoen and M. J. Zweng (Eds.), *Estimation and mental computation* (1986 Yearbook, pp. 31–44). Reston, VA: National Council of Teachers of Mathematics.

Reys, B. J., & Reys, R. E. (1986). One point of view: Mental computation and computational estimation: Their time has come. *Arithmetic Teacher, 33*(7), 4–5.

Reys, B. J., & Reys, R. E. (1990). Estimation: Directions from the standards. *Arithmetic Teachers, 37*(7), 22–25.

Sawada, D. (1985). Mathematical symbols: Insight through invention. *Arithmetic Teacher, 32*(6), 20–22.

Sowder, J. T. (1990, March 7). Mental computation and number sense. *Arithmetic Teacher, 37,* 18–20.

Stanic, G. M. A., & McKillip, W. D. (1989). Developmental algorithms have a place in elementary school mathematics instruction. *Arithmetic Teacher, 36*(5), 14–16.

Usiskin, Z. (1998). Paper-and-pencil algorithms in a calculator-and-computer age. In L. J. Morrow (Ed.), *The teaching and learning of algorithms in school mathematics* (1998 yearbook, pp. 7–20). Reston, VA: National Council of Teachers of Mathematics.

Young, J. L. (1984). Uncovering the algorithms. *Arithmetic Teacher, 32*(3), 20.

Chapter 10

Bezuk, N. S. & Bieck, M. (1993). Current research on rational numbers and common fractions: Summary and implications for teachers. In D. T. Owens (Ed.), *Research ideas for the classroom: Middle grades mathematics* (pp. 188–136). New York: Macmillan.

Dossey, J. A., Mullis, I. V. S., & Jones, C. O. (1993). *Can students do mathematical problem solving? Results from constructed-response questions in NAEP's 1992 mathematics assessment.* Washington, DC: National Center for Education Statistics.

Driscoll, M. (1984). What research says. *Arithmetic Teacher, 31*(6), 34–35, 46.

Hiebert, J., & Behr, M. J. (1988). Capturing the major themes. In J. Hiebert and M. J. Behr (Eds.), *Number concepts and operations in the middle grades* (pp. 1–18). Hillsdale, NJ: Erlbaum.

Hollis, L. Y. (1984). Teaching rational numbers: Primary grades. *Arithmetic Teacher, 31*(6), 36–39.

Jensen, R., & O'Neil, D. R. (1982). That's eggzactly right. *Arithmetic Teacher, 29*(7), 8–13.

Kieren, T. E. (1980). The rational number construct: Its elements and mechanisms. In T. E. Kieren (Ed.), *Recent research on number learning.* Columbus, OH: ERIC/SMEAC.

Kieren, T. E., Nelson, D., & Smith, G. (1985, April). Graphical algorithms in partitioning tasks. *Journal of Mathematical Behavior, 4,* 25–36.

Kouba, V. L., Zawojewski, J. S., Struchens, M. E. (1997). What do students know about numbers and operations? In P. A. Kenney and E. A. Silver (Eds.), *Results from the Sixth Mathematics Assessment of the National Assessment of Educational Progress* (pp. 87–140). Reston, VA: National Council of Teachers of Mathematics.

Mack, N. K. (1990). Learning fractions with understanding. *Journal for Research in Mathematics Education, 21*(1), 16–32.

Mathews, L. (1995). *Gator pie.* Littleton, Massachusetts: Sundance. (Grades K–6)

Murphy, S. (1996). *Give me half!* New York: HarperCollins. (Grades K–3)

National Council of Teachers of Mathematics. (1980). *Curriculum and evaluation standards for school mathematics.* Reston, VA: Author.

National Council of Teachers of Mathematics (2000). *Principles and Standards for School Mathematics.* Reston, VA: Author.

Payne, J. N. (1984). Curricular issues: Teaching rational numbers. *Arithmetic Teacher, 31*(6), 14–17.

Peck, D. M., & Jencks, S. M. (1981, March). Share and cover. *Arithmetic Teacher, 28*(7), 38–41.

Pothier, Y. M., & Sawada, D. (1990). Partitioning: An approach to fractions. *Arithmetic Teacher, 38*(4), 12–16.

Skypek, D. H. B. (1984). Special characteristics of rational numbers. *Arithmetic Teacher, 31*(6), 10–12.

Vance, J. (1990, August) Rational number sense: Development and assessment, *Delta-K, 13*(2), 23–27.

Chapter 11

Adler, D. (1996). *Fraction fun.* New York: Holiday House. (Grades 2–6)

Bezuk, N. S. & Bieck, M. (1993). Current research on rational numbers and common fractions: Summary and implications for teachers. In. D. T. Owens (Ed.), *Research ideas for the classroom: Middle grades mathematics* (pp. 118–136). New York: Macmillan.

Hope, J. A., & Owens, D. T. (1987). An analysis of the difficulty of learning fractions. *Focus on Learning Problems in Mathematics, 9*(Fall), 25–40.

Kieren, T. (1976). On the mathematical, cognitive, and instructional foundations of rational numbers. In R. E. Lesh (Ed.), *Number and measurement: Paper from a research workshop.* Columbus, OH: ERIC/SMEAC.

Leedy, L. (1994). *Fraction action.* New York: Holiday House. (Grades 2–5)

Pallota, J. (1999). *The Hershey's Milk Chocolate fractions book.* Needham, MA: Title Wave. (Grades 2–6)

National Council of Teachers of Mathematics. (1989) *Curriculum and evaluation standards for school mathematics.* Reston, VA: Author.

National Council of Teachers of Mathematics (2000). *Principles and Standards for School Mathematics.* Reston, VA: Author.

Chapter 12

Hiebert, J., & Wearne, D. (1986). Procedures over concepts: The acquisition of decimal number knowledge. In J. Hiebert (Ed.), *Conceptual and procedural knowledge: The case of mathematics* (pp. 199–223). Hillsdale, NJ: Erlbaum.

Kieren, T. (1984). Helping children understand rational numbers. *Arithmetic Teacher, 31*(6), 3.

Kouba, V. L., Zawojewski, J. S., & Struchens, M. E. (1997). What do students know about numbers and operations? In P. A. Kenney and E. A. Silver (Eds.), *Results from the Sixth Mathematics Assessment of the National Assessment of Educational Progress* (pp. 87–140). Reston, VA: National Council of Teachers of Mathematics.

National Council of Teachers of Mathematics (2000). *Principles and Standards for School Mathematics.* Reston, VA: Author.

Owens, D. T., & Super, D. B. (1993). Teaching and learning decimal fractions. In D. T. Owens (Ed.), *Research ideas for the classroom: Middle grades mathematics* (pp. 137–158). New York: Macmillan.

Vance, J. (1986a). Ordering decimals and fractions: A diagnostic study. *Focus on Learning Problems in Mathematics, 8*(2), 51–59.

Vance, J. (1986b). Estimating decimal products: An instructional sequence. In H. L. Schoen (Ed.), *Estimation and mental computation* (1986 Yearbook pp. 127–134). Reston VA: National Council of Teachers of Mathematics.

Chapter 13

Brown, C. R. (1973). Math rummy. *Arithmetic Teacher, 20*(1), 44–45.

Cramer, K., Post, T., & Currier, S. (1993). Learning and teaching ratio and proportion: Research implications. In D. T. Owens (Ed.), *Research ideas for the classroom: Middle grades mathematics* (pp. 159–178). New York: Macmillan.

Dewar, A. M. (1984). Another look at the teaching of percent. *Arithmetic Teacher, 31*, 48–49.

Hart, K. (1989). Ratio and proportion. In J. Hiebert and M. Behr (Eds.), *Number concepts and operations in the middle grades* (pp. 198–219). Reston, VA: National Council of Teachers of Mathematics.

Hoffer, A. R., & Hoffer, S. A. K. (1992). Ratios and proportional thinking. In T. R. Post (Ed.), *Teaching mathematics in grades K–8: Research-based methods* (pp. 303–330). Boston: Allyn & Bacon.

Karplus, E. F., Karplus, R., & Wollman, W. (1974). Ratio: The influence of cognitive style. *School Science and Mathematics, 74*(6), 476–482.

Kouba, V. L., Zawojewski, J. S., & Struchens, M. E. (1997). What do students know about numbers and operations? In P. A. Kenney and E. A. Silver (Eds.), *Results from the Sixth Mathematics Assessment of the National Assessment of Educational Progress* (pp. 87–140). Reston, VA: National Council of Teachers of Mathematics.

Lesh, R., Post, T., & Behr, M. (1989). Proportional reasoning. In J. Hiebert and M. Behr (Eds.), *Number concepts and operations in the middle grades* (pp. 93–118). Reston, VA: National Council of Teachers of Mathematics.

National Council of Teachers of Mathematics (2000). *Principles and Standards for School Mathematics.* Reston, VA: Author.

Quintero, A. H. (1987). Helping children understand ratios. *Arithmetic Teacher, 34*(9), 17–21.

Vance, J. H. (1982). Individualizing instruction through multi-level problem-solving activities. *The Canadian Mathematics Teacher*, pp. 3–9.

Chapter 14

Baker, A. (1994). *Brown rabbit's shape book*. New York: Scholastic. (Grades K–2)

Billstein, R., Libeskind, S., & Lott, J. W. (1990). *A problem-solving approach to mathematics for elementary school teachers* (4th ed.). New York: Cummings.

Blackstone, S. (1998). *Bear in a square*. New York: Scholastic. (Grades K–2)

Burns, M. (1994). *The greedy triangle*. New York: Scholastic. (Grades K–6)

Burns, M. (1997). *Spaghetti and meatballs for all*. New York: Scholastic. (Grades 5–6)

Crowley, M. (1987). The van Hiele model of the development of geometric thought. In M. M. Lindquist and A. P. Shulte (Eds.), *Learning and teaching geometry, K-12*. Reston, VA: National Council of Teachers of Mathematics.

Dodds, D. A. (1994). *The shape of things*. Cambridge, MA: Candlewick Press. (Grades K–3)

Eperson, C. B. (1982a). Puzzles, pastimes, problems. *Mathematics in School, 11*(1), 15.

Eperson, C. B. (1982b). Puzzles, pastimes, problems. *Mathematics in School, 11*(2), 10.

Eperson, C. B. (1983). Puzzles, pastimes, problems. *Mathematics in School, 12*(2), 20–21.

Friedman, A. (1994). *A cloak for the dreamer*. New York: Scholastic. (Grades K–6)

Geddes, D., & Fortunato, I. (1993). Geometry: Research and classroom activities. In D. T. Owens (Ed.), *Research ideas for the classroom: Middle grades mathematics* (pp. 199–222). New York: Macmillan.

Haak, S. (1976). Transformational geometry and the artwork of M. C. Escher. *Mathematics Teacher, 69*(8), 647–652.

Henderson, G. L., & Collier, C. P. (1973). Geometric activities for later childhood education. *Arithmetic Teacher, 20*(10), 444–453.

Hoban, T. (1996). *Shapes, shapes, shapes*. New York: Mulberry. (Grades K–3)

National Council of Teachers of Mathematics (2000). *Principles and Standards for School Mathematics*. Reston, VA: Author.

Owens, D. T. (1990). Research into practice: Spatial abilities. *Arithmetic Teacher, 37*(6), 48–51.

Piaget, J., Inhelder, B., & Szeminska, A. (1960). *The child's conception of geometry*. New York: Basic Books.

Pothier, Y., & Sawada, D. (1990). Students value time and a patient teacher. *Mathematics in School, 19*(3), 38–39.

Rahim, M. H., & Sawada, D. (1986). Revitalizing school geometry through dissection-motion operations. *School Science and Mathematics, 86*(3), 235–246.

Robinson, G. E. (1975). Geometry. In J. N. Payne (Ed.), *Mathematics learning in early childhood*. Reston, VA: National Council of Teachers of Mathematics.

Sgroi, R. J. (1990). Communicating about spatial relationships. *Arithmetic Teacher, 37*(6), 21–24.

Struchens, M. E., & Blume, G. W. (1997). What do students know about geometry? In P. A. Kenney and E. A. Silver (Eds.), *Results from the Sixth Mathematics Assessment of the National Assessment of Educational Progress* (pp. 165–193). Reston, VA: National Council of Teachers of Mathematics.

Tompert, A. (1990). *Grandfather Tang's story: A tale told with tangrams*. New York: Crown. (Grades K–6)

Turpin, L. (1990). *The sultan's snakes*. New York: Child's Play International. (Grades K–6)

Chapter 15

Bright, G. W., & Hoeffner, K. (1993). Measurement, probability, statistics, and graphing. In D. T. Owens (Ed.), *Research ideas for the classroom: Middle grades mathematics* (pp. 78–98). New York: Macmillan.

Cathcart, W. G. (1971). The relationship between primary students' rationalization of conservation and their mathematical achievement. *Child Development, 42*, 755–765.

Hart, K. (1984). Which comes first: Length, area, or volume? *Arithmetic Teacher, 31*(9), 16–18, 26–27.

Hiebert, J. (1984). Why do some children have trouble learning measurement concepts? *Arithmetic Teacher, 31*(7), 19–24.

Hightower, S. (1997). *Twelve snails to one lizard*. New York: Simon & Schuster.

Horak, V. M., & Horak, W. J. (1982). Making measurement meaningful. *Arithmetic Teacher, 30*(3), 18–23.

Horak, V. M., & Horak, W. J. (1983). Teaching time with slit clocks. *Arithmetic Teacher, 30*(5), 8–12

Inskeep, J. E. 91976). Teaching measurement to children. In D. Nelson (Ed.), *Measurement in school mathematics* (pp. 60–86). Reston, VA: National Council of Teachers of Mathematics.

Jensen, R., & O'Neil, D. R. (1981). Meaningful linear measurement. *Arithmetic Teacher, 29*(1), 6–12.

Kastner, B. (1989). Number sense: The role of measurement applications. *Arithmetic Teacher, 36*(6), 40–46.

Kenney, P. A., & Kouba, V. L. (1997). What do students know about measurement? In P. A. Kenney and E. A. Silver (Eds.), *Results from the Sixth Mathematics Assessment of the National Assessment of Educational Progress* (pp. 141–163). Reston, VA: National Council of Teachers of Mathematics.

Lindquist, M. M. (1987). Estimation and mental computation: Measurement. *Arithmetic Teacher, 34*(5), 16–17.

Lindquist, M. M. (1989). The measurement standards. *Arithmetic Teacher, 37*(2), 22–26.

Myller, R. (1990). *How big is a foot?* New York: Dell.

National Council of Teachers of Mathematics (2000). *Principles and Standards for School Mathematics*. Reston, VA: Author.

Newton, J. E. (1988). From pattern-block play to Logo programming. *Arithmetic Teacher, 35*(9), 6–9.

Shaw, J. M. (1983). Exploring perimeter and area using centimeter squared paper. *Arithmetic Teacher, 31*(4), 4–11.

Shaw, J. M., & Cliatt, J. P. (1989). Developing measurement sense. In P. R. Trafton (Ed.), *New directions for elementary school mathematics* (pp. 149–155). Reston, VA: National Council of Teachers of Mathematics.

Steffe, L. P., & Hirstein, J. J. (1976). Children's thinking in measurement situations. In D. Nelson (Ed.), *Measurement in school mathematics* (pp. 35–39). Reston, VA: National Council of Teachers of Mathematics.

Thompson, C. S., & van de Walle, J. (1981, April). A single-handed approach to telling time. *Arithmetic Teacher, 28,* 4–9.

Thompson, C. S., & van de Walle, J. (1985). Learning about rulers and measuring. *Arithmetic Teacher, 32*(8), 8–12.

Wilson, P. S., & Adams, V. M. (1992). A dynamic way to teach angle and angle measure. *Arithmetic Teacher, 39*(5), 6–13.

Wilson, P. S., & Rowland, R. E. (1993). Teaching measurement. In R. J. Jensen (Ed.), *Research ideas for the classroom: Early childhood mathematics* (pp. 171–194). New York: Macmillan.

Chapter 16

Bankard, D., & Fennell, F. (1991). Ideas. *Arithmetic Teacher, 39*(1), 26–33.

Bohan, H., Irby, B., & Vogel, D. (1995). Problem solving: Dealing with data in the elementary school. *Teaching Children Mathematics, 1*(5), 256–260.

Brahier, D. J., & Speer, W. R. (1995). Investigations: Nuts about mathematics. *Teaching Children Mathematics, 2*(4), 228–232.

Bright, G. W., Harvey, J. G., & Wheeler, M. M. (1981). Fair games, unfair games. In A. P. Shulte and J. R. Smart (Eds.), *Teaching statistics and probability* (pp. 49–59). Reston, VA: National Council of Teachers of Mathematics.

Bright, G. W., & Hoeffner, K. (1993). Measurement, probability, statistics, & graphing. In D. T. Owens (Eds.), *Research ideas for the classroom: Middle grades mathematics* (pp. 78–98). New York: Macmillan.

Brosnan, P. A. (1996). Implementing data analysis in a sixth grade classroom. *Mathematics Teaching in the Middle School, 1*(8), 622–628.

Browning, C. A., Channell, D. E., & Meyer, R. A. (1994). Preparing teachers to present techniques of exploratory data analysis. *Mathematics Teaching in the Middle School, 1*(2), 166–172.

Burbank, I. K. (1987). Probability without formulas and equations. *Delta-K, 26*(2), 32–39.

Cartland, P. (1996). What's in a glyph? *Teaching Children Mathematics, 2*(6), 324–328.

Dessart, D. J. (1995). Randomness: A connection to reality. In P. A. House and A. F. Coxford (Eds.), *Connecting mathematics across the curriculum* (1995 Yearbook, pp. 177–181). Reston, VA: National Council of Teachers of Mathematics.

Ewbank, W. A. (1987, December). Readers' dialogue: Accurate pie graphs. *Arithmetic Teacher, 35,* 4.

Fennell, F. (1990). Implementing the standards: Probability. *Arithmetic Teacher, 38*(4), 18–22.

Harbaugh, K. (1995). Glyphs? Don't let them scare you! *Teaching Children Mathematics, 1*(8), 506–511.

Hitch, C., & Armstrong, G. (1994). Daily activities for data analysis. *Arithmetic Teacher, 41*(5), 242–245.

Hofstetter, E. B., & Sgroi, L. A. (1996). Data with snap, crackle, and pop. *Mathematics Teaching in the Middle School, 1*(9), 760–764.

Kader, G., & Perry, M. (1994). Learning statistics with technology. *Mathematics Teaching in the Middle School, 1*(2), 130–136.

Litton, N. (1995). Graphing from A to Z. *Teaching Children Mathematics, 2*(4), 220–223.

Loewen, A. C. (1991, March). M and M and Ms: An alternative context for teaching mean, median, and mode. *Delta-K, 29,* 36–40.

National Council of Teachers of Mathematics. (1989). *Curriculum and evaluation standards for school mathematics.* Reston, VA: Author.

National Council of Teachers of Mathematics (2000). *Principles and Standards for School Mathematics.* Reston, VA: Author.

Paull, S. (1990). Not just an average unit. *Arithmetic Teacher, 38*(4), 54–58.

Rubenstein, R. N. (1989). Building statistical concepts through visualization and verbalization. *Ontario Mathematics Gazette, 28*(2), 10–15.

Russell, S. J., & Friel, S. N. (1989). Collecting and analyzing real data in the elementary school classroom. In P. R. Trafton and A. P. Shulte (Eds.), *New directions for elementary school mathematics* (1989 Yearbook, pp. 134–148). Reston, VA: National Council of Teachers of Mathematics.

Russell, S. J., & Mokros, J. (1996). What do children understand about average? *Teaching Children Mathematics, 2*(6), 360–364.

Sacco, W., Copes, W., Sloyer, C., & Stark, R. (1987). *Glyphs: Getting the picture.* Dedham, MA. Janson

Shannon, B. K. J. (1995). Our diets may be killing us. *Mathematics Teaching in the Middle School, 1*(5), 376–382.

Shulte, A. P., & Smart, J. R. (Eds.). (1981). *Teaching statistics and probability.* Reston, VA: National Council of Teachers of Mathematics.

Smith, R. F. (1986). Let's do it: Coordinate geometry for third graders. *Arithmetic Teacher, 33*(8), 6–11.

Vissa, J. M. (1987). Coordinate graphing: Shaping a sticky situation. *Arithmetic Teacher, 35*(3), 6–10.

Wilkinson, J. D., & Nelson, O. (1966). Probability and Statistics: Trial teaching in sixth grade. *Arithmetic Teacher, 13*(2), 100–106.

Wilson, M. R., & Krapfl, C. M. (1995). Exploring mean, median, and mode with a spreadsheet. *Mathematics Teaching in the Middle School, 1*(6), 490–495.

Young, S. L. (1991). Ideas. *Arithmetic Teacher, 38*(8), 26–33.

Zawojewski, J. S. (1988). Teaching statistics: Mean, median, and mode. *Arithmetic Teacher, 35*(7), 25–26.

Zawojewski, J. S., & Heckman, D. S. (1997). What do students know about data analysis, statistics, and probability? In P. A. Kenney and E. A. Silver (Eds.), *Results from the Sixth Mathematics Assessment of the National Assessment of Educational Progress* (pp. 195–223). Reston, VA: National Council of Teachers of Mathematics.

Chapter 17

Battista, M. R., & Van Auken, C. (1998). Using spreadsheets to promote algebraic thinking. *Teaching Children Mathematics, 4*(8), 470–478.

Bippert, J., & Vandling, L. (2001). *Into the unknown: Algebraic thinking and reasoning.* Carlsbad, CA: Interact.

Blume, G. W., & Heckman, D. S. (1997). What do students know about algebra and functions? In P. A. Kenney and

E. A. Silver (Eds.), *Results from the Sixth Mathematics Assessment of the National Assessment of Educational Progress* (pp. 225–277). Reston, VA: National Council of Teachers of Mathematics.

Booth, L. R. (1988). Children's difficulties in beginning algebra. In A. F. Coxford (Ed.), *The ideas of algebra, K–12* (pp. 20–32). Reston, VA: National Council of Teachers of Mathematics.

Chang, L. (1985). Multiple methods of teaching the addition and subtraction of integers. *Arithmetic Teacher, 33*(4), 14–19.

Cohen, L. S. (1965). A rationale in working with signed numbers. *Arithmetic Teachers, 12*(7), 563–567.

Crowley, M. L., & Dunn, K. A. (1985). On multiplying negative numbers. *Mathematics Teacher, 78*(4), 252–256.

Demana, F. D., & Waits, B. (1990). Instructional strategies and delivery systems. In E. L. Edwards (Ed.) (pp. 53–61), *Algebra for everyone.* Reston, VA: National Council of Teachers of Mathematics.

Erickson, R. (1977). The old integer game. *Mathematics Teacher, 70*(2), 140–141.

Falkner, K. P., Levi, L., & Carpenter, T. P. (1999, December). Children's understanding of equality: A foundation for algebra. *Teaching Children Mathematics*, 232–236.

Grady, M. B. (1978). A manipulative aid for adding and subtracting integers. *Arithmetic Teacher, 26*(3), 40.

House, P. A. (2001). *Navigating through algebra.* Four volumes: *Navigating through algebra in Prekindergarten–Grade 2, Grades 3–5, Grades 6–8, and Grades 9–12.* Reston, VA: National Council of Teachers of Mathematics.

Howden, H. (1989). Patterns, relationships, and functions. *Arithmetic Teacher, 37*(3), 18–24.

Kaput, J. J. (1998). Transforming algebra from an engine of inequity to an engine of mathematical power by "algebrafying" the K–12 curriculum. *The nature and role of algebra in the K–14 curriculum: Proceedings of a national symposium* (pp. 25–26). Washington, DC: National Academy Press.

Kieran, C. (1988). Two different approaches among algebra learners. In A. F. Coxford (Ed.), *The ideas of algebra, K–12* (pp. 91–96). Reston, VA: National Council of Teachers of Mathematics.

Kieran, C., & Chalouh, L. (1993). Prealgebra: The transition from arithmetic to algebra. In D. T. Owens (Ed.), *Research ideas for the classroom: Middle grades mathematics* (pp. 179–198). New York: Macmillan.

Lappan, G. (1998). Capturing patterns and functions: Variables and joint variation. In *The nature and role of algebra in the K–14 curriculum: Proceedings of a national symposium* (pp. 57–60). Washington, DC: National Academy Press

Nasser, R., & Carifio, J. (1995). Algebra word problems: A review of the theoretical models and related research literature. Paper presented at the Annual Meeting of the American Research Association, April 5–6, 1994.

Nibbelink, W. H. (1990). Teaching equations. *Arithmetic Teacher, 38*(3), 48–51.

Peck, D. M., & Jencks, S. M. (1988). Reality, arithmetic, and algebra. *Journal of Mathematical Behavior, 7*(1), 85–91.

Phillips, E. (1991). *Patterns and functions: Curriculum and Evaluation Standards for School Mathematics Addenda Series, Grades 5–8.* Reston, VA: National Council of Teachers of Mathematics.

Sanfiorenzo, N. R. (1991). Evaluating expressions: A problem-solving approach. *Arithmetic Teacher, 38*(7), 34–38.

Schultz, J. E. (1991). Teaching informal algebra. *Arithmetic Teacher, 37*(3), 34–37.

Silver, E. (1998) *Improving mathematics in middle school: Lessons from TIMSS and related research.* Washington, DC: US. Department of Education, Office of Educational Research and Improvements.

Smith, M. S. (forthcoming). *Balancing on a sharp, thin edge: A study of teacher learning in the context of mathematics instructional reform.* Elementary School Journal.

Sulza, J. S. (1998). The function box and fourth graders: Squares, cubes, and circles. *Teaching Children Mathematics, 4,* 442–447.

Usiskin, Z. (1988). Conceptions of school algebra and uses of variables. In A. F. Coxford (Ed.), *The ideas of algebra, K–12* (pp. 8–19). Reston, VA: National Council of Teachers of Mathematics.

Usiskin, Z. (1992) Where does algebra begin? Where does algebra end? In *Algebra for the Twenty-first Century: Proceedings of the August 1992 Conference.* (pp. 27–28). Reston, VA: National Council of Teachers of Mathematics.

Vance, J. H. (1995). Developing and assessing understanding of integer operations. *Delta-K, 32*(3), 10–14.

Wagner, S. (1981). Conservation of equation and function under transformation of variable. *Journal for Research in Mathematics Education, 12*(2), 107–118.

Willoughby, S. S. (1997). Functions from kindergarten through sixth grade. *Teaching Children Mathematics, 3,* 314–318.

Additional Readings

Adams, B. J. (1992) *The go-around dollar.* New York: Simon & Schuster. (Grades 2–5)

Anderson, L. (1998). *Tick-tock.* New York: R & S. (Grades K–3)

Anno, M. (1997). *Anno's math games.* New York: Paper Star. (Grades 1–6)

Atherlay, S. (1995). *Math in the bath (and other fun places, too!)* New York: Simon & Schuster. (Grades 1–4)

Axelrod, A. (1994). *Pigs will be pigs.* New York: Simon & Schuster Childrens. (Grades K–6)

Barret, J. (1978). *Cloudy with a chance of meatballs.* New York: Atheneum. (Grades 1–3)

Bartch, M. (1999). *Math and stories.* Palo Alto, CA: Celebration. (Grades K–3)

Braddon, K., Hall, N., & Taylor, D. (1993). *Math through children's literature: Making the NCTM Standards come alive.* Englewood, CO: Teacher Ideas Press. (Grades K–6)

Bresser, R. (1995). *Math and literature.* Sausalito, CA: Marilyn Burns Education Association. (Grades 4–6)

Briggs, R. (1970). *Jim and the beanstalk.* New York: Coward-McCann. (Grades K–6)

Brisson, P. (1995). *Benny's pennies.* New York: Yearling. (Grades K–2)

Burns, M. (1993). *Math and literature: Book one.* Sausalito, CA: Marilyn Burns Education Association. (Grades K–3)

Carle, E. (1996). *The grouchy ladybug.* New York: Harper Collins. (Grades K–3)

Dale, E. (1998). *How long?* London: Orchard Books. (Grades K–3)

Dee, R. (1990). *Two ways to count to ten: A Liberian folktale.* New York: Holt. (Grades K–3)

Ernst, L. C. (1992). *Sam Johnson and the blue ribbon quilt.* New York: Mulberry. (Grades K–6)

Geringer, L. (1987). *A three hat day.* New York: Harper Trophy. (Grades K–3)

Griffiths, R., & Clyne, M. (1988). *Books you can count on: Linking mathematics and literature.* Portsmouth, NH: Heinemann. (Grades K–6)

Harshman, M. (1993). *Only one.* New York: Cobblehill. (Grades K–3)

Hightower, S. (1997). *Twelve snails to one lizard.* New York: Simon & Schuster. (Grades 2–6)

Hong, L. T. (1993). *Two of everything.* Morton Grove, IL: Whitman. (Grades K–3)

Kaye, P. (1997). *Afterwards: Folk and fairy tales with mathematical ever afters.* White Plains, NY: Cuisenaire. (Grades 1–4)

Lionni, L. (1960). *Inch by inch.* New York: Astor. (Grades K–4)

Maestro, B. (1999). *The story of clocks and calendars: Marking a millennium.* New York: Lothrop, Lee & Shepard. (Grades 4–6)

McKissack, P. (1996). *A million fish . . . More or less.* New York: Dragonfly. (Grades 4–6)

McMillan, B. (1989). *Time too . . . .* New York: Scholastic. (Grades K–3)

Merriam, E. (1993). *12 ways to get to 11.* New York: Simon & Schuster. (Grades K–3)

Morozumi, A. (1993). *One gorilla.* Pleasantville, NY: Sunburst. (Grades K–2)

Moss, L. (1995). *Zin! zin! zin! a violin.* New York: Scholastic. (Grades K–4)

Murphy, S. (1996). *Too many kangaroo things to do!* New York: Harper Trophy. (Grades 2–6)

Myller, R. (1991). *How big is a foot?* New York: Young Yearling. (Grades K–6)

Reid, M. (1995). *The button box.* New York: Puffin. (Grades K–3)

Satariano, P. (1997). *Storytime, mathtime: Math explorations in children's literature.* Palo Alto, CA: Seymour. (Grades 1–3)

Schwartz, D. (1989). *If you made a million.* New York: Mulberry. (Grades 2–6)

Sheffield, S. (1994). *Math and literature: Book two.* Sausalito, CA: Marilyn Burns Education Association. (Grades K–3)

Slobodkina, E. (1987). *Caps for sale.* New York: Harper Trophy. (Grades K–4)

Viorst, J. (1978). *Alexander, who used to be rich last Sunday.* New York: Atheneum. (Grades 1–4)

Wells, R. (1993). *Is a blue whale the biggest thing there is?* Morton Grove, IL: Whitman. (Grades K–6)

Wells, R. E. (1995). *What's smaller than a pygmy shrew?* Morton Grove, IL: Whitman. (Grades 4–6)

Whitford, A. (1991). *Eight hands round.* New York: HarperCollins Juvenile. (Grades K–3)

Williams, V. (1982). *A chair for my mother.* New York: Greenwillow. (Grades K–4)

Williams, V. (1986). *Cherries and cherry pits.* New York: Greenwillow. (Grades K–3)

Wise, W. (1993). *Ten sly piranhas: A counting story in reverse. (A tale of wickedness-and worse!)* New York: Dial. (Grades K–3)

Zimelman, N. (1992). *How the second grade got $8,205.50 to visit the statue of liberty.* Morton Grove, IL: Whitman. (Grades 1–4)

Index

Teaching mathematics today means using a variety of manipulative materials to help children understand math concepts. The ETA/Cuisenaire® Start with Manipulatives Kit offers a selection of the manipulatives and overhead projector materials most widely used in classrooms today, and at a huge savings!

The Start with Manipulatives Kit is your opportunity to learn how twelve different materials are used to introduce math concepts from kindergarten through ninth grade. A 92-page resource book, *Start with Manipulatives*, by Rosamond Welchman, comes complete with a three-ring binder to encourage addition of classroom notes and information from other resources. This clearly written guide begins with an overview of each manipulative, then focuses on its pedagogical usefulness, indicating which math concepts are most appropriately taught with each model.

Equipped with this excellent resource—and using the manipulatives from the kit—you will have everything you need to teach mathematics with methods and materials that support the standards set by the National Council of Teachers of Mathematics.